THE GLOBAL BUSINESS ENVIRONMENT

meeting
the challenges

THE GLOBAL BUSINESS ENVIRONMENT

meeting the challenges

3rd edition

Janet Morrison

palgrave
macmillan

First published 2002
Second edition published 2006
Third edition published 2011 by
PALGRAVE MACMILLAN

Palgrave Macmillan in the UK is an imprint of Macmillan Publishers Limited,
registered in England, company number 785998, of Houndmills, Basingstoke,
Hampshire RG21 6XS.

Palgrave Macmillan in the US is a division of St Martin's Press LLC,
175 Fifth Avenue, New York, NY 10010.

Palgrave Macmillan is the global academic imprint of the above companies
and has companies and representatives throughout the world.

Palgrave® and Macmillan® are registered trademarks in the United States,
the United Kingdom, Europe and other countries.

ISBN: 978–0–230–21025–7

This book is printed on paper suitable for recycling and made from fully
managed and sustained forest sources. Logging, pulping and manufacturing
processes are expected to conform to the environmental regulations of the
country of origin.

A catalogue record for this book is available from the British Library.

A catalog record for this book is available from the Library of Congress.

CONTENTS IN BRIEF

CONTENTS

x

LIST OF CASE STUDIES

LIST OF FIGURES

LIST OF TABLES

ACKNOWLEDGEMENTS

Writing a book of this size and scope is a daunting task, especially for a sole author. The challenges facing businesses, highlighted in the book's subtitle, are, in a sense, mirrored by those which confronted me as its author. Foundation knowledge and skills, much like the basic nuts and bolts of a business, risked being overwhelmed by the convulsive events taking place in the business environment over the last few years. Of course, I was not starting from scratch, as this is the third edition of the book. But my approach to the task, as in the last edition, has not been to leave the edifice in place and simply make adjustments around the edges. The momentous changes taking place in today's world demand a more sweeping response. At the same time, I was aware that much of the strength of earlier editions lay in their lucid explanations of foundation material, which remain the best basis on which to understand the environmental shifts taking place, along with their impacts on organizations. Hence, foundation concepts are still core to the book, interpreted in new contexts and explored in new case studies and thought-provoking critical themes. I hope that this approach will prove stimulating, both to those familiar with previous editions and to those new to the text.

Although the conception and writing of this book fell to me alone, I am greatly indebted to a number of people whose help was indispensable in seeing this large project through to completion. I owe the deepest gratitude to my husband, Ian Morrison, for his support and encouragement. The book's production relied on the professional skills of several people who deserve many thanks. My editors, Ursula Gavin and Joanna McGarry, aided by the staff at Palgrave Macmillan, have overseen the project from the beginning. Jim Weaver designed the page layout. Linda Norris and her team at Aardvark Editorial transformed the manuscript into the finished book. Bryony Allen was the copy-editor. Annette Richards has again produced the index, which readers of earlier editions have found invaluable.

Numerous anonymous reviewers have helped to shape the outline and content of this third edition. They include those who gave me helpful insights and feedback on the second edition, and those who commented on this new edition at the manuscript stage. I appreciate all their remarks, and have endeavoured to incorporate as many as possible of their ideas. I hope the finished book will measure up to their expectations, and I hope especially that student readers will find it enjoyable as well as illuminating.

The author and publishers are grateful to the following companies for kindly granting permission to use the images in this book: CEMEX, Nokia, Volkswagen, Sony UK, Tullow Oil, SAB Miller, Applied Materials, BYD Auto, Carlsberg, Mitsubishi, Autonomy, Nomura, Biocon, Saudi Aramco and Unilever. Additional images were supplied by the Press Association and by IStockphoto.

All maps in this book are copyright of Maps in Minutes 2010, and are reproduced with kind permission.

ABOUT THE AUTHOR

 Janet Morrison, now retired, was a senior lecturer in strategic and international management at Sunderland University Business School in the UK, where she enjoyed a long career in teaching, research, curriculum development and course administration. She taught international business modules at undergraduate and postgraduate levels, including International Business Environment, Management in a Global Environment, Japanese Business and the Social and Cultural Environment of International Business. She was programme leader for undergraduate international business degrees and the MBA in International Management.

Janet's academic background goes back to her first degree (in political science and history) at Mary Washington College of the University of Virginia in the US (now the University of Mary Washington), followed by a master's degree from the University of Toronto in Canada and, later, a law degree from the University of Newcastle-upon-Tyne in the UK. She also studied in Chicago and Nagoya in Japan.

Her published research includes articles in a range of areas, including corporate governance, Japanese business and corporate social responsibility. She is the author of the textbook *International Business*, published by Palgrave Macmillan in 2009.

PREFACE TO THE THIRD EDITION

The first edition of this book, entitled *The International Business Environment*, which was published in 2002, was pioneering in its international sweep and multidisciplinary approach. Looking back now, nearly a decade later, these guiding principles – rare in business studies texts at the time – have demonstrated their enduring value. This third edition reaffirms the relevance of this approach, in opening up new frontiers, both geographically and in terms of outlook. Globalization, a theme of this text from the outset, has remained pivotal in understanding and grappling with the changing business environment. A new title, *The Global Business Environment: Meeting the Challenges*, reflects both the expanding geographic scope of international business and the emergence of global issues, such as climate change and social responsibility, which are central to the challenges facing tomorrow's international managers.

New challenges can be daunting but can also bring excitement and rewards. The successful enterprise rests on skills, vision and resources, to be sure, but it also increasingly depends on knowledge and understanding of factors such as international consumer markets, political currents, financial systems and differing national cultures. Recent events, such as the global financial crisis, have shown that understanding these seemingly more mundane aspects of business is as crucial to business success as having a great idea or product. As in previous editions, I have attempted to present the basic business concepts clearly and logically for students, bearing in mind that many readers will have little or no background in business studies. Also in keeping with the aims of previous editions, I have highlighted changes and trends in societies which, while difficult to capture in quantitative terms, shape events and perceptions of the world, for businesses, governments and individuals alike.

New case studies and new features, such as Meet the CEO, which gives an insider's view of an enterprise, engage the reader in the real world of business. In writing the Meet the CEO features, I have attempted to convey both the joys and disappointments of the international business rollercoaster. In addition, new critical themes enable the reader to cast a critical eye over unfolding events, government policies and business strategies, assessing long-term trends and their impacts. Concepts and explanations are presented clearly, making this book accessible and valuable for students on both undergraduate and postgraduate courses. I am pleased that students and lecturers in a wide range of countries have found this book helpful, and that international students have found the text easy to read. This new edition has been written with this wide readership in mind. I hope that it will again prove stimulating, relevant and enjoyable for readers.

Janet Morrison

INTRODUCTION

The first edition of this book, in 2002, was forward-looking in its international approach, aiming to open up vistas of international business around the world, both geographically and culturally. Since then, international interactions among countries and organizations have multiplied beyond what most people would have thought possible. The third edition of this book continues in the spirit of earlier editions, stressing an underlying international approach, and aiming to acquaint readers with the themes and trends now shaping the global environment. These aims, for both author and student, have become more challenging as the years have passed. New players come on the international scene virtually every day, including companies, countries, international organizations and individual people – each of whom is capable of making a difference in the way business is conceived and carried on. New complexities can be exciting, but can also be daunting to take on board. Why and how does the Chinese entrepreneur now find the funding he needs from an American investment fund? This and many other intriguing aspects of the current international environment are explained and explored in this new edition. New, more highly focused, themes are introduced, and new features are presented which capture both the changing environment and the challenges it poses for international managers.

Critical themes

The last edition of this book revolved around two major themes. The first was globalization, encompassing deeper integration among businesses, governments and societies. And the second was diversity – among societies, peoples, regions and organizations. These themes remain relevant, and much of the discussion in the unfolding chapters will highlight them. However, the new evolving contours of the global economy call for more highly focused themes, which, at the same time, invite critical thinking. These critical themes are described below. For each chapter, relevant critical themes, usually three or four, will be flagged up at the beginning. 'Critical thinking' boxes throughout the chapter will provide opportunities to delve into particular themes in context.

There are eight critical themes, each explained briefly below:

- *Multilayered environment* – Businesses operate in an external environment that includes local communities, regions within countries, sovereign states, regional groupings of states and international groupings. Managing interactions in this increasingly complex international environment depends on understanding the dynamics of each.

- *Multidimensional environment* – Dimensions of the business environment include political, legal, economic, cultural, technological, financial and ecological. A separate chapter is devoted to each of these dimensions, and interactions are highlighted within each.

- **Role of the state** – States are now playing more active roles in business and society contexts than ever before, in both the developed world and developing countries. In some countries, this represents a radical departure from traditional views of what governments should be doing. Their impacts, both direct and indirect, are highlighted throughout the book.

- **Emerging economies** – Why single out emerging economies when the large western economies and Japan have been influential for longer in international business? Emerging economies, notably the Bric economies (Brazil, Russia, India and China) are catching up fast, and are now the greatest source of growth in the global economy. Their companies and governments are growing in confidence and economic power in international business, and their societies are the fastest-growing markets for consumer products.

- **Changing societies** – This theme echoes that of diversity among societies of earlier editions. However, we widen the focus to taken in changes taking place in developing countries, often due to globalization processes.

- **Globalization of industries** – Globalization remains a dominant theme, highlighted here by industries driven by global production networks. Many are highlighted specifically in the new feature, 'Exploring the global business environment'.

- **International risks** – Events in recent years have demonstrated the risks in globalized business activities across a range of sectors. Finance is perhaps the most prominent, as the 2008 global financial crisis alerted businesses and governments to the risks of volatility in globalized markets. But there are others, such as food and commodities, which will also come under the spotlight in the chapters.

- **Corporate social responsibility (CSR) and sustainability** – These topics are typically dealt with in separate chapters of business environment texts, and this book is no exception. However, these themes are now seen as core in business strategy, particularly in interactions with consumers and employees worldwide. Hence, these themes are introduced in Chapter 1, and run through the entire text. There is a grid at the end of this introduction, showing which themes feature most prominently in which chapters.

These eight themes are intended to promote critical thinking, prompted in part by the 'Critical thinking' questions which appear at intervals. They also serve to highlight recurring issues which confront international managers. The eight themes are not to be seen in isolation. In this text, as in real business situations, they are likely to appear in clusters, in which interrelationships will be illuminating. Critical thinking features and case studies will often involve considering cross-cutting themes. Here are two examples: sustainability in an emerging economy such as Brazil (case study in Chapter 11); and the risk of state intervention, as Google experienced in China (case study in Chapter 8).

Plan of the book

The book has been reorganized since the last edition, to bring globalization more into focus at the heart of the enterprise. Globalization now features in Part 1, highlighting impacts on the enterprise in the global environment. Economies and markets are grouped in a second part. The dimensions of the environment, formerly Part 2, have become Part 3. And Part 4, as in the last edition, focuses on global issues, and these have been expanded to include the global financial crisis; ecology and climate change; and issues of ethics and CSR. The following is a brief summary of the four parts, indicating the overall focus of the part and the content of each chapter.

Part 1: The business in the global environment

There are two chapters in this part. **Chapter 1** provides an introduction to the business organization, outlining key concepts and organizational features. The chapter introduces the key dimensions of the business environment and the multiple layers of the environment in which businesses operate. The chapter shows that internal aspects of the business, such as corporate governance, shape its interactions in the external environment, whether at local or global level. **Chapter 2** pursues these themes in a context of globalization. It stresses that globalization is not one but many processes, which proceed at differing paces in different business sectors, different countries and different dimensions of the environment. The chapter highlights globalization as both a reality and a challenge for businesses, pointing to the ways in which multinational companies are meeting the challenges of new markets.

Part 2: Economies and markets

This part centres on the competitive environments in which businesses operate, including national, regional and global. **Chapter 3** introduces national economies and economic systems. Understanding global forces depends crucially on grasping how national economies function, along with the ways in which decision-makers form policies. Global economic integration is proceeding apace, but there remains huge diversity among national economic systems. **Chapter 4** takes us more broadly into the international environment, looking at the ways in which competitive forces, many of them from emerging economies, are shaping the competitive landscape. We examine the nature and patterns of international trade from a range of perspectives, including nation-states and business organizations. **Chapter 5** pursues MNE strategy in greater detail, looking first at the broader issues of strategy formation, including theories highlighting both internal and external factors. Corporate strategy is conceived in the international context, looking at divergent internationalization strategies in terms of the firm's long-term goals.

Part 3: Societies in the global environment

This part marks a shift from markets and strategy to broad areas of the international environment relating to societies – their cultures, how they are governed and how their legal systems impact on people. **Chapter 6** explores the cultural and social environments. For most businesses, as for people, a national culture is an anchoring point, but in today's globalized world, companies are constantly encountering new cultures, whether in markets or in new production locations. Managing in diverse cultural environments has become complex, made more so by the changes rapidly taking place in emerging economies. But opportunities abound as never before, for both firms and societies. In **Chapter 7**, on the political environment, we take a more formal and institutional view of societies, looking at the structures by which they are governed. These, too, change over time, especially in the context of newly independent states and those which are rebuilding their political systems following the collapse of communism. Managing political risk, especially evident in countries where the state plays a major role, is a major challenge for international business. These considerations are taken up again in the following chapter, **Chapter 8**, on the legal environment. Here we look first at national legal systems and their differing approaches to civil and criminal law. For international business, legal risks arise in numerous types of activity, including forming joint ventures, making contracts with suppliers and customers, and employing people in different countries. Legal systems, like other dimensions of the environment considered in this part of the book, are changing. Some of those changes mark a greater awareness of cross-border legal issues and the need for global co-ordination.

Part 4: Global issues and business

This part focuses on areas of the business environment in which global issues and risks are the major features. In **Chapter 9**, we explore global financial markets, a sphere of business activity which has seen rapid growth associated with globalization, but which has also seen increased risks. Following a number of financial crises, regulatory changes at both national and international level aim to create a more stable global environment. **Chapter 10** also examines the impact of globalization, this time in the changing technological environment. Innovation has long been recognized as a key to competitiveness, and with more and more countries building greater innovation capacity, the scope for innovative technology now encompasses a wide range of countries, notably the large emerging economies.

In **Chapter 11**, we take an overview of the impacts of industrialization and globalization in terms of the natural environment. Paramount among these impacts is climate change, a global issue, but one which can have devastating effects in local environments, especially severe in the poorest and most vulnerable countries. Although many governments have been slow to take up the challenges, business initiatives abound, pointing the way with sustainable business strategies. These lead naturally to the topics of **Chapter 12**, ethics and corporate social responsibility. Multinational companies are becoming increasingly involved in the communities and countries in which they operate. The challenges facing today's firms, whether in developed or developing countries, involve multiple stakeholders and issues of social responsibility. In **Chapter 13**, the last chapter, we take an overview of the critical themes, highlighting how they are intertwined in the preceding chapters. We also take the opportunity to look forward at how some of the forces featured in the critical themes are changing.

Chapter features

This book is designed to present the content in a logical and easily accessible manner. Although ideally a reader would begin with Chapter 1 and read each successive chapter in order, the book has been designed so that any chapter can be read independently, and the reader is guided by references to earlier relevant material, such as definitions of key concepts. Chapter features are outlined below, divided between those at the beginning of the chapter, those in the body of the text, and those at the end of each chapter.

At the beginning of each chapter ...

- An **Outline** of the sections in the chapter.
- The **Learning objectives** of the chapter clarify particular outcomes which the reader can expect.

- A list of the chapter's **Critical themes** follow, showing how each theme is illustrated in the text.
- An **Opening case study** sets the scene for the chapter, raising issues which will arise in the text. This case study usually features a company and raises issues of corporate strategy in the changing environment. Questions for discussion and references for further exploration are given.

In the body of the chapter ...

- **Key words** are defined in the text, and definitions appear in the margins alongside the relevant section in which they are introduced (this is a new feature). These include concepts, principles and major international institutions. (They also feature in a glossary at the end of the book.)
- **References** are given in parentheses in the text, for example (Tellis, 2009). The References section at the end of the book lists all references in the main text. References within case studies are given at the end of each case study.
- **Summary points** boxes appear at the end of each major section. These consolidate the main points, and can be used as an aid to revision.
- Web references in **More online** ... These refer to further information available on the internet, relating to the topic under consideration. Most refer to companies which illustrate the point being discussed.
- **Exploring the global business environment** – This is a new case study feature. This case study focuses on an industry, country or group of countries, highlighting challenges in the global environment. Questions for discussion and references are given.
- **Meet the CEO** – This is a new case study feature. Here, there is an opportunity to find out how the CEO of a real company sees his/her job and views the challenges ahead, from a personal point of view. The CEOs are from large and small companies, and from a number of different countries.
- **Critical thinking** boxes appear throughout the chapter. They raise questions and issues which invite the reader to examine the topic critically, often exploring further implications. These boxes highlight the critical themes in each chapter.

At the end of the chapter ...

- **Conclusions** – Each chapter ends with a list of conclusions, which are drawn from the major sections.
- **Review questions** are designed to cover all the topics in the chapter. They are an aid to learning for self-study or discussion. They are also a revision aid.
- **Key revision concepts** – This is a new feature, listing the key concepts and their page numbers in the chapter. These are aids to understanding the themes, discussing case studies and revising for examinations.
- Two **assignments** are given after the review questions. These are broader in scope than the review questions. They require some independent research and offer opportunity to present a considered analysis in a structured way.
- **Further reading** gives an indication of other sources to read that provide both further information and differing critical perspectives on the topics in the chapter.

- **Closing case study** – This is a new feature. This case study focuses on a company, raising issues that have featured in the chapter, and posing strategic questions for the firm. Questions for discussion and references for further exploration are provided.

Other learning aids

Other learning aids are listed below:

- **Grid of critical themes** – This grid, which is at the end of this introduction, shows which critical themes are featured in each chapter.
- **Case study grid** – Also at the end of this introduction, this is a guide to the content of the many case studies in the book, making it easy to see at-a-glance the geographical focus, industry, and critical themes of each case study.

Features at the end of the book

- **Maps** section – Identifying and understanding the geographical location of countries and regions might seem incidental, but is immensely useful in understanding the substantive issues discussed in the text.
- **Glossary** of key words – This contains all the key words highlighted in bold in the text.
- **References** – This section provides details of the references cited in the text, listed alphabetically by author or organization.
- **Index** – This is divided into three sections: Organizations, People and Subjects.

The global business environment is constantly changing, and along with it the individuals, firms and countries that shape events and pose future challenges. This book deliberately focuses on corporate and national actors that are at the forefront of change: some large companies are familiar names, but there are many smaller ones looking to make their mark and shape global markets. No one knows which will be tomorrow's winners, and which will be superseded by friskier, more innovative competitors. However, as this book highlights, the emergence of winners is not as haphazard as a casual observer might think. The global business environment in its many dimensions and different locations provides abundant lessons for the astute international manager eager to take on the challenges.

CRITICAL THEMES IN EACH CHAPTER

	Multilayered environment	Multidimensional environment	Role of the state	Emerging economies	Changing societies	Globalization of industries	International risks	CSR and sustainability
1 Introduction	✓	✓		✓			✓	✓
2 Globalization	✓			✓	✓	✓		
3 Economies and markets	✓	✓	✓	✓				
4 Trade and global competition	✓		✓	✓				
5 Strategies in a globalized world			✓	✓		✓	✓	
6 Cultural and social environment	✓	✓		✓	✓			
7 Political environment	✓	✓	✓				✓	
8 Legal environment	✓		✓				✓	✓
9 Financial markets	✓		✓			✓	✓	✓
10 Technology and innovation	✓	✓	✓	✓		✓		
11 Ecology and climate change	✓		✓	✓	✓			✓
12 Ethics and CSR	✓				✓	✓		✓
13 Critical themes in perspective	✓	✓	✓	✓	✓	✓	✓	✓

CASE STUDY GRID

Ch	Short title	Geographical focus, including home country of company	Industry/ies	Critical themes/topics
1	Facebook	US; global	Social web	Globalization Changing societies CSR
	The Brics	Brazil; Russia; India; China	Various – manufacturing; natural resources	Globalization Emerging economies Multidimensional environment
	CEO of Zegna	Italy; global	Retailing; fashion	Globalization Changing societies Emerging economies
	Cemex of Mexico	Mexico; global	Building materials; construction	Emerging economies Globalization CSR
2	Geely of China acquires Volvo	China; Sweden	Automotive	Emerging economies Globalization
	Global car companies	US; global	Automotive	Role of the state Globalization Multidimensional environment
	CEO of Nestlé	Switzerland; global	Food	Globalization Emerging economies
	Nokia	Finland; global	Mobile phones; telecommunications	Globalization Emerging economies
3	Polish entrepreneur, NG2	Poland	Retailing; shoe manufacturing	Changing societies Emerging economies
	Ireland's rollercoaster economy	Ireland; EU	Pharmaceuticals; computers	Role of the state International risks Globalization
	CEO of Kingfisher	UK	Retailing	Globalization Changing societies CSR
	Tata of India	India; global	Various – manufacturing	Globalization Emerging economies
4	BHP Billiton	Australia	Mining	Role of the state Multilayered environment CSR
	CEO of Procter & Gamble (P&G)	US; global	Consumer goods	Globalization Emerging economies
	Ghana	Ghana	Oil; gold	Emerging economies Role of the state International risks
	Volkswagen	Germany; global	Automotive	Globalization CSR Role of the state

Ch	Short title	Geographical focus, including home country of company	Industry/ies	Critical themes/topics
5	South Korea's Kepco	South Korea; Middle East	Nuclear power stations	Multilayered environment Globalization
	CEO of Carlsberg	Denmark	Brewing	Globalization Role of the state CSR
	Mexico: the lagging OECD economy	Mexico	Various – manufacturing	Role of the state Changing societies Multidimensional environment
	Sony	Japan; global	Electronics	Globalization International risk
6	Vale of Brazil takes over Inco of Canada	Brazil; Canada	Mining	Changing societies Multidimensional environment
	CEO of Mitsubishi, the Japanese trading group	Japan; global	Trading activities	Globalization Emerging economies International risks
	The Arab world	Middle East; North Africa	Natural resources	Changing societies Multidimensional environment
	McDonald's	US; UK	Fast food outlets	Changing societies Globalization
7	SAB Miller	UK; South Africa; emerging markets	Brewing	Emerging economies Globalization Multidimensional environment CSR
	CEO, Soho China	China	Property	Role of the state Emerging economies CSR
	Hungary	Hungary; EU	Various – manufacturing	Role of the state Changing societies Multidimensional environment
	Gazprom	Russia	Energy	Role of the state Globalization
8	Fake iPhones	China; global	Telecommunications	International risk Globalization
	Barriers on the rise in the 'borderless' world of the internet	China; global	Internet services	Role of the state Changing societies
	CEO of Autonomy, a British software company	UK	Software	Globalization CSR
	The Concorde crash	UK; France	Aviation	Role of the state Multilayered environment
9	Microfinance goes global	Bangladesh; global	Finance; social enterprise	Changing societies CSR
	Britain	UK; global	Finance	Globalization Role of the state
	CEO of Nomura, the Japanese investment bank	Japan	Finance	Multilayered environment International risk Multidimensional environment
	Kraft takes over Cadbury	UK; US	Food	Globalization CSR

Ch	Short title	Geographical focus, including home country of company	Industry/ies	Critical themes/topics
10	Applied Materials	US; global	Solar energy	Globalization CSR
	Pharmaceutical industry	Global	Pharmaceutical	International risk Globalization CSR
	Managing Director of Biocon, the Indian biotechnology company	India	Pharmaceutical; biotechnology	Emerging economies Globalization Multilayered environment
	Samsung	South Korea	Electronics; telecommunications; microchips	Globalization CSR Changing societies
11	BYD batteries	China	Batteries; automotive	Emerging economies Globalization
	Brazil	Brazil	Natural resources; agriculture	Emerging economies Multidimensional environment Changing societies
	CEO of Saudi Aramco	Saudi Arabia	Petroleum	Changing societies CSR Globalization Role of the state
	Oil companies in Iraq	Iraq	Petroleum	Globalization Role of the state
12	Cargill	US; Indonesia; global	Agriculture	Globalization CSR
	Food security	Global	Agriculture	Multilayered environment Changing societies Role of the state
	CEO of Unilever	UK; Netherlands	Consumer goods	Emerging economies CSR
	Walmart	US	Retailing	Multidimensional environment Multilayered environment CSR
13	Foxconn of China	China	Manufacturing	Changing societies CSR Globalization
	Oil spill in Gulf of Mexico	US	Oil industry	CSR Role of the state Multilayered environment International risks

TOUR OF BOOK

Outline of chapter and learning objectives

The opening page of each chapter provides a quick guide to what is covered in the outline of chapter. The learning objectives will help you organize your study and track your progress

Outline of chapter

Introduction
What does the business enterprise exist to do?
Purpose and goals
Markets and consumers
Stakeholders and corporate social responsibility (CSR)

How does the enterprise carry out its goals?
Entrepreneurs
Companies
The multinational enterprise (MNE)
Who controls the organization?
Functions within the enterprise
The firm's view on the world

The enterprise in the international environment
Multiple dimensions
The multilayered environment

The enterprise in a dynamic environment
Conclusions

Learning objectives

1 To identify the range of purposes pursued by business enterprises in the changing environment, highlighting the ro
diverse stakeholders
2 To appreciate the differing types of ownership and decision-making structures through which enterprises pursue their o

Critical themes in this chapter

- Emerging economies – an introduction to the Brics
- CSR and sustainability – an introduction to these concepts along with that of stakeholders
- International risks – the role of the entrepreneur
- Multilayered environment – an overview
- Multidimensional environment – an overview

Critical themes

Clusters of critical themes at the beginning of each chapter highlight the overarching issues that you should be aware of as you read on

Critical thinking

Within each chapter, the 'Critical thinking' features encourage debate on critical themes and other key issues facing managers and businesses in the global business environment

Critical thinking

What and who does the business exist
The preceding sections have focused
making money and offering great pr

4 Business in the global environment

OPENING CASE STUDY

The rise of the social web sees Facebook soar in popularity

The founding father of the internet, Tim Berners-Lee, has said, 'the web does not just connect machines, it connects people' (Berners-Lee, 2008).

and to othe
Facebook
creative ta

Questions for discussion

- How did Cemex build its domin
- How was Cemex able to expan markets? Are its prospects bright f
- What are the shortcomings of C governance?

Opening and closing case studies

Case studies at the beginning and end of each chapter feature businesses of all sizes, from every corner of the globe. Questions at the end of each case study, on-page weblinks, and updates on the book's companion website give you the chance to explore further

Glossary

There are definitions of key new terms in the page margin, and an alphabetical glossary of all those terms in the back of the book

market a location where exchange transactions take place, either with formal standing or informally

The **market** as a
actions take plac
market is used i
all stem from th
four main way

Guido Zegna CEO of Italian luxury group, Zegna

As the fourth-generation head of his family's
luxury menswear group, Guido Zegna attributes
the company's success to discipline and respect

2009). A cousin is the group chairman, and
sister, Anna, is the company's image direct
nearly a dozen younger family members

Meet the CEO

How do the CEOs of companies operating in the
business environment today see their roles, and
what are some of the challenges they face? This
case study feature gives you the chance to
explore the work of a diverse range of CEOs

Exploring the global business environment

Focusing on an industry, country or group of
countries, this case study feature highlights some
of the central issues of the globalized business
environment

10   Business in the global environment

EXPLORING THE GLOBAL BUSINESS ENVIRONMENT

The Brics take the stage

The 'Brics' is a term first used by economists at the
US bank Goldman Sachs, who highlighted the
large emerging markets for future growth (Goldman

▶ More online ... For corporate information on Apple, go to www.ap
Research in Motion's website is www.rim.net. Interesting headings
Asus's website is www.asus.com. Click on 'about asus' for corpora

More online

Look out for the 'More online' bar at
the top of many of the pages in this
book: it will point you to websites of
companies featured, and sources of
further information

Summary points

At the end of each section, you will
find a short list of summary points,
which will help you to consolidate
your understanding

Summary points **Business purpose and goals**

❖ The business enterprise has a
broad purpose in society, as well
as shorter-term goals of providing
products or services for customers.

❖ Over time, the business will
need to rethink its goals as the
competitive environment changes
and the firm evolves.

❖ Firms stem from roots in national
environments, which influence their
culture even when they serve global
markets.

Conclusions

1 Globalization comprises processes by which
   resources are able to move around the world
   interconnectedness.
2 MNE internationalization strategies have been
   production and of markets.
3 Theories of FDI highlight the use of location a
   production, a leading example being Dunning
   ownership, location and internalization advan

Review questions

1 What are the defining characteristics of globa
2 What are the leading schools of thought on th
3 What are the main motives behind MNE intern
4 Compare modes of internationalization in terr
   host country.

Key revision concepts

Acquisition, p. 51; Developed/developing country,
Joint venture, p. 51; Industrialization, p. 46; Locatic
Product life cycle, p. 54; Supply chain, p. 67; Sustai

Assignments

❖ Examine the major globalization processes at w
assess their impact on the international business e
❖ Assess the extent to which MNEs' FDI strategies
and local factors.

Further reading

Dicken, P. (2007) *Global Shift*, 5th edn (London: Sa
Giddens, A. (2000) *Runaway World: How Globaliza
Routledge).
Held, D., McGrew, A., Goldblatt, D. and Perraton, J
Politics, Economics and Culture (Cambridge: P
Held, D. (ed.) (2000) *Globalizing World? Culture, E
Hirst, P., Thompson, G. and Bromley, S. (2009) *Glo
(Cambridge: Polity Press).
Keane, J. (2003) *Global Civil Society?* (Cambridge:
Lechner, F. and Boli, J. (2007) *The Globalization R
Publishing).
Reich, R. (1991) *The Work of Nations: Preparing O
(London: Simon & Schuster).
Sklair, L. (2004) *Globalization: Capitalism and Its A
Press).
Waters, M. (2001) *Globalization*, 2nd edn (London:
Zysman, J. (1996) 'The Myth of a "Global" Econ

Review and revise

The end of each chapter has a
number of features to help you to
review and revise what you have
studied, from conclusions and
review questions to key concepts
for revision, assignments and
suggestions for further reading

Companion website

www.palgrave.com/business/morrisongbe3
In the student zone of the companion website, you will find
regular updates on many of the case studies featured in this
book, a fully searchable glossary, and an ever-changing list of
weblinks to guide further study

THE GLOBAL BUSINESS ENVIRONMENT
Meeting the Challenges
Janet Morrison | 3rd Edition

home   about this book   lecturer zone   student zone   order title

About this book

What makes this book so
special?
What's new for the third
edition?
Guided tour of book and
website (pdf)
Book contents
Book case studies
Contact Palgrave

Welcome to the companion website for
**The Global Business Environment:
Meeting the Challenges**
3rd edition
by Janet Morrison

On this website you'll find detailed information about this
book, together with an extensive range of teaching and
learning resources.

LIST OF ACRONYMS

Bric	Brazil, Russia, India and China
CEO	chief executive officer
CPI	consumer price index
CSR	corporate social responsibility
EU	European Union
FDI	foreign direct investment
FSA	Financial Services Authority
GATT	General Agreement on Tariffs and Trade
GDP	gross domestic product
GNI	gross national income
HRM	human resource management
IMF	International Monetary Fund
IT	information technology
ILO	International Labour Organization
IP	intellectual property
IPO	initial public offering
LSE	London Stock Exchange
M&A	merger and acquisition (activity)
MDG	Millennium Development Goal
MNE	multinational enterprise
Nafta	North Atlantic Free Trade Agreement
NGO	non-governmental organization
NYSE	New York Stock Exchange
OECD	Organisation for Economic Co-operation and Development
Opec	Organization of Petroleum Exporting Countries
PEST	political, economic, social, technological
PPP	purchasing power parity
PR	proportional representation
RTA	regional trade agreement
R&D	research and development
SEC	Securities and Exchange Commission
SME	small or medium-size enterprise
SWOT	strengths, weaknesses, opportunities, threats
UK	United Kingdom
UN	United Nations
UNDP	United Nations Development Programme
US	United States of America
WEF	World Economic Forum
WHO	World Health Organization
WTO	World Trade Organization

PART **1**

BUSINESS IN THE GLOBAL ENVIRONMENT

The two chapters in this part form a foundation for the book as a whole. In any study of business, there is a distinction between matters relating to the enterprise itself, often termed the internal environment of the business, and matters relating to the external environment, such as markets where it aims to sell its products. Although this division is oversimplified, as we will find in later chapters, it helps to use these contexts for the initial formulation of concepts and issues, which will become nuanced in later chapters.

Chapter 1, 'INTRODUCTION TO THE BUSINESS ENTERPRISE', focuses on the business itself, its goals and how it goes about achieving them. The chapter begins by looking at the most basic question of all: what does the business exist for? Many issues come into play, including what it is offering customers, the kind of organization it should set up, and how to run it. People who start a company do not take these decisions in a vacuum. As soon as they embark on a new business venture, they become involved in legal and regulatory frameworks, not just in their home countries, but in all the countries in which they wish to sell products or run operations. Today's global environment, while posing these seemingly daunting obstacles at the outset, also offers unprecedented opportunities. For individual firms, a crucial element of success is an organization with clear goals, an efficient, smooth-functioning structure and people committed to organizational goals, whatever function they carry out in its overall operations. The last sections in Chapter 1 introduce the business in its external environment, setting out the dimensions which will form the basis of separate chapters.

In Chapter 2, 'GLOBALIZATION AND THE BUSINESS ENVIRONMENT', we change focus to the external environment, with rapidly changing markets and production based on global supply chains. The many processes which are grouped together under the broad heading of 'globalization' are examined critically, assessing impacts on business organizations, governments and societies. Globalization represents a range of different processes, from high-speed communications to converging consumer tastes. These processes are unfolding unevenly, some bringing about rapid change and some emerging only gradually. Regional and country factors come into play. Globalization has proceeded rapidly in some countries, but more slowly in others. In some countries, globalization has actually receded in recent years. Companies with international operations are attuned to the global/local distinctions, aware that national and local differences are still influential in markets and strategy.

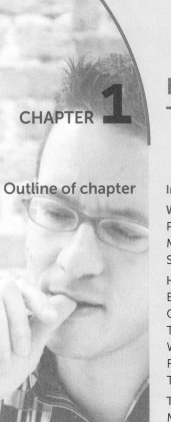

CHAPTER 1

INTRODUCTION TO THE BUSINESS ENTERPRISE

Outline of chapter

Introduction

What does the business enterprise exist to do?
Purpose and goals
Markets and consumers
Stakeholders and corporate social responsibility (CSR)

How does the enterprise carry out its goals?
Entrepreneurs
Companies
The multinational enterprise (MNE)
Who controls the organization?
Functions within the enterprise
The firm's view on the world

The enterprise in the international environment
Multiple dimensions
The multilayered environment

The enterprise in a dynamic environment

Conclusions

Learning objectives

1 To identify the range of purposes pursued by business enterprises in the changing environment, highlighting the role of diverse stakeholders
2 To appreciate the differing types of ownership and decision-making structures through which enterprises pursue their goals
3 To gain an overview of dimensions and layers of the international business environment, together with an ability to see how their interactions impact on firms

Critical themes in this chapter

• **Emerging economies – an introduction to the Brics**
• **CSR and sustainability – an introduction to these concepts, along with that of stakeholders**
• **International risks – the role of the entrepreneur**
• **Multilayered environment – an overview**
• **Multidimensional environment – an overview**

The world at his feet: starting a business is daunting but exciting for the young entrepreneur

Source: Istock

The rise of the social web sees Facebook soar in popularity

The founding father of the internet, Tim Berners-Lee, has said, 'the web does not just connect machines, it connects people' (Berners-Lee, 2008). The phenomenal rise of social networking in just a few years, allowing people to keep in touch and share information with friends, demonstrates the power of the internet as a social medium. In 2010, Facebook, founded in 2004 by a youthful Mark Zuckerberg in his Harvard student days, became the world's second most popular website, behind Google. Facebook is the world's largest online social network, with hundreds of millions of users, accessing it in 50 languages. Seventy per cent of these are outside the US. However, in the fast-moving world of social interaction, companies like Facebook can experience not just meteoric rise, but also precipitous falls. New competitors, such as Twitter, seem to spring up overnight, while MySpace, once considered the star of social networking, saw its popularity evaporate with the surge of Facebook. Is Facebook now threatened by Twitter? Facebook and Twitter are distinctive in their business models. Facebook allows people to keep in touch with their friends, and Twitter is a 'micro-blogging' site, allowing people to speak via 140-character tweets to anyone who cares to follow them. Twitter thus sees itself as more of an information company than a social networking one, according to its founder, Biz Stone (*The Economist*, 2010).

Facebook has become a global business. Its technological expertise and innovativeness, while not immediately obvious to users in the concrete way that an iPhone's attributes are visible to its customers, are nonetheless far-reaching. Its software engineers have been skilful at building systems that can handle increased volume quickly and efficiently, allowing the network to add millions of new users easily. Its innovations encourage greater sharing of data. Facebook Connect, launched in 2009, lets users take their identity and network of friends to other websites

and to other devices, such as game consoles. Facebook has also been skilful in tapping into the creative talent of independent developers of new applications, or 'apps'. The developers benefit from gaining access to a huge audience of users, and users enjoy a directory containing over 500,000 apps.

Although the cost of hardware for storing and processing data has fallen sharply, investment in new technologies is costly. Being relatively young companies started by enthusiasts, where are Facebook and other social networks finding the money needed to propel social networking to global

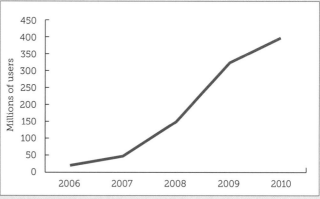

Facebook users worldwide

Source: Facebook website, at www.facebook.com

success? Developing a sustainable business model, which will provide services that users desire and generate profits in the long term, is the dream of every young business. A social networking platform such as Facebook, which holds huge amounts of personal data and is widely accessed globally, would seem to be in a commanding position to be a successful international business. But translating popularity among users into profits is a major challenge. Although Facebook had not yet made a profit, Microsoft invested $240 million in the company in 2007, and a Russian company, Digital Sky Technologies (DST), invested $200 million in 2009. DST thus acquired a 1.9% stake, which would imply

▸ More online ... For information about the company, go to Facebook's website at www.facebook.com and click on 'about'.

that Facebook is worth $10 billion. Facebook aimed to take in $500 million in revenues in 2009, but it was spending more than that on its technology (Gelles, 2009a). In contrast to Google, which has grown rich on selling the targeted advertising that appears alongside its search results, a site such as Facebook faces hurdles in attracting advertising. Because the content is user generated, and possibly in doubtful taste, many advertisers are reluctant to sign up to advertising on social networks. On the other hand, the Facebook audience is far bigger than that of any television network in the world, and, because of the enormous amount of personal data Facebook holds, advertisers can target particular groups of possible customers precisely. Moreover, users often recommend products to friends, and this can be a powerful marketing tool – which costs far less than a traditional marketing campaign.

Although the business prospects look bright from the owners' perspective, an international business strategy depends on numerous other factors – many external to the organization. As other software and internet companies have found, legal regulation must, sooner or later, be taken into account. Microsoft and Google were both founded by young, talented individuals with an ambitious focus on building a global force. Both have encountered regulatory hurdles and setbacks. Facebook has soared to fame, but faces down-to-earth regulatory hurdles, such as privacy laws which protect users' personal data. The company encountered resistance from users when it relaxed its privacy rules, allowing updates of personal data to be viewed publicly unless the user chose to restrict access. Mark Zuckerberg has said that privacy is no longer a 'social norm' (*The Telegraph*, 2010). However, the imposition of stricter privacy settings by regulators, including the European Commission, is a possibility. The world of social networking is helping to democratize the web, but it is also, perhaps paradoxically, concentrating power in the hands of new corporate actors, presenting challenges as well as opportunities for the 25-year-old head of Facebook and others following in his footsteps.

Sources: *The Economist* (2010) 'Profiting from friendship', 30 January; Gelles, D. (2009a) 'What friends are for', *Financial Times*, 3 July; Gelles, D. (2009b) 'Facebook draws criticism for privacy changes', *Financial Times*, 11 December; *The Telegraph* (2010) 'Facebook's Mark Zuckerberg says privacy is no longer a "social norm"', 11 January; Berners-Lee, T., speech before the Knight Foundation, Washington, DC, 14 September 2008, at www.webfoundation.org

Questions for discussion

◆ Why has Facebook grown so rapidly and become an international force so quickly?
◆ What are the risks to the continued success of Facebook?
◆ What are the impacts of social networking for international business?

Introduction

Business activities shape the daily lives and aspirations of people all over the world, from the farmer in rural Africa to the executive of a large American bank. Business enterprises present a rich variety of different organizations and goals, catering for customers ranging from the shopper purchasing a loaf of bread to the giant oil company agreeing to carry out exploration for a government. Business enterprises and their environments have become more complex in recent years, with expanding and deepening ties between societies and between the many organizations within those societies. Many organizations now see themselves as global players, in both their outlook and operations. Yet even the global company must adapt to differing environments and changing circumstances. These changes may be subtle adjustments or radical overhauls, altering the organization's goals, structure and ways of doing things. Understanding the dynamic interaction between the organization and the changing environment is key to business success in today's global competitive landscape. All business organizations, whatever their size and geographical scope, are faced with key questions to which they must respond, whether consciously or simply by carrying on.

We begin this chapter by identifying these key questions behind the business enterprise, which are, 'What do we exist to do?' and 'How should we be carrying out our goals?' We find that goals and means to accomplish them are intertwined, and that success for the enterprise depends on being able to deliver value to customers in a variety of different ways in differing environments. Increasingly, companies are looking at international expansion, to reach more customers and to deliver more efficient performance. We find that operating internationally does not mean simply copying a formula that has worked successfully in the home country. It promises great rewards, but presents new challenges, risks and organizational uncertainties.

Why do some firms falter internationally despite being successful in their home countries? Differences in culture influence how firms engage with organizations and communities in other countries. Similarly, responses to the changing environment differ from firm to firm. There is now a wider range of companies and countries engaged in global business, and changes, especially those involving technological advances, proceed at a rapid pace. We highlight two cross-cutting views of the international environment. The first is the differing dimensions of the environment, including economic, cultural, political, legal, financial, ecological and technological. The second is that of spheres, from the local, through to the national, regional and global. We thus provide a practical framework for understanding how enterprises interact through each dimension in multiple geographical environments.

What does the business enterprise exist to do?

business any type of economic activity in which goods or services (or a combination of the two) are supplied in exchange for some payment, usually money

international business business activities that straddle two or more countries

Business refers to any type of economic activity in which goods or services (or a combination of the two) are supplied in exchange for some payment, usually money. This definition describes the basic exchange transaction. The types of activity covered include trading goods, manufacturing products, extracting natural resources and farming. **International business** refers to business activities that straddle two or more countries. Businesses nowadays routinely look beyond the bounds of their home country for new opportunities. Moreover, although it used to be mainly firms in the more advanced regions of the world (such as North America, Europe and

Japan) which aspired to expand into other countries, now we see businesses from a much wider range of countries 'going global'. These include Chinese, Indian, African and Latin American firms. Consequently, in most countries, there are likely to be both domestic and foreign companies competing alongside each other.

Business has been around a very long time. Ancient societies grew prosperous largely because of thriving business activity, chiefly through trade with other countries, which brought economic power. The urge to do business seems to be universal, taking place in all societies, even under communism, which is avowedly against private enterprise. The small business that operates informally is very different from the ambitious company that seeks to compete in the cut and thrust of today's market economies. The basic questions and concepts that follow help to illuminate how businesses work in a variety of different contexts.

Purpose and goals

A business enterprise does not simply come into existence of its own accord. It is created by people, who may emerge in any society or geographic location, and who bring their own values and experience to bear on it. Businesses are founded in particular national environments, with their distinctive values and social frameworks. The founders could well envisage an overarching purpose or mission of contributing to society through employment and wealth creation. They will have some idea of what type of entity they wish to create in terms of organization. They will also focus on more immediate goals of providing specific goods or services to customers. These goals might change frequently, while broader goals are more enduring. Both the decision-makers and the circumstances will change, but the continuing question confronting them is 'What purpose are we fulfilling or should we be fulfilling?' Most of the world's businesses aim to make money, and are sometimes referred to as **for-profit organizations**, to distinguish them from **not-for-profit organizations**, such as charities. A third category exists, the **social enterprise**, which lies somewhere between the two: it aims to make money, but the money is mainly for social causes. (The social enterprise is discussed in Chapter 12.)

Although for-profit enterprises aim to make a financial gain, most founders would say that the profits are for some other purpose. Admittedly, in some businesses, the purpose might be crudely expressed as simply to enrich the owners. But most businesspeople would describe their goal as, for example, offering products which will satisfy customers. It need not be a wholly new product, but one that is more innovative technologically, a better design or cheaper than rivals'. It could be a 'greener' product than those of rivals, such as a more fuel-efficient car. No firm would realistically aim to outperform competitors on all criteria. Goals can be mutually exclusive: the low-cost product is unlikely to have the latest technology. These are issues of strategy, which are discussed more fully in Chapter 5. There is considerable variety in the way the company can position itself competitively, which tells us much about its expertise, culture and broader goals in society.

In today's global consumer markets we find competing companies from a variety of national backgrounds. One of the most rapidly growing products globally is the 'smartphone', which offers a variety of mobile internet services. The iPhone, made by US company Apple Computers, took the world by storm with its launch in 2007. But a number of competitors have entered the smartphone market, eyeing the good prospects for growth. They include Nokia, the Finnish company which has long dominated the mobile handset market (see the closing case study in Chapter 2); the

for-profit organizations businesses that aim to make money

not-for-profit organizations organizations such as charities, which exist for the purpose of promoting good causes, rather than to make a profit

social enterprise an enterprise that lies somewhere between the for-profit and not-for-profit organization, aiming to make money, but using it mainly for social causes

▶ More online ... For corporate information on Apple, go to www.apple.com/investors
Research in Motion's website is www.rim.net. Interesting headings are 'company' and 'investors'.
Asus's website is www.asus.com. Click on 'about asus' for corporate information.

Canadian firm Research in Motion, with its Blackberry products; and the Taiwanese firm Asus. These firms differ markedly in background and culture: their origins are in different continents (America, Europe and Asia), and their organizations have evolved in distinctive national cultures, while growing into global businesses. Apple, famous for its design and technology, has been guided by the vision of its charismatic founder, Steve Jobs, a veteran of tough competitive battles with larger rivals in North America. Nokia has built a position of dominance in global mobile phone markets, relying on a strong corporate culture rooted in its Scandinavian environment. By contrast, Research in Motion focuses on the Blackberry, which is a premium product favoured especially by business customers. Asus, with its rapidly growing strength in the computer market, is aiming to combine technological expertise with low-cost production in Asia to offer the consumer better value than global rivals.

Summary points Business purpose and goals

◆ The business enterprise has a broad purpose in society, as well as shorter term goals of providing products or services for customers.

◆ Over time, the business will need to rethink its goals as the competitive environment changes and the firm evolves.

◆ Firms stem from roots in national environments, which influence their culture even when they serve global markets.

Markets and consumers

market a location where exchange transactions take place, either with formal standing or informally

The **market** as a concept is an old one, referring to a location where exchange transactions take place, either with formal standing or informally. Today, the notion of a market is used in many contexts, and can cover a number of phenomena, although all stem from the core notion of exchange transactions. A market can be defined in four main ways:

- *A country, in terms of its consumers* – A country's consumers usually have similarities in product preferences, due to shared culture and history. National markets are the mainstay of the many companies which focus on their home markets.
- *A type of trading* – Trading can take place globally and not be confined to a specific place. Financial markets, for example, exist to carry out financial transactions, such as the stock market.

emerging economies/ markets fast-growing developing countries

Bric countries collective reference to Brazil, Russia, India and China, which are grouped together loosely as emerging economies

- *A country in terms of its economy* – This rather recent use of the word usually occurs in the context of **emerging markets**, a term that has become widely used, but is rather loosely defined. It refers to fast-growing developing countries, the most notable of which are the **'Bric'** countries (Brazil, Russia, India and China). Their rapid economic rise has made them the centre of attention for many businesses, largely because of their growing ranks of middle-class consumers (see the case study on them which follows).

segment in marketing, a group of identifiable consumers, such as an age group, socio-economic group or culturally distinct group

- *A group of consumers with similar characteristics and preferences* – In marketing, a group of identifiable consumers, such as people aged 18 to 30, is known as a **segment**.

The Brics take the stage

The 'Brics' is a term first used by economists at the US bank Goldman Sachs, who highlighted the large emerging markets for future growth (Goldman Sachs, 2003). Looking at trends extending until 2050, they concluded that the size and growth of the four economies – Brazil, Russia, India and China – were overshadowing today's developed nations, thus representing a shift in the balance of power in the world. The bank's economists did not see them necessarily forming a bloc which would become cohesive in itself, like the EU. In fact, apart from size and growing influence, they have little in common with each other, but in a twist of fiction becoming reality, the four have begun organizing their own summit meetings to discuss global issues. Do the Brics as a group represent a new force in the global economy, or is the term simply a way of drawing attention to four emerging markets?

The four are all large countries and economies. Together they occupy over 25% of the world's land area, and are home to 40% of the world's people. Their economies and political systems are very different. China and Russia are authoritarian states, while India and Brazil are turbulent democracies. All four countries have histories of closed economies and strong state guidance, and all have put in place reforms which have made them more market oriented and more welcoming to foreign investors, to varying degrees. However, in all, there are tensions between market reforms and the role of the state. Of the four, China is the most authoritarian, but its communist leaders have also been highly successful in guiding liberal market reforms. Its export-oriented economy has benefited from foreign investment and know-how. It is moving up the economic ladder, from the low-level, labour-intensive industries that are prevalent in developing countries, to higher technology industries. China's economy is by far the largest of the four, and its growth rate is the most impressive. Its ranks of growing middle-class consumers are now the fastest growing markets for consumer goods. Furthermore, the wealthy Chinese consumer is younger than in Japan or the US (see figure), splashing out on aspirational lifestyle purchases, such as luxury home furnishings and luxury

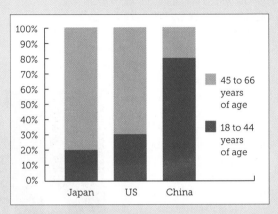

Wealthy consumers by age group
Annual household income of over $70,000, 250,000 renminbi, 8 million yen

Source: *Financial Times*, 10 October 2009

cars, in contrast to the more conservative spending habits of rich Japanese consumers.

India, with its billion-plus inhabitants, aspires to emulate China, but its still predominantly rural population, poor infrastructure and lumbering bureaucracy pose challenges for its democratically elected government to raise economic growth above 6–7% annually. Its exports pale beside China's, and it remains ambivalent about foreign investors in numerous sectors, such as retailing. Brazil, like India, is a democracy, characterized by social and cultural divisions, in addition to widespread poverty. Brazil's government has done much in recent years to improve the lives of its 200 million inhabitants. And Brazil has been active in international forums, voicing the concerns of developing nations and urging rich countries to bring down trade barriers which keep out imports from developing countries like itself.

Of the four countries, Russia is arguably the one which seems out of place. It is officially classified as an industrialized economy under the Kyoto climate change treaty, while the other three are developing economies. Historically, Russia was the superpower rival of the US during the cold-war era following the Second World War. Cold-war ideology has been buried, but the legacy of rivalry with the US lives on. Russia remains one of the world's heaviest military spenders, but behind China; and both are far behind

► More online ... The OECD's website is www.oecd.org, which offers a range of topics and country focus features.

the US, whose military spending is more than quadruple that of the other two combined. Russia's economy has slumped in recent years, and the state has taken greater control of key industries such as gas, which had been privatized in a wave of economic reforms. Despite hopes that a new democratic system would take firm root following the collapse of communism in 1989, the state has taken a stronger grip on political life. Russia possibly views inclusion among the Brics as an opportunity to revive its global political ambitions. Russia was happy to host the first summit meeting of the Brics in 2009.

Are the four countries likely to act as a coherent group? There are conflicts and rivalries among them. All four are cultivating trade and investment relations with countries in the developing world, particularly those rich in natural resources, such as African nations. Brazil and India aspire to become permanent members of the UN Security Council, but Russia and China, as existing members, have resisted. China and India fought a war in 1962 along their common border, which remains tense. Of the three, only Brazil is not a nuclear power, but it is moving in that direction. All four can be targeted for poor environmental records. China is the world's largest carbon emitter, but India and Russia are also among top emitters. Brazil is the leader in deforestation, although it is taking steps to regulate environmental degradation.

The Brics represent a shift in global economic power away from the developed world, in which the US was dominant. With the exception of Russia, their continued growth has stood out against recession in the rich world in 2008–9, helping to substantiate their claims for

Getting a buzz from shopping: These young Chinese shoppers carry the hopes of many of the world's leading brands. What other products are these shoppers likely to be buying?

Source: Istock

global recognition. Relations with the US and other developed nations are evolving as the Brics' political leaders forge new roles on the global political stage.

Sources: Barber, L., and Wheatley, J. (2009) 'Brazil keeps its economic excitement in check', *Financial Times*, 26 October; *The Economist* (2010) 'The trillion-dollar club', 17 April; Hille, K., Lau, J., and Waldmeir, P. (2009) 'Scramble to slake Chinese thirst for high-end brands', *Financial Times*, 10 October; Lamont, J. (2010) 'A good crisis brings greater influence', *Financial Times*, 29 January; Clover, C., and Belton, C. (2009) 'Crisis could be a catalyst for change', *Financial Times*, 13 October; Goldman Sachs (2003) 'Dreaming with BRICs: The Path to 2050', Global Economics Working Paper No. 99, at http://www2.goldmansachs.com

Questions for discussion

◆ Why are the Brics the new forces to be reckoned with in the world economy?

◆ In what ways are the Bric countries different from each other?

◆ In your view, are the Bric countries likely to co-ordinate their action on global policy issues?

An important market for many companies is urban, middle-class consumers, numbers of whom are growing fastest in the large emerging markets. There are probably one billion middle-class consumers globally, but there are over four billion other people further down the 'pyramid' whose needs also matter. Their importance has been highlighted in C.K. Prahalad's book, *The Fortune at the Bottom of the Pyramid* (2009). Increasingly, companies have broadened their focus to include products for this much broader spectrum of consumers, often living in poor countries where infrastructure is weak and levels of education are low. In these markets, price is crucial: a few cents more or less representing a major factor in the consumer's ability to buy a product. Why would a global company such as Procter & Gamble (P&G), whose beauty products cultivate a glamorous image, seek to sell basic soap in difficult conditions in Africa? Part of the answer lies in the dilemma faced by many large companies: weighing up the tremendous growth possibilities of new markets against the safety of existing mature markets where growth is minimal.

Summary points **Markets and consumers**

- A market can be a whole country, but it is usual, especially in a large emerging market such as China, to target particular products to identifiable groups of consumers, such as the urban middle class.

- Many large companies, finding expansion possibilities limited in the developed economies, are targeting consumers in developing countries. In these countries, economic growth and changing lifestyles create business opportunities for both domestic and foreign firms.

- A large company might design products to serve different markets, from basic goods in developing countries to premium branded products in developed countries.

Stakeholders and corporate social responsibility (CSR)

In answer to the question posed at the end of the last section – on why P&G would target African markets – we could simply cite the response suggested earlier: to make money. But this is only part of the story. The large company seeks success in a number of markets, both in terms of countries and types of consumer. It is driven by a desire to satisfy those consumers' needs, and also to provide worthwhile economic activity for its employees. These considerations are part of the answer to the question, 'What do we exist to do?' In recent years, companies have come to recognize that they are participants in society generally.

In the same vein, managers have become more aware of the interrelationships between the internal and external environment of the company. These perspectives bring the company into relationships with stakeholders. Figure 1.1 identifies a variety of stakeholders across home and foreign environments. A **stakeholder** may be anyone, including individuals, groups and even society generally, who exerts influence on the company or whom the company is in a position to influence (Freeman, 1984). The impacts may be direct or indirect, identifiable people or a more general notion of the community as something distinct from its current members. Stakeholders who have direct relations with the company include owners, employees, customers, suppliers and business partners. These might be located in any country where the firm does business. The government can be a direct stakeholder, especially if it has an ownership stake (discussed in the next section), or it can be an indirect stakeholder, framing the legal environment in which the firm operates.

stakeholder broad category including individuals, groups and even society generally, that exerts influence on the company or that the company is in a position to influence

▶ More online ... Nike's corporate website is www.nikebiz.com
Gap's corporate website is www.gapinc.com

Indirect stakeholders, while they affect and are affected by the company's operations, cover a range of broader societal interests which enjoy fewer direct channels
of communication with managers. They include the local community, society generally and the ecological environment affected by the company's operations. On the
other hand, the rapid rise of social IT has seen social networking, on websites such as
Facebook and Twitter, expand into business activities and impact on companies.
People anywhere can voice their views to a potentially large audience. Companies
wishing to retain a tight control on stakeholder relations might see these developments as a threat, whereas more enlightened companies would see opportunities to
gain valuable information on the views of customers and other stakeholders.

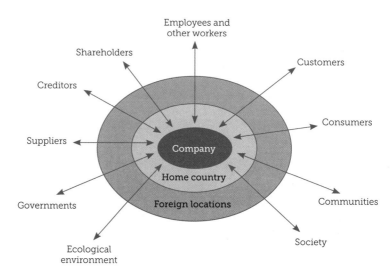

Figure 1.1 **Stakeholders,
home and abroad**

In a company that operates mainly in its own domestic market, managers have a
fairly clear idea of their main stakeholders. Their employees and customers are readily
identifiable. In a company that operates internationally, identifying stakeholders is far
more difficult – and more challenging. The company's branded products might be
made by workers in far-flung locations, who are employed by a different company
and have little contact with the company whose brand appears on the products. This
type of operation, known as **outsourcing** or manufacturing under licence, has
become common. It is exemplified by Nike, Gap and other familiar brands.
Outsourcing, usually in order to manufacture products in a lower cost location than
the firm's home country, is one of the major trends associated with globalization,
which we discuss in the next chapter. The firm that decides to go down this route is
impliedly making a statement about its view of its overall purpose and strategy.

In recent years, companies have increasingly tended to frame their purpose and
goals in terms of stakeholders, a tendency that reflects a recognition of a broader role in
society than the simple economic one. The approach to business activities that accords
with this view rests on a belief in **corporate social responsibility (CSR)**. CSR as an
approach recognizes that the business has wider responsibilities in society, extending
to legal, moral, ethical and social roles. CSR, however, has become rather an umbrella
term, covering a spectrum of approaches to business objectives, which are highlighted
throughout this book and are brought together in a broad assessment in Chapter 12.

outsourcing the
process by which an
owner contracts out to
another firm a business
process, such as
product manufacturing
or a business service,
usually under a
licence agreement

**corporate social
responsibility (CSR)** an
approach to business
which recognizes that
the organization has
responsibilities in society
beyond the economic
role, extending to legal,
ethical, environmental
and philanthropic roles

Whereas some companies prioritize CSR as their guiding strategy, others see CSR as voluntary activities separate from their mainstream businesses. The approach of many companies that fall between these two extremes is one of integrating business objectives with CSR goals. Known as an 'integrated strategy', it is the basis of the 'business case' for CSR (Husted and Salazar, 2006). This approach holds that, although a firm seeks profit maximization as a goal, purely economic motives are rather short term, and the firm would be smarter to look at long-term value creation, maintaining its capacity to generate profits in the future. This longer term perspective involves the **sustainability** of the firm's business, which is the notion that today's business should be carried out in ways which do not cause a detriment to the ability of future generations to fulfil their needs. Sustainability takes into account the firm's impacts on communities and the natural environment (see Chapter 11). In a sense, the principle of sustainability encourages a business to think of stakeholders in the future, not just the present. Most firms would probably say they uphold goals of stakeholder involvement, CSR and sustainability, but firms differ markedly in their commitment of resources to these goals.

sustainability the principle that business should be carried out in ways which do not cause a detriment to the ability of future generations to fulfil their needs

Summary points Stakeholders

- Stakeholders interact with the firm at all levels, although companies differ in their responsiveness to stakeholder interests.

- CSR as an approach views economic goals as only one aspect of the firm's existence, and stresses social and ethical obligations which arise for the firm because it is part of society.

- In contrast to short-term economic goals, a longer term approach looks at the sustainability of the firm's business.

Critical thinking

What and who does the business exist for?

The preceding sections have focused on business goals, from basic ones such as making money and offering great products, to more idealistic ones such as serving society. In your view, which of these goals are the most important in today's world, and why? List them in order of priority.

How does the enterprise carry out its goals?

Although we speak of a *firm* forming goals and carrying them out, it is actually the *people* running the firm who take the key decisions. In this section, we look at the players and processes which make it function. We focus here initially on the forms, structures and processes which constitute a legal framework; this is a necessary consideration before the firm can get on with what it is 'really' about, such as manufacturing. Most businesses start in a small way, with founders who become the first owners. They bear considerable responsibility, especially in the early stages of the business. Having a great idea for a business is only the beginning, however. They must create a legal and organizational structure to carry it out, and decide on how it will be financed and managed. Each of these aspects of the business now has an international dimension for many enterprises, adding to the possible complications, but also offering tantalizing opportunities.

▶ More online ... The Global Entrepreneurship Monitor provides much
comparative country data on entrepreneurs, at www.gemconsortium.com
McDonald's corporate website is www.aboutmcdonalds.com

Entrepreneurs

entrepreneur a person who starts up a business and imbues it with the energy and drive necessary to compete in markets

sole trader the person who is in business on his or her own account, also referred to as a self-employed person

A person who starts up a business, usually with his or her own money, is known as an **entrepreneur**. The successful entrepreneur has a vision of the firm's goals, a great deal of energy and an appetite for a moderate amount of risk (Zimmerer et al., 2007). Not everyone would savour this prospect, often because cultural factors come into play, making some people more reluctant to take on personal risk than others. The founder of a business typically begins as a **sole trader**, also referred to as a self-employed person. The business of the sole trader has no independent existence from its owner. In practice, this means that if the business fails, the personal wealth of its owner can be used to cover the business's debts. In the worst scenario, the owner's resources could be wiped out in order to pay business debts. This risk is known as 'unlimited liability', and is one of the major drawbacks of being self-employed. The business at this stage might have only one or two employees, or even none, although it is common for family members to help out. It is a **small-to-medium size enterprise (SME)**. This category covers the vast majority of the world's business enterprises. It derives from the classification given below:

small-to-medium size enterprise (SME) business ranging from micro-enterprises of just one person to firms with up to 249 employees

- Micro: 0–9 employees
- Small: 10–49 employees
- Medium: 50–249 employees
- Large: 250 or more employees

SMEs range from informal micro-enterprises to firms with up to 249 employees, making this a highly diverse category. These firms provide an important source of employment and economic activity in all countries. Although most are local firms such as family-owned restaurants, many SMEs have set their sights on becoming global in scope from the outset. These ambitious **born-global firms** tend to be in high-technology sectors. Whereas a firm traditionally grows gradually, expanding from local to a national and international business, the born-global firm's owners think from the outset in terms of international markets (Knight and Cavusgil, 2004: 124). Such firms tend to be the ones we think of when visualizing global business. Many well-known firms have grown from start-ups into global organizations.

born-global firm SME which aims to become global from the outset, often in a high-technology sector

McDonald's, founded as a single hamburger outlet in the 1950s, is an example, as is Microsoft (founded in 1975) and Google (founded in 1998). Of the three, it is striking that Google, the most recent, has grown the quickest, becoming the world's dominant internet search engine in just a few years. The fact that these firms are all American is indicative that the cultural environment, as well as the legal and financial institutions, is favourable to entrepreneurs.

franchising business agreement by which a business uses the brand, products and business format of another firm under licence

For individual entrepreneurs, the franchise provides a less risky route to starting a business. The **franchise** agreement allows a businessperson to trade under the name of an established brand, backed by an established organization (the 'franchisor'), while retaining ownership of the business. Under the agreement, the business owner ('franchisee') pays fees to the franchisor organization for the right to sell its products or services. The franchisee does not have the freedom over the business that an independent owner would have, but stands a greater chance of success due to the strength of the established business 'formula' of the brand. Besides McDonald's, Burger King and other fast-food chains, there are numerous other goods and services providers, such as car rental companies, which have grown through the use of franchising.

▶ More online ... Bosch's website is www.bosch.com, where much corporate information is available

Summary points **Entrepreneurs**

◆ For an entrepreneur who starts a business, the enterprise can be highly personal, involving commitment of energy, funds and some risk.

◆ The born-global firm, often in high-technology sectors, aspires to global markets from the outset.

◆ In a franchise arrangement, the business trades under the name of a well-known brand, so that the franchisee enjoys a greater chance of success.

◆ SMEs employ more people globally than larger firms. Although

some are born-globals, with aspirations to global markets from the outset, most are local or national, making them important in national economies.

Companies

company a legal form of an organization which has a separate legal identity from its owner(s); also called a 'corporation'

shareholders legal owners of a company, known as 'members', who enjoy rights such as receiving dividends from company profits

equity in corporate finance, the share capital of a company

limited liability principle that the shareholder is liable up to the amount invested in the company

private limited company company whose shares are not publicly traded on a stock exchange

public company company which lists on a stock exchange and offers shares to the public

initial public offering (IPO) first offering by a company of its shares to the public on a stock exchange; also known as 'flotation'

rights issue for a company, a means of raising capital whereby existing investors are asked to increase their investment

A business can carry on indefinitely as an unincorporated association or enterprise, that is, without formal corporate status. However, when it grows beyond a size that can be managed personally by the owner, it is usual for the owner to register it as a company, to give the business a separate legal identity and separate financial footing. The **company**, also called a 'corporation', is a legal entity separate from its owners. Registration with the correct authorities in each country (or individual state in the US) constitutes its creation, drawing a line between the company's finances and legal obligations and those of the owner(s). It is also possible to register as a European company within the EU, although for purposes such as taxation, the company is still considered a national entity. The company takes on a separate existence from its owners at the point when it is registered, by filing documents of its purpose and constitution with national authorities. This need not mean that the owner becomes distanced from the everyday running of the business, although some owners do decide to hire professional managers to take over the reins of the company, and confine themselves to making the bigger decisions on strategy.

Any registered company is legally owned by its **shareholders**, also known as stockholders. The whole of a company's shares are its share capital, also known as its **equity**. The shareholder is liable up to the amount invested, and therefore enjoys **limited liability**. Historically, shareholders faced more risk than they do now, as they could be liable for all the firm's debts. The introduction of limited liability made owning shares more attractive as an investment, and paved the way for widespread share ownership by the investing public.

Registered companies may be private or public companies. The **private limited company** resembles the family business in which the owner retains control. It has few shareholders, and these are 'insiders', often related. It is not allowed to sell its shares to the public. It faces fewer requirements for disclosure of its financial position than the public company. Although most are SMEs, many large international businesses are private companies. An example is Bosch, the German engineering company. Private companies are key economic players in Germany and many other countries.

The **public company** offers shares to the public, first in an **initial public offering (IPO)** on a stock exchange. It may call for further capital (in a **rights issue**) when it needs to grow its capital. Its shares are openly traded, and it faces considerable scrutiny of its accounts by national regulators in the country in which it is registered, and in which it lists on a stock exchange. The large, well-known companies that are

▸ More online ... Corporate information about Google is found at http://investor.google.com

major global players are mainly listed public companies, such as Microsoft, Nestlé, BP and Toyota. We tend to think of the large public company as one run by professional managers, but even in these companies, founders' families or other investors can exert control through stakes in the company's equity and board membership, the latter of which is exemplified by Cemex, featured in the closing case study of this chapter. In general, the businessperson who wishes to maintain ownership and control will prefer the advantages of a private company, while one who wishes to attract a wide range of investors will probably convert the business into a public company after a few years as a private company. This was the pattern with Google, which listed after six years. However, Google adopted a dual share structure which kept control in the hands of the founders (see later discussion).

Summary points Companies

◈ Founders of businesses tend to register as limited companies, to gain the benefits of limited liability.

◈ Owners wishing to maintain ownership and control, without the requirements of extensive financial disclosure, choose to do business as private companies.

◈ Because of their publicly traded shares, public companies tend to have a higher profile.

Critical thinking

From entrepreneur to established company

The entrepreneur must think ahead in today's environment, envisaging the kind of company and people that will help the company to stay competitive. Becoming a public company is one of the big decisions, but not necessarily the right route for every company. How does the entrepreneur decide whether and when to go public?

The multinational enterprise (MNE)

Both private and public companies abound in the international environment. As they extend their operations outwards from their home countries, their organizations become more complex. A company can grow 'organically' by increasing its capacity and going into new markets without making major structural changes to the organization. When company executives become more ambitious internationally, they contemplate changes with deeper structural implications. A result has been a thriving global market in corporate ownership and control. As its strategy evolves, a company may buy other companies and sell those it no longer wishes to own. It may also buy stakes in other companies, often as a means of participating in a network of firms, rather than for purely ownership motives. This constant reconfiguration of companies and businesses has become a prominent feature of the international business environment. In these ways, companies can grow relatively quickly internationally and adapt their businesses organizationally as changes in the competitive environment occur. The main organizational arrangement through which these changes take place is the multinational enterprise.

multinational enterprise (MNE) an organization which acquires ownership or other contractual ties in other organizations (including companies and unincorporated businesses) outside its home country

The **multinational enterprise (MNE)** is a broad term signifying a lead company (the parent company) which has acquired ownership or other contractual ties in other organizations (including companies and unincorporated businesses) outside its home country. The parent company co-ordinates and controls (in varying

► More online ... ArcelorMittal's website is www.arcelormittal.com

transnational corporation (TNC) a company which owns and controls operations in one or more countries other than its home country

degrees) the international business activities carried out by all the organizations within the MNE's broad control. The term **transnational corporation (TNC)** is often used interchangeably with MNE, and has been used in previous editions of this book. The TNC is defined as a company which owns and controls operations in one or more countries other than its home country, including both companies and unincorporated enterprises (United Nations, 2008a). MNE has been the favoured term in this edition, as the notion of 'enterprise' is broader than 'corporation', recognizing the growing organizational diversity of international business.

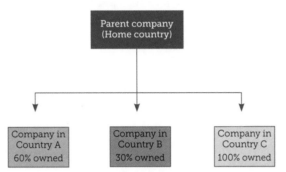

Figure 1.2 **The multinational enterprise (MNE)**

The MNE as an organizational form is not a strictly legal category, but it is recognized as central in international business organization and has been a key driver of globalization, discussed in the next chapter. The term covers businesses of all sizes, from SMEs to global companies with hundreds of thousands of employees. It covers private companies as well as public ones. Typically, the parent company located in the home country co-ordinates the activities of other companies in the group, known broadly as **affiliates**. The parent company can exert strong control, or it can operate on a loosely co-ordinated basis, delegating much decision-making to local managers. Its approach depends largely on the ownership structure of affiliates. A simple MNE is shown in Figure 1.2. In the figure, only the company in Country C is wholly owned and controlled. It is thus a **subsidiary company**. The parent has a 60% equity stake in the company in Country A, making it also a subsidiary, as this gives the parent a controlling stake. If a parent company holds a stake of at least 10% in another company, that other company is generally considered to be an affiliate. Thus, the 30% stake in the company in Country B makes this company an affiliate. MNEs can have quite complex webs of affiliates, and in some countries, especially in Japan and South Korea, affiliates own shares in each other, known as 'cross-shareholding', thereby giving the parent company effective control over an affiliate even though it might own only a small stake itself.

affiliates organizations connected through ownership or other strategic ties to an MNE

subsidiary company a company owned wholly or substantially by another company, which is in a position to exert control

The MNE parent company is likely to be registered in its home country, and its subsidiaries registered in the countries where they carry out their activities. Hence, the subsidiary can be viewed as a 'local' company, even if controlled by a foreign parent. In some countries, foreign investors are not permitted by law to own 100% of a local company, but a sizeable stake can bring considerable power. In another twist, a private parent company can control subsidiaries which are publicly listed in their countries of operation (an example is the steel company ArcelorMittal). Managing subsidiaries in different country environments is one of the major challenges for today's international managers. The rise of MNEs from developing and emerging economies is one of the trends highlighted in this book, beginning with the closing case study of this chapter on Cemex of Mexico.

Next, we look at the roles and responsibilities within these different types of organization, which help us to understand the dynamic processes in play in these enterprises.

Summary points **The MNE**

● The MNE covers a range of organizational arrangements, but is usually organized as a parent company and subsidiaries.

● A subsidiary is a company which is at least 50% owned by a parent company.

● An affiliate company is one in which a parent company has a significant equity stake, but short of majority ownership.

Who controls the organization?

The sole trader or sole owner of a company may well take all the major decisions regarding the business, unfettered by the wishes of other owners and not account-able to anyone else within the business. Still, even a micro-enterprise has stake-holders, in that it exists in a community, has customers, makes an environmental impact and must comply with regulatory authorities. In the private company, there are typically only a few shareholders, often members of the same family. This does not necessarily make for smooth decision-making. Some of the fiercest corporate battles are between family members inside companies. In a public company, the public is invited to subscribe for shares. However, only a small proportion of the share capital need be offered to the public, and it is not uncommon for even a public company to be family dominated. This is often achieved by having a dual share structure whereby founders' shares carry more voting rights than ordinary shares (they are weighted ten to one in Google, for example). The shareholder who buys the company's shares is providing capital to enable it to function. The larger the stake (that is, holding of shares), the more influence the shareholder will expect to exert, although in practice, controlling interests may make this difficult. A share in a company carries certain rights, including the right to receive dividends and (normally) vote in annual general meetings. Importantly, the shareholder is a 'member' of the company, whereas the creditor of the company is not.

The shareholder can be an individual or an organization. A company can be a shareholder in another company, as is often the case with parent companies and subsidiaries. Financial institutions, such as pension funds, are some of the largest global shareholders, with huge sums to invest. A recent trend has been the increase in government ownership of companies, both directly and through investment companies formed for the purpose. In the recent past, it was relatively easy to distin-guish between the state-owned enterprise and one in private hands. Nowadays, the boundaries have become blurred. We see state players acting through a range of companies, including public companies whose shares are traded on stock exchanges. The main ways in which governments own and control enterprises are:

- *Full ownership and control* – This is the traditional state-owned company, which acts like a limb of government and whose finances are managed by the govern-ment. These are sometimes referred to as nationalized industries. State-owned

▶ More online ... EDF's corporate website is www.edf.com/the-edf-group
The OECD's Principles of Corporate Governance can be found at www.oecd.org

companies have been major players in the economic development of many countries, including China and India. It should be remembered, however, that their political systems are very different: China is governed on authoritarian lines, and India is the world's largest democracy (see discussion in Chapter 7).

- *Partial ownership and degrees of control* – The government may choose to **privatize** a state-owned enterprise by registering it as a public company and selling off a proportion of shares to the public, while retaining a large stake and a controlling interest. This process creates a hybrid organization in culture and outlook, neither wholly public sector nor wholly commercial. An example is Electricité de France (EDF), which is now registered as a public company in which 13% of the shares are owned by private investors. Gazprom, the former Russian gas ministry, is another example. It is now majority-owned by the Russian government, and its free-floating shares are traded on the London Stock Exchange.

- *Creation of* **sovereign wealth funds** *and other investment vehicles* – Many governments operate through sovereign wealth funds to invest in a range of global companies, examined further in Chapter 9. Asian countries and oil-rich Middle Eastern countries are prominent among the states that have created these investment vehicles, which are active in global financial markets.

- *Government purchase of stakes in failing companies* – Some governments have become shareholders almost by default, through bailouts of troubled firms with public money. The US government felt compelled to pump taxpayers' money into some banks and car manufacturers during the financial crisis of 2008–9. In these cases, the government had no positive wish to run these enterprises, and would greatly have preferred that their managers could have found market solutions to their problems. The bailouts were a last resort, and these companies, including the carmaker General Motors (GM), are restructuring themselves as leaner, more competitive, companies. As the world's pre-eminent market economy, the US has had to rethink issues of market regulation and accountability of managers.

Accountability of managers in any company is ultimately to its owners, the shareholders. This underlying principle is the basis of the company's decision-making at the highest level, known as its **corporate governance**. Corporate governance differs from business to business, and is influenced by national economic, social, cultural and legal environments. It reflects broader perspectives on the company's role in society, which have come under the spotlight in the wider debate on corporate governance and CSR in recent years. A company's own heritage and corporate culture influence its corporate governance, both formally and informally. National governments are in a position to set legal requirements for corporate governance, as part of their company law and financial regulation frameworks. However, many would prefer to lay down broad principles rather than prescriptive frameworks, in the belief that a one-size-fits-all approach is not appropriate. The UK's Combined Code of Corporate Governance takes this approach. The **Organisation for Economic Co-operation and Development (OECD)**, which was established by representatives of the world's main developed economies in 1960, has been active in giving guidance on corporate governance. The OECD's overarching principles support market economies and democratic institutions. It has published Principles of Corporate Governance, which are intended to guide MNEs generally on best practice (OECD, 2004). These appear in Table 1.1.

privatization process of transforming a state-owned enterprise into a public company and selling off a proportion of shares to the public, usually while retaining a stake and a controlling interest by the government

sovereign wealth fund entity controlled by a government, which invests state funds and pursues an investment strategy; often active global financial markets

corporate governance a company's structures and processes for decision-making at the highest level

Organisation for Economic Co-operation and Development (OECD) organization of the world's main developed economies, which supports market economies and democratic institutions

directors people
appointed by the
company to bear
ultimate responsibility for
the company's activities

Although the senior executives are probably the most influential people in the company, the highest legal authority is its board of directors. **Directors** bear ultimate responsibility for the company's activities. Collectively, they constitute the board of directors accountable to the company's shareholders. Structures differ from country to country. In Germany and other European countries, a two-tier board of directors is the norm. A supervisory board holds the ultimate authority for major decisions, while a management board is the 'engine of management' (Charkham, 1994). The single board is the norm in the Anglo-American type of structure. It is based on the belief that shareholders' interests are the primary focus of the company. The supervisory board in the two-tier system includes employee representation, reflecting the principle of **co-determination** The two-tier model is often said to represent a stakeholder approach to governance, in contrast to the focus on shareholder value which characterizes the single-tier model. However, co-determination in practice reflects the interests of groups of employees in the home country of the company (through their trade unions), rather than a broader stakeholder perspective.

co-determination
principle of stakeholder
participation in corporate
governance, usually
involving a two-tier
board, with employee
representation on the
supervisory board

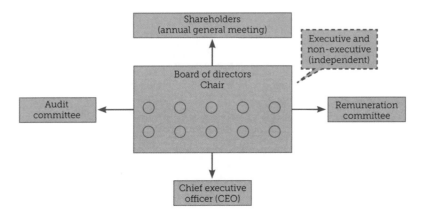

Figure 1.3 **The single-tier board of directors**

executive directors
directors who actively
manage the company

**chief executive officer
(CEO)** the company's
senior executive, who
oversees its management
and is accountable to
the board of directors

non-executive directors
part-time company
directors who are
independent of the firm's
management and owners

The directors who actively manage the company are its **executive directors**, headed by a **chief executive officer (CEO)**. The CEO occupies a pivotal role in decision-making and management of the company. The CEO must answer to the board, maintain the confidence of shareholders, inspire the company's workforce and deal with an array of stakeholders. Whenever the company's fortunes take a turn for the worse, the CEO is in the firing line. We highlight a wide variety of CEOs, in differing corporate and market environments, in the feature 'Meet the CEO' in each chapter of this book.

The boardroom is more relaxed for the **non-executive directors**, who are independent of the firm's management and owners. The non-executive director occupies a part-time role and, in theory, exerts more objective judgment on the company's activities than working managers do. On the other hand, knowledge about the business is now seen as necessary, following the 2008 financial crisis, in which directors' collective failure to curb excessive risk has been highlighted (Kirkpatrick, 2009). The onus is on non-executives to take their responsibilities seriously, and actively query the CEO over strategy. Nowadays, non-executives are keenly aware that, as board members, they are equally liable legally for corporate wrongdoing which they ought to have been aware of. There has been a tendency to appoint other CEOs and retired CEOs as non-executive directors. This approach is now changing as uncritical boards have been implicated in a number of situations where misguided strategies and excessive executive rewards were allowed to go unchecked. An example is Enron, the energy trading company which collapsed in 2001. Enron had a corporate governance system which looked admirable on paper. However, its senior executives were able to steer the company towards their own goals, and the bodies that should have provided a check on their actions (such as the board and its committees) failed to do so. Legislation in the US, in the form of the Sarbanes-Oxley Act of 2002, focused on liability and penalties for false financial reporting, but did not address structural issues of governance. More recently, excessive risk-taking is blamed in a series of bank failures in 2008, including Lehman Brothers of the US, once the country's fourth-largest investment bank, which collapsed under a mountain of $60 billion in bad debts (see Chapter 9 for a further discussion). Other banks, deemed to be too big to fail, such as Citigroup, were rescued by government bailouts, but public confidence in corporate governance had suffered, and regulatory reform was again perceived as necessary.

It is generally thought that a 'balanced' board, consisting of both executive and independent directors, representing both insider and outsider perspectives, constitutes best practice. A proportion of independent directors is usually recommended in national codes of corporate governance and in the OECD's Principles of Corporate Governance (see Table 1.1). It is usually thought to be good practice to separate the roles of chairman of the board and CEO, and to appoint a non-executive director as chairman. However, many companies, particularly American ones, combine the roles in a single person. An example is Cemex, featured in the closing case study, where the current chairman and CEO, who is the grandson of the founder, has held both offices since 1985.

Table 1.1 **Corporate governance principles recommended by the OECD**

Principle	The corporate governance framework should:
I	• Promote transparent and efficient markets • Be consistent with the rule of law • Identify responsibilities of different regulatory and supervisory authorities
II	• Protect and facilitate the exercise of shareholder rights
III	• Ensure the equitable treatment of all shareholders, including minority and foreign shareholders
IV	• Recognize the rights of stakeholders established by law or through mutual agreements • Encourage active co-operation between corporations and stakeholders in creating wealth, jobs, and the sustainability of financially sound enterprises
V	• Ensure that timely and accurate disclosure is made on all material matters regarding the corporation, including the financial situation, performance, ownership, and governance
VI	Board responsibilities: • Monitor management effectively • Align key executive and board remuneration with the longer term interests of the company and shareholders • Consider a sufficient number of non-executive board members capable of exercising independent judgment

Source: OECD (2004) OECD Principles of Corporate Governance, at www.oecd.org

Although shareholders as owners are, in theory, paramount in corporate decision-making, ordinary shareholders themselves have tended to have little direct influence in a number of important matters, such as executive remuneration and appointment

MEET THE CEO

▸ More online ... Carlsberg's website is www.carlsberg.com

Guido Zegna CEO of Italian luxury group, Zegna

As the fourth-generation head of his family's luxury menswear group, Guido Zegna attributes the company's success to discipline and respect among the numerous family members who continue to run the company. Founded by his grandfather, the first Ermenegildo Zegna, in 1910, Zegna was originally a textile company and still has a weaving business. It expanded into the ready-to-wear sector in the 1960s, and now offers a number of different brands for differing consumer markets. Recent additions are sportier lines, Z Zegna and Zegna Sport, which are aimed at affluent under-30s in global markets. The company also offers womenswear and home furnishings. Eighty-eight per cent of the company's sales are exports. Zegna sells most of its products through its own retail outlets, which number over 500 worldwide. In recent years, established markets, such as the US and Japan, have seen sales slump, and sales in Russia have also been weak. On the bright side, sales in China grew 30% in 2008, and in the Middle East, 50%. Asia is now 40% of the company's global business, up from 25% in 2007. Zegna says: 'What we used to call the emerging markets have emerged' (Menkes, 2009).

Zegna views the presence of family members in key posts as responsible for the company's long success. He speculates that, were the company a public one, payouts might have been greater in the boom years of the early 2000s, but he says: 'Because we are all family we were very thrifty and kept the money for the business. We have a very long-term view' (Friedman, 2009). A cousin is the group chairman, and Guido's sister, Anna, is the company's image director. There are nearly a dozen younger family members eyeing jobs in the family business, but Guido Zegna says: 'We have adopted the corporate governance of a public company, and one of our rules is that before any member of the family can even begin at the family company they must have a college degree, they must speak one other language other than Italian – English – fluently, and they must have worked for eight years outside the family business' (Friedman).

The company has also adopted market research methods which are usually employed by public companies. This way, they can see customer preferences in different markets, and respond quickly. Guido Zegna says they find that menswear brands are more stable than womenswear brands, as customers are more loyal (Menkes). Listening to the customer is crucial to continued success. But, he says, 'our core values are our people. And we have to react quickly to change of lifestyle' (Menkes). Zegna celebrated its centenary in 2010, but the family remains focused on the future. Guido Zegna maintains that after the newer emerging markets such as Egypt, Morocco and India, 'luxury's new frontier is Africa' (Menkes).

Sources: Menkes, S. (2009) 'Zegna explores new markets in face of downturn', *New York Times*, 23 June; Friedman, V. (2009) 'Men's wear champion sets trend', *Financial Times*, 6 July; Zegna, A. (2010) 'Ethics and quality can go hand-in-hand', *Financial Times*, 20 February

Looking good, whatever the setting. As a family business, Zegna has prided itself on designs for changing lifestyles and new markets

Source: Istock

of directors. The CEO of Lehman Brothers, who received remuneration of $484.8 million between 2000 and 2008, when the company went bankrupt, faced stern questioning from US legislators in public hearings, mirroring widespread public disgust. European companies are required to hold a vote on executive remuneration, but this requirement is weak, as the vote is not binding. The practice of paying huge rewards to executives of poorly performing (or even failed) companies is now coming under the spotlight. The OECD is reviewing its Principles, last revised in 2004, strengthening those on accountability of directors and checks on executive pay (Kirkpatrick, 2009). The trend that has seen growing share ownership by governments, whether by design or default, is a factor in the corporate governance debate. A government is not an 'ordinary' shareholder, but is usually expected to uphold public interest. However, governments differ, just as countries and political systems differ, and these differences are reflected in how active a role they play and for what purposes.

Summary points Corporate decision-making

◆ Decision-makers in a company are its directors, who are accountable to the shareholders as owners.

◆ In practice, the CEO and other executive directors are the main decision-makers.

◆ Non-executive directors, in theory, play an important independent role in monitoring decision-makers. However, in practice, their willingness to stand up to executives can sometimes be questioned.

Critical thinking
Power and responsibility within the company
Boards of directors have been the targets of criticism in recent years, as having been 'asleep on the job' when managers were pursuing risky strategies which undermined shareholder value. What steps should companies take to give boards more effective oversight of corporate decision-making?

Functions within the enterprise

functions activities of a business which form part of the overall process of providing a product for a customer

Every business, whether large or small, involves a number of different types of activity, or **functions**, which form part of the overall process of providing a product for a customer. Physical resources, including plant, machinery and offices, must be organized and functions such as finance, purchasing and marketing must be co-ordinated, to enable the entire enterprise to function smoothly as a unit. Every business carries out basic functions, such as finance, even though in a small business, it is unlikely to hire specialists in each area, whereas a large organization has separate departments. The importance of particular functions depends in part on the type of business. Product design and production, along with research and development, feature mainly in manufacturing firms, whereas all firms have need of finance, HRM and marketing functions. They cover the entire life of a product, from the design stage to the delivery of a final product to the customer. They even extend beyond the sale, to include after-sales service and recycling. The main functions are set out in Figure 1.4.

In Figure 1.4, the headings in the rectangles represent the co-ordinating activities. The company's overall strategy determines what its goals are, and central managers must co-ordinate all the firm's activities to achieve those goals. We look at the part played by each of these functions in turn:

finance and accounting
business function which concerns control over the revenues and outgoings of the business, aiming to balance the books and to generate sufficient profits for the future health of the firm

operations the entire process of producing and delivering a product to a consumer; covers tangible goods and services, and often a combination of both

human resource management (HRM) all aspects of the management of people in the organization, including recruitment, training, and rewarding the workforce

marketing satisfying the needs and expectations of customers; includes a range of related activities, such as product offering, branding, advertising, pricing, and distribution of goods

- **Finance and accounting** – This function concerns control over the revenues and outgoings of the business, aiming to balance the books and to generate sufficient profits for the future health of the firm. This function is far more complex in large public companies than in SMEs. Trends towards more innovative finance and international operations have called for considerable professional expertise. At the same time, as discussed earlier, legal duties of financial reporting and disclosure are now increasingly under the spotlight. The company's chief financial officer (CFO) is a board member, and many go on to become CEO.

- **Operations** – Operations cover the entire process of producing and delivering a product to a consumer. It covers tangible goods and services, and often a combination of both. Production focuses on the operational processes by which products are manufactured. Production increasingly relies on sophisticated machinery and computerized systems. Quality, safety and efficiency are major concerns of production engineers and managers. A recent trend has been for manufacturing to take place in low-cost locations, often outsourced by a large MNE. The MNE, however, will still wish to maintain quality, even if a licensed manufacturer is making the product. Quality and safety have become more challenging as manufacturing has shifted to diverse locations (discussed in the next chapter).

- **Human resource management (HRM)** – Formerly known as 'personnel management', HRM focuses on all aspects of the management of people in the organization, including recruitment, training, and rewarding the workforce. In the large, hierarchical organization, these activities are formally structured, whereas in the small organization, they tend to be carried out informally, with less paperwork and less reliance on formal procedures. Organizations have become sensitive to the need to take into account the individual employee's own goals and development, as well as the needs of the company. An issue that arises in the MNE is how to adapt HR strategy and policies to differing countries where its subsidiary employees are located. Each country has its own set of employment laws, and in each country, social and cultural factors play important roles in work values and practices. International HR managers increasingly realize the fact that motivating staff in different locations requires differing approaches and reward systems.

- **Marketing** – Marketing focuses on satisfying the needs and expectations of customers. Marketing covers a range of related activities, including product offering,

Figure 1.4 **Business functions in the organizational environment**

branding, advertising, pricing, and distribution of goods. The large MNE might be assumed to devise a global marketing strategy for all markets, but, in fact, MNEs now tend to adapt products and marketing communications to differing country markets. Language, religion and values are all aspects of culture which affect consumer preferences in different markets (discussed further in Chapter 6). As MNEs turn their focus to the large emerging markets, especially China and India, they encounter considerable cultural diversity. These are some of the greatest challenges in international marketing, but their market potential makes them attractive opportunities.

research and development (R&D) seeking new knowledge and applications which can lead to new and improved products or processes

innovation activities which seek improvements and new ways of doing things

- **Research and Development (R&D)** – R&D is the function of seeking new knowledge and applications which can lead to new and improved products or processes. R&D activities are part of the larger focus on innovation in the company. **Innovation** covers the full range of activities carried out by all within the organization to seek improvements and new ways of doing things, which can enhance competitiveness. (Innovation is discussed fully in Chapter 10.) R&D tends to focus on scientific and technical research, which is key to new product development. Pharmaceutical companies typically spend huge sums on R&D, as new medicines are their chief source of profits. For the media or internet company, innovation relies on creating new content (often adapted to new markets) and new ways of delivering content to the consumer.

Each of the business functions adapts and changes as a business expands internationally, as shown in the following examples:

- Financial reporting will involve different regulatory environments and accounting standards. Operations will be linked in global production networks.
- HRM will adapt to different cultures and laws.
- Marketing strategy will be designed for differing markets.
- R&D will be configured in different locations according to specialist skills in each.

For the international manager, understanding the differing cultural environments where the company operates, together with the various functional activities that take place in each unit, is crucial to the overall achievement of the company's goals. A company's approach to these challenges depends heavily on its own background and ways of engaging with other cultures, as we find in the next section.

Summary points Business functions

- The main business functions are finance and accounting, operations, HRM, marketing and R&D.
- In a small firm, functions are typically carried out by staff who are mainly generalists, but the large organization has specialist departments.
- Functional strategies and policies in the MNE tend to be determined by the head office, but in the decentralized organization, there is much autonomy at local level.
- Some functions, such as R&D, are now seen as best located in the environment where the research skills are located.

The firm's view on the world

A company might aspire to be a global leader in its field, and might have technologically superior products, but it must still organize global production efficiently and offer attractive products to consumers at keen prices in a wide variety of different national markets. Some companies have proved themselves to be adept in meeting these challenges, while others struggle. The company tends to see the world at least

▶ More online ... The transnationality index can be found at the website of the
UN Conference on Trade and Development (UNCTAD) at www.unctad.org

partly through the eyes of its own country's national culture. How does this affect its success internationally?

Perspectives on other cultures, held by both individuals and organizations, vary from the ethnocentric at one extreme to the polycentric at the other. The **ethnocentric** organization has an unquestioning belief that its own national culture and ways of doings things are the best. A strong sense of national power can be a source of this outlook, along with a view that the country's culture and history have helped to make it a world leader. Companies based in the US and Japan are usually cited as ethnocentric. The ethnocentric company tends to be dominated by the head office in its home country, which takes the major strategic decisions. Japanese companies have been noted for modelling all their foreign operations on those in their home country, overseen by experienced managers sent from Japan. However, these companies have adapted their manufacturing methods to differing cultures as their operations have become internationalized. This apparent shift might reflect the focus in Japanese management practices on harmony and employee involvement.

ethnocentric an unquestioning belief that one's own national culture and ways of doings things are the best

The **polycentric** organization is one which is open to other cultures and ways of doing things. It accepts that its own cultural assumptions are a part of its background, but strives to understand and work with those in other countries as it becomes international in scope. The polycentric company appreciates the need for cross-cultural skills in international business (discussed in Chapter 6). Small, open countries are often cited as those which tend to have more polycentric organizations. A transnationality index has been compiled by the UN Conference on Trade and Development (UNCTAD) every year since 1995. It surveys the relative importance of foreign assets, employees and revenues for individual companies. Those ranked the highest have the highest proportions of foreign over home weightings in each category. The top ten companies are shown in Table 1.2, with the addition of a few other notable companies in the rankings.

polycentric openness to other cultures and ways of doing things

Table 1.2 **Transnationality index**

Transnationality ranking	Company	Home country	Industry	Transnationality index (%)
1	Barrick Gold Mining	Canada	Mining	94
2	Xtrata	UK	Mining	92
3	Linde	Germany	Industrial and construction	89
4	Pernod Ricard	France	Beverages	87
5	WPP	UK	Business services	87
6	Liberty Global	US	Telecommunications	85
7	Vodafone	UK	Telecommunications	85
8	Philips Electronics	Netherlands	Electricals and electronics	85
9	Nestlé	Switzerland	Food and beverages	83
10	Hutchinson Whampoa	Hong Kong (China)	Telecommunications	83
Selected others				
11	Honda	Japan	Motor vehicles	82
71	General Electric	US	Electricals and electronics	53
87	Toyota	Japan	Motor vehicles	45
92	Walmart	US	Retailing	41

Source: UN (2008) *World Investment Report 2008* (Geneva: UN)

As can be seen, only one US company is in the top ten, and no Japanese companies, although Honda, the Japanese carmaker, is ranked eleven. Honda has been highly successful internationally. It is generally felt that the polycentric firm is better able to succeed in international business than the ethnocentric one, as its managers are better able to adapt to local conditions. These firms, however, tend to be more decentralized, giving latitude to local managers, which can make it more difficult for them to pursue global strategic goals. In this respect, therefore, the ethnocentric firm might have an edge, as it imposes its own systems on all subsidiaries, and maintains a strong corporate culture, which tends to override the national cultures of local subsidiaries.

A third category is the geocentric organization, which lies between the ethnocentric and polycentric approaches. The **geocentric** organization aims to focus on global corporate goals, but allowing for local responses and adaptation (Perlmutter, 1969). The geocentric approach sees the differing local environments as a potential source of value, rather than as an obstacle to be overcome, and aims to recognize local inputs within a global perspective.

geocentric organization which aims to focus on global corporate goals, but allowing for local responses and adaptation

Summary points **The firm's view on the world**

● The ethnocentric firm views the world through the values and norms of its own national culture, tending to impose these ways of thinking on foreign operations and markets.

● The polycentric firm is open to different cultures, seeking to understand foreign operations and markets in terms of their distinctive cultural environments.

● The geocentric firm aims to balance central control with adaptation to cultural differences in diverse locations.

Critical thinking

The company's world vision

Think of some companies you are familiar with, for example as a frequent customer. Which ones are ethnocentric, and which are polycentric? Which of these companies are more successful in the current competitive environment?

The enterprise in the international environment

The opening case study of this chapter featured a number of aspects of the environment which impact on companies and pose challenges for managers. Among these were the cultural and political environments. These dimensions of the environment stem largely from the characteristics which go to make up societies: every society has a cultural heritage, a social makeup, distinctive economic activities, political arrangements, one or more legal frameworks and technological capacities. A description of each of these aspects of a society gives a picture of the society as a whole. However, these dimensions do not stop at national borders. Any dimension will have a layered perspective in terms of geography. For example, the political environment is made up of local community, national government and international relations. These are shown in Figure 1.5. For enterprises, it is necessary to see both the small picture, such as local politics, as well as the big picture, which might be the country's position in relation to trading partners. In fact, understanding the big picture sometimes helps in understanding local currents, and vice versa. Thus, local political leaders could well be influential in attracting a foreign investor wishing to build a factory, from a country with which the national government has concluded a trade and investment agreement. We first identify the dimensions and layers.

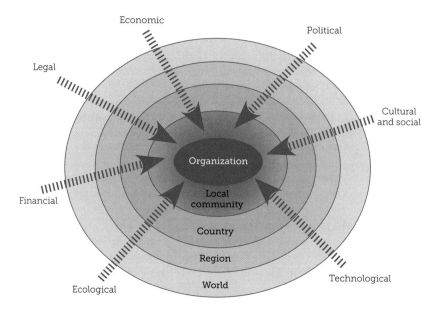

Figure 1.5 **The dimensions and layers of the international environment**

Multiple dimensions

PEST analysis of a national environment which stands for political, economic, social and technological dimensions

Dimensions of the environment are shown in Figure 1.5. These key dimensions can be grouped in a **PEST** analysis, which stands for political, economic, social and technological dimensions. Detailed elements of the PEST framework are shown in Table 1.3.

To make the PEST analysis more complete, the legal environment is considered with the political, and the cultural environment is taken with the social, making it the sociocultural environment. This book recognizes the usefulness of the latter combination, as reflected in Chapter 6. However, we focus on the political and legal environments separately (in Chapters 7 and 8), highlighting the interconnections between the two dimensions. We also add the financial environment and ecological environment, in Chapters 9 and 11. They occur in Part 4, on global issues, as these are areas which have grown in global significance. The technological environment, also highly globalized, falls in Part 4 for the same reason. All these dimensions interact to some extent. The PEST analysis, therefore, is a blunt tool for understanding societies. It also tends to take a rather static view, not capturing changes over time. In this book, we aim to do both: to look at background forces and changes taking place. In many instances, there is tension between established norms and institutions, on the one hand, and, on the other, newer forces seeking to bring about changes – often changes emanating from outside the country. Bearing these dynamics in mind, we describe each of these dimensions below:

- *Cultural and social environment* – covers values, attitudes, norms of behaviour and social relations among people who can be identified as a coherent group. Cultures are usually grouped as national cultures, which are held together by language, a historical sense of belonging and a loyalty to a national homeland. As

Table 1.3 **PEST Analysis in the international business environment**

Political and legal
• Political stability • Form of government, for example democratic, authoritarian • Level of freedoms, for example freedom of expression and association • Incentives to foreign investors • Competition law and policy • Employment law
Economic
• Level of economic development • Trends in GDP • Rate of inflation • Wage levels and level of unemployment • Strength of currency and convertibility • Rates of taxation
Sociocultural
• Growth rate of population, and age distribution of population • Language(s) • Main religious and cultural groupings • Educational attainment levels • Level of social cohesion • Role of·women
Technological
• Government spending on R&D • Legal regime for patent protection • Energy availability and costs • Transport infrastructure and costs • Innovation system, including availability of skilled workforce • Level of technology transfer

indicated above, however, national cultures are only part of a person's identity. Religions, which have adherents worldwide, may play an important part. Lifestyle, such as modern consumer lifestyle is also relevant to people, and lifestyle reflects many aspects of a person's life apart from national culture, such as age, education, and whether he or she lives in an urban or rural setting.

• *Economic environment* – covers the kind of economic activities that make up people's livelihoods, the country's sources of wealth and the extent of the country's industrialization. The economy's growth rate is an indicator of the economy's overall health, as is its ability to provide new jobs for those coming into the labour market each year. Key to creating jobs is whether the country is attracting foreign companies wishing to set up business. This foreign direct investment (discussed in the next chapter) has been a major driver of globalization, which has brought economic growth to many developing economies.

• *Political environment* – covers the country's system of government and the powerful groups and individuals who shape the way it operates in practice. All businesses, domestic and foreign, seek a stable political environment, preferably one which encourages enterprise activities. In some countries, political power is concentrated, and in others, democratic processes are more influential in determining who wields political power. The existence of freedom of expression for individuals and media is also an indication of the type of political environment in a country.

- *Legal environment* – covers the system of laws within a country, backed up by the authority of the state. It covers how laws are made and how they are enforced in practice. In any country, businesses look for clarity and predictability in the laws that pertain to them, with fair, impartial implementation and enforcement. These characteristics indicate the existence of the rule of law in a country. Where a country is fragmented, with differing law-making authorities in separate regions, instability can result, making it more difficult to do business in the country, especially for foreign firms unfamiliar with the differing authorities.

- *Technological environment* – covers the nature and extent of applied scientific knowledge, which is used for practical purposes. The depth of a country's scientific education and training, and the extent of government funding for R&D are indicators of the country's technological environment. It is important for businesses that new products and inventions are protected in law. These assets are referred to as **intangible assets**, as they represent rights over products, which can be exploited. They can be contrasted with **tangible assets**, which are physical assets such as machinery and stock. Intangible assets are protected by laws relating to **intellectual property (IP)**. They include patents for the firm's inventions, copyright for written works, music, film and software, and trademarks, such as company logos. As countries climb the technological ladder, the protection and enforcement of IP rights are demanded by businesses (discussed in Chapter 10).

- *Financial environment* – covers banking and other financial services which serve other businesses as well as consumers. National financial systems differ in their openness to outsiders, their transparency and their levels of regulation. Most countries' financial systems have become more open in recent years to outside investors such as foreign banks wishing to set up operations in the country or invest in domestic companies. However, financial markets are prone to volatility, and investors look to well-capitalized banks and sound regulatory systems to maintain confidence and stability. When confidence wanes in one part of the world, it can quickly spread across financial institutions in other parts of the world, as the crisis of 2008 demonstrated.

- *Ecological environment* – covers all living things and relationships between them in their natural habitats. Environmental degradation in today's world has been caused substantially by human activity, especially through industrialization, urbanization and modern large-scale agriculture. Businesses are gaining greater knowledge and awareness of the environmental impacts of their operations in differing locations, as well as their impacts on global phenomena such as climate change.

intangible assets rights over products, such as trademarks and patents, which can be exploited commercially; they can be contrasted with tangible assets

tangible assets physical assets such as machinery and stock

intellectual property (IP) property in intangible assets, such as patents, copyrights and trademarks, which can be legally protected from use by others unless permission is obtained from the owner

Summary points Multiple dimensions

- The PEST analysis takes in four essential aspects of the environment, which can be supplemented by additional elements, including the legal environment as a separate dimension, the financial environment and the ecological environment.

- Each of the dimensions of the environment covers a range of phenomena, including institutions, processes and historical legacies.

- The PEST analysis is a rather blunt instrument in that it underestimates changes over time and interactions with other dimensions.

The multilayered environment

It is common to speak of *global* firms facing competition in the *global* environment, but in fact, global competition is frequently played out in local environments. Local companies, with their intimate knowledge of local markets, can be some of the toughest competitors which global companies encounter. The international environment can be conceived as layered spatial areas, visualized as concentric circles, beginning with the smallest unit, the local community. Local communities exist in the larger unit of the country, which is itself part of a geographic region, and beyond that, the world. These layers are shown in Table 1.4. The table gives examples of key phenomena as well as relevant institutions and organizations in each sphere. There is considerable interaction and interdependence between these different spheres as countries and regions become more interconnected. Growing connectedness

Table 1.4 **Dimensions and layers of the international environment**

Layers and dimensions	Local community	Country	Region	World
Cultural and social	Families; local customs; schools; urban or rural	National culture; language; sense of shared history	Cultural affinity across the region; movement of people between countries	Human rights; world religions; consumer culture
Economic	Local businesses; predominant industries	National industries; industrial structure; national income and economic growth	Degree of economic integration; regional trade relations	Global economic integration; WTO and multilateral trade agreements; global companies and industries
Political	Local government and politics	Political system; degree of civil and political freedoms	Degree of political co-operation; shared institutions (for example the EU)	International governmental co-operation (for example the UN)
Legal	Delegated law-making; planning; health and safety	Rule of law; independent judiciary and court system; national legislation	Legal harmonization; mutual recognition of court judgments	International law and the International Court of Justice (ICJ)
Technological	Schools and colleges; research centres	National school system; universities; government funding for R&D	Cross-border research ties; co-operation among universities	Global spread of breakthrough technology; global R&D networks
Financial	Penetration of banks and financial services	National financial system; regulatory system	Cross-border financial flows; regional regulation (for example the European Central Bank)	Global financial flows; international institutions (for example the IMF and World Bank)
Ecological	Ecosystems; pollution levels; air quality	Areas of environmental stress; environmental protection laws	Regional institutions; co-operation over regional resources (for example rivers)	Climate change; international co-operation on emissions reduction

between people and organizations is a quintessential aspect of globalization, discussed in the next chapter. It is tempting to fall for the view that all aspects of the business environment are inevitably moving towards the global, but this would be a mistake. Some aspects of the international environment seem to be moving towards global governance, such as financial regulation, but each layer of the environment has its own characteristics and players. Although they are becoming interconnected, they are not melding together into a whole, but retain distinctiveness, which business strategists ignore at their peril.

We look at each of these layers from the perspective of the business:

- *Local community* – Wherever the MNE operates, there will be a local community in which its impacts are immediate. A factory or other industrial process impacts on local people and the natural environment in the area. As an employer, it can bring jobs and wealth, but its impact on the environment is potentially damaging. These are stakeholder issues which involve dialogue within local communities.
- *Country* – The national environment is probably the most influential for a business. National laws cover company regulation, employment conditions and the environment. A country's national culture is influential in strategic decisions about potential markets and location of operations. A country's political system and leadership decide the policies which determine how stable it will be for foreign business investors.
- *Region* – Every country is located in a region and is drawn into relations with neighbouring countries. These relations can give rise to conflicts – regional wars are sadly not uncommon. But relations are more often beneficial. Regional trade agreements have flourished in recent years, allowing for free movement of goods between countries in the region. The European Union (EU) is the most highly developed regional grouping (discussed in Chapter 3). Regions can pool resources to deal with common threats such as climate change.
- *World* – There is increasing awareness of global phenomena, such as climate change, which require co-operation among all players, both businesses and governments, at all levels. To co-ordinate this co-operation, global regulatory frameworks are emerging. This is happening in respect of climate change. It is also happening in the area of human rights and financial regulation. Although national structures have been dominant in these areas, international frameworks are gaining authority. The international organizations highlighted in Table 1.4 are introduced in the next chapter. Business strategists are now looking beyond national regulation to rule-making at international level.

Summary points Multiple layers

- The international enterprise encounters a range of distinctive geographical environments, beginning with the community and moving outward to the country, region and global environments.

- There is interaction and inter-dependence between these layers.
- Each environmental dimension, such as the political environment, is observable in each of these layers.

- In some areas, such as financial regulation, international rule-making is becoming more important, but national and regional institutions remain pivotal, often acting in conjunction with international organizations.

Critical thinking

The multilayered environment

The MNE must be attuned to the changing environment at local, national, regional and global levels. In many areas, such as climate change, there is potentially conflict between the signals coming from these differing sources. Which should have priority for the MNE, or can it balance all of them?

The enterprise in a dynamic environment

Decisions about what the firm ought to be doing, and how, were discussed in the early sections of this chapter. Here we revisit that process, focusing on the environmental context. The firm's purpose is derived largely from its expertise and experience, usually beginning in its home market. The experience it gains from international expansion can contribute to a redefining of its aims as it grows. This evolution depends, too, on its activities in foreign countries, and the extent to which foreign partners play a part in strategy formation. As we have seen, the polycentric company is likely to be more outward looking and decentralized than the ethnocentric company. On the other hand, ethnocentric companies number among the world's largest and most famous brands. Coca-Cola and McDonald's are two, both of which are in food and beverages, sectors which are noted for differing national preferences. These companies, both US American, grew internationally as their products typified American lifestyle, which has been influential in the growth of consumer societies across the world. They have adapted to local differences in different countries, while maintaining a focus on their global brands. These companies are now pursuing growth strategies in the large emerging markets of China and India. In their home market, where growth has slowed, they are seeking innovations in healthier alternatives to their traditional products, the Big Mac and Classic Coke. As these changes show, strategy is closely linked to the changing environment. When established markets slow, companies aim to pursue new opportunities worldwide.

Large firms have become adept at designing global strategy which takes account of local differences. Indeed, local differences can be turned into a source of competitive advantage for the MNE. We see this thinking behind the decisions of large MNEs to outsource manufacturing in low-cost countries. This trend, discussed further in the next chapter, has had significant impacts in both home and host countries. Consumers in developed countries have benefited from a huge range of products at lower prices than those manufactured in their own countries. Host economies have benefited from the investment of foreign companies, the employment created, and the opportunities to gain valuable technological expertise. The greatest beneficiaries have been the large emerging economies, China in particular.

The geographical scanning of MNEs has had consequences in the ways companies perceive the international environment. Developing countries that host outsourced manufacturing are no longer perceived as remote by brand owners and consumers. Workers in outsourced factories are stakeholders of the MNE, even though not employed by it. The host country's government, too, is a stakeholder, whose law and policies are influential for the MNE. In addition, growing concern at international level regarding human rights has heightened awareness of this issue among the company's most valued stakeholders – its shareholders. For the student of international business, the coming together of global and local forces is one of the aspects of the business environment which is becoming most challenging. International markets offer opportunities for the MNE, but they also pose risks. When rethinking long-term strategy, especially in times of economic downturn, some MNEs find it prudent to curb international expansion and focus on familiar markets close to home. For others, the lure of international expansion, especially in emerging markets, is perceived as a golden opportunity when home markets are becalmed. These divergent approaches are explored in the next chapter.

Summary points The business in its environment

- The company evolves as it branches out into new environments. This is true even of ethnocentric companies.

- Global corporate strategies take account of local conditions and preferences.

- Manufacturing in low-cost countries has boosted economic growth in the large developing countries, and has led to abundant low-cost consumer goods in developed countries.

A symbol of modern consumer society: the glistening new shopping mall is a magnet for shoppers, and can now be found in many different countries, especially the large emerging markets

Source: Istock

Conclusions

1   The business enterprise exists to provide goods or services of value to its customers. It interacts with a range of stakeholders, including employees, consumers, the community and society in general.

2   A business typically starts life as the project of an entrepreneur, who invests energy, creativity and resources into the new enterprise.

3   Owners of businesses register them as companies to obtain the advantages of limited liability. Many remain private companies, especially family firms, but many go on to become public companies, attracting outside investors.

4   The multinational enterprise (MNE), consisting of a parent company and subsidiaries, has become a favoured organizational model for international expansion.

5   The company's chief executive officer (CEO) is accountable to the board of directors, which in turn is accountable to the company's shareholders for how the business is run.

6   Accountability mechanisms within companies are the focus of current debate, prompted by public concerns on issues such as risk strategy and executive pay.

7   The key business functions are carried out by all businesses, but in large companies they take the form of specialist departments. As businesses grow and expand internationally, possibilities emerge for changing location and policies in each functional area.

8   Companies differ in their perspectives on the world. The ethnocentric firm sees the world in terms of its own values, while the polycentric firm is more open to ideas from other cultures. The geocentric firm focuses on both corporate goals and local responses.

9   Multiple dimensions of a national environment can be expressed in terms of the PEST analysis: political, economic, sociocultural and technological environments. However, other important dimensions would include financial, legal and ecological.

10   The firm's external environment can also be visualized in layers: local, national, regional and global. Environmental dimensions, such as the political environment, manifest themselves at each of these levels.

Review questions

1   How does a business decide what its goals will be, and in what markets?

2   Define stakeholders and explain the stakeholder approach to corporate strategy.

3   What is CSR, and why is it becoming more important in the formation of corporate goals?

4   What are the advantages and disadvantages of being a sole trader?

5   What are the aspects of the limited company which distinguish it from other types of business ownership?

6   What is distinctive about the entrepreneurial enterprise?

7   What is distinctive about the MNE as a type of organization?

8   Explain the reasons behind the adoption of multidivisional structure for large companies.

9   How does corporate governance differ from the day-to-day management of a company?

10   Why are independent (non-executive) directors considered essential in corporate governance?

11 Explain the shareholder and stakeholder perspectives on corporate governance.

12 Describe each of the main functions within the business enterprise.

13 The polycentric organization might be thought to be advantageous in international operations, but many successful MNEs have been ethnocentric. Why might this be the case?

14 What are the advantages and limitations of a PEST analysis?

Key revision concepts

Company, p. 15; Corporate governance, p. 19; Corporate social responsibility (CSR), p. 12; Emerging economy/market, p. 8; Entrepreneur, p. 14; Ethnocentric/polycentric organization, p. 26; Intellectual property, p. 30; Market, p. 8; Multinational enterprise, p. 16; PEST analysis, p. 28; Privatization, p. 19; Public company, p. 15; Shareholder, p. 15; Stakeholder, p. 11

Assignments

◆ Offer advice to the following CEO: Tom is the CEO of a large retailing company whose recent financial performance, especially in its established western markets, has been lacklustre. Competitors are gaining ground in large emerging economies, but these can be costly to enter. Tom's board of directors is dominated by members of the founding family who are very risk-averse.

◆ The PEST analysis was designed to illuminate specific dimensions of a national environment. How can it be adapted to take into account other dimensions and broader scope, bringing in regional and global impacts?

Further reading

Bartlett, C. and Ghoshal, S. (2002) *Managing Across Borders: The Transnational Solution*, 2nd edn (Boston: Harvard Business School Press).

Brown, A. (1998) *Organisational Culture*, 2nd edn (London: Pitman).

Johnson, G., Scholes, K. and Whittington, R. (2004) *Exploring Corporate Strategy*, 7th edn (London: Pearson).

Kay, J. (2000) *Foundations of Corporate Success* (Oxford: Oxford University Press).

Mintzberg, H. (2000) *The Rise and Fall of Strategic Planning* (London: Financial Times Prentice Hall).

Monks, R. and Minow, N. (2003) *Corporate Governance* (Oxford: Blackwell).

Mullins, L. (2004) *Management and Organizational Behaviour*, 7th edn (London: Financial Times Prentice Hall).

Prahalad, C.K. (2009) *The Fortune at the Bottom of the Pyramid* (Philadelphia: Wharton School Publishing).

Pugh, D.S. (ed.) (1995) *Organization Theory: Selected Readings*, 4th edn (London: Penguin Books).

Quinn, J., Mintzberg, H., James, R., Lampel, J. and Ghoshal, S. (eds) (2003) *The Strategy Process* (London: Financial Times Prentice Hall).

Wheelen, T. and Hunger, J. (2009) *Strategic Management and Business Policy*, 12th edn (New Jersey: Addison Wesley).

Cemex constructing a brighter future

The opening case study featured a youthful entrepreneurial company, Facebook, which, based in the US, has shot to fame in the fast-moving internet world. Here we turn to an established company, over a hundred years old, based in a poor country, Mexico, in a sector perceived as unglamorous: construction and cement. Perspectives on the sector differ, however. Whereas the rich world views cement as a commodity, and a highly pollutant one at that, in the developing world cement is more valued as a branded product, resonating with people aspiring for improved housing and more comfortable lives. Cemex has long focused on low-cost housing in its home market, alongside financing schemes to bring better housing within the reach of the poor. But it attracts attention mainly for its ambitious global expansion.

Although Cemex's predecessor company was formed in 1906, the formation of Cementos Mexicanos, later changed to Cemex for short, dates from the 1931 merger of two companies under the leadership of Lorenzo Zambrano. The company remained national in scope and relatively unambitious for 35 years, enjoying a privileged position in the rather closed Mexican market for cement and construction materials. But when the Mexican economy gradually opened up in the 1970s, creating more competitive markets, Cemex decided the time was right to embark on expansion by acquisition, both in Mexico and internationally. It listed as a public company on the Mexican stock exchange in 1976. Domestic acquisitions in Mexico propelled it to domination of the Mexican cement market by 1990. But the Zambrano family, which still runs the company, had far greater ambitions in mind. Lorenzo Zambrano, the founder's grandson, took over as chairman and CEO in 1985, posts he still held in 2010.

Cemex is now the world's third largest cement company, after Lafarge of France and Holcim of Switzerland. Cement as a sector relies on building activity to flourish, and its fortunes, along with those of its rivals, can dive when economies slow down and construction declines, as happened in the rich world in the recent recession. As an emerging-market multinational, Cemex has benefited from its experience in a poor developing country to gain advantages in other developing countries.

It has acquired businesses in Spain, throughout Latin America and in Asia, but its most ambitious acquisitions have been in the US and UK (see figure). It has long targeted the US market, where its advantages of an efficient, low-cost approach help to build market share. It purchased Southdown, a Texas company, in 2001, which it combined with existing American operations, making it the largest cement maker in the US. Cemex went on to buy RMC of the UK in 2005. The purchase of Rinker Group of Australia in 2007 was a turning point for Cemex. Cemex had to borrow in the region of $14 billion from banks to finance the purchase, which Zambrano felt was worth it because of Rinker's strong presence in the US. This was despite the fact that the US Justice Department required Cemex to shed 39 ready-mix concrete facilities in the US because of its potentially dominant market position in some localities. The takeover of Rinker was a huge gamble, and the aftermath proved to be a difficult period for the company, as the US housing slump soon followed. Cemex's share price, by now quoted on the New York Stock Exchange, plunged from $37

A business empire built on cement: Cemex has pursued its global ambitions from its solid foundation in Mexico

Source: Cemex

in 2007 to just $4 in 2009. Cemex had to sell Rinker's Australian operations to Holcim in 2009, to help pay down the debt.

A setback occurred in 2008 when Venezuela nationalized Cemex's operations in the country. Other cement makers settled compensation terms with the Venezuelan government, but Cemex held out for a better deal. Despite the setbacks, in 2010, Zambrano was upbeat about the company's ability to manage the debt and revitalize the business. He has contemplated selling minority stakes in some of the company's many wholly owned subsidiaries around the world. One of Cemex's chief advantages in global markets has been its skill in utilizing information technology (IT), bringing efficiency to all its operations, which competitors find hard to match. Cemex has been conscious of the challenges posed by climate change, and has made strides in reducing emissions and incorporating sustainability goals into its strategy.

Although a public company, Cemex remains in the control of the founding family. Family members do not hold the bulk of the company's shares, but they dominate its corporate governance. Only one of the thirteen members of the board of directors is independent; six are members of the Zambrano family. One might question whether the company's governance structure is able to provide the independent oversight needed for running a public company. In particular, risky acquisitions and excessive

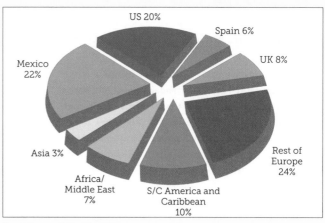

Breakdown of Cemex sales

Source: Cemex Annual Report, 2009, at www.cemex.com

debt have arguably been problematic from a strategy perspective, but the insider-controlled board was not in a position to question the running of the company. Cemex is now eyeing new acquisitions in the large emerging markets, where it feels its competitive advantages can be exploited. Lessons of the recession for many MNEs have been to strengthen independent corporate governance structures and to pay greater heed to the interests of stakeholders. For now, Cemex is not going down this road of corporate reform.

Sources: Cemex Annual Report, 2009, at www.cemex.com; Thomson, A. (2010) 'Cemex to cut debt in stakes sale', *Financial Times*, 26 April; Patalon, W. (2007) 'Global Cement Giant Cemex looks to cut costs, debt after Riker Buyout', *Money Morning*, 14 December, at http://moneymorning.com; Lapper, R. and Wheatley, J. (2008) 'Higher ground', *Financial Times*, 11 March

Questions for discussion

◆ How did Cemex build its dominance in Mexico?
◆ How was Cemex able to expand so rapidly in global markets? Are its prospects bright for future expansion?
◆ What are the shortcomings of Cemex's corporate governance?

GLOBALIZATION AND THE BUSINESS ENVIRONMENT

CHAPTER 2

Outline of chapter

Introduction

What is globalization?

Country differences

MNEs and internationalization
Why do companies internationalize?
Modes of internationalization

FDI and the global economy
Theories of FDI
Trends in FDI
FDI in developed and developing countries

Globalization in the balance
Impacts of globalization in the international environment
Rethinking global business strategy

Conclusions

Learning objectives

1 To gain an overview of globalization
2 To discern and interpret differing impacts of globalization in differing national environments, including developed and developing countries
3 To identify the main modes of internationalization, together with their underlying rationales
4 To gain a critical appreciation of the issues connected with globalization of the business environment

Critical themes in this chapter

- **Globalization – globalized production; internationalization strategies**
- **Emerging economies – location advantages**
- **Changing societies – impacts of globalization**
- **Multilayered environment – interactions between local and global factors**

Geely of China acquires iconic Swedish carmaker, Volvo

Volvo is famous the world over for its safe, well-built cars, albeit slightly boring in design and image. A long and illustrious history and a solid reputation for quality were factors which persuaded Ford of the US to purchase the company in 1999, for $6.5 billion. However, the famous brand was no guarantee of market success or financial performance. Volvo has not made a profit since 2005 and, by 2009, Ford, then in financial difficulties itself, sought a buyer for the company. Volvo still had much to offer: it had sales of over 300,000 vehicles a year, mainly in America, where it enjoyed a strong reputation and loyal customers, although it lacked an American manufacturing base. In a period of global downturn in car markets, the one bright area has been sales of cars in China, up 50% in 2009. It was not surprising, therefore, that a Chinese carmaker, Geely, was interested in buying Volvo. Also unsurprising was the fact that Ford suffered a huge loss on the sale, selling the company for $1.8 billion.

Mergers and takeovers of car companies have a mixed record, especially when differing cultures and operating systems are combined, as in the ill-fated merger of Daimler of Germany and Chrysler of the US. The polar opposite of Volvo, Geely concentrates on manufacturing cheap cars mainly for the Chinese market. Dating from 1986 as a refrigerator parts manufacturer, it started making cars only in 1997. It has six plants in China, and others in Ukraine, Russia and Indonesia. Acquiring a quality brand would seem to offer it a strategic opportunity in more upmarket cars, but it lacks experience and technological expertise at this level.

Geely intends to keep the brands and operations separate. It aims to continue manufacturing Volvo in Sweden, and to build new plants in China making Volvo models for the Chinese market. As Chinese consumers seek more premium brands and become more safety-conscious, Geely's CEO sees a bright future for his new acquisition. However, the road ahead could be bumpy. Intellectual property was one of the stumbling blocks that had to be negotiated, involving both Ford and Volvo ownership of technology. Chinese manufacturers have acquired a reputation for copying design and parts rather than building their own. Geely has said it will keep R&D in

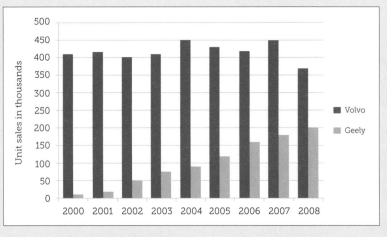

Comparison of Volvo and Geely car sales

Source: *Financial Times*, 29 March 2010

Sweden for the time being. It has also said it will keep the existing management in place, but under a new board. Geely's CEO sees good prospects for Volvo, but turning round the loss-making operation will be a challenge.

Geely has one advantage which might help it towards its goal of restoring Volvo's former glory. That is its strong connections with the Chinese government. Although an independent company, it would not have

▶ More online ... Geely's website is www.geely.com
Volvo's website is www.volvogroup.com

**Geely's takeover of Volvo signals
the ambitions of China's car
companies to expand both at home
and abroad**

Source: Istock

been able to mount such an ambitious takeover by itself. On its own Geely raised about half the money needed to buy Volvo. Government backing and backing from provincial governments provided the rest, and will be crucial in helping it to build new Volvo plants in China. Will suburban Americans retain their affection for Volvo cars even though the company is owned by the Chinese? Geely's head of international operations says: 'We want to be careful not to damage the Volvo brand. We don't want the image of a luxury car made in a third world country. We want the image of a European luxury car, owned by a Chinese' (Waldmeir, 2010).

Sources: Reed, J. (2010) 'Volvo's heart will "remain in Sweden"', *Financial Times*, 29 March; Waldmeir, P. (2010) 'Premium car deal fills a hole at Geely', *Financial Times*, 29 March; BBC News (2010) 'Volvo sale signed by Geely and Ford', 28 March, at http://news.bbc.co.uk

Questions for discussion

◆ Why had Volvo lost its way in the years leading up to the takeover?
◆ What are the risks for Geely in trying to turn around a premium European brand such as Volvo?
◆ In your view, was the purchase of Volvo a brilliant strategic decision, or a mistake? Explain.

Introduction

Since about the second half of the twentieth century, the world has experienced changes in all dimensions of the environment, which have come to be grouped together under the heading 'globalization'. These changes have by now touched nearly everyone, from city dwellers in the rich economies to farmers in rural Africa. Every type of business activity and all sizes of organization have been affected. Industries such as oil, which are self-evidently global, have been affected, but so too have industries such as textiles and clothing, which have traditionally been local and national. MNEs have been the main drivers of these changes, but SMEs, too, have benefited from opportunities to broaden their horizons in numerous sectors. Hallmarks of globalization is interconnectedness and interdependence between people, organizations and governments. These ties have been facilitated by improvements in technology, especially in telecommunications, the internet and transport. Yet, while all would agree that the global economy is a reality, the extent and depth of its reach, along with its impacts, are continually debated. Globalization is often praised for its role in economic development, but criticized for social and environmental impacts. There have been winners and losers, in terms of countries, industries and employment, as this chapter will highlight. It will also join the debate on the future of globalization and its impacts in differing contexts.

The chapter aims, first, to examine the forces of globalization in perspective, and, secondly, to assess changes that are taking place in the context of international business. Focus will inevitably fall on MNEs, which have been the driving forces. Their global strategies, centred on overseas production, have been key factors in the interrelationships we now see between economic, political, cultural and technological environments in the global economy. MNEs are now also playing a role in assessing and handling the negative impacts of globalization, such as environmental degradation. However, they are not lone actors, but involved in networks of organizations – governmental and non-governmental, international as well as local – which are tackling negative impacts in a more connected manner unimaginable in earlier generations. Globalization is often envisaged as inevitable processes linked to the spread of MNEs and markets, but their inevitability is now in question. From the very forces that have driven the processes there has been a growth in organizational linkages which can tame and direct globalization's future.

What is globalization?

We are constantly being reminded that we live in a globalized world. People in the world's richer countries have become accustomed to low-cost consumer goods, internet access from just about anywhere, and worldwide travel as a routine occurrence. These benefits of modern consumer life are all linked to globalization. At the same time, people are fearful for their livelihoods, living conditions and natural environment, in both richer and poorer countries. These aspects of globalization cast a shadow over future prosperity. How can all these impacts, desirable and undesirable, be linked? In this chapter, we take the approach that identifying the interconnected forces and players will aid in forming future strategies for spreading the benefits to all the world's people while reducing the negative impacts.

globalization processes by which products, people, companies, money and information are able to move quickly around the world

globalized production MNEs' ability to locate different stages of production in the most advantageous location

value chain concept which identifies the value created at each stage in a production process

globalization of markets MNEs' ability to serve consumers across the world, taking account of different products for different national markets

Globalization can be defined as a mixture of processes by which products, people, companies, money and information are able to move quickly around the world as decision-makers desire, with few cross-border impediments in their way. The driving processes have seen changes in both production and markets. **Globalized production** refers to MNEs' ability to locate different stages of production in the most advantageous location. The different stages of production can be seen as forming a **value chain**, from sourcing of materials through to production, distribution and delivery to the end consumers. Each stage in the chain contributes value to the final product. Globalized production has become highly developed, with MNEs now able to co-ordinate complex supply chains thanks to advances in IT and communications technology. **Globalization of markets** refers to MNEs' ability to serve consumers across the world with their products, in contrast to an approach which views national markets as essentially separate. Globalized markets have developed in standardized products, but in many sectors, such as food, national differences are still marked. Globalization in these sectors has taken the form of global strategies to deliver specific products to local markets.

Although international trading links and colonialism in the eighteenth and nineteenth centuries connected nations around the globe, these earlier eras did not see the depth of interaction which characterizes globalization as we experience it today. It was only in the post-Second World War period, with the deepening of economic ties through trade and cross-border investment, combined with improved communications and transport, that the current era of globalization began. The use of the term began only in the 1960s and gained common currency only in the 1980s (Waters, 2001: 2). Historians and other commentators have diverged on the nature and extent of these trends. Some commentators are persuaded that globalization has fundamentally changed the world in which we live, including the social and cultural makeup of people as individuals. They observe that we now live in a global age, in which societies, cultures and states are melding into a global community made up of global citizens. This extreme view, which gathered momentum in the late 1990s, is known as 'hyperglobalization' (Ohmae, 1995). It painted a rather idealistic picture of all countries and communities connected through the spread of free market capitalism. It envisaged a 'borderless' world, in which the autonomy of individual countries would gradually shrink and global civil society would emerge (Ohmae, 2000). Although this seemed to sound a rather optimistic note to advocates, it did not ring true to many sceptics, who pointed to the tenacity of deep-rooted cultural values, and it rang alarm bells to others, who feared the consequences for societies, their cultures and the natural environment.

A debate on the pros and cons of globalization ensued, in which both the globalizers and their critics have been highly vocal. Some took an equally radical stance, denying that globalization was taking place and pointing to the continued strength of large sovereign players and differing cultural environments. Other critics were persuaded that globalization was a reality, but that it was unleashing more harm than good, resulting in the concentration of economic power in the hands of large corporate forces to the detriment of societies and the environment. This line of thinking focused particularly on the post-war economic power of the US, evidenced in the might of its multinationals and the influence of the US in international relations. The debate moved to the streets, as anti-globalization protests became a regular occurrence at international governmental conferences, such as that of the WTO in 1999 in Seattle, Washington.

In the decade since then, a more balanced debate emerged, recognizing that globalization is a reality, but moving on to focus on the local impacts, both good and bad, and what can be done about remedying the harms. This perspective, which is the one adopted here, is that globalization is not a single, all-encompassing process sweeping the globe, but processes which reflect the independent actions of many different players in different places.

Figure 2.1 **Globalization processes and their outcomes**

Globalization processes are set out in Figure 2.1. The two overarching themes are interconnectedness and interdependence. The first, **interconnectedness**, is facilitated mainly by advances in technology, computing and the internet, which allow networking to take place routinely between people in different geographical locations. Although we are focusing on business connections, we should bear in mind that social networking sites are now part of this process, reaching out increasingly to firms and their staff. Advances in transport, such as container shipping, have facilitated trading ties. MNEs have become the drivers of globalized production, evolving supply chains to deliver products to consumers in an ever-increasing range of markets. Financial flows have also benefited from the internet and IT, allowing cross-border investments and transactions to be made quickly and easily.

interconnectedness improved communications across national borders, facilitated mainly by advances in technology, computing and the internet

interdependence links based on complementarities and co-operation between two or more countries or organizations

Turning to the second theme in Figure 2.1, growing **interdependence** among countries has taken place. It might appear that countries would thereby lose their autonomy, but more subtle processes are taking place. Rather than the withering away of national autonomy, we are seeing countries both retaining a sovereign right to act and willingly co-operating with other countries for common goals. In processes not unlike those transforming companies, countries are seeing themselves as linked together in their pursuit of prosperity and well-being. As economic integration deepens, so does interdependence, between countries and between business enterprises. A gradual opening up of national economic and financial systems to outside investors has occurred, accompanied by the liberalization of trade. These trends towards market liberalization have been seized on by some as indicators of the spread of global capitalism, a central tenet of the hyperglobalizers. However, market reforms

▶ More online ... The IMF has a page on its website devoted to 'globalization – key issues'. Topics include labour, finance and trade. Go to its website at www.imf.org, and search under globalization.

have varied in both their substance and pace among countries. Countries with authoritarian systems, such as China, have used market tools to achieve national aims, rather than to transform themselves into free market systems. Governments see foreign investment as leading to economic growth, especially in the form of domestic jobs, but are wary of allowing the loss of control over these economic forces. In this respect, the hyperglobalization thesis probably underestimated the tenacity of nations and peoples, and failed to appreciate that interdependence did not automatically lead to a withering away of the state as an economic and political player.

Globalization processes have taken place unevenly, affecting different dimensions of the environment in different ways. These processes have also affected countries in differing ways, leading to gaps emerging both within and between countries, between those who have benefited and those who have not. Beneficiaries have included the favoured locations for low-cost production, while low-skilled jobs in advanced economies have been rapidly disappearing. Globalization has, perhaps ironically, accentuated country differences rather than diminished them.

Summary points Globalization processes

◆ Globalization consists of growing interconnectedness and interdependence among organizations and countries.

◆ For international business, there has been a shift towards global production networks and globalized markets.

◆ Although some observers see globalization as progressing inevitably towards a single global community, in which local identities are subsumed, the evidence suggests that countries and national cultures persist.

Critical thinking
Globalization of production
What is meant by globalization of production, and why is it seen as one of the most highly developed, and beneficial, features of globalization?

Country differences

primary production
agriculture, mining and fishing

secondary production
industrial production, concentrated in factories

tertiary sector the third type of economic activity (following primary and secondary) which consists of services, such as financial services

Every country has distinctive characteristics that influence the nature of the economic activities which make up its national economy. Economic activity can be divided into three broad sectors: **primary production**, which includes agriculture, mining and fishing; **secondary production**, which is industrial production; and the **tertiary sector,** which consists of services, such as financial services. All three types of activity are carried out in every economy, but there are big differences in their proportions. It is usual for countries to progress economically in stages, from primary industries to manufacturing and then to services, which are considered more advanced. There are exceptions to this pattern. Some countries rich in natural resources rely mainly on these activities to generate wealth, but this can be a short-sighted policy, as the day will come when the resources run out. Seeking to diversify to maintain steady growth is more advisable, although not always easy to achieve in practice. We will look at national economic systems closely in the next chapter, but here we take a comparative view of globalization in the context of country differences.

▸ More online ... LG's investor relations homepage is www.lg.com/global/ir
Samsung's home page is www.samsung.com
Hyundai's home page for corporate information is http://worldwide.hyundai.com/company-overview

industrialization
transformation of an economy from mainly agricultural production for domestic consumption to one based on factory production, with potential for export

economic development
can refer to any change in a country's overall balance of economic activities, but usually refers to industrialization and resultant changes in society

developed countries
countries whose economies have become industrialized and have reached high income levels

triad countries advanced economies of North America, the EU and Japan; Australia and New Zealand are also in this category

developing countries
countries in the process of industrialization and building technological capacity

transition economies
economies such as those of Eastern Europe and the CIS (Commonwealth of Independent States, including Russia) which are making the transition from planned economies to market-based economies

Globalization is closely linked with industrialization, which normally drives economic development. **Industrialization** is the process of transformation of an economy from mainly agricultural production for domestic consumption to an economy based on factory production, with potential for export. Industrialization enhances a country's potential for wealth creation and economic growth, especially if its industries grow into successful MNEs. Industrialization is therefore seen as key to economic development.

Although **economic development** can refer to any change in a country's overall balance of economic activities, it usually refers to industrialization and resultant changes in society whereby jobs are increasingly concentrated in industrial sectors. Britain was the earliest country to industrialize, from the early nineteenth century onwards, followed by other European countries and the US. Many inventions, such as the steam engine, electric turbine and railway locomotive, originating in Britain, spread to Europe and the US. Following the Second World War, when many European countries and Japan faced the task of rebuilding infrastructure and industrial capacity, the US was well placed to forge ahead with large-scale manufacturing, meeting growing demand for consumer goods. By the late 1960s, however, Japan's industrial development was gaining momentum, turning it into a global industrial power in sectors such as car manufacturing. By the 1980s, Japanese manufacturers threatened American industrial domination. By then, South Korea was gaining ground in some of the same sectors as Japan, such as electronics and cars. Samsung and LG have become global forces in electronics, and Hyundai has become a global carmaker. More recently, China and India enjoyed the rapid growth associated with economic development.

The world's **developed countries** are mostly those whose industrialization processes reached maturity by the 1980s. The UN classifies 24 countries as high-income OECD countries, which roughly equates with developed economies. They are mainly in North America, the European Union (EU) and Japan, known as the **triad countries.** Australia and New Zealand are also in this category.

Countries changing from agricultural to industrial production fall within the broad category of **developing countries**, which is the UN's second category. These countries have often been referred to as the 'third world', but this term is now seldom used as it reflects the polarized thinking of the post-war period known as the 'cold war' era, which was dominated by tension between the western capitalist countries, the 'first world', and the communist bloc countries, the 'second world'. These cold-war categories have rather been superseded by events, mainly the fall of the Soviet Union and the rise of market economic reforms around the world. The vast majority of the world's countries are within the category of developing countries. There are huge variations in levels of development among these countries. Some are already industrial forces globally, such as South Korea, and some, at the opposite end of the ladder, only in the early stages of industrialization. The UN broadly classifies 137 countries as developing. These are mainly in South America, Africa and Asia. Perhaps confusingly, South Korea is classified as developing, although it is an OECD high-income country. The UN has a separate category for the **transition economies** of Central, Eastern Europe and CIS (Commonwealth of Independent States, including Russia) which have been making the transition from the planned economies of the former Soviet Union to market-based economies from 1991 onwards. These transi-

▸ More online ... The UN Development Programme's Human Development Reports are at http://hdr.undp.org

tion economies number 27, and show considerable variation in the extent of development and market reforms. Ten have become essentially market economies and transition democracies. These are members of the EU and OECD, but the others have retained the more authoritarian structures which are a legacy of their past.

Table 2.1 **Economic development: UN classification of countries**

Category	Countries
Developed – OECD high income (24 countries)	Australia, Austria, Belgium, Canada, Denmark, France, Finland, Germany, Greece, Iceland, Ireland, Italy, Japan, Luxembourg, Netherlands, New Zealand, Norway, Portugal, Spain, South Korea, Sweden, Switzerland, UK, US
OECD members (30 countries)	As above, plus Czech Republic, Hungary, Mexico, Poland, Slovakia and Turkey
Transition economies of Central and Eastern Europe and CIS (27 countries)	Albania, Armenia, Azerbaijan, Belarus, Bosnia and Herzegovina, Bulgaria, Croatia, Czech Republic, Estonia, Georgia, Hungary, Kazakhstan, Kyrgyzstan, Latvia, Lithuania, Macedonia (TFYR), Moldova, Poland, Romania, Russian Federation, Serbia, Slovakia, Slovenia, Tajikistan, Turkmenistan, Ukraine, Uzbekistan
Developing (137 countries)	(*selected*) Algeria, Angola, Argentina, Bangladesh, Bolivia, Botswana, Brazil, Burkina Faso, Cambodia, Cameroon, Chad, Chile, China, Columbia, Democratic Republic of Congo, Costa Rica, Cuba, Cyprus, Ecuador, Egypt, Equatorial Guinea, Ethiopia, Gambia, Ghana, Mongolia, Morocco, Guatemala, India, Indonesia, Iraq, Kenya, South Korea, Kuwait, Lesotho, Malaysia, Mali, Mexico, Nicaragua, Nigeria, Pakistan, Peru, Philippines, Saudi Arabia, Singapore, Somalia, South Africa, Thailand, Tunisia, Turkey, Uganda, United Arab Emirates, Uruguay, Venezuela, Vietnam, Zambia, Zimbabwe
Least developed (50 poorest countries from the above)	(*selected*) Afghanistan, Angola, Bangladesh, Benin, Burkina Faso, Cambodia, Chad, Comoros, Equatorial Guinea, Democratic Republic of Congo, Ethiopia, Gambia, Guinea-Bissau, Haiti, Malawi, Mali, Mozambique, Myanmar (Burma), Nepal, Niger, Rwanda, Sierra Leone, Somalia, Sudan, Tanzania, Togo, Uganda, Yemen, Zambia

Source: UNDP (2007) *Human Development Report 2007* (Basingstoke: Palgrave Macmillan)

least developed countries the world's poorest developing countries, mainly in sub-Saharan Africa

The UN's last category is the **least developed countries**, which are the 50 poorest countries of the group of developing countries. These are mainly in sub-Saharan Africa, but also in South Asia. These countries, which have the world's fastest-growing populations, are mainly primary agricultural producers, with little industrialization. Most have been adversely affected by globalization, suffering from volatility in global commodities markets, weak transport infrastructure and poor communications networks. These societies have fallen behind other developing countries, experiencing extreme poverty, poor health conditions and limited educational systems. Moreover, these countries, which are those most at risk from the effects of climate change and extreme weather, are those with the least resources to meet the challenges. Recent investments in Africa by the Bric countries are having impacts economically, but social challenges remain.

A final category of country is the emerging economy, or emerging market, defined in Chapter 1. As noted there, these countries, although key players in globalization processes, are not a well-defined category, and do not appear separately in the UN classification. They are generally considered to be the fast-growing developing economies, but this is itself a fluid category, as countries' growth rates vary over time. For this reason, a fast rate of economic growth alone would seem to be unhelpful as a criterion. More qualitative criteria are hard to pin down, except that all are important developing economies, becoming economically integrated with the developed countries. We discussed the Bric countries (Brazil, Russia, India and China) in Chapter 1. Other emerging economies include the transition economies of Central and Eastern Europe; the other developing countries in Asia, such as South Korea and Indonesia; and the oil-rich Middle Eastern states.

The emerging economies have all gained from globalization, for varying reasons. In Asia, China has led the world in manufacturing mass-produced goods, and South Korea's electronics and carmaking companies have become global players. The transition economies of Central and Eastern Europe have attracted manufacturing investment due to their proximity to Western European markets. Russia has been dependent on natural resources, mainly gas. The Middle Eastern states have been dependent on oil, which, like gas, is subject to price volatility and is a non-renewable resource. Some of these states have diversified into financial services, but this sector, which is highly globalized, is also volatile. Emerging markets are thus exposed to the opportunities of globalization, but also to the risks.

So far, China has been the star performer in terms of globalization. It has attracted many foreign investors, lured by its huge potential market and abundant labour. Many western MNEs have reaped rewards from China's development, and their home countries have benefited from their earnings. When demand for Chinese goods faltered due to economic downturn in western markets in 2008, especially the US, China was able to weather the storm, looking to home demand. As the next section shows, foreign investment bestows benefits on both home and host countries.

Summary points Differing development profiles among countries

● The industrialization phase of economic development in today's developed economies occurred over decades, and even generations. These countries are seen as modern consumer societies.	● For developing countries, the fastest growing of which are termed emerging economies, economic development depends on natural advantages (such as abundant labour) and becoming integrated into global supply chains.	● The least developed countries, mainly in sub-Saharan Africa, have seen little benefit from globalized production, and risk falling behind the developing countries, which have benefited from globalization.

Critical thinking

Country differences and globalization

What factors determine whether a country wins or loses from globalization? What are the risks associated with globalization, which can imply that even the winners are vulnerable?

MNEs and internationalization

The company that seeks to expand internationally eyes the potential gains from production and markets outside its home country. The internationalization of its activities offers opportunities which greatly exceed those offered at home, even if its home is a large country such as the US or China. Most MNEs do not simply go on a shopping spree, acquiring ownership of foreign assets, but build strategic ties with other organizations, such as suppliers, which enhance their ability to create value. In his book, *Global Shift*, Dicken defines the MNE as an organization able to 'coordinate

and control operations in more than one country, even if it does not own them'
(Dicken, 2003: 198). He goes on to highlight three characteristics of the MNE:

- Co-ordination and control of stages of production chains within and between
  countries
- Ability to take advantage of differences between countries, including geographical differences, natural resources, availability of labour and government policies
- Geographical flexibility to shift resources and operations between locations at
  international level

This definition stresses that control over assets is as critical to internationalization
as ownership of them. MNEs have grown in number as global interconnectedness
has become easier. The MNE is therefore seen as a driver of globalization. The UN
estimates that there are now some 79,000 TNCs worldwide (United Nations, 2008a).
Most of these are from the developed countries. Indeed, 85 of the world's top 100
non-financial TNCs are from the triad countries. Companies from a wide range of
countries have now become players in global supply chains and markets, challenging
the established MNEs in both mature consumer markets and newer emerging
markets. SMEs, once seen as essentially local, can now become part of worldwide
supply chains, raise capital from foreign investors and recruit talented people
globally. In this section, we look at why and how companies internationalize.

Why do companies internationalize?

A company does not decide to branch out internationally on the basis of rather
abstract observations that we now live in a global economy, but because the firm
itself stands to gain financially. For companies, as for people, the grass might seem
greener on the other side, but there is much at stake. For a business, a failed foreign
venture can lead not just to financial loss, but can bring down the entire company.
We highlighted the high-risk acquisition of Rinker Group by Cemex in the closing
case study of the last chapter, which saddled Cemex with a huge debt burden.
Companies therefore need good reasons to venture abroad, and reasonable confidence that the potential benefits outweigh the risks. There are both **pull factors**,
which attract the company to a foreign location, and **push factors**, which drive the
company out of its home country or other countries where it currently does business.
The following motives come into play:

pull factors factors in
a country which attract
foreign investors

push factors factors
in a company's home
country which persuade
it to seek growth
potential overseas

- *New markets* – The new market is a strong pull factor for a company, especially if its
  growth in its home market begins to slow. However, the new market needs to be one
  where the firm's products are likely to be popular and lead to growth in market share.
- *More efficient production* – Companies are constantly seeking ways of producing
  products and delivering services more efficiently, and benefiting from scale economies, that is, savings which come with large-scale production. The country with
  relevant skills and low labour costs is thus attractive, but transport costs and long
  delivery times must be taken into account.
- *Proximity to key resources* – The company that relies on abundant supplies of a
  key raw material is likely to choose a location close to supply. For this reason, food
  processing plants are often located in agricultural areas.
- *Access to technology and skills* – The company that relies on specialist technology tends to seek out locations where these activities are flourishing, and
  where skilled researchers are available. For this reason, SMEs in life sciences often
  locate in the proximity of large pharmaceutical companies.

▶ More online ... Information about Zara can be found at www.inditex.com. This is the website of the Inditex group, owner of Zara.

- *Proximity to customers* – The company that has traditionally exported its products might find it can deliver a better, more customized, service if it establishes a presence near its customers. It thus learns more about the market firsthand.
- *Deterioration in the home business environment* – There are many possible push factors which influence companies to look beyond their home country or to shift from a foreign country where they have become established. Market saturation is one. For the large retailer, market saturation could be reached if availability of large sites becomes limited or planning regulations become stricter. Changes in taxation and regulation in a country can contribute to an exodus of companies to more advantageous locations.

Economic downturn in a country can lead a firm to look for opportunities elsewhere. For example, emerging economies did not suffer as severe recession as the developed economies in the global downturn of 2008. Zara, the fashion retailer, thus halted store openings in its home country of Spain and focused its efforts on opening more stores in China.

Summary points Motives for internationalization

◈ The prospect of sales growth in new markets is a strong motive for international expansion.	◈ The prospect of reduction in production costs attracts companies to low-cost countries to carry out manufacturing activities.	◈ Better access to resources, both physical resources and skilled workers, can justify a shift to a different country.

Modes of internationalization

modes of internationalization methods by which companies expand internationally, such as FDI

export selling products in a country other than the one in which they were made

foreign direct investment (FDI) mode of internationalization in which a firm invests in productive assets in a foreign country, acquiring them wholly or partly and using this ownership stake to exert control on operations

MNEs choose from a variety of methods to internationalize, known as **modes of internationalization**, shown in Figure 2.2. They are not strictly alternatives, as a firm might choose different modes in different locations, and at different stages in its internationalization experience. Here we look broadly at the theories, and we will explore these strategic alternatives in greater detail in Chapter 5. The firm embarking on international activities for the first time tends to choose a low-risk strategy, such as **exporting** its products from its home country. If foreign demand is promising, it might establish a sales office in selected foreign markets, giving it a presence in the market and allowing it to control activities such as customer service.

By means of **foreign direct investment (FDI)**, the company invests in productive assets in a foreign country, acquiring them wholly or partly and using this ownership stake to exert control on operations. The investing company thereby acquires deeper involvement in the host country than the company which simply relies on exporting its products to foreign markets, without a physical presence in them. FDI is generally considered to be the main driver of globalization (Dunning, 1993), as it is characterized by this deeper level of integration in global production networks.

As Figure 2.2 shows, the MNE contemplating FDI has a number of options. The first shown is the foreign subsidiary. As we found in Chapter 1, a parent company might set up a foreign subsidiary which it wholly owns, or it might take a lower stake, still aiming to control operations. The subsidiary gives it a legal footing in the country, from which it can grow. If the MNE is a manufacturing company, with the prospect of good sales in a particular foreign market, it might decide to invest in building a plant on a greenfield site. This type of project is typically carried out by a

greenfield investment FDI which focuses on a new project, such as a factory, in a foreign location

subsidiary set up for the purpose. The **greenfield investment** represents a significant commitment to the country as it involves a large capital outlay, with probably little prospect of immediate profits. This is a long-term strategy that the MNE might consider for a variety of reasons, including lower costs than in its home country, availability of skilled labour in the host country and the existence of trade restrictions which deter exporters from building a presence in the host country's market.

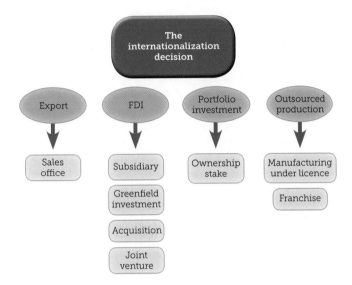

Figure 2.2 **Modes of internationalization**

acquisition type of FDI in which an investor purchases an existing company in a foreign location

joint venture an agreement between companies to form a new entity to carry out a business purpose, often an FDI project

portfolio investment buying shares or other securities in a number of companies internationally, with a view to making financial gains on the investments

The MNE in a hurry to gain a foothold in a foreign market often chooses to purchase an existing business. **Acquisition** allows the MNE to start operations in the country almost immediately, and is common in sectors such as retailing and mining. In acquiring a manufacturing business, there might be a time lag, while the plant is adapted to make the new owner's products, but this is shorter than would be possible on a greenfield site, where the plant is built from scratch. Some acquirers purchase the whole business, including the brand, and carry on production under the new management. The opening case study featured this type of acquisition, in which Geely acquired a brand, Volvo, which is better known in global markets than its own. Acquisition in new markets can also be advantageous in that the MNE can gain local knowledge and expertise from the acquired firm, as Geely hopes to gain from Volvo. In emerging economies, many of the companies that have been sold are through government privatizations of old, inefficient businesses. In this situation, the MNE takes on an ambitious project, needing to inject capital and retrain staff.

The company that is reluctant to enter a foreign market on its own, or is barred from doing so by state controls, can form a **joint venture**, whereby it works with a partner firm to carry out FDI. The MNE's partner in the joint venture tends to be a local firm, whose local knowledge will enhance their chances of success. The partners form a new company, each taking an equity stake. In many emerging economies, foreign companies are required to go down the joint-venture route, as foreigners are legally barred from wholly owning a locally registered company. This restriction is gradually being relaxed as countries open their markets.

The next option, portfolio investment, is also subject to restrictions in some countries. **Portfolio investment** consists of buying shares or other securities in a foreign company, with a view to making financial gains on the investment. These gains are often viewed as short term. The portfolio investor usually acquires small stakes in companies, and can be restricted legally or politically from big purchases. Sovereign wealth funds, mentioned in Chapter 1, are familiar portfolio investors in many sectors, usually keeping investments below 10% stakes. Where an investor is able and willing to acquire a large stake, usually 30% or more, it gains a strong position from which it can exert considerable control in both corporate governance and management. In this case, its role would shift closer to that of the foreign direct investor, who combines ownership and control.

outsourced production agreement between a brand owner and a manufacturer to make the firm's branded products under licence

manufacturing under licence production of products by a firm by agreement with the owner of their patents, trademarks or other intellectual property

The final range of options in Figure 2.2 is **outsourced production**, which, it will be recalled from Chapter 1, has become common among brand owners. Outsourcing rests on agreement by the MNE with a local company that the latter will produce the goods or deliver the service with the permission of the MNE. For MNEs in clothing and other consumer products, the outsourcer **manufactures under licence** from the MNE brand owner, being required to produce the products as needed to the specifications laid down in the licence agreement. The aim of outsourced production tends to be to reduce costs by locating production in a low-cost country, from where products are exported to other markets. This strategy has been key to MNE investment in China and other Asian economies. In some sectors, such as fast food and hotels, companies have opted for franchising (defined in Chapter 1), which also involves a licence agreed with a producer to make and deliver the product in accordance with the brand owner's instructions. The local businessperson who owns the franchise makes a considerable capital investment, but is able to attract customers on the strength of the brand. The brand owner, in turn, is able to expand internationally through a network of franchises, without the burden of significant capital outlay in each country. We tend to think of franchises in connection with global brands, but a national company, such as the Polish company featured in the opening case study of the next chapter, has successfully developed franchise operations in its national market and the Czech Republic.

Companies design internationalization strategies to derive the greatest potential from each market, using different entry modes in different countries, influenced by the local conditions and government policies in each. Their choice also depends on the strengths of the firm itself. (These factors are considered in greater detail in Chapter 5.)

Summary points Modes of internationalization

- Exporting is often chosen as an entry mode for companies with little foreign experience, as it involves a minimum of involvement in the foreign country.
- FDI involves ownership and control of foreign assets, differing in their nature and extent in each country context. Greenfield

investment signals an intention to make a long-term commitment to the country, and is often carried out via a joint venture, in which the risk is shared with a partner firm.
- Outsourcing, utilizing the manufacturing capabilities of a local firm, which produces under licence, has been a favoured

internationalization strategy in some sectors, such as mass-produced consumer goods.
- Firms seeking primarily financial investment choose portfolio investments overseas. Such investments can lead to greater involvement if the firm builds up its stake in the foreign company.

> **Critical thinking**
>
> Choosing market entry mode
>
> What mode of entry would you recommend for each of the following, and why?
>
> - A clothing manufacturer in a developed country whose sales at home are stagnant, and who wants to expand into emerging markets
> - A large retailer from a European country, who wishes to enter the Chinese market
> - A Chinese manufacturer of appliances such as refrigerators and washing machines who wishes to enter the American market

FDI and the global economy

FDI has been a major contributor to globalization. As we have just seen, it is by no means the only mode of internationalization, but it is the one that represents the deepest commitment in a host country, in which the investor and host society develop the deepest interactions. In this section, we analyse these cross-border activities and their impacts.

Theories of FDI

Why firms choose one mode of internationalization over another and one country over another are questions which theorists and researchers have long sought to explain. Theories are constantly being devised and adjusted as global interactions have deepened over time. Discerning the relationship between trade and FDI has been a theme in these theories. Trade has taken place since ancient times, while FDI is a relatively new phenomenon. Why did FDI come to be considered a better strategic option for the firm, and how has trade changed in a world of deepening FDI? We attempt to glean some historical perspective in this section by looking at how the main theories have evolved.

Foreign investment by companies flourished in the nineteenth and early twentieth centuries. Although transnational manufacturing took place in the Victorian era, the big overseas investors were in primary sectors such as mineral extraction and agricultural products. In the period before 1914, the UK was the largest holder of foreign capital assets, the majority in developing countries where British colonial rule provided an institutional umbrella (Dunning, 1993). The interwar period saw the rise of protectionist barriers between countries, which discouraged trade and encouraged companies to focus on home markets. However, the political leaders who met to devise a framework for new co-operative agreements after the Second World War paved the way for an era of growing prosperity which we now link to globalization.

Until about the 1960s, firms tended to carry out manufacturing activities in their home countries. But FDI was beginning to take off, leading early theorists of the phenomenon to ask why. One of these was Stephen Hymer, who sought to explain what advantages would be gained from the firm perspective (Hymer, 1975). Hymer spoke of **location advantages** of some countries over others. These are advantages of country or region, such as access to transport and lower costs than in the firm's home country. Such advantages are not an unqualified benefit, though, as the firm would be entering a foreign environment where it had little knowledge. Why would a firm undertake the risk, rather than simply investing in shares? The answer lay in the ability of the foreign firm to make the most of its **ownership advantages** in the host country. The foreign firm would have resources such as technology, production skills

location advantages
inherent advantages of country or region, such as access to transport and low labour costs

ownership advantages
resources specific to a firm, such as patents, which can be exploited for competitive advantage

and organizational skills which local firms lacked. These ownership advantages were firm-specific, giving the foreign firm a competitive advantage.

A second relevant theory is the **product life cycle theory** of Raymond Vernon (see Figure 2.3). Writing in the 1960s, when American companies were in the ascendant, Vernon envisaged all new products as originating in the US. He wrote particularly about the growing American appetite for mass-produced consumer goods such as televisions and washing machines. He traced the life cycle of the new product from its launch in the US, through to export to other markets, and, finally, its manufacture in cheaper locations for export to US consumers. In the early phase, demand at home leads to expansion, and demand overseas, which is limited to high-income groups, is satisfied by exports. As the market matures and overseas demand grows, foreign production begins to take off, and these products supplant US imports in overseas markets. At the same time, cost factors come into play, the product becomes more standardized and production is increased. US producers are likely to shift production overseas, first to the higher-income markets (such as Europe). These production facilities are able to export to other countries, and even back to the US, but as costs rise in Europe, companies shift production again, this time to low-cost locations, such as Asian developing countries.

product life cycle theory
theory of the evolution of a product in stages, from innovation in its home market to dissemination and production in overseas markets

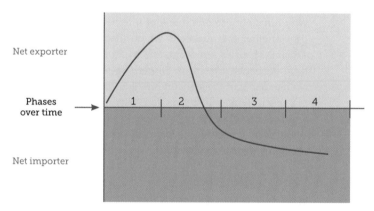

Figure 2.3 **Vernon's product life cycle theory**

Source: Adapted from Wells, L.T. (ed.) (1972) *The Product Life Cycle and International Trade* (Boston, MA: Harvard Business School Publishing)

Phases:
1   All production in home market, for domestic consumption and export
2   Production abroad (import substitution)
3   Overseas producers expand exports, displacing home market exports to emerging markets
4   Production in low-cost locations for export to global markets

Vernon combined concepts of location advantages and ownership advantages. In his rather US-centric view of the world, innovation capacity was an ownership advantage enjoyed by US companies, and other countries were not as competitive. Nonetheless, the core idea that companies will locate production in the most advantageous place was to be influential in later theories. Most notable among these has been Dunning's **eclectic paradigm**, also known as the 'OLI paradigm', based on three sets of advantages: ownership (O), location (L) and internalization (I) (Dunning, 1993). The OLI paradigm, shown in Figure 2.4, was designed to explain FDI, mainly focusing on foreign production, from the firm's perspective. It was called 'eclectic' because the three variables derived from diverse theories and disciplines. The ownership and location variables were to be found in trade theories, and internalization derived from transaction cost economics. The three variables are summarized below:

eclectic paradigm
theory of FDI devised by Dunning, based on three sets of advantages: ownership (O), location (L) and internalization (I); also known as the 'OLI paradigm'

- *Ownership-specific advantages* – These include property rights over assets, broadly defined to include both tangible resources (such as plants) and intangible resources (such as intellectual property rights). Ownership of capital and natural resources strengthens the firm's competitive position. The firm's technology in the form of patents reflects its innovative capacity, which generates future innovations. Crucial to the exploitation of these resources are the firm's organizational and entrepreneurial skills.
- *Location-specific advantages* – These include the economic, cultural and political environments of a country as a potential location in which the firm is contemplating investment, compared to its home country. Low-cost labour as a location advantage was highlighted by earlier theorists, but Dunning expanded the notion in the FDI context. In addition to low-cost labour, access to raw materials, transport and infrastructure, he highlighted political policies such as government incentives to foreign investors. The size of the potential market for the firm's products in the country (and region) is another location advantage, although one which might involve a longer term horizon in the case of developing countries. More recently, technological capacity in a country such as India is a location advantage, as R&D activities there are less costly than in developed countries.
- *Internalization advantages* – These look to the reduction in transaction costs through hierarchical organization as an alternative to reliance on markets. A firm might find it advantageous to gain control of the supply of raw materials or components by buying the supplier outright. The firm thus avoids the transaction costs associated with obtaining supplies on an exchange basis in markets. Taking over the supplier leads to **vertical integration**, which gives the firm greater control over supplies. This can be advantageous from several viewpoints. It allows the firm to monitor quality more closely than would be possible dealing with an independent supplier. The firm can also keep tighter control of intellectual property, which can be a risk in countries where legal protections are weak. In this respect, there is overlap between ownership and internalization advantages.

vertical integration
acquisitions of firms in successive stages of production

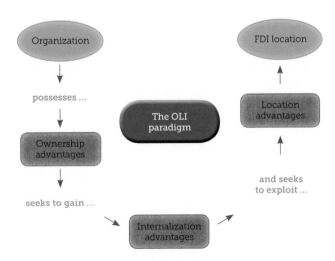

Figure 2.4 **Dunning's OLI paradigm**

The OLI paradigm aids firms contemplating FDI by highlighting the different variables and their interactions. It can thus help to weigh up the likely benefits against the risks and costs. Dunning's theory coincided with rapid growth in FDI, as firms were seeking greater efficiencies of globalized production. These MNEs were mainly from the developed countries. In today's world, MNEs are emerging from a wide range of countries, but the theory remains relevant. For example, a manufacturer of mobile phones based in a developed country is now almost certain to manufacture them in a low-cost country, as is every company in this sector, including large players from South Korea.

What impacts do sizeable inflows of FDI have on a host economy, and what about the countries which do not attract FDI? Perhaps the latter countries are better off in the long term, as they can develop their own home-grown industries, noting that the more opportunistic foreign investors might decide to leave for more advantageous locations in a few years. Certainly, the latter possibility is implied in Dunning's theory, but what are the impacts? These are explored in the next section.

Summary points **Theories of FDI**

◆ Early theories of FDI focused on location and ownership advantages in foreign locations.	◆ Product life cycle theory offered an explanation of how production of standardized products can shift from high-cost to low-cost economies.	◆ Dunning's OLI paradigm explained FDI from the point of view of the firm, in terms of a mixture of location, ownership and internalization advantages.

Critical thinking

Applying the OLI paradigm

Using the principles set out in the OLI paradigm, explain how a high-technology manufacturer from a European country would choose a location for foreign investment. The company makes specialized imaging equipment. It needs a new R&D facility and an outsourced manufacturing facility (which need not be in the same location). It is considering the US, Japan, mainland China and India. Which should it choose, and why?

Trends in FDI

The movements of FDI around the world can be measured in terms of types of investments, their origins and destinations. This information provides valuable insight into globalization processes. **FDI inflows** are the aggregate value of investments that flow into a country, and **FDI outflows** are the aggregate value of investments from a country's organizations to overseas destinations. These are calculated on an annual basis. The total value of foreign investments that a country has attracted is its **FDI inward stock**, and the total value of investments made by its nationals is its **FDI outward stock**. The extent of a country's firms' involvement in FDI is a good indicator of its economic integration and interdependence with other countries. Where a country's outflows and inflows are unbalanced, say, by strong outflows and weak inward investment, it might be an indication of a weak domestic business climate. Japan is an example. Where the balance is tipped towards inward investment, it might be an indication that the country enjoys location advantages, but its domestic firms are not globally competitive – as yet. China is an example. Japan is a developed economy, whereas China is a developing one, and it is tempting to generalize that outward movements are dominated by developed economies and inflows mainly

FDI inflows aggregate value of investments that flow into a country

FDI outflows aggregate value of investments from a country's organizations to overseas destinations

FDI inward stock the total value of foreign investments that a country has attracted

FDI outward stock the total value of foreign investments made by a country's nationals

target developing economies. Such a generalization would be an overstatement, but it does point to one of the trends that have occurred in the changing pattern of FDI, which is the shift of production of a huge range of products from the high-cost countries to the low-cost countries. For this reason, China's economy overtook Japan's in size in 2009.

From the early 1970s, when FDI surged ahead, developed countries have been the leading forces in both outward and inward flows of FDI, as shown in Figure 2.5. Developed countries' attraction for foreign investors is based, among other factors, on their affluent consumer societies, advanced communications networks, skilled workers and high-technology capabilities. These attractions are evident in the strong growth in inflows in the late 1990s, shown in the figure. The year 2000 saw the bursting of the 'dotcom bubble', with the collapse of many overvalued internet companies. A general weakening in economic activity ensued.

The post-2000 decline in FDI flows was dramatic in the developed economies. Inflows into the US declined 90% in 2002. Declines in the developing economies were not so steep, thanks mainly to the record inflows in FDI into China. Other countries that attracted growing inflows were the Central and Eastern European countries, especially those which joined the EU in 2004 (discussed in the next chapter). The flows into these countries have come mainly from other EU countries. The drop in FDI in 2008 reflected the global economic crisis, which started in the developed world. FDI inflows into developed countries fell 32% that year, seriously affected by the drying up of debt finance to fund investment. But flows to developing countries withstood the crisis better, rising 3.6%.

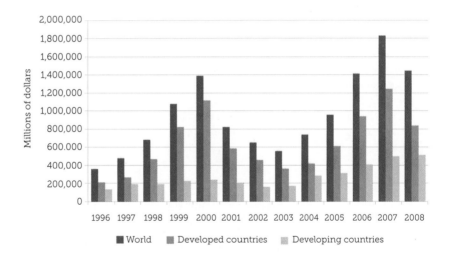

Figure 2.5 **World inflows of FDI**

Source: United Nations, *World Investment Reports 2004–2009* (Geneva: United Nations)

Both outward and inward investment has been dominated by the triad countries (the US, EU countries and Japan). Between 1985 and 2002, the triad countries accounted for about 80% of outward stock and 50–60% of inward stock (United Nations, 2003). In 1980, the EU and US were roughly equal in outward FDI stock, but a gap opened up over the next two decades, as shown in Figure 2.6. By 2002, EU stock was more than twice that of the US. This gap widened in the following years. FDI stock owned by firms in developing countries increased to 12% of global totals in 2002. MNEs from emerging economies increased their outward FDI more dramatically between 2003 and 2007. These emerging MNEs, often state owned or controlled, have gained confidence from their own fast-growing economies. These companies have found success through FDI in developing countries, benefiting from their familiarity with issues common to most developing economies, such as a weak institutional environment. As they have gained in confidence, they have increasingly targeted developed countries, asserting their global competitiveness.

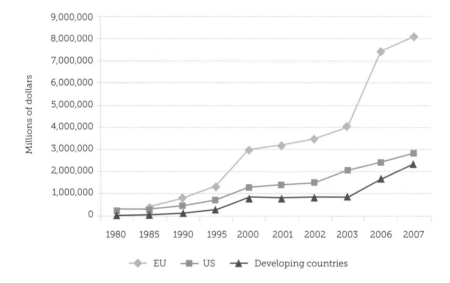

Figure 2.6 **Comparisons in ownership of FDI outward stock**

Source: United Nations, *World Investment Reports 2004–2009* (Geneva: United Nations)

Summary points Trends in FDI

● Developed countries have been the major source of outward FDI and the major destination of FDI inflows, but the trend is now shifting towards greater participation of developing economies.

● Emerging economies, such as China and the countries of Central and Eastern Europe, have seen increasing inflows of FDI, due to their location advantages.

● Global FDI flows diminished in 2008 due to the global financial crisis, but those to the developing countries held up better than those to the rich countries.

---

technology transfer process of acquiring technology from another country, especially in manufacturing, whereby skilled workers in the host country are able to learn from the foreign technology

spillover effects benefits to local firms in host countries from FDI, including technological capabilities and local supply contracts

FDI in developed and developing countries

FDI inflows can be highly beneficial to host economies, both developed and developing. FDI projects bring jobs, wealth creation and greater choice for consumers. For developing countries, the benefits can be transformational, bringing a shift towards an industrial economy. FDI can boost economic development and promote **technology transfer**, whereby skilled workers in the host country are able to learn from the technology of the foreign investor. These **spillover effects** from FDI are also possible where the foreign investor, for example in a greenfield project, uses local suppliers and service providers. The latter companies can gain both technological and managerial skills, which can be valuable in building domestic innovative capacity. Developing countries can see rapid economic growth and increasing wealth from FDI. However, FDI inflows are not without risks for the recipient country.

Host-country governments should bear in mind the investing firm's perspective and motives, discussed above. Location advantages are constantly shifting, and inward investors migrate as the balance of advantage shifts to new locations. Manufacturing companies invested in four Asian 'tiger' economies (Hong Kong, Singapore, Taiwan and South Korea) in the 1980s, promoting industrialization and high growth. But by the 1990s, they were shifting their attention to mainland China, which enjoyed cost advantages. The four Asian tigers had to shift to more high-value manufacturing and R&D to sustain economic growth. As we noted earlier, South Korea is now a high-income OECD country. Singapore, Hong Kong and Taiwan are now benefiting from continued strong growth in mainland China, leading to growing economic integration between these economies (Whipp, 2009).

FDI inflows to developed countries are typically market oriented. The investor seeks to manufacture or assemble products in or near large markets. Furthermore, local manufacturing can bypass tariff barriers which would apply to imports. Arguably, the increased competition leads to both foreign and domestic companies' improving their products to grab the consumer's attention. However, it does not always work out like that. In the US, Japanese car manufacturers built 'transplant' factories to sidestep trade barriers in the 1970s, locating in areas outside the large centres such as Detroit, Michigan, where American car manufacturers were entrenched. From these factories, they (and many other businesses) were able to serve US customers. So competitive were the newcomers that they oversaw a gradual decline in the fortunes of the three large American car companies (see the case study in this chapter).

In some countries, FDI plugs gaps due to the lack of financial resources or skills to exploit location advantages. Foreign investors can transform potential into actual benefits in sectors such as mining and energy resources, notably in developing countries. Despite resource riches, these countries often suffer from poverty, poor governance and corruption. Major oil companies such as Royal Dutch Shell and BP are long established in developing countries, and have built up expertise in oil and gas exploration and extraction. These skills are vital in today's world, in which large remaining reserves are located in difficult environments, both geologically and politically. Resource-rich countries are highly diverse, including Nigeria, Russia, Iran, Iraq, Sudan and Venezuela. Their governments – which, with the exception of Nigeria in this list, tend towards the authoritarian – wish to realize gains from ownership and control over energy assets, awarding exploitation rights and production contracts. Although energy-rich countries have turned to western expertise in the past, they are now attracting the Bric countries.

Chinese FDI has flowed heavily into Africa in recent years, especially in the energy sector (see Figure 2.7). Much of this FDI is combined with trade deals and infrastructure projects, in which the Chinese provide much-needed funding. But the benefits to these sub-Saharan African countries, among the world's least developed societies, are not readily apparent (Collier, 2008). Bric countries' trade with Africa grew from $22.3 billion in 2000 to $166 billion in 2008 (Kynge, 2009). China accounts for two-thirds of this trade. The mainly state-owned Chinese investors are thinking in terms of the benefits which will flow back to China. This approach is not new: foreign investors naturally look for the advantages they can gain, as we noted above. But Chinese investors often bring their own workers from China, rather than employing local people. At the same time, host countries are obliged to buy imported Chinese goods as part of their overall trade and investment packages. Will these deals ulti-

▶ More online ... Information about Zambia can be found on the World Bank's website, at http://web.worldbank.org.
Click on 'Zambia' in the list of countries.
China Non-ferrous Metal Mining Company's website is www.cnm.com.hk

mately deliver the economic development and improved human well-being that the host countries desire?

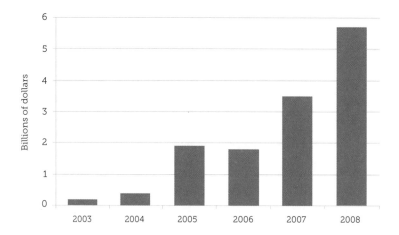

Figure 2.7 **Chinese FDI into Africa**

Source: *Financial Times*, 24 February 2010

The example of Zambia is illustrative. Zambia is a poor country dependent on copper mining to bring in revenues, enabling it to maintain economic growth of about 5% annually. But despite large inflows of FDI into the mining sector in recent years, Zambia remains one of the world's poorest countries, where more than half the population live in extreme poverty. A joint venture between Bein Stein Group Resources of Israel and International Mineral Resources of Switzerland bought the Luanshya Copper Mine (LCM) from the Zambian government in 2003. The government retained a 15% stake in LCM. However, when the price of copper fell dramatically on world markets in January 2009, LCM closed down operations abruptly, leaving 1,700 workers jobless. In July 2009, the Zambian government, desperate to reopen the mine, signed an agreement with the Chinese Non-Ferrous Metal Mining Company, which took over the 85% stake formerly held by the joint-venture company. Although the Chinese company promised sizeable investment, it was met with scepticism and dismay in much of Zambia, as the Chinese had a poor record on working conditions and low pay in its other operations in the country: even though it had promised schools and health facilities, these had not been maintained.

What options were open to Zambia, or any country where vital operations are closed down by foreign investors? Two factors in the Zambian case are influential in numerous other resource-rich developing countries. First, it is heavily dependent on a single sector, in this case, primary products subject to price volatility in global markets. Zambia would need to diversify its economy, building enterprises in other sectors. Secondly, it is dependent on foreign investment to exploit its resources, and the investor holds a strong bargaining position in respect of the terms of the agreement.

FDI has been a major driver of globalization, but local factors help to determine the behaviour of investors, and host-country governments play a crucial role. Also influential have been an array of international organizations and agreements, which are discussed in the next section.

Summary points FDI in developed and developing countries

◆ FDI brings benefits of employment and wealth creation to host economies, but investors tend to shift to other locations which offer more advantageous conditions, such as lower costs.

◆ Technology transfer and spillover effects help the host country to develop domestic industrial and technology capabilities.

◆ FDI is necessary in some countries, such as those rich in natural resources, due to the expertise of foreign investors in mining and energy sectors.

Globalization in the balance

In this section, we first take a broad look at the impacts of globalization across the dimensions of the international environment, taking into account the players involved in national, regional and international spheres. We then turn to their impacts on business strategy, looking at how the issues are being readdressed in a world where emerging economies are becoming increasingly influential.

Impacts of globalization in the international environment

The fast-growing emerging economies have seen the most dramatic benefits from globalization, but, as we have seen in the case of Zambia, globalization processes engulf poorer developing economies too, sometimes in ways which have long-term detrimental consequences. In Zambia, a succession of investors – African, European, Middle Eastern, Asian – were involved over a period of six years, and LCM is now under Chinese control. Meanwhile, Zambia has remained near the bottom of the UN's human development rankings. In the UN's human development index, which assesses health, education and standard of living, Zambia – despite its mineral wealth – ranks 164 out of a total of 177 countries (UNDP, 2009).

In this section, we discuss globalization in the context of each of the dimensions of the environment, highlighting local, national, regional and international aspects.

Economic environment

Countries' economies have their own distinctive economic systems, which have evolved over long periods, some more market oriented and others more state controlled. Globalization has had profound impacts on these national systems as they have become linked through trade and the international activities of firms and governments. Some countries have benefited greatly from globalization: the fast-growing emerging economies are examples, as their manufacturing prowess (in the case of China) and abundant natural resources (in the case of Brazil) serve global markets. But globalization processes may touch a wide range of countries, even those not highly integrated in global networks, simply because so many industries are now global. The oil industry is an example: a severe hurricane in the Gulf of Mexico can affect supply and prices worldwide. Similarly, economic conditions in one country impact on the economies of other countries with which it has ties, both neighbouring countries and trading partners worldwide. MNEs' global strategies have resulted in many countries, such as those with low labour costs, being targeted for their location advantages. A resulting inequality between countries has been a consequence. Moreover, inequalities have arisen

Bumpy road for global car companies

In the heyday of America's post-war car industry, the big companies – Ford, General Motors (GM) and Chrysler – launched new models every year, eagerly awaited by families in America's sprawling suburbs. So great was the growth in car ownership in the following decades that two-, three- and even four-car families became commonplace. That all changed abruptly in 2008, when US new car sales started to tumble, but the roots of the crisis in the US car industry go much further back, and the changes – some painful – now unfolding are indicative of changing global car markets.

America's big three car manufacturers were clustered in a region epitomized by Detroit, the country's motor city. The car companies were not the only beneficiaries of Detroit's boom years. The carworkers' trade union, the United Auto Workers (UAW), was highly successful in achieving beneficial terms for its members and their families. They could point to a range of victories over management resulting in high wages, generous healthcare, pensions and even pay when no work was available (the so-called 'jobs club'). But for their employers, the accumulation of liabilities would have long-term effects, especially due to the rising costs of healthcare in the US. Foreign car companies eyeing the American market, including Japanese and German manufacturers, began setting up greenfield operations in the 1980s, in non-unionized operations which did not offer employees gold-plated benefits. They built up market share and gained reputations for reliability and cost benefits to consumers. Arguably, the home-grown manufacturers should have started adapting to the changing competitive landscape, but they counted on the American consumer to buy more and more of their typically 'gas-guzzling' models. The big three companies' competitive positions were adversely affected by generous deals agreed with the UAW, from which there seemed no way out. Car sales were boosted by discounts and easy credit, often secured on houses. However, the collapse of the housing market in the US in 2008, which led in turn to financial crisis and recession, changed the car industry forever, bringing the big three companies to the edge of bankruptcy.

Cries for government funding to prop up the car industry were heard not just in the US, but also in European countries, as consumers decided to keep

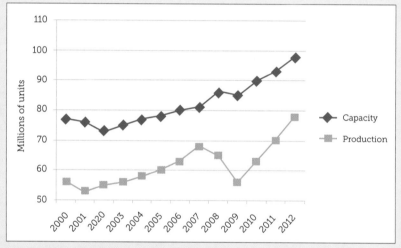

Capacity and production in the global car industry

Note: Forecasts for 2010–2012

Source: *Financial Times*, 26 February 2010

their old cars and the motor industry had to face serious overcapacity. But European manufacturers were not in as perilous a financial state as American counterparts. Nonetheless, France and Germany pumped government money into car companies, and introduced (temporary) scrappage schemes, which encouraged consumers to trade in old cars for new. Production was cut back at Peugeot and Renault, but no factory closed. In the US, only Ford did not need a bailout. GM and Chrysler did, and the government was determined to impose radical restructuring of their businesses. GM received $50 billion in bailout funds, and Chrysler, $7 billion. Both companies were liquidated, and new, leaner companies were formed, in

▶ More online ... Corporate information about the new GM website is at www.gm.com/corporate/investor_information
Ford Motor Company's website is www.ford.com/about-ford/investor-relations

efforts to make them fitter to compete globally than they had been pre-crisis. Chrysler was 20% acquired by Fiat of Italy, whose CEO seemed to welcome the opportunity to revive the brand, targeting new emerging markets.

GM's 47 plants in North America are being reduced to 31, employing 185,000 people, as compared to 266,000 in 2008. Five of its twelve brands are disappearing or being sold. However, legacy issues are evident in the new company. The bailout terms were stringent. The US government became the largest shareholder, with a 60% stake, although it stressed that it would not take over the board or run the company. Importantly, wages and work rules would have to be 'competitive' with non-union, foreign-owned plants in the US (Simon, 2008). The healthcare scheme would henceforth be the responsibility of a new, union-managed, healthcare trust. Half the company's contribution to the new trust would be paid in shares, making the healthcare trust a major shareholder (at 17.5%). In a bizarre twist, the UAW thus gained a seat on the GM board, simply because it had taken over healthcare liabilities.

By 2010, although scrappage schemes were being wound up, new car sales were regaining momentum in mature markets, and production was being increased from the lows of 2009 (see figure). However, any excitement about future growth was focused on China. For newly affluent Chinese consumers, the car as a status symbol has great allure, and sales of luxury models are bringing cheer to their manufacturers, including BMW and Daimler. Are there clouds on the horizon? Government incentive schemes played a part in the rise of 50% in car sales in China in 2009. Overcapacity still prevails in the global market, as the figure shows. Much new demand, especially in mature markets, is for smaller, greener cars, on which profit margins are thinner than at the luxury end. Green technology and reduction in emissions have become imperatives for the car industry, and governments are pressing car companies down these routes. Worrying concerns for manufacturers are rising prices of steel, plastics and other raw materials, which would squeeze profits. Coming at a time when credit deals for consumers still look thin, there is little talk of a new golden age.

Sources: Reed, J. and Sakoui, A. (2009) 'A fork in the road', *Financial Times*, 11 December; Reed, J. and Simon, B. (2009) 'The thrill is gone', *Financial Times*, 3 February; Simon, B. (2008) 'Detroit given three months to find salvation', *Financial Times*, 20 December; Simon, B. (2009) 'UAW gears up to join boards of carmakers', Financial Times, 30 April; *The Economist* (2009) 'Small isn't beautiful', 19 September

Questions for discussion

◆ Why is the post-war era in America viewed retrospectively as a golden era for American car manufacturers?
◆ What were the causes of the near-collapse of the American car industry?
◆ How have global car markets changed in recent years, and what are the regional differences?

within countries favoured by internationalizing firms, as globalized sectors and appropriately skilled workers benefit, while other workers lose out (ILO, 2008).

Political environment

There is no political equivalent of the global economy, probably reflecting the fact that political systems remain mainly country oriented in their structures and players. Political integration across borders has been fostered within the European Union, which has EU-wide political structures, but this example is exceptional. Political integration, in general, has not followed from economic integration. What *has* taken place, which could be attributed to globalization, is greater co-operation among sovereign states, largely through the **United Nations (UN)** and its agencies. The UN was formed in the aftermath of the Second World War, chiefly to prevent future threats to global security and promote peaceful co-operation among member states. It does not operate as a government, but seeks to achieve agreement among sovereign players. Some might lament that the UN cannot coerce members to come into line with resolutions that represent the majority of its members, but this limitation reflects a widespread wariness of countries to cede powers to supranational organizations. On the other hand, international public opinion – as well as long-term self-interest – can be effective in persuading governments to co-operate with others to solve global problems.

United Nations (UN) the world's largest and most authoritative intergovernmental organization

Also dating from the post-war period, the **General Agreement on Tariffs and Trade (GATT)** has sought, through successive rounds of negotiations, to promote agreements among countries to dismantle trade barriers. The **World Trade Organization (WTO)**, created in 1995, became a successor to the GATT, reinforcing the belief that freer trade benefits all countries, both large and small. The WTO's banner of freer and fairer trade has become somewhat tattered, however, as many governments have tended to pay only lip service to its goals, putting national economic and political concerns first (see discussion in Chapter 4).

General Agreement on Tariffs and Trade (GATT) series of multilateral agreements on reducing trade barriers

World Trade Organization (WTO) successor organization to the GATT, set up to regulate world trade and settle trade disputes among member countries

Legal environment

National legal systems are closely connected to sovereign national political systems. In countries where there is a strong sense that the law should operate independently of political influences, an independent judicial system, open to all, is considered an important institution in the safeguarding of civil and political rights. In countries where the legal system is controlled by political elites, the legal system lacks independence. This is considered a significant risk factor for firms doing business in these locations. Firms doing business in China, where legal institutions are weak and politicized, are well aware of the risks. However, there is a growing body of international law, to which countries willingly commit themselves, in a process which is inching towards global legal standards. Central to this process is the **International Court of Justice (ICJ)**, founded in 1920, which is headquartered in The Hague, in the Netherlands. In the area of human rights in particular, international law is the benchmark, and is now incorporated in the national law of many countries, as well as the EU. Regional law-making in many areas, most developed in the EU, is also influential for cross-border businesses, affecting numerous areas of law, including employment, competition and consumer rights. Microsoft and Intel, two giant American companies, have both been fined by the EU court for breaches of competition law. A global company would be unwise to believe that because it is large and dominates its sector worldwide, it is somehow above national and regional law.

International Court of Justice (ICJ) UN-sponsored international court which hears legal cases relating to member states

▶ More online ... Coca-Cola's corporate website is www.thecoca-colacompany.com
McDonald's corporate website is www.aboutmcdonalds.com

Financial environment

Globalization of financial markets has progressed swiftly, due to advances in communications technology and liberalization of national financial systems. Banks and other financial services companies became global players, prospering from innovative financial instruments, a liberalized financial sector in many countries, and light regulation in key financial centres (discussed further in Chapter 9). While governments welcome capital flows, many have become susceptible to the risks of liberalization, highlighted in recurring financial crises of the last two decades. The Asian financial crisis of 1998 showed the risks of opening up fragile domestic financial systems to volatile capital flows from foreign investors. A mismatch emerged between huge globalized financial markets and the predominantly national structures which regulate finance in each country. Excessive risk-taking, especially in investment banking, led to a global financial crisis in 2008, which saw some large banks fail and others, deemed to be too big to fail, bailed out by the governments of their home countries, even though the banks had larger operations abroad than they did at home. A global regulatory framework is now being contemplated. The **International Monetary Fund (IMF)** and **World Bank**, both established in the aftermath of the Second World War, exist to aid countries in financial distress and maintain international financial stability (see Chapter 9 for a further discussion). Their roles could be enhanced, but, as with international bodies generally, this will require agreement by sovereign member states. Nursing massive public debt incurred in propping up failing banks, governments could now be more amenable to arguments in favour of global regulation.

International Monetary Fund (IMF) agency of the UN which oversees the international monetary and financial systems

World Bank organization established in the aftermath of the Second World War, to fund development projects and broader development programmes

Cultural and social environments

The decline of separate cultural identities, especially national cultures, is one of the aspects of globalization that has aroused fears among critics of globalization. They point to the rapid growth of the 'global middle class', which shares similar tastes and lifestyles, oblivious of national borders. These new, mostly urbanized, consumers are changing from traditional cultures, based on rural and family ties, towards a culture based more on material consumption and individualist values. A fear is that people are becoming 'rootless', disconnected from traditional attitudes and values which have ensured stability and observance of norms of social behaviour within societies over the centuries. An undercurrent is disquiet that the new consumer society is essentially shaped by American culture. The international expansion of companies such as Coca-Cola and McDonald's can be perceived as Americanization, which is a more culture-laden concept than globalization. On the other hand, traditional cultural values can persist even though people acquire the trappings of consumer society. Certainly, large American companies now aim to satisfy differing consumer needs and tastes in different countries, implying that localization is an adjunct of globalization. Products, too, are adapted for national markets, although their makers are global MNEs.

Technological environment

It was once assumed that technological advances, especially in high-technology industries, would come from America and be diffused through the rest of the world. Much innovation *has* emanated from America, and American entrepreneurs have stood out in exploiting new ideas. However, as other countries have improved scientific education and technology infrastructure, technological excellence has become more widespread. A factor has been the diffusion of technology through FDI, whereby local workers gain skills through technology transfer, which can boost domestic firms. Technology transfer has been a major positive aspect of globalization, benefiting developing countries. The internet is hailed as a truly global medium, which can be cited as having revolutionized the way businesses and individual people carry out daily activities. But, paradoxically, internet technology has also facilitated greater localization. Global companies now habitually design websites for consumers in many different languages, with marketing communications targeted at particular markets. However, new technology also facilitates governmental controls over content and access within national borders (see case study on internet barriers in Chapter 8).

Ecological environment

Globalization is often blamed for environmental degradation, but the processes taking place are complex. Industrialization, which got under way long before the current era of globalization, is a direct cause of pollution, the depletion of natural resources and destruction of natural ecosystems. Industrialization is itself associated with urbanization, industrialized agriculture, the growth in transport and growing need for energy, all of which contribute to environmental degradation. Where globalization comes into play is in the mounting speed of these destructive processes in the post-war era. China's rapid industrialization, driven by an insatiable appetite for energy and natural resources, has resulted in a particularly woeful toll on the environment, with record levels of air pollution and dangerous depletion of water supplies. China is now the world's largest emitter of greenhouse gases, which are largely responsible for climate change (see Chapter 11). Climate change is a global issue, and the UN's **Climate Change Panel** has been active in urging all countries to sign up to emissions reductions through global agreement, first in the Kyoto Protocol of 1998, and now in a successor to Kyoto. However, as in other dimensions highlighted in this section, countries are slow to sign up to global solutions that they perceive could damage national interests. Again, we find that global problems have local impacts, and governments tend to see global issues through national lenses.

Climate Change Panel UN body which brings together research on climate change and makes recommendations for action by member states

Moves towards international co-operation seem to show that both organizations and governments are conceiving their goals in terms of wider societal values. However, this does not imply that globalization is progressing unimpeded in each of these spheres. The financial and technological environments have globalized rapidly, whereas the cultural and political environments, which are more value oriented, have not. Financial globalization suffered a reversal in 2008, when global financial flows rapidly seized up, spelling disaster for many banks and other companies in the sector, but also spreading into national economies generally. The global crisis that ensued shook confidence in global financial markets, and also raised broader doubts about globalization. Some governments have been inclined to reform their country's banking system to make it more national, thus turning back globalization. Critics might lament this approach, arguing that the crisis showed that what is needed is more, not less, globalization, but in the form of global regulation. The World Economic Forum, which brings together governmental and business leaders, highlights 'global governance gaps' in the areas of financial stability,

▸ More online ... The World Economic Forum is at www.weforum.org

world trade and climate change (World Economic Forum, 2009a: 7). Key to reshaping regulatory institutions at international level is the role of national governments, which are embedded in their countries' distinctive economic, political and cultural environments.

Summary points Globalization and environmental dimensions

● The global economy rests on economic integration of both countries and organizations, implying a willingness to co-operate to achieve goals.

● Political and legal environments are based essentially on national systems, although growing international institutions and international law are impacting on governments and firms.

● National cultures have shown themselves to be persistent, despite economic and political changes within society. Industrialization and urbanization are changing people's lifestyles, but underlying cultural values are changing much more slowly.

● The technological environment has become globalized in that new technology rapidly develops global momentum. However, national factors play a role in the absorption of technology in different countries.

● Environmental degradation and climate change have risen rapidly up the list of threats to global well-being mainly because of rapid industrial development driven by globalization.

● Financial globalization proceeded rapidly in the last two decades, but the global financial crisis in 2008 disrupted these processes, leading to a rethink of how financial stability can best be achieved, by both organizations and governments.

Critical thinking

Globalization and societies

Some societies have seen gains from globalization, in the form of increased prosperity, but the benefits are not evenly shared. Which groups in society are likely to lose out despite the gains from globalization?

Rethinking global business strategy

The period of financial turmoil and economic downturn experienced in 2008–9 has led MNEs to rethink their strategies. Aspects of globalization that are being scrutinized are extended supply chains across continents, reliance on global financial markets, global marketing strategy and sustainability. A more reflective and measured assessment of the risks in the international environment has ensued. We look at each of these aspects in turn.

Extended supply chains

Locating each stage of production in the most advantageous place has become widely accepted in theory, but in practice is difficult to organize and is susceptible to delays and setbacks. These include transport, extreme weather conditions and financial difficulties, which can occur at any point in a supply chain. For example, Porsche, the German luxury carmaker, was forced to close down production for a time because the manufacturer of a thread used in the stitching of its seatbelts went out of business. MNEs are now looking to reduce such risks, some by taking back in-house activities they have outsourced, recalling the benefits of internalization. They are also monitoring carefully the financial health of different organizations in their supply chains, even providing loans to keep them in business if necessary. Long transport links are vulnerable, and relocating production closer to markets is a solution. This

MEET THE CEO

▶ More online ... Nestle's website is www.nestle.com/InvestorRelations, for corporate information

Paul Bulcke CEO of Nestlé, the Swiss food company

Paul Bulcke, a Belgian who took over as CEO of Nestlé in 2008, joined the company as a 25-year-old in 1979. Although quiet and understated in manner, he has not enjoyed what one might consider a quiet life in terms of his career. For the first 16 years, he worked in South America, which included working in Peru at the time of the Shining Path guerrilla movement. He later held positions in Portugal, the Czech Republic, Slovak Republic and Germany. He speaks six languages. Given that Nestlé products are sold in every country of the world except North Korea, his travels within the organization are indicative of Nestlé's global reach. That reach has held the company in good stead during times of economic downturn. Despite the global recession, Nestlé saw a 4.1% increase in sales in 2009. Scale economies and extensive product range have helped. Bulcke says that when times become harder, 'people don't have to trade out of our brands. You have Nescafé, and Nescafé Gold and Nescafé Classic and Nescafé Sachet ... and then you have the offerings of Nespresso' (Simonian and Wiggins, 2009).

He also points to Popularly Positioned Products, a strategy that has been successful in developing markets. The strategy involves pricing, packaging (often in small packets) and distribution adapted to local conditions. For example, for Hispanic consumers in the US, Nestlé imports chocolates made in Mexico. They are sold in small, affordable packets, helping to 'show empathy for the consumer' (Simonian and Wiggins). He feels that maintaining the consumer's trust is crucial. However, food companies such as Nestlé face increasing challenges as they source ingredients more widely, making it difficult to monitor safety.

Bulcke stresses Nestlé's long-term perspective, saying: 'What we are is long-term inspired. We're never going to give up on the long term in pursuit of short-term gain' (Sibun, 2010). Of Nestlé's strategy, he says: 'We don't do revolutions, we are evolutionary' (Sibun). His comments, in 2010, come at a time when many MNEs are rueing decisions made to embark on risky strategies, including ill-conceived acquisitions made in the recent past. Nonetheless, Nestlé's purchase of Kraft's frozen pizza business for $3.7 billion in 2010 puzzled some investors, as it hardly seemed to reflect the current trend towards healthy eating. Nestlé has always been rather guarded in making public statements about its strategy. This approach is reflected by Bulcke, who does not discuss whether the company considered bidding for Cadbury (taken over by Kraft in 2010), or whether it is planning to increase its 30% stake in L'Oréal, the beauty products company. Bulcke highlights the many constituencies that he must address: 'You have the board, stakeholders, financial analysts, investors, governments; authorities, press. It scares and invites' (Simonian and Wiggins).

Sources: Simonian, H. and Wiggins, J. (2009) 'Belgian rock who scaled a Swiss peak'; *Financial Times*, 4 May; Sibun, J. (2010) 'Nestlé chief executive Paul Bulcke is not one for a break, but he loves his KitKat', *The Telegraph*, 21 February

Coffee is popular around the world, and Nestlé's strategy rests on offering a range of coffee products for different consumer tastes and budgets

Source: Istock

strategy is also supported on environmental grounds, as reducing transport results in lower harmful emissions.

Global financial markets

Companies once looked to the domestic banks and shareholders in their home countries for capital. In recent years, however, both debt financing and equity have become open to outside players. Companies now list in countries other than their own, and seek to borrow in financial markets which have become globalized. The global banking crisis of 2008 sent shivers through corporate boardrooms, as banks were caught in a 'credit squeeze': their own ability to borrow drastically contracted, and they were unable to lend on to businesses. Many MNEs had to sell assets to stay in business, and have become more cautious borrowers. Expansion plans financed by either debt or equity are now being scrutinized more carefully than was the norm in the last decade, when large companies had relatively easy access to funds.

Global marketing

Even in global markets, MNEs have focused on national differences as crucial to marketing strategy. It is arguable that, with the growth of the middle classes in the large emerging economies, consumer tastes are becoming similar, but, as mentioned in the last section, local differences remain potent. Many companies are seeking out markets in an array of developing countries, such as those in Africa, where the challenges are greater than in the large emerging economies. Targeting these developing markets offers new opportunities and also highlights ethical issues for MNEs. Nestlé has struggled for a number of years to overcome the damage to its reputation from a scandal over baby milk formula which it marketed in Africa. In focusing on a wider range of markets, companies are facing an increasing array of local conditions. Mistakes can come back to haunt them in their more familiar home markets.

Sustainability

As the last chapter stressed, companies must constantly ask themselves what their guiding purpose or mission is, and how they should best pursue it. Some MNEs became overstretched in global product markets and global production. A period of financial uncertainty and falling demand has caused them to ask again what their core business should be. As noted above, some are rethinking extended supply chains. Some are slimming down, selling subsidiaries in non-core businesses. By focusing on core activities, they aspire to retain competitiveness, which ensures a sustainable economic performance. But companies are also questioning how sustainable their businesses are from an environmental point of view. If their activities are highly pollutant or heavily reliant on natural resources, they face increased costs and possible shortages of raw materials in the future. They also face the prospect of legal regulation, at national or international level. A company can embark on a 'greening' of its strategy for various reasons. In a period of falling demand, simple contraction is not necessarily the best strategy for the future. Economic downturn can be an opportunity to reshape corporate strategy along greener lines and CSR principles.

Companies are rethinking global strategy in a context of financial uncertainty, heightened concern over climate change and heightened awareness of the negative aspects of globalization. They are now wiser and more realistic about international expansion, and more careful to take local factors into account. Globalization was about opening economies and unleashing market forces. The benefits are well exemplified in the rise of emerging economies, but there is now a realization of the risks of unbridled market forces, for businesses and societies. Is a new era of sustainable capitalism emerging? We will seek to answer this tantalizing question in the next chapter, which looks at the international economic environment.

Summary points Strategy in an era of global risks

- MNEs are rethinking global strategy as new risks emerge.
- Among risks associated with globalization are vulnerabilities in extended supply chains and financial risks from volatile financial markets.

- MNEs are refocusing on markets and operations in the context of global risks such as climate change and depletion of natural resources.

- A new focus on sustainability is emerging as a strategic response to global risks

The international airport terminal: a familiar sight for these jet-setting businesspeople, but corporate strategists are now taking a more critical view of international business activities

Source: Istock

Conclusions

1 Globalization comprises processes by which products, people, information and resources are able to move around the world quickly, leading to greater interconnectedness.

2 MNE internationalization strategies have been at the forefront of the globalization of production and of markets.

3 Theories of FDI highlight the use of location advantages to internationalize production, a leading example being Dunning's OLI paradigm, which stresses ownership, location and internalization advantages.

4 FDI has been largely responsible for the deepening of economic integration among countries, particularly benefiting the large emerging economies such as China, Brazil and India.

5 Globalization has proceeded unevenly in the different dimensions of the international environment and in different countries. Economic, financial and technological environments have become highly globalized, whereas political and cultural environments remain centred on national diversity.

6 Global financial crisis in 2008–9 has caused businesses to re-examine strategies in light of increased global risks, including financial volatility and climate change.

7 A focus on sustainability, both economic and in broader societal terms, is emerging as a beacon in managing in a world of increased global risks.

Review questions

1 What are the defining characteristics of globalization?

2 What are the leading schools of thought on the extent and depth of globalization?

3 What are the main motives behind MNE internationalization strategies?

4 Compare modes of internationalization in terms of degrees of involvement in the host country.

5 What are the advantages of FDI as an entry mode?

6 How have the post-war shifts in international power led to (a) growing FDI; and (b) changing patterns of FDI?

7 What does the product life cycle theory contribute to our understanding of FDI?

8 What are the elements of Dunning's eclectic paradigm of FDI?

9 Looking at the impacts of globalization in differing dimensions of the international environment, which are the most globalized, and why?

10 How are MNEs rethinking global strategy in terms of supply chains?

Key revision concepts

Acquisition, p. 51; Developed/developing country, p. 46; FDI, p. 50; Globalization, p. 43; Joint venture, p. 51; Industrialization, p. 46; Location advantages, p. 53; Outsourcing, p. 52; Product life cycle, p. 54; Supply chain, p. 67; Sustainability, p. 69; Technology transfer, p. 58

Assignments

◆ Examine the major globalization processes at work in today's world economy, and assess their impact on the international business environment.

◆ Assess the extent to which MNEs' FDI strategies have generated rethinking of global and local factors.

Further reading

Dicken, P. (2007) *Global Shift*, 5th edn (London: Sage).

Giddens, A. (2000) *Runaway World: How Globalization is Reshaping our Lives* (Andover: Routledge).

Held, D., McGrew, A., Goldblatt, D. and Perraton, J. (1999) *Global Transformations: Politics, Economics and Culture* (Cambridge: Polity Press).

Held, D. (ed.) (2000) *Globalizing World? Culture, Economics, Politics* (London: Routledge).

Hirst, P., Thompson, G. and Bromley, S. (2009) *Globalization in Question*, 3rd edn (Cambridge: Polity Press).

Keane, J. (2003) *Global Civil Society?* (Cambridge: Cambridge University Press).

Lechner, F. and Boli, J. (2007) *The Globalization Reader*, 3rd edn (Oxford: Blackwell).

Reich, R. (1991) *The Work of Nations: Preparing Ourselves for 21st Century Capitalism* (London: Simon & Schuster).

Sklair, L. (2004) *Globalization: Capitalism and Its Alternatives* (Oxford: Oxford University Press).

Waters, M. (2001) *Globalization*, 2nd edn (London: Routledge).

Zysman, J. (1996) 'The Myth of a "Global" Economy: Enduring National Foundations and Emerging Regional Realities', *New Political Economy*, 1(2): 157–84.

Nokia rises to the challenge of the changing mobile phones market

Finland's best-known company has long been a **global leader in the mobile phones market. Perhaps improbably, from its beginnings as a paper mill in 1865, this now-venerable company, whose culture and management remain rooted in Finnish values, has become one of the most resilient,** globalized MNEs in an era dominated by globalization of markets. Indeed, the company attributes its staying power in markets largely to Finnish values of courage and tenacity. But it will take more than perseverance to maintain market leadership in today's mobile phone markets. Stagnation in the handset market generally, in which Nokia has long been dominant, has presented a mammoth challenge, and it has encountered stiff challenges in the smartphone market, which is the only subsector that saw healthy growth in 2009 (see figure). In smartphones, Nokia has fallen behind in technology, its Symbian operating system now showing its age. However, the fightback has long been a Nokia speciality.

In the 1990s, it was caught unprepared as new 'clamshell' handsets were launched by rivals, but soon recovered market leadership with new products. Its ability to respond rested in large part on its ability to exploit economies of scale and its efficient supply chains, which can produce 1.2 million handsets a day. Its production has shifted to low-cost locations, but it has excelled in the planning and logistics necessary to maintain efficient operations. Its design teams have contributed hugely to the company's success, designing phones for all possible types of customer worldwide.

But it must stretch beyond its core strengths in handset design and production to meet the challenges in the smartphone market, in which, because the devices are computer-like, software and services are becoming crucial. Sales of smartphones globally are shown in the figure. Apple's iPhone and the BlackBerry, made by Research in Motion, which are dominant in the American market, have shown impressive growth. Nokia was late in launching mobile phones with touchscreen technology, and its Symbian software needed upgrading. Also entering the market strongly has been Google, whose Android operating system is used in phones made by HTC of Taiwan. Nokia has responded with new smartphones and improvements to Symbian. It has also launched services such as Comes with Music, a digital-music service, and Ovi store to offer services. But they hardly compete with Apple's iTunes or its phenomenally successful App store. Nokia faces an uphill task in building greater expertise in software and services. In these areas, operators are influential, as they sell packages of phones and services directly to customers, which compete with Nokia's own services.

Attracting consumers through design and innovation, but will Nokia continue to shine in the fast-moving mobile phone market?

Source: Nokia

Nokia has risked losing its way as it attempts to compete in all markets and all product categories. It launched a Booklet mini-computer in 2009, recognizing the convergence between computing and mobile phones. The following year, Apple launched its iPad, a 'tablet' positioned between the smartphone and laptop. Nokia has long targeted not just rich countries, but emerging markets. In India it offers Nokia Money, a mobile payments system. Another service aimed at developing countries is its Life Tools, which provides agricultural information (such as prices and weather), and educational tools. This has been marketed in India. Nokia is thus well placed to improve its already-strong position in emerging markets. Its main challenge is likely to be linking hardware and innovative services which outshine its younger, agile competitors.

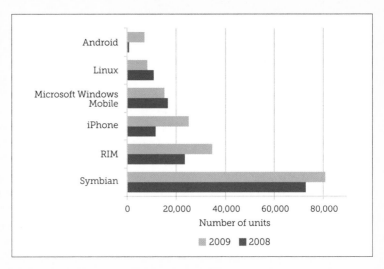

Worldwide smartphone sales by operating system

Source: Gartner's worldwide mobile phone sales data, 2010, at www.gartner.com

Sources: Ward, A. (2010) 'Nokia in smartphone fightback', *Financial Times*, 29 January; Parker, A. (2009) 'Nokia vow to exact revenge on rivals', *Financial Times*, 2 January; Parker, A. and Taylor, P. (2010) 'Different tones at mobile telecoms showcase', *Financial Times*, 15 February; *The Economist* (2010) 'Bears at the door', 9 January; Gartner (2010) Worldwide mobile phone statistics, at www.gartner.com

Questions for discussion

◆ What are Nokia's strengths in global mobile phone markets?
◆ What have been Nokia's competitive weaknesses in the past?
◆ What competitive threats to Nokia are likely to be the most damaging to its global position?

PART 2

ECONOMIES
AND MARKETS

In this part, we focus on the competitive environments in which businesses operate, including national, regional and global.

Chapter 3, 'NATIONAL ECONOMIES IN THE GLOBAL ENVIRONMENT', introduces national economies and economic systems. Understanding global forces depends crucially on grasping how national economies function, along with the ways in which decision-makers form policies. Global economic integration is proceeding apace, but there remains huge diversity among national economic systems. Although the spread of market values has grabbed universal attention in recent years, market reforms are themselves taking on distinctive national characteristics, reflecting divergent histories and values. Understanding the dynamics of national environments and their interactions is essential for today's international manager.

Chapter 4, 'INTERNATIONAL TRADE AND GLOBAL COMPETITION', takes us more broadly into the international environment, looking at the ways in which competitive forces, many of them from emerging economies, are shaping the competitive landscape. We examine the nature and patterns of international trade from a range of perspectives, including nation-states and business organizations. Economic integration at global and regional levels is creating greater interdependence among economic actors, but we find that national forces are still powerful influences, both in the developed and developing parts of the world. In taking strategic decisions such as deciding on a new location, MNEs are able to take advantage of more liberalized markets, but must also be prepared for government intervention.

Chapter 5, 'STRATEGIES IN A GLOBALIZED WORLD', pursues MNE strategy in greater detail, looking first at the broader issues of strategy formation, including theories highlighting both internal and external factors. We focus in particular on corporate strategy in the international context, looking at divergent internationalization strategies in terms of the firm's long-term goals. Globalization has seen the development of extended supply chains, especially in the context of locating activities in low-cost environments. Current MNE strategists are now re-examining these links and rethinking the firm's core competences, with a view to evolving business models which create value over the long term. The last section, on rethinking globalization, brings together these themes and issues.

Learning objectives

1 To define and apply the major concepts used to analyse the macroeconomic environment
2 To identify the distinguishing features of different economic systems and how they impact on international business
3 To assess the strength and content of regionalization and economic integration in the context of national economic pathways
4 To discern the ways in which changes in national economies affect business strategy

Critical themes in this chapter

- **Multidimensional environment – economic and political dimensions**
- **Role of the state – the state as an economic player**
- **Emerging economies – market reforms and mixed economies**
- **Multilayered environment – the EU and eurozone in relation to member states**

Steelworkers in India are fuelling strong economic growth and forging a brighter future for India's billion-plus population
Source: Istock

Polish entrepreneur puts best foot forward

Poland's image to outsiders has tended to be an unflattering picture of a drab, poor country with terrible roads, a harsh climate and rampant bureaucracy. Perhaps not very inspiring to young entrepreneurs, but for a fresh Polish engineering graduate in 1989, just after the fall of communist rule, the country looked bright and opportunities beckoned. Dariusz Milek saw that Poles were eager to buy western consumer goods, but, as yet, supplies were limited and outdoor markets were the norm. That year, he set up his business selling shoes off a metal bedstead in the Lubin market. He soon found he could improve his business by going into manufacturing, and bought a bankrupt shoe factory in Polkowice. From here, his business grew, and he gradually opened franchised shops selling low-cost footwear. Price was crucial to his typical customer, who would be put off by any hint of upmarket trappings. Many of his franchisees sold out of converted shipping containers.

Milek now has a range of shops and many brands, catering for different segments, but he mainly focuses on the lower end of the spectrum. His company, NG2, which stands for New Gate Group, has become one of Poland's most illustrious post-communist success stories. NG2 listed on the Polish stock exchange in 2004. It operates 699 stores, about half of which are company owned, the remainder being franchises. He has expanded into the Czech Republic, but has been cautious in entering new markets because of their unfamiliarity. Although he has become one of Poland's richest individuals, his apparent lack of ambition to expand into international markets has surprised some analysts. He says, 'Analysts did not always understand why I wasn't expanding abroad, but it's not that simple to enter foreign markets' (Cienski, 2009). He notes that many companies which expanded too rapidly regretted it when the global downturn struck.

On the other hand, Milek's supply chain has become internationalized, as he relies largely on imports of shoes manufactured abroad, mainly in China and India (see figure). The company maintains control of its overseas manufacturing facilities, rather than dealing with intermediaries. NG2 prides itself on its design team, attuned to fashion trends and aware that it must present attractive and well-made products to its increasingly affluent customers. As the average Polish customer buys 3.5 pairs of shoes a year, compared with the 5 pairs a year purchased by a Western European consumer, the Polish market offers scope for further growth.

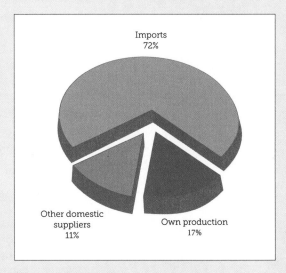

NG2's sources of supply

Source: NG2 website, at http://new-gate-group.ngw.pl

Although his company's profits were down in 2008, Milek felt confident. The weakness of the Polish currency, the zloty, was a factor that made it more expensive to import shoes. However, because his market is mainly in the low-cost segment, he stood to gain from customers 'trading down'.

▶ More online ... NG2's website (in English and Polish) is http://new-gate-group.ng2.pl/

He can now point to a gleaming new shopping centre, which he built on the site of the market where he started his business. In fact, modern shopping malls are now common in Poland, and should help to erase the grim image of the country, which no longer reflects reality. Poland was the only country in the EU that registered economic growth in 2009, albeit at just 1.2%. Foreign bond investors have been attracted to Polish government bonds, in contrast to some of the other EU member states, such as Greece, which did not have to experience the market transition that confronted the post-communist states. The Polish government has prioritized road-building, which it hopes will enhance the country's appeal to foreign investors.

Sources: Mattack, C. (2008) 'NG2 is Poland's footwear superstar', *Business Week*, 12 November, at www.businessweek.com; Cienski, J. (2009) 'Big strides for a market trader', *Financial Times*, 3 June; *The Economist* (2010) 'Horse power to horsepower', 30 January; NG2 website, at http://new-gate-group.ngw.pl

Stylish and practical? Shoe manufacturing has become globalized, but national markets are still the key to success for retailers such as NG2 of Poland

Source: Istock

Questions for discussion

◆ What have been Milek's chief attributes as an entrepreneur?

◆ In what ways has the market for shoes in Poland changed in the post-communist years?

◆ What aspects of Poland's national environment have aided NG2 in growing to its current size?

Introduction

The economic activity of every nation-state makes up its national economy. There is considerable diversity among national economies. This is in large part due to the fact that the world's nearly 200 nation-states differ widely in their size, geography, population, climate and natural resources. These differences have direct effects on the types and intensity of economic activity that are viable. For example, trade is traditionally more likely to prosper in a coastal state than in a land-locked one. States rich in natural resources, such as minerals and oil, have developed national economies built around these natural endowments, whereas labour-intensive manufacturing industries have gravitated to states with large populations offering abundant labour. No country has unlimited resources. In each, the national economy represents the processes that determine how to allocate scarce resources so as to satisfy the needs and wants of those within its territory.

This chapter will begin by looking at the tools with which economists measure and compare national economies. The data generated in these ways allow policymakers to assess economic performance and design national policies. We will examine the major types of national economic system which characterize most of the world's economies. They range from market capitalist models to those in which state controls predominate. A trend observable across all continents in recent years has been the shift towards more open markets, bringing greater opportunities for the expansion of business enterprises globally. Open markets have also created risks, as noted in the last chapter. In an economic environment that has become highly interconnected, the role of national governments has evolved, retaining a pivotal position domestically, and also taking on regional and international perspectives.

The macroeconomic environment

macroeconomics the study of national economies

microeconomics the study of economic activity at the level of individuals and firms

Economists study both the overall activity in the national economy and the lower-level economic activity which takes place between businesses and consumers. **Macroeconomics** is the study of national economies, while **microeconomics** refers to the study of economic activity at the level of individuals and firms. The two areas of economic study are related. A country's macroeconomic environment consists of its national output, employment levels and consumer prices generally. These are known as economic indicators, which allow comparisons across economies to be made. The data are compiled by aggregating data from individuals and firms, so that microeconomic data feed into macroeconomic analysis and policymaking. As an example, microeconomic analysis may focus on motor vehicles in particular, including the market and prices, and this information forms part of the macroeconomic picture of total employment and prices in the economy as a whole.

Flows of economic resources in the economy can be depicted as a model based on circular flows. While this type of model is greatly oversimplified, it does serve to show the interaction between the main groups, businesses and consumers, as can be seen in Figure 3.1. Businesses provide employment and wages to households, while consumers spend earned income on goods and services. At the same time, both businesses and individuals pay taxes to government, which are used to fund public spending and social security. By increasing or decreasing public spending or by altering the tax regime, it is possible for government to influence spending by firms

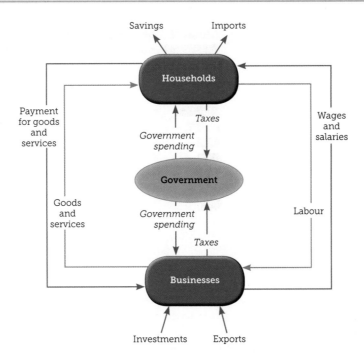

Figure 3.1 **Circular flows of income in the economy**

and consumers. For example, public spending on government projects will provide firms with more orders and greater need for workers. These workers, in turn, will purchase consumer goods. Therefore, the 'injection' of government funds will have had a general effect on the economy, referred to by economists as a 'multiplier' effect, because of its ripple effects across the economy. It should also be noticed that effects of international flows are taken into account in Figure 3.1. Consumers buy imported products, which is depicted as a 'leakage' from the circular flow. Similarly, when firms export products, the income that arises is an injection, as is overseas investment.

In this section, we look at a range of economic indicators revealing the nature and vibrancy of a national economy. We then look at the role of government in managing the national economy. It is telling that, although we live in an era of global economic integration, the role of national governments, far from withering away, has increasingly come into the frame in shaping national economies.

Gross national income and gross domestic product

gross national income (GNI) the total income from all the final products and services produced by a national economy within a single year

gross domestic product (GDP) the value of the total economic activity produced within a country in a single year, including both domestic and foreign producers

The economy of a country is capable of being measured in a number of ways. One of these is **gross national income (GNI).** GNI represents the total income from all the final products and services produced by a national economy, including income that national residents earn from overseas investments, in a given year. It is the broadest measure of a nation's economic activity. **Gross domestic product (GDP)** represents the value of the total economic activity produced within a country in a single year, including both domestic and foreign producers. GDP and GNI vary enormously from one country to another. As can be seen in Figure 3.2, the US is by far the world's largest economy, with a GNI of over 14 billion dollars in 2008. The twelve largest economies now include the large emerging economies – China, Brazil, Russia and India.

For comparisons between countries, GDP or GNI per head (per capita) can give a better idea of a society's prosperity, as it takes the population into account. There are

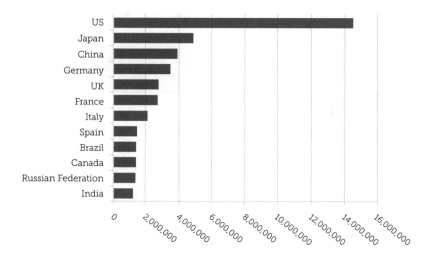

Figure 3.2 **Gross national income of the world's 12 largest economies in 2008** (in millions of US dollars)

Source: World Bank (2009) Data and statistics, at www.worldbank.org

purchasing power parity (PPP) means of estimating the number of units of the foreign currency that would be needed to buy goods or services equivalent to those that the US dollar would buy in the US

huge differences in per capita GNI across the world, as Figure 3.3 shows. The calculations in Figure 3.3 are based on **purchasing power parity (PPP)** calculations. PPP estimates the number of units of the foreign currency that would be needed to buy goods or services equivalent to those that the US dollar would buy in the US. The advantage of using PPP estimates to measure GNI per capita is that they more accurately reflect relative living standards in different countries. Even so, there are huge discrepancies among countries. The US has a GNI per head of over $46,000. Per capita GNI is also relatively high in other advanced economies. But there is wide gap in between these countries and the developing and emerging countries. There is also considerable variation among the Bric countries. India is by far the poorest, its citizens enjoying a GNI per capita of less than $3,000, less than half that of the Chinese

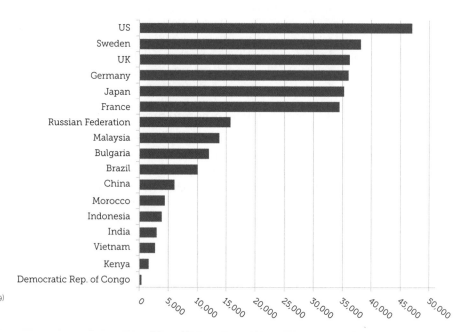

Figure 3.3 **GNI per capita of selected countries for 2008** (based on PPP in US dollars)

Source: World Bank (2009) Data and statistics, at www.worldbank.org

► More online ... World Bank statistics can be found on their website, at www.worldbank.org, under 'Data and research'.

citizen. African countries, especially those in sub-Saharan Africa, are among the world's poorest in terms of GNI per capita. In these countries, poverty is widespread and economic development issues are a priority being addressed by governments.

GNI per capita represents an average figure. It does not take account of the distribution of wealth within the country. Some countries have extremes of wealth between the rich and poor, while others are more egalitarian, although their GNI per capita could be similar. India has a low GNI per head, but is nonetheless seen as a huge potential market because of its large middle class of an estimated 150 million consumers, wanting to buy products such as televisions and mobile phones that middle-class consumers all over the world desire. This information is valuable for companies whose marketing strategy is targeted at emerging markets, as well as for foreign investors. On the other hand, India's government has not been as open as that of China to foreign investors. India has a history of rather heavy-handed state controls, which has played a role in its rather slower economic development than China's. We look at economic growth in the next section.

Summary points **Measuring economies**

● GNI represents the broadest measure of economic activity within a country, and GNI per capita provides a means of comparing prosperity of a country's inhabitants with those of other countries.

● The large emerging economies are now among the world's top 12 largest economies, but their GNI per capita is much lower than that of the advanced economies.

● Even in countries where GNI per capita is relatively low, such as India, the growing middle classes are forming an important market for global businesses.

Economic growth

economic growth a country's increase in national income over time; negative growth occurs where the economy is contracting

Economic growth refers to a country's increase in national income over time, reflecting expansion in the production of goods and services. Capital investment and technological innovation are important factors in theories of economic growth (Coates, 1999). A range of institutions, both formal (such as legal protections) and informal (such as a bureaucracy based on meritocracy) are also important (Rodrik, 2009). A high growth rate in GDP is taken to indicate rising living standards and healthy capital investment. Development policies in low-income countries revolve around fostering economic growth. Growth is highest in periods of industrialization and investment, as experienced by European economies in the 1950s and 60s, and Japan in the 1970s and 80s. As these economies became mature, growth slowed, whereas in recent years the large emerging economies have enjoyed higher growth. China has been the outstanding performer, as shown in Figure 3.4, achieving consistently high growth rates.

After a period from 2005–7, during which the developing and emerging economies enjoyed healthy growth, the global economy declined in 2008, as Figure 3.4 shows. The steep downturn triggered by financial crisis affected all economies, although developing countries, including China, still enjoyed healthy growth. Fluctuations from periods of prosperity to downturn are part of what economists refer to as the business cycle.

Longer cycles can be distinguished from shorter term fluctuations, which are more closely identified with the business cycle. Although economists differ in their

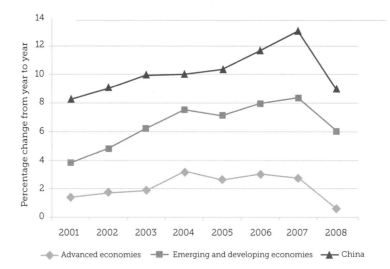

Figure 3.4 **Trends in world GDP growth**

Source: IMF (2009) *World Economic Outlook*, October 2009 (Washington, DC: IMF Publications)

recession two consecutive quarters of negative economic growth in an economy

depression situation in which an economy deteriorates significantly, diminishing by one tenth in size

explanations of causes and indicators, four phases can be identified: prosperity, recession, depression and recovery. A **recession** can be narrowly defined as two consecutive quarters of negative economic growth, although economists prefer to look at the broader picture of the economy. Declining output in a recession is usually accompanied by rising unemployment and weak demand in the economy, as both consumers and businesses spend less. If these indicators continue to deteriorate, and the recession is prolonged, it can become a **depression**, which occurs when the economy has diminished by one tenth in size. The Great Depression of 1929, in which societies experienced severe hardship from high unemployment and inflation, provides a warning for later generations. When an economy is either in recession or on the verge of it, the government faces pressure to devise policies to steer a recovery. It can turn to a number of policy measures, such as reducing interest rates, which will be discussed shortly.

Summary points The cyclical nature of economic change

◆ Economic growth is an indicator of prosperity in an economy, including living standards and levels of investment.

◆ High growth rates are associated with industrialization and economic development within an economy.

◆ Recession, or negative growth, is usually accompanied by high unemployment and weak demand in the economy.

Other economic indicators

In this section, we look at three key national economic indicators: inflation, unemployment and balance of payments. The three are interlinked, and in a healthy economy, we would expect to see low inflation, low unemployment and a positive balance of payments. In today's world, we find a rather more mixed picture among national economies.

Inflation

inflation the continuing general rise in prices in an economy

Inflation can be defined as the continuing general rise in prices in the economy. Its effect is to make the country's currency worth less. The opposite phenomenon is

deflation decline in prices in an economy, associated with recession and falling demand

'deflation', or a general fall in prices. **Deflation** is likely to occur in periods of recession, reflecting falling demand. This occurred in 2008, as Figure 3.5 indicates. The figure also reveals that Japan has relatively long acquaintance with deflation, having endured a protracted economic recession dating from the 1990s.

The rate of inflation is expressed as a percentage rise or fall in prices with reference to a specific starting point in time. These rises and falls are tracked in the **consumer price index** for every country, usually making allowances for seasonal adjustments, such as seasonal variations in food prices. Each country has its own consumer price index, including a diversity of components in its calculations. For this reason, making comparisons between countries is imprecise and can give only an approximate picture of inflation. There is a single, harmonized Consumer Price Index (CPI) used within the EU, which enables more accurate comparisons between member states. The European Central Bank (ECB) set 2% as its target rate of inflation in 2004, when inflation was generally higher, but many EU states experienced inflation rates at near zero in the recession of 2008–9. Recovery in these economies is being accompanied by rising inflation.

consumer price index (CPI) index which tracks the percentage rise or fall in prices, with reference to a specific starting point in time

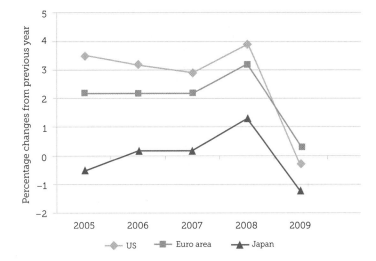

Figure 3.5 **Changes in the consumer price index**

Source: OECD (2009) OECD Economic Outlook, November 2009, at www.oecd.org

Rising inflation is a concern for governments. Economists point to a number of causes of inflation. 'Demand-pull' and 'cost-push' arguments are two of the most commonly advanced causes. The demand-pull explanation holds that demand in the economy is the key factor, which may be the result of cheap borrowing or tax cuts. It encourages producers to raise prices, and these then lead to rises in wage demands as workers strive to maintain their standard of living. The cost-push argument holds that rising costs drive up prices. As a significant element of costs is accounted for by wages, this theory becomes linked with the demand-pull argument. Rising wage costs tend to be passed on to consumers in the form of higher prices, thus creating what is known as the 'wage–price inflationary spiral'.

The damaging effects of high inflation can be widely ramified. A country's domestic producers will find their goods less competitive in global markets, and foreign investors may turn to countries where inflation is lower. High inflation tends to force up interest rates, to enable investors to achieve a real return on their investments. However, high interest rates may adversely affect growth rates, by reducing domestic demand.

The importance of energy costs as a driver of inflation was highlighted in the oil price shocks of the 1970s, which quadrupled the price of oil. Resultant increases in energy and transport costs affected all industrial sectors and sent inflation soaring in developed economies. To bring down inflation, governments can resort to imposing controls on prices or wages, but these measures can be damaging. In particular, they can lead to rising unemployment, as employers cut back on costs. In an environment of relatively low inflation, monetary policy seeks to prevent inflationary pressures arising.

Summary points **Inflation**

◆ Inflation is a continuing rise in prices, which in turn is likely to cause wage inflation, as workers strive to maintain standard of living.

◆ It is expressed as an annual percentage rise in prices.

◆ Increasing costs (such as the price of energy) and increasing demand in the economy are two related causes.

Unemployment

'Full employment', contrary to what it implies, is used by economists to refer to a country's natural rate of unemployment, which exists in all societies. What we commonly refer to as **unemployment** reflects the percentage of people in the country's labour force who are willing to work but are without jobs. National governments use differing definitions of unemployment. There is a generally accepted definition, which dates from the 1982 International Conference of Labour Statisticians and is recognized by the International Labour Organization (ILO). This 'ILO definition' (ILO, 2009a) includes people who are:

unemployment the percentage of people in the country's labour force who are willing to work but are without jobs

- without work in either paid employment or self-employment
- seeking work (by taking specific steps) within a specific reference period
- currently available for work

Specific rules about who is included and excluded from national statistics differ from country to country, making comparisons hazardous. Moreover, in every country, there are probably significant numbers of people who are 'hidden' from the statistics, such as 'discouraged workers', who have ceased to look for a job, and casual workers, who were not registered employees in the first place.

Unemployment may be 'structural', meaning that jobs have been lost due to changing technology or industries relocating in other regions – or other countries. Or it may be 'frictional', which refers to the usual turnover in the labour force that happens, for example, when people are out of work looking for new jobs. When demand in an economy falters and economic growth slows, unemployment tends to rise, as firms cease hiring and lay off workers. Government policies are influential. A government cannot simply 'create jobs', but policies that promote innovation and training can help to mitigate the impacts of unemployment in particular sectors. Governments can also make it easier for new businesses to start up, fostering an entrepreneurial culture. Such policies reflect the impact of globalization, which has seen the migration of many jobs, especially those in low-skilled activities, from high-cost economies in western countries to low-cost emerging economies, especially China.

▸ More online ... The homepage of the International Labour Organization (ILO) is http://www.ilo.org

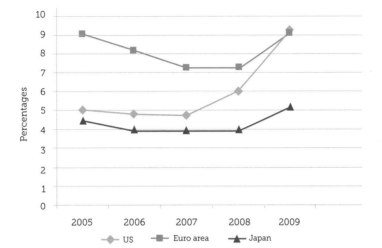

Figure 3.6
Unemployment in selected countries

Source: OECD (2009)
OECD Economic Outlook,
November 2009, at
www.oecd.org

Long-term unemployment is a cause of concern to governments: social security payments will rise, or, in countries that lack extensive state benefit schemes, the burden of individual hardship may fall on families. Moreover, social and political unrest can be triggered by problems associated with high unemployment. It should be borne in mind that overall rates of unemployment tell only part of the story. Almost all countries experience regional disparities in unemployment, differing rates between age groups and differing rates between men and women. In 2008–9, the ILO reported on a global rise in unemployment (ILO, 2009b). The trends in major OECD economies appear in Figure 3.6. Note that unemployment in the US, which had been relatively low, rose steeply as a result of the financial crisis. As the world's largest economy, the crisis in the US impacted on the rest of the world. European countries, which had experienced higher levels of unemployment, had made progress in halting its rise, but in the recession, rising unemployment became one of the major worries for governments.

Summary points Unemployment

◆ Unemployment is the measure of the section of the population willing to work, but unable to find employment.

◆ Unemployment may rise if shifts in the industrial structure leave some workers without the skills needed for the jobs available.

◆ Government policies are important in reducing unemployment, through policies of innovation, training and help for small businesses.

Critical thinking
Unemployment and government policies
Governments might be tempted to say that higher unemployment in some sectors is due to globalization, which has resulted in the shift in jobs to low-cost countries. What can a government do to encourage higher levels of employment in the population and to reap benefits, not just negative impacts, of globalization?

Balance of payments

balance of payments
credit and debit
transactions between
a country's residents
(including companies)
and those of other
countries

current account in
connection with an
economy, account
based on trade in goods
(the merchandise
trade account),
services (the services
account), and profits
and interest earned
from overseas assets

capital account in
connection with an
economy, account
based on transactions
involving the sale and
purchase of assets, such
as investment in shares

The **balance of payments** refers to credit and debit transactions between a country's residents (including companies) and those of other countries. Transactions are divided into the current account and capital account. The **current account** is made up of trade in goods (the merchandise trade account), services (the services account), and profits and interest earned from overseas assets. The **capital account** includes transactions involving the sale and purchase of assets, such as investment in shares. If a country has a current account deficit, this means it imports more goods and services than it exports. If it has a current account surplus, it exports more than it imports. It is clear from Figure 3.7 that in recent years China and Germany have had the healthiest balance of payments, whereas the UK and US have current account deficits – massive in the case of the US. Of course, the US economy is larger than any of the others in this chart, but the trade deficit is equivalent to about 3% of its GDP. The UK's trade deficit is equivalent to about 2% of GDP, whereas China's trade surplus is over 6% of GDP. Improvement in the US trade deficit in 2009 can be accounted for largely by a weakening of the dollar.

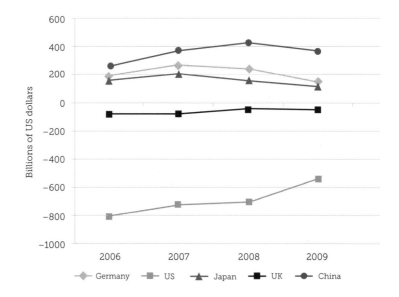

Figure 3.7 **Balance of payments in selected economies**

Source: OECD Statistics: International trade and balance of payments, at www.oecd.org

The balance of payments reflects demand both at home and abroad. It also reflects exchange rates (which will be discussed in Chapter 9) and the relative costs of domestic production. Governments can exert influence by varying the exchange rate, raising interests rates (to slow down growth), or by imposing tariff barriers such as import duties and quotas. China, whose currency is pegged to the US dollar, has come under pressure to allow its currency to appreciate. Raising interest rates is a means of decreasing demand, but possibly deterring future investment. The world's main trading countries are now linked in regional and multilateral trade groupings, which, as will be discussed later, have brought down trade barriers, so that governments are no longer able simply to restrict imports. Nor would they be advised to do so, at the risk of retaliation by trading partners. On the other hand, WTO rules, discussed in the next chapter, allow a number of exceptions, permitting countries to restrict imports in their national interest.

▸ More online ... Balance of payment data are available from the OECD's website at www.oecd.org. Go to 'topics', then 'trade'.

Summary points   **Balance of payments**

◆ An economy's balance of payments indicates the relative strength of its exports and imports. It reflects demand both at home and abroad for goods and services produced by the economy.

◆ Trade deficits have grown to huge proportions in some advanced economies, such as the US and the UK, indicating high domestic production costs.

The role of government in the economy

Governments seek policies that ensure economic growth, low inflation, and low unemployment, but there is considerable divergence of opinion on the extent to which they should intervene, or, alternatively, allow market forces to prevail. The role of government varies considerably between different types of economic system, which will be discussed in greater detail in the following sections. For present purposes, we broadly define the ways in which governments act in the national economy. Governments may act directly as economic players, or indirectly in regulating the environment in which businesses operate. In Chapter 1, we noted that governments in many countries play a direct role in state-owned and state-controlled companies. Governments are also ultimately responsible for the legislative and regulatory systems with which businesses in the country must comply.

fiscal policy budgetary policies for balancing public spending with taxation and other income

monetary policy economic policies for determining the amount of money in supply, rates of interest, and exchange rates

Policymaking falls under two headings. **Fiscal policy** refers to the budgetary policies for balancing public spending with taxation and other income, whereas **monetary policy** refers to policies for determining the amount of money in supply, rates of interest, and exchange rates. In many economies, a major role in monetary policy lies with the country's central bank, which is at the pinnacle of the country's financial system. It is responsible for issuing the country's notes and coins, and sets basic interest rates. It is also the banker to the government and the lender-of-last-resort. Most central banks, including the European Central Bank, are institutionally independent of government, to help to ensure that policy will not be based on short-term political considerations.

At international level, the International Monetary Fund (IMF), which will be discussed further in Chapter 9, has oversight of international exchange-rate stability, and has also considerably expanded its role into areas of economic policy once thought to be purely 'domestic' national policy. The institutional framework has thus become more complex as globalization has impacted on national economies. This intervention is received differently in differing countries. IMF intervention in the Asian financial crisis of 1998 was widely perceived as misjudged (Stiglitz, 2002), whereas in the recent global financial turmoil, several economies have received emergency IMF loans. They include Iceland, Ireland and Hungary – all countries which had enjoyed considerable growth from globalization, but whose exposure to global capital flows put them at risk from sudden financial shocks (see case study on Ireland in this chapter).

Governments raise and spend huge sums of money. Their priorities and means differ according to the country's political system. Especially relevant is the concentration or dispersal of political power: in countries where political power is concentrated in an elite, priorities are likely to be different from countries where leaders are democratically elected. In democratic systems, governments must present annual budgets to elected legislators, who scrutinize how the money is being raised and how the government proposes to spend it. These can be heated debates! In every national economy, there are pressures to prioritize spending in one area over another, and there are also differences of opinion on how best to raise the money needed for public spending.

Public spending is funded in the main from direct and indirect taxation, social security contributions, and borrowing. Income tax is a direct tax, while taxes on goods and services, such as consumption tax and VAT, are indirect taxes. Money taken in by governments from taxation is often expressed as a percentage of GDP. This percentage can be high. It is nearly 45% in France, 40% in Germany, and 32% in Brazil. In China and India, on the other hand, it is lower: 16% in China and 19% in India. The balance between direct and indirect taxation is a sensitive issue. Income tax falls on both individuals and companies, and most countries derive more income from individual income tax than from corporation tax. China and India are exceptions, deriving more tax from companies than from individuals. Some comparisons between different countries appear in Figure 3.8. China stands out as an example of a country where revenues from consumption tax exceed those from income tax. Consumption tax is disproportionately burdensome for poorer people, but is more efficient as a means of taxation than taxation of income (Arnold, 2008). In this respect, the US tax system is less efficient than the others in the figure.

social contributions charges levied by governments on businesses and other taxpayers to help finance social spending

A marked difference among countries is in **social contributions**, the charges which fall heavily on businesses and other taxpayers to help finance government social spending. Looking at Figure 3.8, these charges are highest in Germany and relatively low in the US, but they are virtually non-existent in China and India. The US, which has a tradition of private healthcare, rather than a national health service, took the momentous step of legislating for a national insurance scheme for healthcare in 2009. Governments in Europe, under pressure to keep social spending at high levels, are seeking to reduce social contributions, partly because spending cuts are needed to reduce budget deficits, and also as a way of alleviating burdens on businesses. The global financial crisis has strained government finances everywhere, and budget deficits have become a major worry, whatever the political system and size of national income.

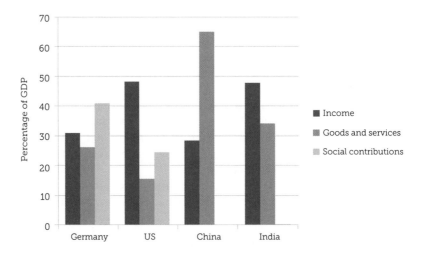

Figure 3.8 **How governments raise money from taxes**

Source: *The Economist*, 'The state's take', 21 November 2009

Governments enjoy a budget surplus when they receive more in revenue than they spend. 'Good housekeeping' principles would suggest that governments, like households, should not spend more than they take in. It is common, however, for governments to be in deficit, spending more than they receive in revenue. The debt that accumulates over the years is known as the **national debt.** National debt, expressed as a percentage of GDP, can grow to large proportions, causing considerable problems for government finances, and in extreme cases even the payment of interest becomes problematic. The **national budget balance** is the extent to which public spending exceeds receipts from taxes and other sources. Governments are more likely in today's world to have budget deficits rather than surpluses, as Figure 3.9 shows.

national debt the total debt accumulated by a central government's borrowings over the years

national budget balance the extent to which public spending is balanced by receipts from taxes and other sources; budget deficits are common

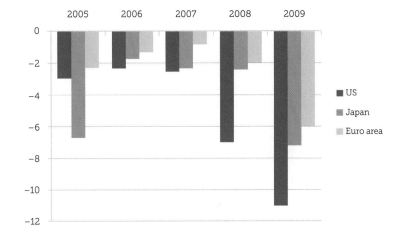

Figure 3.9 **General governmental financial balance** (as a percentage of GDP)

Source: OECD statistics at www.oecd.org

All the economies featured in Figure 3.9 saw a marked deterioration in government finances in 2009, associated with recession. Several factors can be highlighted.

Tax revenues and revenues from other sources diminish when incomes fall, so that tax receipts fall short of expectations which have fed into budgets. Raising taxes might be seen as an obvious solution, but during a recession governments fear that tax rises could further deepen the woes of individuals and businesses. Unemployment rises in a recession and governments must meet the payments of entitlements to these unemployed people for the length of time provided by law; it can be six months or a year. Governments can go further than this, however. Some subsidize companies to keep workers even though falling demand has meant there is not enough work for them to do. The governments of France, Spain and Germany make up wages from public money when companies might otherwise be forced to lay workers off. Similarly, governments help to prop up businesses through loans and other injections of money, which have come to be known as government bailouts, if the company is in danger of collapsing. AIG, America's largest insurance group, was rescued by the US government, as were large carmakers General Motors and Chrysler (see case study in Chapter 2). In the US and Europe, bailing out the banks absorbed huge sums of public money in 2008–9 (see Chapter 9).

The economic indicators discussed in this section are intertwined, both in times of prosperity and times of downturn. Economic growth depends heavily on rising consumer demand, which helps to provide employment. When demand is low, businesses struggle and unemployment rises. In the economic upheavals of recession,

Ireland's rollercoaster economy

Ireland became one of the world's most remarkable success stories for globalization's benefits. From an economy based mainly on low-cost production in the 1980s, it transformed itself into a global player. Ireland's so-called 'miracle' growth took place between 1986 and 2001. It attracted FDI in high value-added sectors such as pharmaceuticals. American companies led the rush to Ireland, with its educated, English-speaking workers, low costs and low taxes. Computer companies such as Dell built factories. Numerous American pharmaceutical companies piled into the country in the early 2000s, establishing multiple sites: Pfizer (5 sites), Abbott (7 sites) and Schering Plough (4 sites). State grants and access to the EU single market were additional attractions. Called the 'Celtic Tiger', Ireland enjoyed buoyant growth, which seemed to be sustainable (see figure). The country gained rapidly in global competitiveness, reaching a rank of third, behind only Hong Kong and Singapore (Krugman, 2009). How the Irish boom turned to bust offers lessons to other small, open economies exposed to global forces in all their manifestations.

A construction boom went hand in hand with economic growth, resulting in a huge expansion in numbers of houses, office blocks and retailing outlets. Builders and developers, along with home buyers, enjoyed easy access to credit from banks which in turn were able to borrow easily in global markets. By 2007, construction accounted for 20% of Ireland's GDP (IMF, 2009). Ireland's growing financial sector benefited from global financial flows. Its major domestic banks flourished, as did numerous foreign banks which set up in the country, attracted by the openness of the economy and low interest rates that prevailed, thanks to Ireland's membership of the eurozone. Exposure to global financial forces, however, made the country vulnerable to global shocks (IMF, 2009).

Ireland had long prided itself on a 'social partnership' between business, workers, trade unions and the government, in which there was a consensus on moderate wage growth. However, wages escalated during the boom, both in the private and the public sectors. Lax fiscal policy on the part of the government contributed to soaring public spending. A cut in income tax, while welcomed by taxpayers, left government finances in a perilous position. When the property bubble burst and financial crisis struck in 2008, the economy went into reverse. Construction companies were left with unsold properties, leading to widespread insolvency in the sector. Banks were left with bad loans connected with the domestic

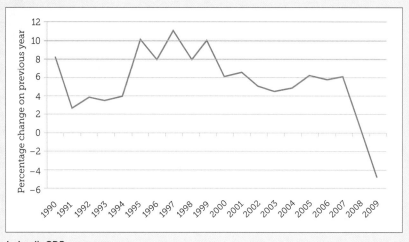

Ireland's GDP

Source: *The Economist*, 21 March 2009

construction industry, as well as their expansion into unregulated global financial markets. In September 2008, in order to avert a bank run, the Irish government offered to guarantee most bank deposits and debts, which would have amounted to two to three times the country's GDP. A number of the banks involved were foreign owned, leading many to question the policies that allowed the country to descend into this disastrous situation (Krugman, 2009).

▸ More online ... The Irish government's website is www.gov.ie and has links to a number of sites, including government departments.
GlaxoSmithKline's website is www.gsk.com

Government finances went dramatically into the red as revenues from taxes dried up but commitments on public spending continued to rise, including welfare payments for the mounting numbers of unemployed people. The Irish government had little prospect of borrowing its way out of difficulties, as potential bond investors had lost confidence in its bonds, especially in light of its bank guarantee policy. From a slight budget surplus in 2001, it plunged into a budget deficit of nearly 12% of GDP in 2009. The government was compelled to bring in drastic austerity measures, effectively cutting public-sector pay and reducing welfare payments. By 2010, the painful measures of wage freezes and reduced public spending appeared to be working, and the economy was forecast to be slowly recovering. However, unemployment, especially severe in the construction sector, was still expected to reach 14% of the workforce. Foreign investors such as pharmaceutical companies were expected to stay, but with slimmed-down workforces. Dell closed down its Irish factory and moved to Poland. Ireland was not expected to restore its budget deficit to the 3% set by the EU stability pact until 2014. Late in 2010, a bailout package of 85 billion euros was put in place by the EU, in support of the Irish economy, but austerity measures remained core to Ireland's economic recovery.

Ireland became one of globalization's success stories, reflected in the gleaming new buildings lighting up Dublin's skyline, but the image dimmed as financial crisis gripped the Irish economy

Source: Istock

Sources: IMF (2009) *Report on Ireland* (Washington, DC: IMF); Krugman, P. (2009) 'The lessons of Ireland', *The Guardian*, 21 April; Brown, J. (2010) 'Ireland finds tough measures paying off', *Financial Times*, 3 February; *The Economist* (2009) 'The party is definitely over', 21 March; Brown, J. (2009) 'Ireland meets economic crisis head on', *Financial Times*, 24 December

Questions for discussion

◆ How did globalization promote Ireland's stunning growth?
◆ What were the causes of Ireland's shattered economy?
◆ What lessons can other economies learn from the Irish example?

governments reach for 'stimulus' measures to bring about recovery. Injecting public money into the economy, in the form of subsidies to particular industries or groups, is one. Maintaining low interest rates is another. Stimulating demand by measures such as payments to people to scrap old cars and buy new ones is short term. Government support for banks has just been mentioned, and extends to other measures such as guaranteeing bank lending. Confidence in the banks is essential for any economy, and a banking collapse, as numerous financial crises have shown, can lead to economic recession in the wider economy. The need for government regulation in the financial sector rose to the top of the agenda following the global crisis of 2008. It also fuelled debate about the deeper issue of the role of government in the economy generally, along with the wider issue of international regulation, which might bring greater stability to the globalized financial environment. Differing economic systems offer differing perspectives, as we find in the next section.

Summary points Government and the economy

● Governments use fiscal policy to balance public spending with income from taxation and other sources.
● Governments raise money from both direct taxes, such as income tax, and indirect taxes, such as consumption tax.
● Through monetary policy, national authorities determine the amount of money in the economy, interest rates and exchange rates.
● As demands on government spending rise, growing national debt has become a worry in many countries.

Critical thinking
Feeling the impacts of budget deficits
Governments often justify their borrowing by stating that it is needed to stimulate the economy, as in the bailouts of failing companies in recent years. But a huge budget deficit is costly in the long term. What are the long-term impacts of high levels of national debt on the country's businesses?

Classifying national economic systems

In the period following the Second World War, the major economic systems were classified as polar opposites, with capitalism at one end and socialism at the other. This outlook reflected political as well as economic views in the cold-war period, when economic systems were seen in the context of dominant ideologies – complete world pictures of societal structures and human values. The socialist states were the state-planned, collectivist economies, ruled by communist party dictatorships. The Soviet Union and China were dominant among the main **planned economies**. The capitalist states were free market economies and also free societies. Among them were the US, European countries and Japan. With the crumbling of the Soviet Union and market reforms taking place in the other major socialist power, China, this dualistic view has given way to a much more fragmented spectrum of contrasting economic systems. Post-communist countries are making the transition from socialism to capitalism. There are now hardly any avowedly communist states left, as Cuba is now gradually liberalizing its economy. On the other hand, while all systems

planned economy economic system based on total state ownership of the means of production, in which the state controls prices and output

now seem to have some elements of capitalism, there are significant differences between them, and market economies are themselves evolving towards a greater emphasis on regulation and social values. National economic systems are not static, but evolve over time, moving towards greater liberalization in some periods and shifting towards stronger government control in others. Nevertheless, there are conceptual differences underpinning the different types of economic system.

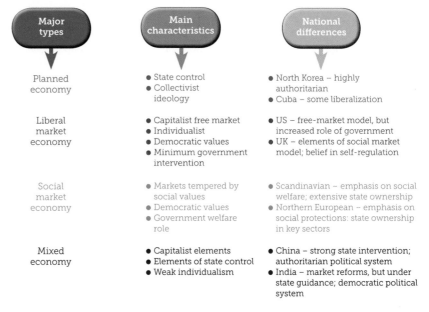

Figure 3.10 **Overview of different economic systems**

A national economic system is not just about a country's economic activities, but about its society. In any society, cultural values and social structures impact on economic activities. Therefore, in classifying economic systems, we are also pointing to social and cultural aspects of the country. Figure 3.10 provides an overview of the main types of economic system, along with the chief characteristics and examples of diverse countries within each. Note that the main characteristics highlight the role of the state and also the cultural values that support economic life.

As Figure 3.10 shows, the planned economy is probably the only distinctively 'pure' model, and even these closed economies are now opening up somewhat to outside influences. The two types of market economy have varying degrees of open markets, and in all, governments play a role, although this role varies greatly. The liberal market economies view state intervention as a necessary evil, while the social market economies take a positive view of the state's promotion of social cohesion. Note that all the market economies emphasize democratic values. It is common to define the mixed economy in the broad sense as one in which both state ownership and markets exist side by side. This definition is so broad that it would encompass just about every economy in the world, and is therefore not very helpful. Here, we take the view that the mixed economy is one in which capitalist elements, including free enterprise, competition and private property, are weaker than in the market economies. The mixed economy, while recognizing private enterprise, lays less stress on individual freedoms and democratic values. Some, such as China, retain the legacy of communist planned economies. India has a democratic political system and a vibrant market economy, but its roots in socialism have left a legacy of the

▸ More online ... Economies can be classified by their degrees of economic freedom.
A well-known index of economic freedom is at www.heritage.org/index/

strong state. Many countries, such as transitional economies and Latin American countries, fall into the same broad category, which can lead to some tension between the state's vested interests and newer market forces.

Summary points Classifying economic systems

◆ Economic systems can be classified according to degrees of state control: strong control at one extreme, as in the planned economy, and free reign of market forces at the other, as in the liberal market model of capitalism.

◆ Social, cultural and political dimensions influence the classification of countries' economic systems.

◆ All economic systems evolve over time, experiencing shifts between liberalization and state control.

Market economies

Market economies encompass a wide range of systems, with diverse cultural backgrounds. While they would all subscribe to capitalism in some form, they differ in the extent they would make market forces subordinate to other values, mainly through governmental regulation. Capitalism was the force behind nineteenth-century industrialization in Europe and the US, but their paths have diverged, reflecting differing cultural backgrounds.

The liberal market model

liberal market economy
capitalist economic system in which supply and demand, as well as prices, are determined by free markets

The **liberal market economy** refers to capitalism in what is considered to be its purest form, or laissez-faire capitalism. Commentators often refer to this model misleadingly as the 'Anglo-Saxon' model, but 'Anglo-American' is more appropriate, in view of the fact that the US is the pre-eminent exponent. Capitalism rests on principles of private enterprise and freedom of individuals to carry out businesses as they wish. The underlying assumption of capitalism is that, through each individual's pursuit of self-interested economic activity, society as a whole benefits. The main examples of the laissez-faire model are Britain and the US. These economies are characterized by high individualism, following Hofstede's cultural dimensions (discussed in Chapter 6). Other examples are Australia and Canada, suggesting that the spread of this model in the English-speaking world was linked to shared historical roots. As Figure 3.10 indicates, democratic values go along with the individualist culture of these countries. In these societies, civil and political freedoms are commonly thought to be linked to economic freedom. This assumption has been questioned, however, in economies such as China, where market liberalization has proceeded independently of political liberalization.

The economist Adam Smith envisaged an 'invisible hand' guiding the market system in his *Wealth of Nations* (Smith, [1776] 1950), implying that markets are self-regulating. The principle that governments should refrain from intervention came to be enshrined in much economic thinking, but in practice, governments have frequently felt compelled to intervene on a number of public-interest grounds. Markets are deemed to be inherently competitive. Businesses compete on the basis of supply

Ian Cheshire CEO of Kingfisher plc, the
British home improvement retailer

When Ian Cheshire joined Kingfisher in 1998, the company had the feel of a decentralized conglomerate. Although B&Q do-it-yourself (DIY) stores were the main business of the group, it also included Comet electronics and Woolworths stores. The subsequent development of Kingfisher into a global home improvement retailer owes much to Ian Cheshire's vision of what Kingfisher should be focusing on in the long term. The non-DIY businesses are now sold, and, under his leadership, the company has become more internationalized and more efficient in managing global supply chains. B&Q in the UK remains a key business, as is the Castorama chain in France, but Kingfisher now has 840 stores in eight countries. They include Poland, Russia, China, Turkey and Spain. Achieving success in these disparate markets has posed some of the sternest challenges that Mr Cheshire has faced since he moved from his job as head of B&Q to become CEO of the whole group in 2008.

Kingfisher has played a key role in the internationalization of the DIY industry, expanding in both emerging and mature markets

Source: Istock

The impacts of economic downturn and especially weakness in the housing market are soon felt in the home improvement sector, as consumers typically shop for new furnishings and fittings when moving into a new home. Economic downturn in the UK has led to rather lacklustre performance at B&Q. But Mr Cheshire has taken the view that the DIY market offers much potential for consumers in terms of value, even if family budgets are squeezed. If products are of good quality, attractively priced and easy to install, then consumers will respond. He says, 'Although the theme of "make it easy" will be a strategic theme, the actual application is slightly different market by market' (Cheshire, 2010). A focus on innovation has been one of his guiding themes, especially relevant in the context of an industry that might be perceived as boring. He has overseen the appointment of the company's first innovation director. A recent initiative has been to introduce room-style display areas, which chime with lifestyle aspirations of consumers, whether they are in the more mature markets of Europe or the emerging markets such as China and Russia.

Another of Cheshire's themes is sustainability, including innovative products designed along ecological principles, or 'eco-products'. An example is a natural paint that is sold as a powder, to be mixed up by the customer, thus avoiding shipping bulky liquids long distances. Kingfisher now offers 4,000 eco-products, and by 2010 its eco-product sales had risen to over £1 billion, representing 10% of its total turnover. Sustainability extends to operations as well as products: in 2009–10, the company reduced its emissions of CO_2 equivalent from energy and transport by 8%. The CEO says that the threat of climate change demands that businesses must adapt to survive, taking in a time frame which extends up to 40 years: 'If you're running a business on a five- to ten-year time frame, you can't simply have an unsustainable business model. Unless we're sustainable, we don't have a long-term future' (De Vita, 2010). Mr Cheshire is a thoughtful and analytic CEO, conscious of the competitive challenges in global markets, but also the long-term sustainability of the business.

Sources: De Vita, E. (2010) 'MT Sustainability Visions: Ian Cheshire on his 40-year plan', *Management Today*, at www.managementtoday.co.uk; Cheshire, I. (2010) Presentation to investors in New York, 7 October 2010, at www.kingfisher.co.uk; Kingfisher plc (2010) Corporate Responsibility Summary Report 2009–10, at www.kingfisher.com/responsibility; Felsted, A. and Stern, S. (2010) 'A makeover man with fresh designs in mind', *Financial Times*, 6 September

monopoly domination by one firm of the market for particular goods or services, enabling the firm to determine price and supply

oligopoly an industry dominated by a few very large firms

and demand: producers supply goods and services to consumers, whose demand is thus satisfied. It is well known, however, that if one supplier becomes dominant in market, squeezing out smaller rivals, that firm, known as a **monopoly**, is able to dictate prices. Similarly, control by two or more firms, known as **oligopoly**, allows these firms to co-ordinate pricing. In these cases, most countries accept that regulation is needed to control market abuse and restore competition. In other words, governments intervene to *maintain* markets (Rodrik, 2009). Competition law (discussed in Chapter 8) has become integral to the smooth functioning of market economies.

Contrary to the image of stability implied by the invisible hand, markets can be volatile and unpredictable. Stock markets and individual companies are susceptible to swings in levels of confidence which can seem to verge on the irrational. A listed company might look sound financially and have good products, but its stock values might suffer if its CEO is perceived to lack vision, or because sentiment within the sector as a whole is pessimistic as to the future. Stock market crashes bring down the well-managed companies along with the reckless ones. The rise of highly risky investments and imprudent financial practices was a cause of the financial crisis in 2008–9, which spread to the wider economy. Citigroup, the US banking and financial services company, came close to ruin in 2008, from excessive debt and risky investments. When the spotlight was shone on corporate governance, weak accountability to boards and excessive executive pay were also highlighted. Citigroup, like other large American companies, received rescue packages from the US government. Why were they not just allowed to fail, as befits a free market economy?

Government bailouts might seem to have little place in the free market model. Critics would say that the model has shown itself to be flawed, but advocates would say that government intervention in market economies has been a persistent feature of capitalism (Phelps, 2009). Indeed, Adam Smith himself recognized that markets cannot stand alone (Sen, 2009). Concern has grown over the sustainability of any economic system in the long term. Sustainability as a concept includes not merely economic factors, but also issues such as whether the environment and non-renewable resources are being managed sustainably. Regulation has long been recognized as essential to ensure openness and fairness in markets, helping to retain public confidence and long-term viability. Other aspects of the government's role are subsidies to specific industries, funding of large infrastructure projects and welfare spending. Although all these areas of spending might seem contrary to capitalist orthodoxy, they have evolved as essential to social well-being and stability. It is now recognized that the ecological environment is another priority. Governments in these countries favour market mechanisms in principle over direct intervention, but in some areas, such as environmental protection, it is arguable that market mechanisms are insufficient. This is one of the crucial points of principle that distinguish the free market model from the social market model.

Summary points The liberal market model

◆ The liberal market model values free enterprise and the legal protection of private property as economic cornerstones.

◆ Although government intervention is perceived as necessary, its role should be as limited as possible, according to liberal market advocates.

Critical thinking

Capitalism: a flawed model?

The financial crisis that occurred in late 2008 revealed a spectacular failure of markets to maintain stability. Does this indicate that capitalism is fatally flawed, or just in need of regulatory adjustments?

Social market models

The concept of the welfare state dates from the aftermath of the Depression of 1929, when western governments introduced systems of social security, unemployment benefit and other welfare programmes which are now perceived as necessary. To many, mainly those on the political right, these measures are seen as an essential social safety net in the market economy, while to those more to the left, social justice is seen as a goal in itself. The **social market economy** gives a social-justice dimension to the capitalist model. Its main features are state ownership or control in key sectors and extensive social welfare programmes, which reduce the inequalities inherent in the pure capitalist model. State ownership and private ownership exist side by side. Major enterprises such as heavy industry, banks, oil companies and airlines are likely to be state owned. Seen as national champions, they are naturally protected from take-over bids, making them less prone to the volatilities which private-sector companies experience. On the other hand, state-owned enterprises are a drain on the public purse, and have gained reputations as being less efficient than private-sector firms. A hybrid solution has been to 'privatize' public-sector enterprises by listing them as public companies, in which the state retains a large shareholding and private investors are invited to take up a minority of 'floating' shares.

The social market model has evolved differently in the diverse societies which have adopted it. In Sweden, the emphasis is on an extensive welfare state to reduce social inequalities (Pontusson, 1997). France and Germany also have extensive social welfare policies, but they differ in the role played by the state in economic life. In France, the centralized state has created a more 'statist' model, while the German model is more 'corporatist', based on co-operation between the state, business and labour (Vitols, 2000). In Germany, workers are legally entitled to a say in company management through 'co-determination' (see Chapter 1). Germany is a more decentralized state than France. As such, it contrasts with the laissez-faire model of the US and the statist model in France (Streeck, 1997). Many tiers of government in Germany, however, have tended to create complex regulatory regimes for businesses to navigate through.

The Scandinavian countries tend to come near the top of rankings for human development, which take in life expectancy, health and education indicators (UNDP, 2009). Their societies have lower inequality than those in the Anglo-American tradition. On the other hand, high taxation and high social contributions are drawbacks for businesses in these countries. Sustaining a large public sector along with extensive social programmes entails huge public expenditure, risking budget deficits. Moreover, the rising costs of social policies in a context of rising unemployment and an ageing population have led these governments to cautiously embrace market reforms, including privatizations, noted above. There have also been pressures from the EU Commission to open markets to greater competition, reflecting its commitment to market reforms and a reduction in the role of the state.

The social market model is more attuned to issues of environmental protection and depletion of natural resources than the more liberal market economy, as these issues are encompassed in the model's recognition of ethical principles as an adjunct

social market economy
capitalist market economy with a strong social justice dimension, including substantial welfare state provisions

▸ More online ... The UNDP human development index is at www.undp.org

to market considerations. In liberal market economies, the 'business case' for environmental protection is that, ultimately, productivity and profitability will fall if environmental considerations are ignored, whereas the social market economy espouses action on the environment as an imperative on both ethical and business grounds.

Summary points Social market economies

◆ In social market economies, the social justice dimension is grafted onto the capitalist model through welfare-state measures and employment protection.

◆ These economies tend to have high human development and greater equality among inhabitants, but they can be high-cost environments for businesses.

◆ Strong government and a centralized state are features of many social market economies, for example France.

Critical thinking

Triumph of the social market model?

These systems achieve high rankings in human development, but at a cost in high social contributions and taxes. On the other hand, some countries with more liberal market models have larger budget deficits. To what extent does this suggest that more countries should shift to the social market model?

Asian capitalist systems

The East and South East Asian market economies are often grouped together as representing variations on the free market model. Japan and South Korea can be highlighted as offering distinctive economic systems. Though different, they share key characteristics. Both were later to industrialize than the economies of Europe and America, and in both, economic development has been guided by the state. They also share a democratic political system, with civil, political and economic freedoms. For these reasons, we place these countries in the broad category of market economies. Although they share with the social market economies a strong state perspective, theirs is not the western welfare-state model of the European countries. Both have far less developed welfare systems than would be the norm in western economies. These countries are more in the collectivist than individualist cultural tradition. Their Asian cultural heritage emphasizes the role of the family and of the company as a kind of family, looking after the whole person, rather than taking the narrow view of the worker as an employee.

Japan, like Germany, faced the task of rebuilding its industries after the Second World War. The state provided economic guidance, and hence Japan is looked on as exemplifying the 'developmental state' model (Johnson, 1982). The use of industrial policy, rather than outright state ownership, has been a chief feature of its economic development, relying on co-operation between the three centres of power – the bureaucracy, politicians and big businesses. Business in Japan has traditionally been organized around groups of companies, or **keiretsu**, linked by cross-shareholdings and informal networks with suppliers and customers. The reliance on interlocking corporate structures as a source of economic strength has given rise to the notion of 'alliance capitalism' as a category to cover the range of economic systems in which inter-firm relations, rather than free market exchange, predominate (Gerlach, 1991). From a position of economic powerhouse in the 1980s, the Japanese economy

keiretsu grouping of Japanese companies, characterized by inter-firm ties and cross-shareholdings

▶ More online ... Toyota's corporate website is www.toyota.co.jp
Sony's website is www.sony.net
Hyundai is at http://worldwide.hyundai.com

descended into stagnation in the 1990s, following a collapse in the banking and financial system, brought on by a collapse in asset values and imprudent lending. Recovery came belatedly, in about 2004, but has been hesitant. Japan's leading companies, such as Toyota and Sony, have remained globally competitive, despite newer competitors, such as South Korea, Taiwan and, of course, China. However, Toyota's reputation has recently suffered from high-profile quality problems, entailing large recalls of cars in major markets.

chaebol family-dominated industrial conglomerates characteristic of business organizations in South Korea

South Korea, too, has taken its own distinctive development path. Here, economic development owes its impetus to the large family-owned conglomerates, or **chaebol**, which expanded aggressively overseas during the 1980s. These groups include Hyundai, Samsung and LG. South Korea was severely affected by the Asian financial crisis of 1997–8, its companies having accumulated excessive debt in a business environment where family considerations mattered more than objectively sound business practices. Restructuring these companies along more transparent lines of governance was one of the reforms that later governments have undertaken, although the strong cultural heritage has worked against radical reforms. On the other hand, a strong cultural heritage can be viewed as an 'anchor' against the more flambouyant characteristics of free markets (Mahbubani, 2009).

Lastly, China, the largest Asian country, is also undertaking market reforms, but still within the framework of the one-party state bequeathed by the communist revolution. We therefore classify China as a mixed economy, discussed in the next section.

Summary points An Asian model of capitalism

◆ Strong state intervention and bureaucratic regulation are features of Asian capitalism, although these countries tend to have weak welfare-state provisions.

◆ A corporate culture based on the company as analogous to the family is characteristic of Asian firms.

◆ Groups of companies, both informal and equity-based, have been a feature of Asian capitalism, often held to have been crucial to Japan's and South Korea's economic development.

Mixed economies

mixed economy economic system which combines market elements with state controls

The **mixed economy** is the last category in Figure 3.10, combining market elements with institutional structures remindful of state-planned economies. Many emerging economies fall into this category. China is the main example, with its embrace of two systems: capitalism as an economic system and a political system still controlled by the communist party. Many post-communist transition economies fall into the broad category of mixed economy, undertaking market reforms and combining these with political democratization. In this section, we highlight the different national examples of the mixed economy, assessing the impacts of globalization. In particular, we look at China, India and the transitional economies of Central and Eastern Europe.

China

China is an ancient civilization and, although later than other Asian countries in economic development, is now asserting itself as a regional and global power –

economically, militarily and politically. The current state of China (its full name is the People's Republic of China) dates only from the communist revolution of 1949 led by Mao Zedong. The ruling party structures were roughly modelled on the Soviet system (McGregor, 2009), and remain so six decades on. However, the underpinning ideology has seen numerous shifts. The Maoism of the early years (based on the teachings of Mao Zedong), loosely based on Marxism–Leninism, has given way to a more nationalist perspective, and only in 1979 was the shift towards liberal economic reforms introduced, under the leadership of Deng Xiaoping.

Thereafter, China's economy grew dramatically, achieving 10% average growth rates for the next two decades, thanks largely to the booming private sector. The prosperity of its people has also grown, although there are wide variations between the rural standard of living and that enjoyed by the new urban dwellers. Liberalization is being contemplated in sectors still under state domination, such as banking. Three of the country's four large state-owned banks were listed on the Hong Kong stock exchange in 2006 and 2007, suggesting that commercial rather than political interests would be paramount, but the government clearly retains the upper hand. The impact of the global crisis was less pronounced in China than had been feared, largely because the government could simply order the banks to increase lending when confidence was evaporating. The manufacturing centres of Guangdong, which have led exports of consumer goods to western markets, were forced to slow down production, resulting in the return of many migrant workers to their rural homes. However, the upheaval was less pronounced than feared. The Chinese government reached for a variety of stimulus measures and increased public spending on infrastructure, in order to sustain domestic demand. The stimulus package is estimated to have amounted to four trillion yuan, the equivalent of $586 billion (*The Economist*, 2009a). Economic growth slowed over 2009, but at over 8% was highly impressive (see Figure 3.11).

China's economy remains dependent on investment and exports. Job creation and innovation have come from the small, private-sector firms, but the centralized, state-controlled financial system has not favoured these companies. China's economic model has featured an opening up to foreign investors and greater

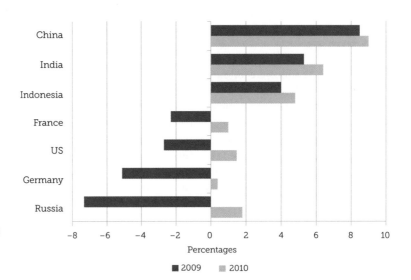

Figure 3.11 **Forecasts for GDP growth in selected developed and emerging economies**

Source: *Financial Times*, 6 October 2009

► More online ... Vodafone is at www.vodafone.com
Jaguar Land Rover is at www.jaguarlandrover.com

economic freedom for individuals. However, these reforms have taken place in a country where the levers of power are controlled by the communist party, which controls appointments to all important positions in both government and industry. Lack of transparency and a weak legal system are drawbacks to further genuine market reforms.

India

Compared to China, India would seem to be closer to a genuine market economy. There is considerable economic freedom, and its government is accountable through democratic elections. It also has a legal tradition resting on the rule of law. However, India was founded as a socialist state in 1948, and retains a legacy of the strong state, prone to heavy-handed regulation. Its market reforms have been guided by the government, which, for many years, was reluctant to welcome FDI. In the past decade, India has become more open to foreign investors, but the western investor must enter the market through a joint venture with an Indian partner. A number of foreign investors have been deterred, including Vodafone. India's poor infrastructure, social tensions and bureaucracy remain obstacles for potential foreign investors (see case study at the end of this chapter).

India's companies have expanded globally, becoming important players in sectors such as IT and outsourcing. Some, for example Tata, have made high-profile acquisitions, such as the purchase of UK car company Jaguar Land Rover from Ford of the US in 2008. India has only recently become important in manufacturing, much later than China, its slowness accounted for largely by its reluctance to welcome FDI. India's economic growth has maintained momentum despite the financial crisis, indicating that, like China, the country feels confident of its internal strengths which help to shield it from financial crisis originating in the US. As Figure 3.11 shows, growth in Asian emerging economies held up well during global economic turmoil. Russia, however, was severely affected by the financial crisis.

The transition economies of Central and Eastern Europe

These economies have enthusiastically sought foreign investors to drive economic development. They embarked on modernization and liberalization programmes following the fall of their communist regimes in the early 1990s. The transition from a planned economy to a market economy can take place rapidly, through 'shock therapy', in which privatizations and market structures are set up as quickly as possible. Alternatively, a longer timeline and gradualist shift can be implemented. Whatever the timescale, four interrelated processes can be identified:

- *Liberalization* – In a planned economy, wages and prices are determined by the government. When state control was removed and prices were freed, the result was a price shock for consumers, who were accustomed to paying prices for commodities which were less than world market levels. Liberalization was perceived as a threat to industrial and agricultural workers in particular. In Poland, for example, the movement to overthrow Soviet rule was led by the Solidarity trade union, supported by the Polish Catholic Church, both representing widespread scepticism about liberal reform policies.
- *Stabilization* – The process of withdrawal of the state from running the economy, while welcomed by consumers eager to purchase new goods in the open market,

inevitably led to economic upheaval. Segments of the population, such as agricultural workers, the unemployed and pensioners, were left vulnerable. Pressures from disadvantaged groups can lead to political instability and even unrest. In these circumstances, the prospect of economic growth from liberalization is perhaps the key factor in helping to bring long-term prosperity across societies.

- *Internationalization* – Crucial to the transition economies is their opening up to trade and investment, relying on private-sector firms to gain in competitiveness. The state-owned industries in post-communist states were largely uncompetitive, leading to protectionist pressures. However, liberalization opened the way for FDI, taking advantage of lower costs – particularly lower wages – than in the advanced economies. Strong economic growth ensued, bringing economic integration with European neighbours, which was the strongest force behind EU accession, discussed below.

- *Privatization* – Privatization involves the conversion of state enterprises to privately owned and operated companies, and also the fostering of new start-up enterprises. SMEs were some of the earliest and easiest enterprises to privatize, as they could be taken over by their managers and workers. Medium and large-scale enterprises proved more difficult, and public opinion was hostile towards handing them over to former communist managers. Sales to foreign firms also met resistance. The leveraged buy-out (LBO) by workers, financed by loan capital from the government, was a favoured route. Another option was to allow takeover by a joint venture between a foreign firm and a local partner.

These processes were put in motion when the Soviet bloc started to break up in 1989. East Germany was united with West Germany in 1990. In the early 1990s, the states of Hungary, Poland, Czechoslovakia, Romania, and Bulgaria became sovereign states. Further fragmentation resulted in the creation of separate Czech and Slovak Republics, as well as the separate Balkan republics of Slovenia, Croatia, Bosnia and the Yugoslav Federation. The Soviet Union itself broke up into 15 separate republics. The three Baltic republics – Estonia, Latvia and Lithuania – went their own way, eventually becoming EU member states in 2004, along with Poland, the Czech Republic, Hungary, Slovenia and Slovakia. They were joined by Romania and Bulgaria in 2007.

Russia, which had been the largest of the Soviet republics, opted for the shock therapy approach to privatizations, unleashing a new powerful capitalist class, but without the regulatory institutions which are common in mature market economies. A result was the growth of a class of powerful oligarchs in major industries, creating political tensions. Russia adopted a new constitution in 1993, but its democratic aspirations have only been partially fulfilled. The rise of Vladimir Putin was responsible for reining in the oligarchs and restoring stability following a financial crash in 1998, but this process resulted in a consolidation of leadership in the all-powerful ruling party. Hence, Russia's economic and political transition has been fraught with uncertainties.

Other states that emerged following the breakup of the Soviet Union have taken a more gradualist approach to transition. It is important to remember that the former Soviet republics had experienced the socialist planned economy since 1928, whereas the states of Central Europe and the Baltic states were 'sovietized' only in 1948, and thus had recent memories of real independence and a market economy (Bradshaw, 1996). These countries embarked on privatizations and opened their doors to foreign investors, although bureaucracy and corruption were continuing drawbacks for investors. Proximity to the western consumer markets made these countries key locations for manufacturing. They also took advantage of global financial markets for funding, but heavy reliance on debt left these economies vulnerable when the global financial crisis struck. Their governments are now facing huge budget deficits and general decline in regional GDP. Latvia came to the brink of bankruptcy, requiring a bailout from the IMF and EU, which also assisted Hungary and Romania.

Summary points Mixed economies

● The mixed economy combines market elements within the context of state controls.
● Many mixed economies are making the transition from a socialist, planned economy to one based on market forces.

● Large emerging markets, such as China and India, are mixed economies, benefiting from globalization to foster economic development.

● The post-communist transition economies of Central and Eastern Europe have combined economic liberalization with new democratic political systems, but have experienced instability both economically and politically.

Critical thinking

China versus India

China and India, both characterized here as mixed economies, are very different. List their similarities and their differences. Which factors can be highlighted as weighing most heavily with foreign investors?

Regionalization: focus on the EU

regionalization growing economic links and co-operation within a geographic region, both on the part of businesses and governments

Regionalization has been taking place throughout the world, despite the forces of globalization. By **regionalization**, we mean growing economic links and co-operation within a geographic region, on the part of both businesses and governments. Economic ties, such as trade, can lead to what is termed 'shallow' integration, in that there need be little physical presence of the foreign company in its destination market. FDI, which entails establishing operations in the foreign location, represents a deeper involvement in local economies as stakeholders, although foreign investors, too, can withdraw from markets as their strategies change. Regionalization at a deeper level involves not just liberalized trade and investment, but deepening institutional ties and political co-operation. The extent of regionalization differs among the world's regions. In many, diverse economies and disparate cultural and political backgrounds of states tend to limit the deepening of ties. Regional trade agreements, discussed in the next chapter, have sprung up in every continent. Examples include the North America Free Trade Agreement (Nafta) and the Asean agreement of South East Asia. These agreements have focused mainly on reducing trade barriers between member economies.

European Union (EU) regional grouping of European countries which evolved from trade agreements to deeper economic integration

The **European Union (EU)**, by contrast, has progressed beyond trade deals to take on regional governmental functions, becoming a supranational structure, potentially challenging the sovereignty of member states. However, the vision of the EU from its foundation in the 1950s, when the memories of the Second World War were still fresh, included creating a closer political union as a force for peace, co-operation and security. This was an ambitious project, as, even among the original members (shown in Table 3.1), there was diversity among economic systems. Diversity became much greater as more states joined, including poorer states and former communist states.

Map of EU and
eurozone

The economies of the EU and eurozone

The EU now has 27 member states; of these, 16 are members of the single-currency eurozone (see map and Table 3.1). A turning point came in 2004, when the union absorbed 10 new states, often referred to as the 'accession 10', distinguishing them from the pre-2004 states, which make up the 'EU 15'. The EU encompasses a population of over half a billion people, and, taken as a whole, it is the world's largest economy, with a GDP of $16.1 trillion in 2009, coming ahead of the US in second place, with a GDP of $13.8l trillion (IMF, 2009). EU GDP per capita varies markedly, from Luxembourg, where GDP is 276% of the EU average, to Bulgaria, where it is just 41% (European Commission, 2008). We will look at the development of the institutions in detail in Chapter 7. Here we focus mainly on the economic impacts in the individual countries, the region and the global economy.

Table 3.1 **Membership of the EU and eurozone**
Members of the eurozone are shown by an asterisk (*)

Date of EU entry	State
1957	Belgium*, France*, Germany*, Luxembourg*, the Netherlands*, Italy*
1973	Denmark, Ireland*, the UK
1981	Greece*
1986	Portugal*, Spain*
1995	Austria*, Finland*, Sweden
2004	Cyprus*, Malta*, Czech Republic, Hungary, Poland, the Slovak Republic*, Slovenia*, Latvia, Lithuania, Estonia
2007	Bulgaria, Romania

The EU project aimed to create a single market in which goods, people, information and capital can move freely. The process has been mapped out in a series of treaties, beginning with the Treaty of Rome in 1956. The opening up of trade in goods and FDI among member states has been a success story, but other aspects of integration, such as services and transport across national borders, have not yet been liberalized. The EU is committed to liberal goals of free markets and rolling back the state, which, as we have seen, is a strong player in a number of European economies, notably those which fall within the broad category of social market systems. Any liberalization or harmonization of rules involves co-operation of national governments, willingly ceding powers to EU structures. National governments are politically highly sensitive to groups and interests within their own countries, and, despite wishes to commit to Europe-wide open markets, are constantly under pressure to protect domestic industries. The EU's history to date has been one of member governments pursuing domestic policy objectives within EU structures, rather than taking an EU-wide perspective.

In theory, governments remain responsible for the prudent management of their own economies, where national economic systems retain their distinctive characteristics. They retain control of fiscal policies such as spending and taxation, but in matters of monetary policy, the EU plays an important role, especially in view of the authority of the European Central Bank, set up to oversee eurozone members.

Central to the process of economic integration was the introduction of the single currency, the euro. The elimination of exchange-rate risk and reduction in transaction costs have contributed greatly to growth in trade and FDI. The **eurozone** came into existence in 1999. Membership of the eurozone involves relinquishing power over exchange rates and interest rates to the European Central Bank. In times of economic downturn, governments can use the policy of devaluing their currency – one used extensively by Italy before the eurozone came into being. A government within the eurozone relinquishes this power. In addition, a government might raise interest rates when the economy appears to be overheating, but a government within the eurozone gives this power to the European Central Bank.. Although these policy restrictions might seem unappealing, and governments could take the drastic step of withdrawing from the eurozone, the benefits of the euro are usually perceived to outweigh the disadvantages. Slovakia, the latest state to join the eurozone, had seen a flourishing of car manufacturing, which, despite the slowdown in demand, has not experienced drastic economic implications and pressure on the currency, largely because the country is in the eurozone. Italy's car industry, dominated by Fiat, has weathered the economic crisis, even absorbing one of America's ailing carmakers, Chrysler. The euro, although a weak currency during its early years, is now relatively strong, for example in relation to the US dollar. For a small member state accustomed to a floating currency, the stability of the euro is a benefit, especially in a context of volatile markets.

Any EU member state wishing to join the eurozone must first fulfil a number of criteria, known as the Maastricht convergence criteria, set out in the Maastricht Treaty, which came into effect in 1993. A cornerstone of the Maastricht Treaty is the stability and growth pact, which commits all EU governments, whether in the eurozone or not, to keep budget deficits in check. As budget deficits have mounted in most European countries, this is one of the important hurdles for prospective eurozone members. An applicant country must become part of the EU's **European Monetary Union (EMU)**, and comply with the Exchange Rate Mechanism (ERM) system, by which its currency is loosely pegged to the euro. This means that its

eurozone member states in the EU which have satisfied the Maastricht criteria and joined the EMU

European Monetary Union (EMU) EU programme centred on the single currency and an independent central bank, which sets monetary policy for eurozone member states

▶ More online ... The EU's portal is at http://europa.eu and has links to the EU's institutions.

currency fluctuation against the euro must remain within relatively tight bands. The EMU dates from 1979, and the ERM was updated in 2004, to become ERMII, with which current applicants must comply. The full convergence criteria are listed below:

- *Price stability* – The rate of inflation must be no more than 1.5% higher than the three member states with lowest inflation rates.
- *Sound public finances* – The government's budget deficit must be below 3% of GDP.
- *Sustainable public finances* – National debt should not exceed 60% of GDP.
- *Exchange rate stability* – The country should have been in the ERM for two years, without having devalued its currency within that time.
- *Long-term interest rates* – The country's interest rate must not be higher than that of the three countries with the best performance in terms of price stability in the EU.

These criteria have been somewhat overtaken by events in recent years. Some existing eurozone members would not meet the limits on budget deficits and national debt. Ireland has seen its economy come near to collapse, forcing it to make radical cuts in public spending, to the consternation of its inhabitants. Greece has been an even more dramatic example, with a budget deficit of nearly 13% and national debt reaching 125% of GDP in 2009 (*The Economist*, 2009b). A bloated public sector combined with profligate finances and corruption has rocked this eurozone country, raising the prospect of other eurozone countries mounting a bailout. Four countries (Latvia, Estonia, Lithuania and Denmark) are in the ERM at present. One of these, Latvia, has seen a 12% contraction in its economy in 2009, leading to financial aid from the EU and IMF. The accession countries which joined the EU in 2004 were all committed by their treaties of accession to joining the EMU as soon as possible. Hungary's huge budget deficits would, in principle, preclude it from eurozone membership. It is struggling to reduce public spending and bring the budget deficit within 3% of GDP. Given the financial difficulties of some member states, both in the eurozone and waiting in the wings, it is not difficult to see why the appetite for enlargement among existing EU members seems to have waned. In 2010, only Estonia was approved by the European Commission for eurozone membership in 2011.

Summary points The EU and eurozone

- Creation of a single market is at the centre of the EU, but economic integration has not led to convergence among member states.

- The eurozone has benefited businesses through the introduction of the single currency, but the economies of eurozone member states have remained divergent, some struggling with excessive debt.

Enlargement and the future of the EU

The process of enlargement has been at the heart of the EU since its inception, bringing the prospect of greater prosperity and stability to the wider region. However, the debate over the EU has been ongoing almost as long, and enlargement is now at the crossroads. Current applicants include Turkey, a Muslim country traditionally seen as straddling Europe and Asia. Closer to 'old Europe', Croatia is in the forefront of current applicants. Will the EU continue to expand, playing a global role that befits its status as the world's largest economy? Or will it become more fragmented, mired in the strains between competing national powers?

Tension over future enlargement was one of the factors that held up the Lisbon Treaty, which took seven years to be finalized (coming into force in 2009). The treaty represents an amended version of a constitutional treaty which failed ratification hurdles in several member states. The difficulties encountered in securing ratification of the Lisbon Treaty reflect member states' scepticism about the benefits of the EU in terms of national interests. The spectre of national economic protectionism is one that has long haunted the EU, especially in the context of countries in which nationalist politicians have long criticized the EU's liberal reform policies as threats to national sovereignty. EU enlargement has been about the prospects of economic gains winning out over these inward-looking forces. These gains have been real enough in new member states: businesses have flourished from greater cross-border activity, and governments have welcomed the structural funds which have flowed into poorer economies. The 'cohesion' funds, along with subsidies of agriculture, amount to a large proportion of the EU's budget, as Figure 3.12 shows.

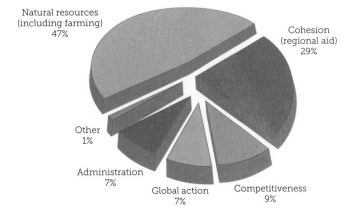

Figure 3.12 **Breakdown of the EU's 2010 budget**
Total budget is 122.9 billion euros

Source: European Parliament (2010) 'Making sense of the 2010 EU budget', at www.europarl.europa.eu

The EU Commission has remained committed to market reforms, but these have taken place only very gradually, and governments have tended to retain a mindset that ranks countries as winners or losers in terms of EU funding. Poorer countries have been winners in this respect, as the lion's share of its budget is devoted to aiding poorer regions and vital sectors. The extent to which this provides the basis of a definable regional capitalism is much debated. A model of European capitalism closer to the free market model has been a beacon for many within the EU, but national governments have retained a strong grip on institutional direction within its structures. Proponents of the social market model can point to the fact that their focus on social priorities and state intervention in markets has helped them to avoid the worst of the recession which started in the US. The fact that the financial crisis struck Ireland, a leader in market reforms, has clouded prospects of further market liberalization. Iceland, which has now applied to join the EU, had emulated the Irish example, and was also a casualty of crashing global financial markets. Will it find the hand of welcome extended?

The EU is unlikely to repeat the ambitious enlargement exercise that took place in the mid-2000s. Both the Netherlands and France voted 'no' in referendums on the constitutional treaty which preceded the Lisbon Treaty, largely for fear of paving the way for further enlargement. Inhabitants of the richer member states shoulder the greatest financial burdens of the EU, which have grown to huge proportions. They question why they should be burdened with propping up member states which, they feel, have failed to act responsibly in managing their internal economies. They point to weak governance, out-of-control public spending, corruption and lack of transparency in some member states, which, they fear, could threaten the whole edifice. A stronger regulatory role for the European Commission is a possible outcome. Restoring stability to individual economies will help to restore confidence in the EU as a whole.

Summary points EU enlargement at the crossroads

- Successive enlargements have brought greater economic diversity to the EU, and have resulted in burdens on the richer countries in supporting the poorer countries, which are mainly in Central and Eastern Europe.

- The Lisbon Treaty introduced new institutional arrangements designed to accommodate the newly enlarged union. However, the protracted ratification process revealed a lack of consensus on the EU's future enlargement.

- In the economic fallout of the global financial crisis of 2008–9, it is possible that the EU institutions will play a stronger regulatory role.

Critical thinking
The EU at the crossroads
Divergent national perspectives and goals have clouded prospects of EU enlargement. Further doubts have arisen in connection with financial woes in individual economies, such as Greece, Ireland and Portugal, compounded by the possibility of 'contagion' spreading to other eurozone members. Are these temporary difficulties, or are they signs that the EU is unworkable in its present form?

Implications for international business strategy

The economic environment is a key dimension in the PEST analysis (introduced in Chapter 1). In this chapter, we have covered a variety of aspects of national economies, as well as regional and global factors. Looking first at comparisons between national economies, it is clear that economic indicators are interdependent. A firm considering an FDI project in a new location will look not just at current GDP data, but at economic growth over a long period. It will also study levels of unemployment and its preponderance in regions or segments of the workforce. The prospective investor will take account of the state of government finances. If the country is heavily in debt, this does not bode well for investors looking for growing markets in the future. Many countries opened their economies to foreign investors, financing their growth through borrowing, but they found that when markets deteriorated, investors fled.

To what extent does the national economic system influence the prospective foreign investor? Foreign investors seek good returns, whether the investment is purely financial or in production capacity. The mature western economies, which are mainly market economies, are among the costliest locations, and, in some cases, businesses incur high social costs. Consumer markets in these countries are lucrative, and these economies are relatively stable. Growth in these mature economies, however, has been lacklustre for many years. The highest rates of growth in recent years have been in emerging economies. These economies, including the large Asian

▶ More online ... Ikea's corporate website is www.ikea-group.ikea.com

countries and the post-communist countries, have liberalized their economic systems, and, on the whole, welcome foreign firms. These are not mature market economies, however. Many are transition economies with shaky regulatory systems, building market institutions, but in a context of state controls. Although large potential markets await the investor, these are not as stable or predictable as the mature economies. Ikea, the Swedish furniture and furnishings firm, called a halt to opening new stores in Russia in 2009. Although Ikea had become accustomed to operating in the uncertain environment, the difficulties had become even greater, as the government found itself having to bail out failing banks. The company does not plan to exit the country, still believing that there is much scope for growth in Russia as a consumer market.

The example of Ikea in Russia is similar to dilemmas faced by western MNEs in numerous emerging markets: there is huge potential in both production and markets, but instability and uncertainties abound, hampering business operations. Internationalization strategy will observe that these countries have maintained high growth rates, pointing to rising consumer incomes, which indicate a growing market for consumer goods. Some MNEs now have large market shares in emerging markets. Nokia, the Finnish mobile phone company, is both a global market leader and well established in China. These successful Nordic companies are highly competitive internationally while retaining strong roots in their home countries. One of the challenges that has faced Nokia in particular has been the rise of competitors from emerging markets. Companies from the large emerging economies of China, India, Brazil and Russia have become global players, their aspirations reflecting their countries' new global status. These emerging MNEs do not set their sights merely on other emerging markets, but also on markets in the advanced economies, as seen in the closing case study.

Emerging MNEs have typically spent their formative years building strength in their domestic market. Recall that emerging MNEs tend to be from mixed economies in which the state is a major player. In these transitional and developing economies, personal ties can be more important than legal or contractual relations. Many of these companies are state controlled, and others have benefited from connections with government, and are able to access capital provided by state banks. Many are family firms and, despite being listed companies, tend to have weak corporate governance in terms of western standards of transparency. Their managers are accustomed to opaque and bureaucratic business environments and weak legal protections, including weak environmental laws. Chinese firms, mainly state controlled, have been at the forefront in investing in the developing world, securing valuable natural resources for its vast economy.

As the issue of sustainability becomes more important, companies, like governments, are now compelled to look at their economic activities in environmental terms. As we have seen, the liberal market model in its pure form lacks a defined social-conscience dimension. Still, British and American companies have taken a lead in corporate social responsibility (CSR), even when their governments have shown only reluctant support for measures such as controlling greenhouse gas emissions. Would a company choose to invest in production in a developing country with weak environmental standards, or a costlier location with higher standards? Many would choose the former on economic grounds, but this could be rather short-sighted. Technological improvements could bring down costs, making the costlier country a more competitive location over time, whereas the operations in many developing countries might not be sustainable long term, due to dangerous depletion of key resources, usually combined with rising prices. The investing firm is wise to look beyond size of market to the broader economic picture, including demands on resources, when surveying comparative economic environments.

Summary points Strategic implications for business

◆ Economic growth has been stronger in emerging markets than in the mature economies, making these countries attractive markets for consumer products.
◆ The mixed economies of emerging markets, while developing market institutions, can be unstable,

and are prone to intervention by the government.
◆ MNEs from emerging economies have learned to operate in the uncertain environments of their home countries, and are able to adapt in their forays into other developing countries.

◆ As sustainability becomes central to business strategy as well as government policy, firms and locations that design sustainable strategies are likely to win out over those that do not.

Critical thinking
Strategy choices for MNEs
Emerging markets are now the focus of many MNE strategies, but they pose challenges in terms of sustainability. On what principles should today's MNEs design emerging-market strategies?

And there are more features inside ... Car showrooms are buzzing with prospective buyers, especially in emerging markets, where the dream of buying your own car is becoming a reality
Source: Istock

Conclusions

1   The macroeconomic environment can be depicted in terms of flows of resources, income, production and expenditure.

2   Gross national income (GNI) and gross domestic product (GDP) are used to measure the size of national economies.

3   Controlling inflation and unemployment are major concerns of modern governments, in order to achieve sustained growth in the economy.

4   Balance of payments calculations are used to assess a country's trade with other countries. A trade deficit indicates that it imports more than it exports.

5   While the fluctuations of the business cycle affect all economies, governments use monetary and fiscal policies to avoid the damaging effects of severe swings.

6   Economic systems range from the planned economy to capitalism, reflecting society's values regarding production and the accumulation of wealth.

7   The liberal market economy, with an emphasis on free markets, is exemplified by the US and UK, although state intervention and welfare-state measures have become a feature of modern capitalist systems generally.

8   Social market capitalism, as exemplified by France and Germany, has relied on greater state ownership and more extensive social welfare programmes.

9   Asian capitalist models, including Japan, have also relied on strong state guidance. The Asian model, however, is underpinned with Confucian values of the strong family and the company itself as family.

10 The planned economy as a system is giving way to market forces, as exemplified by China, where private enterprise has become the chief driver of the economy.

11 Post-communist transitional economies of Central and Eastern Europe, while they have struggled to overcome the problems of restructuring outdated industries, have become increasingly integrated into the advanced western economies.

12 Economic integration between national economies has been facilitated by liberalization measures. At the same time, regionalization, which is most advanced in the EU, is becoming an increasingly important force in international business.

13 As emerging markets grow, sustainability and environmental concerns are becoming significant strategic concerns for MNEs.

Review questions

1   In what ways is the circular flow diagram useful to show overall economic activity in the national economy?

2   How are GDP and GNI per capita used to compare countries, and what are their limitations?

3   Define inflation, and explain what its damaging effects can be on a national economy.

4   Why is the balance of payments important to policymakers, and why are governments concerned if there is a current account deficit?

5   What factors cause economic growth, and which countries at present show the strongest rates of growth?

6   Describe the stages of the business cycle. How do they impact on business activities?

7   In what ways do governments control monetary policy, and how has their room for manoeuvre become more limited with economic integration?

8   What are the distinguishing characteristics of the liberal market economy?

9   Which countries are considered strongholds of the social market model of capitalism, and how are their economies evolving at present?

10   What are the specific strengths of the Asian model of capitalism? In the case of Japan, how did these strengths seem to translate into weaknesses in the 1990s?

11   What are the elements of the transition process towards a market economy in (a) China; and (b) the transition economies of Central and Eastern Europe?

12   What are the implications of European Monetary Union (EMU)? Is EMU bringing about convergence between member states?

13   What are the forces behind the growth in regionalization? How does the economic profile of the enlarged EU in 2004 differ from that of the EU made up of 15 member states?

Key revision concepts

Balance of payments, p. 88; Economic growth, p. 83; Fiscal policy, p. 89; GDP, p. 81; Inflation, p. 84; Liberal market economy, p. 96; Mixed economy, p. 101; National debt, p. 91; Social market economy, p. 99; Unemployment, p. 86

Assignments

◆ Looking at the key indicators of the macroeconomic environment, what policy instruments are available to national decision-makers, and to what extent are they now limited by factors beyond their borders?

◆ Assess the potential benefits and drawbacks of the liberal market economic model. To what extent does a more statist economy such as China now offer a valid alternative that can be emulated by other developing economies?

Further reading

Amable, B. (2003) *The Diversity of Modern Capitalism* (Oxford: Oxford University Press).

Begg, I. and Ward, D. (2009) *Economics for Business*, 3rd edn (New York: McGraw-Hill).

Bootle, R. (2010) *The Trouble with Markets: Saving Capitalism From Itself* (London: Nicholas Brealey Publishing).

Coates, D. (1999) *Models of Capitalism* (Cambridge: Polity Press).

De Grauwe, P. (2003) *Economics of Monetary Union*, 5th edn (Oxford: Oxford University Press).

Dunning, J. (ed.) (1997) *Governments, Globalization and International Business* (Oxford: Oxford University Press).

Fisher, M. (2009) *Capitalist Realism: Is There No Alternative?* (Ropley, Hampshire, UK: O Books).

Gros, D. and Steinherr, A. (2004) *Economic Transition in Central and Eastern Europe: Planting the Seeds* (Cambridge: Cambridge University Press).

Hall, P. and Soskice, D. (2001) *Varieties of Capitalism: The Institutional Foundations of Comparative Advantage* (Oxford: Oxford University Press).

Landes, D. (1998) *The Wealth and Poverty of Nations* (London: W.W. Norton & Co.).

Maddison, A. (1991) *Dynamic Forces in Capitalist Development* (Oxford: Oxford University Press).

Parkin, M., Powell, M. and Matthews, K. (2007) *Economics*, 7th edn (New Jersey: Addison Wesley).

Piggott, J. and Cook, M. (2005) *International Business Economics* (Basingstoke: Palgrave Macmillan).

Schnitzer, M. (2000) *Comparative Economic Systems*, 8th edn (Cincinnati: South-Western Publishing).

Whitley, R. (1999) *Divergent Capitalisms* (Oxford: Oxford University Press).

Yasheng Huang (2010) *Capitalism with Chinese Characteristics: Entrepreneurship and the State* (Cambridge: Cambridge University Press).

Tata's prospects mirror those of India

Tata is India's largest corporate conglomerate, spanning diverse business sectors from chemicals to hotels to steel. Founded by the Tata family during British rule, its history has unfolded with the upheavals of India itself. It continued to expand in India's post-colonial period, beginning in the 1950s, when the country was officially a socialist republic. This period was characterized by a closed economy, with heavy regulation, protectionist policies, and an emphasis of self-sufficiency. As imports were limited and companies were not allowed to invest abroad, domestic firms focused on import substitution. Much of what was available to consumers, however, was perceived to be of poor quality in comparison to foreign equivalents, which were barred.

With the opening of the economy from 1991 onwards, more foreign goods and foreign companies gained access to the Indian market. FDI was cautiously welcomed, although regulation and restrictions remained obstacles. Similarly, capital controls were lifted, allowing Indian companies to expand abroad. From 2004 onwards, they were allowed to borrow money from foreign banks. As India became a more open, market-oriented economy, the prospects for Indian companies brightened. Since 1991, the Tata group has been headed by Ratan Tata, the fifth generation of his family to take the helm. Tata companies began expanding internationally, almost as a defensive move, anticipating greater competition in the Indian market (*The Economist*, 30 May 2009). Many Tata companies are now becoming global forces, reflecting their international ambitions, which echo those of India's government.

Among the Tata companies that are considered the jewels in the family crown, there are Tata Steel, Tata Motors and Tata Consultancy Services (TCS), the last of which has been a star in India's most recent development phase, promoting computing and business process outsourcing. Tata's foreign acquisitions include the purchase by Tata Steel of Corus, the UK steelmaker, in 2007. In 2008, Tata Motors purchased Jaguar Land Rover of the UK. This last acquisition proved to be somewhat ill-timed, as it coincided with economic recession, but Ratan Tata was resolute that the luxury brand would be successful under Tata ownership. His most eye-catching announcement that year was the introduction of the Tata Nano, a small, cheap car at the opposite end of the market. The Nano, billed as the 'people's car', caught the imagination of India's growing ranks of consumers who could now aspire to car ownership (see figure). It also grabbed headlines globally. A European version was envisaged, the Nano Europa, which would meet European emissions standards, and even an American version was envisaged.

Following the euphoria of the Nano launch, Tata came back down to earth when production difficulties set in. It is often the case in India that land for industrial use is compulsorily purchased by the government. In this case,

A proud new owner: suburban apartments like these are designed for India's growing middle class, but the government must also focus on development issues for the country's millions of poor rural inhabitants

Source: Istock

the government of West Bengal, although communist, was keen to have the estimated 10,000 jobs that the Nano factory would bring. It held out incentives to attract Tata, including a site that was nearly free and low taxes. The proposed site, over which some 12,000 peasant farmers had separate titles, was compulsorily purchased, to pave the way for the factory. However, the government underestimated the hostility of the displaced farmers. Violent protests ensued, ultimately making it impossible to complete the factory. Tata abandoned the site, along with the nearly finished factory, and started again in the state of Gujarat, which, with its existing industrial base, proved a more amenable environment. The shift in location was costly in terms of time and money, and the suppliers who had invested in facilities near the West Bengal site also suffered. People in West Bengal had mixed feelings: the opportunity for factory jobs looked attractive to many, as being more secure than subsistence farming, but many others felt they were not being offered enough money to compensate them for the compulsory purchase of their land.

The travails of getting the Nano into production, some seven months late, are indicative of the strains which prevail in India. Some 60% of the population is still agricultural, although agriculture is just 20% of the country's GDP. India's government is now focusing on building manufacturing capacity, conscious of rivalry with China as a manufacturing superpower. But there remain many obstacles, including poor infrastructure. Poverty and poor education continue to hold back development. India grew at an impressive 7.9% in 2009, and was relatively unscathed by the global financial

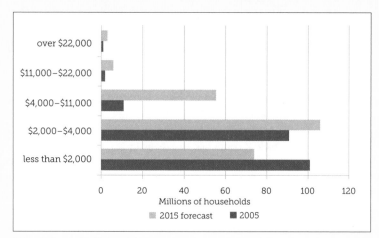

Indian households' income

Source: *Financial Times*, 20 January 2010

crisis. This was partly fortuitous: India's dominant state-owned banks have not become globalized and were not exposed in risky financial markets. Liberal reforms, including privatizations, have stalled in recent years. The state-owned sector remains huge, ranging from food to telecommunications. These state-owned companies employed 1.8 million people in 2008, and accounted for 8.3% of GDP. The government could sell stakes in these companies, encouraging them to become more efficient. Such sell-offs could yield valuable cash to deal with the country's budget deficit of nearly 7% of GDP.

Meanwhile, Tata has moved on to another headline-grabbing launch, the Tata Swach, a water filter device at 1,000 rupees (about $21) which caters for people without running water and electricity in their homes – a category which covers about 400 million of India's inhabitants.

Sources: Lamont, J. (2010) 'Building Brics', *Financial Times*, 20 January; Lamont, J. (2010) 'Potholes in the road', *Financial Times*, 9 February; Leahy, J. (2008) 'Journey into conflict', *Financial Times*, 15 September; *The Economist* (2009) 'Gone shopping', 30 May; *The Economist*, 'Stakes and mistakes', 14 November 2009

Questions for discussion

◆ In what ways has Indian economic policy benefited companies such as Tata, or harmed them?

◆ How has Tata benefited from globalization?

◆ What development issues are the major concerns for India?

CHAPTER 4

INTERNATIONAL TRADE AND GLOBAL COMPETITION

Outline of chapter

Introduction

Trade and economic growth

Theories of international trade
The theory of comparative advantage
Product life cycle theory from the trade perspective
Newer trade theories
Porter's theory of competitive advantage

National trade policies
Government perspectives on trade
Tools of governmental trade policy

Global and regional trade patterns

International regulation of trade
GATT principles
WTO and the regulation of world trade
Multilateral trade agreements and the WTO

Regional and bilateral trade agreements
Categories of regional trade agreements
Focus on regions – Europe, The Americas, Asia, Africa

Multilateralism at the crossroads

Globalization and world trade

Conclusions

Learning objectives

1 To appreciate the contributions of theories of international trade to an understanding of the ways in which companies, industries and nations compete in the global environment
2 To understand the rationale and mechanisms of national trade policies
3 To understand the evolution of the multilateral trading system, in terms of its structures, processes, and issues to be resolved
4 To assess the impact of regional integration on the business environment

Critical themes in this chapter

• **Multilayered environment – national trade policies; bilateral, regional and multilateral trade agreements**
• **Emerging economies – growing influence in international trade**
• **The role of the state – national trade policies and tools; protectionism**

The growth in container shipping reflects the importance of trade in the global economy
Source: Istock

BHP Billiton digs deep in global markets

BHP Billiton is the world's largest diversified natural resources company. Mining is its core activity, with divisions in minerals, coal and iron ore, but it is also a significant oil and gas producer. This diversity has helped the company to withstand the instability of commodities markets. Although its profits for many metals fell steeply in 2009, its iron ore and petroleum divisions performed well. Its other great advantage has been its sheer size, which gives it a strong market position, especially in iron ore, which is our focus here. Iron ore is the main ingredient in steel and one of the key commodities associated with industrialization, whether in manufacturing cars or building skyscrapers. Demand for iron ore has surged ahead from the fast-growing emerging economies, such as China, Brazil and India. All are big producers of iron ore, although China is by far the largest, producing 770 million tonnes in 2008, nearly double the amount produced in Brazil. But China's domestic demand exceeds its own production, forcing it to import from abroad (see figure). In addition, China's low-grade iron ore and dwindling production have been other factors leading it to shift to importing, in both its large state-run steel producers and smaller private firms. This is good news for the seaborne iron ore sector, in which BHP Billiton ranks third in the world, behind Vale of Brazil (first) and Rio Tinto of the UK (second). China imported only 20% of its iron ore in 2000, but by 2009, the proportion had jumped to 70%, much of it from Australian mines controlled by Rio and BHP Billiton.

BHP Billiton was formed from a merger in 2001 of BHP (formerly Broken Hill Proprietary Co.) of Australia and Billiton, a UK company, both companies dating back to the nineteenth century in their origins. The merged company is listed in both the UK and Australia, where there are separate groups of shareholders. In theory, there are separate boards, but they consist of the same people. The management is also unified, and

the company's headquarters are in Melbourne. The merged company has become a powerful force, accounting for 18% of Australia's GDP. China is now Australia's largest export market, and mining exports account for 37.9% of its total exports.

Ambitious expansion strategies have led BHP Billiton to make acquisitions around the globe. It now has 100 sites in 25 countries. But its most audacious move was a bid for its rival, Rio Tinto, in 2007. Had the merger gone ahead, the combined company would have controlled about 75% of the seaborne iron ore market, effectively creating a duopoly. Although competition authorities in the US and Australia approved the deal, the EU took a critical view, largely due to the potential to control prices. The European

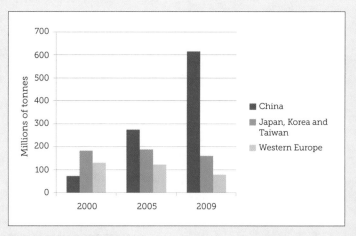

Seaborne iron ore imports
Source: *Financial Times*, 31 March 2010

Commission set a condition for approval which required BHP Billiton to dispose of other assets. Discouraged from going ahead, it dropped the bid. However, in 2009, BHP executives came forward with another proposal, this time to create a 50-50 joint venture with Rio Tinto, which would operate the rich Western Australia iron ore field. It would be a 'hands-off', independent company, with its own management. The parent companies argued that this would be a 'production-only' deal, combining infrastructure, but not pricing power (*Financial Times*,

▶ More online ... BHP Billiton's website is at www.bhpbilliton.com

1 April 2010). This proposal, too, attracted the attention of competition authorities, including those in Australia, Japan and the EU. Few believe that the joint venture would be autonomous in practice, given its powerful owners. Pricing was again a key issue. The two companies gave up plans for the joint venture late in 2010.

For 40 years, global iron ore pricing has been based on a system of annual contract negotiations which set 'benchmark' prices. But with rising demand, these prices have lagged behind 'spot' prices which obtain in commodity markets. The mining companies have argued, therefore, that they have lost money, as their prices were effectively capped when dealing with major customers. They have proposed a new system based on quarterly spot market prices, and they have persuaded steel customers in China and Japan to change to the new system. The result is likely to be steep price rises in iron ore globally. Although for Asian economies, with their healthy industries, these rises could possibly be absorbed, for European manufacturing, with its fragile steel industry, the price rises would be damaging. The European steel industry complained in 2010 to the EU Commission about possible 'illicit co-ordination of price increases' by the big mining companies (*Financial Times*, 1 April 2010). The Chinese government has also announced an investigation into iron ore pricing.

BHP Billiton has said in the past that it wished to see a system of market-based pricing in iron ore, as for oil or coal (MacNamara, 2009). However, these other global industries are not as concentrated in the hands of a few players. In 2010, Australia's Labour government announced the impending imposition of a 40% mining supertax, which would fall heavily on BHP Billiton. Although rebates and a lower corporation tax would help to soften the blow, the company still felt the tax would be unfair. It waged a public media campaign against the measure, which was perceived as largely to blame for the toppling of the government. The prime minister, Kevin Rudd, was replaced by Julia Gillard, who was more sympathetic to BHP's arguments; a temporary deal for a lower rate of tax, at about 30%, was reached. However, Labour did not achieve an outright majority in the elections that followed, leaving the issue of the mining tax still in doubt. BHP Billiton has prided itself on its corporate citizenship, but paying a windfall tax was probably not one of the elements it had in mind.

Sources: *Financial Times* (2010) 'Iron ore deal sparks European steel fury', 1 April; MacNamara, W. and Waldmeir, P. (2010) 'Ore struck', *Financial Times*, 6 April; MacNamara, W. (2009) 'BHP in plea over iron ore pricing', 13 August; Wachman, R. (2010) 'BHP and Rio Tinto hit by Australian supertax', *The Guardian*, 4 May; Blas, J. (2010) 'Annual contract system collapses', *Financial Times*, 31 March; Jolly, D. (2010) 'EU opens antitrust investigation into mining deal', *New York Times*, 25 January; BHP Billiton Annual Report, 2009, at www.bhpbilliton.com

Questions for discussion

◆ Why is the iron ore market a crucial one in today's global economy?

◆ What impacts to the iron ore market would have resulted from a successful takeover of Rio Tinto by BHP Billiton?

◆ Would it be preferable for iron ore to be priced on the old benchmark system, or on the new spot-price model, and why?

Introduction

Businesses seeking markets have across the ages looked to trade beyond their home country. Growth in international trade has been a major contributor to the rise of the industrialized countries, stretching back to the Industrial Revolution. Indeed, when we look at the flourishing trade between Asia and Europe as far back as the medieval era, we are tempted to think that globalization has been happening a long time. However, both the volume of trade and the patterns of trade between nations have changed greatly over the years. In the decades following the Second World War, the dominant trading powers were the US, Japan and Europe. From the 1990s and into the twenty-first century, there has been a shift towards Asia, in which the large emerging economies have become leading traders. Two major factors can be highlighted in this shift towards Asia: globalization of production by MNEs and the opening up of national economies. Understanding the impacts of these factors on the global trading system, including particular regions and national economies, is key to formulating business strategies in the changing environment.

We begin this chapter with an overview of international trade, highlighting shifts in trading relations now taking place. We look at the major theories that help to explain changing patterns of world trade. We then analyse divergent views on the issues of free trade and protectionism, which have shaped national perspectives. Belief in the benefits of free trade has underpinned co-operative agreements to open markets, guided particularly by the World Trade Organization (WTO). We examine the role of the WTO as trade envelops more developing and emerging economies. Multilateralism is coming under threat from the growth in regional and bilateral trade agreements. These developments have taken place in a context of globalization, highlighting the interdependence of national economies. Nonetheless, governments continue to focus on national perspectives, leading to fears that protectionist pressures are gaining ground.

Trade and economic growth

Since the end of the Second World War, trade has grown at a remarkable rate: from 1950 to 2002 the volume of world exports tripled, and production doubled. In the 1990s, trade grew on average 6.5% annually, while output grew at 2.5% annually. The following decade showed similar growth, but sharp declines occurred towards the end, as the global credit crunch and recession affected trade and economic activity generally (see Figure 4.1). Extended supply chains across national borders should be taken into account when looking at trade data in relation to GDP. Over 40% of world trade is accounted for by **intermediate goods**, components and parts which might cross national borders more than once before being made into final products. These goods are counted each time they cross national borders. Trade in intermediate goods is particularly relevant for Asian countries, where the proportion can be over half. China's imports are 57% made up of intermediate goods which are destined for factories, to be made into final products for export to other countries. Similarly, about 42% of its exports are made up of intermediate goods. It is because of this double counting that swings in trade growth appear to be greater than changes in GDP growth.

intermediate goods components and parts which cross national borders before being made into final products

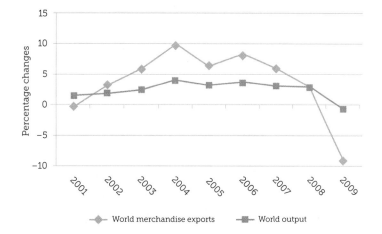

Figure 4.1 **Changes in world merchandise exports and GDP**

Source: IMF, Data and statistics, at www.imf.org

Three major trading regions, Europe, North America and Asia, account for over 80 per cent of global trade. From Figure 4.2, it can be seen that in the post-war period, Asia's share in global merchandise exports has grown and North America's share has decreased. Europe remains the best-performing region, but its share has declined from over 50% in 1973 to 41% in 2008, largely due to the gains by Asian exporters.

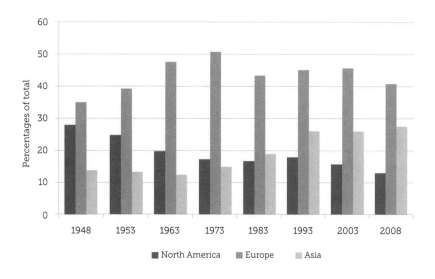

Figure 4.2 **Shares in world merchandise exports by region**

Source: WTO, International trade statistics 2009, at www.wto.org

China is now challenging Germany as the world's largest exporter of merchandise, as Figure 4.3 shows. In exports of manufactured goods, China became the global leader in 2008. China's exports of manufactured goods grew at a rate of over 25% a year from 2000 to 2008 (WTO, 2009). Of the four leading traders, the US stands out as being the largest importer by far, but it shows the greatest imbalance between exports and imports. The trade deficit of the US is mirrored by the trade surplus of China. The US had a trade deficit with China of $268 billion in 2008 (US Trade Representative's Office, 2009).

▸ More online ... The WTO's trade statistics are at www.wto.org
The US Trade Representative's Office provides trade data for the US, at www.ustr.gov

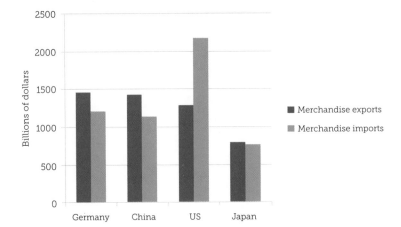

Figure 4.3 **The world's four leading trading countries in 2008**

Source: WTO, International trade statistics 2009, at www.wto.org

China's development model has been based on manufacturing for export. Favourable tax treatment of foreign investors, including tax-free export zones, has helped to turn the country into a powerhouse for exports of consumer goods globally. In the early stages of development, basic advantages such as low labour costs help to ensure this success. These advantages are particularly evident in low-technology sectors in which labour is a major component. The bulk of China's trade surplus has been derived from sectors such as toys, textiles and footwear. As we have seen, globalization has been characterized by the shift of much manufacturing to low-cost environments. As an economy matures, its advantages tend to slip away to developing countries which can undercut it in costs. For this reason, countries whose advantages are mainly based on low-cost labour seek to move up the value chain. South Korea and Taiwan, which industrialized prior to China, have moved up to higher value-added goods such as high-technology products. China's growth in the export of higher technology products, such as electronics, has been linked to the growth in imports of components, many from Taiwan and South Korea. For China, building its own technological and innovative capacity will propel it up the value chain.

Summary points Trade and economic growth

◆ Trade has grown faster than GDP in the post-war period, although both declined in 2008–9 as economic downturn affected global markets.

◆ China has become the world's largest exporter of manufactured goods, and the second largest exporter of merchandise generally.
◆ Crucially for developing countries, trade aids economic

growth. Initially, developing countries benefit from a low-cost manufacturing environment. Rising up the value chain in terms of technology contributes to economic development.

Critical thinking

Trade and economic growth

Although trade is boosting growth in developing countries, often in conjunction with FDI, these economies can become entrenched in low-cost manufacturing activities, which can damage growth prospects in the long term. How does this happen, and what can be done about it?

Theories of international trade

import the purchase of
goods or services from a
buyer in another country

In Chapter 2, we found that exporting, the selling of goods abroad, is a favoured
internationalization strategy of many firms. **Imports** are goods bought from abroad,
and, as we saw, growth in imports is associated with globalization. The first major
theorist of international trade, Adam Smith, believed that all countries benefit from
unrestricted trade. Free trade is said to exist where citizens can export and import
without restrictions or barriers imposed by governments of either the exporting or
the importing country. In his book, *The Wealth of Nations* (published in 1776), Smith
argued in favour of the 'the invisible hand' of market forces, as opposed to government intervention (discussed in the last chapter). When countries produce the products in which they are the most efficient producers, they are said to have an **absolute
advantage** in these products. A country may then sell these goods overseas, and
purchase from overseas goods that are produced more efficiently elsewhere. Thus,
both countries benefit from trade.

absolute advantage
enjoyed by a country
which is more efficient
at producing a
particular product than
any other country

The theory of comparative advantage

comparative advantage
enjoyed by a country
where production of
a particular product
involves greater relative
advantage than would be
possible anywhere else

Starting from the principle of absolute advantage, David Ricardo ([1817]1973), writing
some 40 years after Adam Smith, developed his theory of **comparative advantage.**
His theory contends that, if Country A is an efficient producer of wheat and Country
B an efficient producer of clocks, it pays A to purchase clocks from B, even if it could
itself produce clocks more efficiently than B. According to Ricardo, if countries
specialize in the industries in which they have comparative advantage, all will benefit
from trade with each other; consumers in both countries enjoying more wheat and
more clocks than they would without trade. According to Ricardo's theory, therefore,
trade is not a 'zero-sum' game, that is, where one side's gain is the other's loss, but a
'positive-sum' game, that is, one in which all parties benefit.

In reality, most countries do not specialize in ways envisaged by Ricardo's theory.
Further, the model does not allow for dynamic changes that trade brings about.
Economists base the benefits of free trade on 'dynamic gains' that contribute to
economic growth. Free trade leads to an increase in a country's stock of resources, in
terms of both increased capital from abroad and greater supplies of labour. In addition, efficiency may improve with large-scale production and improved technology.
Opening up markets and creating more competition can provide an impetus for
domestic companies to become more efficient. Trading patterns are also influenced
by historical accident, government policies, and the importance of MNEs in the
global economy – all of which have been incorporated into newer trade theories.

Summary points **Theory of comparative advantage**

◆ Ricardo's theory of comparative
advantage holds that countries will
ultimately benefit by concentrating
on the industries in which they

hold efficiency advantages over
other countries.
◆ The theory presents a static
view of trade, and Ricardo could

not have envisaged the role of the
modern MNE in international trade.

Product life cycle theory from the trade perspective

Raymond Vernon's theory of the international product life cycle was introduced in
Chapter 2, for its early contribution to our understanding of FDI and the location of

production. The theory also helps to explain trade from the perspective of the firm (Wells, 1972). It traces the product's life from its launch in the home market, through to export to other markets, and, finally, its manufacture in cheaper locations for import into its original home market. The theory observes that, over the cycle, production has moved from the US to other advanced countries, and finally to developing countries, where costs are lower.

This simple outline of the product life cycle rests on a view of manufacturing which has been rather overtaken by globalization. In modern supply chains, a firm may use components from various locations, and choose yet another for assembling the final product. Because of the rapid pace of technological innovation and shortened product life cycles, a company in industries such as consumer electronics may well introduce a new product simultaneously in a number of markets, wiping out the leads and lags between markets. The model is useful in explaining production patterns for some types of products, such as standardized consumer goods, but is less useful in predicting future patterns, especially in industries dominated by a few global players. Moreover, the theory takes little account of trade barriers and government trade policies. Trade barriers of various kinds (discussed later in this chapter), are typically imposed to block imports or protect local industries.

Summary points Product life cycle theory

● This theory envisages a new product as passing through four phases from launch to maturity. Initially, it is exported abroad, but as it ages, it becomes more standardized and less costly to produce, eventually leading to production in low-cost locations around the globe.

● Vernon's theory can be helpful in analysing how trade has evolved in conjunction with production in low-cost economies.

Newer trade theories

More recently, theorists have turned their attention to the growing importance of MNEs in international trade, taking into account the globalization of production and trade between affiliated companies (see Chapter 2). Krugman, in his book, *Rethinking International Trade* (1994), emphasized features of the international economy such as increasing returns and imperfect competition. More precisely, he said, 'conventional trade theory views world trade as taking place entirely in goods like wheat; new trade theory sees it as being largely in goods like aircraft' (Krugman, 1994: 1). For companies, innovation and economies of scale give what are called **first-mover advantages** to early entrants in a market. This lead increases over time, making it impossible for others to catch up. For firms able to benefit in this way, the increased share in global markets has led to oligopolistic behaviour in some industries, such as the aircraft industry. For countries, there are advantages to be gained from encouraging national firms which enjoy first-mover advantages. There are clear implications here that government intervention can play a role in promoting innovation and entrepreneurship, thereby boosting competitive advantage of nations.

first-mover advantages precept that countries or firms which are first to produce a new product gain an advantage in markets that makes it virtually impossible for others to catch up

Summary points Newer trade theories

● Newer theories take account of globalization of production and the manufacture of complex products.

● First-mover advantages contribute to gains in industries where innovation and economies of scale are important, making it impossible for later entrants to catch up.

Porter's theory of competitive advantage

In his book, *The Competitive Advantage of Nations*, published originally in 1990, Michael Porter developed a theory of national **competitive advantage**. His considerable research, which is set out in the book, attempts to find out why some countries are more successful than others. Each nation, he says, has four broad attributes that shape its national competitive environment (Porter, 1998a: 71):

competitive advantage
theory (devised by Porter) that international competitiveness depends on four major factors: demand conditions, factor conditions, firm strategy and supporting industries

- *Factor conditions* – The nation's position in factors of production, such as skilled labour or infrastructure and natural resources necessary to compete in a given industry.
- *Demand conditions* – The nature and depth of home demand for the industry's product or service.
- *Related and supporting industries* – The presence or absence in the nation of supplier industries and related industries that are internationally competitive.
- *Firm strategy, structure, and rivalry* – The conditions in the nation governing how companies are created, organized, and managed; and the nature of domestic rivalry.

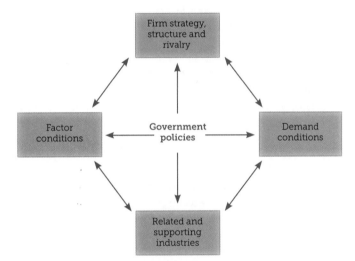

Figure 4.4 **Porter's Diamond: the determinants of national advantage**

Source: Adapted from Porter, M., *The Competitive Advantage of Nations* (Basingstoke: Macmillan Press, 1998), p. 72

The four attributes, or determinants, form a diamond shape, as shown in Figure 4.4. The first two determinants, factor conditions and demand conditions, relate to the national environment, which, for Porter, includes social and cultural environment as well as natural resources and labour market attributes. The third and fourth determinants relate to the nation's firms and industries. Porter stresses that the four determinants are interdependent. Favourable demand conditions, for example, will contribute to competitive advantage only in an environment in which firms are able and willing to respond. Advantage based on only one or two determinants may suffice in natural resource-dependent industries, or those with lower technological input, but to sustain advantage in the modern knowledge-intensive industries, advantages throughout the diamond are necessary.

Porter adds that there are two additional variables in his theory. They are chance and government. Chance can open up unexpected opportunities in a variety of ways: new inventions, external political developments, and shifts in foreign market demand. He cites the fall of communism, which resulted in the opening of Central and Eastern

Europe, as an example. His categorization of these occurrences as happening as if by chance is perhaps unfortunate, and it would be preferable to see them from the business perspective as simply opportunities. On the other hand, government policies can be highly influential, and these are therefore shown in the centre of Figure 4.4. Government policies highlighted by Porter include a strong antitrust policy, which encourages domestic rivalry, and investment in education, which generates knowledge resources. Government policies can play a crucial role in building national competitive advantage. Porter stresses that this role, however, is indirect rather than direct (Porter, 1998b: 184–6). Government remains an 'influence' rather than a 'determinant' in his model. However, government probably plays a larger direct role than his model suggests. Governments in market economies are taking on a more directly interventionist role, including ownership stakes in companies, in addition to a regulatory role. In countries climbing the economic ladder, the role of government has been a key to international success. Both these dimensions of government action are indicative of an enhanced role of the state, which is a critical theme in this book. Government guidance was crucial in Japan (see Chapter 3). In the more recent case of China, economic development has been directed by government. An important policy has been to attract FDI with business-friendly taxation regimes and the setting up of special economic zones. In addition, state-owned organizations have been instrumental in natural resources, energy, banking and the development of infrastructure. China and India provide contrasting examples. Transport and other infrastructure have developed rapidly in China, but have progressed slowly in India, largely because of lack of government impetus and complex rights over land (see closing case study in Chapter 3). On the other hand, the Indian government has prioritized investment in high-technology education, in order to attract computing and IT services industries, which have driven the country's economic growth.

Porter emphasizes that the diamond is a tool not just for explaining past competitive advantage, but also for predicting how industries will evolve in the future. The theory is useful in demonstrating the interaction between different determinants of national competitive advantage, but it probably underemphasizes world economic integration. For example, both capital and managers are now likely to be mobile. Similarly, related and supporting industries are increasingly internationalized, thanks largely to cheaper transport, reductions in import duties, and the advances in communications technology. By the 1990s, an estimated one-third of all manufactures trade involved intermediate goods (World Bank, 2000), and this proportion has now risen to 40% (UNCTAD, 2009). Intra-firm trade between MNEs and affiliates accounts for a high proportion of world exports. Intra-firm exports make up 60% of the total exports from firms under control in the US, 70% in Sweden and 20% in Japan (Onodera, 2008). It should be noted, however, that the low proportion for Japanese MNEs is probably due to the fact that Japanese firms trade heavily in *inter*-firm networks, where firms are legally distinct. Internet growth has contributed to both the growth in global sourcing of components and the growth in international trade in services.

There is an essential difference between comparative advantage, which pertains to the national *economy*, and competitive advantage, which pertains to the *companies* that make it up (Hirst and Thompson, 1999). Competitive advantage in areas such as manufacturing and services can be deliberately created and maintained (through government policy and corporate strategy), whereas comparative advantage obtains where natural factor endowments are paramount, as in agricultural and extractive industries (Hirst and Thompson, 1999; Gilpin, 2000). Hirst and Thompson

▸ More online ... Highlights of the WEF competitiveness league table may be found at http://www.weforum.org/

go on to suggest that, on the whole, it makes more sense to speak of companies, rather than countries, competing with each other. Countries do compete in, for example, attracting FDI, but here, location advantages often focus on particular regions and cities, rather than on whole countries. And competition is based on many aspects of the business environment, such as social and cultural values, which are not measurable in the same ways that relative cost structure, productivity and exchange rates are measurable (Hirst and Thompson, 1999: 122). Nonetheless, international competitiveness 'league tables', which have been compiled annually for a number of years, assess countries in terms of competitiveness. Table 4.1 shows rankings compiled by the World Economic Forum (WEF), along with the criteria used.

Table 4.1 **WEF global competitiveness rankings for 2010–2011**

The WEF criteria	WEF competitiveness ranking 2010–2011	
12 pillars 1 Institutions 2 Infrastructure 3 Microeconomic stability 4 Health and primary education 5 Higher education and training 6 Goods market efficiency 7 Labour market efficiency 8 Financial market sophistication 9 Technological readiness 10 Market size 11 Business sophistication 12 Innovation	**Top 15** 1 Switzerland 2 Sweden 3 Singapore 4 US 5 Germany 6 Japan 7 Finland 8 Netherlands 9 Denmark 10 Canada 11 Hong Kong 12 UK 13 Taiwan 14 Norway 15 France	**The Brics** 27 China 51 India 58 Brazil 63 Russia

Source: World Economic Forum (2010) Global Competitiveness Index 2010–2011 (Geneva: WEF)

The WEF ranked a total of 139 countries in its 2010 survey. It defines competitiveness in terms of institutions, policies, and other factors (World Economic Forum, 2009b: 4). The criteria contained in the twelve pillars focus on various indicators of a country's level of development; economic indicators are only part of the picture. An established institutional framework, high levels of education at all levels, a sound financial system and technological strengths are all attributes which propel a country up the rankings. These are more likely to be found in the advanced economies than in the developing ones. For this reason, the Brics' rankings are relatively low. It is notable that seven EU member states are in the top 15, whereas Greece (83) and Bulgaria (71) fall well below them in these rankings, highlighting variations within the EU (see Chapter 3). The US slipped from second in 2009 to fourth in 2010, reflecting institutional weaknesses.

Summary points The theory of competitive advantage of nations

◆ Porter's theory of competitive advantage is based on four sets of attributes: factor conditions, demand conditions, structure of domestic industries, and related industries.

◆ Other factors highlighted by Porter are chance and government policies. Together with the four sets of attributes, they form a diamond shape, which is a tool for analysing a nation's competitive advantage.

> **Critical thinking**
> Porter's theory of competitive advantage
> Porter's theory has been criticized for underestimating the role of government poli-
> cies. How can the rise of China be explained in terms of Porter's diamond of compet-
> itive advantage of nations? What weaknesses in the theory have become evident?

National trade policies

protectionism
government trade
policy of favouring
home producers and
discouraging imports

National economic prosperity for almost all countries is more than ever tied in with
international trade. However, benefits are not spread evenly, either between countries
or between groups within individual countries. Richer countries are in a stronger
position than poorer countries to use trade to foster national goals, such as food security, or benefit particular industries, such as the car industry (see case study on food
security in Chapter 12). Governments face innumerable political and social, as well as
economic, pressures to intervene in trade. **Protectionism** is the deliberate policy of
favouring home producers, for example by subsidizing home producers or imposing
import tariffs. Figure 4.5 summarizes the pros and cons of free trade which are
discussed in this section. The term 'free trade' is misleading. There has never been
'free' trade in the sense of no cross-border barriers at all. 'Trade liberalization' is therefore more accurate, to indicate measures *towards* free trade, which involve reducing
border controls and reducing governments' scope for curtailing imports. In this
section, we look first at national priorities and then at policy tools for promoting them.

The free trade debate

In favour of free trade:

- Free trade benefits all countries
- A country risks falling behind if it is
  isolated from global markets
- Costs of protecting industries can be
  high, and tend to go to uncompetitive
  industries

In favour of protectionism:

- Protection of national industries promotes
  independence and security
- It protects domestic employment
- It supports national industries, allowing
  them to compete globally, and adding to
  national wealth

Figure 4.5 **The pros and
cons of free trade**

Government perspectives on trade

Governments are perceived as ultimately responsible for the safety and well-being of
those within their borders, including individual citizens, groups of people, industries
and companies. We highlight below four major policy areas in which trade policy is
shaped by national interests.

Promoting industrialization

Industrialization may be promoted by restricting the flow of imported products,
thereby encouraging domestic manufacturing. We have seen in Chapter 3 that
industrialization in many countries, such as Japan and the newly industrialized
countries of South East Asia, has been guided by government, through industrial

policy. These countries have made rapid transitions from mainly agricultural to industrial economies. The 'infant industries' argument holds that developing countries should protect infant industries in which they have potential comparative advantage until they are strong enough to survive when protections are removed. Japan is an example of both successful infant industry support and industrial policy (Gilpin, 2000). For Singapore and other tiger economies, foreign direct investors provided the impetus for development. Industrialization may focus on **import substitution,** that is, producing goods for domestic consumption which otherwise would have been imported. India is an example, featured in the closing case study of Chapter 3. Domestic industries nurtured through protective measures in this way do not always become competitive in world markets. Export-led development, by contrast, focuses on growth in export-oriented goods. Industrialization in China has taken this route.

import substitution approach to economic development which favours producing goods for domestic consumption that otherwise would have been imported

Protecting employment

By restricting imports, governments aim to safeguard domestic jobs. However, the situation is seldom as simple as this. A common fear of US workers in manufacturing industries is that their jobs have gone to lower-paid overseas workers. Work in lower-skilled jobs, as in the textile industry, is particularly vulnerable to being lost to low-cost imports. Proponents of trade liberalization would argue that protectionist measures are damaging to the economy in the long term. They assert that restricting imports may lead to retaliation, so that a country's exporters in profitable sectors may suffer, causing job losses in those sectors. Import restrictions may also have a dampening effect on *foreign* workers' incomes, which translates into a decrease in jobs in domestic export industries. Workers in industrialized countries who are displaced by global competitive forces are usually those without the skills to benefit from the newer job opportunities. Whole regions can suffer as a result. In the long term, it could be argued, governments need to look at education and training needs of the economy to enhance competitive advantage. Nonetheless, protectionist pressures are very strong; special interests' regional strongholds are often effective in mobilizing political support.

Protecting consumers

Conventional wisdom holds that consumers benefit from free trade in that competition in markets brings down prices and increases choice among all products, from agricultural produce to televisions. Both agriculture and consumer electronics have become global industries. The industrialization and globalization of the food chain have resulted in agricultural produce and livestock being transported hundreds – even thousands – of miles to markets. An outcome is that any health and safety concerns, such as contamination from BSE in beef, can have wide ramifications.

Governments have at their disposal a variety of regulatory measures in respect of consumer products such as food and medicines, whether produced at home or abroad. However, levels of regulation and quality controls differ from country to country. With the rise in world trade, it becomes difficult in practice for governments and port authorities to keep out dangerous imported toys or contaminated food.

Promoting strategic interests

Strategic interests cover a number of considerations. It is often thought that the strategic sensitivity of defence industries dictates that domestic suppliers are preferable to foreign ones, and thus should be protected. The strategic necessity argument can

MEET THE CEO

▸ More online ... P&G's website is www.pg.com

Robert McDonald CEO of Procter & Gamble (P&G)

If P&G wished to signal to the world that it is shifting its focus to emerging markets, it could have found no better way than to appoint Robert McDonald as CEO in 2009. Taking over from A.G. Lafley, who had continued a long-term restructuring of the company, as well as presiding over notable acquisitions such as Clairol beauty products, McDonald represents a shift in focus more towards emerging markets and lower-end products. McDonald describes his appointment as 'continuity with change' (Birchall, 'Analysis ...'). P&G has always appointed new CEOs from within, and McDonald is no exception, having been with the company 29 years. Before joining the company, he was in the US Army, specializing in managing in rough terrains. A decade-long stay in Asian markets (the Philippines and Japan) led him to see the scope for designing products for lower-income customers, especially in the developing world. He allegedly travelled by canoe to outlying Philippine islands to ask villagers what detergent and soap they were using. He says of the private label competition, 'There is no reason for anyone to have to use a private label. We should be able to innovate at multiple price points' (Birchall, 'Analysis ...'). In 2009, only about half of P&G's product lines had a lower-priced version, and he wishes to see this proportion rise to 75%. His refocusing is not just on developing countries. He points out that minority communities of Hispanics and African Americans in the US are likely to become the majority before 2045. Designing products and packaging to suit recent Mexican immigrants, with lower prices than the company's mainstream products, is a way of attracting Hispanic consumers.

McDonald argues that a free trade environment is most conducive to global growth and prosperity. It has also facilitated the company's expansion of its international business: 20% of P&G jobs in the US depend on the company's international business, which represents 60% of its annual sales revenues of $79 billion in total. He is concerned that the US government is becoming more protectionist, saying, 'It is short-sighted for the US government to think they can create jobs at home by hurting our ability to

P&G has become adept at designing products and packaging, such as laundry detergent, for poorer consumers

Source: Istock

compete internationally' (Birchall, 'P&G warns ...'). He points to the situation in India and China, where half a billion people have come out of poverty. The impressive growth figures of their economies have rested, he says, on free trade. And he urges that P&G's strategy must focus on these markets because this is where future growth will lie.

Sources: Birchall, J. (2009) 'Analysis: tumble cycle', *Financial Times*, 18 December; Birchall, J. (2009) 'P&G warns over growth of global protectionism', *Financial Times*, 18 December; Birchall, J. (2009) 'P&G sales drive targets Hispanics', *Financial Times*, 28 December; Wolf, C. (2009) '"Very Procter" McDonald reached top job with canoe and parachute', Bloomberg news, 11 June, at www.bloomberg.com

▸ More online ... The Airbus website is www.airbus.com

be extended to a great number of products. It was used to provide federal funding for the semiconductor industry in the US in the 1990s, as semiconductors are crucial to defence systems. Food production is one of the most heavily protected industries, because of the strategic importance of safeguarding food supply and also agricultural employment. On this reasoning, subsidies and import restrictions have long bene-fited Japanese farmers, while Japanese consumers have paid well above world prices for their food. These barriers are only slowly coming down. In 2008, after 20 years of price stability, sharp rises in global prices of basic commodities, including wheat and rice, caused shortages around the world, leading to food riots in some countries. As a result, food security has risen up the agenda, and a number of countries, including China and Saudi Arabia, are acquiring farmland in poor developing countries, mainly in Africa, where food is being grown to feed their home populations. This practice is being monitored by the UN's Food and Agricultural Organization, for its long-term implications, especially in the developing countries which are giving over land for this purpose (see case study in Chapter 12). These countries themselves have a growing problem of food security.

Strategic industries are also a target of policymakers. Strategic trade policy holds that governments can assist their own firms in particular industries to gain competi-tive advantage. This theory mainly applies to oligopolistic industries such as the aerospace industry, in which the US helped Boeing by providing it with lucrative defence contracts, while European governments helped Airbus through subsidies. Both sides have accused each other of breaching WTO rules restricting state aid, resulting in a long-running legal action under the WTO's dispute procedure.

Trade policies may be linked to foreign policy objectives, as was clearly demon-strated during the cold war, when trade followed political and military alliances. Government overseas aid packages to developing countries may be tied to trade. Trade policies are often based on historical relationships between countries, for example those between the former colonial powers of Europe and their former colonies. This resulted in another long-running dispute between the EU and US. The so-called 'banana dispute' had its roots in the preferential treatment that former colonies in the Caribbean have continued to receive, which were found to contravene WTO rules.

Protecting national culture

For governments, maintaining national culture and identity is an important aspect of social stability. This covers literature, film, music and other cultural products. The growth of the internet and global media has led to fears of cultural globalization, prompting some national authorities to limit foreign content and foreign ownership in these sectors. Internet censorship, which has become highly elaborate in some countries, is based in some measure on the perception by the government that the free flow of content from abroad can undermine national cultural and social values (see case study in Chapter 8).

Summary points **Why governments intervene in trade**

◆ Governments have differing priorities within their domestic economies. For developing countries, industrialization can be promoted through export-led FDI.

◆ Protecting domestic employment is a concern of all governments, as it is closely linked to social stability.

◆ Governments see trade as strategically important, and aim to safeguard strategic industries, both for domestic security and to create globally competitive industries.

▸ More online ... Japanese carmakers have a US association, the Japan Automobile Manufacturers Association, at www.jama.org, where there is information on their role in the US car industry.

Critical thinking

Government intervention in trade

Although governments pay lip service to free trade, protectionist pressures abound. Weigh up the possible benefits to the national economy against the risks when governments intervene in trade to foster national strategic objectives. Give examples.

Tools of governmental trade policy

Government policies affect trade in numerous ways, both directly and indirectly. Of direct impact is the manipulation of exchange rates. Devaluing a country's currency will have the immediate effect of making exports cheaper and imports more expensive (see Chapter 9). However, governments now have less scope for manipulating exchange rates in increasingly interlinked currency markets. Similarly, most governments are now party to multilateral and regional trading arrangements which curtail their ability to control trade. We will therefore look at government policy options in the context of changing global and regional contexts. The traditional tools for controlling trade are tariffs, quotas, subsidies, and other non-tariff barriers to trade.

tariff tax imposed by governments on traded goods and services, usually imports but can also be on exports

The classic tool of trade policy is the **tariff**, or duty payable on goods traded. Tariffs are usually imposed on imported goods, but they can also be imposed on exports. When we think of protectionism, we think naturally of tariff barriers. The tariff raises the price of an imported product, thereby benefiting domestic producers of the same product. Japanese whisky producers have been protected in this way by huge import duties levied on foreign whisky. The sums collected also swell government coffers. The main losers are the consumers, who pay higher prices for the imported product. While tariffs on manufactured goods have diminished dramatically, thanks to the multilateral GATT (discussed later), tariffs on agricultural products are still common.

import quota a barrier to trade which consists of limiting the quantity of an imported product that can legally enter a country

The **import quota** limits the quantity of an imported product that can legally enter a country. Licences may be issued annually to a limited number of firms, each of which must stay within the amounts specified in its import licence. Limits are set so as to allow only a portion of the market to foreign goods, thus protecting the market share of domestic producers. Restricting supply in this way is likely to result in higher prices for consumers. Import quotas are sometimes evaded by companies shipping goods via other countries with quota to spare when their home country's quota is used up. An exporting firm may ultimately set up production in a country to avoid the imposition of quotas.

voluntary export restraint (VER) tool of government trade policy by which trading partners wishing to export into a country are encouraged to limit their exports, or else incur the imposition of tariffs or import quotas

An alternative to the import quota is the **voluntary export restraint (VER)**, which shifts the onus on the exporting country to limit its exports, or possibly risk the imposition of quotas or tariffs. A leading example of the VER has been Japanese car exports to the US. In the 1980s, when the Japanese motor industry was growing apace and making rapid inroads in the American market, the US government persuaded Japan to agree to a VER. A way around these restrictions is to set up local production, which Japanese manufacturers have done in the US and other markets. The protectionist urge, however, is still strong, as governments have imposed **local content requirements**, to insure that local component suppliers gain. Japanese motor manufacturers have responded by locating associated Japanese component manufacturers near to assembly plants in the overseas location, thus facilitating just-in-time operations and maintaining high levels of local content.

local content requirements trade policy which requires foreign investors to use local component suppliers in, for example, manufacturing

subsidies payments from public funds to support domestic industries; can also be export subsidies to home producers to bolster a country's exports

Government **subsidies** are payments from public funds to support domestic producers. Some subsidies to domestic producers are justified by governments as a strategic need. For example, they maintain the livelihoods of farmers who provide basic domestic food supplies. This justification can be distinguished from the argument used to justify programmes to boost farmers' incomes for the purpose of enabling them to export cheaply. The latter line of reasoning is that the extra funds, which are export subsidies, will boost the local producers' competitive position in global markets, and can be helpful across many sectors, including agricultural products and cars. Export subsidies run counter to WTO rules as they distort markets. Some types of state funding fall into a more nebulous, 'grey' area. For example, R&D grants can help local producers indirectly, and funds to promote green technology are viewed as legitimate. There are other types of state aid, including loans at preferential rates and tax concessions. Although countries within a 'strong state' tradition, such as France, are more likely to favour state aid than the US and UK, which are in the liberal market tradition, all three – and many others, including the Brics – have pumped public funds into domestic industries.

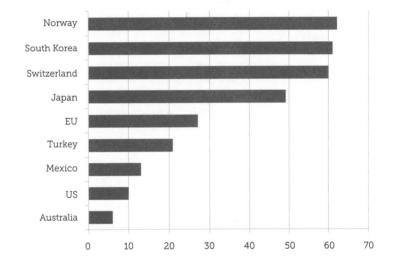

Figure 4.6 **Subsidies to agricultural producers as a percentage of gross farm receipts in selected OECD countries, 2008**

Source: OECD (2009)
Agricultural Policies in OECD Countries: Monitoring and Evaluation (Paris: OECD)

Advocates of trade liberalization criticize subsidies on several grounds. Subsidies work against a 'level playing field' for trade, as unsubsidized foreign firms claim that they face unfair competition. And, although subsidies aim to increase the competitiveness of domestic firms, they do not encourage local firms to be more efficient. Often, they protect inefficient producers (and jobs), creating a culture of dependence on subsidies. Agriculture is a traditionally heavily subsidized sector (see Figure 4.6). The EU, through the Common Agricultural Policy, has provided substantial subsidies for farmers since 1962, creating considerable trade friction with other nations. The extent of EU support diminished in the 1990s, but agriculture continues to be a highly politically sensitive sector. Across the OECD, the level of support was 21% in 2008, the lowest level it has been since the 1980s (OECD, 2009a). The reason, however, is not a general shift of government policy away from subsidies, but the fact that world prices for agricultural commodities rose sharply in 2008, following two decades of relative stability.

As trade in the post-war period has expanded, tariff barriers have generally come down, largely as a result of multilateral initiatives (discussed below). On the other hand, many non-tariff barriers have proliferated, in both developed and developing countries. Countries have increasingly used the WTO's anti-dumping rules to block imports. These are discussed in the next section.

Summary points **Tools of government trade policy**

◆ Government trade policies can be aimed at protecting the country's producers, through programmes such as state

subsidies, or discouraging foreign producers, through import duties and import quotas.

◆ Although formal tariff barriers have tended to come down, non-tariff barriers still proliferate, indicating the strength of protectionist pressures.

Global and regional trade patterns

Figure 4.7 shows merchandise trade flows within and between regions. Europe is the largest of these regions, accounting for 41% of world merchandise exports. It is a significant exporter to the other three regions, as the figure shows, but the bulk of European countries' trade (69.7%) is with other European countries. Europe is Asia's largest export market, but Asian countries' main markets are other Asian countries: 55.9% of Asia's trade is intra-regional. North America is another important destination for Asian exports, amounting to $775.02 billion in 2008. Goods from Asia account for 28.6% of North America's imports, whereas goods from North America account for only 9.6% of Asia's imports. North America's intra-regional trade flows amount to only 37.5% of the region's trade. Of the three countries in North America, both Canada and Mexico are dependent on exporting to the US, whereas most of the exports from the US go to destinations outside the region.

African countries are less economically integrated than other regions: only 11.7% of their trade flows are within the region. As we discuss later in this chapter, efforts towards regional integration are helping to increase cross-border trade within Africa. Africa's largest export market is Europe, while European countries supply the largest portion of Africa's imports (40.5%). Asian exports to Africa, however, are on the increase. China's exports to Africa rose from $26.19 billion in 2006 to $50.16 billion in 2008, nearly doubling in two years.

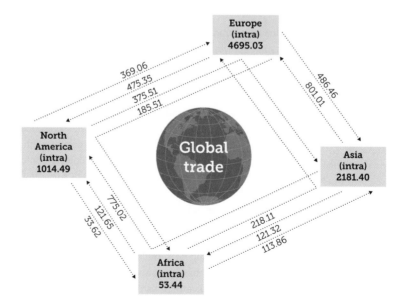

Figure 4.7 **Merchandise trade flows between and within selected regions, 2008** (in $US billions)

Source: WTO, International trade statistics 2009, at www.wto.org

Africa's natural resources: the example of Ghana

Ghana has long been blessed with gold reserves, valuable and relatively easy to mine in comparison with the metal found in other gold-rich African countries, such as South Africa. And Ghana has been fortunate: although mines in other countries have become dangerous or unproductive, it registered a 10% increase in production in 2008. The price of gold surged following the financial crisis of 2008, as investors sought safe havens. Ghana's mining companies have benefited, and so has the country, but the government is now looking at whether the country is getting a fair return. President John Atta Mills was elected in 2008, marking the second peaceful transfer of power in the country, an example that stands out in Africa's turbulent political scene. The new government is now looking at how best to exploit further gains for the country while continuing to encourage foreign investors.

Ghana introduced incentives to attract foreign mining companies to invest in 1986. Mining companies have invested $6.7 billion in the country since 1994. Seven companies altogether made $2.1 billion in revenues, $146 million of which (about 7%) went to the Ghanaian state, mainly through royalties and taxes. Mining multinationals, Newmont of the US and South Africa's AngloGold Ashanti, have led the investment in Ghana's goldmines, but both have been implicated in cyanide spills and human rights violations.

Ghana remains a very poor country. Although the numbers living in poverty have diminished to just under a third of the population, progress in poverty reduction has been disappointingly slow in rural areas (IMF, 2009). Ghana ranks a lowly 152 out of 182 countries in the UN's human development index (UNDP, 2009). With gold prices now rising, the Ghanaian parliament voted to raise the royalties from 3% to 5% in 2010. However, the companies have resisted stoutly. They argued that their agreements were sacrosanct, incapable of being overridden by new law (Burgis, 2010). They also said that planned future investments would be jeopardized if the government altered their terms. Ghana's government is well aware that its reputation with foreign investors could be dented if it imposed more onerous terms, and the country depends on gold for 40% of its exports. But it is also aware that environmental damage, particularly from cyanide spills, has been an issue for communities, leaving the perception that mining companies take the profits with minimal accountability to communities. In a report of 2009, the IMF found Ghana to have 'weak institutional capacities for environmental management' (IMF, 2009).

The government's resolve is facing another challenge in that oil discoveries off its coast in 2007 look set to usher in an oil boom. The Jubilee field is forecast to pump 120,000 barrels of oil per day from 2010 onwards. Oil earnings could eclipse those of gold and cocoa, its other primary natural resource. The government is firm that the oil investments must take into account benefits to all sectors of the economy. The world's large oil companies have eyed the prospects in Ghana, which look inviting in comparison to the resource nationalism evident in countries such as Russia and Venezuela. Tullow Oil of the UK, which acquired three exploration licences from the government, has been successful in its oil explorations in a number of offshore sites. It has worked with other specialist foreign companies in the field, including Kosmos Energy of Texas. ExxonMobil came forward in late 2009, agreeing to buy the stake held by Kosmos in Ghana's oil fields. However, Ghana's government initially blocked the bid by ExxonMobil, and was said to favour a deal with CNOOC, the Chinese state-owned oil company.

US President Barack Obama, on a visit to Ghana in 2009, praised the country for its governance, but warned that the oil issue could detract from its success (Hoyos, 2009). Ghana's oil seemed to be a prize dangling between an established superpower and an aspiring one: the strategic interests of both were at stake. Ghana's government had many factors to consider. Which potential investors had the technology and development expertise needed over the long term? How can the benefits for Ghana as a country be maximized? Ghana's president said, 'We must make sure oil and gas become a blessing. We must get

> ▸ More online ... Newmont Mining is at www.newmont.com
> ExxonMobil is at www.exxonmobil.com
> Tullow Oil is at www.tullowoil.com

Turning the prospect of oil riches into reality: Tullow's employees are shown at work in Ghana's Jubilee oil field

Source: Tullow Oil

competent people to manage the resources, to account for the resources and we must use them to build a stronger economy and invest in our people' (Wallis, 2009). Ghana's president remained reluctant to allow the deal with ExxonMobil to go through. In August 2010, the agreement Kosmos had signed with ExxonMobil was ended.

Sources: Burgis, T. (2009) 'Gold-diggers boost production to help meet world demand', *Financial Times*, 4 December; Hoyos, C. (2009) 'Ghana moves to block Exxon bid for stake in Jubilee field', *Financial Times*, 13 October; Burgis, T. (2010) 'Mining money fails to usher in golden era for Ghana', *Financial Times*, 23 March; Wallis, W. (2009) 'Finds put Ghanaians on a roller coaster of expectations', *Financial Times*, 4 December; *The Economist* (2010) 'Carats and sticks', 3 April; IMF (2009) *Ghana: Poverty Reduction Strategy Report* (Washington, DC: IMF); UNDP (2009) Human Development Index, as www.undp.org

Questions for discussion

◆ Why are natural resources in Ghana, as in other African countries, considered a curse as well as a blessing?
◆ What is the role of foreign oil companies in exploiting Africa's resources, and how is it changing?
◆ What advice would you give to Ghana's government in deciding which foreign investors to welcome and on what terms?

▸ More online ... The WTO website is http://www.wto.org
The International Monetary Fund (IMF) website is http://www.imf.org
The World Bank's website is http://www.worldbank.org

Summary points Global trade patterns

◆ Intra-regional trade is more significant in Europe and Asia than in the other continents.

◆ Asian countries export largely to the EU and North America, but the US has a large trade deficit with Asian countries, as its imports far exceed its exports.

◆ Africa is becoming integrated in world trade, its major trading partners being in Europe. However, trade relations with Asia, especially China, are increasing.

‖ **Critical thinking**
‖ Neighbours first?
‖ Which regions have the greatest disparity between intra-regional trade and trade with the rest of the world? In your view, would countries be best advised to foster greater regional ties or to trade more with other world regions, and why?

International regulation of trade

Bretton Woods agreement agreement between Allied nations in the aftermath of the Second World War, which was intended to bring about exchange rate stability; established the IMF and World Bank

multilateral agreement international agreement signed by many countries, usually in the form of a treaty which creates legal obligations

Institutional arrangements put in place in the immediate aftermath of the Second World War have played a major role in establishing a global trading order. The preceding era, scarred by the Great Depression of the 1930s, had seen protectionism and a decline in world trade. Under the **Bretton Woods agreement**, reached at a conference of the allied nations in 1944, exchange rate stability would be achieved by pegging every currency to gold or the US dollar (see Chapter 9). Negotiators envisaged the **multilateral agreement** involving many countries as a means of dismantling barriers to trade. They also laid plans for an international trade organization (ITO) to bring down tariff barriers, but the charter eventually drawn up in 1948 met with little enthusiasm from nations, still reluctant to endorse free trade. Instead, a more modest set of proposals for a weaker institutional framework was formulated, in the General Agreement on Tariffs and Trade (GATT), which we introduced in Chapter 2. Under the GATT, successive rounds of negotiations have brought about global trade liberalization, leading to the establishment in 1995 of the WTO, reminiscent of the stronger body envisaged in early days after the war. The WTO now has 153 member states. Two other institutions set up as a result of post-war initiatives were the International Monetary Fund (IMF) and the International Bank for Reconstruction and Development (the World Bank), both of which are discussed in Chapter 9. The Bretton Woods system disintegrated in the early 1970s, bringing about a resurgence of protectionism. The period 1945–70 has been called the 'golden age of capitalism' (Michie and Kitson, 1995). In this section, we examine how the WTO's regulatory framework has evolved.

GATT principles

most-favoured-nation principle (MFN) GATT principle by which the most favourable tariff treatment negotiated with one country is extended to similar goods from all countries

The GATT provided the principles and foundation for the development of a global trading system, which were carried forward into the WTO. Perhaps the most important of these is non-discrimination, or the **most-favoured-nation principle (MFN)**. There are two aspects to this principle:

1 Favourable tariff treatment negotiated with one country will be extended to similar goods from all countries.

► More online ... The WTO has a gateway on anti-dumping issues, at www.wto.org/english/tratop_e/adp_e/adp_e.htm

2 Under the principle of 'national treatment', imported goods are treated for all purposes in the same way as domestic goods of the same type.

MFN status is negotiated between countries, and while it is the norm among trading partners, there are exceptions. US legislation has linked MFN treatment with human rights record. Because of its poor human rights record, China was granted only temporary MFN status from 1980 onwards, which was renewed annually. Unconditional MFN status came in 2000, paving the way for China's WTO member-ship. Russia is the one Bric country which is not a WTO member.

Other GATT principles include reciprocity, requiring tariff reductions by one country to be matched by its trading partners; and transparency, ensuring that the underlying aims of all trade measures are clear. The principle of fairness allows a country that has suffered from unfair trading practices by a trading partner to take protectionist measures against that country. Defining fair practice is at the heart of many trade disputes, as countries naturally have differing perspectives on what is and is not fair. An example is **dumping**, or the sale of goods abroad at below the price charged for comparable goods in the producing country. The GATT **anti-dumping** agreement of 1994 allows anti-dumping duties to be imposed on the exporting country by the importing country, in order to protect local producers from unfair competition. The country making allegations of dumping against another asks the WTO to investigate the matter. The number of investigations initiated by the WTO increased from 163 in 2007 to 208 in 2008. China was the most frequently cited country alleged to be engaged in dumping, and the countries that launched the most anti-dumping complaints were India and Brazil, not – as one might expect – the advanced western economies.

dumping sale of goods abroad at below the price charged for comparable goods in the producing country

anti-dumping rules WTO rules which allow anti-dumping duties to be imposed on the exporting country by the importing country, in order to protect local producers from unfair competition

The Uruguay Round, culminating in the 1994 GATT, laid the groundwork for future trade liberalization, while allowing countries to take limited steps to safeguard national industries. It resulted in worldwide tariff reductions of about 40% on manu-factured goods. Less spectacularly, it made strides in the more difficult areas of reducing trade barriers in agricultural products and textiles. It also initiated agree-ments on intellectual property rights and services, both crucial areas in growing world trade. Finally, the GATT 1994 created the WTO as its successor institution.

Summary points GATT principles

◆ Under the most-favoured-nation (MFN) principle, a favourable tariff agreed on a specific product with

one country applies to all member countries.

◆ Other important GATT principles are transparency and fair practices.

WTO and the regulation of world trade

Whereas in 1947 the GATT created only a weak institutional framework, the WTO, which came into being in 1995, was designed on firmer legal footing, with a stronger rule-governed orientation. This approach is reflected in its organizational structure. A Ministerial Conference, consisting of trade ministers of all member states, is the main policymaking body, meeting every two years. A Dispute Settlement Body over-seas the dispute settlement procedure for specific trade disputes between countries. This new legal procedure for resolving disputes marks a sharp departure from the GATT procedure, which had no power of enforcement.

► More online ... The Office of the US Trade Representative is at www.ustr.gov

The WTO's dispute settlement procedure aims to resolve trade disputes through impartial panels before they escalate into damaging trade wars in which countries take unilateral action against each other. A country that feels it has suffered because of another's breach of trading rules may apply to the WTO, which appoints an impartial panel for hearing the case within a specified timetable. A country found to be in breach of trade rules by a panel may appeal to the Appellate Body. If it is again found to be in the wrong, the WTO may authorize the country whose trade has suffered as a result, to impose retaliatory trade sanctions.

For the WTO's procedure to succeed, countries must adhere to its decisions, even when they disagree with them. All countries enjoy a recognized right to safeguard national interests, but this principle, as well as interpretation of WTO rules themselves, is subject to considerable latitude in interpretation. If countries impose unilateral sanctions, bypassing the WTO, then WTO procedures, and the authority that underlies them, could be eroded. The US law known as Section 301 is such a provision. Originally enacted in the Trade Act 1974, it authorizes the US to retaliate unilaterally against other countries (as opposed to specific companies) that it judges are violating a GATT provision or unfairly restricting the import of US goods or services. Section 301 was strengthened in 1988, authorizing the US Trade Representative (USTR) to identify 'priority trade practices' of other countries that pose the greatest barriers to US trade, and to single out particular countries which have a history of trade discrimination. Under this legislation a country could lose access to the entire US market, not merely that of the offending product. The legislation has been criticized for its aggressive unilateral approach, which, some argue, is in breach of WTO rules (Sell, 2000). In February 2000, a WTO panel ruled, in what was seen by a number of developing countries as an unsatisfactory decision, that Section 301 is not incompatible with WTO rules, so long as the US refrained from taking unilateral action. Recent monitoring by the USTR has focused on intellectual property rights, relevant to medicines under pharmaceutical patents and copyright material, which are frequently cited as areas in which there is thriving trade in counterfeit goods, produced without permission of legal owners (discussed further in Chapter 10).

Summary points **The WTO**

◆ Following in the footsteps of the GATT, the WTO provided a structural and institutional framework for applying multilateral trade rules and negotiating trade agreements.

◆ The WTO's dispute settlement procedure depends on its perceived fairness and on countries' continued adherence to its rules.

Multilateral trade agreements and the WTO

The WTO has made a dramatic impact in focusing international attention on issues of world trade, but it has also sparked considerable controversy. Since its creation in 1995, issues of globalization and the rise of developing nations have come to the fore, involving the WTO in wider debates. Its meetings have been targeted by demonstrations, from anti-capitalist protesters to environmental activists. In addition, NGOs have been instrumental in vocalizing environmental and human rights issues. Within multilateral negotiations themselves, national interests have remained divergent. Developing and emerging countries seek the opening of markets in rich countries,

▶ More online ... Doha Round issues can be found under 'trade topics' on the WTO's website at www.wto.org

while rich countries wish to export more easily to markets in the developing world. Both developed and developing countries fear that the removal of barriers will open their economies to damaging competition which could jeopardize local industries; hence, all are reluctant to make concessions.

In 2001, a new round of multilateral trade negotiations, known as the Doha Round, commenced in Doha, Qatar. Negotiations continued at several ministerial conferences which followed, but the major policy areas, which had been carried forward from the Uruguay Round, generated sharp divergence of perspectives, mainly between developed and developing countries. It was intended that the new Doha agreement would be in place by the end of 2008, but negotiations faltered once again, and the deteriorating global economic situation at the time seemed to dampen national leaders' appetites for further multilateral talks. Areas in which agreement was sought included agriculture, opening of markets, and access to patented drugs. Other issues were labour standards, environmental protection, and competition policy. Doha was described as a 'development' round, focusing on issues central to developing countries. These countries have been firm in their view that progress must be made by rich countries in reducing farm subsidies and tariffs. A framework agreement on the principle of reducing farm subsidies was reached in 2004, but it lacked detailed provisions. A draft accord on measures to ease access to cheap medicines for poor countries was also agreed in 2004. Welcomed by developing countries, it caused alarm in the pharmaceutical industry.

The Doha Round placed issues of labour standards and the environment on the agenda for future consideration. Environmentalists argue that if issues such as global warming and protection of the rainforests are not brought into the equation, commercial goals will win out and the environment will suffer. Trade unionists in industrialized economies, fearful of job losses, argue for the inclusion of labour standards in trade policy. Moreover, labour standards, including condemnation of practices such as child labour, have come to be included in human rights principles generally. These issues crystallized over China's application for WTO membership: its poor human rights record and weak environmental protection regulation were major hurdles to its eventually gaining WTO membership in 2002. Since then, China's growing strength as a trading superpower has tended to overshadow ethical and environmental concerns in the many countries with which China is developing trading ties. A rift between developed and developing countries seemed to cast a cloud over future multilateral negotiations.

Summary points The Doha Round

● Intended to be a 'development' round, the Doha multilateral negotiations reached only tentative agreements on development issues such as reducing tariffs on agricultural products.

● Other agenda items were labour standards and the environment, but different perspectives of developed and developing countries cast doubt on the future of multilateral negotiations generally.

Regional and bilateral trade agreements

Although the WTO has promoted a multilateral approach to trade liberalization, countries have been active in making their own agreements to liberalize trade with trading partners, both within their own geographical regions and beyond. It is common to make a distinction between a **bilateral agreement**, between just two countries, often just called a **free trade agreement (FTA)**, and a **regional trade agreement (RTA)** among a number of countries in the same broad geographic region. However, from the WTO's perspective, both types of agreement, which lie outside the multilateral system, are treated broadly as regional trade agreements. The RTA is often referred to as a 'preferential trade agreement' (PTA), reflecting the fact that its terms give preference to goods and services from countries which are parties to the particular agreement. The number of RTAs (including bilateral agreements) notified to the WTO has grown dramatically in recent years, now reaching over 400, as Figure 4.8 shows. Although they are not all active, this rise shows a marked trend towards trade initiatives outside the multilateral system. Here, we look at these initiatives, distinguishing between regional and bilateral agreements, and then assess their impacts on the global economy.

bilateral agreement an agreement between two countries, often for reciprocal trade terms

free trade agreement (FTA) any agreement between countries which aims to liberalize trade among them; often bilateral or regional

regional trade agreement (RTA) free trade agreement among a number of countries in the same broad geographic region

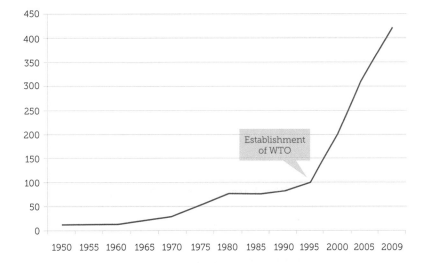

Figure 4.8 **Regional trade agreements notified through the GATT and WTO in the post-war era**

Source: WTO (2009) RTA notifications, RTA portal at www.wto.org

Categories of regional trade agreement

Countries look naturally to trade with their neighbours. Not only does regional trade make sense in terms of costs, firms are likely to have greater familiarity with firms and industries in their own region than with those oceans away. RTAs are designed to bring down trade barriers among their member states, thus opening up regional markets for national producers. A group of countries that have joined in an RTA are sometimes referred to as a **free trade area or bloc**. The RTA can cover a range of issues besides trade, including investment, intellectual property protection and environmental protection. Political considerations can play a key role, as economic integration is inseparable from the political power balance within any region, and regional trading blocs are influential in global politics. We begin by looking at the categories of regional groupings, expanded from the one originally devised by Bela Balassa in *The Theory of Economic Integration* (Balassa, 1962). They can be categorized accordingly:

free trade area or bloc a group of countries which have joined in a regional trade agreement

- **Free trade area** – Member states agree to remove trade barriers among themselves, but keep their separate national barriers against trade with non-member states.

- **Customs union** – Member states remove all trade barriers among themselves and adopt a common set of external barriers.
- **Common market** – Member states enjoy free movement of goods, labour and capital.
- **Economic union** – Member states unify all their economic policies, including monetary, fiscal and welfare policies.
- **Political union** – Member states transfer sovereignty to the regional political and law-making institutions, creating a new 'superstate'.

Most of the world's nations belong to at least one regional grouping, the vast majority of which fall into the first two categories – free trade area and customs union (see Table 4.2). The categories can be seen as successive steps towards deepening economic integration. Only the EU has reached the stage of economic union. Political union is still some way off, but reforms in 2009 have enhanced the role of the European Parliament, discussed in Chapter 7. Free trade areas are now in place in all the world's regions, although with less regional economic integration than in Europe.

Table 4.2 **Regional trade groupings**

Region	Group	Current member countries	Date of formation	Type of agreement
South America	Mercosur (Southern Common Market)	Argentina, Brazil, Paraguay, Uruguay	1991	Common market
South America	Andean Community	Bolivia, Colombia, Ecuador, Peru	1969	Free trade area
Asia-Pacific	Apec (Asia-Pacific Economic Cooperation Group)	21 countries: Australia, Brunei, Canada, Indonesia, Japan, South Korea, Malaysia, New Zealand, Philippines, Singapore, Thailand, US, China, Hong Kong, Taiwan, Mexico, Papua New Guinea, Chile, Peru, Russia, Vietnam	1989	Free trade area to be in place by 2020
South East Asia	Asean (Association of South East Asian Nations)	Indonesia, Malaysia, Philippines, Singapore, Thailand, Brunei, Cambodia, Laos, Myanmar (Burma), Vietnam	1967	Co-operation agreement, free trade by early 2010
Caribbean	CARICOM (Caribbean Community)	15 Caribbean nations: Antigua and Barbuda, Bahamas, Barbados, Belize, Dominica, Grenada, Guyana, Haiti, Jamaica, Monserrat, St Lucia, St Kitts and Nevis, St Vincent and the Grenadines, Suriname, Trinidad and Tobago	1973	Common market
Europe	EFTA (European Free Trade Area)	Iceland, Switzerland, Norway, Liechtenstein	1960	Free trade area
	EU (European Union)	Austria, Belgium, Denmark, France, Finland, Germany, Greece, Ireland, Italy, Luxembourg, the Netherlands, Portugal, Spain, Sweden, UK, Czech Republic, Poland, Hungary, Slovenia, Slovakia, Estonia, Lithuania, Latvia, Cyprus, Malta	1957	Economic union, moving towards political union
North and Central America	Nafta (North America Free Trade Agreement)	Canada, Mexico, US	1994	Free trade area

▶ More online ... The WTO has a web page on regional trade agreements, under 'trade topics' at www.wto.org

Region	Group	Current member countries	Date of formation	Type of agreement
Africa	Ecowas (Economic Community of West African States)	15 members: Benin, Burkina Faso, Cote d'Ivoire, Gambia, Ghana, Guinea, Guinea Bissau, Liberia, Mali, Niger, Nigeria, Senegal, Sierra Leone, Togo, Cape Verde	1975	Customs union
Africa	East African Community (EAC)	Kenya, Tanzania, Uganda, Rwanda, Burundi	2001	Common market

Summary points Levels of regional integration

● The free trade area, in which customs barriers are reduced among member states, is the commonest type of regional free trade agreement.

● The RTA can, and often does, cover many areas in addition to trade, including investment and intellectual property protection.

● Moves to achieve greater integration, involving economic and political union, have occurred mainly in the EU.

Focus on regions

In this section we look in turn at the major geographic regions of the world, describing the free trade groupings in each, along with regional variations and prospects for the future.

Europe

As early as the Treaty of Rome in 1957 the founding six members of the European Economic Community, later the EU, envisaged both economic and political integration (see Chapter 3 for a discussion of EU economic goals). The institutions set up, dominated by the Commission and Council, have remained the structural foundations, and the European Court of Justice has established its legal supremacy (see Chapters 7 and 8). No other regional grouping begins to approach this level of structural autonomy. However, the goal of Single European Market, which was the cornerstone of European economic integration, has come about only gradually, and amid a good deal of political and bureaucratic stalemate. The Single European Act of 1987 aimed to dismantle internal barriers and establish a single market by 1992. Businesses would be able to move seamlessly from one member country to another without bureaucratic frontier procedures. Product standards would be recognized between member states. Financial services would be liberalized, so that firms such as banks and insurance companies could compete across national borders.

In reality, progress in internal liberalization has been neither as swift nor as easy as many predicted back in 1987. Liberalizing of financial services began in the mid-1990s. Banks and investors urged speeding up of the necessary legislation, which has taken years, and there are still national barriers to cross-border financial services. Telecommunications deregulation and deregulation of utilities such as water, gas and electricity have been uneven. Histories of protected industries and varying degrees of state ownership have slowed progress. Deeply rooted national cultural differences were underestimated, and domestic political considerations have loomed large. The latter have sparked continuing debate on principles of sovereignty and national identity, and also the economic interests of groups of workers affected by liberalization.

▸ More online ... The EU's main portal is http://europa.eu.int
Mercosur is at http://www.mercosur.org

For agriculture, the effect of the GATT Agriculture Agreement of 1994 was to reduce the CAP budget, but it is still nearly half the EU's annual budget (see Chapter 3). Liberalization has taken on renewed urgency in negotiations on EU enlargement, as the countries waiting in the wings are concerned to protect farming interests, creating more strain on the CAP in propping up relatively inefficient agriculture.

As Table 4.2 shows, Europe has long had a free trade area co-existing with the EU. The **European Free Trade Area (EFTA)** was formed in 1960 by countries not signed up to the Treaty of Rome. They were Austria, Denmark, Norway, Portugal, Sweden, Switzerland and the UK. They were later joined by Iceland and Finland. As most of these countries joined the EU, EFTA has four remaining members, as shown in the table. With the exception of Switzerland, EFTA members have joined the EU in a wider **European Economic Area (EEA),** which is a free trade area.

The Americas

The Andean Pact, later changed to the **Andean Community**, is the oldest of the regional trade groupings in the Americas. Political instability in the 1970s set back plans to establish a customs union. With the upsurge in global commodities markets, which occurred in the 1980s, South American countries saw economic gains from commodity exports. The two largest traders, Brazil and Argentina, joined forces in 1988 to form a grouping which became **Mercosur**, with the addition of Paraguay and Uruguay. These countries are all associate members of the Andean Community. Similarly, Andean Community member countries are associate members of Mercosur. Efforts to bring the two groupings together in a Free Trade Area of the Americas have taken place partly as a response to US moves to expand Nafta southwards. Venezuela, one of the continent's largest trading nations, and also an oil exporter, applied to join Mercosur in 2006. Its application had to be approved by member states, the key to which has been approval by Brazil, the region's largest economy. Within Brazil, there was considerable opposition to Venezuela's membership, for fear that Venezuela's outspoken left-wing president, Hugo Chavez, well known for his anti-US sentiment, would jeopardize free trade initiatives. Approval by Brazil's Senate came in 2009, removing a major hurdle to full membership for Venezuela.

The **North American Free Trade Agreement (Nafta)**, which came into effect in 1994, comprises the US, Canada and Mexico. While Nafta does not envisage the degree of economic integration of the EU, its provisions and future developments raise similar issues, including political concerns and the question of sovereignty. In contrast to the EU, Nafta is centred on one dominant power, the US, whose GDP is ten times that of Mexico – a much bigger gap than that between the rich and poor EU members. Fear of economic dependence on the US has bred nationalism in both Canada and Mexico, although rather more virulent in nature in its Mexican form. In the post-war period their economies became increasingly integrated with that of the US, as US companies set up branch plants and subsidiaries to export to US markets. A free trade agreement, securing free access to markets, offered advantages to all three countries. The US looked for advantages of low-cost labour in Mexico, the opening of Canada and Mexico to US financial services, and improved access to oil in Canada and Mexico. For the two smaller states, the main advantage consisted of negotiated rules to put their access to US markets on a more secure footing, replacing the informal relationships of the past. Still, some Canadians have considered that their trade relations with the US are being constrained by having to work within a tripartite arrangement with Mexico, which is a

European Free Trade Area (EFTA) grouping formed in 1960 by countries not signed up to the Treaty of Rome (which created what is now the EU)

European Economic Area (EEA) grouping of the European Free Trade Area (EFTA) and the EU

Andean Community South American free trade area

Mercosur South American common market

North American Free Trade Agreement (Nafta) free trade area comprising the US, Canada and Mexico

▶ More online ... The Nafta website is http://www.nafta-sec-alena.org/en/view.aspx

much poorer country than itself. They would like to see Canada negotiating a bilateral agreement with the US (*The Economist*, 2009c).

Market access provisions were the main substance of Nafta, by which the parties agreed to eliminate tariffs on most manufactured goods over a 10-year period. Nafta's investment rules allow investors from any of the three countries to be treated in the same way as domestic investors. These rules apply to both FDI and portfolio investment. For matters other than investment, Nafta introduced a dispute settlement procedure. While it aimed to satisfy the worries of the smaller partners that the stronger partner always has the upper hand, there is still the problem for smaller countries that US pressure may be backed up by retaliatory actions such as anti-dumping measures to restrict imports into the US. Two 'side accords' of Nafta concern labour standards and environmental standards, stemming from concern in the US over firms moving production to Mexico in order to avoid the higher US standards. Commissions were set up in both areas to monitor and enforce national standards (rather than international ILO standards), but enforcement procedures are weak.

Unlike the EU, Nafta operates no common external trade policy. Also in contrast to the EU, it has no institutions for dealing with exchange rates. The Mexican peso crisis of the mid-1990s was left to individual governments to resolve. At its inception, Nafta aimed to increase exports between partners, who already traded heavily with each other, and to create jobs in all three countries. Fifteen years later, Mexico remains a poor country, with GDP per capita only one-fifth that of the US. More than 80% of Mexico's exports are to the US, making it vulnerable to economic downturn in America. An additional concern has been rising protectionism in the US. During the recession of 2008–9, Canada and Mexico feared that their exports would be adversely affected by the 'Buy American' law introduced by the US Congress. American proposals to expand Nafta to include South American countries made some progress, but have been rather stalled since 2006, having met resistance from leading players such as Brazil.

Asia

Asia's economies vary from the small city-state (Singapore) to the industrial giants (China and Japan). Despite some cultural affinities among the many Asian countries, they are diverse in their economies and political systems. The **Association of South East Asian Nations (Asean)** brings together ten South East Asian countries (see Table 4.2). Even among these economies, there is considerable diversity and differing levels of economic development. Singapore has developed as an FDI-oriented market economy with rather autocratic political rule, while Vietnam is a poorer country, whose communist leadership is keen to foster economic growth and market reforms. For these countries, links in global supply chains are key to development. A new free trade agreement has been made between China and the six founder members of Asean (Brunei, Indonesia, Malaysia, Philippines, Singapore and Thailand). This agreement, which came into effect in January 2010, is the world's largest free trade agreement, covering a population of 1.9 billion people. It eliminates tariffs on 90% of imported goods. The smaller countries have concerns that they will be unable to compete with China. China will benefit from the free flow of raw materials from Asean countries to its factories. Asean countries also stand to gain, specifically from the flow of parts and components from China to their own assembly plants.

The **Asia-Pacific Economic Cooperation Group (Apec)** is the other large regional grouping, although it lacks the coherence of most free trade areas. It is hardly regional, as its members, all bordering the Pacific, are located on three different continents. As

Association of South East Asian Nations (Asean) co-operation agreement of South East Asian countries

Asia-Pacific Economic Cooperation Group (Apec) co-operation agreement of economies bordering on the Pacific

▶ More online ... Apec's home page is http://www.apecsec.org.sg/
The Asean Secretariat is at http://www.aseansec.org/
The Ecowas Commission is at www.ecowas.int
The East African Community is at www.eac.int

yet, it does not function as a free trade area, and its large size, encompassing more than half of the world's economic output, makes it rather different from regional groupings. Its members attend regular summits, at which bilateral agreements are negotiated. The presence of the US, China and Japan in Apec have led some to see it as a kind of multilateralism, or 'open regionalism', potentially rivalling the WTO (Bhagwati, 2006). As with all RTAs, the preferential status afforded to members contrasts with the treatment of non-members, which would amount to discrimination within the WTO's framework. A free trade area of the Asia-Pacific which would exclude the EU, India and Brazil, would be viewed by many as a threat to multilateralism.

Africa

African countries, many of which are rich in oil and other natural resources, are becoming increasingly important in world trade. Co-operative agreements focusing on regional trade in the western, southern and eastern regions, have not as yet led to deepening regional integration. Poverty and poor governance have combined with internal instability in many countries, which has spilled over into regional conflicts. These have all been factors in slowing the economic development that Africans had hoped for in their post-colonial period. A number of regional co-operative agreements have been entered into, often with overlapping membership. One of the oldest and most developed at the institutional level is the **Economic Community of West African States (Ecowas)**, which has a Commission, Parliament and Court of Justice. The Commission's specialized agencies focus on development projects in areas such as health and sport. A first-ever Ecowas cycling tour, modelled on famous western tours such as the Tour de France, was held in 2009. It went through 12 countries and featured 12 national teams.

Economic Community of West African States (Ecowas) organization for co-operation among West African states

The **East African Community (EAC)**, which started as a free trade area, became a customs union and is now being transformed into a common market. From mid-2010, goods have flowed tariff-free across the national borders of five of its member countries (Burundi, Kenya, Rwanda, Tanzania and Uganda). Kenya is the largest of these economies, with well-positioned retailers, manufacturers and banks, which hope to gain from the common market. The smaller countries also stand to gain, with better transport and the opportunity to build more competitive manufacturing industries than they could achieve individually. By coming together, these countries' manufacturers could begin to compete with imports from China. EAC members hope to set up a monetary union as a next step, and envisage joining free trade blocs in western and southern Africa in the future.

East African Community (EAC) common market of East African countries

Summary points **Region-by-region focus**

◆ The EU is an economic union, and EFTA is the wider free trade area.
◆ In the Americas, two important free trade areas are Nafta and Mercosur. There have been proposals to combine these into a north–south free trade area.

◆ In Asia, there are two main groupings, Asean and Apec, but the growth of China as a regional superpower, challenging Japan's longstanding strength, is a major factor in future free trade initiatives.

◆ Among African countries, the creation of regional free trade areas is gradually taking place, with potential for cross-border business which could aid economic development.

Critical thinking

Regional integration: some more equal than others?

Free trade agreements are generally applauded for bringing down barriers to trade, benefiting all members. But where the member countries are unequal, as in Nafta, this assumption does not necessarily hold. What are the benefits and drawbacks of free trade agreements from the perspective of a weaker partner?

Multilateralism at the crossroads

As bilateral and regional initiatives proliferate, the multilateralism promoted by the WTO has foundered, calling into question its future for the regulation of world trade. The breakdown of the Doha Round, economic recession in many countries, and rising protectionist sentiments have weakened governments' commitment to the WTO's multilateral trade agenda. In this context, governments see bilateral agreements as more attractive and potentially more advantageous in terms of their own national interests. There has been a proliferation of free trade agreements (FTAs), usually bilateral in conception. Pascal Lamy, the WTO's Director-General, concerned about the threats to multilateralism, has highlighted some of the aspects of bilateral agreements which appeal to governments (Lamy, 2007):

- They can be concluded much more quickly than multilateral agreements.
- They can go into areas beyond trade, such as investment, technical standards and environmental standards, which can be designed for the interests of the countries involved.
- In circumstances of inequality, such as agreements between a poor developing country and a rich one (which is common in bilateral agreements), development assistance and other benefits to the developing country can be written in.

Lamy argues that, despite these apparent benefits, the rise of preferential trade agreements constitutes a threat to global trade. He cites four causes for concern:

- The preferential terms contained in a bilateral agreement discriminate against outsiders. A country outside such an agreement will try to conclude an agreement with one of the partners inside, to avoid discrimination, leading to a 'bandwagon' effect of multiplying bilateral agreements. The result is that the preferential positions contained in the first agreement tend to be short-lived: 'the more agreements you have, the less meaningful the preferences would be' (Lamy, 2007).
- Many issues cannot be dealt with at the bilateral level. These include antidumping and subsidies to farmers, which must be agreed on a multilateral basis.
- The proliferation of bilateral agreements greatly complicates the international business environment, creating a 'spaghetti bowl' effect for companies to wade through.
- The inequality of bargaining power between a small, weak country and a large, powerful one can be immense. The smaller country will have neither the legal and technical expertise of the more powerful partner, nor the in-depth resources to support negotiating teams to match those of the richer partner. The small partner is likely to be at a greater disadvantage in negotiating than it would be in multilateral talks.

Lamy concludes that a strong multilateral trading system should be at the centre of world trade, and that RTAs should complement, rather than undermine, the WTO

▸ More online ... See the G20's website at www.g20.org

approach. In practice, the major economies, including the large emerging economies, are expending considerable effort in forging bilateral ties while multilateral
negotiations to conclude the Doha Round are on hold.

The US has concluded FTAs (including bilateral and regional agreements) with 17
countries: Australia, Bahrain, Canada, Chile, Costa Rica, Dominican Republic, El Salvador,
Guatemala, Honduras, Israel, Jordan, Mexico, Morocco, Nicaragua, Oman, Peru and
Singapore. A number of others, including one with Columbia, are pending. The foreign
partner in all these agreements is a weaker partner, which is targeted by the US largely as
an export market for US business. However, many of these agreements have not been as
quick and uncomplicated as one might expect in a situation where there are only two
partners, in contrast to the WTO's 153 members. The American trade agreements with
Peru and Columbia were signed in 2006. Both run to over 20 chapters and nearly 1500
pages of text, challenging even technical and legal experts to fathom. The US–Peru
agreement came into force in 2009, and the Columbia agreement was still pending in
2010. The presence of US military bases in Columbia, with defence agreements pending
for their expansion, suggests that military and trade considerations are connected.

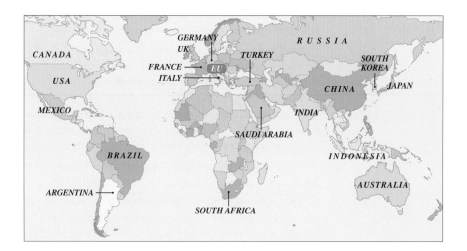

Figure 4.9 **G20 members**

G20 grouping of 20
developed, developing
and emerging
economies, brought
together by the IMF
in 1999, which meets
regularly, focusing mainly
on financial stability

Group of Seven (G7)
grouping of 7 advanced
economies (US, Canada,
UK, France, Germany,
Italy, and Japan); with
the addition of Russia,
it is known as the G8

The future of multilateralism will be influenced by the relatively recent grouping
of countries known as the **G20**. Brought together by the IMF in 1999, in the wake of
financial crises, this grouping is more representative of the current global economy
than the **Group of Seven (G7)**, which represents only the advanced economies (US,
Canada, UK, France, Germany, Italy and Japan). The G20 is a diversified group, with
members representing all continents, as shown in Figure 4.9. These countries
account for 80% of world trade. Although advanced economies are heavily represented and the EU is a member in its own right, emerging economies are also well
represented. The IMF and World Bank are also involved.

Envisaged initially as a gathering of finance ministers, the G20 members attend
regular summit meetings on both finance and wider issues, but have no permanent
secretariat. Meeting in the aftermath of the global financial crisis of 2008–9, member
countries raised concerns that rising protectionism could jeopardize economic
recovery. Nonetheless, their governments implemented numerous protectionist
measures in the months that followed, in efforts to aid their individual economies'

recovery. As the emerging economies were not as severely affected by the financial crisis as the US, it is possible that protectionist pressures are receding and governments will once again recognize the importance of multilateral agreements on trade and other issues. Larger members of the G20 featured in the climate change conference held in Copenhagen in 2009 (see Chapter 11). Although environmentalists were disappointed because no binding targets were set, the meeting did establish that governments of the large economies, both developed and developing, recognize the need for multilateral solutions.

Summary points The future of multilateralism

◆ The rise of regional and bilateral trade agreements poses threats for future multilateral agreements. However, their proliferation has occurred partly as a reaction to the failure of the Doha Round of multilateral talks.

◆ Although bilateral agreements look an attractive alternative in principle, they tend to be lopsided, favouring the stronger country.

◆ A prospect for future multilateral agreements could lie with the G20 countries, which represent a wide range of developed and developing countries.

Critical thinking

Bilateralism and international business

For international managers, which type of trade agreements would be preferred: multilateral or bilateral?

Globalization and world trade

Trade, as this chapter has highlighted, involves both political and economic considerations. Nation-states have traditionally relied on tariffs, quota restrictions and other policies which rested on the assumption that protection and economic development naturally went together. In modern economies, the levels of productivity, technological innovation and investment are more than ever dependent on participation in the global economy. Participation no longer simply means increasing trade, although expansion of trade has been one of the major trends of the post-war era. Increasingly, through the global strategies of MNEs, foreign investment has been the driver of trade. The processes of globalization in integrating national economies can largely be attributed to MNEs' global production networks.

The 1980s and 90s saw a tension between two apparently contradictory trends: trade liberalization, sponsored by the WTO, on the one hand, and growing regional and bilateral arrangements on the other. Economists have argued that regional agreements put up barriers to free trade with outsiders, but predictions of a regionalized world economy have not yet come to fruition (see Castells, 2000). As we have seen, few of these groupings are homogeneous or cohesive. Apart from the EU, institutional structures are limited. And even in the EU, which is the most economically integrated, nation-states have not yet been superseded as defining units for a population's economic interests. But those interests are now played out in regional, as well as multilateral, institutions. Moreover, bilateral free trade agreements are a continuing trend.

Conclusions

1 The post-Second World War period has seen a growth of international trade and a trend towards liberalization of the world trading system.
2 A recent trend has been the rise of China as a trading superpower.
3 International trade theories offer explanations of why countries, as well as companies, compete, and how comparative and competitive advantages can be exploited.
4 Government policies, highly influential in international trade, rest on concerns of national producer and consumer interests.
5 Tools of government trade policy include exchange rate manipulation, tariffs and non-tariff barriers to trade. However, the growth of the multilateral trading system, initiated by GATT, has limited the scope of governments to act unilaterally in managing trade.
6 The World Trade Organization, successor to GATT, has strengthened the rule-governed system of international trade regulation, particularly in regard to dispute settlement. Tensions nonetheless remain over the processes and implementation of WTO decisions in trade disputes.
7 The Doha Round of negotiations has made progress in some respects, such as a framework for reductions of agricultural subsidies, but differences between developed and developing countries have slowed negotiations. Outstanding issues facing the WTO remain whether to link issues such as core labour standards and environmental protection to trade policies.
8 The trend towards regional trade agreements since the Second World War represents growing regional economic integration. However, regional groupings differ considerably in their internal cohesiveness and structures, the European Union being the most integrated.
9 Bilateral free trade agreements, which have proliferated in recent years, raise questions of the benefits to the two parties, especially where they are unequal in bargaining power and resources.
10 World trade can best be viewed in the context of globalization, in which the large MNEs with globalized production capacities have been major players.

Review questions

1 How relevant is the theory of comparative advantage to modern trade patterns?
2 What are the main contributions of Porter's theory of competitive advantage?
3 What is meant by strategic trade policy?
4 Outline the motivations underlying government trade policy.
5 Summarize the arguments for and against free trade.
6 What are the main tools of government trade policy?
7 Define the GATT principles of most-favoured nation and national treatment.
8 In what ways does the WTO represent a step on from GATT?
9 What progress has been made in the Doha Round of trade negotiations?
10 What are the outstanding issues facing the WTO, and why has it struggled to arrive at a consensus?
11 Why have regional trade groupings become popular, and in what ways, if any, do they undermine multilateral trade liberalization efforts?
12 Contrast the European Union and Nafta in terms of regional integration.
13 Why do developing countries have ambivalent feelings about trade liberalization?

Key revision concepts

Comparative advantage, p. 123; Competitive advantage, p. 125; Export/import, p. 123; Free trade agreement (FTA), p. 141; Multilateralism, p. 137; Protectionism, p. 128; Subsidies, p. 132; Tariffs, p. 132; Voluntary export restraint (VER), p. 121

Assignments

◆ Assess the contrasting perspectives and interests of developed countries, the large emerging economies and the weaker developing countries with respect to global trade liberalization.

◆ Is regionalism a 'stepping stone' or 'stumbling block' to free trade? Compare the progress of regional integration in three regions: Europe, North America and Asia.

Further reading

Berry, B., Conkling, E. and Ray, D. (1997) *The Global Economy in Transition*, 2nd edn (New Jersey: Prentice Hall).

Frieden, J. and Lake, D. (1999) *International Political Economy: Perspectives on Global Power and Wealth* (Oxford: Routledge).

Gilpin, R. (2000) *The Challenge of Global Capitalism* (Princeton: Princeton University Press).

Gilpin, R. (2001) *Global Political Economy: Understanding the International Economic Order* (Princeton: Princeton University Press).

Hirst, P. and Thompson, G. (1999) *Globalization in Question*, 2nd edn (Cambridge: Polity Press).

Mattli, W. (1999) The *Logic of Regional Integration: Europe and Beyond* (Cambridge: Cambridge University Press).

Oatley, T. (2009) International Political Economy, 4th edn (New Jersey: Pearson Education).

Michie, J. and Kitson, M. (eds) (1995) *Managing the Global Economy* (Oxford: Oxford University Press).

Volkswagen builds on strengths in global markets

Volkswagen (VW) once toyed with the idea of building a 'global car', one model suited for all markets, whether Europe, the US, China or India. Those days are now gone, and the company's strategy is to build cars tailored to consumer needs in each market, using its strengths as a global company to be competitive in each. Its engineering strengths are formidable, centred in its home market in Germany. It is headquartered in Wolfsburg in the State of Lower Saxony, where it operates six factories. As Lower Saxony is also one of its main shareholders, VW's strategy is partly influenced by domestic political concerns. It operates 15 factories altogether in Germany, employing 195,000 people, 47% of its global workforce. Its factories have built up specialist expertise in component manufacturing for the whole network: they include specialist makers of engines, gearboxes and steering units for the group. Its strengths in component manufacturing – some for other car manufacturers – have helped Germany to gain pre-eminence in export markets. Germany is a high-cost location, but the company has implemented agreed cost reductions, including wage freezes. VW has also maintained its competitiveness by globalizing

production in lower-cost locations, from where it exports to other markets.

Mexico is home to the largest VW plant outside Germany. It has been manufacturing cars in Puebla, Mexico since 1965, but the focus of these operations has changed over the years. Initially, it produced small cars mainly for the Mexican market, but it gradually shifted to production for export: 80% of its output is now exported. Following the Nafta agreement of 1995, VW was able to export its Mexican-made cars freely into the US. Puebla now manufactures a range of models, including the New Beetle and Jetta models, for export globally. Europe remains VW's biggest market, and it has trailed behind other foreign manufacturers in the US (see figure). Japanese carmakers, as well as German luxury rivals, such as BMW, invested in greenfield sites in the US from the 1980s onwards, and have built market share. VW has now, belatedly, followed in their footsteps, with a factory in Chatanooga, Tennessee. Its location is close to a network of supplier companies which serve existing BMW and Mercedes plants. The current climate in the car industry, which has seen falls in global sales, is perhaps not the best time for new greenfield

On show at the Shanghai Expo: Volkswagen sees a bright future in emerging markets such as China

Source: Volkswagen

▶ More online ... Volkswagen's corporate website is www.volkswagenag.com

investments, but VW feels in a strong position. It has been less exposed than its rivals to the downturn in the US market, and the shifts in consumer tastes in America, towards smaller, cleaner cars, have opened up opportunities for VW. It is also optimistic about growing sales in the large emerging markets, Brazil, China and India. In India, it set up a Skoda plant, its first in the country, in 2001. It now has another new plant in India, producing the Polo model.

VW has become adept at producing a range of models that share design and engineering, using 'platforms' which can form the basis of a number of models, from the modest to the luxurious. For example, it can use the Polo small-car platform to build a bigger car for the American market. The Skoda and the Seat utilize basic parts found in the more expensive VW Golf, but these more modest brands have their own distinctive fittings and finishes. At the more luxurious end of the market, the Audi brand also benefits from VW's platform strategy. VW is now seeking to expand the Audi brand, hoping to topple BMW as the world's largest premium brand. The strength of VW's formidable expertise in other consumer segments will be an asset.

VW's strategic focus in recent years has been clouded by ownership and corporate governance disputes, which now seem to be resolved. VW's roots go back to Ferdinand Porsche, who designed the original Beetle, which became symbolic of Germany's post-war development. The Porsche family also founded the sports-car company, which became a major VW shareholder. In a series of audacious moves, Porsche attempted to take over VW in 2008, but the attempt failed, and the sports-car company was left nursing large debts. VW then orchestrated a merger of the two companies, also involving an investment by a Qatari sovereign wealth fund. The merger would see all VW and Porsche brands under the same roof, in an

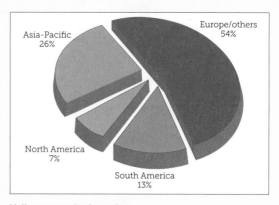

Volkswagen sales by region
Total: 6,310,000 vehicles
Source: Volkswagen Annual Report 2009, at www.volkswagenag.com

'integrated car-manufacturing group' (Schafer, 2009a). The dominant families will own 40% of the newly merged company, and Lower Saxony will retain its 20% stake, from which it is able to influence strategic and operational decisions. Lower Saxony's stake has long been a subject of contention, having been enshrined in Germany's so-called 'VW law', which deters a would-be takeover by capping any shareholder's voting strength at 20% regardless of the size of its shareholding. Although the German government had contemplated relaxing the law as part of its liberal market reforms, the law has remained in place. In addition, employee representation of 50% of VW's supervisory board helps to ensure that domestic employment remains a strong element of future VW strategy.

Sources: Schafer, D. (2009a) 'Saxony firm on keeping its blocking power at VW', *Financial Times*, 8 May; *The Economist* (2009) 'My other car firm's a Porsche', 22 August; Schafer, D. (2009b) 'VW flexes its muscle ahead of Porsche merger', *Financial Times*, 13 May; Schafer, D. (2009c) 'VW small vehicle focus to take on Toyota in the US', *Financial Times*, 16 September; Kierman, P. (2009) 'Workers strike at VW plant in Mexico', *Wall Street Journal*, 19 August; Volkswagen Annual Report 2009, at www. volkswagenag.com

Questions for discussion

◆ What are Volkswagen's main strengths as a company?
◆ How has Volkswagen managed to expand into differing national markets, even in times of economic downturn?
◆ To what extent do Volkswagen's ownership and corporate governance suggest German protectionism?

CHAPTER 5

STRATEGIES IN A GLOBALIZED WORLD

Learning objectives

1 To appreciate the ways in which corporate strategy is formulated and implemented in the international context

2 To assess internationalization strategies of MNEs from a variety of national environments

3 To identify organizational structures through which MNEs achieve their aims

4 To critically assess corporate strategic objectives in terms of the changing global environment, including opportunities and risks

Critical themes in this chapter

- **Globalization – internationalization strategies of MNEs**
- **Multilayered environment – corporate structures and strategies for managing subsidiaries in differing locations**
- **International risk – market entry strategies; joint ventures**
- **Multidimensional environment – entry strategies and operations in different cultural environments**
- **Emerging economies – emerging-market MNEs**

Shanghai has become an emblem of China's growing prosperity and global ambitions

Source: Istock

South Korea's Kepco: the new global force in nuclear power stations

Building nuclear reactors is a complex, specialist business, in which projects can last many years and cost billions. Only a handful of companies worldwide can offer a full service, designing, building and running nuclear power stations. Yet, because of its low emissions, most governments now see nuclear power generation as having a vital role in meeting energy needs of the future. The dominant companies in the nuclear industry have tended to travel in groups, or 'consortiums', which come together in joint ventures to bid for large projects. The two main groups have been a GE-led one, which includes Hitachi Heavy Industries of Japan, and a French one, which includes Areva and EDF, both French national champions, and both largely state owned. Now, a newcomer has arrived on the scene: Korean Electric Power Company (Kepco). Kepco sprang a surprise by beating its two heavyweight rivals and winning a $20 billion contract to build and run nuclear reactors in the United Arab Emirates (UAE), the oil-rich state now seeking to develop peaceful nuclear power. The bidding process was led by Abu Dhabi, the richest of the emirates, and the project was for four nuclear plants. A simple explanation for Kepco's success would be that its bid was cheaper, but this explanation would overlook the other benefits which the Koreans brought to the table.

For 20 years, Kepco has been building and running nuclear power stations in South Korea, where it is the state-owned monopoly electricity provider. It has an enviable safety record and a history of building quickly, efficiently and within budget. Its CEO says, 'We're cheap, durable and dependable' (*The Economist*, 2 January 2010). This is in contrast to some of its rivals. Japanese reactors have a weaker safety record, for example. In addition, there are perhaps organizational and managerial explanations for Kepco's success. Kepco works with a consortium that includes Hyundai and Samsung, two of the country's big conglomerates,

and also uses Westinghouse technology. The Kepco group has worked together for many years, and has expertise not just in building the reactors, but in running them. South Korea's president, Lee Myung-bak, was a knowledgeable advocate for the Korean group, being himself formerly of Hyundai Construction. His travelling to the UAE to encourage the bid did no harm. The French president, Nicholas Sarkozy, also stepped in to back the French bid. But by contrast, the two French companies involved, Areva and EDF, although in the same consortium, offer rival reactors in global markets. Similarly, GE and Hitachi are promoting separate reactors, and have also developed a third design. Meanwhile, Areva and Mitsubishi Heavy Industries, although each has its own design, have come together in a joint venture to promote yet another different design. The web of alliances and joint ventures in the industry makes it difficult to discern where ownership and control lie. In this environment, Kepco's relative simplicity and government backing are assets.

Kepco has gone on from its success with the UAE contract to take part in a consortium that won a $6 billion wind and solar farm project in Canada. It now has its eyes focused on Vietnam, where there is a big project. And, further ahead, it hopes to invest in countries such as Turkey, Indonesia and South Africa – all middle-income countries. Kepco has become an emerging-market national champion, signifying its country's new confidence in international business. South Korea's car companies, such as Hyundai, and electronics firms, such as Samsung, are notably gaining competitive advantage, while Japanese counterparts, Toyota and Sony, have seen their reputations suffer due to quality problems. South Korea's conglomerates have restructured and revitalized their organizations, and are now focusing on global markets.

▸ More online ... Kepco is at www.kepco.co.kr/eng

The UAE is the first Gulf state to invest in civilian nuclear power, but other Middle Eastern countries might follow, especially in light of Iran's nuclear programme, which is looked on with some disquiet in the region. The UAE has pledged not to engage in domestic nuclear enrichment or reprocessing – technologies which can lead to nuclear weapons. The UAE is an ally of the US, which keeps a careful eye on Middle East relations. US and Japanese companies in the nuclear industry now realize there is a formidable new competitor in building nuclear capacity globally. The South Korean government also feels more confident of its global role, hosting the G20 in 2010.

Sources: England, A., Hollinger, P. and Song, J. (2009) 'South Korea wins $20bn UAE nuclear power deal', *Financial Times*, 28 December; Oliver, C. and Pilling, D. (2010) 'Into position', *Financial Times*, 17 March; *The Economist* (2010) 'Unexpected reaction', 6 February; *The Economist* (2010) 'Atomic dawn', 2 January

Nuclear energy is becoming crucial for governments seeking to meet future energy needs, offering opportunities for energy companies to compete for large projects such as this nuclear power station

Source: Istock

Questions for discussion

◆ Why is nuclear energy gaining more attention from governments?

◆ What were the strengths of Kepco and its partners in their UAE bid?

◆ In what ways does the success of the South Korean company symbolize the shifting international competitive environment?

Introduction

A now-familiar aspect of globalization is the driving force of MNEs seeking competitive edge. They juggle with a number of aims: to reduce production costs (including raw materials and operations), to improve efficiency, to improve technology and to respond quickly to changing demand from customers. In fact, many of these goals overlap. For example, improving efficiency often involves improved technology, which brings down costs. For the MNE, the ability to shift location relatively easily has become a key factor in achieving these goals. Using the concept of the value chain (introduced in Chapter 2), the MNE can identify priorities for each stage of production, and is then in a position to choose locations and design operations to meet corporate goals. This journey from identifying corporate objectives to delivering products to customers depends crucially on the right strategy. We have already stressed the importance of environmental factors in strategy formation (in Chapter 2). Here, we focus on strategy from the firm's perspective.

The chapter begins with a broad overview of corporate strategy. We highlight influential theories which provide the guideposts for decision-makers within companies generally. We then turn to internationalization strategies, looking at alternative entry modes in the context of different environments. Because MNE strategies are closely linked to organizational issues, we discuss organizations in the international environment. Is there one best type of business organization for international operations, or must organizations respond constantly to changing environments? While the network organization and an array of inter-organizational networks have been generally thought to present the optimum balance between control and flexibility, networks are being rethought in the constantly changing global environment. The rise of emerging markets and emerging MNEs is changing the competitive landscape, as these new players becoming catalysts for all international businesses to refocus on strategy. In particular, the impact of differing corporate cultures on strategy and organizations is making for a richer range of strategic perspectives, and posing new challenges for MNEs.

Overview of strategy

Back at the start of Chapter 1, we posed the question, 'What does the business enterprise exist to do?' We found that enterprises aim to achieve a variety of purposes, among them, to satisfy customers, to make money and to contribute to communities in which they operate. At the broadest level, strategy is about the firm's goals and means to achieve them. A large MNE is guided by its global corporate strategy, which sets overall goals and envisages how each of the units in different locations contributes to achieving them. Strategy of the subsidiary is linked to that of the parent company, which has an overall framework for allocating roles to different subsidiaries in its global activities. Companies differ considerably both in their ultimate goals and in the means to achieve them, that is, the organizational and operational aspects of their business.

No firm sets out with a completely 'blank slate' to formulate strategy. Both internal and external factors play a part, as the following discussion of theories will show. Even in a start-up firm, the owners will bring their own cultural background and ways of doing things into the business, along with their technical expertise. In some firms, the owners determine strategy and exert a firm grip on operations, through which a strategic plan is implemented. One might expect SMEs to be the main type of business that is centred on the owner, but some large MNEs are also run in this way, especially where the founder's strategic vision is strong and shapes the corporate culture of the firm. The home country of the company is also important, as we have seen in Chapter 1. Some countries and companies are more likely to look beyond their home environment and values, whereas others seek to stamp their national values and ways of doing things on operations worldwide.

Formulating strategy in a changing external environment is one of the supreme challenges of the MNE. A number of 'balancing acts' must take place. It must strike a balance between flexibility and control. It desires the benefits of customization, but these must be weighed against the scale economies of standardized products. The firm seeks to carry out activities in the best location for production costs, but manufacturing in China for western markets, although low-cost in terms of production, involves higher transport costs: the risks associated with shipping and the need for a long lead time, make it difficult to respond quickly to changes in demand. Every company chief executive probably dreams of the 'killer' product in global markets, produced in low-cost locations with high quality standards and able to adapt to changing demand at short notice. Turning the dream into reality is partly a matter of luck and having talented people in the company, but mainly it is about strategy.

Summary points Strategy overview

◆ Strategy is about the firm's goals and ways of achieving them.

◆ Firms must strike a balance between flexibility and control, and between customization and standardization.

Theories of business strategy

Theorists of strategy offer a variety of perspectives on both how businesses should formulate strategies and what they should focus on. Generally, these theories concentrate on one or more of the following perspectives: the external dimension, the internal dimension and the process of strategy formation. The discussion here will roughly follow these categories. In Chapter 1, a common analytical tool, the PEST analysis, was presented. The PEST analysis is a good starting point for assessing the external environment, especially for companies looking for the best location for international expansion. However, internal capabilities are also important, and these are highlighted in the SWOT analysis.

SWOT analysis

SWOT analysis
strategic tool used by businesses to assess the organization's strengths, weaknesses, opportunities and threats

The **SWOT analysis** is a familiar analytical tool, highlighting a firm's strengths, weaknesses, opportunities and threats. Strengths and weaknesses relate to the firm itself (the internal environment), while opportunities and threats relate to the external environment. The SWOT analysis is usually depicted in the form of a matrix, as shown in Figure 5.1. The top boxes represent the internal environment, and the bottom boxes, the external environment.

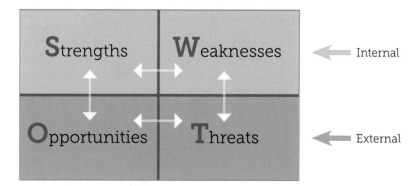

Figure 5.1 **SWOT analysis**

The interactions that are highlighted by arrows in the figure show how the firm can glean strategic insight, aiming to build distinctive competencies, which will enable it to gain competitive advantage.

Some of the key issues addressed in a SWOT analysis are listed below:

1   *External environment: opportunities and threats:*

- What are the main factors in the societal environment (political-legal, economic, sociocultural and technological)?
- What is the market strength of competitors?
- What new products or services, including both those of the firm and those of competitors, are in the pipeline?
- What is the level of consumer demand, and can it be expected to remain stable?
- What is the likely threat of new entrants in the market for the firm's products?

2   *Internal environment: strengths and weaknesses:*

- Does the organization have a structure that helps it to achieve its objectives?
- Does it have clear marketing objectives and strategy?
- Does the organization use IT effectively in all aspects of its activities?
- Does its investment in R&D match or exceed that of competitors?
- Does the organization meet its financial objectives?
- To what extent does the firm have clear HRM objectives and strategies in areas such as employee motivation, turnover of staff, and provision of training?

The SWOT analysis can be carried out in teams or by groups of executives (Piercy and Giles, 1989), and their impressions can be quite different. It has been found that higher-level managers tend to take a broad overview, seeing organizational factors as strengths, while lower-level ones single out marketing and financial factors (Mintzberg, 2000: 276). This suggests that people's views are influenced by their own position in the business. The SWOT exercise can serve to widen the perspectives of participants, which raises awareness of strategy for all employees of the company. However, it is rather limited in that it does not give any direct pointers as to how a firm should achieve its goals.

Summary points SWOT analysis

- The SWOT analysis focuses on both internal environment (strengths and weaknesses), and external environment (opportunities and threats).

- The theory is limited in that it does not address the process of strategy formation.

Porter's theory of competitive strategy

Porter's approach to firm strategy concentrates on the competitive forces in any industry. Analysis of these forces is necessary to achieve profitability (Porter, 1998c; 2008). The five forces are industry competition, buyers, suppliers, potential entrants and possible substitute products. They are depicted in the **five forces model**, shown in Figure 5.2.

five forces model in Porter's theory of competitive strategy, an analysis of an industry based on buyers, suppliers, potential entrants and possible substitute products

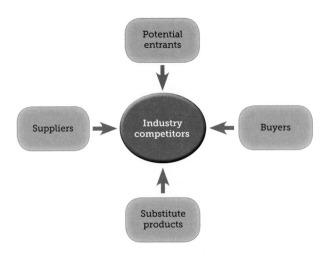

Figure 5.2 **Porter's five forces model**

Source: Adapted from Porter, M. (1998) *Competitive Strategy: Techniques for Analyzing Industries and Competitors* (New York: Free Press)

In Porter's model, buyers and suppliers are key players, with ability to exert bargaining power on the firm. The supplier might be in a strong bargaining position because there are few who can meet the firm's needs for quality or quantity. Alternatively, if there are many potential suppliers of a standardized product, the firm will be in a relatively strong position vis-à-vis any one supplier, and be able to negotiate more favourable terms. Similarly, the purchasing firm will be in a strong position if it is a large company with a large order to place and there are many possible suppliers. In this situation, the buyer is seeking economies of scale and is looking for the lowest cost in the marketplace. On the other hand, the buyer with specialized requirements might find there are few potential suppliers, and will therefore be compelled to pay a premium price. As these examples show, the existence (or absence) of substitute products is a factor which helps to determine the market. Where substitute products are usable and available, buyers are in a stronger position; where a substitute product will not work, the company selling the desired product has the upper hand.

Industry rivalry is at the centre of Porter's model. In every industry, there is a changing scenario of competitors – newcomers, established businesses, some gaining market share and some losing market share. Corporate performance is often envisaged in terms of market share. In Porter's model, the ease (or difficulty) of entry into a market is one of the forces. There can be a variety of barriers to entry. For example, if large capital expenditure is required, as in the oil industry, potential entrants could be deterred. The opposite is the case where little capital outlay is necessary to get started, as in software design. If there are strong global brands in a sector, such as carbonated drinks, then a new entrant will find it difficult to make inroads in markets. For a new entrant in this sector, offering a product to appeal to local tastes in specifically targeted markets could be a better strategy. In this situation, the newcomer would be designing a strategy with a particular focus, to gain competitive advantage.

▸ More online ... Coca-Cola's corporate website is www.thecoca-colacompany.com

A firm's overall strategy, for Porter, must be based on an analysis of the five forces, addressing the competitive pressures which exist under each heading. This is the highest level of strategy within the company, and is referred to as competitive strategy or generic strategy. Porter sees generic strategies falling into three main types. The first is 'low-cost' positioning, and the second, 'differentiation', referring to the attributes of the product offered. A third type, 'focus', brings the strategic target into the equation. A strategic target can be industry-wide (broad) and a particular segment (narrow). The focused strategy can be based on low cost, differentiation or a combination of the two. We have just seen an example of the focused strategy, in the example of a new carbonated beverage. By targeting a 'niche' market, the competitor can win over a particular group of consumers. Health-conscious or environment-conscious consumers are niche markets, for example. Of course, large MNEs such as Coca-Cola cater for different groups of consumers, offering healthy alternatives to sugary carbonated drinks. It can be all the more difficult, therefore, for niche companies to compete, even if their products have been established for longer. Such a company might pursue one of the other two strategies, but what would be its chances of success?

A low-cost strategy aims to undercut the competitor on price, usually bringing in economies of scale, which act as an entry barrier. In emerging markets where the new middle-class consumers are highly cost-conscious, this is a key strategy. But this does not necessarily mean that only the large MNEs are competitive. On the contrary, smaller local companies are often able to compete on price, which is the main source of competitive advantage in the consumer markets of China and India. They probably do not compete on quality, but that does not matter so much for consumers living on $2 to $10 a day. And this is the fastest growing segment of middle-class consumers globally (Ravallion, 2009). Where consumers have more money to spend and seek out products above the basic level, companies with a differentiation strategy can gain competitive advantage. Not just quality, but brand image, design and high-tech features can give a product a competitive edge in this market.

As an aid to strategy formation, Porter's model is focused on the external competitive environment. Assessing the five forces in an industry can help a firm to identify whether to enter a market or not, and how to position the product. However, national markets must be distinguished from global markets, and in this respect, the model is possibly less helpful. There are not many products in which the market is truly globalized. The oil industry is one. For most products, companies formulate national strategies based on national conditions. Although these are co-ordinated at the global level (as discussed below), the MNE does not pursue a single competitive strategy, such as low-cost positioning, in all markets. The large MNE could well have a portfolio of many brands, and it might well develop a low-cost brand for sale in emerging markets (as we found in the P&G 'Meet the CEO' feature in Chapter 4). Making these decisions involves assessment of the company's own internal strengths as well as external environments.

Summary points   Porter's five forces model of competitive advantage

◆ Competition in any industry, according to Porter, can be assessed by examining the five forces he highlights, which are competitor rivalry, potential entrants, buyers, suppliers and substitute products.

◆ Competitive strategies fall into three broad categories: low cost, differentiation of products and focused strategy on a particular group of customers.

Critical thinking

Porter's five forces model

To what extent is Porter's model too narrowly focused on national markets, underestimating other aspects of a country's environment which are relevant for corporate decision-makers?

Resource-based and competence-based theories

resource-based theory
theory of the firm based on analysis of three sets of resources: physical, human and organizational

A number of theories can be grouped in this category. They share a focus on attributes of the firm itself, from its buildings to its skills. In **resource-based theory,** the starting point is that every firm has three sets of resources: physical resources, such as plants; human resources, such as skills and insight; and organizational resources, such as its formal structures and networks (Barney, 1991). Barney argued that assessment of the firm's strengths in each area will help it build competitive advantage. A set of criteria aids in assessing each resource. These are shown in Figure 5.3.

Figure 5.3 **The resource-based view of the firm**

Source: Adapted from Barney, J. (1991) 'Firm resources and sustained competitive advantage', *Journal of Management*, 17(1): 99–120

The four key attributes of each resource are shown in Figure 5.3. To take an example, firm Q might view its informal network with SMEs as a resource. It is valuable, in that it can generate new ideas to exploit. It is relatively rare, as Q's competitors tend to rely on in-house generation of new ideas. It is not easily imitable, in that the links have been cultivated over time and rely on personal relations between individuals, who have become accustomed to each other's ways of thinking. Such relations would be difficult for a rival firm to put in place mechanically. But would there be another way of achieving the same benefits? The fourth criterion is that there is no strategic equivalent which would yield the same firm-specific benefits. A rival firm with in-house R&D can seek new ideas from outside the company, and, like many large pharmaceutical companies, develop products under licence from their inventors. But it will not be replicating the network benefits enjoyed by Q.

For Q, its network links are a source of *sustainable* competitive advantage, in that new ideas will be likely to flow from this resource over the long term, even in the midst of a changing competitive environment. Indeed, its network links will probably help it to keep to the forefront of advances in technology – one of the major weaknesses of large companies, which can become bureaucratic and fall behind in innovation.

core competencies
capabilities of a firm
to maintain innovative
and competitive edge

Q's competitive advantage could equally be viewed from the perspective of the theory of the firm which focuses on core competencies. Developed by Prahalad and Hamel (1990), the theory rests on the belief that a firm's most important resources are the organization's specialist skills and learning, or **core competencies.** Ideally, a firm will build a portfolio of core competencies. Competencies can be distinguished from products: competencies enable the firm to maintain a pipeline of new products, whereas a product's success could be disappointingly short-lived, especially in fast-moving markets. Three criteria help the firm to identify its core competencies. First, they are critical to a number of the firm's product markets. Secondly, they add value to the end product which reaches the consumer. Thirdly, they are difficult for rivals to imitate. If the company produces a successful product, rivals are certain to imitate it, but, the authors argue, the real source of the product's competitive advantage is not the product itself, but the portfolio of competencies lying behind it, which rivals cannot manufacture overnight.

The implications for strategy contained in these theories are that, first, firms should identify their key resources and competencies at present, assessing which technologies and skills they are strong in, and which are weaker. No firm can build expertise in every relevant aspect of its product development and operations. But, looking at its people and organizational history, it will emerge which activities are more worthwhile concentrating on. Building core competencies takes place over a long period, and corporate strategy can be focused towards these goals. This rather general focus, however, provides only a rough 'roadmap' (Prahalad and Hamel, 1990: 89). There will be relevant specialist areas in which the company has little expertise and which it is not worth investing resources in. There will also be supply-chain issues, such as the need for standardized parts or components which are not worth the company's energy and resources to produce itself. Hence, it will look to a range of suppliers and collaborators outside the company, and probably outside its home country. Building competitive advantage, therefore, relies on these non-core activities as well as the core activities. And these strategic considerations bring us back to the external environment.

Summary points Resource-based and competence-based theories

◆ These theories focus on the internal environment of the organization, mainly on its resources in the broadest sense, as key to strategy formation.

◆ Identifying and building core competencies is held to be the route to sustaining competitive advantage.

Critical thinking

Core competencies

Recalling some of the case studies of earlier chapters, identify the core competencies of the following companies: Volkswagen, BHP Billiton, Nokia. To what extent have these companies rethought their strategies to sharpen their focus on core competencies?

Process-based theories

In a sense, the theories already discussed in this section would fall under this heading. Porter's theory sees analysis of the external environment as a process, and firm-based theories see development of resources over time as crucial to business strategy. However, these theories mainly focus on the key dimension as they see it, rather than on the process itself. Here, we turn to two theoretical approaches in which the process is central. These are Mintzberg's theory of emergent strategy, and stakeholder management theory.

Mintzberg's theory of emergent strategy

Mintzberg considers a number of ways in which strategy can be envisaged (see Mintzberg et al., 2009). A common view of strategy is found in the 'strategic plan'. This notion of making a plan and simply following it is highly prescriptive and leaves little flexibility for changes in response to external factors. A more flexible approach is to see strategy as a position, that is, to formulate a position in the prospective market for the firm's products. This view takes account of the changing external environment, allowing for strategy to be adapted accordingly. However, Mintzberg criticizes both of these approaches as being too inflexible. Strategy is formed deliberately in both the planning and positioning approaches, which tend to undervalue the need to adapt strategy over time. They also take little account of strategic learning constantly taking place in the firm (Mintzberg et al., 2009). In **emergent strategy**, by contrast, 'a pattern is realized that was not expressly intended' (Mintzberg et al., 2009: 12). Business decisions taken by the firm, when looked at as a series of actions, form a pattern over time.

emergent strategy
theory devised by Mintzberg, which focuses on firm strategy adapting over time, rather than following a deliberate plan

The firm is advised to evolve a combination of deliberate and emergent strategies, recognizing the need to plan for likely eventualities, and also the need to be responsive to changes in the environment. How managers combine these two approaches depends heavily on the company's organizational culture and its approach to organizational learning. For example, the firm might have an open corporate culture, in which people are constantly adapting strategy in small ways. In this type of firm, strategy can emerge from anywhere in the organization: employees feel empowered to take part in strategy formation, and subsidiaries in varied locations contribute to the debate. This broad view of strategy formation, in contrast to Porter's five forces model, takes account of the firm's internal capabilities, giving it an affinity with the resource-based and competence-based theories. Our next theoretical approach builds on this broad view of organizational learning.

Stakeholder management theory

The second of the process-based theories is stakeholder management theory. The concept of the stakeholder was introduced in Chapter 1. Recalling that discussion, we found that stakeholders cover a large and potentially divergent group of interests. It is common to think of stakeholders as external to the firm, when in fact stakeholders are both internal and external. Stakeholder management theory aids in (a) identifying stakeholders; and (b) bringing stakeholders into the strategic management process. It is because of this latter element that we look at stakeholder management in this section.

In Chapter 1, we considered Freeman's definition of stakeholders as those who influence the company or are influenced by it. Direct stakeholders were identified as those who have direct links with the company, such as owners and suppliers, whereas indirect stakeholders are more remote, often resembling aspects of the external environment, such as community groups. Because the first group consists of people and organizations with whom the firm has regular relations, both formal and informal, stakeholder management theory tends to focus on them. This is not to say that the second group of interests is less important, but they are more diffuse, and tend to fall more naturally into theories of ethics and CSR, which will be discussed in Chapter 12.

Stakeholder management theory urges that involving stakeholders in strategy formation can make sense for firm competitiveness and performance (Harrison et al., 2010). In a 'managing for stakeholders' approach, the firm can benefit from allocating value and decision-making influence to its primary stakeholders, both individuals and organizations. Investing in stakeholder relations, by, for example, providing health benefits to part-time employees, involves costs. And some might see this as a waste of money, or 'overinvestment', as the firm is paying more than it would need to simply to keep the stakeholder relationship in existence. However, it can be argued that performance in the long term will be enhanced, leading to sustainable competitive advantage. The authors cite the following ways in which value can be created through managing for stakeholders (Harrison et al., 2010: 67):

- Information gained from stakeholders such as customers and suppliers can lead to improvements in demand and efficiency
- Interactions with stakeholders can lead to innovation and evolving innovation networks
- The firm will be better able to deal with unexpected events, such as changes in technology, if it has built up relationships of trust with stakeholders

The last of these points suggests a link with strategic flexibility. Recalling the example of firm Q above, the firm that has invested in stakeholder relationships possesses a resource which is rare and difficult for rivals to imitate. The rival will not know exactly which relationships yielded advantages and how they functioned. The 'nuanced information' that derives from these relations is not readily quantifiable and becomes blended into its corporate culture. Similarly, the value created is not necessarily reflected in the firm's economic data, as relations are not captured using accounting measures. Market share that a firm enjoys today may be fleeting, as the competence-based theories point out, because today's successful products will soon be superseded. The benefits of managing for stakeholders accrue over time, making this approach a sounder footing for sustainable advantage.

Summary points Process-based theories of strategy

◈ Mintzberg stresses that strategy can be both deliberate and emergent, and that it involves the whole organization.

◈ A managing-for-stakeholders approach holds that nurturing stakeholder relations can create

value and enhance competitiveness over the long term.

Levels of strategy

The journey through theories of strategy has highlighted numerous important factors: internal capabilities, analysis of industry competition, corporate culture and organizational learning. In an SME with only a few employees, decision-making can be informal, and all can participate in discussion of the way the business is being run, roles, products and locations. In a large organization, however, each of these topics is complex and interlocking with the others. The MNE with multiple subsidiaries requires a coherent strategy for all its operations and markets. It desires the flexibility to make strategic adjustments as needed in differing conditions, but it needs co-ordination at the centre, to ensure that all the units are singing in at least some semblance of harmony, rather than entirely different tunes.

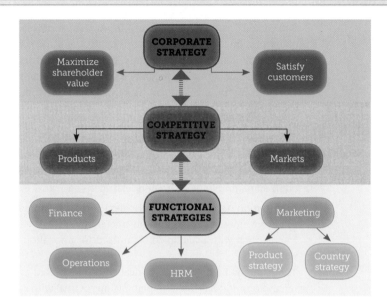

Figure 5.4 **Levels of strategy**

corporate strategy
strategy which focuses on the overriding goals of the company, embracing its values and culture

competitive strategy
a firm's business strategy which focuses on advantages of particular products and particular markets

For the MNE, it is helpful to view strategy in levels, beginning with the highest level, which is corporate strategy. Levels of strategy are shown in Figure 5.4. Corporate strategy is the unifying theme, which provides guideposts for lower-level strategies. **Corporate strategy** can be envisaged as the overriding goals of the company, embracing its values and culture. In a sense, the answers to the question we posed in the overview early in this chapter – 'What does the company exist to do?' – form its corporate culture. The answer could be satisfying customers, creating value for stakeholders, or any other goal which gives the company its distinctive character. In liberal market economies, the goal of maximizing shareholder value is often held up as paramount. Corporate goals are set out in company 'mission statements', which typically mention all these goals. However, looking beyond the mission statement, it becomes clearer what the firm's ultimate values are. We therefore turn to further levels of strategy which are less abstract.

Competitive strategy, or business strategy, has been discussed in the context of Porter's five forces model. The firm's competitive strategy concerns its products and markets, which generate its competitive advantage. Porter highlights two generic strategies, differentiation and price, warning that firms are at risk of being 'stuck in the middle' if they do not concentrate on one of these strategies (Porter, 2008). However, there are risks in overspecializing, in that a firm might not be in a position to exploit new opportunities. Many companies target particular markets with low-end products, and target more affluent consumers with high-end products. As markets and competitors change over time, a test of business strategy is whether it is sustainable. Core competencies therefore come into play. If the firm has developed core competencies, these will equip it with the innovation capacity and technological skills to improve its offering, launch new products and meet challenges from competitors' new products. In addition, it must consider the opportunities in new markets. Internationalization strategies, considered in the next section, have profound implications for the way a company is run, including its organizational structure.

As we found in Chapter 1, the firm's activities can be roughly divided into separate business functions. In small firms there are probably no organizational divides. But in a large MNE, these functions take on organizational reality and a feeling of cultural

functional strategies a firm's strategy pertaining to each functional area, such as marketing, which contributes to achieving corporate goals

distinctiveness, based partly on the professional or management culture involved in each. Ideally, these functions are all co-ordinated, through **functional strategies**. Hence, the marketing strategy will reflect the firm's competitive strategy regarding products and markets; it will also help the firm to achieve its overall goals. For a large MNE, marketing strategy can be designed for its various products and for differing national markets, as Figure 5.4 shows. Hence, a country-specific marketing strategy would need to 'fit' the three strategic levels above it, which are functional, competitive and corporate strategies.

Summary points Levels of strategy

◆ Corporate strategy, representing the company's broadest goals, is the highest level of strategy.

◆ Competitive strategy relates to products and markets, while functional strategies support

both competitive and corporate strategies.

Internationalization strategies

A shift in strategy occurs when a business that has been operating only in its home country decides to add an international dimension to its enterprise. In particular, its competitive strategy changes. Internationalization involves outward expansion in markets and/or production. The firm contemplating a new market or the shift of production to a foreign location can consider a variety of entry strategies. These strategies are often referred to as modes of internationalization, which were introduced in Chapter 2. Here, we look in greater detail at each. The choice of entry strategy depends on both internal and external factors. Internally, the firm's corporate culture influences how it goes about international expansion and also what locations it chooses for foreign operations. External factors include the competitive environment in differing locations as well as country-specific factors, which the PEST analysis reveals.

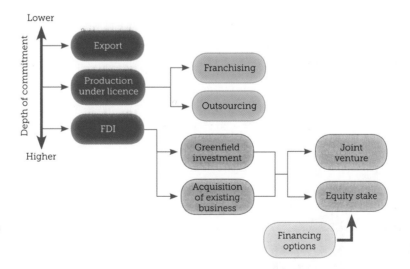

Figure 5.5 **Foreign integration in modes of internationalization**

Entry strategies can be compared according to the depth of involvement that the firm envisages in the new location. This commitment is usually reflected in the

MEET THE CEO

▸ More online ... Carlsberg's website is www.carlsberg.com

Jorgen Buhl Rasmussen CEO of Carlsberg, the Danish brewer

Carlsberg's chairman and CEO, Jorgen Buhl Rasmussen, although Danish by birth, had worked mainly outside the country, in Asia, Eastern Europe and the UK, before joining Carlsberg. These jobs, chiefly with Duracell batteries, were unrelated to brewing, but his focus was always on marketing – an expertise which helped to propel him into the top job at Carlsberg in 2007. He was plunged straight into the 'deep end' at Carlsberg, as the company was in the process of negotiating a huge takeover of Scottish & Newcastle (S&N). That acquisition, mounted jointly with Heineken, was a strategic turning point for the company. S&N was strong in Russia, where it owned the leading brand, Baltika. Acquiring the brand presented an opportunity for further growth in this large market, although Rasmussen realized it also brought challenges. Investors were concerned that the Russian market would now account for about 40% of Carlsberg's overall profits.

Although a large emerging market, Russia has not enjoyed the economic growth of the other Brics, and it was more affected by the global financial crisis. Carlsberg had an impressive market share of 39.1% in the quarter to 31 March 2010, but this was actually down on its market share a year earlier. From his depth of experience in marketing, Rasmussen says, 'Pricing in a big place like Russia is a delicate task ...

This will be different based on brand, packaging, type and region. It will vary from St. Petersburg to Vladivostok' (Anderberg, 2010). The financial crisis has had a negative impact in all the company's markets, in many of which it is competing with strong local brands. He says, 'in Carlsberg we often talk about being "glocal", and for us that's being global and local. Ideally, we need strong, local power brands – as we call them – and then some international, global brands on top' (*Financial Times*, 2009).

Carlsberg is famous for its advertising – 'probably the best lager in the world' – as well as for its brands, which, apart from Carlsberg itself, include Tuborg and Kronenbourg. With sales lacklustre in western markets, Rasmussen is banking on growth in Russia, but is also making acquisitions in Asia. He is alert to the fact the Russian government is concerned about alcohol consumption, and is intending to regulate advertising and sales more closely. Rasmussen feels the key to success is keeping in touch with people, whether employees or consumers. Marketing has been the force that drives him, but he welcomed the opportunity to take on greater responsibility for the business. He says, 'Having responsibility for the business, working with a team ... it becomes more important than just doing marketing because this is suddenly people' (Wiggins and Anderson, 2008).

Sources: Anderberg, J. (2010) 'Interview: Carlsberg to up market share in Russia – CEO', *Wall Street Journal*, 11 May; Wiggins, J. and Anderson, R. (2008) 'Brewery chief's thirst for success', *Financial Times*, 24 November; *Financial Times* (2009) 'View from the top: interview with Jorgen Buhl Rasmussen', 5 June

Jorgen Buhl Rasmussen
Source: Carlsberg

▸ More online ... Chery's website is www.cheryinternational.com
Carrefour is at www.carrefour.com

extent of ownership and control that the firm exerts over foreign assets. A comparison of entry modes is shown in Figure 5.5. It is common for a firm to begin with export, and to expand through other modes which involve greater presence in the foreign location.

Exporting

The manufacturing firm contemplating foreign expansion for the first time will be attracted to the relatively low-risk option of exporting. It will need to choose carefully which products to export to specific markets, for the greatest chance of success. A PEST analysis of likely markets will be an aid. Recall from the last chapter that barriers to imports can be an important external factor: tariffs or non-tariff barriers can make imported goods appear expensive alongside domestic goods in consumer markets. The firm will be relying heavily on the services of other organizations. It must arrange freight and distribution with specialist export companies, and it must choose the retailer carefully, to obtain the best possible exposure for its products.

Although exporting is a low-risk option in terms of financial commitment, with minimal organizational impact on the firm's home activities, there are numerous pitfalls due to the heavy reliance on others in the supply chain. Without a presence in the market, designing marketing strategy is likely to be contracted out to a local company. Because of the distance between the home production and the end consumers, after-sales service will probably be handled by other firms, again adding a potential weakness in the delivery of value to the consumer. The use of external organizations adds to transaction costs, which must be factored in when considering the firm's pricing policy. There are also foreign exchange risks to be considered. Nonetheless, if the firm's products prove successful, it will probably contemplate setting up a sales office in the country, establishing an organizational presence. It could then think about establishing production in the country, depending on its assessment of the market potential. An example is Chery Automobile of China, which has been exporting vehicles, and now plans FDI projects on greenfield sites in Eastern Europe, the Middle East and South America.

Exporting is an obvious entry mode for a manufacturing company with operations concentrated in its home country. Is there an equivalent of the export option for firms in other sectors? The retailer wanting to expand abroad is almost compelled to establish a presence in the foreign location. An example is Carrefour, the French hypermarket retailer, which has expanded in Asia. Similarly, the service provider, in, for example, financial services, must usually have some presence in the target country, even if its computing system is integrated with that in the home country. For firms in these other sectors, international expansion can involve the acquisition of assets (such as buildings) in overseas locations, but there are other legal alternatives available, such as the franchise, considered in the next section.

Summary points Exporting

◆ Exporting as an entry mode offers the firm possibilities of wider markets with minimal investment in assets and operations in the foreign location.

◆ The exporter will entail considerable costs, especially over long distances, and could face trade barriers in some markets.

▶ More online ... Danone is at www.danone.com

Licensing

Operations in a foreign location are often carried out through organizations linked by contractual arrangements short of outright ownership. In manufacturing sectors in today's globalized world, even SMEs consider foreign production as a strategy from early on, carried out by other companies under licence. The **licence** is a legally enforceable agreement by which a firm (the licensor) grants permission to use its property (mainly intellectual property such as patents and trademarks) to another firm (the licensee). The owner of a patent essential to the manufacture of a product can license a firm to produce the product in a foreign location, either the relevant market or a low-cost country. This is the typical arrangement with outsourced production. A manufacturing company that has operated its own factories in a high-cost country might decide to shift manufacturing to a low-cost country, in order to become more competitive in global markets.

licence legal agreement by which a firm (the licensor) grants permission to another firm (the licensee) to use its property, notably intellectual property such as patents and trademarks

The company need not set up a greenfield operation in the new location, but can license a locally registered company (which could be foreign owned) to manufacture the product. This type of strategy is often called **offshoring**, which carries rather negative connotations, as it suggests that jobs are being lost in the firm's home country. The firm might also face allegations that local people are being exploited in the production of its branded products, even though they are employed by an independent company. Clothing and sportswear are industries in which the cost of labour is a major factor, and these industries are often relocated to low-cost economies, as we saw in Chapter 2. Where the firm licenses a manufacturer in a country near to a major market, such as manufacturing in Mexico for the US market, this arrangement is known as **nearshoring**. Nearshoring, similarly, can be seen as a cost-reduction exercise. Perceptions vary according to the prevailing approach to stakeholders. Where maximizing shareholder returns is the guiding goal, reducing costs of production is welcomed, whatever the location of manufacturing.

offshoring contracting out of a business process, usually to a low-cost location; often carrying negative connotations

nearshoring type of FDI or outsourcing by which a firm invests in operations in a lower-cost location near to a major market

Although it might be assumed that the licensor has the upper hand in licence arrangements, the relationship can be quite complex, requiring trust and co-operation on both sides. In the pharmaceutical industry, the licensor can be an SME, which licenses a large MNE to manufacture and market a medicine. This occurs where the SME's researchers have come up with a product that is patentable, but lack the resources to exploit the patent. The reverse situation is also possible: large pharmaceutical companies license local companies to manufacture their medicines for local markets. In these situations, both the patent and the brand are involved. However, there are inherent risks with any licensing of IP rights. The licensor is concerned that quality of production is maintained and that no misuse of its brand takes place. These are difficult to monitor from a distance. Similarly, there could well be problems where the local company is accused of misusing the brand or patent for its own purposes. Danone, the French food company, endured a number of years of difficulties, including lengthy legal proceedings against a Chinese firm, Wahaha, which made its products in China. Finally, in 2008, the disputes were settled and the relationship was dissolved.

The franchise is a particular type of licensing agreement, whereby the franchisee, or business owner, agrees with the franchisor, the owner of a branded product, to deliver the product in the franchisee's local market. This type of arrangement is often suitable for entrepreneurs, as mentioned in Chapter 1. The entrepreneur benefits from the brand, know-how, marketing and quality proceedures of the brand owner. Some companies specialize in the franchise, acquiring numerous outlets from the same franchisor. McDonald's decided to pull out of Iceland in 2009, following the country's financial collapse. The owner of its three outlets in the country decided to carry on in business. Although no longer able to brand his products with the McDonald's logo, he was confident he could produce appetizing meals for less money by using Icelandic ingredients. His franchise agreement had required him to import basic products such as onions from Germany, which became prohibitively expensive when the Icelandic currency collapsed.

Nonetheless, McDonald's reported healthy profits for 2009, growth stemming largely from foreign markets. The benefits of licensing, from the MNE's point of view, are that it can exit the country relatively smoothly, as the investment commitment is made by the local business owners rather than the brand owner.

Summary points Licensing

- ● Licensing agreements cover a wide range of international business situations, including manufacturing and service provision.

- ● Licensing allows MNEs to deliver products and services in local markets based on contractual relations with firms in the target market.

- ● Production under licence in low-cost economies is associated with globalization.

Critical thinking
Licensing and globalization
Manufacturing under licence in low-cost locations has acquired a negative image in many consumer markets. How can it be criticized from a stakeholder perspective?

FDI

FDI represents a deeper level of commitment to a foreign location than the alternatives discussed above. In Figure 5.6, greenfield investment and acquisition of an existing business are highlighted as examples of FDI. Both involve capital investment and a planned long-term commitment to the foreign location. Recalling the discussion of motives for FDI in Chapter 2, MNEs are influenced by both push factors and pull factors, which can be mutually reinforcing. Saturation in the firm's home market might be felt by companies in the western advanced economies. At the same time, the large emerging markets attract investors because of the good prospects of growth. But how does the investor choose which route to follow? Figure 5.6 gives a breakdown of the advantages and disadvantages of each.

The ability to design and control operations is an advantage of the greenfield project, but there could be a long wait before production becomes a reality. It will have required patient dealing with regulatory and planning bodies, and it will be an even longer wait before the firm begins to see profit from the investment. It is not difficult to see, therefore, why acquisition of an existing business is an attractive option. The acquired company can be integrated into the acquirer's strategy for the region, and could well have an existing customer base on which to build. Acquisition thus seems like a lower-risk alternative to greenfield investment. However, integration of the two firms can be slow, requiring give-and-take on both sides.

Greenfield investments

The type of industry is one of the main factors in choosing an entry strategy. Where the manufacturing process involves specialist plant and skills, the greenfield site is

Greenfield or acquisition?

Greenfield	Acquisition
• Customized design of plant	• Quicker to get up and running
• Control over build and operations (including IP), *but ...*	• Local company has local knowledge, existing workforce and customer base, *but ...*
• Slow to get going	• Cultural tension between acquirer and local firm
• Large capital investment	• Weaker control over quality, delivery and IP
• Lack of local knowledge a drawback	
• No pre-existing customer base	

Figure 5.6 **FDI options**

attractive. Some governments, keen to attract greenfield investors, offer incentives such as tax concessions. Southern states in the US attracted foreign carmakers through incentives, hoping to create new jobs as the region shifted away from agriculture to industrial activities. The carmaking industry in the US has been transformed by the success of foreign manufacturers setting up production on greenfield sites outside the traditional carmaking regions of the country, notably Michigan, where American carmakers were strong. Japanese, South Korean and German companies, in particular, set up to serve the US market. They benefited from being close to the consumer. They were able to undercut American car companies on price partly because they set up in regions without the strong trade unions which have dominated the American motor industry (see case study in Chapter 2).

Greenfield investment is appropriate in manufacturing industries that require new plants to be built, but FDI in the extraction industries is similar, requiring large capital investment in the foreign location before production can begin. This entails dealing with governments and other stakeholders, and complying with local environmental laws. The greenfield investor becomes part of the local community in a way that the brand-owning company which outsources production does not. Still, putting down roots does not mean that the MNE will stay permanently in the country. There are numerous examples of companies that have built factories in countries for cost savings, and, when the costs grew and new markets opened up, moved on to build factories in these newer markets. Spain's car industry, which attracted FDI for its proximity to European markets and relatively low costs in the 1990s, saw the departure of a number of these companies in the 2000s, to Slovakia and other lower-cost destinations. Similarly, Slovakia must compete with countries where costs are even lower, such as Romania, Turkey and India, all of which have growing car industries.

Where the MNE contemplates greenfield investment in a new environment, the joint venture can provide a means of sharing the financial burden – and the risk. If a local partner is chosen, its local knowledge can be beneficial in navigating the process of building up a business from scratch. The joint venture can be a new company, with participating investors each contributing capital. If successful, the joint venture company can gradually become more independent of its parent companies. However, success depends not just on environmental factors in the new market, but on relations between the parent companies, which must develop a coherent strategy for the venture. The joint venture must have a clear position in the strategy of the parent companies, as the opening case study showed. A company that invests in a number of joint ventures risks blurring its strategic vision.

Acquisitions

In many industries, acquiring a local company is an attractive alternative to the greenfield operation. The local company can be wholly bought out by the acquirer, but it is also possible for the investor to acquire a sizeable equity stake, which can be raised at a later date. In many industrial and extraction industries, acquisition is a common expansion strategy. The growth of ArcelorMittal, the steelmaking company, has been largely by acquisition. The MNE wishing to expand by acquisition is looking for quick growth, and benefits from the fact that the acquired company already has a presence in the market. It has local knowledge and knows local business practices. It might also have good links with governmental authorities, which can be important. However, there are disadvantages in expansion by acquisition, as Figure 5.6 highlights. If the corporate cultures of the two companies are quite different, the acquirer must decide what type of integration strategy to pursue. It might attempt **integration** of the companies, blending the cultures of both. Alternatively, if the acquiring company's culture is paramount, the acquired company will be compelled to conform with the new owner's culture and practices, through an **assimilation** process. However, assimilation can be difficult if the two cultures are very different: sensitivity and a willingness to adapt can be needed to smooth the process. The polycentric organization is more likely to be successful in managing integration than the ethnocentric organization. (These issues are discussed in Chapter 6.) Productivity can suffer in the meantime, as the participants focus on internal issues, and give less attention to the market.

Growth by acquisitions has been a widely used strategy in the era of globalization. In sectors ranging from banks to telecommunications, some MNEs, such as General Electric (GE), have built business empires largely through acquisition (see Figure 5.7). Acquisition strategy varies from sector to sector, and company to company. It is common for companies to buy up smaller rivals in the same industry. In this way, industries become **consolidated** over time. With fewer players, economies of scale are achievable. In such industries, for example mining and shipping, which are globally consolidated, the size of the players can act as a barrier to entry.

A **diversification** strategy is also favoured, whereby MNEs acquire companies in other sectors, often those which are complementary to their existing portfolio of products. For example, Google, the search engine company, diversified into operating systems for mobile phones, then into its own branded phone. This would seem to be akin to an emergent strategy in the case of Google: one product succeeds, and the firm then thinks of ways of building on this success (Mintzberg et al., 2009). From the marketing perspective, diversification is a means of brand extension, whereby success with one branded product can be transferred successfully to a range of others. This strategy does not always work: the products in the newer categories must live up to the reputation of the first one, or the brand as a whole could suffer. If the company is starting from scratch in the new product area, it must learn quickly to compete against existing specialist players, and it will take more than simply a well-known brand to maintain consumer loyalty.

integration in an acquisition of one firm by another, the blending of the two cultures into a single organizational culture

assimilation in an acquisition by one firm of another, compelling the acquired company to conform to the culture and practices of the new owner

consolidation in an industry, a pattern of larger firms taking over smaller ones, which results in a few large companies

diversification corporate strategy whereby a company acquires businesses in a range of different sectors

▸ More online ... GE is at www.ge.com

Figure 5.7 **General Electric (GE) businesses in 2009**

Some firms possibly take diversification too far, losing sight of core competencies. The highly diversified multidivisional company might benefit if there is a downturn in one sector, as it can compensate with healthy earnings in other sectors. The strategy is thus defensive to some extent. The large, diversified company is often referred to as a **conglomerate**, indicating that there is no one single identifiable core business. General Electric (GE) of the US, whose separate businesses are shown in Figure 5.7, is essentially an industrial company, having been founded to produce light bulbs. As the figure shows, it now produces a wide range of industrial products for businesses and consumers. Some might find its industrial range alone rather too diverse to be coherent. It should be remembered, too, that GE is involved in numerous joint ventures. GE's financial and media businesses are the sectors that stand out as not fitting with its industrial legacy. The financial business, once part the GE Capital division, has been largely scaled back. The media and entertainment businesses, shaded in Figure 5.7, retain their own brand identities. In late 2009, GE decided to gradually reduce its stake in these businesses by placing them in a joint venture with Comcast, a media company.

Conglomerates are not confined to western MNEs. MNEs in many emerging markets, India in particular, have grown to become sprawling conglomerates, whose businesses are only tenuously linked to each other. We look next at emerging MNEs and ask in what ways their internationalization strategies are distinctive.

conglomerate large, diversified company, in which there is no single identifiable core business

Summary points **FDI strategy**

◆ Greenfield investment indicates a desire to commit extensive resources in the new location, reflecting its importance as a potential market for the firm.

◆ Acquiring companies in new markets is a relatively quick means of market entry, and benefits from existing operations of the acquired company.

Emerging-market MNEs and internationalization

Ford Motor Company of the US purchased Jaguar, the upmarket British carmaker, in 1989 and Land Rover in 2000. Both companies were sold to Tata Motors of India in 2008 (see closing case study in Chapter 3). In 1990, developing countries accounted for 5% of outward FDI in the world. This percentage was up to 14% in 2006, and 18.9% in 2008. And this figure does not include companies like ArcelorMittal, the steel-making empire of Lakshmi Mittal, whose roots are in India, although the company is registered in Luxembourg. Mittal bought steelmaking plants in developing countries around the world, many of which, such as those in Mexico, were privatizations. His largest acquisition, however, was the purchase of Arcelor, the European steelmaker, in 2006. How does emerging MNEs' expansion compare with that of existing globalized MNEs, in whose footsteps they are following?

The history of MNE expansion, along with the theoretical insights which have developed simultaneously, provides guidance for today's emerging-market MNEs. They are probably more acutely aware of the risks of rapid expansion, and will have bigger and better resources for researching potential markets than their predecessors. But these advantages are true of *any* company internationalizing today. For emerging-market companies, there are some distinctive aspects of the home environment which can be viewed as advantages. Their MNEs have grown quickly in fast-growing economies which combine large potential markets with low costs. These are ideal platforms for future growth. Most of them, including Brazil, India and China, have seen liberalization in their home markets, bringing in foreign competitors, which have forced them to sharpen up their products and performance. Hence, there are both push and pull factors at work. As they have gained in competitiveness, they have felt better able to take on rivals in both developing and developed countries, including the home markets of their biggest competitors.

Emerging MNEs have also learned the lesson of the importance of innovation in global markets. They have been early to see the importance of collaborative partnerships in R&D, often with other MNEs. Western MNEs, in comparison, were slow to internationalize R&D, this function often remaining concentrated in the home country long after the parent company had become globalized.

The home background in a developing country can be frustrating. Poor infrastructure, heavy-handed regulation, weak skills in the workforce and lack of supporting services pose challenges for new businesses, especially those in the private sector in countries which have widespread state ownership, as in China. However, the skills developed in coping with the difficulties can make managers more resilient, adaptable and imaginative in facing problems. In particular, companies in developing countries are accustomed to the need to keep costs and prices low – disciplines which hold them in good stead in global markets. On the other hand, these companies are entering markets in which globalization is already advanced, and existing MNEs enjoy economies of scale, along with well-oiled global supply chains. Breaking into this competitive landscape is a huge challenge. Often, the lack of management expertise and experience is a stumbling block, and these competencies are difficult to acquire overnight. Years of organizational learning in global markets benefit the western MNE, but the emerging MNEs are catching up quickly. Recall Cemex of Mexico (featured in the closing case study of Chapter 1), which has become globalized rapidly.

We have noted that the emerging MNEs aim to grow quickly, implying ambitious acquisitions in diverse locations, seemingly undaunted by the cultural differences

EXPLORING THE GLOBAL BUSINESS ENVIRONMENT

Mexico: the lagging OECD economy

In recent years, Mexico has tended to capture media headlines for a disparate variety of reasons, many unfavourable. The billion-dollar drugs cartels, whose violent activities are regularly reported, lead to perceptions of general lawlessness, although their activities are mainly concentrated in the area along the US border. Mexico stresses that, in fact, it has a lower murder rate than its Latin American neighbours. Brazil, often applauded for its improvements in social development, has a murder rate twice that of Mexico. Mexico also features in development data for its high levels of inequality and poverty. This picture contrasts sharply with the 2010 ranking of a Mexican tycoon, Carlos Slim, as the world's richest individual, overtaking Bill Gates, the Microsoft founder. Slim's fortune, estimated at $53.5 billion, about 5.4% of Mexico's GDP, grew $18.5 billion in the previous year, largely thanks to the financial performance of his telecoms empire. In

that year, Mexico's economy shrank about 6.5%. To add to a bad year, Mexico's coastal resort area was struck by a swine flu epidemic in 2009.

The year 2010 is Mexico's bicentenary as an independent country, and the centenary of Mexico's 1910 revolution, which marks the beginning of modern Mexico. But Mexicans might feel there has been little to celebrate of late. A severe contraction in the economy followed recession in the US, as four-fifths of its exports are destined for the US. As the US economy resumed growing in 2010, Mexican firms stood to benefit. Another source of optimism is that, as costs have risen in China, Mexico, which had lost out to Chinese imports in some sectors in the US, is now becoming more competitive again. This is largely thanks to the effects of Nafta, which has led to a burgeoning of export-oriented businesses in the northern regions of the country. On the other hand,

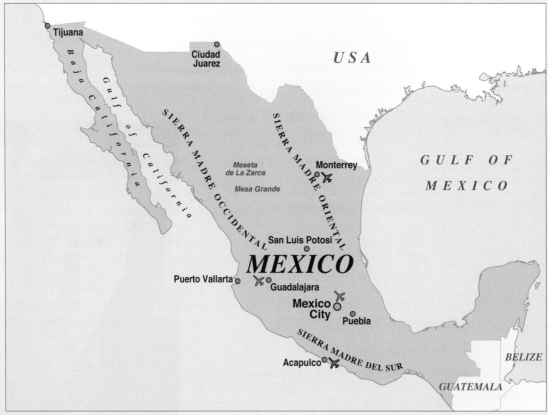

Map of Mexico

► More online ... See the World Bank's page on Mexico, under 'countries' on the World Bank's website at www.worldbank.org

Mexico's finance minister has stressed that the country still needs to diversify the economy, away from the reliance on American exports. Mexico's business environment is ranked only 51 in the World Bank's 'Doing business' rankings of 183 countries, whereas Brazil is ranked 26 (World Bank, 2010). Mexican SMEs, in particular, find it difficult to get bank loans and cope with bureaucratic regulation. The government is also concerned that oil, which has been a valuable source of income for Mexico, is now a contracting industry as the oil is running out. Diversification, however, remains more an aspiration than a reality. Part of the reason has been the structure of Mexico's economy.

Mexico's economic development has been dominated by large state-owned enterprises. Although privatization has helped to open the economy, the result in some cases has been to perpetuate near-monopolies in the hands of a few individuals, such as Carlos Slim. Income inequality and poverty are the highest of all OECD countries (OECD, 2008). The percentage of Mexican inhabitants living in poverty (defined as less than 50% of the median income) has fallen to 18%, from a high of 22.5% during the 'peso' financial crisis of the mid-1990s, but this is double that of the OECD generally. Worryingly, there are significant differences between the more prosperous north and mainly rural south of the country. The Mexican government does calculations on a broad measure of poverty, *pobreza de patrimonio*, which is the ability to afford basic food, clothing, health, education, housing and public transport. On this measure, 54.7% of rural inhabitants fall below the poverty line, a reduction from nearly two-thirds in 1992, but still over half the rural population. In urban areas, 35% live in poverty, a reduction from 44.3% in 1992 (CONEVAL, 2008). While the impacts of Nafta were beneficial to firms in the north, the grain producers in southern Mexico have suffered, especially small farmers, who have lost out to large producers and imported grains from subsidized US producers.

Mexico's tourist industry has been a source of optimism. In the 1970s, the government invested large sums in developing the Yucatan peninsula, with aid from the Inter-American Development Bank. The resort of Cancun became the country's largest, but suffered a devastating setback in May 2009, with an outbreak of swine flu, which grabbed media headlines around the world. It was particularly unfortunate, occurring in the same year as the US recession. The authorities closed all hotels and services, emptying the beaches, which should have been packed with visitors. The tourism sector is gradually recovering, and there are plans for more developments. Are there more clouds on the horizon? Violent storms are a risk in coastal areas, and the oil slick in the Gulf of Mexico in 2010, which BP struggled to control, illustrated another kind of risk to which coastal resorts are susceptible.

Sources: OECD (2008) *Growing Unequal? Income Distribution and Poverty in OECD Countries* (Paris: OECD); Thomson, A. (2010) 'Eager to shut the door on a bad year', *Financial Times*, 31 March; Buchanan, R. (2010) 'Business unfazed by drugs bloodshed', *Financial Times*, 31 March; Forbes (2010) World's richest rankings, at www.forbes.com; World Bank (2010) Doing Business rankings, at www.doingbusiness.org; CONEVAL (Consejo Nacional de Evaluación de la Política de Desarrollo Social) (2008) 'Informe de Evaluación de la Política de Desarrollo Social en México 2008', at www.coneval.gob.mx

Questions for discussion

◆ How would you rank Mexico's economy in terms of economic sustainability?

◆ Why does Mexico receive a rather low rating in the 'Doing business' rankings?

◆ What should be the Mexican government's priorities for diversification of the economy and social development?

which arise. Can their organizations keep up with their strategic ambitions, and are there lessons to be learned in this respect from the more traditional MNEs? Corporate governance is perceived as a crucial issue in western MNEs, as it is gradually becoming accepted that structures and processes should comply with best practice internationally (see Chapter 1). However, MNEs from emerging markets are often perceived as close-knit and opaque in their governance, despite their growing international presence. Some are largely state owned and seen as 'national champions' in their home countries. As these companies become more internationalized, it is arguable that their structures and governance should reflect this diversity. MNEs from developed countries present a variety of organizational models, discussed in the next section.

Summary points Emerging-market MNEs go global

- MNEs from fast-growing emerging economies are new global players, showing ambition
and agility in the fast-changing competitive environment.
- These MNEs are keen to establish
themselves globally, often pursuing acquisition strategies to enter new markets.

MNE structures

organization two or more people who work together in a structured way to achieve a specific goal or set of goals

An **organization** may be defined as 'two or more people who work together in a structured way to achieve a specific goal or set of goals' (Stoner and Freeman, 1992: 4). This broad definition encompasses many types of organization. It includes, for example, police forces, hospitals and schools, as well as all types of business enterprise. The structure and operations of an organization within national borders are much less complicated than those of organizations which operate across borders. The MNE parent company, introduced in Chapter 1, is at the pinnacle of its organization, usually located in the company's home country. Structures of subsidiaries and links between them must be co-ordinated through structures designed to serve the organization's corporate strategy. Physical resources, including plant, machinery and offices must be organized, and functions such as finance, purchasing and marketing must be co-ordinated, to enable the entire enterprise to function smoothly as a unit.

While every organization wishes to make the most of its expertise and resources, there is no one type of organization which can be said to be an ideal model that suits all businesses. There is a large body of organization theory, which studies 'the structure, functioning and performance of organizations and the behaviour of groups and individuals within them' (Pugh, 1997: xii). **Structure** has been defined as 'the design of organization through which the enterprise is administered' (Chandler, 1990: 14). It includes both formal and informal lines of authority. Organizational structures can be divided into three broad categories. The first is organization based simply on function. The second is the divisional structure, based on products, brands or regions. Thirdly, there is the organizational structure based on a matrix, the aim of which is to bring together the benefits of the other types. We look at each in turn.

structure the design of organization through which the enterprise is administered

The functional approach

functional approach organizational structure based on business functions, such as finance, HRM and marketing

Business functions were introduced in Chapter 1. In the **functional approach** to organization, business functions determine organizational structure. The importance of particular functions depends in part on the type of business. Product design and production, along with research and development, feature mainly in manufacturing firms, whereas all firms have need of finance, HRM and marketing functions.

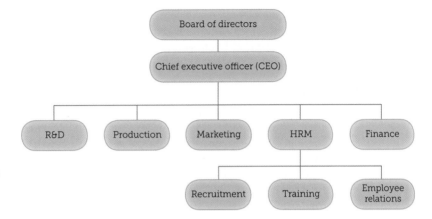

Figure 5.8 **Organization based on functional departments**

The functional organizational approach is depicted in Figure 5.8. There is a risk in this type of structure that each functional department will become inward-looking, evolving its own culture and losing sight of organizational goals. Within the formal structure, the functional specialists must blend into a smooth-running whole. Central management and, in particular, its chief executive officer (CEO) is at the pinnacle of the organization, and is therefore crucial in co-ordinating the departments. This is one of the main management challenges. **Management** is the:

management
process of planning, organizing, leading and controlling the work of organization members

> process of planning, organizing, leading and controlling the work of organization members, and of using all available organizational resources to reach stated organizational goals. (Stoner and Freeman, 1992: 4)

Head-office managers seek to reap the benefits of specialized staff in each functional area, but must also keep organizational goals in focus, which can mean making tough decisions on budgets of particular departments. For example, the marketing budget could be cut in order to boost spending on R&D, or vice versa. The larger the company, the more cumbersome this structure becomes. This type of structure is suitable for domestic companies, but does not necessarily lend itself to companies which are becoming internationalized. The MNE that produces a number of different products for different markets will require a structure accommodating these aspects of the business – one that combines central guidance and local responsiveness. The more decentralized divisional structure has developed in conjunction with international expansion.

Summary points The functional structure

● A structure based on separate functional areas is commonly adopted by companies which operate in a limited range of activities and in a single national environment.

● The functional structure risks becoming inward-looking, each function evolving its own culture, and losing sight of organizational goals

▶ More online … DuPont is at www.dupont.com
PepsiCo is at www.pepsico.com

The divisional structure

When a company has grown to the extent that it has a number of successful products in different regions, it tends to structure the organization into business units or divisions, which may be based on product, brand, or geographical region (see Figure 5.9). Known as the **multidivisional structure**, this has been one of the major structural innovations of modern corporations, seeking to solve the problems of how to decentralize a large company while still maintaining overall co-ordination of the parts. A full account of its development is given in Alfred Chandler's *Strategy and Structure* (1990). In it he recounts the experiences of General Motors and the American chemical corporation DuPont, which adopted the multidivisional structure in the early 1900s. The principle is that each division is headed by a division manager who has responsibility for managing the division as a profit centre in its own right. The division itself may be a subsidiary company whose major shareholder is the parent company. The company's executives at the head office concentrate on the broader corporate aims, leaving the divisions considerable independence. The head office will house centralized functional departments, such as finance, for the group as a whole.

multidivisional structure organizational structure with decentralized divisions based on product lines or geographical areas

A divisional structure based on **product divisions** has been adopted by a number of global companies, including General Electric (GE), British Telecom (BT), and Ericsson. An advantage of this approach, in theory, is the ability to co-ordinate activities to produce and market a particular line worldwide, but a drawback tends to be that its standardized approach overlooks differences in national markets (Birkinshaw, 2000). Some companies combine product divisions and an international division, which is responsible for the firm's products in all markets other than its home country. PepsiCo is an example.

product divisions company divisions based on products, which co-ordinate product strategy globally

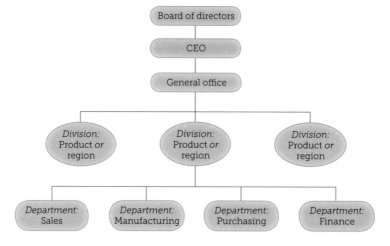

Figure 5.9 **The multidivisional structure**

The **area division** is a way of addressing different regional conditions. In this type of organization structure, country or regional managers preside over area divisions, and are responsible for all of the company's activities in that area. The area may be, for example, Asia-Pacific, in which case the area manager has charge of operations in that region, including control over resources. For many US companies, Europe, the

area divisions company divisions based on geographical regions of the world, adapting strategy to local conditions

Middle East and Africa (EMEA) form a division, although these markets are highly diverse. A main advantage of the area division structure is that it is able to respond to regional needs. It also lends itself to decentralization, that is, the delegating of decision-making down to the divisions. Many global companies, including Nestlé and Unilever, have been organized in this way, although they have found that it is difficult to achieve economies of scale in development and production (Birkinshaw, 2000). They have tended to move towards global product divisions or a combination of geographical regions plus product divisions, as Unilever has done.

holding company
company, often referred to as the 'parent' company, which owns a number of subsidiaries

The **holding company** may also be said to be based on divisions, in that a parent company is the owner of a diverse array of subsidiary companies. However, unlike the multidivisional companies described above, the holding company usually exerts little control over the separate companies and provides few general functions for the group as a whole. The companies within the group operate, in effect, as independent organizations.

Summary points **The divisional structure**

◆ The divisional structure facilitates decentralized product units or regional units.

◆ This structure has been widely adopted by MNEs, and adapts to expanding international operations.

The matrix structure

matrix structure
organizational structure involving two lines of authority, such as area and product divisions

The **matrix** is a way of structuring the organization to incorporate the benefits of other types of structure, including the functional organization, product divisions and area divisions. It involves two lines of management, as indicated in Figure 5.10. The product manager must co-ordinate with the area manager for the launch of a new product in that region. In theory, this allows the company to respond to local trends, and also to derive the benefits of globally co-ordinated product management. In

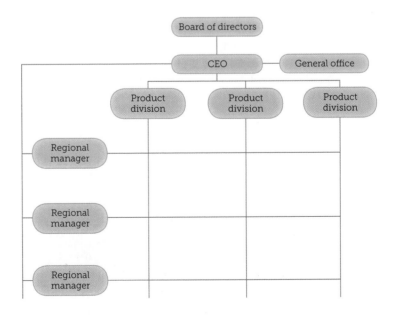

Figure 5.10 **The global matrix**

practice, however, it is difficult to reconcile these different lines of authority, and the system can lead to deadlock in decision-making (Bartlett and Ghoshal, 1990). Thus, although the matrix should theoretically provide flexibility, it can lead to inefficiency.

Some companies adopt a compromise, using product divisions, but adding country management where it is specifically needed (Birkinshaw, 2000). In the early 1990s, the Swiss-Swedish electrical engineering company ABB put in place a matrix structure, but changed to a divisional structure based on products and technologies in 1998. The company has undergone further restructuring since then, in which the divisions were replaced by four 'consumer segments', aimed at developing a greater customer orientation. The structural design journey of ABB reflects the challenges of MNEs in balancing the need for central control with local responsiveness.

Summary points The matrix structure

◆ The matrix structure aims to combine co-ordinated product management and regional centres.

◆ In practice, the matrix structure is difficult to manage, due to crossing lines of communication.

Critical thinking

Growing too big?

The large, often highly diversified, MNE has come in for criticism for being so unwieldy that it is unable to make efficient use of the economies of scale which its large size should bring. Think of some large organizations that you know or that have featured in this book. What have they done to enhance their competitiveness in recent years?

Evolution of the transnational organization

As experiments with matrix structures suggest, designing organizational structures is only part of the story for an organization to achieve its aims. The parts must function efficiently, focusing on corporate goals while remaining agile in local markets. Degrees of autonomy of local units vary from one company to another: some are highly centralized while others are decentralized. Bartlett and Ghoshal have devised a typology of international organizations that highlights these features and emphasizes the importance of the firm's own corporate culture and legacy in influencing its structures (Bartlett and Ghoshal, 1998). These models are shown in Figure 5.11.

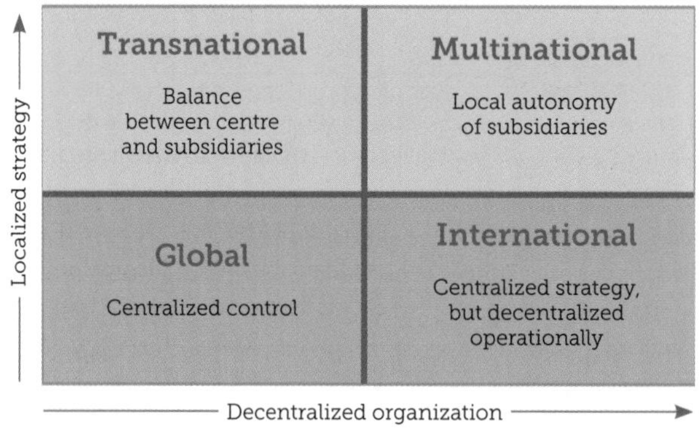

Figure 5.11 **Models of the international organization**

Source: Based on Bartlett, A. and Ghoshal, S. (1998) *Managing Across Borders: A Transnational Solution*, 2nd edn (London: Random House)

▶ More online ... IBM's website is www.ibm.com/investor

multinational model in Bartlett and Ghoshal's typology, a model of the international company based on autonomous national units

international model in Bartlett and Ghoshal's typology, a model of the international company based on decentralized subsidiaries

global model in Bartlett and Ghoshal's typology, a model of the international company based on centralized control

Fordism approach to an industrial organization based on large factories producing standardized products for mass consumption, named after the automobile magnate Henry Ford

Looking at the models shown in Figure 5.11, the **multinational model** (sometimes called the 'multidomestic' model) is the most decentralized. Subsidiaries are managed as autonomous units, with strategy-making powers for their areas. The **international model** decentralizes operations, but maintains central strategy formation. This model has proved successful for many European companies which have expanded through acquisitions. These businesses have considerable managerial latitude, which allows for local responsiveness, but the lack of strong global strategy might be considered a drawback. By contrast, the global model is highly centralized strategically and operationally. Resource allocation and planning stem from the centre, with little scope for local responsiveness.

The **global model** is typified by the management system known as **Fordism**, deriving its name from the top-down management associated with the Ford Motor Company in its post-war heyday. Ford aimed to produce a basic standardized product in large volumes and at prices affordable by the new middle classes in America's booming post-war period. This vertically integrated system relied on assembly-line processes operated by large numbers of semi-skilled workers. In Ford's River Rouge plant, which employed 35,000 under one roof, coal and iron went in at one end, and complete Ford cars rolled out the other. The Fordist system was highly bureaucratic and inflexible. Poor industrial relations characterized Fordist factories, where adversarial relations between highly organized trade unions and inflexible managers lingered long after Fordism as a manufacturing system was superseded.

To meet changing consumer tastes and a diversity of consumer needs, mass manufacturing was compelled to become more flexible, no longer based on a single mammoth factory, but on networks of smaller specialist organizations linked in supply chains. The use of integrated networks characterized the last of the four models, the **transnational model**. The thinking behind this model is similar to that underlying the matrix structure, in that it emphasizes local responsiveness. IBM's CEO speaks of the 'globally integrated enterprise'. He says:

transnational model in Bartlett and Ghoshal's typology, a model of the international company balanced between the centre and subsidiaries

> Unlike the multinational – which created mini versions of itself in markets around the world – this new kind of organization locates work, skills and operations wherever it makes sense, based on access to expertise, on superior economics and on the presence of open environments and technologies. (Palmisano, 2008)

flexible mass production model of manufacturing which combines the benefits of flexibility with those of scale economies

lean production systems and techniques of production enabling companies to reduce waste, leading to greater flexibility in production processes

just-in-time (JIT) manufacturing system of manufacturing which relies on a continuous flow of materials

Organizational flexibility and decentralized management, relying on more highly skilled workers to share responsibility, characterized the post-Fordist factory. Japanese companies are credited with the most successful examples of these manufacturing innovations. The Japanese model has been called one of '**flexible mass production**' (Sabel, 1994: 122). The large Japanese manufacturing companies, such as Toyota, the leading automaker, allow for flexibility in production and organization. While producing for mass markets, the system of centralized product development is nonetheless able to respond to changes in demand, making use of technology to reduce development time. New automated manufacturing equipment facilitates the rapid implementation of changes and variations in the product. **Lean production** techniques aim to reduce waste of all types, including time, and rely on a **just-in-time** supply of components, reducing the need for large amounts of stock. This flexibility is reflected in a workforce trained to understand the entire process involved in the new technology, enabling workers to change tasks with ease. High levels of knowledge and training are also essential to the Japanese philosophy of quality control, which emphasizes worker involvement and contribution (summed up in the

▸ More online ... Information on *kaizen* can be found at www.lean-manufacturing-japan.com
Toyota is at www.toyota.co.jp

kaizen management philosophy of continuous improvement, involving the entire workforce

concept of **kaizen**). A consensus-based system of worker participation is a long way from the confrontational labour relations of classical mass production.

Summary points **The transnational organizational structure**

◆ Corporate structures differ in the extent of centralization of both strategy and operations.

◆ The transnational model aims to benefit from global strategy and

decentralized networking at the operational level.

Inter-organizational networks

Supply chains depend on co-operation among numerous organizations in the value chain, in which personal relations and ease of communication are crucial. As these ties, both formal and informal, evolve, the boundaries of the firm become 'fuzzy': people might have greater day-to-day relations with key people in other organizations than with people in their own firm. These network ties require a sharing of knowledge and thinking, which can benefit all the firms in the chain. But how does the notion of the network fit into traditional notions of competitive strategy?

Strategic alliances have become important aspects of corporate strategy. By co-operating in R&D, for example, two firms can make greater headway than each would achieve separately (see Chapter 10). In this way, both firms can benefit. The firm that co-operates with a competitor in this way can help to build competitive advantage, translating the knowledge into performance, which enhances the firm's core competencies. The idea of benefiting from ties with other firms is not new. Japanese firms have long nurtured inter-firm ties in the loosely formed keiretsu groups (see Chapter 3). Japanese manufacturing companies rely on a constellation of smaller firms to supply components and expertise. As western companies adopted Japanese management principles of lean production and just-in-time systems, they have become more open to co-operative strategies and inter-firm ties. However, just as there are risks in the highly centralized, hierarchical organization, there are risks in the decentralized, networked organization. Toyota has experienced problems in maintaining quality in its global production networks. Having built up expertise in quality management in its domestic production, it has encountered challenges in adapting these systems to globalized production.

The company that works closely with a number of suppliers and customers enhances its ability to satisfy customer needs, but also risks losing sight of its own core competencies. It can even find that its partners are benefiting from shared technology to gain a competitive lead. Hence, perhaps paradoxically, the firm must focus more strongly on its own core competencies, lest its competitive position becomes undermined. On the other hand, if it goes to the opposite extreme and is very reluctant to share technology with partners, it could well find that co-operative agreements bear little fruit. The balance must be struck between openness and control. Where firms are from differing cultural backgrounds, inter-firm networks face challenges in working smoothly and achieving collective goals, as the next chapter will show.

Summary points Inter-organizational networks

◆ The spread of supply chains, involving different companies, has led to the development of inter-organizational networks, involving the sharing of information and operational co-ordination.

◆ Networks are characteristic of post-Fordist organizations, especially in manufacturing based on Japanese-pioneered flexible mass production.

Rethinking globalization

MNEs from the developed economies have been at the forefront of globalization in the post-war period. Various strategies have played a part. Some companies have focused on vertical integration, acquiring ownership of key assets in a variety of locations. Others have acquired a diversity of different businesses, building sprawling conglomerates. More recently, companies have become more 'asset light', collaborating in complex supply chains. All three responses reflect globalization processes, as communications technology makes cross-border business easier to manage. National governments have played a big role, too, bringing down obstacles to cross-border business activities. However, national governments have revealed rather ambivalent approaches to globalization. They have liberalized trade and facilitated cross-border capital movements and FDI. However, in times of domestic economic stress, some governments have reacted by raising barriers to trade and investment, in order to protect domestic industries and jobs. At the same time, they express disappointment when foreign MNEs, once welcomed for their FDI, have exited countries in which performance has been disappointing.

For MNEs, keeping ahead in the global competitive environment requires a willingness to seize new opportunities and seek new markets. However, firms can find that they become overstretched, hanging onto units and activities which are not viable. Inevitably, from time to time, they will close factories or sell whole businesses, as part of their ongoing realignment of corporate strategy. If an acquired business or joint venture turns out not to be a good fit with the parent company's product portfolio, or if problems of integration emerge, the company must take hard decisions on where to let the axe fall. CEOs must take into account the views and interests of stakeholders. Key shareholders, in particular, are vigilant in cases where they feel the overall value of the parent company might be eroded.

In periods of rapid expansion, some MNEs have enjoyed acquisition sprees, acquiring dozens of companies around the globe in a single year. Nowadays, MNEs from developed countries are inclined to weigh up expansion plans more carefully, thinking more of the long-term benefits – and possible drawbacks. MNEs from emerging economies, keen to catch up with more established competitors, are approaching internationalization from slightly different perspectives. Their foundations in strong-performing economies encourage them to internationalize quickly. Some are family empires, unencumbered by the concerns of diverse shareholders and other stakeholders which have helped to shape western MNEs' approaches to strategy. In addition, many emerging-market MNEs are backed by state governments and approach internationalization as national champions. The notion of the globalized national champion might seem a contradiction. However, as we noted in Chapter 2, the truly global company, with little sense of national roots, is a rarity. Most reflect to some extent the cultural background in which they have emerged, even when their operations take place mainly outside their home countries. The cultural dimension remains strong in MNEs, as we discuss in the next chapter.

Summary points **Rethinking globalization**

- Expansive MNE strategies have propelled globalization, largely through FDI and the growth of global supply chains.

- National governments have facilitated MNE expansion, for example by welcoming FDI, but can show a reverse side, by discouraging and constraining investment when domestic interests are perceived to be at stake.

- Emerging-market MNEs have expanded quickly, often encouraged by generous state support and the underpinning of strong domestic economies.

Critical thinking

Globalization perspectives

In what ways do the perspectives of established western MNEs and emerging-market MNEs differ in respect of globalization?

Companion website

Remember to check the companion website at www.palgrave.com/business/morrisongbe3 where you will find a searchable glossary, updated weblinks, video interviews with CEOs and extra guidance on the case studies in this book, all designed to help you get to grips with the global business environment.

Conclusions

1 Formulating strategy involves examining the organization's goals and how to achieve them.

2 The SWOT analysis, highlighting the firm's strengths, weaknesses, opportunities and threats, is an aid to formulating strategy, which takes in both internal and external aspects of the firm's environment.

3 Porter's five forces model focuses mainly on the competitive environment in a particular industry.

4 The resource-based view of the firm assesses the firm's internal strengths, including core competencies, in relation to those of competitors and potential competitors.

5 The emergent strategy approach allows for a firm's strategy to evolve as it grows and responds to the changing environment.

6 The stakeholder management approach focuses on the need to involve a range of stakeholders in the strategy process.

7 Strategy can be viewed at three different levels: the highest is corporate strategy, involving the firm's ultimate goals. Competitive strategy focuses on achieving success in different markets. Both help to determine functional strategies, such as marketing strategy.

8 Of internationalization strategies, export is the mode that entails the least involvement in the host environment, while FDI involves greater integration in the host country.

9 Greenfield investment can be contrasted with acquisition, the latter of which is a quicker way to gain a foothold in the host country, often implying existing market share.

10 Licensing, especially to outsourcers, is a favoured option in many manufacturing sectors, but terms of agreements and management relations need to be carefully handled, in order to succeed.

11 Emerging-market MNEs have become powerful players in global markets, demonstrating ambition and flexibility in adapting to changing environments.

12 MNE organizational structures vary according to the degree of latitude which foreign subsidiaries enjoy. In the multinational structure, they enjoy considerable latitude, while the global model is highly centralized.

13 The transnational model combines centralized strategy with local responsiveness.

14 The benefits of inter-firm networks, which develop relational ties between firms, have become more apparent with the advances in global supply chains.

15 Some MNEs have embraced globalization by going on acquisition sprees, especially when financing posed few obstacles. Now, as finances have become tighter and the competitive environment has become more challenging, firms are rethinking global strategies with a view more focused on core competencies.

Review questions

1 What factors must a firm balance in formulating strategy?

2 Explain the different elements of the SWOT analysis, giving an example of each.

3 In what ways does Porter's five forces model aid the firm in identifying strategic opportunities?

4 Define the key attributes of a resource according to the resource-based view of the firm.

5 Give an example of a core competence, and explain how it would help to achieve competitive advantage.

6 What are the advantages of an emergent-strategy approach, as opposed to a strategic-planning approach?

7   What long-term benefits are arguably achievable through the stakeholder management approach to strategy?

8   Explain the different approaches to competitive strategy.

9   What type of firm and product would be likely to benefit from export as an internationalization mode?

10   What are the advantages and disadvantages of licensing as an entry mode?

11   What are the advantages of acquisition over FDI as an entry mode? What are the drawbacks?

12   What degrees of decentralization are associated with each of the following organizational structures: (a) the multinational model; (b) the global model?

13   Why are multidivisional companies increasingly opting for global product divisions?

14   The matrix organizational structure is often held up as ideal in theory, but unworkable in practice. Why?

15   What advantages and disadvantages do emerging-market MNEs have in their internationalization strategies?

Key revision concepts

Core competencies, p. 163; Diversification, p. 173; Emergent strategy, p. 164; Five forces model, p. 160; Flexible mass production, p. 183; Fordism, p. 183; Integration, p. 173; Management, p. 177; Multidivisional structure, p. 180; Resource-based theory, p. 162; SWOT analysis, p. 158

Assignments

◆ The large conglomerate has traditionally relied on its diverse businesses as a strength in global markets. These supposed benefits are now not so obvious. Assess the advantages and disadvantages of the large diversified organization in today's global environment.

◆ Assume you are the CEO of a large retailer in a western country. Your shareholders wish to see the company expanding into large emerging markets. How would you go about formulating an internationalization strategy to maximize the chances of success and minimize the risks?

Further reading

Barney, J. and Hesterley, W. (2007) *Strategic Management and Competitive Advantage: Concepts and Cases*, 2nd edn (Prentice Hall).

Bartlett, C.A. and Ghoshal, S. (2002) *Managing Across Borders: The Transnational Solution*, 2nd edn (Boston, MA: Harvard Business School Press).

Johnson, G. and Scholes, K. (2006) *Exploring Corporate Strategy*, 7th edn (Financial Times Prentice Hall).

Lasserre, P. (2007) *Global Strategic Management*, 2nd edn (Basingstoke: Palgrave Macmillan).

Mintzberg, H., Ahlstrand, B. and Lampel, J. (2009) *Strategy Safari*, 2nd edn (Harlow: Pearson Education).

Mullins, L. (2009) *Management and Organizational Behaviour*, 8th edn (Financial Times Prentice Hall).

Wheelen, T. and Hunger, J. (2009) *Strategic Management and Business Policy*, 12th edn (Pearson Education).

Sony seeks to revive profitability

Few brands in electronics have the enduring brand reputation that Sony enjoys. Yet the Japanese company has found it difficult to maintain profits in an increasingly competitive environment. Its history of innovative products goes back to the Walkman in 1979. It invested heavily in flatscreen televisions, but competitors such as Samsung and LG have challenged it in quality and price. Sony has not been an inward-looking company. It was among the first Japanese companies to have foreign board members, and its chairman and CEO, Sir Howard Stringer, is British. It has globalized production and sought to locate manufacturing facilities near markets. However, competitive pressures and global economic downturn have taken their toll. Sony's CEO has embarked on a widespread restructuring programme, targeting its television factories in particular.

Sony started manufacturing televisions in Slovakia in 2006, and built up production capacity, but it has now decided to slim down its operations to save costs. Overall, Sony's electronics business, which includes audio, video and televisions, is being reduced from 57 factories to 42. It is shedding four of its eight TV factories. The Nitra plant in Slovakia was sold to Hon Hai (Foxconn) of Taiwan, an outsource manufacturer making TVs under licence (although Sony retained a 10% stake). Hon Hai also bought Sony's TV factory in Mexico. Hon Hai's attractiveness as an outsourcer stems partly from its acquisition of an affiliate specializing in liquid crystal display (LCD) panels. Hon Hai should thus be a strong competitive position in TV assembly, as it can

benefit from transaction costs savings. Still, competition from Samsung is stiff, and Samsung has an in-house supply of LCD panels.

Sony's loss-making Barcelona factory posed another challenge. The Barcelona operation is small in comparison to Nitra, and therefore a natural candidate for closure, but it would be costly. The factory is unionized, and Spain has strong employment protection laws. Who would buy the Barcelona factory? An outsourcing manufacturer would be deterred by the small scale and high costs. Late in 2010 a provisional deal was done to sell the Barcelona factory to two local Spanish firms, one concentrating on manufacturing operations and the other on development and engineering. Sony had thus disposed of all its European TV plants. It is still intent on keeping the 'mother factory' in Japan, which is important in design and feedback. Its factories in Brazil and China, both growing markets, will also be kept: these are large markets and both countries have high import duties on TVs.

Small LCD panels for use in mobile phones and digital cameras are still manufactured at Sony factories in Japan, even though they are not profitable. It sold one of these factories to Kyocera, but has kept two. Its reasoning is that it wishes to

Watching the screen: Sony has become a global leader in technology, but despite its fame as a global brand, it faces stiff global competition

Source: Sony

develop display technologies for the future, as these help to differentiate its products. Sony has faced criticism that it has lost its leadership role in innovation as other companies, such as Apple, with its iPad, have taken the limelight. Sony is producing a rival to the iPad, and it has been somewhat cheered by increased sales of its Vaio PCs. However, quality problems with the new PS3 PlayStation were disappointing, especially coming at a time when Toyota was also experiencing quality problems. Production of the PS3 is outsourced to China. Sony has traditionally justified its premium prices on its reputation for quality. With its TV manufacturing increasingly outsourced, will consumers still be willing to pay for the Sony brand, even though someone else has made the product? Sony executives are hoping the answer is 'yes'.

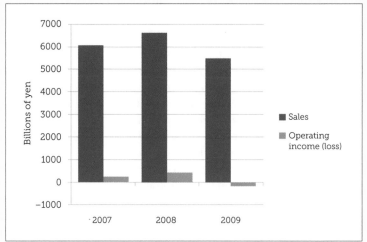

Sales and operating income (loss) in Sony's electronics division

Source: Sony Annual Report 2009, at www.sony.net

Sources: Harding, R. and Soble, J. (2010) 'Japanese fret over quality of manufacturing', *Financial Times*, 3 March; Harding, R. (2010) 'Stringer's Sony restructuring has unfinished business', *Financial Times*, 1 April; Harding, R. and Gelles, D. (2010) 'Sony plans to compete against the Apple iPad', *Financial Times*, 5 February; Sony Annual Report 2009, at www.sony.net

Questions for discussion

◆ What trends are apparent in the global electronics industry, which are having adverse effects on Sony?
◆ What are Sony's core competencies?
◆ What are the risks of outsourcing from Sony's perspective?

PART 3

SOCIETIES IN THE INTERNATIONAL ENVIRONMENT

In this part, we shift from markets and strategy to broad areas of the international environment relating to societies – their cultures, how they are governed and how their legal systems impact on people.

The first is Chapter 6, 'CULTURAL AND SOCIAL ENVIRONMENTS'. For most businesses, as for people, a national culture is an anchoring point, but in today's globalized world, companies are constantly encountering new cultures, whether in markets or in new production locations. Understanding underlying values and norms in differing national environments helps international managers to achieve better performance in international operations. At the same time, MNEs are becoming enmeshed in the societies in which they operate, and a new focus on communities and localization is now informing strategy. MNEs are thus better able to adapt to unfolding changes in societies, especially those associated with economic development.

In Chapter 7, 'THE POLITICAL ENVIRONMENT', we take a more formal and institutional view of societies, looking at the structures by which they are governed. These, too, change over time, especially in the context of newly independent states and those that are rebuilding their political systems following the collapse of communism. Spreading democratic institutions has been a trend in the post-war period, notably in the post-communist countries of Central and Eastern Europe. But democratic setbacks and the strengthening of authoritarian governments have led to a rethink of democratic values and institutions. Political stability is valued by businesses as well as by individuals. A turbulent democratic system, in which social tensions sometimes boil over, can be detrimental to the business environment, but businesses have cause to be wary of the stability offered by repressive authoritarian regimes, where tensions exist under the surface. The chapter also examines the widening scope of intergovernmental institutions which impact on businesses.

These considerations are taken up again in the following chapter, Chapter 8, 'THE LEGAL ENVIRONMENT'. Here we focus first on national legal systems, and their differing approaches to civil and criminal law. For international business, legal risks in areas of contract law arise in numerous types of activity, including forming joint ventures, making contracts with suppliers and customers, and employing people in different countries. Liabilities are incurred, for example, when an accident occurs in operations under the firm's control. Court proceedings, whatever the location, can be slow and costly, and firms are increasingly taking account of legal risk when entering new markets. As in the political environment, legal considerations are increasingly taking on an international dimension. MNEs now recognize that international law, notably in the area of human rights, creates obligations that stakeholders expect to be applied.

CHAPTER 6

CULTURAL AND SOCIAL ENVIRONMENTS

Outline of chapter

Introduction

What is culture and how is it relevant to business?

National cultures

Languages
English: the global language?

Religions
Christianity
Islam
Asian religions – Hinduism, Buddhism, Confucianism
How religion impacts on business life

Culture theories
Hofstede's cultural dimensions
Trompenaars' theory of relationships

Organizational culture

Changing societies
Migration
Urbanization
Changing populations

Conclusions

Learning objectives

1 To understand the nature and origins of cultural diversity in societies
2 To identify cultural dimensions as an aid to comparing national cultures
3 To assess the role and impacts of different organizational cultures in the business environment
4 To appreciate the ways in which societies change over time, together with the implications for international managers

Critical themes in this chapter

- **Multidimensional environment – MNEs operating in differing cultural environments**
- **Multilayered environment – national culture and subcultures within countries**
- **Changing societies – how societies change in response to factors such as industrialization and urbanization**
- **Emerging economies – impacts of rapid economic growth on populations**

Too hot or just right? Hundreds of different types of peppers are grown around the world, adding distinctive qualities to a huge diversity of national cuisines

Source: Istock

When cultures collide: Vale of Brazil takes over Inco of Canada

Nickel mining in Sudbury (Ontario) in Canada goes back to the nineteenth century, in a history dominated by one company, Inco, which became one of Canada's largest mining companies. Sudbury's mining community has evolved a strong local ethos, reflected in the belligerence of its trade union, the Canadian limb of the United Steelworkers of America (USW), which can point to miners' high wage levels and generous pension scheme as proud achievements. A profit-sharing scheme has helped to boost miners' wages, and they enjoy a defined-benefits pension scheme in an era when many companies globally are going over to defined-contributions schemes, with no assurance of levels of benefits. However, these achievements looked to be under threat when Inco was taken over by Vale of Brazil. Vale is the world's largest iron ore producer, and its purchase of Inco in 2006, for about $18.9 billion, represented a strategic departure into a more diversified mining operation. It was the largest acquisition ever made by a Brazilian company, signalling the rise of emerging economies in global business.

As a former state-owned company, Vale has shone as a Brazilian national champion since its privatization in 1997. Its charismatic CEO, Roger Agnelli, is eager to take on new challenges and further rapid expansion, describing Vale as 'a company with attitude' (Simon and Wheatley, 2010). Inco, by contrast, had become rather complacent and lacking in a strong sense of direction. It presented itself as a takeover target with investment potential, involving the prospect of more jobs and improved productivity. These aims found favour with the federal government of Canada, which approved the takeover. However, Vale immediately ran into difficulties with its Canadian acquisition, renamed Vale Inco. Inco had a well-established way of working, but Vale had ambitious plans to make the operations globally competitive. A meeting of the two sets of executives a few weeks after the purchase

finished in acrimony, with one of the new owners asking: 'How come, if you're so smart, you didn't take *us* over?' (Simon and Wheatley, 2010 [authors' italics]). Of the 29 executives present that day, only six remain.

Since the takeover, Vale has invested in new plant for the acquired nickel operations in Canada, but it has made little progress in relations with the workforce. In 2009, Vale proposed a modification of the profit-sharing scheme and an end to the existing pension scheme – contract changes which the company viewed as reasonable in terms of the industry globally. However, a bitter labour dispute ensued. A strike was called in July 2009. Striking workers took against what they saw as the dictatorial style of the new owners, who 'just want to show us that they're the boss' (Austen, 2010). The clash has been depicted as one between Brazilian and Canadian cultures – the one of an aggressive emerging market and the other of an old-world company with inward-looking values. Certainly, Vale has taken a robust line against the trade unions, which it perceives as obstructive, launching several disciplinary actions against union members. The clash of cultures has also been attributed to the differences between nickel mining, which relies on skilled workers, and iron ore production, Vale's main business, which is technologically less sophisticated and relies on low-skill workers.

The first CEO brought in by Vale to run Vale Inco was a technical expert, who spoke English poorly. In 2008, he was replaced by Tito Martins, a more amenable executive, with greater communication skills and appreciation of the strong feelings on both sides. Vale's CEO has said, 'it can't be easy to have me as a boss', but now admits of the labour dispute, 'It is a question of cultures that have to adjust' (Simon and Wheatley, 2010).

The strike was finally settled in July 2010, with the help of government mediators, nearly one year after it started, making this one of the longest strikes in

▶ More online … Vale Inco's website is www.inco.com

Canada's mining industry. A five-year agreement was reached, involving compromises on both sides. The unions agreed a less generous pension scheme for new workers, and agreed to a capping of their bonus payments under the profit-sharing scheme. Vale offered wage rises and a cap on bonus payments which was more generous to workers than the terms they had offered at the outset of the long dispute.

Sources: Simon, B. and Wheatley, J. (2010) 'Heading in opposite directions', *Financial Times*, 11 March; Austen, I. (2010) 'Some in Canada say strike shows risk of foreign control', *New York Times*, 13 January; Statement by Tito Martins, 18 March 2010, at http://valeinconegotiations.com

Striking Canadian miners resisted changes brought in by the new Brazilian owners of their company, but the gulf between their cultures – which seemed unbridgeable – was resolved through give and take on both sides

Source: Press Association

Questions for discussion

◆ Why was Inco considered to be an attractive takeover target?

◆ Describe the culture clashes between Vale and Inco.

◆ What recommendations would you make to Vale for managing future takeovers?

Introduction

Globalization has brought people from different parts of the world and from different cultural backgrounds into routine contact with each other, and with each other's cultures. But does greater interaction imply that people are drawing closer together and becoming more like each other? An international businessperson will argue on the basis of personal experience that negotiating a business deal in Morocco is very different from negotiating a similar deal in Japan or Germany. In each case, achieving a successful outcome, in both the initial agreement and the long-term business relationship, will depend on sensitivity to differences in languages, value systems and norms of behaviour between themselves and their hosts. In short, being attuned to cultural differences can directly affect the success or failure of the project.

This chapter has two broad aims. The first is to gain an understanding of how culture influences business activities and organizations across the globe. The second aim is to understand how societies are changing, including population changes and the impacts of globalization. While there is abundant evidence, such as the explosive growth of internet use, pointing to an emerging global culture, there is also considerable evidence that local cultural identities are not withering away, as some expected, but are adapting and persisting in the new global environment. The dynamic between the global and the local is helping to shape corporate strategy. For international business, grasping this dynamic interaction is the key to 'riding the waves of culture' (Trompenaars, 1994). We begin by defining culture, looking at the dimensions of culture in society, and the makeup of specific cultural identities among the world's peoples.

What is culture and how is it relevant to business?

Culture has been defined in many different ways, reflecting the variety of cultural phenomena that can be observed. Language, religious ritual, and art are just a few examples of cultural symbols whose shared meanings form the unique fingerprint of a particular society. **Culture** can be broadly defined as, 'a learned, shared, compelling, interrelated set of symbols whose meanings provide a set of orientations for members of a society' (Terpstra and David, 1991: 6). Inevitably, we all view and interpret the world around us through a cultural 'filter' to some degree. As we highlighted in Chapter 1, ethnocentrism denotes the inflexible approach of relating to the world only in terms of our own culture, while polycentrism is the approach of attempting to overcome our own cultural assumptions and to develop an openness and understanding of other cultures. Successful international business relationships depend in large measure on developing a polycentric approach in situations where cross-cultural issues arise, such as joint ventures.

culture shared, learned values, norms of behaviour, means of communication and other outward expressions which distinguish one group of people from another

Figure 6.1 presents many common aspects of culture. Culture includes values and beliefs shared by a group, and also norms of behaviour expected of group members. Values relate primarily to notions of good and evil, right and wrong. Values also include notions of the individual in relation to the group. An important distinguishing characteristic of particular western value systems, for example, is the intrinsic value accorded to the individual. Where individualism is highly valued, the society's institutional and governance structures will seek to guarantee individual freedoms. The growth of democracy in countries with strong individualist cultures is no coincidence, but an outcome of value systems. By contrast, societies that place greater value

▶ More online ... Coca-Cola is at www.coca-cola.com

on the collectivity, such as the family or the kinship group, are likely to develop institutional structures which are more paternalistic, that is, dominated by a father figure. These societies are likely to value group loyalty more highly than individual freedoms. These dimensions are further discussed in the section on culture theories.

Values and beliefs
Moral values,
aesthetic values

Language
Written, spoken,
gestures

Religion
Organized religions,
religious practices

Customs
Festival, national
celebrations

Culture

**Societal
characteristics**
Family roles,
attitudes to
education

**Norms of
behaviour**
Dress, etiquette

**Geographic
homeland**

Music, art,
dance

**National symbols
and myths**

Figure 6.1 **Aspects of
culture**

Norms relate to patterns and standards of behaviour. They shape what is considered normal and abnormal behaviour. Manner of dress, food and the etiquette associated with eating and drinking are also obvious distinguishing features of a culture. Norms within societies relate to the family, education and gender roles. Norms often reflect values, and, like values, can derive from religious beliefs and take on religious significance in many societies. Norms may also reflect customs which distinguish societies one from another. For businesspeople in a foreign environment, an understanding of local culture is needed not just in the context of doing business, but in general social relations with hosts. Indeed, in Asian cultures, doing business is not confined merely to working hours, but blends into social occasions such as meals together. Here the bonds of trust are sown which are crucial to a successful business relationship.

Values and norms of behaviour are learned in the social context – we are not born with them. For this reason they are not fixed and static, but are capable of change. Societies may evolve over time, and individuals may change when they move to a new environment. Organizations, too, change as they expand internationally. One of the themes of this chapter is the extent to which growth in interactions between cultures, and the growth of international markets and global brands such as McDonald's and Nike are leading to a global or 'cosmopolitan' culture. The Big Mac and Coca-Cola epitomize the uniform standard product for all markets. But in fact, McDonald's has long been sensitive to differing local tastes, offering the teriyaki burger in Japan, for example, although relying on their core brands as the mainstay of the business. Waning enthusiasm for hamburgers in their mature markets, however, has given impetus to changes in strategy (see closing case study). Coca-Cola, too, has revised its global strategy, offering different products to suit consumers in different markets, under a variety of brand names. Similarly, entertainment and media industries, including music and film, present a mixed picture: the emergence of large global companies, but also much local output designed for local tastes. We live in a world in which emerging economies are becoming increasingly influential culturally as well as economically. India's thriving film industry, usually referred to as 'Bollywood' as it is centred in Bombay (Mumbai), was founded to cater for local tastes, but, not surprisingly, is going global. Bollywood companies are now financing much of the output of Hollywood, home of America's film industry.

Summary points Aspects of culture

* Values, beliefs and norms of behaviour are central to culture. They are acquired through social interactions which give members of a group a sense of identity.

* Cultures can change over time, and the impact of global brands has arguably changed patterns of consumption, but local differences remain potent.

National cultures

national culture
distinctive values and behavioural norms which distinguish one nation from other

Peoples or nations are distinguishable from each other by language, religion, ethnic or racial identity, and, above all, by a shared cultural history. Together, these distinguishing characteristics blend into a **national culture**. Research has shown that people have acquired their basic value systems by the age of ten (Hofstede, 1994). It is during these formative years that national culture exerts its strongest influence, through family and early schooling. National culture influences family life, education, organizational culture, and economic and political structures. The sense of belonging to a nation is one of the most important focal points of cultural identity. In the course of time, myth mixes with historical events in the collective memory, and the associated symbols serve as powerful emotive links between present and past, and even future.

nation-state social, administrative and territorial unit into which the world's peoples are divided

The **nation-state** combines the concepts of cultural bonds created by the nation with the territorial and organizational structures of the state. The world's peoples comprise many more nations than states, and hence most states contain multiple cultural and national identities. There are two main reasons. First, through immigration, people move to other countries, usually in search of betterment and security. Secondly, in many countries there are indigenous peoples whose communities pre-date the arrival of colonizing outsiders who later founded the state. Historically, nations have sought self-determination for their own people, often through nationalist movements. New nation-states thus represent the culmination of national aspirations. Largely as a result of the break-up of colonial empires, the number of nation-states has grown dramatically since the end of the Second World War. However, many of these states have proved to be ill-fitting administrative containers for the multiple social and ethnic groups within their borders.

Internal social tensions characterize many of the world's states, especially where minority ethnic groups feel disadvantaged by the state's institutions and laws. In times of economic stress, these tensions can come to the fore, as minority groups are typically poorer and less well educated than fellow citizens in mainstream groups associated with the national culture. For example, Spanish-speaking, or 'Hispanic', people resident in the US are largely of immigrant background, mainly Mexican. They are less

► More online ... Information from the US Census Bureau is at www.census.gov
In the UK, the Office for National Statistics has population data at www.statistics.gov.uk

well off than non-Hispanic groups. Real median income in the US fell between 2007 and 2008, but the fall was greater for Hispanics, at 5.6%, while the fall in non-Hispanics' income was 2.6% (US Census Bureau, 2009). Worryingly, poverty rose in 2008, and the rise was steeper among Hispanics, from 21.5% in 2007 to 23.2% in 2008. The rise in poverty among non-Hispanics was from 8.2% to 8.6% (US Census Bureau, 2009).

Almost all countries have minority groups. In most South American countries, indigenous peoples form sizeable groups and have distinctive cultures, which co-exist uneasily with the Spanish-speaking or, in the case of Brazil, Portuguese-speaking, majority. In both cases, the dominant language is a legacy of the colonial era. Discrimination against minority cultures is a common phenomenon, despite efforts by governments to promote social cohesion. Language is one of the most distinctive attributes of a people, signifying cultural heritage and a person's sense of belonging.

Summary points **National cultures**

● National cultures distinguish different peoples or nations. A shared language, history national symbols and sense of homeland help to give nations a sense of cultural identity.

● Majority cultures and minority cultures characterize most nation- states, causing some tension, especially where minorities are discriminated against.

Critical thinking

Identifying with the nation-state

Think of a nation-state which you are familiar with. Does it have a strong national culture, or is there a mixture of diverse cultural identities within its borders? If the latter, explain what they are.

Languages

Language is the basic means of communication between people, which facilitates social interaction and fosters a system of shared values and norms. Language is much more than the vocabulary and grammar that make up written and spoken expression. The researchers E.T. and M.R. Hall distinguish between 'low-context' and 'high-context' cultures (Hall and Hall, 1960). In a **low-context culture**, communication is clear and direct; speakers come straight to the point and say exactly what they mean. The US is a good example of the low-context culture. In the **high-context culture**, much goes unsaid; depending on the relationship between the speakers, each is able to interpret body language and 'read between the lines'. In this type of culture, ambiguity is the norm, and directness is avoided. Asian cultures fall into this type. For Americans, meeting with people from high-context cultures can seem frustrating, as they are unsure where they stand, while their Asian counterparts are unsettled by their directness of approach, which may come across as insincerity.

low-context culture
culture in which communication is clear and direct, rather than relying on patterns of behaviour

high-context culture
culture in which communication relies heavily on the behavioural dimension, such as 'body language'

In terms of numbers, the linguistic family of Chinese is spoken by the largest number of people. As Figure 6.2 shows, Chinese speakers far outnumber any other language group, amounting to about 20% of the world's population. It is notable that five of the ten most widely spoken first languages are from the Bric countries. The large number of Portuguese speakers is due to the size of Brazil. Hindi and Bengali are both Indian languages.

► More online ... Ethnologue's website is www.ethnologue.com

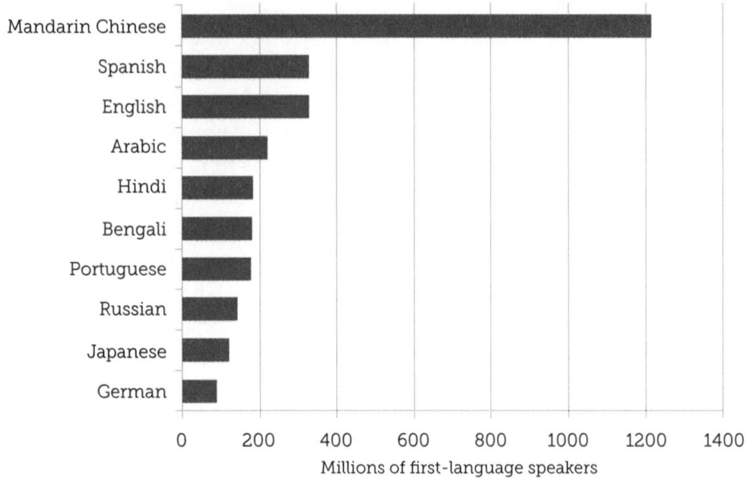

Figure 6.2 **The world's ten most widely spoken languages**

Source: Lewis, M.P. (ed.) (2009) *Ethnologue: Languages of the World*, 16th edn (Dallas, Texas: SIL International)

In most countries, one or more dominant languages exist alongside minority languages, which may be concentrated in specific geographical regions. Canada has two official languages, English and French, and the minority French speakers have a history of separatist activism. Switzerland, by contrast, has four official languages (German, French, Italian and Romansh) which co-exist in harmony. Linguistic diversity within a state may arise in several different ways:

- A minority language may represent a native culture, such as the Indian nations which inhabited North and South America before the arrival of European settlers. The US, Australia and South Africa are all settler societies where tensions erupted between the new arrivals and existing native cultures. These tensions are still observable today, as evidenced by the second-class citizen status of which Native Americans complain.

- Colonizing states introduced their own language into their colonies. The western imperial powers of the sixteenth to the nineteenth centuries included the British, French, Dutch, Belgians, Spanish and Portuguese. All left their national languages in their colonies, where the colonial language became that of the elites, as well as that of government and administration. The many indigenous peoples spoke native languages, but struggled to maintain their cultures against the tide of colonialism. Today, most of South America is Spanish-speaking, and Spanish companies in recent years have expanded in the region, attracted by a perceived affinity with these markets, derived from a common language.

- Immigration can create linguistic diversity. Immigrants are faced with the difficulties of **assimilation** in a new culture, or maintaining a separate identity. Where immigrants are concentrated geographically, they may form a **subculture** in which they speak their home language.

assimilation of cultures process by which minority cultures become integrated into the mainstream culture of a nation

subculture minority culture in a society, often associated with immigrant communities

Governments' education policies can be directed towards protecting minority languages or, more commonly, compelling schools to teach the dominant language in order to facilitate assimilation of minority cultures into the mainstream culture. In countries that have decentralized authority in regions or provinces, the regional authorities may wish to maintain the local language in the school system as a means of maintaining the local culture. In Spain, there are several 'autonomous regions', where regional languages, such as Catalan, are strongly in evidence.

▶ More online ... Statistics about internet usage are at www.internetworldstats.com

English: the global language?

The importance of English as a global language extends far beyond the number of native speakers. English is the commonest language for the global media and the internet (see Figure 6.3), and the commonest second language. For the many people who travel internationally, English is a recognized means of communication, often when neither of the parties speaks English as a first language. These globetrotters include not only businesspeople and diplomats, but tourists, sportspeople, academics, and students. The English language in these contexts is an intercultural means of communicating. Businesspeople are likely to use English in their international business activities, but speak their own first language at home. By the same token, while Hindi is the official language of India, English as an associate national language facilitates communication between the many non-Hindi-speaking groups. India is one of the world's most multilingual countries, with fourteen major languages and many more minor ones. English is spoken by about 50% of India's population. Moreover, in the booming information technology industry, the predominance of the English language is proving a location advantage.

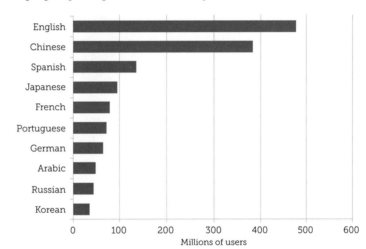

Figure 6.3 **The top ten internet languages**

Source: Internet World Statistics, 2009, at www.internetworldstats.com

---

Summary points **Languages**

◆ Some languages are considered low-context, in which direct speaking prevails, whereas others are high-context, where personal relations and body language are more important.

◆ In most countries there is linguistic diversity, reflecting multiple cultures: a dominant language prevails, but minority languages, signifying distinctive subcultures, indicate persisting linguistic diversity.

◆ Although Chinese is the world's most commonly spoken first language, English is the dominant language of the internet.

Religions

In many cultures, values and beliefs are dictated by religion. There are many thousands of distinct religions and religious movements among the world's population.

religion set of beliefs and moral precepts which guide people in their lives; often contained in sacred scriptures and propounded by spiritual leaders

They range from simple folk religions to highly refined systems of beliefs, with set rituals, organized worship, sacred texts and a hierarchy of religious leaders. A **religion** calls on its followers to believe in supernatural forces that affect their lives, and to follow prescribed moral rules. Religion may exercise considerable secular and political – as well as religious – influence, and can form a major unifying force in society. Religious divides, both within states and between states, can also be a source of friction. Research suggests that a large proportion of terrorism stems from religious groups, many of these either independent or on the fringes of mainstream religions (Juergensmeyer, 2003).

Most of the world's states adhere in principle to the right of religious freedom, allowing multiple religions to worship freely. But in practice, there are exceptions, where the observance of particular religions is prohibited by state authorities. States may have a dominant or even an official religion, although most modern states follow the principle of separation of church and state. Religious affiliation may coincide with a sense of nationhood, as in Poland, where being a Pole and being Roman Catholic are integrally linked in the nation's sense of identity. The church in Poland is still a potent force, but the government stepped back from a national church in its new constitution in 1997, and opted instead for an expression of the importance of the church in national life. In countries where religion is a major element of the cultural environment, sensitivity to local religious beliefs and practices is particularly important in building business relations.

Religions with the largest following globally are shown in Figure 6.4. The two major religions are Christianity and Islam (whose adherents are called Muslims). Both are 'monotheistic', that is, believing in one God, in contrast to polytheistic religion such as Hinduism, in which there is a panoply of gods. Christianity and Islam are both 'proselytising religions', which means that they deliberately aim to expand numbers and convert new followers. Both are organized religions. However, as indicated below, under the general umbrella of Christianity there are numerous organized religions, many specific to countries or regions. Note the importance of indigenous and traditional African religions in this figure, representing numerous types of religious groupings, often tribal and highly local, lacking the organizational structures of the major religions. We look at the major organized religions in this section.

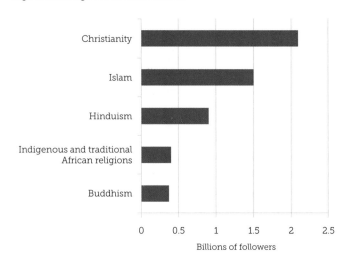

Figure 6.4 **Religions with the largest numbers of followers**

Source: Major religions of the world, 2007, at www.adherents.com

Billions of followers

▶ More online ... Statistics on many religions can be found at www.adherents.com

Christianity

Christianity
monotheistic religion
based on belief in Jesus
Christ, whose teachings
are in the Bible

About two billion people, or 33% of the world's population, identify with Christianity in some way. Through missionary activity, **Christianity** has spread from Europe and America to all parts of the globe. While all Christians believe in the divinity of Jesus Christ and regard the Bible as authoritative, differences of interpretation have emerged, leading to a great deal of fragmentation among Christians. The first of Christianity's major splits occurred in the eleventh century, between the Orthodox church and the Roman Catholic church. The Roman Catholics are now by far the more numerous, numbering about 1.13 billion people (Catholic News Agency, 2009). Followers of the Orthodox rites, numbering some 300 million, are still very influential in many countries, including Greece and Russia.

The second major split in the Christian world occurred in the sixteenth century, when the Protestant churches separated from Rome. Protestants went on to establish themselves throughout Europe and America, through different denominations, such as Methodists and Baptists. Protestantism is associated with the principle that individual salvation is achievable independently of the institutional church. Recent trends in both Protestantism and Roman Catholicism have been the growth of more evangelical groups, with growing numbers of followers outside traditional centres. Numbers of Catholics and Protestants have risen substantially in Latin America and Africa.

Summary points Christianity

◆ Christianity has the greatest overall number of adherents globally, although they are divided among a number of different organized churches.

◆ About half of all Christians are Roman Catholics. Catholicism is growing in Latin America and Africa more strongly than in traditional European centres.

Islam

Muslims number about 1.15 billion globally, spread among many different countries, ranging from the Middle East and Africa to areas now part of Russia, and extending as far as China and Malaysia in East Asia. They make up a majority of the population in over 30 countries, and large minorities in others. Through immigration, they now form significant minorities in most European countries. Founded by the prophet Muhammad in the seventh century, **Islam** unites its followers through shared faith, shared ritual in everyday life, and belief in the words of the Koran, the sacred book. There are two major branches of Islam: Sunni and Shiite. For the Muslim, religious ritual is part of everyday life, not confined to worship on a particular day of the week. While codes of conduct form part of the values of all religions, Islam is particularly endowed with formal prescriptive guidance in all aspects of life, including social relations, social behaviour, rules for the consumption of food and drink, and the role and appearance of women in society. Religious leaders play an important guiding role and are influential, particularly in education (see case study in this chapter).

Islam monotheistic
religion based on the
teachings of the prophet
Muhammad, as revealed
in the Koran; followers
are referred to as Muslims

An enterprise culture is fostered in Muslim societies, and economic development is promoted. However, it is forbidden to earn a profit based on the exploitation of others. Interests payments are seen as sinful, and therefore the common forms of financing used in western countries violate Islamic law, known as Sharia law, or the

▸ More online ... The BBC is a good source for general information about world religions, at www.bbc.co.uk/religion

Shari'a (defined in Chapter 8). Islamic banking has developed systems complying with Sharia law, and western businesses are able to make financial arrangements that accommodate both sides. These arrangements show the adaptability of Islamic institutions to modern business conditions. Similarly, state courts have grown up in Muslim countries, where traditionally there were only religious courts. State courts can apply both religious law and western-style commercial law, signifying an accommodation with western legal forms. The issue of westernization divides Muslims. 'Westernization' refers to a society's adoption of western culture and values, and is associated with processes of modernization, while 'Islamic fundamentalism' refers to maintenance of the supremacy of Islam in all aspects of society. Westernization has not been universally welcomed by Muslims, many of whom see their religious values being undermined in the process.

Summary points Islam

◆ Islam is the dominant religion in some 30 countries, and a significant minority in many others.

◆ For Muslims, religious practices are part of daily life, impacting on social, economic and political spheres.

Asian religions

Asia has been a rich source of some of the world's oldest religions. Hinduism, Buddhism and Confucianism, among many others, originated in Asia, and still have millions of followers.

Hinduism

Hinduism polytheistic religion whose followers are concentrated in India

Unlike either Christianity or Islam, **Hinduism** is polytheistic, its believers worshipping many different gods through many different rituals. The sheer diversity of Hinduism is a major feature, despite the fact that geographically Hindus are mostly concentrated in the Indian subcontinent. Hindus make up 80% of the population of India. Hinduism is an ancient religion, older than all other major world religions. In keeping with its ancient origins, Hinduism resembles a folk religion, associated with rural communities and accessible to illiterate as well as literate followers. An important social and economic aspect of Hinduism is the **caste system** of rigid social stratification. It holds that a person is born into a particular station in society's hierarchy, which is fixed for life. For example, those at the bottom, the 'untouchables', have no prospect of rising out of this group into a higher caste. Numbering an estimated 160 million people, India's untouchables often suffer discrimination. This system, while officially abolished in the modern state, is still a force in Indian society, as is Hinduism itself. Caste-based political parties, as well as the Hindu nationalist party, the Bharatiya Janata Party (BJP), are active in India's somewhat turbulent democratic political scene.

caste system social stratification system based on birth; associated with Hinduism

Buddhism

Buddhism Asian religion based on the teachings of Buddha

Buddhism also originated in India, where it has some five million followers. Buddhism has also been an important religious influence in China and Japan. A feature of the Buddhist heritage in all these countries has been its assimilation with other religions: in Indian temples, Buddhism and Hinduism mingle; in Japan, Buddhist temples and Shinto shrines rub shoulders. Buddhism does not recognize the many gods of Hinduism; nor does it subscribe to the caste system. The Buddha's teachings form the basis of the religion. They centre on the 'eight-fold-path' whereby the individual goes through a series of rebirths before reaching *nirvana*. As the Buddha's teachings were never written down, Buddhism split into a number of different schools. The two major ones are the Hinayana, which subscribes to a more ascetic lifestyle, and is followed mainly in Sri Lanka, Thailand, and Burma; and the Mahayana, which is less austere, and is followed in China and Japan. From this latter school arose Ch'an Buddhism, or Zen Buddhism, which became a quite distinctive sect, highly influential in the cultures of both China and Japan. Zen's attraction has been its simplicity and directness, with its emphasis on meditation and rejection of dogmatic teaching. Some large Japanese companies send new employees for Zen training.

Confucianism

Confucianism ancient Chinese ethical and philosophical system based on the teachings of Confucius

Confucianism is often considered the foundation stone of Asian values. Founded in the fifth century BC by the Chinese philosopher, Confucius, Confucianism is more a set of moral precepts than a religion. Simon Leys, the modern translator of the *Analects of Confucius*, describes it as 'an affirmation of humanist ethics ... the spiritual cornerstone of the most populous and oldest living civilization on earth' (Leys, 1997: xvii). At the heart of Confucianism is the family and 'filial piety', the paramount value of family loyalty. The countries with a strong Confucian heritage – China, Korea and Japan – have in common the prevalence of family-based social organization. In China, Confucianism was rejected by the communist revolution of 1949, but nationalists fleeing to Taiwan maintained Confucian beliefs, evidenced in temples and religious practices. Confucian heritage links many Asian economies, including Japan and the tiger economies of South Korea, Taiwan and Hong Kong, where Confucian values have been adapted to the needs of modernization.

Summary points Asian religions

* Hinduism, Buddhism and Confucianism are all ancient religions which have to some extent become intermingled in the societies in which they are influential.
* These religions are less hierarchical than the more organized religions of Christianity and Islam, stressing the personal religious journey of each adherent.

How religion impacts on business life

Religious beliefs and practices have direct and indirect influences on many aspects of business life. This is especially true in countries where religious practices, for example daily prayers in Muslim countries, are intertwined with daily living. Doing business is not confined to what happens in corporate meeting rooms. Often the behavioural norms that are observed in business life, such as dress code, reflect religious values. Furthermore, in many countries, social occasions are important aspects of doing business, helping the parties to get to know each other as people. Many pitfalls lie in wait for western businesspeople unfamiliar with the ways in which food and drink are consumed in specific Asian societies.

Some of the aspects of religion that impact on business life are shown in Figure 6.5. Rules about clothing operate in some countries, such as the requirement of long clothing for women in Muslim societies. The consumption of alcoholic drink is also forbidden in these societies. There are restrictions on types of food, such as the

Religious practices
e.g. daily prayers

Restrictions on
trading in keeping
with religious
observances
e.g. particular places
and days

Clothing
requirements
dictated by
religion

**The cultural
environment
of business**

Religious
festivals and
celebrations

Religious law –
restrictions on
business
transactions

Religious
requirements
regarding food
and drink

Figure 6.5 **Religious
influences on doing
business**

prohibition on beef for Hindus or pork for Muslims. Religious festivals, such as Ramadan for Muslims, are periods with their own observances. Similarly, there are restrictions on business hours in many countries, often due to a designated day of religious observance, such as Sunday in predominantly Christian countries. In many countries, there are restrictions on media content deemed to conflict with the main religion. Of direct importance to people doing business in Muslim countries are the restrictions on financial transactions which are not compliant with Sharia law. These countries, however, have established western legal systems specifically for commercial transactions. In Muslim societies, therefore, there is co-existence between many westernized forms and the more traditional religious culture.

Summary points Religion and business

◆ Religious rules regarding social behaviour affect businesses in their dealings with other organizations and with employees.

◆ In societies with a prescribed religion, foreign businesses can find numerous constraints, including legal frameworks, within which they must operate.

Critical thinking
Business and religion
In what ways do business values and traditional religious values tend to clash, and what have the experiences of today's developed countries shown that can be of use to those in developing countries currently experiencing economic development along with changes in culture?

Culture theories

Differences in national values and attitudes have been the subject of considerable research. We consider two main theories here, those of Geert Hofstede and Fons Trompenaars.

Hofstede's cultural dimensions

Hofstede developed a theory of culture which holds that cultural and sociological differences between nations can be categorized and quantified, allowing us to compare national cultures. Hofstede's research was carried out in 50 countries, among IBM employees in each country. An obvious weakness of the research is its reliance solely on IBM employees, who are a special group in themselves and not necessarily representative of the countries in which they live. However, his research does yield interesting comparisons between national cultures, and has served as a benchmark for cultural research.

Hofstede distinguishes four cultural dimensions – to which he later added a fifth – as variables. He uses these dimensions to compare value systems at various levels: in the family, at school, in the workplace, in the state, and in ways of thinking generally. The cultural dimensions are:

- *Power distance*, or the extent to which members of a society accept a hierarchical or unequal power structure. In large power distance countries, people consider themselves to be inherently unequal, and there is more dependence of subordinates on bosses. The boss is likely to be autocratic or paternalistic in these countries – to which subordinates may respond to positively, or negatively. In small power distance countries, people tend to see themselves more as equals. When they occupy subordinate and superior roles in organizations, these situations are just that – roles, not reflecting inherent differences. Organizations in these countries tend to be flatter, with a more consultative style of management. Asian, Latin American and African countries tend to have large power distance, while Northern Europe has relatively small power distance.
- *Uncertainty avoidance*, or how members of a society cope with the uncertainties of everyday life. High levels of stress and anxiety denote high uncertainty avoidance countries. These cultures tend to be more expressive and emotional than low uncertainty avoidance countries. The latter have lower anxiety levels, but their easy-going exterior may indicate simply greater control over anxiety, not its non-existence. High uncertainty avoidance countries are in Latin American, Latin European and Mediterranean countries, along with Japan and South Korea. Ranking relatively low are other Asian countries and other European countries.
- *Individualism*, or the extent to which individuals perceive themselves as independent and autonomous beings. At the opposite extreme to individualism is collectivism, in which people see themselves as integrated into 'ingroups'. High individualism scores occurred mainly in the English-speaking countries, while low individualism was prevalent in Latin American and Asian countries. Hofstede remarks that management techniques and training packages, which almost all originate in the individualist countries, are based on cultural assumptions which are out of tune with the more collectivist cultures (Hofstede, 1994).
- *Masculinity*, or the extent to which a society is inclined towards aggressive and materialistic behaviour. This dimension tends to present stereotyped gender roles. Hofstede associates masculinity with assertiveness, toughness, and an emphasis on money and material things. At the opposite extreme is femininity, which denotes sensitivity, caring, and an emphasis on quality of life. Conflict and competition predominate in more masculine environments, whereas negotiation and compromise predominate in more feminine environments. According to Hofstede's results, the most masculine countries are Japan and Austria, while the most feminine are Sweden, Norway, the Netherlands and Denmark.

- *Long-term vs short-term orientation*, or people's time perspectives in their daily lives. Hofstede added this dimension as a result of work by another researcher, Michael Harris Bond, who found different time orientations between western and eastern ways of thinking. Short-term orientation stresses satisfying needs 'here-and-now', and is more characteristic of western cultures, whereas long-term orientation stresses virtuous living through thrift and persistence, and is prevalent in eastern cultures (Hofstede, 1996).

Table 6.1 **Ranks of selected countries on four dimensions of national culture, based on research by Hofstede**

	Power distance (PD) rank	Individualism rank	Masculinity rank	Uncertainty avoidance rank
Group 1 (high PD + low individualism)				
Brazil	14	26–27	27	21–22
Indonesia	8–9	47–48	30–31	41–42
Malaysia	1	36	25–26	46
Mexico	5-6	32	6	18
Group 2 (low PD + high individualism)				
Finland	46	17	47	31–32
Germany	42–44	15	9–10	29
Netherlands	40	4–5	51	35
Sweden	47–48	10–11	53	49–50
UK	42–44	3	9–10	47–48
USA	38	1	15	43
Group 3 (varying patterns)				
France	15–16	10–11	35–36	10–15
Greece	27–28	30	18–19	1
Japan	33	22–23	1	7

Rank: 1 = highest; 53 = lowest

Source: Hofstede, G. (1994) *Cultures and Organizations* (London: HarperCollins), various tables

Hofstede was able to group countries together in clusters, and also to make correlations between the different dimensions. Some of these are shown in Table 6.1. For countries in Group 1, high power distance combines with low individualism, suggesting that where people depend on ingroups, they also depend on power figures. Conversely, in cultures where people are less dependent on ingroups, shown in Group 2, they are also less dependent on powerful leaders. There are some anomalies, however. France seems to have high individualism, but also medium power distance. Japan seems to be roughly in the middle in both power distance and individualism. Japanese companies are usually depicted as collectivist ingroups, akin to a family relationship. This apparent contradiction in the research could reflect the nature of his survey sample, which focused on employees of a large American multinational company.

Summary points   Hofstede's cultural dimensions

◆ Hofstede classified national cultures on the basis of five dimensions: power distance, uncertainty avoidance,

individualism/collectivism, masculinity/femininity and long-term/short-term orientation.

◆ He grouped national cultures in clusters, observing correlations, for example, between individualism and small power distance.

Trompenaars' theory of relationships

More recent research by Fons Trompenaars also used the individualism/collectivism continuum as a key dimension. Trompenaars' research involved giving questionnaires to over 15,000 managers in 28 countries (Trompenaars, 1994). He identified five relationship orientations. These are:

- *Universalism vs Particularism* – Cultures with high universalism place more weight on formal rules, whereas more particularistic cultures value relationships more than formal rules or agreements. Western countries such as the UK, Australia and USA, Trompenaars found, tend to rate highly in universalism, whereas China rated highly in particularism.
- *Individualism vs Collectivism* – This relationship mirrors one of Hofstede's four dimensions, but the findings were somewhat different. Trompenaars found Japan to be much further towards the collectivist extreme. On the other hand, Mexico and the Czech Republic, which Hofstede had found to be more collectivist, now tend to individualism. This finding could be explained by the later date of the research data, reflecting the progress of market economies in both regions: the impact of Nafta in the case of Mexico, and the post-communist transition to a market economy in the case of the Czech Republic.
- *Neutral vs Emotional* – In a neutral culture, people are less inclined to show their feelings, whereas in an emotional culture, people are more open in showing emotion and expressing their views. In the findings, Japan has the most neutral culture, and Mexico the most emotional.
- *Specific vs Diffuse* – In a specific culture there is a clear separation between work and private life. In diffuse cultures, 'the whole person is involved in a business relationship', not merely the contracting role (Trompenaars, 1994: 9). Doing business in these cultures, therefore, involves building relationships, not simply focusing on the business deal in isolation. The US, Australia and the UK are examples of specific cultures, while China is an example of a diffuse culture.
- *Achievement vs Ascription* – In an achievement culture people derive status from their accomplishments and record. In an ascription culture status is what matters, which could relate to birth, family, gender or age. The US and UK are achievement cultures, whereas China and other Asian cultures are ascription cultures.

The research by Hofstede and by Trompenaars shed new light on the diversity among national cultures, dispelling the assumption that there is 'one best way' of managing and organizing people. International companies had assumed the universal application of management theories, but, in truth, many of their applications, such as pay-by-performance or management-by-objectives, were products of Anglo-Saxon culture, and unsuitable for other cultures with different values and norms. Just as standardized products do not suit all markets, organizations cannot be standardized, but must adapt to local social and cultural profiles.

▶ More online ... Nestlé's website is www.nestle.com

Summary points Trompenaars' theory of relationships

● By using Trompenaars' five relationship orientations, we can understand the ways in which superiors and subordinates interact in organizations based in different cultures.

● The research indicates that there is no one best way of managing people, but adaptation to social and cultural profiles is essential.

Organizational culture

organizational culture
an organization's values, behavioural norms and management style; also known as 'corporate culture'

Organizational culture or 'corporate culture', like national culture, focuses on values, norms and behavioural patterns shared by the group, in this case, the organization. Elements of organizational culture include the following:

- Common language and shared terminology
- Norms of behaviour, such as relations between management and employees
- Preferences for formal or informal means of communication within the company and with associated companies
- Dominant values of the organization, such as high product quality and customer orientation
- Degree of empowerment of employees throughout the organization
- Systems of rules that specify dos and don'ts of employee behaviour

The organization, however, unlike the nation, is an artificial creation, and a corporate culture is one that is deliberately fostered among employees, who may have come to the company from a variety of different cultural backgrounds. As we saw in Chapter 5, companies tend to reflect the national culture of their home country, despite globalization of their operations. Swiss multinationals, such as the food giant Nestlé, are among the most transnational, whereas US and Japanese companies are among the least transnational. Switzerland is highly multicultural, with a mixture of national cultures, including German, French, and Italian. Its organizations are thus well attuned to appreciating cultural differences in overseas subsidiaries. American or Japanese companies, on the other hand, are from countries of a dominant national culture and a single language. Boardrooms in both American and Japanese companies are dominated by home nationals, in contrast to Nestlé, whose board resembles a miniature UN.

Some multinational corporations see a strong corporate culture as a way of unifying the diverse national cultures represented by employees. Others evolve different organizational cultures in different locations, in effect incorporating a multiculturalism within the company. The need to manage cultural diversity may arise through a number of routes: the acquisition of a foreign subsidiary, a merger with another company, or a joint venture. In joint ventures, in particular, the need for co-operation and trust between partners is the key to long-term success. As we saw in Chapter 5, an organizational culture that promotes a unifying vision of where the company is going can be a valuable source of competitive advantage.

Yorihiko Kojima Chairman of Mitsubishi Corporation, the Japanese trading group

Like many Japanese executives, Yorihiko Kojima, who took over as CEO in 2004 and chairman in 2010, has been with the company virtually his entire career. But, unlike many of his counterparts in other Japanese companies, he has always had an outward-looking perspective. Mitsubishi Corporation is a vast trading group, or sogo shosha, whose activities span the globe and extend well beyond trading, involving investment and acquisitions. It has 500 affiliates worldwide, from steelmaking operations to operators of KFC restaurants. The company is part of the wider Mitsubishi keiretsu, the loose grouping which also includes the carmaker of the same name. They were linked in a formal holding company before the Second World War, but are now independent, although informal ties remain. Building large networks of companies gives its executives unique insights into how industries work across supply chains. Mr Kojima joined the company as an engineering graduate, wishing to work abroad, but had to work on improving his English before he got a foreign posting.

His early work within the company was in heavy industry, where the atmosphere was what many consider Japan's traditional corporate culture of

listening to ordinary workers' opinions and achieving consensus. He looks back on this

Yorihiko Kojima
Source: Mitsubishi

experience, in which open communications are the norm, as a kind of benchmark for successful relations between managers and employees.

His first job abroad was in Saudi Arabia, where he was involved in orders for the water treatment and air conditioning systems at Riyadh's new international airport. Here he worked under a Lebanese manager and with fellow workers who included American, British, French and Dutch. The experience was to be eye-opening. He had to learn to work in a multicultural work setting, but in the context of a local culture which was very different from his own.

Mitsubishi Corporation has prided itself on keeping its competitive edge by spotting potential innovations and investing in them. The New Business Initiative Group, started in 2000, has been one such initiative, with Mr Kojima as its head. Looking for new ideas in IT and other businesses, he feels his chief asset is his curiosity, listening as inventors and founders of businesses try to win a contract with Mitsubishi. When he took over as CEO of Mitsubishi Corporation in 2004, his first statement to employees was to slip out on their own 'runways', saying, 'Go out of the Mitsubishi world and talk to people outside' (*Asahi Shimbun*, 2004).

Sources: Sobel, J. (2009) 'A desire to speak up and speak out', *Financial Times*, 23 February; *Asahi Shimbun* (2004) 'Insight into leadership: Yorihiko Kojima', 13 November, at www.asahi.com

Summary points Organizational culture

◆ Organizational culture covers the firm's vision of itself and its pattern of communications within the organization and with outsiders.

◆ A corporate culture that promotes a strong, shared vision of the firm's strategy at the broadest level can help to unify the parts of the MNE, despite locational differences.

Critical thinking

Changing corporate culture

How does corporate culture reflect the national culture of its home country? Give some examples, which can include those in case studies in this book. Is a strong corporate culture based in national values an asset or liability in international business? Explain.

Changing societies

Societies are constantly changing, some in dramatic ways and others in ways that are scarcely perceptible. Industrialization, which has taken place rapidly in some countries, brings changes in people's livelihoods and style of life, which becomes urbanized as people move from the countryside to cities. Mobility also encompasses movements of people to other countries, usually in the hope of a better life. Economic development generally brings growing prosperity, improvements in health and longer life expectancy. The impacts of these changes on whole societies add up to more diverse populations and growing urban populations. Changes also present challenges. Growing populations in developing countries place pressure on scarce resources. Ageing populations in developed countries are a growing concern for future prosperity. We look at each of these phenomena in turn in this section.

Migration

The urge to move to 'greener pastures' is not a recent phenomenon. People have been on the move throughout history. Movements that result in a permanent change of residence are referred to as **migration**, and are a normal aspect of most societies (de Haan, 1999). Migration can be internal, from one place to another within the same country, or it can be international, from one country to another. 'Immigrants' refer to people coming into a country, and 'emigrants' refer to people leaving a country. Push and pull factors are involved. Some push factors are escape from poverty, natural disasters or religious persecution. Often, when these factors are involved, people move en masse across borders. Pull factors include the prospect – real or imagined – of a good job and greater economic opportunities.

migration movement of people from one place to another, which can be within a country or between countries, with a view to making a new life in the new location

The most important historic examples of population outflow have been the movements of European settlers to the new worlds of the Americas and Australia. From about the sixteenth century, people emigrated in search of more space, economic riches, a better life and also, simply, adventure. The exodus of Europeans, mainly to the Americas, in the nineteenth century created the world's largest international population flow, amounting to a million arrivals a year in the years leading up to the First World War. Push and pull factors both played a part. In the early phase, people left the densely populated areas of Northern Europe to seek more space and a better

► More online ... UNDP's Human Development Report of 2009 is on migration, entitled
Overcoming barriers: human mobility and development. It can be found at www.undp.org

living in America, but later immigrants came from the poor areas of Southern and Eastern Europe.

In the period following the Second World War, international migration has been mainly from developing countries to developed ones, chiefly in North America and the industrial areas of Europe. This flow of labour reflects the gulf between richer and poorer economies, as well as the rapid rates of population increase in the developing countries (UNDP, 2009). It might be expected that with globalization processes, including better transport, the numbers of people on the move would rise substantially. However, the rate of international migration has fallen slightly in recent years. The annual rate of change was 2.7% globally in the years 1990 to 1995, and was projected to be 1.7% for 2005–2010 (UN Population Division, 2008). One reason is probably the growth in barriers and administrative hurdles that governments have imposed at their borders, deterring would-be immigrants (UNDP, 2009).

Many countries welcome – and even depend on – immigrant workers, particularly during periods of rapid growth. Post-war economic development in France and Germany depended in large measure on immigrant labour. In Germany, many of these immigrants came as 'guest-workers', on short-term contracts. However, millions of these workers, a large proportion of whom were Turkish, stayed on and have become settled. A recent trend has been migration from countries in Africa and Asia to the oil-rich countries of the Gulf region, mainly Kuwait, the United Arab Emirates and Saudi Arabia. International migrants account for about one in ten inhabitants of developed countries, but in some countries the proportion is much higher, as Figure 6.6 shows.

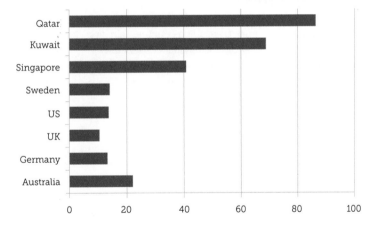

Figure 6.6 **International migrants as a percentage of the population**

Source: UN Population Division database (2008 revision), at www.un.org

Migration impacts on both the sending and receiving countries. Highly skilled workers, such as scientists, doctors, and engineers, come to industrialized regions from developing countries, forming a 'brain drain' which deprives their home countries of their skills, but provides broader individual opportunities for self-betterment. These workers are welcomed by industrialized societies to fill gaps in their own workforces. On the other hand, poor, unskilled migrants, often without legal documentation, enter a country and find work in jobs that local people are reluctant to take (for example in agriculture). These people pose a number of issues for both government and society in recipient countries. Employment, housing, healthcare and education are some of the main areas where they have particular needs, often because of language difficulties. **Remittances** sent by workers back to their home countries

remittances money sent by migrant workers back to their families in their home location

contribute to the economies of many developing countries, as shown in Figure 6.7. Total remittances to developing countries amounted to $328 billion in 2008, up 15% from the previous year. However, late 2008 saw a slowdown in the flow of remittances, with flows continuing to be weak in 2009 (World Bank, 2009).

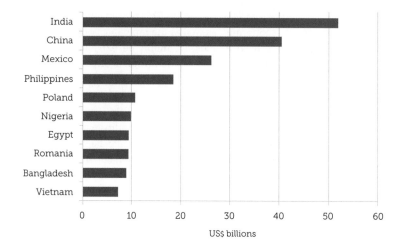

Figure 6.7 **Top recipients of migrant remittances**

Source: World Bank, Migration and Development Brief 10, 13 July 2009, at www.worldbank.org

Summary points Patterns of migration

⬥ Migrants tend to move from poorer areas to richer ones, either in their own countries or to other countries.

⬥ Developing countries benefit from the remittances sent back by migrant workers, but they can suffer skills shortages when highly qualified people emigrate.

⬥ Although migrants contribute economically to their host countries, they pose challenges for welfare and other services. It has become common for governments to keep tight border controls to deter migrants without legal documentation.

Urbanization

urbanization process of large-scale shift of populations from rural areas to cities

Migration from rural areas to cities was commonplace long before industrialization. People were 'on the move' not just for economic motives, but for social and cultural reasons as well. The process by which a growing proportion of the population shifts to the cities is termed **urbanization**. Urbanization is generally associated with industrialization and economic development. However, people also move to the cities from poor regions simply because precarious agriculture can no longer support their families. Western countries, the first to experience urbanization, are now about 75% urban, and are expected to be 77% urban by 2020, as shown in Figure 6.8. Urbanization is taking place much more quickly in less developed regions. From 25% urban populations in 1970, these countries are expected to be 50% urban by 2020. The process has happened even more quickly in China, as Figure 6.8 shows. Some 55 million Chinese people migrate from rural to urban areas each year (see opening case study of Chapter 13).

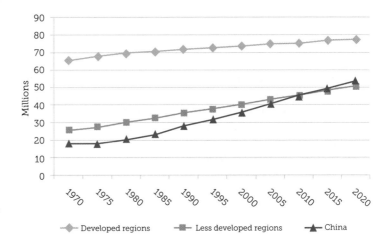

Figure 6.8 **Growth in urban population**

Source: UN (2007) World Urbanization Prospects, 2007 revision, at http://esa.un.org

Whereas the world's largest cities were once concentrated in the developed world, cities in the developing world now predominate in the top ten largest cities, as seen in Table 6.2. The Bric countries, especially India, feature prominently. Only two cities, Tokyo and New York, are in developed countries.

Table 6.2 **The ten largest cities in the world, 2010**

Ranking	City	Country	Population (millions)
1	Tokyo	Japan	36.67
2	Delhi	India	22.16
3	Sao Paulo	Brazil	20.26
4	Mumbai	India	20.04
5	Mexico City	Mexico	19.46
6	New York City	USA	19.43
7	Shanghai	China	16.58
8	Kolkata	India	15.55
9	Dhaka	Bangladesh	14.65
10	Karachi	Pakistan	13.12

Source: UN Population Division, World Urbanization Prospects, 2009 revision, at www.un.org

By 2050, most of the world's urban population will live in Asia (see Figure 6.9). By then, Africa's growing urban population will overtake those of North America and Europe combined. This is by no means unqualifiedly good news. Cities in the developing world struggle to cope with the pressures of huge and growing populations. Traffic congestion, pollution, inadequate sanitation, and poor housing are endemic problems. Slum areas, with their proliferation of shanty dwellings, are particularly vulnerable to disease and natural disasters. Slums are characterized by the absence of one or more of the following: improved sanitation, clean water facilities, durable housing and sufficient living area. About 37% of urban inhabitants in developing regions live in

The Arab world looks to the past and the future

The Arab world encompasses a range of countries spread across North Africa and the Middle East. **The 22 countries belonging to the Arab League, a loose grouping that acts mainly as a co-operative forum, are highly divergent. Although Arab peoples predominate ethnically, other ethnic groups form** significant minorities. In addition, there are large numbers of foreign workers in many Arab states, making these societies culturally diverse, but with accompanying tensions, as foreign workers, many in low-paid jobs, are not assimilated into local cultures. Although Arabic is the dominant language in the region, there are numerous French speakers in some countries, dating from the colonial era. Islam is the dominant religion across the region and, although there are many other practising religions, such as Christianity, Islam is probably the strongest cultural identity. That said, Muslims are themselves divided, as evidenced by violent conflicts between Sunnis and Shiites, for example, in Iraq.

Social and political instability haunts governments in Arab states, both large and small. Their regimes tend to be authoritarian, characterized by restrictions on personal freedom and political debate, and reinforced by religious authorities. Many, such as Saudi Arabia and Syria, have been controlled by ruling families for generations. These ruling families and elites have been economically sustained by the oil wealth over which they have control. Over 60% of the world's proven oil reserves are in North Africa and the Middle East. Although the region's rulers have introduced democratic assemblies and elections, these formal mechanisms have tended to be 'shallow', with little impact on the real processes of governance. Dominant institutions – in government, economic power and religion – seem to be firmly rooted in the past, but changes are taking place, both within their borders and in their outreach towards the rest of the world.

Many social currents exist in Arab societies. There are radical Islamists who wish to see strict religious rule; groups seeking reforms such as economic liberalism and political freedoms; and secularists who see religion as inhibiting modernization. Rulers have reasons to fear all these groups, as all would like to see changes in society, which would threaten their continued grip on power. Some are social movements, while others are political parties, sometimes the one melding into the other, as in the Muslim Brotherhood

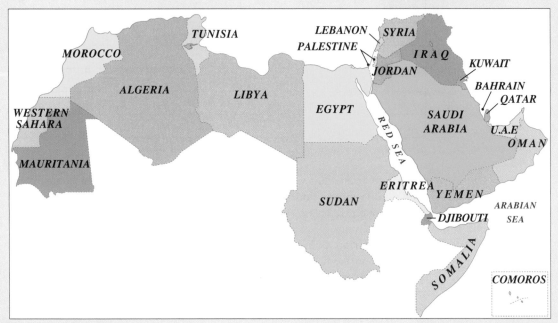

Map of the Arab world

▶ More online ... The Arab League's website is www.arabji.com

in Egypt and Jordan. In Egypt, the Muslim Brotherhood, actively engaged in social services, operates under the authoritarian regime of President Mubarak (in office since 1981). It has members of parliament, who sit as independents, but even this limited recognition has suffered, as new restrictive laws banned the Brotherhood in 2007. Dissidents are also speaking up on the internet, where bloggers have been active, able to organize political opposition, which would be banned if they took to the streets. However, in cyberspace, too, governments have taken repressive measures. Although levels of internet use in the Middle East are generally low, at 28%, this figure looks set to rise, as the majority of people are under 25 years of age, and attracted to the freedoms online which are restricted in other spheres.

These societies are experiencing a population boom. Having doubled in population in the last 30 years, the current population of 350 million inhabitants is expected to grow 40% in the next 20 years. The median age in Egypt is 24; in Morocco it is 26. Levels of education are improving, but creating jobs for millions of young people entering the labour force each year is challenging governments, whose countries have among the lowest employment rates in the world. The presence of many foreign workers, outnumbering the local workers in some states, creates tensions over jobs. Youth unemployment is a major worry, and the participation of women in employment is low, at only 30%, whereas the world average is 55%. These societies are rapidly becoming urbanized, creating strains on infrastructure and causing concerns over social unrest and environmental degradation.

Most governments in the region have recognized the need to diversify their economies, both to create jobs and to be prepared for the oil running out.

However, reforms have had limited success, and when oil prices surge, governments feel less urgency to press diversification. In the United Arab Emirates, Dubai, which has little of the oil riches of its neighbours, embarked on an ambitious policy of transforming itself into a financial centre, but it suffered in the financial crisis of 2008, and had to be rescued by its richer neighbouring emirate, Abu Dhabi. States such as Kuwait and Qatar have become noted for their sovereign wealth funds which invest in markets globally. Islamic finance, designed to comply with Islamic law, has also grown to be important in global markets. Greater integration in the global economy, however, still rests largely on the region's oil wealth. And governmental institutions have remained in control of these developments.

Largely because of the region's oil wealth, the Arab world is seen as strategically important globally. But, just as internal tensions underlie many of its governments, external conflicts also make the region unstable. Conflicts with Israel and, more recently, Iran, have involved the US, which has long seen the Middle East as a matter of its own national security. In 2009, Saudi oil exports to the US dipped below one million barrels a day for the first time in two decades, with declining demand caused by the recession. In the same year, Saudi exports to China rose above this psychologically important threshold. This shift in the balance of Saudi exports might be seen in a context of greater outreach globally, veering towards the rising superpower in the east.

Sources: Meyer, G. (2010) 'China taps more Saudi crude than US as Riyadh turns towards the east', *Financial Times*, 22 February; Saleh, H. (2009) 'Arab dissent finds voice in cyberspace', *Financial Times*, 2 July; *The Economist* (2009) 'Waking from its sleep', special report on the Arab world, 25 July

Questions for discussion

◆ What is the role of Islam in Arab countries?
◆ In what ways is the Arab world rooted in traditional cultures?
◆ What changes are taking place in Arab countries which will potentially lead to culture change?

▶ More online ... The UN's population division is at www.un.org/esa/population

slums that lack one or more of these characteristics. The percentage is 62% in sub-Saharan Africa. Here, over half the slum households lack two or more of these elements, whereas most slum dwellers in Asia suffer from only one of these deprivations. Growing populations in these regions are adding to the difficulties of authorities in attempting to improve slum conditions (United Nations, 2008b).

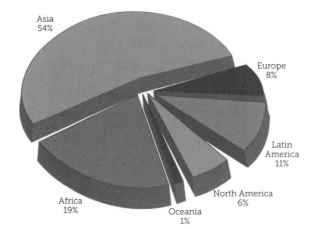

Figure 6.9 **Breakdown of the world's urban population in 2050**

Source: UN (2007) World Urbanization Prospects, 2007 revision, at http://esa.un.org

Summary points Urbanization

◆ Population shift from the countryside to cities is associated with industrialization and economic development.

◆ Most of the growth in urban populations today is taking place in developing countries, creating

strains on infrastructure and services in many poor countries.

Critical thinking
Urbanization in the developing world
Urbanization should make it easier than in rural areas for authorities to deliver health services, organize education and build durable housing, but urbanization in developing countries is often associated with poor conditions and increased health risks. Should businesses shoulder any of the burden for providing improved living conditions and education, and why?

Changing populations

The world's population stands at 6.8 billion people. Asia is by far the most populous continent, with 4.1 billion people, followed by Africa, with just over one billion people. These are the continents with the largest number of developing countries, and it is in these regions that future population growth will primarily take place. As Figure 6.10 shows, projected growth rates for the period 2009 to 2050 in sub-Saharan Africa and in the least developed countries generally are over 100%. These figures contrast with a projected growth rate of just 3.4% in developed regions. By 2050, populations of developing regions will account for 86% of the world's population (see Figure 6.11).

The most common way in which populations grow is the increase in number of births over deaths. Populations change constantly. They change naturally over time

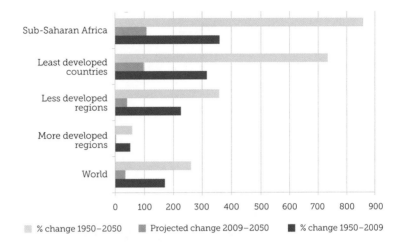

Figure 6.10 **Population growth** (percentage change)

Source: UN Population Division database (2008 revision), at www.un.org

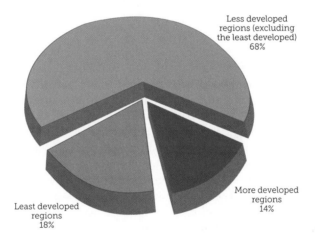

Figure 6.11 **The world's population in 2050**

Source: UN Population Division database (2008 revision), at www.un.org

demographic change changes in whole populations brought about by rises and falls in the birth rate and death rate, as well as by migration of people

and across space. **Demographic change** refers to these population changes. They include births, deaths, and migration. Demographic changes, while they take place at a slow pace, can have profound long-term effects on societies.

Improved health and living conditions have resulted in people living longer than those of earlier generations. But while people welcome the opportunities afforded by an active and healthy life beyond retirement, there are looming challenges associated with ageing societies. Globally, the number of people over 65 is expected to have doubled between 2005 and 2030 (World Economic Forum, 2009c). In developed countries, the funding of pensions and healthcare for swelling numbers of retired people has become a major issue for governments. In the advanced economies in 2000, there were four people of working age for every one over 65, but by 2020 this number will have dropped to 2.7.

Developing countries are also rapidly ageing, and governments in these countries will soon be facing similar challenges, only with considerably larger populations of retired people, as Figure 6.12 shows. By 2030, the number of people over 65 in China will have risen nearly 138% from 2005, to about 240 million people. The percentage rise in India is slightly less, at 135%, but the rise in Brazil will be 158%. Of the developed countries, the one with the largest expected increase is the US, where the increase will be 88%.

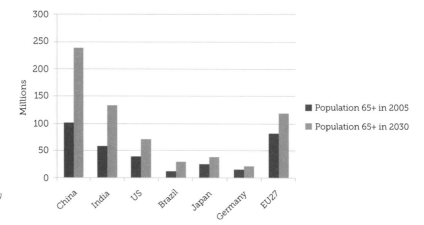

Figure 6.12 **Population aged 65+ in selected countries**

Source: World Economic Forum (WEF) (2009) *Transforming Pensions and Healthcare in a Rapidly Ageing World* (Geneva: WEF)

In a report on pensions and healthcare, the World Economic Forum recommends viewing ageing societies positively as creating opportunities, rather than negatively as creating burdens (World Economic Forum, 2009c). Business organizations and governments are involved in finding ways to utilize the talent that older workers have to offer, as well as finding ways to fund pensions and healthcare. As people are able to remain economically active for longer than in earlier generations, keeping older people at work, possibly on a part-time basis, is a sensible measure businesses can take. Legal retirement ages set by governments tend to reflect shorter longevity than is now the case. In many countries, people carry on working past the legal retirement age, partly out of necessity. In South Korea, the average man works until he is 71, even though the official retirement age is 60. In many countries, most people retire before the legal retirement age, and are able to receive pensions despite their early exit from the labour force. In Austria, the average man leaves work at 59, even though the legal retirement age is 65. Early retirement schemes are expected to be scaled back as governments seek to deal with increasing pension costs. The magnitude of the problem looming is huge. A French worker can expect to live another 24 years after retirement, now taken on average at the age of 58.7.

Companies have a role to play in encouraging older workers to stay on. Training and development, usually targeted on younger employees, can be used to help older workers to play an active role. The experience of older workers can be an invaluable asset to the organization. An HR focus on younger workers tends to overlook the knowledge and experience of the older workers, viewing them negatively as obstacles holding back progress. Business history abounds with examples of entrepreneurs starting business later in life: Ray Kroc was 53 when he founded McDonald's; Harland Sanders was 62 when he founded Kentucky Fried Chicken. Changing attitudes is part of the co-ordinated strategy needed to maximize the potential contribution of older workers. Managing teams of different generations of workers is a challenge, but can bring long-term rewards for firms, as well as helping societies to accommodate growing numbers of older people.

Summary points **Changing populations**

◆ Populations are growing more quickly in developing regions than in developed ones.

◆ Societies are gradually ageing, a process quite advanced in developed countries, and starting to accelerate in the emerging economies.

◆ Although an active retirement is good news for individuals, the necessary rise in public spending on pensions and healthcare is posing challenges for governments.

Critical thinking

Contrasting demographic profiles

Contrast the youthful societies in the Arab world (featured in Exploring the Global Business Environment) and the ageing societies of most of the developed world, in terms of the implications for business management.

This diverse team – of different cultural backgrounds and different ages – is thrashing out new ideas for the enterprise

Source: Istock

Conclusions

1 Culture refers to a society's values and norms, which have developed through shared history and experiences over a period of time. These cultural phenomena, which include language, religion, and ethnicity, give a group of people a distinctive cultural identity.

2 The nation as a group of people is the dominant source of collective cultural identity. However, in most states there are minorities with distinctive cultures.

3 Chinese languages form the largest group among the world's languages, while English is perceived as the most global language.

4 Religious groupings often dominate particular national cultures, and religion is seen as the primary identity of many people. The major religions span many different countries.

5 Research by Hofstede and by Trompenaars, focusing on cultural dimensions as variables, while tending to present static pictures of national cultures, has provided useful tools for cross-cultural analysis, in terms of both organizational and societal profiles.

6 Organizations, while they may develop their own specific values and behaviour, are also highly influenced by the national culture of their home country.

7 Migration of population from poorer to richer regions, both within and between countries, is a trend associated with industrialization.

8 Urbanization, while slowing in the developed world, is still a trend in the developing world, where eight out of the world's ten largest cities are located.

9 While populations in the industrialized world are growing only very slowly, and becoming greyer, populations in the developing world are growing more rapidly and face the challenges of ageing in the near future.

10 Ageing populations have implications for governments and businesses, including skill shortages, pressure on healthcare provisions and pension systems.

Review questions

1 What are the main elements of culture?

2 Explain the essential aspects of national culture. Why are strong national cultures often considered to be those of homogeneous societies?

3 What are the differences between a 'high-context' and 'low-context' language? Why do these differences matter in business negotiations?

4 What are the divergent currents in predominantly Muslim societies?

5 What has been the impact of Confucianism on firms in Asia, including their structures and ways of doing business?

6 What are the essential cultural dimensions described by Hofstede in his research?

7 How do the rankings of national culture produced by Hofstede shed light on international management practices in different locations?

8 List the main elements of organizational culture. Why is 'culture clash' a common problem in mergers between large companies?

9 What are the effects of the 'demographic timebomb' faced by industrialized societies, and what steps can be taken to deal with them?

10 How does the international migration of labour affect businesses in industrialized countries?

11 What are the problems associated with urbanization, and why have they become most acute in developing countries?

Key revision concepts

Assimilation of culture, p. 200; Culture, p. 196; Demographic change, p. 219; Hofstede's cultural dimensions, p. 207; Migration, p. 212; National culture, p. 198; Organizational culture, p. 210; Religion, p. 202; Remittances, p. 213; Subculture, p. 200

Assignments

◆ For a global company from a western economy contemplating a joint venture with a foreign partner in China, what are the cultural difficulties likely to be encountered, and what are your recommendations for how to enable the joint venture to succeed?
◆ Assess the impact of demographic changes on the business environment in (a) advanced economies, and (b) developing economies.

Further reading

Bartlett, C., Ghoshal, S. and Beamish, P. (2007) *Transnational Management: Text, Cases and Readings in Cross-border Management*, 5th edn (McGraw-Hill).

Bartlett, C. and Ghoshal, S. (1998) *Managing Across Borders: A Transnational Solution*, 2nd edn (London: Random House).

Berger, P. and Huntington, S. (eds) (2002) *Many Globalizations: Cultural Diversity in the Contemporary World* (Oxford: Oxford University Press).

Harrison, L. and Huntington, S. (2000) *Culture Matters: How Values Shape Human Progress* (New York: Basic Books).

Held, D. (ed.) (2000) *A Globalizing World: Culture, Economics, Politics* (Andover: Routledge).

Hickson, D.J. and Pugh, D.S. (1995) *Management Worldwide* (London: Penguin).

Hofstede, G. (1994) *Cultures and Organizations: Software of the Mind* (London, HarperCollins).

Patten, C. (1998) *East and West* (Basingstoke: Macmillan – now Palgrave Macmillan).

Schein, E.J. (2004) *Organizational Culture and Leadership*, 3rd edn (London: John Wiley & Sons).

Schneider, S. and Barsoux, J.L. (2003) *Managing Across Cultures*, 2nd edn (Harlow: Pearson Education).

Smith, A.D. (1991) *National Identity* (London: Penguin).

Trompenaars, F. (1994) *Riding the Waves of Culture* (New York: Irwin).

Usunier, J.-C. and Lee, J. (2009) *Marketing Across Cultures*, 5th edn (London: Financial Times Prentice Hall).

Variety is the spice of life for McDonald's

McDonald's has long prided itself on localized menus, designed to suit the local taste preferences in the 120 countries in which it operates, often through franchise operations. Its heart, of course, remains in the US, where about half its restaurants are located. Localization has been the strategy here, too: there are menu items designed for southern tastes, for example. Yet sales have been lacklustre in the US. The company had fondly thought that staples such as the Big Mac would be recession-proof, but found that people were eating at home more to save money. New, low-price items were introduced, to lure people back. American executives could well look at the company's strategy in Europe, which has proved a success despite recession.

Although McDonald's was the first global fast-food chain to offer localized menus, several others have followed their example. Thanks to technological advances not dissimilar to those in manufacturing industries, fast-food kitchens can offer customized products as cheaply and easily as standardized menus. McDonald's found its competitive position slipping in the early 2000s. In 2002, it made its first-ever loss. Its reputation took a number of setbacks due to the unhealthy image of its standard menu, detailed in Eric Schlosser's book *Fast Food Nation*, in 2001. A new CEO, Jim Cantalupo, took over in that year, determined to drive a turnaround. Although he did not live to see the fruits of his strategic changes, the improving sales

that followed in Europe, and especially in Britain, are an indication of the strategy's success.

Britain was one of the bleakest markets for the company five years ago, for a number of reasons. McDonald's had brought a libel action in court against two activists, for a leaflet they had distributed. The company spent £2 million suing them, finally settling out of court. The Morgan Spurlock film *Super Size Me* was targeted at McDonald's. And the company was the subject of negative publicity in its employment practices, where the term, 'McJobs' came to signify any low-paid, poor-quality employment. A first step in turning the British operations around was the replacement of the American who was running them with a British head, Steve Easterbrook, who better understood the local market.

Easterbrook brought in changes, but they were more subtle than simply localizing the menus and offering healthy alternatives, which had already been done. He tapped into consumers' concerns that the food should be local, by using placemats which featured photos of the farmers who supply the restaurants. He aimed to attract more and different customers, but also customers who were watching their spending. Ideally, they would stay longer too. He noticed that mothers would often bring children for 'happy meals', but have only a coffee themselves. His solution was the 'little tasters' menu, featuring a range of 'localized' items, which in fact had a foreign flavour, such as the Ranch Snack Wrap and Little Chorizo Melt, for about £1.50. Other ideas were to offer greater variety in coffees, often through a separate McCafé counter, and to offer more chicken options. These ideas

Universal appeal? Although McDonald's has long catered for differing national tastes, its image remains based on American fast food and lifestyle

Source: Istock

▶ More online ... McDonald's website is www.mcdonalds.com where there are links to national websites.

seemed to catch on. Sales improved, and there seemed to be evidence that McDonald's was eating into the market share of both fast-food chains specializing in chicken and Starbuck's, the coffee chain.

McDonald's localization strategy continues to be one of its strengths. The McArabia, a spicy burger in a wrap, was launched in the Middle East in 2003, the year the US invaded Iraq. Not the best timing for launching an American product, but it has become popular, and a Moroccan version has been introduced. Sales in Europe have outshone the company's other regions, as the figure shows. European sales accounted for 40% of the operating income of the global business, with 30% of the sales and 20% of the restaurants. Sales were weaker in China, where local alternatives are popular, and are 35–40% cheaper. As China has huge potential for growth, McDonald's executives will be revising their localization strategies again, taking account of the fact that getting the pricing right is a large part of going local.

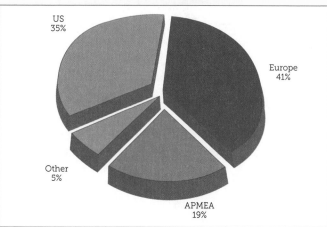

McDonald's total revenues for 2009, by region

Total revenues: $22,745,000,000
Note: APMEA is Asia-Pacific, Middle East and Africa
Source: McDonald's Annual Report 2009, at www.aboutmcdonalds.com

Sources: Wiggins, J. and Anderlini, J. (2010) 'Burger King beefs up in battle with Big Mac', *Financial Times*, 23 January; Birchall, J. (2009) 'McDonald's takes a knife to China expansion', *Financial Times*, 23 April; Wiggins, J. (2009) McCafé concept helps fast food chain', *Financial Times*, 11 August; King, I. (2010) 'McDonald's: the world's local restaurant', *The Times*, 9 February

Questions for discussion

◆ What difficulties has McDonald's faced at home and abroad, in increasing sales?
◆ What are the elements in McDonald's localization strategy?
◆ To what extent does localization simply mean listening to customers?

Learning objectives

1 To appreciate the characteristics of nation-states and how they are evolving in the global environment
2 To gain an understanding of political decision-making structures in different national systems, and how they interact with business
3 To appreciate the dimensions of political risk in business decision-making
4 To assess the extent to which democracy and authoritarian governments are evolving in the current global environment
5 To understand the changing role of transnational and regional forces in political processes worldwide

Critical themes in this chapter

- **Role of the state** – systems of government, including accountability and legitimacy
- **International risk** – political risk
- **Multilayered environment** – local, national, regional and international political institutions
- **Multidimensional environment** – interactions between political, social and economic factors

Democracy at work? The European Parliament, like other representative bodies, has come under scrutiny, as people turn a critical eye towards political leaders

Source: Istock

OPENING CASE STUDY

SAB Miller reaps rewards for investing in emerging markets

SAB Miller, now one of the world's largest brewing companies, is at heart South African. Originally South African Breweries, the company dates from the late nineteenth century. For most of its history, it has existed in a colonial environment. The process of dismantling apartheid began in the early 1990s, culminating in fully democratic elections in 1994. It was only in this period of reform that the company began to expand internationally. Its expansion was targeted mainly at other emerging economies, notably those in Eastern Europe and Latin America. It acquired Hungary's largest brewer in 1993. SAB's listing on the London Stock Exchange in 1999 signalled further expansion, but it was not until 2002 that it made a major acquisition in the US, with the purchase of 100% of Miller Brewing of Milwaukee in 2002, after which it changed its name to SAB Miller. The following year it made its first acquisition in Western Europe, with the purchase of a majority interest in Birra Peroni of Italy. However, its internationalization strategy remained primarily focused on emerging markets. Its purchase in 2005 of Bavaria S.A., a local brewer in Colombia, is indicative. Apart from South Africa, its largest markets are Latin America, Asia and the rest of Africa. It now owns some 200 brands, both global and local, and operates in 75 countries. It has pursued a multi-pronged strategy in its acquisitions, buying some firms outright and taking smaller stakes in others. In some locations, such as China, it has entered via joint ventures.

SAB Miller's expansion has reflected the policies of the South African government, particularly the ruling African National Congress (ANC) party, which has focused on building a southern axis, linking the large emerging nations with South Africa. The policy also reflects its political values. The government has pursued a foreign policy which seeks to move away from the historical dependence on Europe and the US. It also wishes to foster multilateralism as a counterbalance to US dominance.

The focus on emerging markets has proved profitable for the South African brewer, as these are some of the countries with the strongest economic growth. Furthermore, beer drinking is still on the rise in these markets. Beer consumption rose 10.7% in China between 2005 and 2009, and 8.4% over Asia as a whole. In contrast, beer consumption showed only a .5% rise in North America, and it fell in Europe and Australasia (Annual Report, 2009). SAB Miller entered China in 1994, and has continued making acquisitions of regional brewers in this vast market, with its joint-venture partner, China Resources Breweries Ltd (CRB). The CRB joint venture owns the Snow brand, the market leader in China, which enjoys a 20% share of the buoyant Chinese beer market. Although this is good news for SAB Miller executives, they highlight in the company's Annual Report in 2009 that the competitive situation in China is so tight that profit margins are paper-thin.

Cheers! SAB Miller's brands have enjoyed popularity in many diverse markets
Source: SAB Miller

India, the other large emerging market where SAB Miller is seeking to make gains, presents a different set of challenges. Here, beer consumption is low in comparison to China. There are several reasons. Beer has rather a negative image in India, and is heavily taxed. Nearly half the price paid by the customer is tax. Moreover, outlets are thin on the ground, largely because of the Indian government's policy of promoting local suppliers and retailers. Locally brewed beer products, popular throughout the developing world, are thus protected from inroads by the large

▸ More online ... SAB Miller's website is www.sabmiller.com

global brands. Although SAB Miller has been active in India since 2002, its expansion has been slow.

SAB Miller sees itself as having unique skills in operating in emerging markets, building on its experience in the South African environment. It has gained valuable experience in selling products to South Africa's growing numbers of black middle-class consumers, and also offering a range of products to low-income consumers. It has sourced products from local farmers in Africa, reducing distribution costs and enabling it to keep prices low and attract the many consumers who have been accustomed to home brews. Of African customers generally, its regional manager says that breweries 'have to be closer to the market' (Lapper, 2010). The company has shown itself to be adaptive to local cultures, including diverse products and methods. For example, projects in Uganda and Angola have been based on local brewing techniques.

Whether in premium-quality beers or in low-end products similar to home brew, SAB Miller is showing

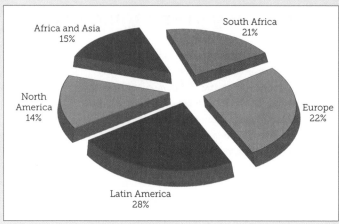

Regional shares of SAB Miller's earnings

Source: SAB Miller Annual Report 2009, at www.sabmiller.com

the way for other South African companies to globalize, seizing opportunities in emerging markets while finding that the best guarantee of success is to adapt to local conditions.

Sources: Lamont, J. (2008) 'SAB Miller in battle to take lid off India's beer market', *Financial Times*, 30 December; Lapper, R. (2010) 'Out of the bottle', *Financial Times*, 1 February; SAB Miller, Annual Report 2009, at www.sabmiller.com

Questions for discussion

◆ How would you describe SAB Miller's internationalization strategy?
◆ What political considerations influence SAB Miller's activities?
◆ In what ways is SAB Miller both global and local in its outlook and strategy?

Introduction

From global corporations down to family-run enterprises, businesses desire a stable and reasonably predictable environment in which to carry on their activities. As interaction between government and business has grown, the importance of political stability has become more apparent. In the political dynamics of every society both internal and external factors come into play. First, internal governmental structures and processes form a political system, responsible for containing and channelling conflict and promoting the collective good of the society. Just as no two societies are identical, no two political systems are identical, and the political system can have a profound effect on the attractiveness of a country as a business location. Secondly, regional and global forces outside its territory impact on a country's ability to control its affairs, and these considerations, too, underpin firm strategy to invest in a particular region. Two themes of this chapter will be the diversity of political institutions and the extent to which political processes at all levels, from the local to the international, are becoming more connected in the wider global environment.

People everywhere wish to see public order maintained, public services function efficiently, and government officers carry out their duties. But they want more besides. A police state can offer security, but it hardly offers an environment conducive to a happy life. People also wish to have a good education, a good job and the material prosperity it brings. Although democracy as a system has spread across the globe, many nominally democratic systems fall short of the stability and legitimacy hoped of them. With large swathes of the globe under non-democratic systems, basic issues such as the merits of democracy are coming into question. This chapter will focus first on national political systems and their public policy implications for business. Secondly, we look at the impact of globalization and the growth in transnational political institutions

The political sphere

politics processes by which a social group allocates the exercise of power and authority for the group as a whole

Politics has been defined in numerous different ways, but all highlight the function of conflict resolution in society. Broadly, **politics** refers to processes by which a social group allocates the exercise of power and authority for the group as a whole. Breaking down the definition into three elements, *first* there is the existence of a social group – the word 'politics' derives from the Greek word *polis*, meaning city-state, a political community. Conflict is inevitable within societies, and politics provides the means of resolving conflict in structured ways. *Secondly*, politics concerns power relations. The contesting of power in society arises from groups and individuals with a wide range of viewpoints – ideological, economic, religious, ethnic or simply self-interested opportunistic. In democratic societies political parties are the most high-profile players on the political scene, but political authorities interact with a range of interests in society, including businesses and numerous interest groups, in arriving at policy decisions.

The *third* element is the terrain of politics – the social group as a whole. While politics occurs in every organization, we are here concerned with agenda-setting for a society as a whole. Its scope is thus public life, rather than particular organizations. For the citizen of ancient Athens, this distinction did not exist: participation in the city-state was both civic and moral in nature, the polis providing the means to the good life.

Later developments, especially the growth of secular states in Europe and increasing emphasis on the worth of the individual, led to a separation between public and private spheres. The sphere of politics is public life, institutions of the state, governmental structures and the process by which individuals come to occupy offices of state.

The private sphere is often referred to as **civil society**, a term that covers the sphere in which citizens have space to pursue their own personal goals. Private individuals and businesses, trade unions, religious groups and the many sub-national associations that exist in pluralist societies are all part of civil society (Linz and Stepan, 1997). Institutions of civil society may be very limited or even banned in some states, but the trend in the post-war period has been towards greater **pluralism**. Pluralism implies a multiplicity of groups – a development which flows logically from liberalism (Sartori, 1997).

civil society sphere of activities in society in which citizens are free to pursue personal goals and form associations

pluralism existence in society of a multiplicity of groups and interests independent of the state, characterized by freedom of association; includes political parties and independent trade unions

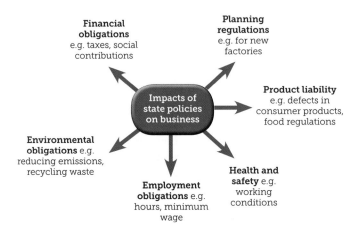

Figure 7.1 **Impacts of state policies on business**

Public and private spheres, however, are not as easily separated as the theoretical distinction suggests, and their distinction has become blurred with the growth of the welfare state in the major industrialized societies since the Second World War, extending the reach of the state into the private sphere. Some of these impacts are shown in Figure 7.1. Governments argue that increased regulation is beneficial, protecting workers, consumers and the environment.

The liberal's view of the public/private divide is that government interference in civil society should be kept to a minimum (see Chapter 3). However, the social and economic problems associated with growing inequalities in industrial societies, such as poverty and unemployment, have brought about a revision of this view, to encompass a more interventionist role for the state. The extent to which governments are justified in intervening to promote social welfare is one of the major issues giving rise to political divisions in all societies. It goes hand in hand with the issue of the extent that governments should intervene in markets. Most governments have undertaken wide-ranging privatization of public enterprises. In addition, we have seen the emergence of public/private partnerships in the provision of public services, such as education, transport, healthcare and prisons. The simple dichotomy of public and private domains, therefore, is being replaced by a less polarized, more interlinking relationship between the state and civil society. Increasingly, businesses are becoming intertwined with government agencies and processes, in activities as diverse as air traffic control, hospitals and prisons.

Summary points   **The political sphere**

● Politics is about the allocation of power and authority within a society.

● The extent to which political authorities should reach into private activities is much debated,

but a relatively high level of state intervention is now recognized as necessary for social well-being.

Nation-states: their scope and authority

The basic unit into which the world's peoples are divided is the nation-state. The concept of the nation-state, introduced in the last chapter, combines the principle of a people's right to self-determination with the achievement of a territorial state ruled by its own government and subordinate to no higher authority. New nation-states are often born of nationalist movements within existing states. The dismantling of colonial empires in the years following the Second World War gave rise to newly independent states. Some 17 new states were born out of the break-up of the Soviet Union in 1990–91.

The nation-state, or just 'state' for short, may be defined as:

> those specialised institutions that exercise a monopoly of law-making and adjudication over a given territory, and of the organised physical coercion necessary to enforce it. (Beetham, 1991: 21)

The definition highlights three defining principles of statehood: territoriality, sovereignty and the monopoly of coercive power. 'State' is a broader term than 'government'. While state encompasses people, territory and institutions, **government** refers to the particular institutions by which laws are made and implemented. It can also refer to the particular individuals in office at a given time, as in 'the government of the day'. The machinery of government may change from time to time while the state is a more enduring, and unifying, concept.

government structures and processes of the state by which laws are made and administered; also refers to the particular officeholders at any given time

Territoriality and the state

The state occupies a geographically defined territory, within whose boundaries it has jurisdiction. Disputes over territory can be particularly bitter, and have led to innumerable wars. Maintaining border controls, all would agree, has become more problematic, as territorial boundaries generally have become more permeable with the processes of globalization, including improved communications, transport, the internet, and the growth of e-commerce. These developments, facilitating growth in cross-border business, are welcomed by firms, but permeable borders are also seen by governments as a source of insecurity.

Although the state is still the legal gatekeeper controlling what crosses its borders, this role has become more daunting with the growing international flows of goods, people, information and money. Importantly from a national economic standpoint, the state also controls access to natural resources such as mineral reserves and oil in its territory. It is not surprising that countries such as Venezuela and Mexico, on gaining independence, nationalized their oil industries, but both have taken steps towards liberalization and privatization. However, residual authority remains with the state in the case of resource rights, giving governments the upper hand: a licence to mine granted to a private-sector firm is always at risk of being withdrawn at a later date (see case study on Ghana in Chapter 4).

The post-colonial states of Africa have generally followed inherited borders from the colonial period, which were artificially drawn and did not reflect ethnic groupings. Except for Rwanda and Burundi, none of the 34 modern African states corresponds to pre-colonial boundaries. Two consequences have followed: historic groupings are divided between states, and a state's population may comprise groups which are historic enemies (Hawthorn, 1993). Ethnic conflict has been an inevitable result. In these situations states struggle to maintain control and a sense of legitimacy over all their inhabitants. The pictures of flows of refugees from conflict into neighbouring countries have become a saddening feature of modern politics, highlighting the vulnerability and interdependence of states.

Summary points Territoriality

● The state occupies a defined geographical territory in which it is the supreme authority.

● Territorial boundaries have become more permeable in the era of globalization, but states remain vigilant in asserting rights over their territory.

Sovereignty

sovereignty supreme legal authority in the state; also mutual recognition of states in international relations

A defining feature of statehood is **sovereignty**, which denotes the supreme legal authority of the state. Sovereignty has an internal and external aspect. A state has 'internal' sovereignty in that it possesses ultimate authority to rule within its borders; all other associations within society are subordinate. The state's legal authority is supported by a monopoly of the use of coercive force in the form of military and police forces. 'External' sovereignty refers to the position of states in the international context, in which all states recognize each other as supreme within their own borders. This principle of mutual recognition, known as the 'sovereign equality of states', governs the conduct of international relations between states, although the growth of numerous other international actors now questions the dominance of state actors (as will be examined in the section on global politics). Internal and external sovereignty are like reverse sides of a coin. Internal sovereignty declares the state master in its own house, whereas external sovereignty prohibits it from interfering in the affairs of another state.

Sovereignty must be distinguished from the actual exercise of power. In many societies real power lies outside formal political structures. An example is the ascendancy of military over civilian rulers. Military regimes, arising through violent seizure of power (the *coup d'état*) are inherently unstable, and there is a constant threat of social unrest and factionalism within the military leadership. In the 1970s and 80s, Latin America's military regimes gave way to democratically elected governments.

Summary points Sovereignty

● Sovereignty has internal and external dimensions: supreme authority within the state and mutual recognition by states of each other's authority.

● Sovereign authority denotes a legitimate claim to make laws within the state, as opposed to the exercise of mere power, as in, for example, a military dictatorship.

Critical thinking

States and nations

Citizenship of states and the sense of belonging to a nation as a cultural identity are different concepts and, in practice, there can be conflict between the two. Give examples of the tension between national culture and citizenship in today's world, explaining the nature of the tension.

Sources of authority in the state

In every viable state there is a source of legitimate authority. Some countries struggle to achieve viability, and where there is a complete breakdown of authority and resulting instability the country is referred to as a 'failed' state. Here we examine the most common sources of legitimacy in states. In a traditional monarchy, such as the Arab state of Saudi Arabia, heredity in the royal lineage is the legitimating principle. In a 'theocracy', religious prerogative is the guiding principle. Iran, which is a Muslim state, while it still has the religious leader (the ayatollah) as supreme leader, now has a dual, religious and secular, institutional hierarchy. Tensions inevitably arise between secular and religious authorities, as contested elections in Iran in 2009 indicated. The disputed elections sparked considerable discontent among the middle classes, who are seeking reforms. The clampdown on dissent by the secular government was a sign of assertion of its authority, making uncertain the extent of sway held by the country's religious leaders.

ideology
all-encompassing system of beliefs and values, or 'world-view'

Ideology as a source of legitimacy is based on a system of beliefs which permeate the whole of society, not just the system of government. 'Ideology' is often used in a broad sense to refer to any set of political beliefs, such as liberalism or conservatism, but both these sets of beliefs embrace political pluralism, whereas the ideological state is monolithic, rejecting any competing belief systems. Fascism, an extreme nationalist ideology, reached its peak in the racist ideology of fascist Germany and Italy. While these fascist states were defeated in the Second World War, fascist groups still form part of the political scene in many states. Historically, communism has been one of the most important ideologies. Communist revolutions take over the state, replacing existing governments with communist party dictatorships, as in China and the Soviet Union. Since the collapse of the Soviet Union, China has been the leading communist country, followed by a dwindling number of smaller states, such as Cuba and North Korea. China's leaders have distanced themselves from their communist ideological heritage in the course of embracing market reforms. Cuba and North Korea are still 'hardline' communist states, but even these are taking tentative steps towards opening their economies. Ideological regimes often rely on charismatic leaders, like Fidel Castro in Cuba, to maintain ideological fervour. As in other non-democratic regimes, political succession can be a destabilizing event, and constitutes an element of political risk for foreign investors.

constitutionalism set of rules, grounded in a society's shared beliefs, about the source of authority in the state and its institutional forms

rule of law principle of supremacy of the law over both governments and citizens, entailing equality before the law and an independent judiciary

In most modern states legitimacy is founded on constitutionalism. **Constitutionalism** implies a set of rules, grounded in a society's shared beliefs, about the source of authority and its institutional forms. Constitutionalism stands for the **rule of law**, above both ruler and ruled. Its underlying principle is that the institutions of government, such as president, prime minister and elected assembly, and bureaucracy, derive their power from these pre-existing rules. Actual officeholders will change from time to time, and, indeed, a vital function of a constitution is to provide for smooth change in the transfer of power. But the constitution, setting out the ground rules, provides continuity and legitimacy. Inherent in constitutionalism are the

▸ More online ... Political resources on types of government can be found at
International Foundation for Election Systems at www.ifes.org/

control by the civilian authority over the military and the existence of an independent judiciary (court system).

Most of the world's constitutions are written. The major exception is the British constitution. However, while the UK has no separate constitutional document, much legislation, which is contained in Acts of Parliament, is constitutional in nature. This trend towards written constitutional law looks set to continue, with European integration, devolved powers for Scotland and Wales, and the impact of the Human Rights Act 1998, which incorporates the European Convention on Human Rights into UK law (see Chapter 8). There are some states where, despite a written constitution, there is only lip service to the rule of law. In some of these, such as Kazakhstan and Uzbekistan, former Soviet republics, the constitution has been amended to allow the existing president to remain in office indefinitely. The mere existence of a constitution is thus no guarantee of accountable government.

A constitutional state can be a constitutional monarchy, where a monarch remains head of state, but where democratic institutions are supreme in government. Some examples are Britain, Japan and Spain. Other constitutional states are republics, where sovereignty rests in principle and in practice with the democratic institutions, usually headed by a president.

Summary points Sources of authority in nation-states

● Monarchy vests authority in a hereditary ruler, and although most monarchies have made the transition to constitutional monarchies, some remain traditional monarchies.

● Rule based on religious authority, or theocracy, is rare. Most countries with strong religious establishments nonetheless have secular governments.

● Ideology is a source of authority in many states in which leaders

are both heads of government and perpetuators of the belief system that underpins their authority.

● Constitutional rule recognizes the rule of law over the will of individual leaders.

Political risk

In the aftermath of the Second World War, political leaders were anxious to put in place an institutional framework at the global level which would ensure peace and security. This was the impetus behind the setting up of the UN, as well as other international bodies, including the IMF and World Bank. The unfolding post-war period saw growing economic prosperity – a good indicator of peaceful co-existence among nation-states. But in the decades that followed, has the world become a safer place in which to live and do business?

Globalization has seen the opening up of markets in Russia and China, where communist legacies have cast a long shadow. Seizing opportunities for expansion, the numbers of foreign companies doing business in these countries have grown. But foreigners face high levels of political risk in entering these markets. The apparent flowering of liberal reforms might suggest that these countries are becoming more like western political environments, where democratization and constitutional governments took hold in the context of economic reforms. However, these large emerging economies have taken different development paths. Both are ruled by closed leadership groups as, effectively, one-party states. Outsiders, including foreign businesses, must tread warily in uncertain legal environments, in which political connections are crucial to business. Heavy-handed bureaucracy, unpredictable government policies, corruption and opaque administrative processes lie in wait for foreign businesspeople. Despite their appeal as large emerging markets, these locations still carry high levels of political risk. It is notable that state intervention in business and industry has become more evident in recent years in both countries.

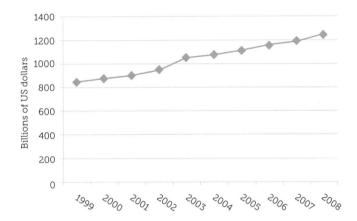

Figure 7.2 **Global rise in military expenditure 1999–2008**

Source: Stockholm International Peace Research Institute (SIPRI) 2009 Year Book, at www.sipri.org

political risk
uncertainties associated with the exercise of governmental power within a country, and from external forces

Political risk for businesses is the extent to which they are affected by disruption and uncertainty from government action or social unrest with political overtones. Despite the benefits of peace, which flowed in the post-war period, there have been numerous regional wars and continuing build-up in military establishments and defence spending. Figure 7.2 shows an increase in military spending of 45% globally in the past decade, amounting to a total of $1.2 trillion. Half of this increase is due to military spending by China, which rose 194% from 1999 to 2008 (SIPRI, 2009). A breakdown of military spending by regions is given in Figure 7.3. North America accounts for 46% of global spending on arms, far ahead of all other continents. However, China's rapid increase in military spending is a sign that it is asserting itself as a global power (Dyer, 2009).

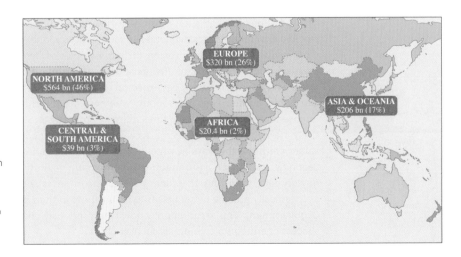

Figure 7.3 **Global military expenditure**
Amounts by region, with percentage of world total in brackets

Source: Stockholm International Peace Research Institute (SIPRI) 2009 Year Book, at www.sipri.org

States invest in military establishments and arms because of a perception of threats to national security. The US has the most widely ramified defence establishment, with armed forces deployed in some 865 bases in 130 countries (US Defense Department, 2007). In recent years, aggressive wars in Iraq and Afghanistan have led to a questioning of its use of military power as well as its moral authority internationally. American political leaders have been concerned uppermost with threats from terrorism, notably flowing from the attack on the World Trade Center in New York in 2001.

Terrorist threats may emanate from numerous sources, including disenchanted groups within a society or from outside the state. **Terrorism** has been defined broadly as action meant:

terrorism action by an individual or group intended to inflict dramatic and deadly injury on civilians and create an atmosphere of fear, generally for a political or ideological purpose

> to inflict dramatic and deadly injury on civilians and to create an atmosphere of fear, generally for a political or ideological (whether secular or religious) purpose. (UN Policy Working Group, 2002)

In the wake of the New York attacks, the then US president, George W. Bush, prioritized the 'war on terror'. But many questioned the legality of the invasion of Iraq in 2003, arguing that it lacked UN authorization and that there was little evidence that Iraq posed a serious threat to peace and security or that it had sponsored terrorist activities. The UK, which was America's main coalition partner in the invasion, encountered considerable anti-war public sentiment at home, helping to undermine the public's trust in its government. According to the World Health Organization (WHO), between 2003 and 2006, some 151,000 civilians were killed in Iraq through violence (Boseley, 2008). The region is only slowly recovering economically and politically. Meanwhile, the terrorist groups associated with militant Islam are still active in the region, and America's focus has shifted to fighting them in Afghanistan, in another protracted military offensive with unclear aims.

Terrorism is a threat in many of the world's regions. Terrorists have access to abundant weaponry and they have become adept at using them to target civilians. Terrorists have become highly mobile, not just in terms of their activities, but also in regard to their funding networks and organization. Businesses face considerable risk in locations which have a history of terrorist attack. For some, especially those involved in mining and extraction industries, working in volatile locations is common. In most of these, such as Nigeria, internal social and ethnic unrest is the cause of political risk. Establishing stakeholder relations with prevalent groups in the society, and maintaining ties with governmental authorities are ways of managing these risks. The oil company Shell has had a long history in Nigeria and has begun investing in Iraq. Its strategy now focuses on stakeholder engagement as a long-term commitment.

A justification for the invasion of Iraq was that of 'regime change': the US-led invaders sought to remove the dictatorial government of Saddam Hussein and replace it with a democracy patterned on western pluralist values. At least two issues can be highlighted. First, it is doubtful whether a set of formal democratic institutions imposed from outside can acquire legitimate authority and an ability to govern effectively. National culture is a factor. As we saw in the last chapter, deep-seated cultural values permeate the ways in which organizations, including governments, function. Secondly, there is an assumption that democratic institutions are naturally the best government, implying that democracies are more stable, more likely to thrive economically and are better places to do business in than countries with other types of government. This assumption is now being seriously challenged by the economic success of emerging economies such as China.

► More online... SIPRI (Stockholm International Peace Research Institute) is at www.sirpi.org

As we have noted, businesspeople desire a stable environment, and some would argue that a stable authoritarian country is better for business than a turbulent democratic one. Political risks, however, arise in both. In the former country, a foreign company can conclude a contract with the current leaders, only to find it altered unilaterally by new leadership at a later date. In a democracy, a change of government usually takes place at regular intervals along constitutional lines, but policy changes can still happen at any time. Furthermore, ethical concerns weigh with many companies. Does the firm wish to be seen doing business in a country with a record of human rights abuses, such as Burma (Myanmar)? A firm could well decide that this apparent acquiescence risks damaging stakeholder relations both within the company and in other markets.

Summary points Political risks

● Businesses face political risks where there are either internal or external threats to the government or within society.
● Terrorist activities represent a major source of risk, and can be difficult to guard against, especially for companies which operate in unstable regions of the world.
● Stability and instability relate to countries rather than simply to political systems: a democracy can be stable or unstable, as can a dictatorship. However, the dictatorship suffers from an inherent instability as clear lines of authority and succession are lacking.

Democracy and authoritarianism

Political systems are often classified along a continuum, with democracy at one end and authoritarianism at the other. Democracy broadly covers a range of political systems falling under the phrase 'rule by the people', but popular sovereignty in theory can issue in a great diversity of institutional forms. In basic terms, **democracy** is rule by the people, through elected governments. **Authoritarianism** is rule by a single leader or small group of individuals, with unlimited power, usually dependent on military support to maintain stability.

democracy system of elected government, based on fair and free elections and universal suffrage

authoritarianism rule by a single leader or group of individuals, often sustained by ideology associated with a one-party state

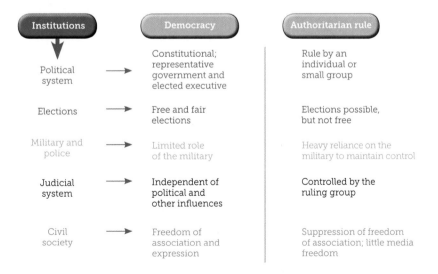

Institutions	Democracy	Authoritarian rule
Political system	Constitutional; representative government and elected executive	Rule by an individual or small group
Elections	Free and fair elections	Elections possible, but not free
Military and police	Limited role of the military	Heavy reliance on the military to maintain control
Judicial system	Independent of political and other influences	Controlled by the ruling group
Civil society	Freedom of association and expression	Suppression of freedom of association; little media freedom

Figure 7.4 **Democracy vs authoritarianism**

Figure 7.4 presents a comparison of democracy and authoritarianism. The political system in a democracy is based on representative institutions, which endure beyond the life of a particular government. Authoritarian rule is based on personal power, which is more precarious. The authoritarian ruler has been likened to a tightrope acrobat, always at risk of being toppled (Nathan, 2009). Note that these two very different systems share many elements, including the military, police, justice system and even elections. The differences lie in their degrees of influence. The military and police elements loom larger in the authoritarian regime, where they are central to maintaining order. By contrast, the justice system and elections are of greater significance in the democracy. Elements of civil society represent a crucial difference. Whereas there is freedom of association and expression in a democracy, these rights are suppressed in the authoritarian regime.

Authoritarianism

In an authoritarian government, power is concentrated in the hands of the few, and this elite is largely unaccountable to the citizens for its actions. Authoritarian regimes vary from overtly repressive military rulers to systems that have some democratic forms, such as elections to choose among state-approved candidates. In all these cases, personal rule by a single leader or small group of individuals is the norm. These leaders have usually come up through the ranks of the military or the party in a one-party state. All independent political forces are banned, and any opposition to the regime is seen as a threat, typically suppressed by military force. Freedom of expression, a free press and freedom of association are all restricted. The judicial system is not independent, but run as an administrative arm of the state. Although rule is personal to the leaders, the strong state is the dominant image that they wish to portray. They take care to keep secret the political infighting and disputes over succession issues which inevitably arise.

The economic success of China has led to a reappraisal of authoritarian governments. It might be thought that the authoritarian regime is inherently rigid, and that sooner or later it will topple. However, China's leadership has proved to be resilient, adapting to changing internal and external conditions, and using market reforms to boost economic growth. The Chinese leadership engages in a balancing act between freedom and control: balancing freedom of enterprise and state regulation, internet freedom and state censorship. It has been called an 'authoritarian capitalist' alternative to democracy (Plattner, 2010). While it had been assumed that authoritarian regimes inherently lack the moral credentials of legitimacy to govern that democratic systems offer, there is now a good deal of admiration for China's accomplishments, leading to a view that authoritarian governments are not as bad for societies as western political observers have depicted them.

The 'economy first' view of development prioritizes economic development, implying that democratic reforms can be left until a later stage. This view is most notably exemplified by China, where the authoritarian regime has used oppressive means to retain its tight grip on power. Many developing countries now see this model as a legitimate alternative to received western views about liberal democracy, apparently unperturbed by the current lack of individual freedoms and weak human rights record. This view arguably rests on a mistaken conception of democracy as simply a set of formal mechanisms such as elections.

Zhang Xin CEO, Soho China

Enjoying a personal fortune estimated at over $3 billion, Zhang Xin has become one of China's richest individuals and an influential member of China's new business elite. She has come a long way from her childhood in the Cultural Revolution. When the economy was opened in 1980, she was 14 and went to work in a garment factory in Hong Kong. She studied part-time and won a scholarship to study economics at Sussex University in the UK. Her first professional job was as an analyst at Goldman Sachs in New York. But opportunities in China beckoned, and she returned to start her property business. As co-founders of Soho China, a property development company, she and her husband, Pan Shiyi (now the chairman), have enjoyed meteoric success in China's building boom. Their company was founded in 1995 and listed in Hong Kong in 2007. Soho's business model initially was based on luxury housing for the rising affluent middle classes. The 'small office home office' concept caught on rapidly, catering for the needs of professionals in new high-technology enterprises, who wanted flexible space for home and office in high-quality accommodation. Soho China became famed for its innovative projects and striking buildings designed by international architects.

The government shifted its housing policy in 2006, restricting luxury developments, which meant that Ms Zhang and Mr Pan had to rethink their strategy. They decided to go into commercial and retail property development, and to move outward from their centre in Beijing to other regions, especially Shanghai. Here, property values have rocketed. Ms Zhang says, 'Strategy? I am afraid we don't have a strategy and we only know we must respond to government initiatives' (Lifen Zhang, 2010). Still, she has raised her voice publicly in questioning the government's policy for stimulating growth, fearing it could lead to a property bubble: 'The government needs to realise how serious the asset bubble is. It cannot control the asset bubble by just saying a few words. The most fundamental solution is to tighten credit' (*China Daily*, 2010).

Her critical comments have come partly from the perspective of her business: Soho China's share price slumped from a peak of over HK$10 to a low of just over HK$2 during the financial crisis of 2008. Her stance is also based on her conscience as member of the Baha'i faith, to which she converted in 2005. She says: 'Being a Baha'i has transformed me. Without [it] I would have blindly pursued profits at any cost. But now I will make choices. For example, I am not prepared to invest in casinos in Macau even if it makes huge returns' (Lifen Zhang, 2010). Still, her company was criticized by some for its involvement in the development of the Qianmen District of Beijing, a traditional area of great cultural significance. The development, aimed to coincide with the 2008 Olympics, seemed to epitomize the clash of values between the modernization and conservation. Still, this too reflected government policy: many traditional areas have been destroyed to make way for modern development, and the Qianmen development was seen as a means of highlighting the country's cultural heritage.

Ms Zhang maintains: 'As long as people want to buy houses, I will continue building them. After all, my personal power is nothing compared with the power of the state' (Lifen Zhang, 2010). She is looking to a bright future for her brand and company on the global stage, but says the Chinese company of the future 'will not be like a US company. There will be a dominant company in China ... which will be very different. Ultimately, US companies are the result of capitalism, but China is neither communist nor capitalist' (von Hase, 2008).

Sources: *China Daily* (2010) 'Soho China's CEO warns of bubble in second-tier cities ,' 4 January, at www.chinadaily.com.cn/bizchina ; von Hase, B., 'Zhang Xin and Pan Shiyi: Beijing's It-couple', *The Times*, 2 August 2008; Lifen Zhang, 'The women helping to build the new China', *Financial Times*, 8 February 2010

Democracy

Most definitions of democracy focus on the formal institutional aspects of government, such as elections and the right to vote. Without these, no democracy. However, democratic institutions go far deeper than formal processes, and it is the gradual building of these foundations which makes democracies durable and stable in the long term. Citizens living in the world's established democracies complain of too much partisanship, corrupt elected officials, and political debate which focuses just on personalities. Many people simply distrust politicians, as evidenced by low election turnouts. But the democratic systems in these countries evoke a legitimacy which weathers the turmoil of everyday politics.

Formal institutions are therefore necessary, but not sufficient, to construct a democracy. Minimal 'electoral democracy' can be distinguished from liberal democracy, which stipulates pluralism and political freedoms for individuals and groups (Diamond, 1996). Beyond liberal democracy, lies 'social democracy', which focuses on the broader social and economic spheres in society. Social democracy is concerned with the underlying social and economic conditions in a society which contribute towards deeper participation than the simple exercise of the vote. A sharply divided or unequal society, in which power is concentrated in an entrenched ruling elite, is not a democracy in this substantive sense, even though it may have a constitution and regular elections. When attempting to measure democracy, the requirements of liberal democracy are generally accepted as the key criteria.

The following is a list of basic principles underlying democracy:

- *Rule of law*, based on a constitution which establishes representative institutions, accountability of governments, and an independent judiciary. Thus, executive power is kept in check.
- *Free and fair elections*, at relatively frequent intervals. These must provide for choice of candidates and the peaceful removal of representatives from office when they fail to secure enough votes, in accordance with the constitution. Reports of outside monitors are usually seen as a guarantee that the election has not been tainted by fraud.
- *Universal right to vote for all adults*. Voting alone is the most minimal form of participation.
- *Freedoms of expression, speech and association*. These political rights are essential to ensure competitive elections, in which all interests and groups may put forward their candidates. There should be independent media providing alternative sources of information to which citizens have access.
- *Majority rule and minority rights*. Most countries have minority groups, who are often fearful that they will be oppressed by the majority. There must be safeguards to protect minorities as an essential element of civil society.

The post-war period saw a surge in countries making transitions to democracy. Some 90 countries have become transitional democracies since 1974. This progress

▸ More online ... The Freedom House surveys are at www.freedomhouse.org

has now slowed. A US research group, Freedom House, conducts an annual survey of the state of freedom in the world. It classifies as 'free' countries that have full political competition, free media and civil liberties; 'partly free' countries have only limited political rights and weak rule of law; 'not free' countries lack basic political rights. The 2010 survey found that declines in freedom have taken place in 40 countries, whereas gains occurred in only 16. This result can be compared to those earlier in the decade, shown in Figure 7.5. Many of the examples of decline are in countries where widespread vote-rigging and bribery have tainted elections, indicative of continuing corruption. Kenya is a sad example of a transitional democracy which has slid into disarray, following disputed elections in 2007. It had been hoped that the country would progress on the road to a consolidated democracy, but it lapsed into ethnic violence, indicating the underlying weakness of its democratic institutions. A new constitution, approved by referendum in 2010, gave renewed hope of restoring institutional stability (see discussion below on the referendum).

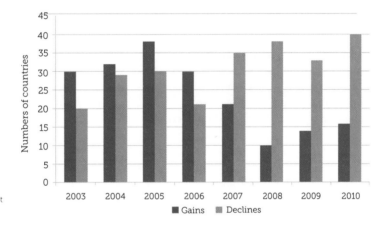

Figure 7.5 **Gains and declines in freedom worldwide, 2003–2010**

Source: Freedom House, *Freedom in the World* 2010, at www.freedomhouse.org

Summary points **Democracy**

● Rule of law and individual rights are at the heart of democracy, and these substantive underpinnings give a democracy its durability.

● Electoral democracies offer a formal choice to voters, but, without freedom of expression, these systems are failing to build the democratic institutions that will withstand challenges in the future.

The democratization debate

It used to be assumed that democracies are always preferable to authoritarian regimes simply because they have a legitimacy which the latter can never have. It has been argued that in resource-rich developing states, such as Nigeria, an autocratic government is more effective and less corrupt than a democratic one, in which electoral competition opens the way for corruption (see Collier, 2008: 45–7). It is true that competitive elections can lead to disunity in countries where political institutions are not soundly established. On the other hand, autocrats unchecked by any democratic institutions would be tempted to take the proceeds of resource riches for themselves personally. State control and opaque institutions provide plenty of scope for corruption (Diamond, 2008). Simmering political dissent and social unrest may destabilize the system as a whole over time, even though security forces keep it in check day-to-day. China's apparent stability has been bolstered by strong economic growth. If incomes decline or jobs disappear, the growing numbers of educated middle-class citizens could conceivably begin to question the system. The Chinese authorities have had to walk the high wire in keeping elements in society, such as minorities and the unemployed, under control. When factory jobs disappeared in the coastal regions in 2009, the workers sent back to rural areas found work in government-sponsored infrastructure projects funded by the government's huge stimulus package. However, this panacea could be short-lived. Moreover, the stimulus measures enhanced state power at the expense of private enterprises, including both domestic firms and foreign investors.

A democracy can be unruly, and an authoritarian state can be relatively stable, assuming the coercive forces maintain order. Every system needs to provide security, justice and an environment in which economic activities can flourish. In the long term, democratic politics is probably better insurance against some of the worst abuses of dictators.

Summary points The democratization debate

- Liberal democracy has seen declining popularity as authoritarian regimes have appeared to offer both stability and economic growth.

- Authoritarian governments, however, are at risk of being toppled by adverse events, such as widespread economic

distress, which could ignite public dissatisfaction.

Critical thinking

A new model emerging?

To what extent is China providing a new model of governance, combining capitalist elements with authoritarian structures?

Unitary and federal systems

unitary system system of authority within a state in which all authority radiates out from the centre

federal system system of government in which authority is divided between the centre and regional units

In a **unitary system** authority radiates out from the centre. There may well be local and regional governments, but they are not autonomous actors, as their authority is delegated from the centre. Whether a state is unitary or federal has a direct impact on the business environment. Regulatory regimes, including planning permissions, health and safety, and legal framework generally, may be regionally governed in federal systems, while they will be centralized in unitary systems. On the other hand, the UK is a unitary system with devolved authority to local authorities, and also now with devolved authority to Scotland and Wales. In a **federal system** authority is shared between the centre and local or regional units, which retain autonomy in specific areas, such as education or regional development. Spain is an example of a state that, while not officially federalist in design, recognizes a high level of regional autonomy, accommodating strong historical regional identities.

Federalism is often seen as a solution for states with strong local identities, which can be incorporated into the larger whole while retaining semi-autonomous status. Thus the separate 'states' of the US have separate legal systems and limited autonomy.

▶ More online ... The Scottish Parliament is at www.scottish.parliament.uk

However, the power granted by the US Constitution to the federal government 'to regulate interstate commerce' has opened the way for an increase in federal regulation. Separate authorities and inconsistencies in business regulation between states can pose headaches for businesses that operate in more than one state. Germany's constitution, too, provides for state governments, called *länder*, which, historically, have had strong identities. For countries such as Canada and Belgium, federalism serves to accommodate separate founding nations, who wish to retain separate identities and languages within the federal structure: English and French in Canada; French and Flemish in Belgium. It is often said that a specifically democratic advantage of federalism is shifting decision-making closer to the people affected. The UK, although unitary in principle, in devolving limited authority to a Scottish Parliament and Welsh Assembly, seems to be taking a step in this direction. Federalism is also seen by many as a solution to the governance of the EU. However, many within the EU see a federal solution as allocating too much power to the central institutions in Brussels.

Summary points Unitary versus federal systems

- In a unitary system, all authority radiates out from the centre; local bodies might have delegated authority, but only within strict parameters.

- In a federal system, power is shared between the centre and regions. This type of system is suitable where there are strong regional identities.

Systems of government

separation of powers in systems of government, the division between legislative, executive and judicial functions, or branches, with checks and balances to prevent one branch becoming dominant

checks and balances system by which the three branches of government (legislative, executive and judicial) share legal authority and accountability

It is customary to think of government as comprising three functions or branches: legislative, executive and judicial. The division of functions between the three is known as **separation of powers**, shown in Figure 7.6. The legislative is the law-making branch. In a democracy, it is located in an elected assembly. The executive is at the head of government, responsible for administration and policy. It carries out functions such as external relations and oversight of defence. It is usually considered responsible for security matters. It is also the source of much legislation in democratic systems, which then passes through the legislative process. The judicial function, located in the court system, interprets the law and thereby keeps a check on the other two branches. The system thus functions through the principle of **checks and balances**. Law and policy emanate mainly from legislative and executive branches, and more specifically from political interplay between the two, depending on the balance of power within the system. In practice, most systems have considerable overlap between these functions, and the main safeguard that no one branch comes to dominate the others is the system of checks and balances between them. We look first at legislative assemblies.

Legislative assemblies and elections

legislative assembly body of elected representatives within a state, which has law-making responsibilities

Most countries have a national assembly of representatives, whether elected or not. In authoritarian systems, the assembly is merely advisory, rubberstamping the decisions made by the ruling elite. This type of assembly has no actual law-making powers. In a democracy, the **legislative assembly** lies at the heart of the political

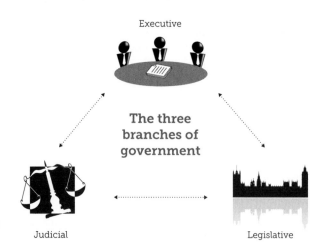

Executive

The three
branches of
government

Judicial

Legislative

Figure 7.6 **The branches
of government**

system, representing the sovereignty of the people. It carries the main law-making function, and, through the ballot box, it is the one tangible way citizens express a say in the makeup and policies of their government. Many countries have legislatures consisting of two houses (bicameral), where the lower house is the main law-making body. In the US, both houses, the House of Representatives (the lower house) and the Senate (the upper house) are directly elected. In the UK, only the House of Commons (the lower house) is elected. The upper house, the House of Lords, has been a subject of much recent debate concerning its future composition and powers. Reforms have converted it from a hereditary chamber to one composed of hereditary and appointed members. Its role has been gradually reduced to one of a revising chamber, and further reform plans were put forward in 1997. The first stage of the reform took place in 1999, with the abolition of 600 hereditary peers, but since then, there has been disagreement on the makeup of the new House of Lords – whether members should be directly elected, indirectly elected, appointed, or a possible combination of these categories. Other parliamentary systems have only a single chamber (a unicameral legislature). Sweden and New Zealand abolished the upper chamber.

Free and fair elections are a key element in political participation in a democracy. The electoral system may be the traditional first-past-the-post system or one of the more recent **proportional representation** (PR) systems, which allocate seats in proportion to the votes obtained. A common type is the 'alternative vote' system, by which voters vote for candidates in an order of preference; votes for candidates with the fewest votes are redistributed to second-choice candidates, so that eventually a winner emerges with a majority of the votes. The first-past-the-post system has predominated in the US and UK, although elections for devolved assemblies in Scotland and Wales are based on PR. Most European countries (and also the European Parliament) have opted for PR. Outcomes in PR systems represent a broader political spectrum, giving small parties a greater prospect of winning seats than a first-past-the-post system, where they may win sizeable voter support but fail to win many seats. The Liberal Democrats in the UK have long campaigned for PR reforms: as a 'third' party in a two-party system, they attracted 23% of the popular vote in the general election in 2010, but won only 8.7% of the seats in the House of Commons. As no party achieved an outright majority, the Conservative Party, which had the most seats, formed a coalition government with the Liberal Democrats (see discussion

**proportional
representation**
system of electoral representation in which seats are allocated in proportion to the votes obtained by each party

▶ More online ... Information on elections, parties and parliaments is at www.electionresources.org/

below on parliamentary systems). The Liberal Democrats have long prioritized the need for electoral reform, and are now in a strong position to press for PR.

PR systems are considered to be friendlier to women candidates. Women world-wide hold just 18.7% of the seats in national legislatures (Inter-Parliamentary Union, 2010). There are wide disparities among countries, from 46.4% of the seats in Sweden to none in a number of countries, mainly Arab states. A selection of countries is given in Figure 7.7. In countries where there are more women legislators, governments have introduced policies directed specifically towards increasing the number of women candidates.

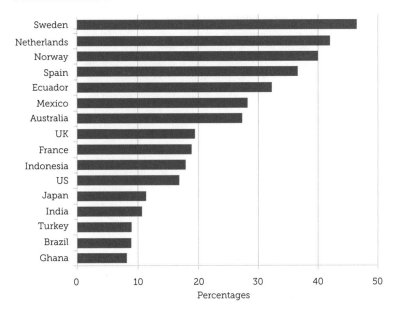

Figure 7.7 **Women in national legislatures in selected countries** (lower or single house)

Source: Inter-Parliamentary Union (2010) at www.ipu.org

A drawback of proportional representation is that in a multi-party system, if many parties secure seats, it may be difficult to form a government, and political instability may result. A common requirement is that a party must obtain a minimum of 5% of the total vote to gain any seats. Poland's first fully free election, in 1991, demonstrates the hazards of extreme PR: 111 parties or groups put up candidates; 29 parties or groups gained seats, including the Beer Lovers' Party, but none gained more than 13% of the total. A series of unstable coalition governments followed, until a 5% threshold was introduced in 1993. Since then, parties have settled into two main blocs. Increasingly popular is the 'mixed' electoral system, combining first-past-the-post and PR systems. The leading example is Germany, in which coalition governments have become usual. A 'grand coalition' of the two major parties was formed following the close result in 2005, led by Chancellor Angela Merkel of the Christian Democrats. The 2009 elections produced a clearer result consisting of a victory for the centre-right parties, giving Chancellor Merkel a stronger mandate.

referendum example of direct democracy, in which electors cast a vote on a particular issue

The **referendum** is an example of direct democracy, and is used to complement the legislative function carried out by the assembly. In a referendum, voters are invited to approve or reject a question on a particular issue. In some states (such as Italy) it is a constitutional requirement; in others (such as the UK) it is optional. Some examples of the varied uses of the referendum are:

- Devolution in Scotland and Wales, 1997
- Decision to join the UN by the Swiss in 2002, following earlier rejection in 1986
- The end of apartheid in South Africa, 1992
- The decision not to join the eurozone by Denmark (2000) and Sweden (2002)

The advantages of the referendum are that it acts as a check on elected governments, giving citizens an opportunity to express a view on an issue of the day. A drawback, however, is that citizens are typically asked to make a yes/no decision although the issues may be complex. Moreover, ordinary citizens are not as well informed of the ramifications of proposed changes as elected representatives are.

Summary points Legislative assemblies and elections

◆ Legislative assemblies have genuine law-making powers in a democracy, their members representing constituencies of voters.

◆ The effectiveness of a democracy depends heavily on free and fair elections. Voting systems, such as the first-past-the-post system, which underrepresent minorities are often perceived as less democratic than proportional representation systems.

The executive

The executive function provides strong leadership in some systems, and only a co-ordinating role in others. We look at three types of system: presidential, parliamentary and 'hybrid'. A summary of their characteristics is shown in Table 7.1. These will now be discussed.

Table 7.1 **Systems of government**

	Presidential	**Parliamentary**	**Hybrid system**
Advantages	Strong executive based on popular mandate; fixed term of office	Executive reflects electoral support in parliament	Strong executive imparts unity; prime minister co-ordinates parliamentary programme
Disadvantages	Possible disaffection among electorate	Thin majority may lead to breakdown of government	Conflict between president and prime minister
Stability	Stable executive, but legislature may be dominated by the opposing party, stifling law-making agenda	Stable if prime minister has a large majority; coalition and minority governments can be unstable	Fixed-term president imparts stability; but successive coalition governments can be unstable in multi-party systems

presidential system
system of government in which the head of the executive branch, the president, is elected by the voters, either directly or through an electoral college (as in the US)

A **presidential system** is thought of as producing a strong chief executive, as presidents are normally directly elected by the people and thus have a personal mandate. The US is the leading example of a presidential system, although the president is technically elected by an electoral college to which each state sends delegates representing its voters' choice. Checks on executive power are provided by the constitution and also by a vigorous two-party system. The other main proponents of the presidential system have been Latin American countries, for whom a strong presidency is more grounded in political culture, in which nationalism and populism have been prominent features. Inherent drawbacks of the 'winner-takes-all' nature of presidential elections are that supporters of the losing candidate may feel alienated, while the winner may overestimate the popular mandate, 'conflating his supporters with the people as a whole' (Linz, 1993: 118).

▶ More online ... Information about UK elections can be found at www.electoralcommission.org.uk

The US presidential election in 2000 was the closest result in the country's history. After five weeks of re-counting and several court cases culminating in a decision of the US Supreme Court, George W. Bush was declared the winner. Despite his wish to bring a sense of national unity after such a protracted and bitter episode, his Cabinet and legislative agenda, including major tax cuts, were distinctly rightist, reflecting traditional conservative Republicanism. A Senate finely balanced between Republicans and Democrats ensured that new laws would be difficult to pass. Securing a majority on any issue in Congress tends to involve deals with individual members which offer benefits to their constituents. Known as 'pork-barrelling', this practice has contributed to lowering the esteem in which legislators are held.

Businesses, including those abroad that do business in the US and those that are indirectly affected by US economic and trade policies, look for a clear and coherent legislative agenda on issues such as trade liberalization and regional trade agreements. However, the system seldom delivers the political mandate that elections promise, and policies emerge piecemeal through negotiation and compromise among numerous competing interests, even when the voters deliver a decisive majority to the president, as happened with the election of President Obama in 2008. Mr Obama prioritized healthcare reform, devising programmes to extend health insurance to the 43 million Americans without coverage, but he struggled to steer the reforms through Congress.

parliamentary system
system of government in which voters directly elect members of parliament, from whom a prime minister is chosen

In a **parliamentary system**, the voters directly elect members of parliament, from whom a prime minister and cabinet are selected, usually from the political party with a majority of seats. This is often called the 'Westminster model' as the leading example is the UK. The efficient running of a parliamentary system depends greatly on the nature and number of a country's political parties. It is usually felt that it works best in a stable two-party system of 'government' and 'opposition' parties, in which the opposition is in effect an alternative government. However, the UK general election in 2010 revealed a more fragmented pattern. The Conservative Party won 306 of the 650 seats, receiving 36.1% of the popular vote. The Labour Party's share of the overall vote was 29%, and they won 258 seats. Liberal Democrats won only 57 seats, despite attracting 23% of the popular vote. The result was said to be a 'hung' parliament, with no party achieving an absolute majority. The Labour Party, having been in power since 1997, admitted it was no longer able to govern, and the Conservatives and Liberal Democrats formed a coalition government.

Figure 7.8 **British general election turnout, 1945–2010**

Note: There were two general elections in 1974, one in February and one in October. Source: UK Political Information (2010), Electoral turnout, at www.ukpolitical.info

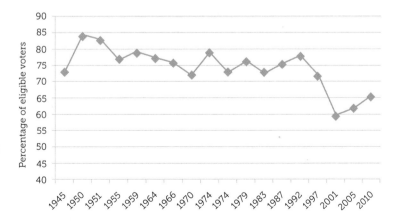

Low turnout in democratic elections is a concern, as it indicates apathy or lack of engagement in the democratic process. Turnout in UK general elections was in the 70–80% region throughout most of the post-war period (see Figure 7.8), and dived to a low of 59.6% only in 2001. The 2005 and 2010 elections represent slight improvements. Also worrying is that the turnout among younger voters was particularly low: less than 40% of people under 25 vote. Apart from the obvious conclusion that people are disillusioned with politics, it is also possible that they are turned off by the mainstream political parties, which seem remote. A trend has been the rising profile of various lobby groups and interest groups, which seek to influence policy on particular issues, rather than to play a direct role in politics. Consultation by government with lobby groups of all descriptions – from animal rights groups to railway users – has become routine, arguably sidelining established political parties.

coalition government
government composed of two or more parties, usually arising in situations where no single party has obtained a majority of seats in legislative elections

In multi-party systems, a **coalition government**, made up of two or more parties, is the likely outcome. Aware of its power to bring down the government, a minor party in a coalition may demand a 'price' for its co-operation in terms of key policies, to keep it on board. Small right-wing religious parties in Israel are an example of this phenomenon, wielding more political power than their number of seats alone would justify. It could be claimed that coalition government is more representative of electoral support, and hence more democratic, but a major disadvantage is its potential instability.

The so-called 'hybrid system' aims to achieve both a stable executive and maximum representation, with an independently elected president and a prime minister who heads the cabinet. The model for this system, also known as the dual executive, is the Fifth French Republic. Apart from Hungary, which has a parliamentary system, the post-communist states of Central and Eastern Europe have adopted the hybrid model. The theory is that the nationally elected president can foster national unity, playing the role of head of state, while the prime minister plays more of a party-political role, maintaining support for the government in the legislature. In practice, these systems may not run as smoothly as envisaged if the two executives are of different parties (called 'co-habitation' in France) or, as is almost inevitable, each sees the other as a rival. In new democracies such as Poland and the Czech Republic, where politics tends to focus on personalities, the role of president can be seen as a strong political platform.

Summary points **The executive**

◆ Presidential systems are associated with a strong executive, but a drawback is that the system could become unbalanced if the executive gets the upper hand and tends towards the authoritarian.

◆ In a parliamentary system, the prime minister is not directly elected, but emerges from the winning party. In this system, accountability of the prime minister to parliament is paramount.

◆ The hybrid system, having both a president and prime minister, can lead to tension and overlap in their positions and responsibilities.

The judicial function

The legal environment in general will be discussed in the next chapter. Here we focus on the judicial function as a branch of government. The judicial function is carried out by the state's system of courts. For firms and individuals, the way that the laws are applied in practice in the country's courts is of utmost importance (as we will discuss further in Chapter 8). The rule of law and an independent judiciary are essential elements of a democracy. These principles imply that the law is above any individual, from an officeholder to simply a rich and powerful individual. To be independent, the members of the judiciary should be seen to be impartial: a judge who is in the pay of an interest group is not suitable for office. In order for the judicial function to act as an effective check on the other two branches of government, procedures must be devised to call officeholders to account if they have acted unlawfully. The member of the legislature who takes money from a firm for helping to secure a government contract is acting unlawfully, although many firms seek such advantages through payment of politicians.

In a constitutional system, the judges are tasked with ensuring that the country's laws passed by the legislature are consistent with the constitution. If there is a doubt, the supreme court of the country can be asked to judge on the issue of constitutionality. The US Supreme Court has dealt with many such cases throughout its history, and in some, changed its mind at a later date. Separate but equal facilities for non-white citizens were held to be constitutional in 1896, but in a landmark case in 1954 (Brown v. Board of Education of Topeka), the Supreme Court overturned its earlier decision, declaring segregation unconstitutional. Tension inevitably arises between the law-making branches (executive and legislative), and the judiciary often finds itself influencing policy, although, in theory, judges are meant simply to apply the law, rather than make it. If judges become 'politicized', this is seen as eroding their independence, and also eroding their standing as a check on the executive. In some cases, judges have asserted independence in delivering their judgments despite the pressures of authoritarian regimes. Late in South Africa's apartheid era, courts struck down some of the country's race laws (*Time*, 1986).

Summary points The judicial function

● A country's judiciary acts as a check on both the executive and legislature.

● Independence from political pressure is a key aspect of the rule of law.

Political parties

political party
organization of people with similar political perspectives, which aims to put forward candidates for office and influence government policies

Political parties form the link between voters and legislative assemblies. In democratic states, they are essential to the pluralism which characterizes civil society. In authoritarian and semi-authoritarian states, they help to cement the ideology of the leadership and mobilize public support. We look at democratic systems first.

In a pluralist society, parties perform several functions:

- They provide candidates for public office, who rely on their organizational machinery and funding to get elected. The independent candidate faces an uphill battle, and needs to be very rich.
- They provide a policy platform, on which voters can decide whom to support. Many voters traditionally are party loyalists, not bothered who the individual candidate is.
- When in office, they provide an agenda for government, against which performance can be judged.

Hungary finds political consensus elusive

Hungary's economic development since the fall of communism has rested heavily on FDI. But the country's socialist government, which came to power in 2002, presided over a period of economic downturn, which eventually led to a political crisis, forcing the prime minister, Ferenc Gyurcsany, to resign in 2009. His government had overseen a period of uncontrolled budget deficits, caused in large part by profligate public spending and corruption. Gyurcsany, a former communist youth leader who became a multimillionaire businessman, had portrayed himself as a modernizer in terms of policy, welcoming foreign investors. He took pride in the decision of Daimler in 2008 to build a large factory in Hungary, winning out over Poland and Romania. However, government finances were spiralling out of control. He later admitted lying about the size of the deficit during the election campaign which his party won in 2006. As the crisis deepened, the public turned against not just the government but also the foreign owners who dominate much of the economy, including the banks. The main opposition

party, the centre-right Fidesz party, was eager for the next general election, seeing the political tide turning their way. In the meantime, an interim, non-party prime minister, Gordon Bajnai, was appointed, who was able to muster a majority in parliament made up of the socialists and two smaller parties.

When Mr Bajnai took over, Hungary's economic position was precarious, having suffered in the recession. Its economy was expected to shrink 7% in 2009. He initiated drastic austerity measures, especially taking an axe to public spending. Social spending and public-sector pay were severely affected. These measures helped to bring the budget deficit down from 9.2% of GDP in 2006 to 3.4% in 2009. Hungary's currency, the forint, seemed to recover, and the threat of a banking crisis receded by the time new elections were called.

Fidesz swept to power in the general election of 2010, giving the new prime minister, Viktor Orban, 53% of the vote, translating into 263 out of the 386 seats. By then socialist supported had evaporated, and they won only 59 seats. To the surprise of many, the

Map of Hungary

▶ More online ... Daimler is at www.daimler.com

far-right Jobbik party won 17% of the vote, giving them 47 seats. A new liberal-green party (LMP, standing for 'politics can be different') won 16 seats. With his big majority, Mr Orban promised reforms such as reducing bureaucracy and cracking down on corruption. The country's ills, including unemployment (at over 11%) and crime, he blamed on the previous regime, in which the business allies of the socialists had flourished. Mr Orban is a vice-president of the centre-right grouping, the European People's Party, in the European Parliament, which has positioned itself as an upholder of democratic and European values. Nonetheless, the party espouses more nationalist values than its predecessors, and sought early on to renegotiate the terms of loans from the EU and IMF, as part of a 'new partnership' (*The Economist*, 1 May).

The electoral support for the far-right revealed many of the tensions in Hungarian society. The plight of the Roma gypsies, mired in poverty and discrimination, is an issue that governments can help to alleviate, but during times of economic crisis, it is not uncommon for extreme nationalist parties to gain support. Extreme nationalism feeds on people's economic anxieties, mixing anti-capitalist messages with a picture of a better life under the protection of the nation-state. The extreme nationalist Jobbik party has been perceived as tapping into veins of anti-Semitism and hostility to Roma people, who they blame for much crime. Although Jobbik has lacked the

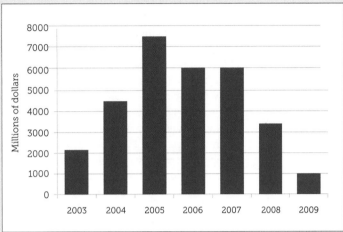

FDI inflows into Hungary

Source: UNCTAD (2010) FDI database, at www.unctad.org

resources to mount media campaigns in the manner of the two main parties, it utilized the internet to put its messages to the electorate, touching in particular discontented young people. The strong electoral showing for the radical right could possibly affect Hungary's future attraction for international investors. It was hoped by many, including socialist and liberal voters, that if Fidesz won a big enough majority, it would halt the apparently rising support for the extreme right. Mr Orban said on his election, 'the better the performance of the government is, the weaker the far right will be in the future' (Bryant, 2010).

Sources: Escritt, T. (2008) 'Daimler picks Hungary for east Europe factory', *Financial Times*, 19 June; Bryant, C. (2010) 'Investment fears on election success of Hungary's far right', *Financial Times*, 13 April; *The Economist* (2010) 'Orban's triumph', 1 May; *The Economist* (2009) 'Gyurcsany goes', 28 March

Questions for discussion

◆ What are the causes of political instability in Hungary?
◆ Why did Hungary's socialists see their support diminish so dramatically?
◆ To what extent will foreign investors be concerned about Hungary's economic, social and political environments?

Parties vary in their political agendas and in their views of society. Some embrace strong ideological positions, such as communist parties. Others are religious in origin, such as Muslim parties and Christian parties. Many countries have rural-based, or peasant parties which exist mainly to foster rural interests. Parties may also emerge from interest groups, such as the Green Party, which concentrates on ecological issues. Most of the narrowly based parties have little hope of gaining a majority of legislative seats and forming a government; instead, they seek publicity and political influence for their views. They are more likely to win seats in multi-party systems with proportional representation. In two-party systems, such as the US and UK, the trend has been towards the 'catch-all' party, with weaker ideological underpinning and greater direct appeal to voters via the media, in which personalities are as important as policies. Political parties depend on funding largely from supporters, and, although many states attempt to regulate funding, this area is a fertile one for corruption scandals, in which politicians and corporate donors can become enmeshed.

Political parties are usually described in terms of left, right and centre, with the modern catch-all parties falling somewhere near the centre. The modern Labour Party in Britain has shifted from being a left-wing socialist party to a broader-based centre-left party. However, pinning down what these labels stand for in terms of policy can be bewildering, especially as their meanings have shifted over time. Parties to the 'left' generally support high public spending on social services, protection of workers, and trade union rights; they tend to oppose privatization. Parties on the 'right', known almost universally as 'conservatives', generally wish to see a minimum of government intervention in business, reduced public spending, and low taxes. They favour more privatization of the economy, reducing the size of government bureaucracy. However, all modern parties, the British Conservatives included, support the welfare state. Nationalist tendencies are associated with the right, but most parties of the right (except extremist right-wing parties) support multiculturalism. With its election in 1997, 'New Labour' in Britain expressly moved closer to business-friendly policies and distanced itself from its working-class ideological roots. However, having lost the general election of 2010, the Labour leadership has moved away from the New Labour agenda towards what are perceived as more traditional trade union values. The new social democratic parties across Europe are said to represent the 'third way', between socialism and market liberalism. Also active in European politics are nationalist parties, which tend more towards the right.

Some states, such as the US and UK, have two major parties, making these essentially **two-party systems**. Both have first-past-the-post electoral systems. Third parties, while they obtain electoral support, are unlikely to gain seats in proportion to their overall support, unless there is a shift to a PR system (see earlier section on legislative assemblies). A **multi-party system** exists in much of Europe, including Italy, Poland and other Central and Eastern European countries. In these states, which have PR systems, parties cover a greater range of ideological positions, from left to right. Centre-left or centre-right coalitions are a typical outcome of elections. Some countries have a single dominant party, but are nonetheless democratic. Examples are Japan and Mexico, but in both these states, the dominant party has seen its electoral popularity decline, leading to a more fragmented political scene, in which other parties have formed governments.

Authoritarian states are typically one-party states, and in these systems, parties not approved by the leadership are banned. In China, the Communist Party is the dominant institutional force, in effect capturing the state. The state's institutions,

two-party system
political system in which there are two major political parties, alternating between government and opposition

multi-party system
system in which many political parties represent a wide spectrum of views, and where the government is likely to be a coalition of parties

while appearing to be autonomous, are in practice controlled by the party. Russia is a more complex example. Here there has been a democratic transition, but the dominant United Russia Party is firmly in control, and other political organizations, as well as non-governmental organizations (discussed below), have little freedom. With little press freedom and precarious freedom of association, elections fall short of being free and fair. Russia's system has been described as a 'managed democracy' (Buckley, 2006).

Summary points **Political parties**

● Political parties are a feature of civil society, with freedom to organize, voice views and select candidates for elected offices in democratic systems.

● Authoritarian systems are often one-party states, in which the leadership of the party and the state come together.

Critical thinking

Are people becoming disillusioned with political parties?

Corruption scandals and the use of public office to gain personal power or riches feature frequently in the media. Trust in politicians is at a low ebb in many countries, and at the same time, people have many new means of making their voices heard, for example, on the internet (which politicians also use abundantly). Are organized political parties ceasing to be relevant?

Global politics

On the international stage, every sovereign state theoretically enjoys equal status with all others, now numbering over 200. But in practice, international politics revolves around power, both economic and military: the most powerful states in any historical period tend to be the richest and strongest militarily. The weight of a country's military helps to ensure that it can assert its will over others, by force if need be. On the other hand, it is increasingly recognized by governments that states no longer have the means to deliver national security and material well-being on their own. By co-operating with other states, a government can boost its country's material well-being, for example through trade, and also reach defence agreements with other countries for their mutual security. In this section we look first at some of the institutions which aim to channel sovereign states towards a more peaceful and prosperous existence. We then discuss the changing power relations which help to determine how these institutions function in practice.

Institutions

non-governmental organization (NGO)
voluntary organization formed by private individuals for a particular shared purpose

Interdependence and co-operation have generated numerous alliances and international organizations, dating mainly from the period following the Second World War. The main legally established institutions are governmental, but **non-governmental organizations** (NGOs) have gained in political influence and become part of the international institutional process in some areas of global concern. These include human rights (for example Amnesty International) and the environment (for example Greenpeace). UN agencies feature regularly in this book, for the research they carry out and global issues they deal with at international level. Here we provide an overview of the UN itself.

The United Nations

The UN was introduced in Chapter 2. Founded in 1945, it has grown from 50 to nearly 200 states, shown in Figure 7.9. The UN acquired 26 new members in the period 1990–95, mainly the post-communist states of the former Soviet Union. The UN's institutions derive their authority from intergovernmental co-operation. They do not constitute a world government. Its Secretary-General, while having none of the executive powers that state leaders possess, commands considerable respect in the international community, and exemplifies the UN's aim of achieving peaceful negotiated settlement of conflicts between states. See Figure 7.10 for a summary of some of the main provisions of the UN Charter.

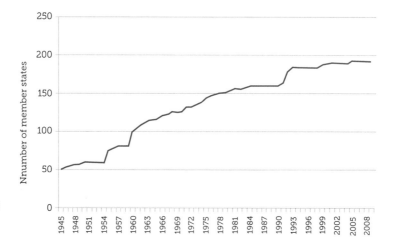

Figure 7.9 **Growth in United Nations membership**

Source: United Nations (2010) Growth in United Nations Membership 1945–2009, at www.un.org/Overview

The General Assembly, in which all member states have one vote, can be contrasted with the Security Council, in which the major post-war powers – the US, UK, France, China and Russia (formerly the Soviet Union) – were made permanent members and given the right of veto. The use of the veto – and threat to use the veto – has hampered the Security Council's effectiveness. The UN has provided a forum for international debate, and expanded its social and economic activities through its many agencies and affiliated bodies. The International Labour Organization (ILO), which actually predates the UN, sets standards for health and safety, workers' rights, and child labour. Its conventions have been ratified by dozens of states, which by doing so, show a commitment to be bound by them. Similarly, the human rights covenants have been ratified by over 140 states (see Chapter 8).

While state practice sometimes falls far short of these commitments, they do represent an acknowledgement of the principles contained in the conventions. The Covenant on Civil and Political Rights (in Article 25) lays down minimum standards for democratic government, including free and fair elections, universal suffrage, and secret ballots. The acceptance by states of the principle that these conventions impose on them a 'higher' duty to comply is an indication of a shift away from the pure theory of state sovereignty.

The UN itself has taken the lead in giving humanitarian aid priority over state sovereignty by intervening in states' domestic affairs in cases of human rights violations in Iraq, Somalia and Bosnia. Under its Charter, the UN can take measures to

▸ More online ... The full text of the UN Charter may be found on the UN's website at www.un.org
The Security Council's website is www.un.org/sc

The United Nations

To maintain international peace and security:

Collective measures to prevent and remove threats to peace, suppress acts of aggression

Settle international disputes which might lead to breach of the peace

To promote friendly relations among nations:

Principle of equal rights and self-determination of peoples

To help solve international problems:

Economic

Social

Cultural

Humanitarian

Upholding basic human rights

Figure 7.10 **Main provisions of the UN Charter**

Source: The UN Charter, at www.un.org

enforce or maintain international peace, including peacekeeping operations and sanctions against particular countries. Sanctions include a range of measures: they may be economic and trade sanctions, arms embargoes, travel bans or financial restrictions. Countries affected have included Libya, Somalia, Sudan, Sierra Leone and Iraq. Sanctions, however, may have negative effects in that ordinary people suffer while regimes find ways of getting round the sanctions, as happened in Iraq under Saddam Hussein. A framework of 'smart' sanctions approved by the Security Council in 2002 against Iraq was designed to target arms exports while allowing goods needed by civilians to enter the country.

Summary points The UN

◆ The UN is the broadest and most highly respected of intergovernmental organizations.

◆ Founded on the principle of state sovereignty, the UN operates through co-operative means to further its

ends, which include maintaining peace and promoting a range of economic and social activities.

The European Union

As we found in Chapter 4, regional groupings of states have grown in numbers in the post-war period. Most of these are trading alliances, but the most advanced, the EU, represents much deeper economic, social and political integration. Originally comprising a group of six states (Germany, France, Belgium, Luxembourg, the Netherlands, and Italy) under the Treaty of Rome in 1957, the European Community, as it then was, envisaged a 'pooling' of national sovereignty. When Britain joined in 1973, the possibility of the erosion of parliamentary sovereignty was a major issue, and it has remained so, particularly among Eurosceptics. Despite misgivings about national sovereignty, perceived economic benefits have made the EU more popular than ever. It has expanded to 27 members. Accession negotiations are taking place with Turkey and Croatia. Other Easter European countries, such as Ukraine, have aspired to membership, but the victory of the pro-Russian party in elections in 2010 seemed to signal a cooling of relations with Western Europe.

The EU's main institutions are the Council, which was envisaged as holding the main law-making authority, the Commission, through which much legislation has originated, and the Parliament, which has acted mainly as a check on the other two bodies. The enlargement debate has raised questions about the effectiveness and democratic credentials of these structures, perceived as unwieldy, over-bureaucratic, and lacking in democratic accountability. A proposed new constitution for the enlarged EU was put forward in 2004, but rejected in referendums in two countries (France and the Netherlands). A revised document was put forward as the Lisbon Treaty. A key aspect of the Lisbon Treaty, which took effect in December 2009, was to enhance the powers of the European Parliament. A summary of the constitutional proposals and Lisbon Treaty appears in Table 7.2. These will now be discussed.

Table 7.2 **Comparison of the EU draft constitution and the Lisbon Treaty of 2009**

Constitutional proposals of 2004	Lisbon Treaty of 2009
Enhances powers of the European Parliament over legislation and EU budget	Yes
Introduces new system of weighted voting in the Council of Ministers: a yes vote requires at least 55% of member states representing at least 65% of EU population	Yes
Reduces size of European Commission: members to be sent from only two-thirds of member states on a rotation basis	Not in force. All member states retain right to send commissioners
Creates new offices of president of the Council (serving a term of up to five years), and high representative for foreign affairs	Yes
Ends the six-month rotating presidency of the Council	Not as yet. Rotating presidency retained in 2010, although the new president was in place
Incorporates an EU charter of Fundamental Rights	Yes

Source: The European Parliament, at www.europarl.europa.eu

The highest law-making authority in the EU, officially renamed the Council of the European Union in 1993, is commonly referred to as the Council of Ministers. Members are ministers in their own states. Under the Lisbon Treaty, a new president of the European Council was appointed. He was intended to replace the previous arrangement of a six-month rotating presidency among member states, but in fact, the rotating presidency continued. Originally, unanimity among council members was required for a proposal to proceed, but this requirement has been relaxed in some key areas (for example agriculture, the environment and transport) by 'quali- fied majority voting' (QMV). A safeguard for small countries is the provision that a vote is carried if it is supported by at least 55% of member states representing 65% of the overall population of the EU (see Table 7.3). National veto is still retained on issues of tax, defence, foreign policy and financing the EU budget. A new office of high representative for foreign affairs has been created, to oversee the diplomatic service. The aim of creating the new foreign affairs post was to raise the EU's foreign relations profile.

Table 7.3 **The Council of the European Union**

Member state	Population (millions)	Percentage of Council votes
Germany	82	16.5
France	64	12.9
UK	62	12.4
Italy	60	12
Spain	46	9
Poland	38	7.6
Romania	21	4.3
The Netherlands	17	3.3
Greece	11	2.2
Portugal	11	2.1
Belgium	11	2.1
Czech Republic	10	2
Hungary	10	2
Sweden	9.2	1.9
Austria	8.3	1.7
Bulgaria	7.6	1.5
Denmark	5.5	1.1
Slovak Republic	5.4	1.1
Finland	5.3	1.1
Ireland	4.5	.9
Lithuania	3.3	.7
Latvia	2.2	.5
Slovenia	2	.4
Estonia	1.3	.3
Cyprus	.87	.2
Luxembourg	.49	.1
Malta	.41	.1

Source: The European Council, at www.european-council.europa.eu

The European Commission is composed of 27 commissioners, one from each member state. The Commission is headed by a president. The Directorates-General of the Commission are the heart of the EU's civil service, responsible for its day-to-day running. Importantly, in addition, the Commission takes the lead in proposing legislation, and thus enjoys considerable political power from its 'agenda-setting' initiatives, such as the Single Market and Monetary Union. The 2004 constitutional plan provided for a reduction in the number of commissioners to 18 from 2014. There have been objections to this streamlining of the Commission, and the proposed reduction in size of the Commission was shelved.

The European Parliament is composed of members from each state roughly in proportion to the state's population. The EU Parliament has grown in size from 78 to 736 members. Although Members of the European Parliament (MEPs) have been directly elected by EU citizens since 1979, the parliament does not play the pivotal

▶ More online ... The EU portal is http://europa.eu

role which is customary in national systems. The Treaty of Rome gave Parliament little direct say in legislation, but with later treaties, it gained greater influence with an increase from 15 to 38 areas in which it has 'co-decision-making' powers with the Council (amounting to two-thirds of all EU legislation). These reforms have come in response to criticism that EU institutions lack sufficient democratic accountability and that they are bureaucratic and inefficient. The new constitutional treaty also provides for increased scrutiny of proposed legislation by national parliaments.

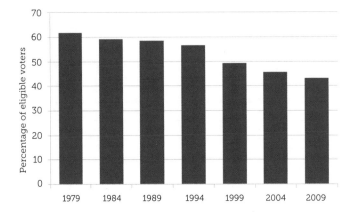

Figure 7.11 **Voter turnout in European Parliament elections**

Source: European Parliament (2009) Turnout trends at European elections, at www.europarl.europa.eu

The European Parliament has not as yet resonated with voters to the same extent that national parliaments do. As Figure 7.11 shows, voter turnout has declined with each successive election, reaching a low of 43% in 2009. It had been hoped that the prospect of a greater role for the parliament in the new European constitution would persuade voters to take greater interest. However, the popularity of Eurosceptic parties in many countries suggests that national issues loom larger with the electorate than pan-European issues. This is suggested in the low turnout in some new member states: Romania, 27.6%; Poland, 24.5% and Slovakia, 19.6%.

Summary points EU institutions

◆ The EU's structure has remained essentially that created by the founding Treaty of Rome, but the balance of authority has shifted over the years, as the European Parliament has gained greater say over legislation.

◆ Reform of the institutions and enlargement have become the major issues for the EU's member states. Progress has been slow in both areas, due in large part to sensitivities to national interests.

Changing world balance of power

At its founding in 1945, the UN was envisaged as an overarching body that would ensure world peace, but it was a peace dominated by sovereign states, notably the major powers which emerged victorious in the Second World War (Mazower, 2010). This world picture was reflected in the composition of the Security Council, which had three western members out of the five with permanent seats (the US, UK and France). At that time, the UN had only 45 member states in total. The crumbling of empires, both political and economic, which occurred in the following years, creating dozens of new sovereign states, could hardly have been foreseen. These developments have transformed the world. The sovereign state is no longer the preserve of a minority of world powers, but claimed by countries large and small, located all over the globe. The bulk of the UN's current membership is made up of developing countries, representing an extraordinary shift. Many would argue that this broad base gives the UN a greater mandate to take action, say, by intervening in human rights abuses in Burma. On the other hand, its enshrining of the principle of sovereignty has led it down the path of persuasion and diplomacy, which in many situations appears to be ineffectual. The UN remains active in many spheres, notably peacekeeping, but in global politics, it now looks more like a debating forum: although it retains moral authority in theory, in practice it is unable to follow through with actions. One of its enduring accomplishments, which should not be underestimated, however, is its work in negotiating treaties (discussed in the next chapter). The role of facilitator in areas such as climate change is a worthy one, although many would see this role as second-best to the political role envisaged by its founders.

The politics of today's world have become more fragmented than in the cold-war period following the Second World War. The G20 (discussed in Chapter 4) is more representative of the current global powers economically than the UN Security Council or the IMF. Indeed, the IMF, by sponsoring the G20, is carving out a broadened role in which the major developing countries are engaged. With the rise of Asian economies in particular, there is a shift in the balance of global power from west to east. But, although the G20 represents the emerging powers on the global stage, this grouping is just that: it meets periodically in summits and discusses major issues, but its pronouncements are not binding on its members, and it has no permanent secretariat or structure. Like the UN, the G20 is a grouping of sovereign states. And global politics is played out not so much in intergovernmental institutions, whether formal or informal, but in the power dynamics between states, including the extent of a country's global economic power and its military strength. Much talk of the emergence of the G2 – China and the US – has focused on both these areas of global power. But both countries are aware that in the fragmented world of global politics, interdependence as a guiding concept is perhaps more relevant than assertions of sovereignty.

Summary points Global balance of power

● The UN has become rather anachronistic as a governance structure; the Security Council in particular is no longer representative of the world's political landscape.

● The growth of developing economies, notably the large emerging economies, has implied a shift in the balance of power from west to east.

● The power relations in global politics remain governed by sovereign actors, although tempered by interdependence.

Critical thinking
The G2
How illuminating is it to discuss global politics in terms of the G2?

Conclusions

1 The political sphere concerns decision-making processes for resolving conflict in society as a whole. Interactions between state and private actors are blurring the traditional distinctions between state and civil society.

2 The nation-state is the basic unit into which all the world's people are divided.

3 Although sovereign states, which are autonomous in theory, predominate across the world, interdependence, both political and economic, encourages intergovernmental co-operation in practice.

4 States vary in their sources of legitimacy. Traditional sources of legitimate authority have given way to constitutionality and democratic forms.

5 Businesses seek stability in business environments, but face political risk from both internal and external sources in the countries in which they operate.

6 Authoritarian governments in today's world often promote market reforms and rely on elections, although only among state-approved candidates.

7 Democratic government may take a number of forms: these include presidential, parliamentary and 'hybrid' systems. A stronger executive is associated with presidential systems, while the legislative is predominant in parliamentary systems.

8 Freedom of association, political parties and pluralistic political debate are characteristic of genuinely democratic systems.

9 Two-party systems are associated with the first-past-the-post type of electoral system, while multi-party systems are more associated with proportional representation. Where no party has a clear majority, parties are inclined to form alliances, which govern as a coalition.

10 The EU represents an attempt to achieve political cohesion at supranational level, but its institutions, often perceived as lacking sufficient democratic legitimacy, do not enjoy the support in member states that national political institutions command.

11 Since the Second World War, the UN has been the most important institutional framework for intergovernmental co-operation. However, large emerging economies are now playing greater political roles at international level.

Review questions

1 What are the defining characteristics of the nation-state? How is globalization threatening state sovereignty?

2 What are the internal and external political risks to international business?

3 What are the characteristics of a constitution, and why is it felt to be stable in the long term?

4 What are the differences between authoritarian states and democratic ones? Why is the line between them becoming blurred?

5 What is federalism, and what are its alleged advantages?

6 How do presidential systems compare with parliamentary systems of government? The hybrid system is said to combine the best of both worlds, but does it?

7 What is the role of political parties, and how are they evolving with changes in the environment?

8 Looking at the main institutions of the European Union, how democratic are they?

9 What are the proposals for reforming the European Union?

10 What are the main trends now occurring in global politics? What institutional changes are reflecting these trends?

Key revision concepts

Authoritarianism, p. 238; Civil society, p. 230; Coalition government, p. 248; Constitutionalism, p. 233; Democracy, p. 240; Elections, p. 243; Government, p. 231; Ideology, p. 233; NGO (non-governmental organization), p. 253; Political party, p. 249; Political risk, p. 234; Politics, p. 229; Presidential/parliamentary system, p. 246; Proportional representation, p. 244; Separation of powers, p. 243; Sovereignty, p. 232

Assignments

◆ Assume that a company is considering moving production to a location in a developing country (for example Mexico), but is concerned about political instability. What particular aspects of the country's political structure and processes should it take into account when assessing political risk?

◆ Authoritarian regimes in today's world, such as China, often see economic development as unconnected to democratic reforms. To what extent can it be argued that economic development logically leads to democracy?

Further reading

Baylis, J., Smith, S. and Owens, P. (eds) (2007) *The Globalization of World Politics*, 4th edn (Oxford: Oxford University Press).

Heywood, A. (2007) *Politics*, 3rd edn (Basingstoke: Palgrave Macmillan).

Hague, R. and Harrop, M. (2007) *Comparative Government and Politics: An Introduction*, 7th edn (Basingstoke: Palgrave Macmillan).

Held, D. (ed.) (1993) *Prospects for Democracy* (Cambridge: Polity Press).

Held, D. and McGrew, A. (2007) *Globalization/Anti-globalization: Beyond the Great Divide*, 2nd edn (Cambridge: Polity Press).

McGrew, A. and Lewis, P. (1992) *Globalization and the Nation-State* (Cambridge: Polity Press).

Gazprom: seeking new markets but weighed down at home

Russian gas giant Gazprom, in common with other natural resource companies, sees its fortunes fluctuate with market demand. When demand is strong, especially in export markets, and prices are high, its revenues soar, but when demand and prices fall off, its financial position can rapidly deteriorate. MNEs in mining and extraction sectors are well aware of these fluctuations, and their executives seek strategic ways to mitigate dependence on volatile markets, for example, by diversification and technological improvements. But Gazprom has relied mainly on selling gas, aware that it is sitting on 26% of the world's gas reserves. However, gas sales at home and abroad have resulted in dwindling profits, affected by financial woes, including scarcity of credit. Its development activities have also been disappointing. Can it find new strategies to turn round its fortunes?

If Gazprom were an ordinary private-sector company, its executives would probably have some difficult questions to answer from shareholders. But as a state-controlled company, it is answerable mainly to the Kremlin in Moscow. It has close links with Russia's political rulers, notably the former president, now prime minister, Vladimir Putin. Mr Putin, constitutionally barred in 2008 from standing for a third term as president, came to power following the financial crisis of 1998, which left the country in political and economic turmoil. His formula for returning the country to stability involved tightening his political and economic grip on power, and placing on hold liberal economic reforms which had been

undertaken in the earlier post-communist years. In the process, Gazprom, the former Soviet gas ministry, which had been privatized, came back under more direct state control.

With state resources to support it, Gazprom embarked on rapid expansion internationally. This strategy was partly dictated by its situation in its home market, where prices were capped and revenues therefore low. One of Gazprom's chief strengths is its control over the pipelines that take gas to customers. It has been a major supplier to European markets, but here demand has fallen in recent years, partly because European governments have become wary of energy dependency on a company closely associated with the Russian state. Sales to neighbouring Ukraine, a former Soviet Republic, have been the subject of regular price disputes. Price rises followed Ukraine's veering towards pro-west policies, but the new pro-Russian government, elected in 2010, agreed to extend the leases of Russian Navy bases in return for a 30% reduction in gas prices.

Russia's Gazprom, the energy giant, has become accustomed to operating in harsh environments in remote regions, but its management remains close to the Russian state

Source: Istock

▶ More online ... Gazprom is at www.gazprom.ocm
GM&T is at www.gazprom-mt.com

Gazprom has sought to explore and develop new gas fields, but these projects, some in harsh climates such as the Yamal peninsula inside the Arctic circle, have stalled. These gas fields were discovered in the Soviet era, but years of underinvestment followed. Now, falling demand for gas, due to economic downturn, has set Gazprom's timetable for development back further. It was constrained to cut back its investments in development in 2009.

The disappointments of the Yamal gas fields are indicative of wider problems in the Russian economy. Although a Bric country, Russia's economy remains precariously dependent on oil and gas exports. A divide has emerged between the prosperous resource-based firms and firms in other sectors, many SMEs, which have struggled to achieve competitiveness and have little access to credit. Russia's GDP shrank nearly 10% in 2009. Although a vast country spanning 11 time zones, Russia's regions have been governed mainly from the centre. Putin formed a kind of 'social contract' to ensure stability throughout the country: people would be content with little voice so long as funds, mainly from oil revenues, flowed to the regional governments, to fund social spending in particular. When oil revenues slowed, the central government provided subsidies to the regions, but these stopped as the financial crisis deepened. As a result, regions had to meet these

obligations themselves, by raising taxes, which triggered social unrest in many distant regional centres.

Although the Russian economy started to recover in 2010, a question remains whether the government will rely simply on rising oil and gas prices, or will seek to introduce liberal reforms to diversify the economy and reduce the influence of the state. There has been talk of allowing independent producers to gain access to Gazprom's infrastructure, over which it has a monopoly, thus introducing competition in the domestic supply of gas. Gazprom itself has formed Gazprom Marketing and Trading (GM&T), a wholly owned subsidiary based in London, which is an energy trader. GM&T is looking to transform its business away from simply supplying gas to other activities that can be more profitable, such as distribution and retail sales. It has now established businesses in numerous countries, including Germany, Singapore and the US, where it is developing carbon trading and other activities. This trading limb seems to be flourishing, aided by more liberal market environments than exist in Gazprom's home economy.

Sources: Clover, C. (2010) 'Strife on the edge', Financial Times, 25 March; Clover, C. (2010) 'Unrest as subsidies and credit dry up', Financial Times, 14 April; Elder, M. (2009) 'Gazprom faces problems at home and abroad', Financial Times, 5 October; Gazprom Marketing and Trading website, at www.gazprom-mt.com

Questions for discussion

◆ In what ways have Gazprom's links with the Russian government been benefits or drawbacks to the company?
◆ Would Gazprom benefit if Russia were to introduce more liberal reforms in the industry? Explain.
◆ To what extent has Gazprom's international strategy been a success?

CHAPTER 8 THE LEGAL ENVIRONMENT

Outline of chapter

Learning objectives

1 To understand the interrelationships between national, regional, and international legal frameworks in their impact on the international business environment

2 To appreciate the divergence in structures, processes and content between national legal systems

3 To assess the impact of evolving regional, in particular, European Union, law-making on enterprises, workers and consumers

4 To apply principles of international law, including human rights, to organizations and their workforces

Critical themes in this chapter

- **Multilayered environment** – national legal systems; legal framework of the EU; international legal environment
- **Role of the state** – state jurisdiction and co-operation at international level
- **International risk** – legal risk in international operations
- **CSR and sustainability** – legal obligations as an aspect of CSR; international human rights

Shaking hands on the deal, but legal pitfalls abound in international business
Source: Istock

Anyone for a fake iPhone?

The phone the customer is buying might look like a gleaming iPhone, but in many markets, the strong likelihood is that it is a counterfeit, manufactured by one of the many small handset manufacturers that have sprung up in China, making phones which fall into the broad category of 'grey market'. It might carry an Apple logo, or it could be a 'HiPhone', one of many clones that were launched soon after the entry of the legitimate iPhone into China. In addition to infringing the brand owner's trademark, the so-called 'bandit' phone will probably run pirated software and have no quality certification. With no guarantee or warranty, if it breaks, the customer has no redress. It will lack an international mobile equipment identity number (IMEI), which is legally required of all phones. The IMEI makes them traceable, especially useful in cases of suspected terrorist and criminal activities. Alternatively, the phone could carry a fake IMEI, which some companies have become adept at providing.

The grey handset market has grown hugely in just a few years. Of the estimated 750 million handsets produced in China, it is estimated that 20% are counterfeit or illegitimate in some way. Although many are sold in China, a large proportion are destined for export markets, favoured destinations being Africa, Latin America and the Middle East. Half the Ghanaian market and nearly half the Indian market are now some shade of grey. The bandit phone is not simply a cheap imitation of a major brand. The large companies such as Nokia have become skilful at producing low-end phones, which are highly competitive, leaving little scope for the grey marketers to make money in this segment. Instead, they often go for models with innovative extras, such as the iPhone which takes two SIM cards, letting the user run two phone numbers on the same phone. Such features have helped to win market share. A crucial element in their success is that they use the same components as legitimate manufacturers: a technological breakthrough in microchips by Mediatek, a Taiwanese company, in 2005, made it cheaper and easier to make a handset. As a result, thousands of new inexperienced handset manufacturers sprang up in China almost overnight. The fact that the grey marketers share a supply chain

with the legitimate producers has created a headache for regulators, blurring the boundary between legitimate and illegal. However, governments are now starting to crack down on the illicit manufacturers.

Highly entrepreneurial, the handset makers have risen to the challenges of the changing legal environment. India has begun to squeeze out the illicit phones from China. This is due in part to the ongoing tension between the two countries, which affects trade relations. A group of Chinese handset manufacturers, eager to retain their Indian market, have taken steps to set up production in India. In addition to establishing better relations in an important market, it is also an opportunity for them to display their technological know-how to best advantage, attempting to shake off the bandit-phone image. They are gradually coming to the realization that if they offer phones with quality guarantees and legitimate identities, they can generate more profits and also start to build up their own brands.

Is the writing on the wall for the counterfeiters? Many of the other target markets of the Chinese counterfeiters are now squeezing out bandit handsets. In China itself, sales are slowing, as consumers begin to weigh up the disadvantages of fake Nokias or iPhones. Some determined counterfeiters are shifting their efforts away from handsets into laptops and digital cameras. How about a fake iPad?

Sources: Farrar, L. 'China's "bandit" phones making big scores', 3 August 2009, CNN news at www.cnn.com; Hille, K., 'China groups eye production in India', *Financial Times*, 17 February 2010; Hille, K., '"Bandit" phone makers build up brands', *Financial Times*, 17 February 2010; *The Economist* (2009) 'Talk is cheap', 21 November

Questions for discussion

◆ Why has China become a favoured location for counterfeit manufacturers?
◆ Why is the grey market so thriving in the technology sector, and how is it evolving?
◆ What can brand owners do to counteract counterfeit products?

Introduction

The legal dimension of international business has grown as business relations across national borders have deepened and become more complex. Historically, the legal environment has been determined by national legal systems. All commercial transactions across national borders, from the simplest export contracts to complex joint ventures, exist within the frameworks of national legal systems. Globalization of markets and production has provided the impetus for harmonization in the legal systems between states. We now see a burgeoning body of international law as well as moves by nation-states to co-operate in drafting and applying laws. Modern international managers, therefore, require an understanding of the workings of international law, as well as familiarity with different national legal systems.

The speed of some developments such as e-commerce has far outpaced the development of the law to cover them. While governments have slowly woken up to the legal implications of advances in technology, they have also realized their own limitations in regulating international transactions. Lawmakers now co-operate in international legal reform and in the reform of national systems to take account of new ways of doing business. Most countries appreciate the need for an efficient, modern, impartial legal system, to attract enterprises (both local and overseas investors) and to retain their confidence in its processes. They also see the benefits of harmonization of laws to facilitate international transactions. The legal environment can be divided into three interacting spheres, as shown in Figure 8.1: national legal systems; regional law-making authorities, of which the European Union is the major example; and international law emanating from recognized international bodies such as the United Nations and its agencies. This chapter will set out the 'boundaries' of each, and explore the ways in which these overlapping spheres of law impact on international business.

Figure 8.1 **The international legal environment**

Classifying law

law rule or body of rules perceived as binding because it emanates from state authorities with powers of enforcement

Law refers to the rules identified as binding because they emanate from state authorities. Groups within a society, such as sports bodies, create rules for their own participants and members, but the distinguishing feature of law is that it creates obligations for society as a whole. Law touches on almost all aspects of business. While business-people are inclined to see legal rules in a negative light, constraining their activities (for example an application for planning permission), in fact, much law is of an enabling nature (for example eligibility to apply for public funding). Market-driven economies aim to strike a balance between freedom of enterprise and sufficient regulation to safeguard the public interest. In the post-war era, with an upsurge in welfare-state provisions, the law has extended to areas such as employment protection, consumer protection, and health and safety in the workplace. More recently, with advances in telecommunications, data protection for personal details has come into the ambit of legal protection.

A number of the main areas of legal obligation, in each of the three spheres, are shown in Figure 8.2. There is overlapping jurisdiction in some of these areas, such as competition and environment. For sheer scope of jurisdiction, the national legal system is the most relevant for any business. However, the regional and international spheres cover some of the global issues that are becoming increasingly important for business, and there is now greater co-ordination between the three sets of authorities.

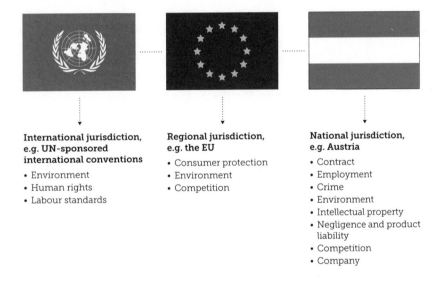

International jurisdiction, e.g. UN-sponsored international conventions

- Environment
- Human rights
- Labour standards

Regional jurisdiction, e.g. the EU

- Consumer protection
- Environment
- Competition

National jurisdiction, e.g. Austria

- Contract
- Employment
- Crime
- Environment
- Intellectual property
- Negligence and product liability
- Competition
- Company

Figure 8.2 **Summary of major areas of law affecting business and relevant authorities**

public law body of law covering relations between citizens and the state

civil (or private) law in any legal system, the law pertaining to relations between private individuals and companies

litigation the use of judicial procedures and the court system to bring claims for damages and other remedies in legal cases

Law may be broadly classified into two categories: **public law**, which concerns relations between citizens and the state, and **civil (or private) law**, which concerns relations between individuals (including companies). Tax and social security fall within public law, whereas contract law and employment law are areas of civil law. The state plays a significant, although less direct, role in civil law. Legislatures enact law regulating employment relations, for example; and the state's courts may be called on to settle disputes between the parties. In a dispute over a contract or an accident at work, the person who has suffered loss or injury (the 'plaintiff') may bring a claim for money compensation ('damages') or a range of other remedies against the 'defendant' in the state's courts. The use of the courts to bring claims for damages and other remedies is referred to as **litigation**. Litigation can be costly and time-consuming. Companies greatly prefer to settle disputes 'out of court', saving costs and achieving an agreement more quickly than waiting for a court hearing. There are now many mechanisms available which help to facilitate settlements through mediation and negotiation short of full court proceedings. One mechanism is arbitration (discussed later in this chapter), whereby the parties agree to allow a third party to step in to settle disputes. An agreement to use arbitration can be included in a contract.

criminal law body of laws which designate offences and set out legal procedure for prosecution of those charged with violations

A major body of public law is the **criminal law**, under which certain types of wrongdoing are designated by the state as criminal offences. In these cases, state authorities initiate proceedings, known as a 'prosecution', in the criminal courts, which, on conviction, will lead to a fine or imprisonment of the offender. While we tend to think of crime in terms of individual crimes, such as assault and theft, companies, as well as their directors, can be guilty of criminal offences. Breaches of health and safety law are a common type of corporate crime. In Britain corporate liability has been extended by a new offence of corporate killing, following unsuccessful prosecutions for manslaughter in relation to ferry and train disasters, including a crash at Paddington, London, in 1999, in which 31 people died. Directors cannot hide behind the facade of the company: they may be personally liable for its crimes. On the other hand, enforcement of the criminal law, which is mainly rooted in national systems, poses major challenges as many criminal activities have become increasingly globalized, and also highly organized. Fraud is an example of a 'white-collar' crime which has been greatly facilitated by global financial networks. See Table 8.1 for a breakdown of the distinctions between civil and criminal law. Note that the 'burden of proof' is higher in a criminal case, which means that a greater degree of certainty is required for criminal guilt than for the judgment as to which party succeeds in a civil case.

Table 8.1 **Outline of civil law and criminal law**

	Criminal law	**Civil law**
What is it about?	Offences against society	Disputes between private individuals or companies
What is the purpose of the action?	To preserve order in the community by punishing offenders and deterring others	To seek a remedy for the wrong which has been suffered, usually money compensation
Who are the parties?	A prosecutor, usually representing the state, prosecutes a defendant, the accused	A plaintiff sues a defendant
Where is the action heard?	State, regional or local criminal courts	Civil courts, at local, regional or state level
Who has to prove what?	The prosecutor must prove a case against the defendant beyond all reasonable doubt	The plaintiff must establish a case on the balance of probabilities
What form does the decision take?	A defendant may be convicted if found guilty, or acquitted if found not guilty	A defendant may be found liable or not liable
What remedies are handed down by the court?	Imprisonment, fine, probation, community service	Damages (money compensation) to the successful plaintiff is the commonest
What are some common types of legal action?	Offences including theft, assault, drunken driving, criminal damage	Actions for breach of contract; actions in negligence for breach of a duty of care owed to the plaintiff

Legal risk for international business

For a business, the bulk of the relevant law stems from national law-making authorities. Each of the world's sovereign states has its own legal system, which has both law-making capacity within its territory ('jurisdiction') and capacity to apply its law to organizations and individuals within its jurisdiction. Legal systems do not exist in a vacuum, but are influenced by the society's social, political and cultural environment. The legal environment, including the content of law and legal processes, is an indicator of attitudes to law in general, as well as the wider values of a society. It also reflects the historical development of the country's institutions.

Figure 8.3 **Legal risk in international business**

legal risk uncertainties surrounding legal liabilities, their implementation in differing legal systems, and the observance of fairness and impartiality in judicial proceedings in differing locations

Legal risk can arise in any situation where a firm engages in business across national borders. Some of the main areas of risk are shown in Figure 8.3. The degree of risk depends on the extent and nature of the firm's involvement in the foreign location. Internet companies operating in China are subject to censorship and other controls, discussed in the case study which follows. Contracts are often the first area in which the firm encounters a foreign legal system. If disputes arise with suppliers

Barriers on the rise in the 'borderless' world of the internet

The global spread of the internet has brought opportunities for individuals and organizations to access virtually limitless amounts of data and also to communicate freely with other internet users, for all manner of reasons, from cross-border business to social networking. But the freedom to surf, once taken for granted, is increasingly subject to constraints imposed by governments. One legal expert from Harvard Business School says, 'It's true of cyberspace as it is of real space – companies have to bow to the laws and customs of the countries they operate in' (Waters and Menn, 2010). Censorship and controls are becoming more sophisticated and more widespread.

There are now more than 40 countries that operate official barriers to the internet, whereas a decade ago, there was only a handful. China and other authoritarian countries, such as Iran, Vietnam and Burma (Myanmar), are well known. Indeed, China has developed such censorship expertise that it claims its web security companies are now gaining export contracts. In countries where political dissent is suppressed, much control of the internet is targeted at people perceived to be opposing the government. Perhaps more surprising, states with elected governments and the rule of law have some of the most stringent censorship in place. In Australia, tough internet filters are imposed to block out offensive content, such as pornography, deemed to be harmful to citizens.

Curbs on the internet take many forms. Software filters act to block traffic from websites that are blacklisted. Much of the filtering technology developed by western companies, including Microsoft and Cisco, is used by governments. Software that detects simple key words like 'democracy', is giving way to more sophisticated data mining technology, which can identify the content of messages. In some countries, MNEs are compelled to engage in self-censorship, or risk being forced out. Google originally complied with China's self-censorship regime when it entered the country in 2006, but became exasperated in 2010, and closed down its mainland search business, directing users to Hong Kong instead, as an offshore alternative. Google has not exited China altogether. It said that its main reason for closing down its Chinese search engine was cyber attacks on it servers, targeted at the email accounts of human rights activists.

The appeal of an internet cafe for these Chinese users is the freedom to surf the web, but for Chinese government authorities, cafes like this represent a threat

Source: Press Association

Google's motto 'Don't be evil' has been highlighted as placing the company in an ambivalent position in respect to China. There was certainly a good business case for entering the country – China has over 300 million internet users. But one of Google's founders,

▸ More online ... Google's investor relations website is http://investor.google.com

Sergey Brin, whose family left Russia during the communist era in 1979, had been uneasy with China's self-censorship requirements.

Responsibility for blocking sites and setting up filters can be placed on internet service providers, as has happened in China, making them effectively agents of the state. Perhaps more worrying was the decree issued by the Chinese government in 2009 that all computers sold in the country would have to come with pre-installed filtering software. Known as the Green Dam Youth Escort project, it was officially intended to block pornography, but could be used to block other content. Manufacturers, including HP and Dell, objected to this ruling, and the blanket ruling was put on hold, but the Green Dam project has gone ahead on a selected basis, for example on PCs in schools and internet cafes.

From governments' points of view, protection of the public is a broad principle which is used to justify censorship and blocking technology. Cybercrime is on the rise, and governments argue that they need equipment for monitoring suspected criminal activity. Increasing attention given to cybersecurity has spurred the development of software which can analyse masses of data. There are many types of activity which governments take an interest in, including illegal file-sharing of copyright films. The US has asked internet service providers to monitor the traffic in copyright material. In the UK, a digital economy bill was passed after just two hours' debate in the House of Commons, in the final days of its session prior to the general election in 2010. The new law gives broad powers for blocking the internet where illegal file-sharing is occurring or even suspected of occurring. To critics, blocking a site simply on assumed intentions represents a serious erosion of liberty.

The line between reasonable restrictions on the internet in the public interest and unjustifiable inroads into freedom has become blurred. In many cases, governments are able to mount justifications for legal controls of the internet based on public interest and national security – in both democratic and non-democratic countries. To date, there have been few companies which have taken high-profile stances on ethical grounds against state interference.

Sources: Waters, R. and Menn, J. (2010) 'Closing the frontier', *Financial Times*, 29 March; Menn, J., Waters, R. and Hille, K. (2009) 'Control, halt, delete', *Financial Times*, 27 June; *The Economist* (2010) 'Failed search', 20 March; Harvey, M. (2010) 'Searching for an answer to the "evil test"', *The Times*, 15 January; Arthur, C. (2010) 'Digital economy bill rushed through wash-up late night session', *The Guardian*, 8 April

Questions for discussion

◆ To what extent are governments justified in imposing controls on the internet?
◆ How would Google explain its apparently inconsistent position in respect of the Chinese government?
◆ Should companies simply go along with government internet controls or make a positive stance against them?

▸ More online ... Toyota is at www.toyota.com
Ranbaxy is at www.ranbaxy.com
Danone is at www.danone.com

or customers, then foreign courts could be involved. The MNE that manufactures in a foreign location incurs several types of legal liability. Its operations are affected by local environmental and employment laws, and its products are subject to the law on product liability in each country. For a global company, different situations can arise in different markets. Toyota had to examine its quality management systems and supply chain in several respects, as faults appeared in its products. It was compelled to recall products in large markets, aiming to put right the faults. Even so, the company faced lawsuits in some markets.

A firm's patents and trademarks, which are aspects of intellectual property law, can be difficult to enforce in some locations, even leading companies to exit particular markets. The food company Danone, for example, engaged in a long legal battle against Wahaha, its Chinese partner in a soft drinks joint venture, and eventually decided to sell out its 51% stake. It accused Wahaha of running parallel businesses which infringed its trademarks. Had Danone taken a 60% stake, giving it greater control, it might have been able to prevent the activities which led to legal action.

Although functioning in an authoritarian environment, China's legal system is becoming more transparent, partly as a result of the influence of foreign investors (McGregor, 2001). Since the 1980s, contract law, intellectual property law and tax law have undergone reforms, which benefit foreign investors. A new competition law (discussed later) is based on the EU model. However, despite western forms, the workings of the legal system lack the transparency and independent judiciary that would be expected in western contexts. In 2010, China charged four Rio Tinto executives with bribery and industrial espionage, for which they were given prison sentences. The arrests closely followed the collapse of negotiations of iron ore contracts, discussed in the case study on BHP Billiton in Chapter 4. Also in the recent past was a failed bid by Chinalco, a state-owned mining company, to take a large stake in Rio Tinto. The Rio Tinto experience shows that commercial transactions do not take place in a vacuum, but are tied up with strategic and political considerations, especially when state-owned businesses are involved.

Legal risk can arise in situations which are difficult to foresee. Sankyo Daiichi, the Japanese pharmaceutical company, took over Ranbaxy of India in 2008. Ranbaxy is a leading producer of generic medicines, that is, medicines not covered by patents, often because the patents have expired. Generics are becoming more popular globally as costs of branded medicines have spiralled. Daiichi would probably not have foreseen that the Indian company's products would be barred from the US market because of suspected patent infringements. An underlying factor in this case was the power of America's large pharmaceutical companies, which face competition from generic products (see case study in Chapter 10).

Summary points Legal risk

● Businesses wish for a stable and predictable legal environment, but there is a degree of legal risk in all countries, mainly attributable to changing laws and policies of government, the tensions which exist within society, and any external threats which the country faces.

● Legal risk is sometimes higher in countries with high levels of political influence in business, and with high levels of corruption.

Critical thinking

The rule of law

Why is the rule of law essential in societies? Think of societies in which the rule of law is weak or non-existent: what are the drawbacks from the business perspective?

National legal systems

The pre-eminence of national legal systems derives from the theory of the sovereign state. Every legal system may be divided into two main sets of functional institutions. These are legislation (law-making) and adjudication (the settlement of disputes). **Legislation**, or statute law, is enacted by state authorities with law-making powers. In a democracy, the elected legislature is a key law-making body. Much law-making follows social and political agendas of elected governments. Legislators can get it wrong, of course. The prohibition law in the US in the 1930s, banning alcoholic beverages, met widespread opposition and had to be repealed.

legislation laws enacted by law-making processes set out in national constitutions; also known as statute law

The system of courts, or **judicial system**, interprets and applies the law in particular cases. The extent to which judges thereby shape legal development, overlapping with the law-making function, differs between systems, and even within systems is a matter of differing opinions. As will be seen below, 'case law' (judge-made law) is more important in some countries than in others. A general rule is that legal systems attempt to draw a line between law-making and judicial functions. Court systems are designed to prevent the intrusion of political and personal considerations, and judges should be seen to be fair and impartial. In its Global Governance indicators, the World Bank assesses the depth of the rule of law in the world's countries. Included in its assessment are the quality of property rights, the police, the courts and the risk of crime.

judicial system system of courts, usually divided between civil courts and criminal courts

An overview for selected countries is given in Figure 8.4.

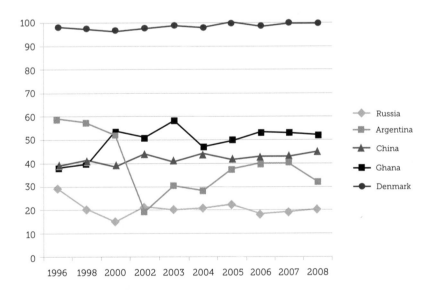

Figure 8.4 **The rule of law rankings of selected countries** (percentage rankings)

Source: World Bank, Governance Matters 2009, World goverance indicators database, at www.worldbank.org

As Figure 8.4 shows, Denmark stands out as the highest example of the rule of law, and this standing has been consistent over a long period. Other selected countries have been less consistent. All the other countries have in common their focus on

► More online ... The full set of global governance indicators can be found on the World Bank's website at www.worldbank.org

economic development. Improvement in the rule of law since 1996 has been only slight in the case of China. Ghana has seen more significant improvement, while Russia and Argentina have gone backwards. These latter two countries have suffered from financial turmoil, straining the rule of law, already fragile in these societies.

The world's legal systems can be classified in terms of legal traditions or legal families. The two major western historical traditions are the civil law tradition and the common law tradition. The **civil law tradition**, prevalent in continental Europe, is founded on a comprehensive legal code, whereas the **common law tradition**, English in origin, emphasizes case law. Both have been adopted in a variety of non-western contexts, as part of modernization processes (see Table 8.2). Newly independent states have tended to adopt the legal tradition of their former colonial power. For this reason, a lawyer from Ghana will find it much easier to understand a lawyer from Kenya or England, than one from the Ivory Coast just next door, which falls within French colonial influence (Zweigert and Kötz, 1998).

civil law tradition
legal system based on comprehensive legal codes which form the basic law

common law tradition
legal system based chiefly on accumulated case law in decided judgments, through a system of binding precedents

Table 8.2 **Selected civil law and common law countries**

Civil law	Common law
Argentina	Australia
Brazil	Bangladesh
Chile	Canada
China	Ghana
Egypt	India
France	Israel
Germany	Jamaica
Greece	Kenya
Indonesia	Malaysia
Iran	Nigeria
Italy	Singapore
Japan	England
Mexico	United States
Sweden	Zambia

Civil law tradition

The civil law tradition is by far the older of the two, and has its origin in the ancient Roman *ius civile*, which in the sixth century was codified in the Justinian Code. Civil law relies on a legal code for the basic groundwork of the system, on which further law-making is built. The legal code is a comprehensive, systematic setting out of the basic law for a country. The modern models of codified law are the French Civil Code of 1804, known as the Napoleonic Code, and the German Civil Code of 1896. Codified law is in fact divided into a number of different codes, depending on the subject matter. The Civil Code, which contains the body of private law (that is, between citizens), is complemented, for example, by a Commercial Code and a Criminal Code. These codes have demonstrated their adaptability by providing models for numerous other countries in Europe, Latin America, Africa, Asia and the Middle East (see Table 8.2). They are adaptable in federal systems, as in Germany, or in unitary systems, as in France. In the UK, Scotland falls in the civil law tradition. Japan's choice of the civil code model coincided with the country's initial industrialization and modernization policies in the late nineteenth century.

The attraction of the civil law model lies in the supremacy of the single authoritative source of the law. The principles and concepts contained in the codes form the basis of legal reasoning. Although the accumulated decisions of judges are useful as guidelines, they are not in themselves a source of law. This is the major distinction between the civil law and common law systems, shown in Table 8.3. The distinction has been described as one between different legal styles. The urge to regulate and systematize has dominated continental legal thinking, whereas English lawyers have tended to improvise, not making a decision until they have to, on the view that 'we'll cross that bridge when we come to it' (Zweigert and Kötz, 1998: 70).

Table 8.3 **Outline of civil law and common law traditions**

	Civil law tradition	**Common law tradition**
Sources of the law	Comprehensive legal codes	Judge-made law and statutes
Role of case law	Guidance, but not binding	System of binding precedent
Legal style	Systematized application of principles	Pragmatic and piecemeal

Summary points **The civil law tradition**

◆ In countries with a civil law system, codified law is the supreme source of law.

◆ In these jurisdictions, judges have less direct influence on the development of the law than in common law systems.

Common law tradition

The common law tradition originated in England some 900 years ago – long before Parliament had become the supreme law-making authority. Common law is essentially judge-made law, known as case law. In deciding a particular dispute, the judge creates a precedent to be followed in similar cases in the future. The body of law builds up through the accumulation of precedents in decided cases. The system has both flexibility and rigidities in practice. Precedents may be applied more loosely or more strictly in later cases, lending flexibility. However, as the court system is hierarchical, the decisions of higher courts form precedents which must be followed by lower courts. Faced with what seems to be a bad precedent, the judge in a lower court has little choice but to follow it. The growth in statute law, in the form of Acts of Parliament, mainly in the past hundred years, has come about largely in response to the complexities of economic and social changes. Modern judges spend a great deal of their time interpreting and applying statute law, including, it should be added, EU law. The growing importance of statute law (also referred to as enacted law) suggests a convergence with the civil law tradition, although, when it comes down to inter-

▶ More online ... The American Law Institute is at www.ali.org

preting the law in particular factual situations – which is what matters to litigants – the judge still holds a good deal of power.

Common law systems have been transplanted to countries as diverse as the US and India. Like all legal systems, the tradition has been adapted to the local environment. The US, with its division between federal and 50 state jurisdictions, has evolved a particularly complex system, with overlapping jurisdictions that can be confusing to outsiders (and even insiders). Each state constitutes a system within a system – Louisiana even has remnants of French codified law from its own colonial past. The individual states have made efforts to achieve consistency in the law in key areas that affect business, notably through the Uniform Commercial Code, which has been adopted by all the states (although only partially in Louisiana). The American Law Institute has spearheaded the efforts to bring about consistency by producing its Restatements of the law in areas such as contract and product liability. These restatements resemble codified law in all but name, but they do not have the status of a statute as they are not passed by Congress. Their aim is to clarify the law and they act as guidance to lawyers and judges.

Summary points The common law tradition

◆ Judges have greater influence in common law systems, although the growing body of statute law tends to suggest that these systems are moving closer to the civil law jurisdictions.

◆ Common law systems differ from country to country, and are adapted to federal systems, as in the US.

Non-western legal systems

The growth in commercial law has reached almost all countries, aware that economic development depends on a sound legal framework and an efficient and accessible court system. As has been seen, the groundwork for modern legal systems in much of the world was the legacy of colonial regimes. Legal traditions in many countries, which are based on customary law, pre-date western systems and continue to form an important part of the overall legal environment. In many countries, therefore, we now find a mixture of pre-modern customs, colonial forms, and newer codes designed to keep up to date with business needs. The study of evolving legal systems in developing countries reveals much about the relationship between law and social change.

Shari'a the authoritative source of Islamic law

Non-western legal traditions include Islamic, Chinese and Hindu law. Of these, Islamic law, called the **Shari'a** (or God's rules), is perhaps the most highly developed. Islamic law can have a direct impact on the way business is conducted in Muslim countries, such as Saudi Arabia and Sudan. Because the *Shari'a* prohibits 'unearned profits', the charging of interest is forbidden. Financing through banks can still be arranged, by devising alternative legal forms to cover transactions, including profit-sharing and loss-sharing by a lending bank. Muslim countries have introduced codes for secular regulation of the formation and enforcement of contracts, foreign investment, and the employment of foreign workers. Accordingly, most now have secular tribunals for these areas.

Both western and non-western legal traditions have evolved and adapted to different cultural contexts, in response to two related forces. *First*, there has been a perceived need to modernize national legal structures as societies have become more complex, and legal relations including consumer and employment contracts have become more common. Most of this development has come through legislation, such the Consumer Protection Act 1987 and Employment Rights Act 1996 in the UK. *Secondly*, the growth of global markets has led to increasing international efforts to achieve uniformity and standardization of laws across national borders. Much of this latter effort has come through multilateral international conventions. These are signed and then ratified by national authorities, ultimately taking on a status similar to the domestic law of the state. In particular, international conventions have played an important role in bringing common legal frameworks for international trade in goods (as will be discussed below). Within the European Union harmonization has gone further, putting in place supranational legal structures for both law-making and adjudication.

Summary points **Non-western legal systems**

- Non-western legal systems are often based on religious law.

- They can constitute the main legal system in the state, but, more often, they exist alongside

the state's legal structures, having jurisdiction in particular cases where religious law comes into play.

Critical thinking

National legal systems

Which of the types of national legal system described here is most likely to be accessible and efficient from a business perspective?

Legal framework of the European Union

For each member state, the EU is a growing source of law, which has become intertwined with national law. The foundation treaty, the Treaty of Rome of 1957, has been followed by a number of treaties creating supranational institutions, that is, institutions above those of domestic law. Under the Maastricht Treaty of 1992, three pillars were designated: the European Communities, the Common Foreign and Security Policy, and the Police and Judicial Co-operation in Criminal Matters. The first of these was supranational, and the other two represented intergovernmental co-operation. The law of the EU was technically referred to as EC law, as it fell under the first pillar. With the Treaty of Lisbon of 2009, the three-pillar system has been abolished, subsuming the second and third pillars. The EU itself now has legal personality: the EU can now make treaties in its own name, and its law is now 'EU law'.

As discussed in the last chapter, EU law-making now extends to a wide range of areas, although not as yet taxation and defence. The legislative function is divided between the Commission, the Council and the European Parliament, through the co-decision procedure (see Chapter 7). EU law falls into two main types: regulations and directives. Regulations are directly applicable throughout the EU, becoming incorporated automatically into the law of each member state. They create individual rights and obligations which governments must recognize. Directives require member states to implement their provisions, usually within a given period of time, typically two years. In some cases, the directive may have direct effect, allowing individuals to enforce rights in EU law, even though the member state has not implemented the law within the required time limit. For businesses, competition law is an area with growing implications for MNEs (see later section). In competition law,

▸ More online ... The European Court of Justice (ECJ) is at http://europa.eu/institutions/inst/justice

high-profile cases, such as the Microsoft case, have involved the Commission taking legal action against a company in the European Court of Justice.

European Court of Justice (ECJ)
highest court for interpreting EU law

The judicial function centres on the **European Court of Justice (ECJ)**. It is the sole interpreter of EU law, and can override national legislation in cases of conflict. Although national supreme courts have ultimate authority in domestic matters, in issues involving EU institutions and EU law, the ECJ is the ultimate authority. The ECJ interprets the treaties and other legislation. It is modelled on courts in the civil law tradition, in that it is not bound by its previous decisions, but its case law has in fact shown consistency. The ECJ is now divided into sections that hear cases at first instance and those that hear cases in an appellate capacity, that is, on appeal.

Summary points Legal framework of the EU

◆ The EU's legislative bodies are the Council, Commission and Parliament. Of these, the Parliament gained greater say in law-making due to the reforms in the Lisbon Treaty of 2009.

◆ The judicial function in the EU is situated in the European Court of Justice.

Cross-border transactions

Laws covering trade between businesses in different countries have existed since the medieval period, when the *law merchant* was born of customary rules used by the merchants of the period. These rules, relating to sale of goods and the settlement of disputes, were gradually incorporated into national bodies of law, codified in the case of the civil law countries, and part of the common law in common law countries. In England, the law became enacted in the Sale of Goods Act 1894, and in the US the Uniform Commercial Code (1951) harmonized the law between the 50 states. Impetus to achieve international harmonization has come from a number of initiatives.

International codification of contract law

Set up in 1966, the UN Commission on International Trade Law (UNCITRAL) attempted to devise a framework to satisfy the needs of businesses from trading nations of all continents. The result was the Convention on Contracts for the International Sale of Goods (CISG) of 1980 (the Vienna Convention), which came into force in 1988. The CISG does not apply automatically to international sales. The convention must be ratified by individual states, becoming incorporated in their domestic law. The number of countries that have ratified the convention (75 by January 2010) continues to rise, accounting for the bulk of the world's trade. Among major trading nations, the US, Germany, France, China and Japan have ratified. Notable among those that have not yet ratified are Brazil, India, South Africa and the UK. The convention applies to contracts falling within its scope that are concluded by firms in countries which have ratified, or to contracts whose performance is carried out in a country which has ratified. For transactions between firms in non-ratifying countries, the rules of private international law apply. (These are discussed below.)

Where the CISG makes a major contribution is in harmonizing rules to do with the formation of contracts for the sale of goods, obligations of the parties and remedies. It attempts to bridge the gap between civil and common law jurisdictions on questions

▶ More online ... The UN's main international law website is http://www.un.org/law/
The UNCITRAL home page is http://www.uncitral.org
The UNIDROIT principles are available in full at http://www.cisg.law.pace.edu/cisg/principles.html

such as the 'meeting of minds' between the parties over the existence of an agreement, and its particular terms. These are the key areas in which disputes arise, and the CISG attempts to compromise between countries that require certainty and those that allow greater flexibility. For example, the requirement that a contract must be in writing is traditional in the common-law countries (although of diminishing importance), whereas civil law countries tend to have no writing requirement. The CISG allows ratifying countries the option, in keeping with their own national law. China, for example, has preserved its writing requirement.

The International Institute for the Unification of Private International Law (UNIDROIT) has complemented the CISG, and approached the need for unification from a different perspective. The UNIDROIT Principles of International Commercial Contracts, published in 1994 and revised in 2004, offer general rules for international contracts, and are broadly similar to the CISG, but of wider application. The Principles are not confined to the sale of goods. Moreover, as they are not embodied in any binding international convention, they can be incorporated into contracts by firms from any country, not just those that have ratified the CISG. It has been suggested that they come closest to 'the emerging international consensus' on the rules of international trade (Moens and Gillies, 1998: 81). Because the Principles do not themselves have any force of law, they can be adopted and modified as needed, and have even provided models for legislators as diverse as Mexico, Quebec and the Netherlands. In particular, they have facilitated the growing trade between Australia and its Asian neighbours.

Summary points International codification of contract law

◈ UN harmonization initiatives have made it easier for businesses to make cross-border contracts.

◈ These include the CISG, now ratified by most countries, and the UNIDROIT Principles, which can be

adopted by MNEs doing cross-border business.

Cultural factors in international contracts

Negotiation of international contracts usually involves use of a foreign language for at least one of the parties. Apart from problems of translating technical terms, the cultural context of negotiations varies considerably. High-context and low-context languages will have different styles of negotiation. Attention to detailed terms and confrontational bargaining are far more significant in the Anglo-American context than in Asian contexts, for example. The formally agreed contract may be in one language, with an unofficial translation in another, which clarifies the terms. Alternatively, the contract may have two official versions in two different languages. An inescapable difficulty is possible misunderstandings in the translation process. The CISG exists in six languages (Arabic, Chinese, English, French, Russian and Spanish), and unofficial translations into other languages must be made for negotiators who need them. Interpretation of terms, even between speakers of the same language, can differ from country to country. Hence, it should be remembered that while the contract creates legal obligations, these are not necessarily interpreted in exactly the same way by all parties, and, in case of dispute, an arbitrator or judge faces an unenviable task of finding out what the parties intended in a particular situation.

The role of the contract itself is viewed differently in different cultures. In individualistic cultures, the detailed formal contract governs business relationships, whereas in the more group-oriented societies, such as Japan and South East Asian countries, business relies more on informal, personalized relationships. **Relational contracting**, as the latter is known, is rooted in societies where personal ties built on trust, often over a number of years, matter more than formal written documents. In these societies, the preferred method of settling disputes is out of court rather than through litigation. In China, this cultural approach is known as *guanxi*, which simply means 'relationships'. In more individualist societies, **arm's length contracting** (in which the agreement is paramount) is more the norm. With the growing numbers of joint ventures and expanding markets across cultural boundaries, an understanding of cultural sensitivities is essential in cross-border contracts. While written contracts are now part of the modern legal systems that have been adopted in non-western societies, the underlying cultural environment is still influential in their negotiation and interpretation. It goes without saying that a 'meeting of minds' over both the terms and the working relationship that flows from the agreement is good insurance against a breakdown which could lead to the courts.

relational contracting business dealings in which personal relations between the parties are more important than formal written agreements

guanxi personal relations which establish trust and mutual obligations necessary for business in China

arm's length contracting business dealings between people who interact only for the purpose of doing business with each other

Summary points Cultural factors in international contracts

- Whatever legal forms are adopted, cultural factors come into play in contract formation and performance.

- These factors can affect interpretation of contractual terms and the way they are carried out.

Critical thinking

When is a contract not a contract?

Discerning who was liable for what when a contractual dispute arises can be costly for all parties, and result in long-term effects which damage corporate performance. What advice would you give to a firm from a western country negotiating a cross-border contract with a firm from an Asian country, with whom it has had no previous dealings?

Negligence and product liability

While obligations under contracts are defined by the particular agreement, obligations in **tort** arise from a range of broadly defined obligations owed by those in society to fellow citizens generally. The plaintiff may suffer personal injury or damage to property in an accident caused by the activities of the defendant. If the plaintiff's reputation has been damaged by something the defendant has said publicly, the claim is in libel. There are many different areas of tort law, but the areas that are of greatest relevance to business are negligence and product liability. In a **negligence** claim, the defendant is alleged to have failed to take reasonable care and so caused the plaintiff's injuries or loss. Negligence can cover injury from defective products, and it can also cover situations where there is a service provided, such as professional services. **Product liability** claims involve a duty that is much nearer to 'strict' liability, in which the defendant (usually the producer) is made liable for defective products that cause harm to consumers. The development of tort law in these areas parallels the growth of modern consumer society. Factory-produced goods, mass transport, advanced pharmaceutical products, medical procedures and industrialized food

tort in common law countries, branch of law which concerns obligations not to cause harm to others in society

negligence breach of a duty to take reasonable care which causes injury or other harm to another person or organization

product liability the liability of a producer of a defective product to consumers harmed by the product; can extend to suppliers

production all carry risks of accidents and injury, sometimes on a wide scale. All industrialized countries have in place laws protecting consumers and other victims in these cases. In the EU, product liability laws were harmonized by a directive in 1985, which has been incorporated into national law (in the UK, by the Consumer Protection Act 1987). The directive, which includes a 'development risks defence', providing an escape route for producers who have achieved an industry-standard level of product testing, is perceived to be less consumer-friendly than US law.

In the US, tort litigation, particularly product liability, has developed into a booming industry. Product liability laws vary from state to state, but generally the legal climate has facilitated litigation in three key ways: (1) the use of the 'class' action, whereby a group of plaintiffs may come together to bring legal proceedings; (2) the award by courts of 'punitive' damages (intended to punish the defendant for the wrongdoing) to plaintiffs, in addition to compensatory damages. Huge sums have been awarded by American juries as punitive damages (although often reduced on appeal, and punitive damages are capped in some states); and (3) the 'contingency' fee system for lawyers' fees, also known as the 'no-win-no-fee' system, whereby the legal fees are an agreed percentage of the damages. With this prior arrangement, the potential plaintiff without huge resources can still bring a claim.

Total tort costs in any jurisdiction include compensation, insurance, lawyers' fees and administrative costs. The cost of the US tort system was nearly 1.79% of GDP in 2008 (Towers Perrin, 2009). This figure is roughly double the equivalent figure for other advanced economies. As Figure 8.5 shows, however, the costs per capita have fallen since a peak in 2004, when tort costs amounted to 2.24% of US GDP.

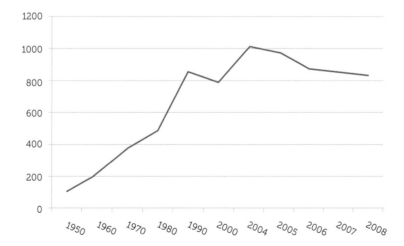

Figure 8.5 **Cost of the US tort system, per capita** (dollars, adjusted for inflation, based on 2008 dollars)

Source: Towers Perrin, 2009 Update on US tort cost trends, at www.towersperrin.com

The successful plaintiff in a negligence or product liability claim in the US stands to gain greater damages than his or her equivalent in most other countries. Plaintiffs, like all consumers of services, shop around, and 'forum shopping' is a continuing issue in the international legal environment. The rules of private international law (discussed below) provide guidelines on where claims in tort should be brought (choice of forum), which hinge on where the damage suffered by the plaintiff took place.

In Bhopal, India, in 1984, a chemical disaster resulted in the deaths of 8,000 people in the first few days, and injuries to several hundred thousand others, including long-

▶ More online ... Information about Bhopal can be found at http://www.bhopal.net and http://www.bhopal.org

term health problems. The victims attempted to sue the parent company, Union Carbide, in New York, arguing that negligence in the design of the plant caused the accident, in which a massive escape of poisonous gases occurred. Their claim failed, as much of the design and engineering that went into the plant was carried out by local engineers in India. The plaintiffs then sought damages in India. A settlement was reached with the Indian government, which took over the case, but where payments were made, they were inadequate, and many victims received no compensation. Meanwhile, contamination remains a blight on the area over two decades later. Criminal cases against those held responsible were also a story of too little, too late, from the point of view of victims. Seven former employees of Union Carbide, all Indian, were found guilty of criminal negligence in 2010, some 26 years after the explosion. They were given prison sentences of two years each, the maximum possible for criminal negligence, as the original charges of culpable homicide against the individuals had been reduced by a previous court. So great was the public outcry at these light sentences, that India's Supreme Court is now reviewing the judgment which reduced the charges against the seven men. The Bhopal case has taken on renewed significance for India, as the country is considering a new nuclear liability law to pertain to equipment for nuclear power generation bought from foreign suppliers such as the US.

When a consumer suffers harm as a result of a product defect, a manufacturing company can find itself on the end of product liability claims, where the damage may be multiplied in relation to the number of consumers. The large corporation that manufactures for global markets may face claims from millions of consumers worldwide. The **product recall** is a means of limiting the damage. An EU product safety directive was implemented in 2004, but there has been a steep increase in dangerous consumer products in EU markets (see Figure 8.6). The data presented in the figure refer to consumer products that are dangerous to health and safety, not including food and medicines. Despite the use of quality management systems in manufacturing supply chains, dangerous products, often imported toys, are on the rise. An issue in the EU has been the proliferation of consumer goods manufactured in low-cost locations where quality standards are weak or not enforced. Checks on imports, highlighting particular products, are a means of tracing products to particular manufacturers.

product recall
withdrawal of a product from the marketplace due to defects which might cause harm to consumers

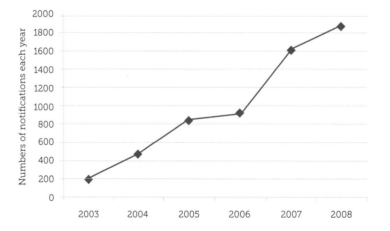

Figure 8.6 **Product safety notifications in the EU**

Source: European Commission, Consumer safety statistics 2009, at http://ec.europa.eu/consumer/safety

Competition law

Where companies compete fairly and are not allowed to manipulate markets, it is assumed that consumers will benefit in terms of price, value for money and innovation. Most governments would probably prefer that markets remain fair and competitive, but history has shown that unfair practices such as price-fixing can occur, either between companies that are ostensibly competitors or where one firm has a dominant market position. Governments step in to regulate uncompetitive behaviour in these situations. This body of law is known as 'antitrust' law in the US, where the large business empires that dominated the end of the nineteenth century relied on the trust as a legal device in corporate ownership. Since the introduction of legislation in the US in the early twentieth century, many countries have felt the need to introduce similar laws and agencies to regulate competition. Some 104 competition agencies now exist, in 94 jurisdictions (Tait, 2009).

competition law area of law which concerns rules against abuse of a dominant position and unfair trading practices by one or more firms

Competition law can be divided into distinct areas, each targeting different types of anti-competitive activity:

- Prohibition on agreements that amount to restrictive practices, such as a price-fixing agreement. This prohibition is aimed at cartels, that is, groups of firms which come together, often informally, to restrict trade or engage in anti-competitive behaviour
- Oversight of mergers, to prevent the creation of a monopoly in a particular market
- In cases where a firm already has a dominant market position, prohibition of behaviour which constitutes abuse of a dominant position in the relevant market

In every country that has competition law, the government sets up specialist agencies to handle competition matters, including investigation and enforcement of the law. There are wide variations in the size and approach of these bodies. Agencies in some countries consist of only a handful of people on a very limited budget, making it difficult to carry out extensive investigations. In others, competition authorities have greater resources and an ability to take on large MNEs such as Microsoft, which themselves are able to spend large sums on defending anti-competitive cases brought against them. The vigour with which cartels and monopolists are pursued differs from country to country, and over time. Although legislation tends to be worded in a similar way in every jurisdiction, interpretation can vary: a merger could be viewed as compliant in one country, whereas in another, one of the firms might be asked by the authorities to divest itself of some parts of its operations. In Mexico, in 2007, Telmex, part of Carlos Slim's empire, was cleared of antitrust allegations despite its 90% domination of the fixed-line telephone market. Historically, competition law has developed in market economies. US and European national competition authorities are examples, as is the EU. The EU has widened its perspective, taking in cases involving state aid to companies, which violates EU competition law.

For international managers, competition law can be an important determinant of strategy. If the firm wishes to take over another in a country where it already has a

▸ More online ... Panasonic is at www.panasonic.com
The EU's competition law website is http://ec.europa.eu/competition

sizeable market share, the takeover would look attractive from the firm's perspective, but the country's competition authorities might take a dim view. Moreover, it might be many months before the firms are given the decision of the government agency. When the decision does come, it might state conditions that must be met before the merger can go ahead. A competition authority's jurisdiction is ostensibly its own territory, but decisions can compel a firm to divest activities in another country. Although this extra-territorial aspect might seem strange, it is being actively used by Chinese competition authorities.

China introduced competition law only in 2008. The new law covers acquisitions, mergers and anti-competitive agreements. The law has caused considerable stir among foreign companies due to its aggressive approach. Coca-Cola was among the first western companies to feel the force of it, when its proposed acquisition of China Huiyuan Juice Company in 2008 was blocked. As well as blocking acquisitions, Chinese competition authorities can compel foreign companies to dispose of assets in China, on the grounds that, without the disposals, the company would have a monopoly position. The most aggressive of Chinese policies is to compel foreign companies to dispose of businesses outside Chinese territory. In 2009, when deciding whether to approve the takeover of Sanyo Electric of Japan by Panasonic, a larger Japanese rival, they cleared the deal, but ordered Panasonic to dispose of production capacity in Japan, and to reduce its stake in a battery joint venture with Toyota from 40% to 20%. In contrast, competition authorities in the US and EU asked Panasonic to dispose of capacity in China, but did not comment on the joint venture. Sanyo was an attractive takeover target largely because of its strengths in battery technology, and Panasonic persisted with the acquisition, ultimately accepting the onerous conditions laid down by the regulators. Following the Panasonic case, large companies will need to review their acquisition strategies carefully where the Chinese market is involved. If they do not wish to incur the legal risk of a Chinese anti-monopoly review, they could exit China altogether. However, given that this is the most important of the emerging markets, they might well decide to accept the regulatory hurdles.

Summary points Competition law

◆ Competition law aims to maintain fair practices in markets. Government agencies oversee a range of laws, including anti-monopoly laws, which are targeted at abuse of a dominant market position, and laws which prohibit anti-competitive behaviour.

◆ Although competition law emanates mainly from national authorities, some, including the Chinese, have imposed conditions on companies for activities outside their national borders.

Which nation's law applies?

Every international business, sooner or later, becomes involved in a dispute with a foreign element. The exposure to legal risk is greater for international businesses than domestic ones, mainly because of multiple jurisdictions. Disputes are likely to arise over contractual terms, licence agreements and in the area of tort, in which the firm either alleges wrongdoing or is the defendant in a negligence or product liability

private international law the body of law for determining questions of which national law prevails in cases between individuals and companies in different countries

claim. The area of the law concerned is **private international law**, which determines which national law pertains between individuals and firms in more than one country. Also referred to as 'conflict of laws', private international law seeks to establish rules for deciding which national law to apply to a particular situation. The rules of private international law give guidance on three broad issues: (1) the choice of law governing transactions; (2) the choice of forum, that is, the country in which a case should be heard; and (3) the enforcement of court judgments. The harmonizing of private international law has been an important aim of international conventions. The Rome Convention on the Law Applicable to Contracts 1980 and the Brussels Convention on Jurisdiction and Enforcement of Judgments in Civil and Commercial Matters 1968 have both been incorporated into English law.

In the basic transaction of buying or selling goods, at least one of the contracting firms is likely to find its rights governed by foreign law, thereby adding to the legal risk in a number of ways. First, there is the question of what contract law in the foreign jurisdiction actually stipulates. Then there is the possibility of having to go through the courts in that country to obtain redress. Finally, the firm may face problems of getting a judgment of the foreign court enforced in its own country.

Litigation is costly, time-consuming, and may bring unwanted publicity if the case is a high-profile one. Added risks in international disputes are the distance, unfamiliarity of the law, and unfamiliar cultural environment. While US businesses have become accustomed to a culture of litigation, the costs in damages can be astronomical, and the high cost of liability insurance is a consequence. In contract disputes, the incentives to find other means of dispute resolution are therefore strong. Practising lawyers, far from suggesting litigation in all cases, emphasize the benefits of 'alternative dispute resolution'. Alternatives to litigation are:

- *Settlement* by the parties 'out of court'
- *Mediation*, in which the parties agree to bring in a third party, who attempts to settle their differences
- *Arbitration*, the submission of the dispute to a named person or organization in accordance with the agreement

arbitration the submission of a legal dispute to a named person or organization in accordance with a contractual agreement; an alternative to litigation

Arbitration has grown in popularity in recent years. It is not a cheap alternative, and can be lengthy, but on both counts is usually thought to be preferable to litigation, especially in complex commercial disputes. Arbitration centres have sprung up around the globe, often staffed by panels of lawyers. In comparison to courts, arbitration processes are informal. They also offer flexibility and privacy which court-based litigation does not. On the other hand, the settlement of disputes out of court, often cloaked in secrecy, might be thought detrimental to the development of the law (Peel and Croft, 2010). Increases in workload of some leading arbitration institutions are shown in Figure 8.7. As the figure shows, all these arbitration centres have seen increases in workload, the rise being steepest in Singapore, where the International Arbitration Centre saw an increase of 153%. Danone's dispute with Wahaha, its joint-venture partner, discussed earlier in this chapter, is one of many cases settled by arbitration.

Contracts between firms based in different countries may specify a 'choice of law' to govern their contract. This choice will also normally govern the forum in which any disputes will be heard. Most countries recognize choice-of-law clauses. For EU member states, the Rome Convention provides that if the parties have not made a clear choice of law, then the contract is governed by the law of the country with which it is most closely connected. In practice, this is likely to be the law of the party who is to carry out performance of the contract. The Brussels Convention provides

► More online ... The London Court of International Arbitration is at www.lcia-arbitration.com
The Singapore Court of International Arbitration is at www.scia.org.sg

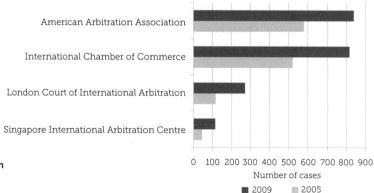

Figure 8.7 **Growth in international arbitration**

Source: *Financial Times*, 16 April 2010

that jurisdiction depends on whether the defendant is 'domiciled' in the EU (which, for a firm, means that it must have a 'seat' of business there). In employment contracts, the employee can sue where he/she carries out his/her duties. In consumer contracts, the Brussels Convention (now an EU regulation) gives the consumer the right to sue in local courts. This regulation has profound implications for online traders, who may be liable to be sued in national courts of any EU member state where their business activities are directed. For enforcement of judgments, most states will recognize the judgment of a foreign court if the foreign law and procedure are broadly compatible with their own. Within the EU this recognition is automatic, as it is between states within the CISG.

Summary points Which nation's law applies?

◆ Choice of law is a basic principle of private international law, which deals with contracts where there are elements of more than one country.

◆ International conventions provide basic rules for determining the applicable law. These are becoming more significant with the growing numbers of cross-border consumer transactions.

Critical thinking

A good place to do business?

What are MNEs looking for in the legal environment of a foreign country in which they contemplate doing business? In what ways is a joint venture a wise strategy from the legal point of view, and in what ways is it a risky one?

Crime, corruption and the legal environment

A body of criminal law forms an important part of every national legal system. However, societies differ markedly on which activities are designated as crimes, and crime prevention and enforcement vary from society to society. Moreover, attitudes towards corruption also differ among countries. What is seen as criminal dealing in one society may be accepted as normal in another. For international businesses, the robustness of criminal law enforcement and the society's attitudes towards corrup-

Mike Lynch CEO of Autonomy, a British software company

Mike Lynch set up Autonomy in 1996, when he was just completing his PhD at Cambridge University. Since then, it has grown rapidly, becoming Britain's biggest software company by market value, overtaking Sage in the process. Autonomy's success has owed much to Lynch's entrepreneurial drive, although he plays down comparisons with Bill Gates of Microsoft. Mr Lynch built the business in the growing sector of enterprise search. Its business is described on the company website as 'meaning-based computing', or software which handles unstructured data. Unstructured data can be text, images, audio and video – anything which is not numerically based. Organizations are accumulating more and more unstructured data, now accounting for 80% of the world's data. With the rise in global communications traffic and interactions on social media, the growth in unstructured data is outstripping that of structured data, such as payrolls and data on financial performance.

Autonomy's software aids organizations in identifying, monitoring and archiving the different types of content, contributing to greater operational efficiency. Importantly, it also enables organizations to meet compliance requirements, which are increasingly important for businesses. Lynch cites new demands for corporate governance as one of the reasons Autonomy is gaining more customers. Firms must now reveal more and more for government and industry regulatory bodies. When firms are involved in lawsuits, it is particularly important to produce all the relevant pieces of information to the court, showing an audit trail extracted from all kinds of data, including email, text and audio. Mr Lynch cites the advantages of his firm's programmes in

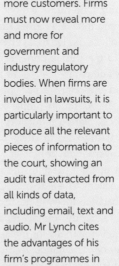

Mike Lynch

Source: Autonomy

complying with the US Federal Rules of Civil Procedure, which lay down the rules for court documentation.

Law firms are among Autonomy's customers, as are financial firms. These areas have brought in new clients in the wake of the financial crisis. Mr Lynch speculated in 2005, 'What happens when the SEC knocks on the door and says we want everything to do with a certain subject?' (Sturgeon, 2005). Or, a CEO might be called before Congress because something has gone wrong. Although not involved directly, the CEO must answer awkward questions at short notice, knowing that the hearings are being aired on global media. These examples he gave five years ago have turned out to be more relevant than even Mr Lynch could have foreseen at the time.

His latest compliance software is in social media, allowing companies to search social media interactions by employees, customers and others. As in other innovations, his development of this software has been in response to regulators who increasingly demand this type of monitoring. In the US, they include the Financial Industry Regulatory Authority (FIRA) and the Federal Trade Commission (FTC). Among Autonomy's customers are firms such as Astra Zeneca and BAE Systems. But government departments have also figured among his clients from his firm's early days. They include the US Department of Homeland Security and the US Department of Energy. Mr Lynch has made a number of acquisitions of smaller specialist software companies, in order to serve a wider range of client needs. Enterprise search is a growing sector, in which he competes against heavyweight rivals, including Microsoft, IBM and Google.

Autonomy was listed as a public company in 1998, when the dotcom boom was riding high. Two years later, the dotcom crash struck, sending the share price of Autonomy down 90%. Mr Lynch was philosophical, saying, 'No one needs a billion pounds' (*The Economist*, 2009). Although not in the Bill Gates league, he is now a billionaire too.

Sources: Vietch, M. (2009) 'Autonomy CEO Mike Lynch is in the search for meaning', *CIO*, 24 July, at www.cio.co.uk; Sturgeon, W. (2005) 'Interview: Mike Lynch, founder of Autonomy', 19 September, *silicon.com* at www.silicon.com; *The Economist* (2009) 'Out on its own', 28 February; Autonomy website at www.autonomy.com

tion are aspects of the location which form part of its legal risk. Corruption can adversely affect the investment climate in a country. Transparency International compiles a Corruption Perception Index each year, assessing countries on a scale of 1 to 10, the higher the score representing the least corrupt. It ranked 180 countries in 2009, and a selection of their scores is shown in Figure 8.8.

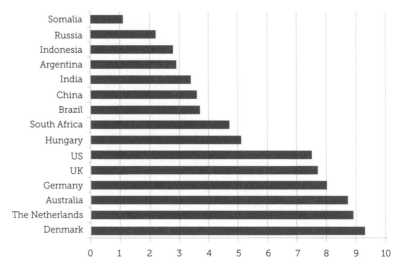

Figure 8.8 **Corruption perception findings for selected countries** (1 = the lowest; 10 = the highest)

Source: Transparency International, Corruption Perception Index 2009, at www.transparency.org

Looking at Figure 8.8, the highest scores were attained by advanced western countries with stable legal and political systems. These are countries in which there are regulations to control conflicts of interest, such as legislators who own companies as private individuals, which are the subject of the laws which they themselves enact. Hungary, a transitional economy, has a score of 5.1, while countries with lower scores are developing and emerging economies. The Bric countries are all in this group, Russia being the most corrupt in this survey. Notably, China is slightly less corrupt than India in this ranking. One might expect that, as India is a democracy with established institutions, it might have a higher ranking than it does, but India's turbulent mix of business and politics has led to an environment in which corruption is often perceived as the way to get things done, especially in the context of the country's unwieldy bureaucracy and paralytically slow judicial system.

Criminal law has become an important aspect of company law and corporate governance in some countries. The 2001 high-profile corporate scandal of Enron, the collapsed energy trader, in the US, alerted regulatory bodies of the ways in which companies that appear to be trading legitimately can avoid financial reporting requirements and corporate governance principles. In Enron's case, off-balance sheet liabilities led to financial disaster, despite the outward appearance that the company's performance was excellent. The Sarbanes-Oxley Corporate Reform Act of 2002 tightened the rules on off-balance sheet disclosure, and required both CEOs and chief financial officers (CFOs) to certify annual reports. Criminal penalties were raised, including the length of jail sentences for reckless certification. An effect has been to raise the cost of regulatory compliance, leading a number of companies to delist from US stock exchanges and list in other countries (discussed further in the next chapter).

▶ More online ... Transparency international is at www.transparency.org

The financial crisis of 2008 highlighted the role of directors, who have a duty to oversee executives, but had become acquiescent in companies' aggressive strategies. Questions of negligence arose in connection with many aspects of the financial services sector, including rating agencies, on which banks and investors depend. Shining a bright light on corporate strategies also revealed issues of ethical behaviour. More generally, underneath outward compliance with the law, there can lurk unethical behaviour which, while seemingly legal, complies only with the letter of the law and not the 'spirit' of the law. Much corruption falls into this grey area. Companies with a strong CSR approach should be less likely to face such accusations, as will be discussed in Chapter 12.

Summary points Crime, corruption and the legal environment

◆ Corrupt activities such as bribery can taint business transactions in any country, and can be difficult for legal authorities to deal with; in some countries, corruption is perceived as normal.

◆ National criminal law can deter fraud, but wrongdoers are facilitated by the ease with which money and goods can cross national borders.

◆ The global financial crisis of 2008–9 indicated a need for concerted efforts to regulate the financial sector more closely.

Impacts of international law on business

international law body of rules recognized by the international community as governing relations between sovereign states

International law covers the body of rules recognized by the international community as governing relations between sovereign states. It is also referred to as 'public international law', to distinguish it from the rules of private international law, discussed above. The world's sovereign states, while recognizing international law, have not (as yet) created a supranational legal system with enforcement mechanisms mirroring those at national level. The functions of law-making and dispute settlement, therefore, rely on the co-operation of states and the willingness of state authorities to submit to international law as a matter of obligation. Since the Second World War there has been an accelerated growth in international law, which has coincided with processes of globalization. Its growth depends on states recognizing that, in the long run, national interests are interdependent. The growth in international law has been largely due to a growing awareness of the following:

- *The need to protect the global environment* – This covers climate change, environmental degradation and the use of natural resources on a sustainable basis (discussed in Chapter 11).
- *Global security* – This covers the handling of regional conflict, aggression by one country against another and terrorism. It also covers efforts to control nuclear and other weapons.
- *Human rights* – Increasingly, human rights are being recognized in international law as transcending the sovereignty of nation-states.

treaties instruments of international law; may be multilateral, involving many countries, or bilateral, between two countries

Most international law comes about through treaties and conventions, and most of these are the result of initiatives by UN-affiliated bodies. **Treaties** may be multilateral, involving many countries, or bilateral, between two countries. An extradition treaty is an example of a bilateral treaty, requiring states to co-operate on the handing

▶ More online ... The home page of the International Court of Justice is http://www.icj-cit.org/
Informative documents about the ICJ can be found at http://www.icj-cij.org/icjwww/ibasicdocuments.htm

over of persons accused of crimes. Major multilateral treaties may take years in the drafting stages, and do not become law until ratified by a given number of individual states specified in the treaty itself. There is no cut-off date – additional states may ratify indefinitely. However, even when a state does ratify, there is no guarantee that it will abide by treaty obligations, especially if national interest seems to conflict. It is in these circumstances that the effectiveness of international law is tested.

An international court, the International Court of Justice (ICJ), which was introduced in Chapter 2, hears a limited range of international cases. Based in The Hague in the Netherlands, the ICJ is a UN body whose authority derives from its governing Statute, attached to the UN Charter. While the ICJ's prestige is acknowledged, its effectiveness is limited by the restrictions to its jurisdiction. The major one is that it hears only disputes between sovereign states. A non-state organization cannot apply to it, although cases can involve activities of individuals and companies. The Hague

International Criminal Court (ICC) court established under the auspices of the UN and the International Court of Justice, which hears cases involving crimes against humanity and war crimes

is also home to the **International Criminal Court (ICC)**. The ICC is complementary to national courts, which have the first opportunity to investigate and prosecute crimes such as genocide, crimes against humanity and war crimes. Cases against individuals can be brought in the ICC. These two major international courts help to raise the profile of international law and exert moral as well as legal authority. In addition, for trade disputes, there is the dispute-settlement procedure established by the WTO for member states, discussed in Chapter 4.

International public opinion, encouraged by the many non-governmental organizations (NGOs), plays an important role in putting pressure on governments. In the area of climate change (discussed in Chapter 11), many businesses have gone further than national lawmakers, and taken their lead from international law, often working with NGOs on climate change initiatives.

Summary points **Impacts of international law on business**

◆ Treaties and conventions impose obligations on governments to bring their domestic laws into line with their international legal obligations.

◆ Businesses can anticipate international obligations in their strategies, adapting operations and

taking initiatives in areas such as climate change.

Human rights

human rights basic, universal rights enjoyed by all individuals, which transcend social and cultural differences

Human rights may be defined as basic, universal rights of life which transcend social and cultural differences. The first general enunciation of human rights came in the Universal Declaration of Human Rights, adopted by the UN General Assembly in 1948. It did not have the legal authority of a convention or treaty, but it did give expression to a consensus on fundamental freedoms, including social, cultural, political and economic rights. These took more concrete form with the adoption of two conventions in the 1960s: the International Covenant on Civil and Political Rights and the International Covenant on Economic, Social and Cultural Rights (see Figure 8.9). These conventions take a broad view of the content of human rights, stretching the concept from principles such as freedom from slavery and torture to the right to vote for governments and bargain collectively in the workplace. A majority of the

► More online ... The two covenants in full can be found on the UN's treaty database at www.unhchr.ch
The Universal Declaration of Human Rights is at http://www.un.org/Overview/rights.html
The Charter of Fundamental Rights of the European Union is at http://www.europarl.eu.int/charter/en/default.htm

world's states have ratified both covenants, committing themselves to implementation. However, subscribing to these goals in principle does not readily translate into practice, especially in developing countries, where economic development has often taken precedence over human rights issues. For example, child labour is tolerated in many developing countries, and large MNEs that have affiliated manufacturers in these countries have been criticized for failing to take a stronger stand against the practice (see Chapter 12).

International human rights covenants

International Covenant on Civil and Political Rights	International Covenant on Economic, Social and Cultural Rights
• Right to life • Right not to be held in slavery • Right against arbitrary arrest or detention • Freedom of movement and freedom to choose place of residence • Freedom of thought, conscience and religion • Right of peaceful assembly	• Right to just and favourable conditions of work • Right to fair wages and a decent living • Right to join an independent trade union • Right to medical attention in the event of sickness • Right to free primary education • Right to take part in cultural life

Figure 8.9 **UN human rights covenants**

Source: UN treaty database, at www.unhchr.ch

A trend in the increasing global awareness of human rights issues has been to place responsibility on companies to answer for their practices and policies, irrespective of the national laws in host countries. What standards should the company apply? While it was once thought that local standards suffice, this view is no longer considered to be tenable. Companies are now expected to maintain consistent standards and policies across their operations, whatever the location. Both legal and ethical issues are involved. As we have seen, companies can be sued in their home countries for alleged wrongdoings in foreign operations. Importantly, too, companies are now perceived as having a duty of social responsibility to the local communities in which they are located. The strategy implications for companies are examined further in Chapter 12.

The European Convention on Human Rights was drafted by the Council of Europe in 1950 and came into effect in 1953. The Council of Europe (which is quite separate from the EU) oversees the **European Court of Human Rights (ECHR)**, which hears cases of alleged breaches of its provisions brought by individuals in member states, now numbering 47. It includes many countries, from Azerbaijan to Switzerland, which are not members of the EU. The court, which sits in Strasbourg in France, has seen a huge growth in its workload in recent years, as citizens of newer member states, mainly in Eastern Europe, bring forward their cases. Most of these relate to human rights abuses and complaints of unfairness in criminal proceedings. So great is the court's popularity that a backlog of 120,000 cases had accumulated by 2010. Some 27,000 of these are from Russia, involving alleged complaints against the security forces. Member states drew up plans to streamline the court's proceedings in 2010, in

European Court of Human Rights (ECHR) court established by the Council of Europe, which hears cases of alleged breaches of the European Convention on Human Rights, brought by individuals in member states

▸ More online ... The website of the European Court of Human Rights is www.echr.coe.int
The website of the Charter of Fundamental Rights of the EU is http://europarl.eu.int/charter/default/en.htm

an attempt to clear the backlog, deciding that three judges, rather than seven, would henceforth constitute a panel. Russia was the only objector, and agreement was reached that a Russian judge would be required for any hearing involving a Russian case. This runs counter to the court's tradition of judicial officers who sit independently. Although all member states are signatories of the convention and support the principle of the rule of law, weaknesses in the practical application of these principles in national legal systems have led to the large increase in complaints to the ECHR.

The EU has also stepped into the human rights arena with the fundamental charter, which enshrines fifty basic rights. This document, entitled the Charter of Fundamental Rights of the European Union, would seem to overlap with the ECHR, and confusion could arise over whether grievances should go to national courts, the European Court of Human Rights, or the EU's European Court of Justice.

Summary points **Human rights**

◆ Human rights, in principle, transcend national boundaries. UN conventions set out the basic human rights, which are also to be found in the national laws of many countries, as well as in EU law.

◆ For European countries, the European Convention on Human Rights has led to national legislation.

◆ Businesses have both responsibilities and rights in respect of human rights, for example in respect of employee relations and work conditions.

Critical thinking

Human rights and business obligations

A business operating internationally might take the view that it need only comply with whatever legal obligations exist in a country's domestic law. Why is this perception now changing?

Conclusions

1   The legal environment may be depicted as interacting spheres, consisting of national legal systems, regional authorities, and international structures.
2   Most of the law affecting business transactions emanates from national legal authorities, but an increasing amount is international in scope, and, for EU member states, a product of EU law-making.
3   Laws can be classified according to their substance: civil law pertains to relations within society, and criminal law pertains to offences against society.
4   Legal risk can arise in almost any type of business activity, and can be higher when a foreign business engages in operations in countries with weak rule of law.
5   Civil law and common law legal systems have been established all over the globe, in many cases existing alongside non-western legal systems such as Islamic and Chinese.
6   European Union law-making increasingly penetrates the national legal systems of EU member states, taking precedence when there is a conflict between EU and national laws.
7   While commercial transactions across national borders are governed by national law, harmonization of national laws through international convention and codification is moving forward apace, in recognition of the global interconnectedness of modern business.
8   Resolution of disputes in contract and tort can lead to lengthy (and costly) litigation. Settlement 'out of court', mediation and arbitration are alternatives to litigation.
9   Law-making and enforcement in the area of criminal law have increasingly encountered the globalization of criminal activity. Corruption can deter investors and create an uncertain legal environment.
10   International law focuses on relations between sovereign states, enshrined in treaties and conventions. Nonetheless, increasingly, individuals and organizations are being brought within their scope, in human rights and environmental law.

Review questions

1   What is meant by the interlocking spheres of national, regional and international law? Which sphere is the most important in the business environment, and why?
2   What are the differences between civil and criminal law?
3   Give three examples of legal risk and how it can be managed.
4   What are the main functions of a national legal system?
5   How do codified legal systems differ from common law systems? What are the difficulties in a federal system such as the US?
6   What international conventions exist for harmonization of national commercial law?
7   Distinguish between arm's length contracting and relational contracting. What are the factors to consider for joint ventures across the two cultural approaches?
8   What factors account for the global growth in negligence and product liability claims?
9   What are the alternatives to settling legal disputes in court?
10   Name at least three examples of human rights law. How does the law on human rights impact on business?

Key revision concepts

Arm's length contracting, p. 280; Civil/criminal law, p. 267; Competition law, p. 283; Human rights, p. 290; International law, p. 289; Judicial system, p. 273; Law, p. 266; Litigation, p. 267; Negligence, p. 280; Product liability, p. 280; Public law, p. 267; Relational contracting, p. 280

Assignments

◆ Emerging markets present some of the greatest business opportunities in today's world, but these countries often pose high levels of legal risk. What steps can foreign companies take on entering an emerging market to minimize legal risk and be prepared for challenges, such as industrial accidents, when they occur?

◆ Human rights law is now enshrined in international, regional and national law. To what extent is it having an impact on the ways in which businesses operate in diverse national environments?

Further reading

Adams, A. (2008) *Law for Business Students*, 5th edn (London: Longman).

Alston, P., Goodman, R. and Steiner, H. (2007) *Human Rights in Context: Law, Politics, Morals*, 3rd edn (Oxford: OUP).

August, R., Mayer, D. and Bixby, M. (2008) *International Business Law: Text, Cases and Readings*, 5th edn (Harlow: Pearson).

Edwards, L. and Waelde, C. (2009) *Law and the Internet*, 3rd edn (Oxford: Hart Publishing).

Harris, D. (2010) *Cases and Materials on International Law*, 7th edn (London: Sweet & Maxwell).

Keenan, D. (2006) *Smith and Keenan's Law for Business*, 13th edn (London: Longman).

Schaffer, R., Earle, B. and Augusti, F. (2008) *International Business Law and its Environment*, 7th edn (Cincinnati: South Western College Publishing).

Shaw, M. (2008) *International Law*, 6th edn (Cambridge: Cambridge University Press).

► More online ... A dedicated website on Concorde is www.concordesst.com

The crash that brought down an aircraft forever: Apportioning blame for the Concorde crash

Concorde, the world's first supersonic passenger jet, which flew its first commercial flight in 1969, had been a stunning achievement in collaboration between French and British engineers. With its distinctive swept-back wings and dropped nose, it was a recognizable sight everywhere it flew. Its flying time across the Atlantic, at about three-and-a-half hours, was half that of a subsonic flight. But just over three decades later, in 2003, it flew its last flight, brought down in the aftermath of a crash, although even after a decade of investigation and research, it remained unclear what was the cause of the crash or who was to blame. A long-awaited court trial opened in France in 2010, in which Continental Airlines of the US and five individuals were prosecuted for causing the crash of the Air France Concorde.

The Concorde took off from Paris Charles de Gaulle Airport in July 2000, carrying mainly German tourists flying out to the US to join a Caribbean cruise. It soon burst into flames, killing 113 people – 109 in the plane and four on the ground. One fact was undisputed: the Concorde hit a metal strip about 43cm (17 inches) in length on the runway, which had come off a Continental DC-10 plane that had taken off earlier. A tyre on the Concorde burst, and the debris flew into a fuel tank, which burst into flames. But was the accident actually caused by the plane hitting the metal strip? The defendants' lawyers argued that the plane caught fire before it hit the metal strip, due to defects in the design and engineering of the Concorde. The prosecutors argued that the metal strip on the runway was the cause, pointing to the design and maintenance of the DC-10 as the cause of the metal stripping falling off the plane.

The defendants were prosecuted for involuntary manslaughter, for which imprisonment of up to five years and fines of up to 75,000 euros could be handed down. The five individuals included the Continental worker who fitted the strip to the DC-10 and the supervisor who checked it. Also prosecuted were the main director of the Concorde programme, who had worked for Aérospatiale, now a division of EADS, between 1978 and 1994. Two other defendants were a chief engineer of Concorde and a French civil aviation official, who was alleged to be liable for not requiring the manufacturer to make changes following earlier incidents, in London and Washington, in which the fuel tanks were damaged by this type of shock.

A French judicial enquiry in 2004 had confirmed that the fuel tanks had insufficient protection, and that Concorde's makers had

The unforgettable sight of the Concorde in flight is how most people remember the world's first supersonic passenger jet

Source: Press Association

known this since the Washington incident in 1979. But their report blamed the metal strip on the runway for causing the accident. Concorde's makers had reinforced the fuel tank cladding of all their Concordes in 2001, but in 2003 both Air France and British Airways decided to ground them all, amid lingering doubts about the plane's safety. Concorde never flew again.

The fateful day in 2000 was the only crash ever to involve a Concorde. In France, civil proceedings take place in tandem with criminal prosecutions. In this case, the families of the passengers who were killed accepted compensation from Air France, EADS, Continental and Goodyear (the tyremaker), in return for agreeing not to take any legal action. The sums they received were kept confidential, and the companies involved accepted no liability for the accident. Although Air France was in control of the Concorde on the day of the crash, it was not named as a defendant in the 2010 trial. Indeed, Air France joined the case as a civil plaintiff against Continental, arguing that it was itself a victim. It sought damages for its expenses and for detriment to its image. Other civil plaintiffs included the families of the four people who were killed on the ground, who had not been offered a compensation deal.

In a judgment delivered in December 2010, the court found two of the defendants guilty: Continental Airlines and the company's worker who fitted the metal strip. Both were fined, and the employee was given a suspended 15-month prison sentence. However, the trial, estimated to have cost three million euros, was not mainly about possible punishment and amounts awarded in damages. Imputations of design defects and poor maintenance can have long-term consequences for corporate reputation. The case is also noteworthy for the fact that ordinary workers who do routine jobs can suddenly find that they are being held personally responsible. Both Continental and the worker intended to appeal against the verdict.

Sources: BBC (2010) 'Concorde crash trial begins in France', 2 February, at http://news.bbc.co.uk; Davies, L. (2010) 'Concorde crash trial: Continental airlines to make final plea', *The Guardian*, 28 May; Schpoliansky, C. (2010) 'Concorde crash trial begins', ABC News, 2 February, at www.abcnews. go.com; *Libération* (2010) 'Procès Concorde: qui est visé?', 2 February, at www.liberation.fr

Questions for discussion

- What are the issues surrounding the cause(s) of the crash?
- Have the victims of the crash achieved fair or unfair redress? Explain.
- What lessons emerge from this case for companies operating in diverse legal environments?

PART 4

GLOBAL ISSUES AND BUSINESS

We now turn to areas of the business environment in which global issues and risks are the focus.

In Chapter 9, 'FINANCIAL MARKETS', we explore a sphere of business activity which has seen rapid growth, but which has also seen increased risks. All businesses rely on financial transactions, not just those in the financial sector. The smoothness and efficiency of cross-border finance has been one of the prominent features of globalization. MNEs have been aided by a liberalization in national financial systems, which has opened opportunities for raising capital in different locations. However, the risks have multiplied with the broadening opportunities. Successive financial crises have pointed to a need for greater regulation, but national governments are aware that regulation needs to facilitate markets, not stifle them, if enterprises are to thrive. Similarly, international financial institutions such as the IMF, are looking at regulatory reforms in the global arena. Internationally, players are looking towards the emerging economies, where new national forces are counterpoised against trends towards greater global outreach.

Chapter 10, 'TECHNOLOGY AND INNOVATION', also examines the impact of globalization, this time in the changing technological environment. Innovation has long been recognized as a key to competitiveness, and with more and more countries building greater innovation capacity, the scope for innovative technology now encompasses a wide range of countries, notably the large emerging economies. Transforming an innovative idea into a successful product requires a range of skills spanning entire organizations. Environmental factors, including the legal protection of intellectual property, are crucial. So too, is the need for a business climate in which entrepreneurs can obtain the resources needed to pursue their new ideas. Technological innovation provides a route towards economic development, notably illustrated by the emerging economies. Governments of both developed and developing economies also look to innovation in meeting environmental challenges such as climate change, the subject of Chapter 11.

In Chapter 11, 'ECOLOGY AND CLIMATE CHANGE', we take an overview of the impacts of industrialization and globalization in terms of the natural environment. Paramount among these impacts is climate change, a global issue, but one which can have devastating effects in local environments, especially severe in the poorest and most vulnerable countries. Combating climate change has become the focus of moves to achieve international agreement on limiting harmful emissions. The Kyoto Protocol of 1998 went some way towards this goal, involving the world's developed countries. However, achieving consensus has become more difficult in a world in which the developing economies are becoming the largest emitters. Diverse national agendas, and political sensitivity towards any measures that might dampen economic growth, have dimmed hopes of achieving a consensus on reducing emissions through a new international treaty. Nonetheless, forward-looking businesses and international organizations are taking initiatives in sustainable development, as we explore in Chapter 12.

Chapter 12 is 'ETHICS AND SOCIAL RESPONSIBILITY'. Although distinguishing ethical from unethical behaviour might seem straightforward in principle, in practice, large areas of grey can make decision-making difficult. In many cases, a business might be faced with 'lesser evils', neither of which it would happily choose in an ideal world. In this chapter, we look at the foundation principles of ethical decision-making, taking the view that understanding how the definitions of good and bad behaviour have evolved aids in handling the practical situations which can arise. Ethics and CSR have become important elements of strategic decision-making for MNEs, not just because of high-profile corporate scandals. Certainly, CSR is compelling companies to look at their own corporate governance and stakeholder responsiveness. But it also leads firms increasingly to see the importance of *how* profits are generated in global operations, not just *how much* money the company is making.

Chapter 13, 'CRITICAL THEMES IN PERSPECTIVE', takes a look back at the critical themes, highlighting how they are intertwined in the preceding chapters. We also take the opportunity to look forward, showing how some of the forces featured in the critical themes are changing. How is the balance of power globally shifting away from the developed world to the emerging economies? Is the sovereign state becoming a bigger player both at home and away? One thing is certain: the trends highlighted by these questions will be some of the major determinants of changes in the global economy in the future.

CHAPTER **9**

FINANCIAL MARKETS

Outline of chapter

Learning objectives

1 To gain an overview of the evolving structures and processes that make up the international financial system, including the extent and implications of financial globalization for international business

2 To analyse the ways in which shifting patterns of global finance have impacted in diverse economic environments, including developed, industrializing and developing countries

3 To appreciate the causes of financial crisis, and the means by which regulation can stabilize financial markets

Critical themes in this chapter

- **Globalization – globalized financial markets**
- **Multilayered environment – international regulation, including the IMF and World Bank**
- **Role of the state – national regulatory frameworks**
- **International risk – volatility of financial markets; financial crises**
- **CSR and sustainability – microfinance**

Numbers change so quickly, they become a blur, but the rises and falls on the stock exchange can signal success or failure for a company

Source: Istock

The base of the pyramid: microfinance goes global

Formal banks generally cater for people in the middle classes and upwards, usually people who have regular incomes and live in urban areas. Large commercial banks have traditionally excluded the people at the base of the pyramid – the four billion people living on less than $2 a day, with no secure job and no assets to speak of. For these billions, the only recourse was to go to local moneylenders with their extortionate rates and unscrupulous practices. That changed with the growth of specialist microfinance institutions (MFIs) from the mid-1970s, providing small loans, or microcredit, as well as a place to deposit small savings. MFIs were established mainly as non-profit organizations. The most famous, Grameen Bank, was set up in Bangladesh in 1976, run by Mohammad Yunus. Grameen Bank, like many other MFIs, was based on a charitable model: most of the funds distributed came from official aid and other donors. ASA (which stands for Association for Social Advancement), also in Bangladesh, took a different approach. Its aim was to develop its own sustainable microfinance model. From its early days of offering microcredit in 1992, ASA aspired to being self-sufficient rather than having to rely on donors.

ASA's strategy was to keep costs down by having a decentralized, lean operation. Borrowers were required to save with ASA as well. The sustainable microfinance model, which included savings in conjunction with microcredit, has been followed by others, including Grameen. Since 2001, ASA has accepted no donor funding.

Seventy per cent of Bangladesh's population are dependent on agriculture. As the country is vulnerable to destructive natural disasters such as flooding, it was thought that the need for borrowers to have some savings to fall back on would reduce the incidence of default. The default rate among borrowers is low, at only about .5%. In Bangladesh, ASA has 3,000 branches and six million borrowers. It provides a package of services designed for clients' needs. Besides savings and credit, there is a member security fund, which is a kind of life insurance, and a service for the safe transmission of remittances. Special loans exist for a range of purposes, varying from small business start-ups to solar energy projects. MFIs in other parts of the world have similarly evolved a range of services designed for client needs. In India, for example, MFIs cater for urban slum dwellers.

In 2007, ASA started ASA International, which operates in a number of other countries, including India, Pakistan, Ghana, Nigeria and Afghanistan. The success of the sustainable banking model has also attracted the attention of the large banks. Although it might seem paradoxical, the large commercial banks have seen that money can be made from microfinance, and many are now involved, including Citigroup. Moreover, for banks struck by financial crisis, microfinance is now perceived as part of a shift towards a sustainable banking strategy The large banks do not operate as microlenders directly, but acquire MFIs and also offer technical assistance and banking services to MFIs. Citigroup now has, improbably, a 'global director of microfinance'. One MFI, Compartamentos in Mexico, transformed itself from a non-profit organization to a for-profit one, with an IPO which raised impressive sums of money. This example of commercialization, which is being followed by other MFIs, alarms the more idealistic microfinance pioneers, such as Yunus. On the other hand, dependence on aid agencies and private investors is not as secure a model as they would like. Although funds flowed into microfinance in the years up to about 2007, since then, MFIs have been affected by the financial crisis. Commercial banks the world over have wobbled, some coming near to collapse, and the finances of most national governments have come under strain, notably from rising needs for social spending. Economic plight in many countries, for example in Africa, could push more people below the under-$2-a-day poverty line.

Because of its policy of self-sufficiency, ASA, although it now has large outside investors, has not

► More online ... ASA is a www.asa.org.bd
Grameen Bank is at www.grameen-info.org

been as dependent on foreign capital flows as other MFIs. ASA's abiding goal has been to reduce poverty, and it is possible that the savings facilities are contributing more to that end than microcredit. Microcredit loans are helping businesses to set up, which, one day, with a good credit record behind them, might be able to access larger sums from commercial banks. ASA has shown that a viable

business model can be sustained by serving the needs of the poor at the bottom of the pyramid.

Sources: Murray, S. (2008) 'Microfinance unlocks potential of the poor', *Financial Times*, 3 June; Chazan, D. (2009) 'Maoism to microfinance: a journey of hope', *Financial Times*, 4 June; *The Economist* (2009) 'Sub-par but not subprime', 21 March; *The Economist* (2009) 'A partial marvel', 18 July; Jenkins, P. (2010) 'Pushing its way on to boardroom agendas', *Financial Times*, 3 June; ASA Annual Report 2009, at www.asa.org.bd

Farmers in the world's developing countries are among the main customers of microfinance organizations
Source: Istock

Questions for discussion

◆ What types of people are served by microfinance?
◆ In what ways does microfinance combine a commercial operation with social goals?
◆ Why are mainstream banks becoming involved in microfinance, and is this a sign that banking is becoming more sustainable?

Introduction

Smoothness and efficiency in financial transactions are valued by all businesses, whether local, national or international. For business dealings that are entirely within national boundaries, these aims are much more easily achieved than they are when dealings cross national borders. With globalization, many more firms, including SMEs, are internationally active. The global financial crisis of 2008, with its origins in the US, soon spread around the world, affecting all business sectors, not merely those directly involved in finance. There is therefore a growing need for businesspeople to grasp essential aspects of the international financial environment. Growing trade networks lead to a demand for cross-border financial services. These include currency exchanges, stock exchanges, banks and other financial intermediaries by which money transfers take place and credit is arranged. Like international trade in goods, cross-border financial flows have existed for centuries. However, the twentieth century saw major changes in international finance. Growing overseas investment, as well as trade, led to the growth of global capital markets and global financial institutions. Facilitated by improvements in communications technology, cross-border capital flows have become more extensive, and national financial systems have become more deeply enmeshed than ever before in global financial networks.

Global financial markets are now 24-hour-a-day, fast-moving and complex processes, whose operations are on a scale which dwarfs many national governments. This chapter will attempt to demystify these processes as they impact on businesses. A major aim is to explain in relatively simple terms how international financial institutions interact with businesses, investors, and national financial systems. As will be seen, sharply differing perspectives have emerged between enterprises, consumers and governments. The growth of international financial institutions, raising broad questions of stability and control in financial markets, has drawn both praise and criticism. From the business point of view, there are huge benefits from integrated markets, which have been particularly evident in emerging markets, but there are also risks of instability and vulnerability to financial shocks. MNEs have been major drivers of financial globalization. Shifting patterns of corporate control, now evident on a global scale, have revealed the differing perspectives of corporate management, shareholders, lenders, consumers and governments. With globalization has come greater awareness of the interactions between markets, national and international forces, that increasingly impact on international business.

International capital markets

Access to capital is essential for every company. Firms may turn to banks and other institutions for loans, raising capital by debt financing. Or they may raise capital through share offerings, known as equity financing. In practice, companies rely on a combination of equity and debt financing, which are discussed in this section. Capital markets refer to flows of capital, including equity investments (portfolio investment) and also bonds, which are loan instruments. Students of international business might expect that the biggest and most influential players in equity and debt markets are the large MNEs, but this would be only partially true in today's world. Some of the largest players are governments, which are active in many global markets, and some of the more influential players have been the world's private investor funds, which act as catalysts in both debt and equity markets. The resounding crash in financial markets in 2008 caused all these players to rethink strategies.

Equity markets

stock exchange market in which shares in public companies and other securities are traded

Shares in listed companies are traded on the world's **stock exchanges**. A rise in the value of a company's traded shares is an indication of market sentiment towards the company, and also towards the sector and the general economic environment. When a company is publicly 'floated', it is listed on a stock exchange, and its shares are offered through an initial public offering, or IPO (defined in Chapter 1). When the investment climate is buoyant, shares can trade at many times their nominal value, but when sentiment declines, corporate values can decline sharply. In one of the most spectacular falls, Citigroup, ranked as the world's largest bank, slumped from a market capitalization of $151 billion in 2007 to $13.7 billion by 2009.

The number and size of IPOs is a good indication of the investment climate. When share prices are rising generally, a company is confident that its IPO will find subscribers, and its value will rise in subsequent trading. In recent years, however, market volatility has led many companies to be cautious. The collapse of high-technology shares in the dotcom crash of 2000 affected numerous sectors, and the recovery in share prices was slow to gain momentum. The financial crisis of 2008 caused many companies to postpone IPOs, especially on western exchanges (see Figure 9.1). IPOs in China have eclipsed those in the more established markets. As confidence returns to markets, the number of flotations rises again.

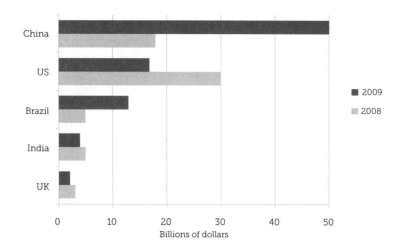

Figure 9.1 **Value of IPOs in selected countries**

Source: *Financial Times*, 22 January 2010

The trend shown in Figure 9.1 reveals a shift of global capital flows towards the main Bric countries. In 2009, there were more funds raised in Hong Kong than in New York, largely because of the listing of a number of large Chinese companies. Brazil's strength was confirmed by the record IPO of Banco Santander of Spain, amounting to $7.5 billion.

In 2009, the total capitalization of the world's publicly traded equity was over $46 trillion, but while this seems an incredible amount, it represents a large drop from $62 trillion global market capitalization in 2007 (World Federation of Exchanges, 2010). Stock exchanges are located in financial centres around the world. Traditional centres are New York and London. The New York Stock Exchange (NYSE) and the Nasdaq

▸ More online ... The New York Stock Exchange is at http://www.nyse.com
New York's Nasdaq exchange is at http://www.nasdaq.com
The London Stock Exchange is at http://www.londostockexchange.com

(National Association of Securities Dealers Automated Quotations system) are the main New York exchanges. The Nasdaq is relatively young, founded in 1971, to trade in technology and other 'new economy' stocks. In the year following the crash in dotcom stocks of 2000, shares traded on the Nasdaq lost half their value. The fastest growing exchanges are now in Asia, as Figure 9.2 shows. The Hong Kong and Shenzhen exchanges are benefiting from the effects of strong economic growth in Asia. These exchanges now have more listed companies than those in the traditional financial centres.

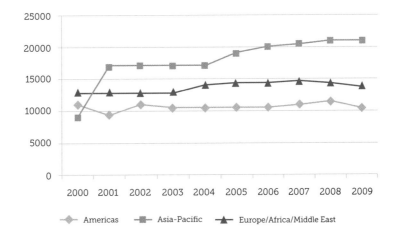

Figure 9.2 **Number of listings on stock exchanges in major regions**

Source: World Federation of Exchanges (2010), 10-year Review, at www.world-exchanges.org

While stock markets historically served the needs of investors within their national borders, global companies now often seek listings outside their home countries in order to attract more international investors. The New York Stock Exchange, Nasdaq and London Stock Exchange all have significant numbers of foreign companies listed. An important trend in capital markets has been the growth of institutional investors, such as pension funds and other investment funds. On the other hand, as noted in the last chapter, some foreign companies have recently delisted from the New York exchanges, following the increase in costs of compliance with new financial reporting regulations. Investment institutions have broadened their horizons from their national markets to international markets. As the likelihood of more onerous regulation – as well as higher corporate taxes – loomed in the UK in 2009, a number of companies considered delisting and moving to other locations.

Summary points **Equity markets**

◆ Shares are traded on stock exchanges, which are regulated by national authorities.

◆ Companies tend to list on stock exchanges in their home countries, but increasingly they are listing

in their key markets, often large emerging markets such as China.

▶ More online ... Financial regulators – the UK Financial Services Authority's website, http://www.fsa.gov.uk, provides a summary of the Financial Services and Markets Act 2000.
The US Securities and Exchange Commission is at http://www.sec.gov/

Regulating equity markets

Stock exchanges are subject to national regulation. Individual investors cannot trade directly on stock exchanges, but buy and sell through licensed brokers who act as intermediaries. Regulatory systems aim to establish transparency and 'market integrity, i.e. ensuring that the market is fair and efficient and warrants public confidence' (OECD, 2000). Cross-border markets present new challenges to national systems of regulation. Integration in capital markets has not been matched by integrated regulatory frameworks. The advent of e-commerce, which facilitates almost instantaneous securities transactions around the globe, benefits investors but is also vulnerable to market abuse. Automated trading, whereby systems are programmed to trade stocks on certain target events, has also become common. There are concerns that such systems could unleash market distortions.

The most recent development in automated trading is 'high frequency trading', whereby large numbers of trades take place in fractions of a second, programmed by algorithms. The software decides when, what and where to buy and sell, without any human intervention. Each trade is designed to generate a profit from the tiniest movement in prices; although each trade is small in itself in terms of value, the volume of trades is immense. A trade can take place in 300 microseconds, which is 1,000 times faster than the blinking of a human eye (Grant and Mackenzie, 2010). As a result, there has been a dramatic increase in the number of trades, and a fall in the value of each. The volume of messages sent by high-frequency traders can almost overwhelm an exchange's trading system. It is estimated that by 2009, 73% of the volume of trades on the NYSE were high frequency. When a mistake occurs, an exchange can be bombarded with false trades, which could cause a breakdown of trading systems. The rapid growth in high-speed trading also poses potential risk to the integrity of markets. Concerns are that machines rather than humans are driving markets, and that the technology is in the hands of a few trading firms. The US regulatory body, the Securities and Exchange Commission (SEC) is examining the impacts of the new technology, including ways of regulating high-speed traders and preventing the system overload that can occur from technology-generated trading.

In the UK, the regulation of financial services was reformed by the Financial Services and Markets Act 2000. Under the new framework, the Financial Services Authority (FSA) took over from nine former regulatory authorities, acquiring wide powers of regulation of insurance, investment activities, and banking. Its philosophy has been one of light-touch regulation, rather than direct oversight. However, regulatory scrutiny suffered a blow with the collapse of a bank, the Northern Rock, in 2007. The bank had taken on excessive risks in mortgage markets, which brought it to the verge of collapse, forcing the government to step in and nationalize it. Other banking disasters followed, which are discussed in the Exploring the Global Business Environment case study in this chapter. The banking crisis has led to a rethinking of the UK's financial services regulatory framework generally. Moreover, it has become clear that a number of apparently national banks had grown into global empires, with businesses scattered across the globe. Co-ordinated regulation of financial services among countries has moved closer to becoming a reality, as we explore further in the discussion of financial crises.

Summary points Regulating equity trading

● Regulation is generally carried out by national authorities for exchanges located within their territories.

● Regulation of trading, especially high-frequency trading, is becoming an important issue for transparency

in market functioning, as technology becomes more influential in stock exchange transactions.

Critical thinking

Global equity markets

Share ownership and corporate IPOs are no longer predominantly national phenomena. As they become increasingly globalized, what are the new opportunities, and threats, for companies contemplating listing on a stock exchange?

Debt markets

bond a loan instrument which promises to pay a specific sum of money on a fixed date, and to pay interest at stated intervals

Eurobond a bond denominated in a currency other than the one of the country in which it is issued

Debt financing has given rise to an international bond market, which facilitates trade in a variety of loan instruments. A **bond** is a loan instrument that promises to pay a specific sum of money on a fixed date, and to pay interest at stated intervals. Bonds are marketable securities which can be issued in different currencies. An 'external bond' is one issued by a borrower in a capital market outside the borrower's own country. The external bond may be a foreign bond which is denominated in the currency of the country in which it is issued. **Eurobonds**, by contrast, are denominated in currencies other than those of the countries in which they are issued. Dollar-denominated bonds issued outside the US are examples of Eurobonds. Their attraction has been that they escape official regulation. Global bonds are the most flexible of bonds, as they may be sold inside as well as outside the country in whose currency they are denominated. Dollar global bonds are regulated by the SEC in the US. The World Bank is the leading issuer of global bonds. Governments have also raised money in this way, with the recent addition of developing countries.

In some countries, government debt, or 'sovereign debt', has grown to huge proportions, as we noted in Chapter 3. Governments have tended to rely on borrowing, feeling confident that economic growth would follow, and that the debt burden would be manageable. However, the economic recession in 2008–9 put extra strain on governments, leading to increased borrowing, as Figure 9.3 shows. Many were compelled to inject huge sums into companies on the verge of collapse, estimated at $14 trillion globally, in 'bailout' money (*The Economist*, 2010a). Government finances were further strained by increasing social payments and decreasing revenues from taxes. As Figure 9.3 shows, government debt for 2009 and 2010 is much higher than in pre-crisis years.

Imbalances have emerged between debtor and creditor nations. China has been a major purchaser of US Treasury bonds, implying that the two economies are interdependent. China and other Asian economies have accumulated vast reserves. China has accumulated $2,400 billion in foreign exchange reserves. About half of this money is invested in US Treasury bonds. In 2008, China's state fund also invested in equities, but this turned out to be poorly timed as a diversification strategy. Government funds that invest globally, via agencies and investment funds, are known as sovereign wealth funds (introduced in Chapter 1). Oil-rich Middle Eastern countries are also notable for the investment activities of their sovereign wealth funds. Sovereign wealth funds have become important players in the global economy. Observers might question whether these funds are acting on instructions of their political masters or are

▸ More online ... Citigroup is at www.citigroup.com

merely behaving like ordinary commercial investors. One of the largest shareholders in Citigroup, the US banking and finance giant, is the investment fund of Prince Walid bin Talal of Saudi Arabia, who owns 4% of the company. However, private investors in Citigroup are now dwarfed by the 36% holding of the US government, which stepped in to rescue the bank in 2008, deeming it too big to fail.

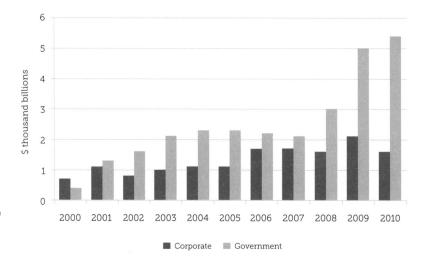

Figure 9.3 **Global bond issuance**

Note: the figure for 2010 is an estimate.
Source: *Financial Times*, 19 February 2010

Overreliance on debt, or 'leverage', was one of the causes of the 2008 financial crisis. Corporate executives were tempted by low interest rates, making borrowing attractive. However, excessive levels of debt can be a risky strategy, especially where companies lack sufficient assets to cover their borrowings. The debt of America's financial-sector firms ballooned from about 2000 onwards, to a figure which, by 2008, was the equivalent of nearly 120% of US GDP. The typical bank had borrowings 37 times its equity (*The Economist*, 2010a). The catastrophic losses that beset Citigroup were symptomatic of a reliance on runaway borrowing and a proliferation of structured debt instruments (see below).

hedge fund investment fund managed by an individual or firm, which is active in all types of securities markets

Hedge funds, which are investment funds in equity and bond markets, have been blamed for their speculative strategies, designed to generate short-term gains, but which, in aggregate, can distort markets. This type of activity must be distinguished from the hedging that non-financial companies engage in on a daily basis, to ensure they are not disadvantaged by, for example, fluctuating exchange rates. Hedge fund managers are active investors, constantly seeking opportunities to generate profits. They are the object of criticism from both governments and corporate leaders, especially when they move, vulture-like, on weak targets, be they governments or companies. Also accused of predatory behaviour are private equity groups. The **private equity fund**, which usually lasts for a fixed term of several years, invests on behalf of wealthy investors. Like hedge funds, private equity groups look for relatively short-term gains, but their strategies have focused on buy-out activities, taking control of companies which are then saddled with large debt burdens.

private equity fund investment fund managed on behalf of wealthy investors, which engages mainly in buy-out activities

Financial instruments generally falling under the heading of **derivatives** have become a large market in their own right. The value of any derivative depends on the value of some asset, such as cash or property. Derivatives have facilitated growth in the securitization of debt, that is, the packaging of debt as securities which can be

derivative financial instrument whose value is dependent on another asset class, such as stock

► More online ... AIG is at www.aig.com
Moody's is at www.moodys.com

traded. There are many classes of securitized debt. The basic form is an 'asset backed security' (ABS). The security for these instruments depends on the repayment of the loans. There are many types of ABS. They can be mortgage-backed securities, either residential or commercial, and there can even be an ABS backed by car and credit card loans. The value of the ABS depends on the value of the underlying assets. A difficulty, however, is that asset values can go down as well as up. Debt instruments thus came to be 'structured', packaging a range of assets, some higher risk than others, which was deemed to be a relatively safe strategy. The likelihood was that if there was a fall in the value of one, the remainder would suffice as security.

Rating agencies, such as Moody's, apply credit ratings to all these categories of debt, commercial and sovereign. A rating of AAA is the highest rating. Their AAA rating of some structured debt products, even though containing bad loans, has been held largely responsible for the boom in these products, despite the risks. The rating agencies reflected perceptions that the risk was low, not foreseeing a collapse in the housing market. The notion of safety through spreading the risk, while plausible in theory, spectacularly failed in 2008.

Summary points Debt markets

- Debt is crucial to financial planning for both businesses and governments.

- Debt markets have become globalized, facilitated in large part by the securitization of debt.

- The growth of hedge funds and private equity buy-outs rested largely on debt finance.

The financial crisis of 2008

With hindsight, the decade preceding 2008 seems like a golden age for finance. Low interest rates, high returns and stable markets were the ingredients of sustained financial growth. Technology and the use of mathematical models were the tools that would ensure markets would police themselves and remain forever immune from financial crashes of earlier eras. Key to this growth was derivatives trading, specifically the securitization of debt, described in the previous section. Banks became skilled at repackaging their loans into bonds, which could be sold, thus removing them from the balance sheet. It was estimated that $2,500 billion of loans were securitized in 2007. This process is depicted in Figure 9.4. The bank providing the mortgage to the householders is funding its lending through inter-bank borrowing. Banks were able to use short-term debt to fund further lending, thus enabling them to lend far more than would have been possible under traditional rules of capital adequacy, which required banks to have a substantial asset base. This type of trading was outside regulated exchanges, generating large sums of money for participants, which included not just banks, but other financial institutions such as the large US insurer, AIG. As shown in the figure, the householder's property is the 'concrete' security on which the chain of transactions depends. If the householder defaults or the house falls dramatically in value, the whole system is at risk.

The financial environment in the US was a factor in the explosive growth of derivatives trading. Government policies encouraged home ownership, making it easier for people to obtain mortgages, which in turn led to a housing boom. But much of the growth in mortgage lending was in 'sub-prime' mortgages, which carried a high

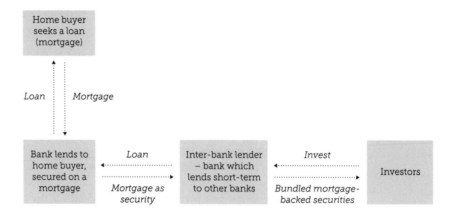

Figure 9.4
Securitization of mortgage debt

risk of non-payment. As long as property prices continued rising, the risk seemed negligible. Moreover, sub-prime mortgages could be repackaged with higher value assets and sold on as securitized debt. Many institutions leapt on the bandwagon of dealing in mortgage-backed securities. Products became so complex that it defied even financial experts to establish the actual value of debt instruments. When the US housing boom collapsed, uncertainty rapidly spread through financial markets. Lending abruptly stopped, and banks were caught in a 'credit crunch'. Suddenly, their access to short-term lending, on which they had come to depend, was cut off, as banks ceased to trust each other. Their asset bases, which in earlier times would have held them in good stead, looked inadequate. As the values of securitized debt evaporated, companies exposed in these markets faced huge potential losses. Moreover, banks and other financial institutions had become global operations, often intertwined with each other and presiding over complex networks of organizations worldwide. A bank collapse could spread to other companies in the same geographic area, and also to affiliated companies around the globe. Suddenly, exposure to 'toxic' assets seemed to have grown from an American phenomenon to a global one.

The US bank Lehman Brothers, whose traditional banking business dated from 1850, became a test case for the handling of a corporate crisis in a financial institution. According to the court examiner's report into its bankruptcy, Lehman Brothers had switched from its traditional banking model to a riskier business model in 2006, engaging in high-risk, high-leverage activities (Valukas, 2010). These it funded through short-term debt: it had to borrow tens of hundreds of billions of dollars each day to keep the business going. As the year 2008 unfolded and confidence in debt markets waned, a similar investment bank, Bear Stearns, came near to collapse. A rescue deal saw it merged into JP Morgan. In September 2008, the US government had to bail out two government-sponsored mortgage insurers, as the housing market deteriorated. This bailout amounted to nearly $100 billion. Lehman was heavily exposed in the same markets. It reported losses of $2.8 billion in the second quarter of 2008 and $3.9 billion in the third quarter. With mounting losses, it needed to raise $6 billion in fresh capital to stay afloat, but was unable to do so in an environment of rapidly shrinking confidence. Would the government bail it out?

After a tense period when its fate rested on a knife-edge, the government refused, and Lehman collapsed in September 2008. It became the largest bankruptcy in US history, involving 27 separate bankruptcies around the world. As Figure 9.5 shows, these were mainly concentrated in the US and UK, both of which had benefited hugely from the growth in global finance, largely due to the rise in derivatives trading.

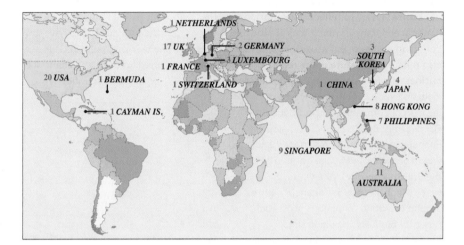

Figure 9.5 **Lehman companies in bankruptcy around the world**

The crisis soon spread to other financial institutions heavily exposed in derivatives markets. The UK government and Bank of England quickly stepped in to rescue two major UK banks, Royal Bank of Scotland (RBS) and Halifax Bank of Scotland (HBOS), discussed in the case study which follows. Stricter regulation to prevent future crises seemed inevitable. Research on financial crises has shown that, whereas there were 38 crises between 1945 and 1971, there were 139 between 1973 and 1997. In the latter period, 44 of the crises were in high-income countries (Eichengreen et al., 2000). The era of globalization, in which interdependencies were assumed to ensure greater stability, seemed to have led to the opposite – greater instability.

Summary points The financial crisis of 2008

◆ A major cause of the financial crisis was uncertainty of underlying values of structured, securitized debt, which became widespread in banking and other financial institutions.

◆ The failure of Lehman Brothers showed the extent to which levels of debt had become unsustainable.

◆ The evaporation of confidence in banking institutions led to extensive bailouts by governments, helping to undermine a belief in self-regulating markets.

Critical thinking

Fallout from the crisis

Although the US government offered lifelines to some financial institutions, Lehman Brothers was allowed to fail, with ramifications of its bankruptcy reaching round the globe. Why was there apparently little political will to save Lehman Brothers, and was this the right course of action, in your view?

Britain loses its shine in global finance

Thriving financial centres that attract international business tend to reflect the importance of the national economy in which they are located. New York is an example. But growth of financial centres also reflects the nature of the regulatory and broader business environment of the particular location, including, for example, the level of taxation of companies and individuals. For decades, Britain's position in global finance has been more important than would be warranted by the position of the British economy in the world. In today's global economy, financial centres around the world compete against each other for business, including stock exchanges, asset management, insurance and other financial services. Britain generally, and the City of London in particular, have grown in importance mainly because of these regulatory and general environmental factors. London has a strategic location geographically, midway between New York and Asia. The fact that business is conducted in English is perceived as an advantage. Over a million people are employed in Britain's financial sector, along with those employed in related professions such as law and accounting, whose financial expertise adds to the attractions of London.

A liberal market economy, the UK is perceived as more business-friendly than the more state-centred economies of other European countries, such as France and Germany. Britain has had a relatively light-touch regulatory regime, which is based on self-regulation by firms, with general oversight by the Financial Services Authority (FSA), rather than a strict, rule-governed bureaucratic system. Investors have welcomed this approach. Some 600 overseas financial institutions operate in the UK. Half the world's top 100 banks have a presence there, along with 67% of the largest asset managers and 45% of top insurers. Half the world's sovereign wealth fund assets are managed from London. London accounts for 35% of global foreign exchange turnover daily, and 70% of all

Eurobond turnover. It has become the leading centre for hedge funds and private equity groups. Rewards in the financial sector have grown spectacularly, forging ahead of growth in GDP (see figure). However, the credit crunch and financial crisis have taken their toll on all these activities.

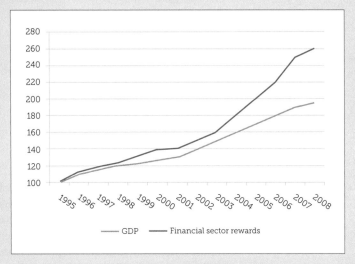

A comparison of financial sector rewards and GDP
1995 = 100

Source: HM Treasury (2009) Risk, reward and responsibility: the financial sector and society, at www.hm-treasury.gov.uk

In part due to the success of Britain's banks in becoming globalized themselves, the banking system came close to collapse in the autumn of 2008. RBS (the Royal Bank of Scotland) had become the world's sixth largest bank. Its acquisition of the Dutch Bank ABN Amro, that autumn, was misjudged. Financing the deal stretched the bank at a time when credit was drying up, and the acquired bank turned out to be harbouring a worrying level of bad loans, which RBS had not fully appreciated. With RBS on the verge of collapse, the British government stepped in to prop it up, and required the CEO to step down. As a result, the government became the main shareholder, owning 70% of the bank.

Similarly, the government played a crucial role in rescuing another Scottish bank, HBOS, whose difficulties stemmed from its lending on mortgages and in commercial property. HBOS was taken over by

▶ More online ... RBS is at www.rbs.co.uk

Lloyds Bank, the combined group now known as Lloyds Bank Group (LBG), in a deal brokered by the government, which had to waive competition rules that would normally have applied. Weighed down by debt, the combined group also needed government help, with the result that the government became a major shareholder in LBG, holding a 40% stake.

The near-collapse of major banks undermined confidence in the self-regulation which had been a hallmark of Britain's financial sector. As large stakes in major banks are now held on behalf of taxpayers, the spotlight inevitably focuses on tighter regulation, reining in the risky strategies which got the banks into trouble. Also in the line of fire are the huge rewards, including bonuses, which those in the financial services sector had become accustomed to.

Proposals for more stringent regulation and higher taxes targeted at the financial services sector might well result in a shrinkage in financial service activities, as well as a departure of the firms which depend on them. But, with 24% of the UK Treasury's corporate tax revenues coming from the financial services sector, the new coalition government under Prime Minister David Cameron would need to think of the likely consequences before taking any drastic action. Moreover, the EU and G20 are both devising proposals for regulating global finance, which would erode London's competitive advantage. In any case, the gradual shifting of economic power from west to east is occurring, and financial services activities are migrating to newer centres such as Hong Kong and Singapore. Both these centres currently have business-friendly regulatory regimes, which London firms are now eyeing for possible relocation.

Storm clouds gathered over the City of London in 2008, as its global financial prowess suddenly showed signs of crumbling
Source: Istock

Sources: Murphy, M. (2009) 'City limits', *Financial Times*, 14 December; Jenkins, P. and Masters, B. (2010) 'Eroded authority', *Financial Times*, 12 February; *The Economist* (2010) 'Scots on the rocks', 27 February; *The Economist* (2009) 'Foul-weather friends', 19 December; HM Treasury (2009) Risk, reward and responsibility: the financial sector and society, at www.hm-treasury.gov.uk

Questions for discussion

◆ What are the sources of Britain's competitive advantage in the financial services industry?
◆ Why did major banks come near to collapse, and does this imply regulatory failures?
◆ What trends now occurring are eroding London's pre-eminence as a financial hub?

The changing international regulatory landscape

When the music stopped for stricken global banks, they split into their legal parts: 'A corporation may be global in life but it becomes national in death' (Hughes, 2009). Unlike a manufacturing company, such as General Motors, which could plan its bankruptcy and restructuring, a bank can crumble overnight. Governments quickly stepped in to bail out some: Citigroup and AIG, the insurer, were quickly fed a lifeline, through the US government's Troubled Assets Recovery Program (TARP), which was rushed through Congress. But unravelling the complex affairs of Lehman Brothers was a long and painstaking process. Inevitably, questions arose. Could or should Lehman executives have foreseen disaster looming, and could they have averted it? Did they act prudently as bankers, or were they negligent, or even fraudulent, in the way they ran the company? These questions arise in all the corporate disaster stories that emerged in the financial crisis.

Regulators have turned their attention to ways in which future crises can be prevented, recognizing that national regulators should co-operate with each other in drawing up proposals. Some of the possible areas of regulatory reforms are listed below:

- *Taxation* – Banks could be taxed according to their liabilities, through a 'levy', to create a rescue fund for helping out crisis-hit banks in future. The taxation of bonuses is also under consideration.
- *Size of banks* – Banks could be compelled to keep within a certain size.
- *Separate banking institutions* – Banks could be compelled to adopt a more traditional banking model, and forbidden to run former investment banking activities such as hedge funds, private equity arms and derivatives trading unconnected with client accounts. These latter activities were the main source of banking losses in 2008.
- *Orderly wind-down* – Leading financial institutions could be asked to write 'living wills', setting out their structures and stating how these businesses can be wound down in the case of failure.
- *Capital adequacy* – Banks could be required to increase significantly the capital they hold, to cover trading losses.
- *Derivatives trading* – Derivatives trading could be compelled to operate through exchanges, to bring these transactions within regulatory systems.
- *Possible regulation of high-frequency trading* – Discussed above, high-frequency trading is thought to disadvantage ordinary investors, and could jeopardize trading systems in cases of overload of message traffic.

Structural reforms at the international level are also being considered, with a view to co-ordinating reforms among the many national players. The Basel Committee on Banking Supervision, which sets standards for the banking industry globally, is adding new members to its committee, bringing the total to 20. Formerly, its members were all European or American, with the exception of Japan. Its new members are Australia, Brazil, China, India, South Korea, Mexico and Russia. The widening of its membership will give it a stronger mandate internationally. Similarly, the G20, which also includes large developing economies, is leading the discussions on regulatory reform at international level (see Chapter 4). The new inclusiveness of these global bodies is seen as making them more representative of the global economy, but adding these new members is likely to slow down the reform process. The Basel II rules on capital took nine years to be agreed, and that was with the committee's former membership.

Although most national governments now recognize that reform is necessary to prevent another global financial disaster, differences of approach are evident among the 'old' economies, not to mention emerging markets. Changing the rules on capital adequacy has been proposed as part of an EU directive. It would need to be phased in carefully, however. If there were a series of huge rights issues by banks to raise capital (defined in Chapter 1), they could well find a dearth of buyers, especially as banks' track records in terms of strategy and long-term profitability have hardly endeared them to investors in the last several years.

Summary points The changing regulatory environment

◆ Among the possible reforms being considered are tighter controls on banking and requirements that banks' asset bases are raised.

◆ National regulators are co-operating in international negotiations for global banking reforms, but governments are unlikely to back reforms which they feel will not be advantageous for their own financial systems.

Development of the international monetary system

We turn now from equity, debt and investment to another crucial aspect of global financial markets: currencies and foreign exchange. Currencies are generally controlled by national central banks, although the European Central Bank is more akin to a supranational institution. Currencies function in global financial networks, which have become more integrated as trade and FDI have grown. For businesses, consumers and governments, stability in international finance is a priority. However, achieving an effective international system has relied on co-operation between sovereign states, which has encountered numerous hurdles. In order to understand the challenges currently confronting international financial institutions, we need to look briefly at how they have evolved.

The gold standard

gold standard the setting of exchange rates based on the value of gold (from the 1870s to 1914)

The rise in trade and financial flows from the late nineteenth century onwards led to growing internationalization of finance. To facilitate these movements, the world's major trading nations adopted a global **gold standard** system, which lasted from the 1870s to 1914, a period in which Britain was the strongest trading nation. Under the gold standard, all currencies were 'pegged' to gold, which removed the uncertainty of transactions involving different currencies. For each currency, a conversion rate into gold ensured stability. The system required countries to convert their currency into gold on demand, and did not restrict international gold flows. Governments willingly endorsed the system even though, in theory, it reduced their control over their own economic policy. In practice, governments did not always play by the 'rules of the game', and there was more national monetary autonomy than supposed (Eichen-green, 1996: 28).

Significantly, national interest rates, while they showed some convergence, were largely influenced by domestic conditions. The gold standard period nonetheless represented the emergence of a global financial order. The maintenance of the gold standard depended on central banks' continuing commitment to external convertibility. This system broke down with the First World War, when governments used

► More online ... The IMF is at www.imf.org

precious metal to purchase military supplies, and restricted movements in the gold market, thus causing currencies to float. The system collapsed despite efforts to resurrect it in the interwar period, during which government priorities had shifted from exchange-rate stability to domestic economic concerns. Moreover, the domination, or hegemony, that Britain had exerted over capital markets had declined, and the rise of US commercial and financial power did not lead to its taking on a similar role in the international system (Eichengreen, 1996).

Summary points The gold standard (1870−1914)

◆ The gold standard was an early example of globalization, requiring countries to peg their currencies to the price of gold.

◆ The instability brought about by the First World War caused the system to collapse.

The Bretton Woods agreement

The Bretton Woods agreement at the close of the Second World War was meant to usher in a new international financial order and a restoration of stable foreign exchange. It was not, however, simply a revamped gold standard system. It differed from the gold standard system in three ways. *First*, currencies were pegged to the US dollar, with the dollar fixed in terms of gold at $35 an ounce. This was an 'adjustable peg'. A country could alter its currency only if it was in 'fundamental disequilibrium', which was not fully defined. *Secondly*, controls were permitted, to limit private financial flows. *Thirdly*, a new institution, the International Monetary Fund (IMF) was created to monitor national economic policies. The IMF could also help out countries with balance-of-payments difficulties. The Bretton Woods system has been described as 'a compromise between the free traders, who desired open global markets, and the social democrats, who desired national prosperity and full employment' (Held et al., 1999: 201). It aimed to liberalize world trade, but also took into account governments' wishes to maintain systems of social protection and other domestic objectives. This meant that governments had considerable autonomy to pursue domestic economic policies.

During the 1950s and into the 60s international capital flows were low, largely because of national capital controls and also because of the limited infrastructure for private international capital flows. This situation was to change dramatically. Events in the 1960s and 70s led to the collapse of the Bretton Woods system. Three factors can be highlighted. *First*, the US in the 1960s was gripped by inflation and a mounting trade deficit, fuelled by increasing imports, largely from the growing economies of Europe. *Secondly*, there arose the 'Euromarkets', which were systems for taking foreign currency deposits, such as dollar deposits in European banks (Kapstein, 1994: 32). The source of the dollars could be individual investors, central banks or firms. From the 1950s, a Eurocurrency market grew, as funds flowed into European banks, and European economies were growing. European banks were able to expand their Eurocurrency business, unrestrained by national regulations and capital controls. *Thirdly*, the quadrupling of the price of oil had the effect of transferring huge sums from the oil-importing countries to the oil-exporting countries.

Opec (the Organization of Petroleum Exporting Countries) was able to control the supply and price of oil. These oil-rich countries, which accumulated large sums from higher oil prices, invested in international money markets, swelling the funds of

▸ More online ... Opec is at www.opec.org

international banks. Much of this Opec surplus was recycled to developing countries, thus contributing to the expansion of global financial flows. The effects of a booming Eurocurrency market, combined with US inflation and a growing trade deficit, led to speculative activities against the US dollar, the linchpin currency of Bretton Woods. In 1971, President Nixon announced that the dollar would no longer be convertible to gold, heralding the collapse of the Bretton Woods system, with its system of fixed exchange rates. This brought about extreme volatility in exchange rates.

Summary points The Bretton Woods system (1944–1971)

◆ The dominance of the US dollar after the Second World War led to a system based on the dollar as the peg for other currencies.

◆ The IMF was created to maintain foreign exchange stability.

◆ The Bretton Woods system broke down during the oil crises of the 1970s, when the US dollar came under pressure.

The exchange rate system

The IMF (introduced in Chapter 2) was originally designed to promote exchange-rate stability. It had a pool of money contributed by member countries, and could provide short-term loans to members suffering from balance-of-payments deficits. The aim was to allow a country to maintain imports, avoid the imposition of controls and thus reduce pressure on its currency and restore equilibrium. The IMF would consider a devaluation of more than 10% if a country's currency was in 'fundamental disequilibrium', according to its Articles of Agreement. Post-Bretton Woods, the IMF was concerned to curb volatility, and adopted a policy of greater exchange-rate flexibility. It recognizes several means by which governments and central banks can determine exchange rates, ranging from a fixed rate to a free-floating currency. Among the free-floating currencies are the US dollar, the Australian dollar, the Japanese yen and the euro.

Many countries adopt a middle position between market valuation and fixed rate, known as the 'managed float' of the currency. This allows the currency to fluctuate within a band. Another option is the **pegged exchange rate**. It has the benefit of a peg to a 'harder' currency, usually the US dollar or euro. The peg is intended to act as a stabilizing factor. It is often seen as an advantageous policy by governments of developing and transitional economies, as it attracts foreign investors. The currency peg helps to facilitate economic growth, but when an economic downturn occurs, the policy can have a deleterious effect on the currency, leading to pressure to devalue. In currency markets, as in financial markets generally, confidence is a crucial element. As we noted in relation to the financial crisis of 2008, confidence in banks and other financial institutions evaporated, resulting in governments stepping in with huge sums to bail them out and restore public trust. Similarly, when a national economy appears to be in trouble, the currency comes under pressure, but when a whole economy is in trouble, the bailout is likely to be beyond the means of a country's national reserves. The IMF has stepped in when national economies are on the brink of disaster, as we will discuss below. Here we look at how financial stability can be maintained by sound policies which can prevent a crisis arising.

The IMF provides guidelines to governments on how best to manage their exchange rates. It emphasizes that governments must not allow their currencies to be either too high or too low in relation to market perceptions. If a country's currency

pegged exchange rate
exchange rate which links the value of a currency to that of another, usually stronger, currency

is perceived to be undervalued, its exporters enjoy an advantage in global markets. The US has accused China of such a policy. China's currency is pegged to the dollar, and China holds huge foreign currency reserves, estimated at $2,400 billion. It also holds gold and other currencies, to shield the domestic currency from any future shocks. The reserves held by China and a few other countries, such as South Korea, Japan, Russia and Singapore, help to create imbalances globally, as we found earlier in this chapter. The IMF therefore warns against accumulating vast currency reserves. It also advises governments not to intervene in efforts to protect their currencies. These efforts usually fail in any case, largely because of the volatility of foreign exchange markets.

Derivatives trading, often by hedge funds and other active investors, affects money markets as well as equity and debt markets. Companies that do business internationally are directly affected by foreign exchange rates. Their transactions thus expose them to financial risk. To protect them from adverse currency fluctuations, they may turn to trading in currency markets. The currency **futures contract** allows a business to buy or sell a specific amount of foreign currency at a designated price in the future. They are therefore said to have a **hedge** against future fluctuations that can adversely affect their business. The company might also find the 'option' a useful tool in hedging against currency risk: the option gives the firm the right, rather than an obligation, to purchase the currency in the future at a specific exchange rate. Futures contracts and options are types of derivatives. For MNEs, importers, exporters, and others, dealings on the currency markets are necessary but incidental to their main business.

By contrast, if a firm's main business is to buy and sell currencies with a view to profit, it engages in **arbitrage**. This is a type of speculation, in which the buying and selling of a commodity, such as currency, contains considerable risk, but also a chance to make handsome profits. Hedge funds are active in these markets. These activities, like their other activities discussed earlier, come in for criticism. Trade in derivatives grew enormously in the 1990s. Hedge funds are associated with fund managers such as George Soros, who acquired a 'troublemaker' image from the point of view of governments, fearful of speculation against their currencies. Currency speculation has been implicated in a number of financial crises since then.

futures contract contract to carry out a particular transaction on a designated date in the future

hedge a financial tool or arrangement which insures a firm against adverse currency movements in its international financial activities

arbitrage financial activities which involve making profits from the buying and selling of currencies, commodities or other assets

Summary points The exchange rate system

- Under oversight by the IMF, countries can adopt an exchange rate system of their preference, from a fixed exchange rate to a free-floating currency.

- Many countries adopt some form of managed currency, sometimes adopting an exchange rate pegged to the dollar or euro.

- IMF guidelines extol governments not to intervene or manipulate their currencies.

The International Monetary Fund and World Bank

Although the Bretton Woods system of fixed exchange rates disintegrated in the 1970s, the IMF and World Bank have grown to become important actors in international finance, as well as in national economies. Both organizations have expanded from their original 44 member states to over 180 today, most of these developing countries. The changes that have taken place in the world economic environment over their more than 50 years in existence have led to very different roles for both organizations from those intended by their founding agreement.

Both organizations have become involved in economic development, including long- and short-term. The IMF has supervised assistance to heavily indebted poor countries. The World Bank was intended from the outset to be more development oriented, beginning with post-war reconstruction. The money would be channelled through governments towards specific development projects. As the organization has evolved, however, it has gone in more for financing broad programmes, in addition to specific projects, bringing it closer to the IMF's changed role of making general-purpose loans. The World Bank spends about $47 billion a year on programmes in Africa, Asia and in the transition economies of Central and Eastern Europe – all areas in which the IMF is also active. The World Bank provides low-interest loans and grants to developing countries. The funding roles of both organizations have led to deeper intervention in recipient countries, aimed at reforming national institutions. Seeking to establish sounder economic and financial systems in the long run, the IMF's preference for instituting free market institutions in developing countries has aroused considerable controversy, as we discuss in the next section.

Like the IMF, the World Bank now imposes a range of conditions attached to loans, including institutional changes such as privatization of banks, legal reforms (including property rights), and conditions regarding foreign investment (Mikesell, 2000). There is thus overlap between the IMF and World Bank, not envisaged by the Bretton Woods agreement, as both organizations have become involved in general economic and social development.

Dealing with crisis-struck national economies

The financial crisis that struck three South East Asian countries and South Korea, in 1997, was to generate a general rethinking of international finance, the relationships between national and international institutions, and the role of the IMF. The crisis that spread from Thailand to Korea, Malaysia and Indonesia, startled the world, largely because it occurred in high-growth economies, against a backdrop of seemingly stable economic conditions. These countries had neither the large budget deficits nor the inflation commonly associated with financial crisis, as had occurred in the peso crisis in Mexico. Interpretations of why it occurred differ widely, but it is generally agreed that, rather than a single cause, there was a mixture of national domestic conditions and global financial movements.

Policies of liberalization and deregulation in the 1990s led to inflows of capital, as investors were attracted to high rates of interest, and trusted that governments would not allow their banks to fail. Net capital inflows more than doubled between 1994 and 1996 in the four countries (Singh, 1999). The investment boom was largely financed by borrowed money, much of the borrowing in US dollars. As in other developing countries struck by financial crisis, banks and businesses across South East Asia borrowed in dollars and then either loaned in local currency or invested in local assets. Asian currencies were pegged to the dollar, and interests rates on dollar loans were generally lower than on local currency loans. The collapse of the Bangkok Bank of Commerce in 1996 started a bank run which led to a banking crisis in Thailand. Thai financial institutions had engaged in imprudent lending on local property development, and found themselves at risk of defaulting on dollar-denominated debt to international financial institutions. The Thai government attempted to defend the currency, the *baht*, by increasing interest rates and buying baht with its own foreign currency reserves, but this effort exhausted the reserves of the central bank. Under increasing pressure, the baht was floated in 1997, and immediately dropped 20% in value.

In Thailand, overinvestment had been followed by a swift deterioration in confidence. Declining confidence caused investors to flee. Banks and businesses found the burden of dollar debts increasingly crippling. The banking crisis was thus directly related to the currency crisis, the combined effect of which was to send the economy into meltdown (Krugman, 1999). Contagion spread to other Asian economies. Large sums, by way of credits, were made available by the IMF to South Korea and Indonesia, to support the currency and meet external debts. IMF conditions to strengthen fiscal and monetary stability were imposed in the hope that confidence in capital and foreign exchange markets would be restored.

In its Asian rescue packages, the IMF has been criticized for exacerbating the problems, rather than curing them. In particular, its one-size-fits-all market-oriented solutions, administered as shock therapy, have been criticized for not taking into account national conditions, which vary from country to country. In giving assistance, it imposed strict monetary and fiscal conditions on recipient countries. This approach, based on what is known as the 'Washington consensus', placed free market principles at the top of the reform agenda, with devastating effect in some unstable countries. This criticism is expressed by Joseph Stiglitz, former chief economist at the World Bank, who has pointed in particular to the fact that the IMF programme in Indonesia helped to cause a recession. Rocketing unemployment and economic hardship in ethnically divided Indonesia contributed to social and political strife, causing the government to fall (Stiglitz, 2000). The experience of Asian economies in dealing with the IMF has led them to accumulate the large currency reserves they now hold, as the best insurance against any future crisis.

The Asian crisis also impacted on Russia, where the 1990s did not bring the economic growth and prosperity that had been hoped for following the fall of the Soviet Union. The IMF was active in Russia in the 1990s, encouraging liberalizing reforms and the growth of the private market economy, which accounted for 70% of Russia's GDP by 1998. But Russia's prosperity depended on natural resources and commodities. When the Asian crisis struck and demand for oil fell, the Russian economy was threatened. The currency, the rouble, was subject to a 'floating peg' with the US dollar, which meant that it had to be maintained within a band of value. When the rouble came under pressure, the central bank intervened, using foreign currency reserves to buy roubles and thus try to sustain the peg. The IMF stepped in with loans, but with confidence in the currency draining away, the peg had to be abandoned in 1998. When the rouble was allowed to float, it lost two-thirds of its value against the dollar. The financial crisis soon spread to a political crisis, with the fall of the government. The new government that emerged, headed by Vladimir Putin, took a more statist approach to the economy, in contrast to the market reforms sponsored by the IMF. A resurgence in the price of oil and other resources helped the Russian economy to recover, although it remains highly dependent on resource wealth (see closing case study of Chapter 7).

More recently, the financial crisis of 2008 has impacted on numerous national economies, as their currencies came under pressure and their levels of debt soared. An example is Iceland, a small, open economy whose banking institutions were over-exposed in financial markets, bringing the country's economy close to collapse. EU member countries in financial difficulties have also had to approach the IMF, including Ireland, Latvia and Greece. Latvia, a former Soviet satellite state, had enjoyed high levels of economic growth following its independence (see Figure 9.6). But much of its growth was based on credit, and its liberalized banks were heavily exposed in real estate markets. Its currency was pegged to the euro, and when confidence deteriorated, the country faced a situation threatening a bank run on the central bank. An IMF bailout package was put together in December 2008. The EU and World Bank have also been involved.

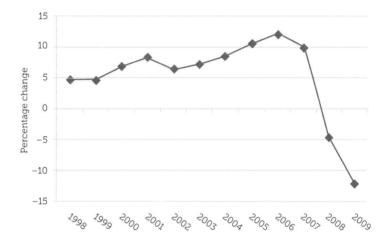

Figure 9.6 **Latvia's GDP**

Source: World Bank
economic indicators (2010) at
www.worldbank.org

The lessons of previous rescue packages seem to have been learned. The long lists of strict conditions attached to loans have disappeared. In broad terms, the recipient economy is compelled to bring public spending under control and reduce the budget deficit. The World Bank is providing social support for vulnerable groups in society, with the aim of ensuring social and political stability. The Washington consensus, inspired by American free market values, is no longer seen as orthodoxy. This is not simply a matter of changing attitudes towards dealing with crises: the fact that the US government was compelled to spend $700 billion bailing out its own financial institutions has shattered the belief that what is good for the US is good for everyone else.

Summary points The IMF and World Bank

• The IMF maintains oversight of global exchange rate stability. Increasingly, it has taken on a role of lender of last resort, involving a more active role in national economies than envisaged at its inception.

• The World Bank was conceived as a development organization, funding specific development projects. Its activities now focus mainly on developing countries. Its development perspective has

become rather more long term than originally envisaged, and also more inclusive, bringing in social and welfare considerations.

Critical thinking

Failing economies and contagion

As cross-border financial flows have grown, there is greater risk that a financial crisis in one country will spread to others. How can contagion be averted, even in a world of globalized financial markets?

▶ More online ... GlaxoSmithKline is at www.gsk.com

Global markets for corporate control

The globalization of financial flows, notably through markets in equities and debt, has facilitated MNEs in their expansion strategies. Cross-border acquisitions and mergers, known generally as 'M&A' activities, forge ahead when markets are buoyant, but can slow down markedly when markets are weak. In this section we look at mergers and acquisitions from a financial perspective, and the impacts of the financial environment on current trends.

Mergers

merger coming together of two or more companies to form a new company

horizontal integration mergers or acquisitions between two or more companies in the same industry

A **merger** occurs where two or more companies agree to come together to form a new company. For example, GlaxoSmithKline was formed by a merger between Glaxo and SmithKlineBeecham, the latter of which was itself born from earlier mergers. Mergers are a feature of consolidation in industries which have become globalized. From the strategic perspective, mergers represent **horizontal integration**, because the merger takes place between companies in the same industry. There have been waves of consolidation in the pharmaceuticals and chemicals sector, for example in the late 1990s. In research-intensive sectors, the main rationale for consolidation is the increasing returns to scale in R&D. There are other reasons at work, too. Pharmaceuticals can be a large and lucrative market in some developed countries, and a merged company is in a stronger position to benefit from the large market, having, for example, greater resources for marketing than the two firms would be able to access independently.

If mergers bring together two large players in a market, there are implications for competition policies in the countries where their businesses are carried out. As we saw in the last chapter, competition authorities can take an aggressive approach towards a proposed merger if they feel there is a possibility that the combined company will be in a dominant position from which it can act anti-competitively. Competition issues are now a major concern in global M&A strategies.

Summary points Mergers

● Mergers typically occur between companies in the same broad sector, allowing companies to complement each other's core competencies.

● Where mergers take place between two players whose combined business would be dominant in an industry, clearance is needed from national competition authorities, which might lay down conditions.

Acquisitions

A favoured growth strategy of MNEs is the acquisition (see Chapter 5). Acquisitions help to build market share quickly in new markets. The acquirer often benefits from the strengths of an existing business, shortening the timescale in which the profits from the acquisition start to flow.

In the case of an acquisition, or takeover, one company takes over another, often turning the target company into a subsidiary. The predator must pay for the firm it buys, which usually means raising money. How to finance the acquisition is a major concern, which can influence whether the purchase goes through at all. The acquirer can raise fresh capital through a rights issue to finance the acquisition. Alternatively,

leveraged buy-out (LBO) acquisition of a company's equity by a firm or group of individuals, financed by borrowing

it can finance the deal through debt, issuing bonds or seeking loans from banks. The **leveraged buy-out**, financed through debt, is a favoured strategy of private equity groups. The right strategy depends on market conditions as well as the existing levels of debt being carried by the companies in question (see this chapter's closing case study on Kraft's takeover of Cadbury).

If equity markets are strong, raising fresh capital is a viable option, but shareholders might have to be persuaded to invest more heavily. Similarly, executives would need to feel confident that investors will purchase their bonds, and when markets are weak, investors often turn away from corporate bonds as being too risky. Debt financing provided by banks is attractive if interest rates are low and loans are readily available. These conditions have prevailed in a number of countries during periods of strong economic development: Japan and South Korea are examples. Companies in China have also benefited in this way. However, the recent weakness of many global banks, suffering in the aftermath of risky lending policies, led to companies have difficulties in borrowing from banks. Bank debt became very costly and in short supply.

Financing a takeover depends in part on the size and status of the target company. If the target is a private company rather than a public one, the acquirer need only buy out the owners. If the target company is a public one, however, the shareholders become involved. The acquirer will make an offer to the board, which will then recommend it to the shareholders. If the board rejects the offer, the bid becomes 'hostile'. A hostile bidder must win over the owners of the majority of shares in order to succeed. In countries where the norm in corporate governance is to adopt a 'one share, one vote' policy, this can be relatively straightforward, assuming the shareholders find the offer appealing. The UK is such an environment. Shareholders are sometimes offered a combination of cash and shares in the acquiring company. In countries where companies operate weighted voting systems, in which a few dominant shareholders control most of the votes, there is an inbuilt barrier to takeovers. This situation prevails in many continental European countries. The takeover of Cadbury of the UK by Kraft of the US in 2009 was facilitated by the ease with which it is possible to accumulate shareholder support in the UK.

Summary points Acquisitions

◆ Acquisition is a favoured strategy for MNE expansion, creating subsidiaries in a variety of locations.

◆ Acquisitions can be financed in a variety of ways, involving equity issuance and borrowing. The investment climate globally is a key factor in deciding what company to acquire and how to finance the acquisition.

Trends in cross-border mergers and acquisitions

Historically, there have been periods of heightened merger activity generally, resulting in the rise of large conglomerates, as happened in the 1960s in the US and Europe. From the 1980s onwards, waves of privatizations in former state-owned industries, such as telecommunications and utilities, have accounted for much acquisition activity, attracting foreign investors, usually global companies keen to expand into new markets.

Privatizations in the post-communist transition economies of Central and Eastern Europe provided many western MNEs with opportunities to acquire former state-owned businesses, among them banks and telecommunications companies.

MEET THE CEO

▶ More online ... Nomura is at www.nomura.com

Kenichi Watanabe CEO of Nomura, the Japanese investment bank

The collapse of Lehman Brothers Bank presented Nomura, the Japanese bank, with what its CEO, Kenichi Watanabe, looks back on as a once-in-a-lifetime opportunity. He had been in the CEO job for under a year, the previous CEO having left behind huge losses incurred in the mortgage market in the US. However, when Lehman collapsed, Mr Watanabe moved within days to buy up the European and Asian assets of the failed bank. Nomura has traditionally relied on the Japanese market, its forays abroad not having yielded any great success in becoming internationalized. Although at knockdown prices – the European operation cost a nominal $2 million – the size of the task and the risk were immense. Nomura had technically to integrate the different sets of operations with its own, and, perhaps more challenging, overcome the cultural gap between the brash style of Lehman, with its relish for big risks and big rewards, with the Japanese emphasis on long-term company loyalty and more modest rewards.

Mr Watanabe was perhaps an unlikely CEO to be thrust so rapidly into the limelight, having spent his entire career at Nomura, none of which was in an overseas posting. Nonetheless, Nomura was not as inward-looking as outsiders might think. In the 1960s and 70s, when the Japanese economy was growing rapidly, the bank sent junior staff to the US and Europe, to look firsthand at banking practices in companies such as Deutsche Bank and Merrill Lynch. Mr Watanabe's vision has always been to transform Nomura into a world-class company, and to move away from a Japanese-oriented management style. In 1998, he initiated a shift of asset management into a separate unit and obtained a listing on the New York Stock Exchange. For Nomura, domestic revenues, however, have traditionally exceeded global revenues. The Lehman acquisition, despite the disheartening circumstances, was an opportunity to make a big acquisition which would change the balance of the company's activities – and its outlook. Watanabe welcomes the latter change. He feels that as Nomura becomes a global bank, it will need to instil a more performance-based culture.

Mr Watanabe faced his first big challenge straightaway, which was how to deal with the Lehman staff who had lost their jobs. Nomura's European operations are now based in London, in Lehman's old offices. Hoping to keep Lehman staff on board, he offered them their bonuses, even though at a cost of $1.5 billion, and a risk of backlash from Nomura's employees, whose rewards are a fraction of those earned by Lehman's. Mr Watanabe has long believed that integration happens best through communication, both with staff and clients. Wary of new Japanese management, the risk was that the former Lehman employees would simply take their bonuses and go, but many decided to stay. One said, 'I have more autonomy at Nomura than I did at Lehman' (Cheng, 2009). Mr Watanabe says the company will not 'Japanify' operations, but become more internationalized. He says, 'Under my new management, we asked ourselves: how do we become a world-class player, with world-class products and services for our clients?' (Jenkins, 2009). His aim is to satisfy clients, and the financial performance will follow, he hopes.

Sources: Cheng, A. (2009) 'Kenichi Watanabe aims to transform Nomura into a global powerhouse', *Institutional Investor*, April 2009, at www.iimagazine.com; Jenkins, P. (2009) 'The architect of a rebuilt Nomura', *Financial Times*, 1 June

Kenichi Watanabe

Source: Nomura

Rapid growth in emerging markets has driven much M&A activity in the past decade. Among the more active acquirers have been Indian companies, such as Tata, which acquired British car manufacturers Jaguar and Land Rover, purchasing the brands from Ford Motor Co. of the US in 2008. The Indian steel magnate Lakshmi Mittal achieved one of the more ambitious takeovers of the decade by purchasing European steelmaker Arcelor, to create ArcelorMittlal, now the world's largest steel company. Mexican cement maker Cemex has pursued a successful acquisition strategy, becoming a global force in the industry. It became the world's third largest building materials company, behind Holcim of Switzerland (first) and Lafarge of France (second) with the acquisition of Rinker Group of Australia in 2007 (see closing case study in Chapter 1). Chinese companies have focused more on acquisitions in the developing regions, pursuing resource-seeking strategies.

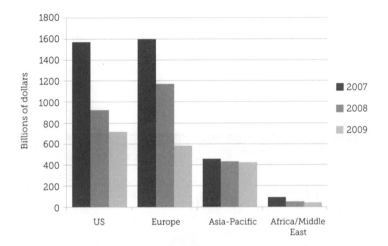

Figure 9.7 **Recent merger and acquisition activity by region**

Source: *Financial Times*, 18 March 2010

The years 2007–2009 saw a slowdown in M&A deals, as Figure 9.7 shows, but this slowdown was most evident in the developed economies of the US and Europe. Much of this activity was takeovers of distressed companies. Although companies purchased might seem like a bargain, their purchasers can face an uphill battle in generating good returns in the long term (as shown in the Meet the CEO feature in this section). What they desire above all is for confidence to return to markets. Asian M&A held up relatively well in 2009, despite turmoil in global financial markets, partly because the large emerging markets were not as exposed to the western, debt-ridden financial institutions. The progress of emerging-market acquisition activity continued into 2010. In the first six weeks of the year, emerging markets led by Brazil, India and China, accounted for $91.2 billion of deals, which was 43% of global M&A.

A recent trend has been for highly diversified companies to slim down to what is conceived to be their core business, and demerge, or spin off, the non-core businesses. The urge to sell weakly performing businesses can arise at any time, but is particularly associated with periods of economic downturn. Indeed, some companies have felt forced to raise money by selling businesses even though they would have liked to retain them. Some highly diversified companies have long histories of success. GE is one. But as competitive pressures mounted in the various different sectors, the company felt compelled to sell off its media business (see Chapter 5). Diageo is another. Although mainly a drinks company, Diageo acquired a packaged

▶ More online ... Diageo is at www.diageo.com

food business and the Burger King chain of restaurants. In the case of Diageo, wine and spirits were seen to be the core business, and it sold off the packaged food and Burger King businesses.

Summary points Cross-border mergers and acquisitions

● M&A activity thrives during periods of economic boom and slows during a downturn, when corporate finances are more strained.

● MNEs from emerging economies are now increasingly active in global M&A, in both developed and developing countries.

Critical thinking
Who gains from the takeover?
Consolidation through takeovers in some industries has resulted in just a handful of global players. An example is the food industry, in which Nestlé and Kraft are dominant players. Who among the relevant stakeholders (such as consumers and shareholders) benefits from this type of market concentration?

Out of a job – the human toll of the financial crisis. What does the future hold for this person's prospects of finding new work in financial services?

Source: Istock

Conclusions

1 All businesses require access to capital. A firm may borrow funds or raise capital by issuing shares. In practice, firms rely on both equity and debt markets.
2 Stock exchanges handle flows of publicly traded shares in systems which are becoming increasingly globalized. Moreover, investors, especially institutional investors such as pension funds, are seeking advantageous investments abroad.
3 Debt financing through bonds is used by companies and governments. The securitization of debt, that is, transforming debt into tradable securities known as derivatives, was a factor in the build-up of risky debt which led to the financial crisis of 2008.
4 Foreign exchange refers to currency dealings across national borders. Exchange rates can be determined in a number of different ways, including fixed exchange rates, 'pegged' exchange rates, and more flexible arrangements.
5 With the collapse of the Bretton Woods fixed-exchange-rate system in the early 1970s, volatility in exchange markets set in. The IMF, founded under the Bretton Woods agreement, has responsibility for maintaining stability in the international monetary system.
6 The IMF and World Bank have evolved considerably since they were established in the 1940s, particularly to address problems of financial crisis, as in the Asian crisis of 1997–8, and the many problems of developing countries.
7 The Asian crisis highlighted the risks of volatile capital flows, and posed challenges for the affected Asian economies in restructuring, to achieve a more stable financial environment.
8 The financial crisis of 2008 was precipitated by the rise of high-risk investment products which relied on mortgage and other types of debt. The value of these debt products tumbled with the collapse in the US housing market.
9 Greater regulation of banks, including their levels of capital, is being carried out at national level and also co-ordinated among governments.
10 MNEs have become drivers of financial globalization, largely through merger and acquisition (M&A) activities. The benefits of global integration, however, must be weighed against the concentration of economic power enjoyed by merged global companies.

Review questions

1 How have capital markets become globalized, and what are the implications for listed companies?
2 How can a company benefit from the issuing of bonds, and how do bondholders differ from shareholders?
3 What were the causes of the financial crisis of 2008?
4 How have governments responded to the 2008 financial crisis?
5 How have banks changed their strategies since the 2008 financial crisis?
6 Explain the benefits that were enjoyed under the gold standard system.
7 What were the aims of the Bretton Woods agreement? What were the reasons behind its collapse in the 1970s?
8 Explain the differences between fixed, floating and pegged exchanged rates.

9 Summarize the initial aims of the Bretton Woods institutions – the IMF and World Bank. How have their roles evolved since their formation?

10 What were the causes of the Asian financial crisis of 1997–8?

11 How have the Asian economies been restructured and reformed since the crisis, and what has been the role of the IMF? To what extent have their combined efforts been a success?

12 Mergers and acquisitions have become increasingly important in the markets for corporate control. What is the driving force behind them?

Key revision concepts

Acquisitions and mergers, p. 322; Bond, p. 307; Bretton Woods agreement, p. 316; Derivative, p. 308; Exchange rate system, p. 317; Financial crisis, p. 309; Hedge, p. 318; Hedge fund, p. 308; Leveraged buy-out, p. 323; Pegged exchange rate, p. 317; Private equity fund, p. 308

Assignments

◈ Globalizing capital markets have provided investment opportunities for outside investors, but have also posed risks both for investors and for national authorities. Assess the lessons that have been learned from the 2008 financial crisis.

◈ Growing through merger and acquisition is one of the main ways in which companies seek to expand internationally. Often, however, expectations outrun reality, and the difficulties of merging two companies are underestimated. Examine a cross-border takeover or merger of your choice, discussing the balance between the benefits that it has generated and the difficulties that had to be overcome.

Further reading

Cable, V. (2009) *The Storm: The World Economic Crisis and What It Means* (Atlantic Books).

Eichengreen, B. (2008) *Globalizing Capital: A History of the International Monetary System,* 2nd edn (Princeton: Princeton University Press).

Eichengreen, B. (2002) *Financial Crises and What to Do About Them* (Oxford: Oxford University Press).

Grosse, R. (2004) *The Future of Global Financial Services* (Oxford: Blackwell).

Kapstein, E.B. (1994) *Governing the Global Economy: International Finance and the State* (Cambridge, MA: Harvard University Press).

Kohn, M. (2003) *Financial Institutions and Markets,* 2nd edn (Oxford: Oxford University Press).

Krugman, P. (2008) *The Return of Depression Economics and the Crisis of 2008* (Harmondsworth: Allen Lane).

Kuttner, R. (1991) *The End of Laissez-Faire: National Purpose and the Global Economy after the Cold War* (New York: Alfred A. Knopf Inc.).

Michie, J. and Grieve Smith, J. (eds) (1999) *Global Instability: The Political Economy of World Economic Governance* (Andover: Routledge).

From cheese to chocolate: Kraft takes over Cadbury

In January 2010, Kraft Foods of the US, a food conglomerate, made headlines on both sides of the Atlantic by making what seemed to be an audacious offer to buy Cadbury, the famous British confectionery company. Cadbury proved to be a more awkward target than Kraft's aggressive CEO, Irene Rosenfeld, had anticipated. The Cadbury board rejected Kraft's advances, which meant that Kraft had to mount a hostile bid, which would have to be voted on by Cadbury shareholders. Its initial offer of £10.5 billion was snubbed by Cadbury's shareholders. Ms Rosenfeld raised the offer to £11.5 billion and eventually, the shareholders were persuaded that this represented a good deal for them. The deal was approved by more than the bare majority of 51% which was needed. However, the deal left a sour taste in the mouths of many stakeholders in Britain as well as in the US.

Kraft and Cadbury have very different histories and cultures. Started as a cheese wholesaler and still identified with processed cheese slices, Kraft has followed the route of mass-produced branded products, from Cheez-Whiz to Kool-Aid. Size, scale economies and efficiencies have mattered more than innovation and quality ingredients. Until 2007, Kraft was owned by the tobacco company Philip Morris (which changed its name to Altria in 2003). Famous for its Marlboro cigarettes, Philip Morris diversified into food in the 1980s, as a buffer against huge liabilities arising from tobacco litigation. With the threat of future tobacco liabilities receding, Kraft was spun off in 2007. The company was now in a freer position to 'rewire its culture', improve its disappointing performance and become more competitive globally. Ms Rosenfeld, CEO since 2006, saw the addition of confectionary as a means to deliver growth, saying 'scale will be an increasing source of competitive advantage in the confectionery and food industry as a whole' (Farrell and Wiggins, 2010).

Cadbury was founded in 1824 by a Quaker, John Cadbury, on principles we would now term corporate social responsibility. However, the company had long ceased to reflect the idealism of its founder. Its CEO at the time of the takeover (and who stepped down a few days later) was an American lawyer, who was more like Ms Rosenfeld than John Cadbury. Cadbury had merged with Schweppes drinks in 1969, and demerged in 2008, after which it started to look like a possible takeover target. Cadbury had reported strong financial performance in the months before Kraft made its offer. Its sales of more products with higher profit margins had been a factor, as had its improvements in efficiency. Its shareholders were mostly institutions, including pension funds, and 49% of its institutional investors

Kraft, makers of Velveeta cheese spread, acquired a sweet tooth, becoming the new owners of Cadbury, famous for its Dairy Milk chocolate brand

Source: Press Association

were American. However, after Kraft's first bid, short-term investors such as hedge funds moved to buy up Cadbury shares, holding 31% of its shares by the time of the final bid. Their concern was mainly to make a profit, having no idealistic attachment to the company as a British icon. Soon after the deal was done, Cadbury was delisted from the London and New York stock exchanges.

On paper, the takeover looked attractive to Kraft, offering a bigger presence in some key markets, such as India, where it has been weak. The deal would shift Kraft's centre of gravity away from its US sales to international sales, especially in emerging markets. The offer was in cash and shares. The issuance of new shares to help pay for the bid was strongly criticized by one of Kraft's main shareholders, the renowned investor Warren Buffett, who complained of the dilution of share value. As the share component was less than 20% of the company's share value, no shareholder vote was required. Kraft sold a profitable frozen pizza business to Nestlé to help fund the bid, which did not help to win over its shareholders. Even so, Kraft had to borrow £7 billion ($11.5 billion) to raise the cash. A month after the deal, Kraft announced a bond issue of $4 billion, and a rating agency, Standard & Poor, downgraded Kraft's credit rating from A- to BBB. New debt, combined with a huge existing debt burden, implied that Kraft would be looking to gain efficiencies by reducing the workforce and closing down factories wherever possible. Kraft assured British negotiators at the time of the deal that Cadbury's main factory at Somerdale near Bristol

would be kept running, but went back on this assurance within a week of the deal.

Britain is one of the easiest locations in which to mount a hostile takeover. British companies have fewer defensive devices to block predators than American companies typically have in place, and shares are mainly free-floating, not controlled by insiders, in contrast to many companies. Moreover, there is little the UK's Takeover Panel can do to stop a takeover on public interest grounds. Following an investigation, the Takeover Panel formally censured Kraft for breach of the Takeover Code, in that the company gave assurances regarding the Bristol plant at a time when plans were underway to close it. This was the panel's first such censure since 2007 and only the third in five years.

Takeovers, and especially hostile ones, seldom deliver the value that is claimed they will achieve. Indeed, research suggests that between 1980 and 2007 American 'mega-mergers' involving a hostile bid resulted, on average, in a loss of nearly 15% in value (Hutton and Blond, 2010). Who are the winners in the Kraft takeover of Cadbury? In contrast to the thousands who are likely to lose their jobs, one winner stands out: Ms Rosenfeld, who received $26.3 million in remuneration in 2009.

Sources: Rigby, E. (2010) 'Kraft's bold ambition means tough task for Rosenfeld', *Financial Times*, 1 April; Farrell, G. and Wiggins, J. (2010) 'Kraft chief says deal will boost growth', *Financial Times*, 20 January; Hutton, W. and Blond, P. (2010) 'End this charter for selling off top British companies', *Financial Times*, 21 January; *The Economist* (2009) 'Food fight', 7 November; *The Economist* (2010) 'Small island for sale', 27 March

Questions for discussion

- Why was the UK a good environment for mounting a takeover?
- Are takeovers such as this justified, even though reliant on debt financing, or is the debt burden detrimental to value creation in the long run?
- What issues of corporate governance arise in this case study?

CHAPTER **10**

TECHNOLOGY AND INNOVATION

Outline of chapter

Introduction

Concepts and processes

Theories of technological innovation
Schumpeter's theory of industrial waves
Product life cycle and innovation

National systems of innovation
Key aspects of a national innovation system
National innovation systems in context

Patents and other intellectual property rights
What is a patentable invention?
Patent rights in practice
The Trade-related Aspects of Intellectual Property (TRIPS)

Technology transfer
Channels for internatioal technology transfer
Technology diffusion and innovation

Technology and globalization

Conclusions

Learning objectives

1 To appreciate the role of technological change in economic progress
2 To gain an insight into the ways in which innovation is generated and diffused in different societies
3 To understand the interactions between national systems of innovation and processes of globalization and technology transfer
4 To gain an overview of the impact of the rapidly changing technological environment on business processes and structures

Critical themes in this chapter

- **Multilayered environment – national innovation systems; national IP protection; international networks**
- **Globalization – globalized R&D**
- **Multidimensional environment – influences of cultural and economic factors in technology diffusion**
- **Role of the state – state guidance in technology development**
- **Emerging economies – technology transfer and spillover**

Could this be a breakthrough discovery?
Scientific breakthroughs can come from
an instant discovery, but are more often the
fruit of long, painstaking laboratory work,
exemplified by these research workers

Source: Istock

Applied Materials: thinking small leads to thinking big

Applied Materials has undergone transformations as a company as it has grown internationally from its beginnings in Silicon Valley in California in 1967. Its changing strategy has tracked its own high-technology expertise, which has centred on uses of silicon, the base material used in semiconductors. Its expertise in thin-film engineering helped it to become the leading maker of equipment for the production of semiconductor and flat screen displays. Although its name is not well known to consumers, its technology is embedded in Apple's iPhone and other devices that have depended on technological innovation in microchips, an important element of which was the reduction in costs resulting from miniaturization. Its expertise has been in providing improved tools to enable others to create innovative end products. But 2006 marked a turning point for Applied Materials, when it decided to apply its thin-film engineering expertise to the solar panel industry.

Alternative energy has gained a foothold among Silicon Valley companies, mainly because semiconductors and solar panels both rely on silicon technology. Applied Materials' research has focused on a combination of chemistry, physics and nanotechnology, with a chest of 7,600 issued patents to its name. But it wanted opportunities to transform its ideas into applications which directly serve customers. Its chief technology officer says, 'What is exciting about solar for our employees is that we feel like it's in our hands, we can play a very big role' (Nuttall, 2008). Solar energy is a young, fast-growing industry, and the company was in a position to make big strides quickly. Only about 1% of the world's energy needs are supplied by solar, so the potential market is huge. And he feels the company's main advantage is that its technology will help to make solar energy cheaper. In 2006, the CEO, Mike Splinter, said the company hoped to be able to cut the cost of

Applied Materials is a pioneer in solar panels, but has a long track record in related technologies behind it

Source: Applied Materials

► More online ... Applied Materials is at www.appliedmaterials.com

generating electricity from solar from
$3–5 per watt to $1.

The fast-changing solar panel industry
is exploring different technologies.
Applied Materials has focused on thin-film
solar, which is based on the photovoltaic
effect of sunlight being absorbed: silicon
only 2–3 millionths of a metre thick is
deposited on glass. However, alternative
developments are occurring in crystalline
silicon, which requires a thicker deposit.
The thin film needs less silicon and is
therefore cheaper, but is less efficient
than crystalline silicon. Applied Materials
acquired two companies specializing in
crystalline silicon, to be able to serve
customers in both technologies.

The solar business is also a departure
for Applied Materials in that it involves providing a
complete solution for customers, as the company
supplies entire factories. Its solar business now
accounts for about 25% of its revenues. In two years, it
had built 14 solar panel factories: 5 are in Germany and
4 in China. Germany now produces half the solar
power consumed globally, and the solar industry there
employs 50,000 people. The country is rapidly
transforming itself into a centre for solar research and
engineering. Yet the US, which has been home to
innovative high-technology companies such as
Applied Materials, lags behind. Splinter says that
environmental factors make a crucial difference.
Certainty regarding the regulatory framework, costs

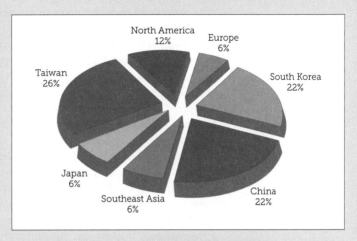

2010 orders for Applied Materials equipment by geography
Total: $2.53 billion
Source: Applied Materials (2010) Company factsheet, at www.appliedmaterials.com

and connectivity are all factors in enabling the industry
to develop. In the US, fragmentation has been the
norm, with start-stop subsidies and regulation
governed by individual states rather than at national
level. Splinter considered the departure into solar to be
a 'huge gamble' for the company: 'We are betting a lot
of shareholders' money as well as our own research
and development' (Nuttall, 2008). But the gamble was
based on a sound history of success in related
technologies, which is now paying off.

Sources: Nuttall, C. (2008) 'Silicon feels the power of the sun', *Financial
Times*, 25 March; Friedman, T. (2009) 'Have a nice day', *New York Times*,
15 September; Applied Materials website, at www.appliedmaterials.com

Questions for discussion

◆ How has technological innovation contributed to Applied
Materials' gaining competitive advantage?
◆ What aspects of the company's strategy and outlook
complement its innovation capacity?
◆ To what extent is solar energy becoming a globalized
industry?

Introduction

Technology is a key driving force in the world economy. Technological innovation and the capacity to sustain a technological lead are crucial to success in the competitive environment, for both companies and countries. No longer the preserve of engineering and design departments, technology now penetrates every aspect of business, linking R&D, design, production and distribution in global networks. In particular, advances in computing, telecommunications and transport have had widespread implications in all sectors, from manufacturing to media. Technological changes have impacted on the ways in which organizations operate, both internally and, increasingly, in interdependent global networks. They have also transformed the daily lives of people around the world, as illustrated by the huge rise in internet and mobile phone use globally in the last decade (shown in Figure 10.1).

'Cutting edge' technology can be an important source of competitive advantage. However, the relationships between knowledge, technological innovation and markets are now recognized to be more complex than was once thought. The growth of international markets has focused attention on differences between national systems of innovation, as well as differences in organizational structures that can promote or inhibit innovation. Social, cultural and political factors in national environments can influence the creation and adoption of technological know-how. Globalization processes have raised these questions particularly in relation to technology transfer and knowledge transfer. Thus, while organizations see the need for a strong focus on technological innovation, they are becoming increasingly aware that technology must be viewed in the context of the wider business environment. In particular, the regulatory environment in many countries impacts on MNE strategies, reminding us that, even in this most globalized of areas, national forces remain potent. This chapter aims to explain and assess the broad processes of technological innovation and diffusion in the context of national and organizational environments.

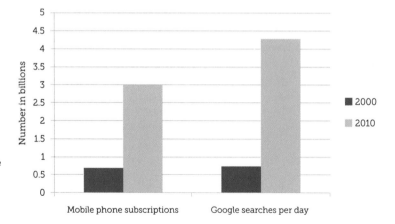

Figure 10.1 **Meteoric rise in mobile phone and internet use**

Source: *Financial Times*, 10 March 2010

Concepts and processes

We begin by defining the basic terms which are used in this chapter. **Technology** can be defined as the methodical application of scientific knowledge to practical

▶ More online ... Citibank's Tap and Pay is at www.online.citibank.co.in

technology methodical application of scientific knowledge to practical purposes

invention product or process which can be described as 'new', in that it makes a significant qualitative leap forward from the state of existing knowledge

innovation activities which seek improvements and new ways of doing things

purposes. It is a concept at the intersection of learning and doing. Throughout history there have been talented, imaginative individuals, able to assimilate scientific knowledge and transform its principles into practical inventions. An **invention** is a product or process which can be described as 'new', in that it makes a significant qualitative leap forward from the state of existing knowledge. Inventions come under the broad heading of **innovation**. However, innovation also includes improvements which are less radical but offer commercial benefits. The OECD defines innovation as 'the implementation of a new or significantly improved product (good or service), or process, a new marketing method, or a new organizational method in business practices, workplace organization or external activities' (OECD, 2005). For example, when Citigroup wished to expand its consumer banking operations in India, it came up against the Indian government's restrictions on foreign banks opening new branches. It therefore introduced a system of banking by mobile phone, tapping into India's booming mobile phone market. The bank launched specially adapted 'Tap and Pay' mobile phones, which enabled customers to bank and purchase goods.

While many inventions, including patented ones, are never commercially produced, innovations, by definition, are economically valuable. Technical innovation has thus been described as the matching of new technology to a market, or 'the first commercial application or production of a new process or product' (Freeman and Soete, 1997: 201). Inventions can be legally protected by a patent, which gives the inventor (or more often, a company) 'ownership' of its rights of exploitation. An innovation may be a less dramatic step forward, for example an improvement that speeds up an industrial process. While not patentable, it is nonetheless significant in that it can lead to scale economies.

Scientific knowledge plays a crucial role in technical innovation. As Figure 10.2 depicts, however, there are many steps along the way from turning a scientific discovery into a workable invention which can be commercially exploited. Figure 10.2, although highly simplified, shows the flow of ideas from science to applied research, and then to development for commercial application. Note that consumer feedback is integrated into the process, helping to generate improved products and further innovation. It is important to remember that this process takes place within distinctive national and corporate environments, which may greatly facilitate the bringing of innovative ideas to commercial fruition (Tellis et al., 2009).

Historians puzzle over two key questions in relation to technology. First, why do science and invention flourish in particular societies during certain eras, but not in others? And secondly, why are some societies with high levels of learning, scientific knowledge and creative inventors, still not able to convert learning into invention, or invention into technological advancement at the level of society? David Landes points to two examples. Islam, in its golden age, CE 750–1100, 'produced the world's greatest scientists, yet a flourishing science contributed nothing to the slow advance of technology in Islam' (Landes, 1998). More remarkable were the Chinese, with a long list of inventions, including the wheelbarrow, compass, paper, printing, gunpowder and porcelain. In the twelfth century, the Chinese were using a water-driven machine for spinning hemp, anticipating English spinning machines by some 500 years. Yet technical progress made little impact on the Chinese economy. The Chinese, it seems, had the scientific knowledge to produce the steam engine, but for some reason that still baffles historians, failed to do it. Summarizing the debate, Landes points to China's lack of 'a free market and institutionalized property rights' as

▸ More online ... The UK's Department for Business, Innovation and Skills is at www.bis.gov.uk/

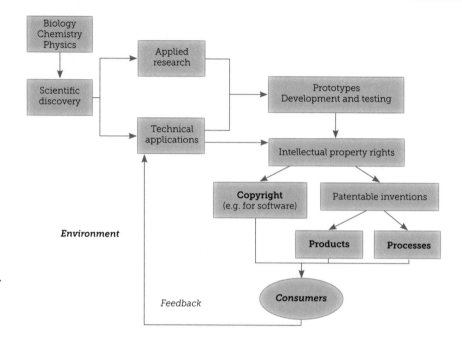

Figure 10.2 **The innovation process for intellectual property**

key factors that discouraged initiative (Landes, 1998: 56). Market reforms in China since 1980 have produced a flowering of innovative capacity.

We generally assume that in societies where learning is valued, a high level of science education will lay the foundations for people with technological talent to flourish, and, further, that their skills will feed into the country's industries, fostering economic prosperity. However, the relative importance of 'demand-pull' and 'science-push' is debated. Both forces play a role in technological innovation. Emphasis on demand-pull factors, as in product life cycle theory, has been criticized as one-sided. How, it might be asked, can consumers judge a revolutionary new product of which they have no knowledge (Freeman and Soete, 1997: 200)? Many of the early inventors, with their scientific backgrounds, had little idea of the economic potential of their innovations, or of the many possible applications of their technology. Science-push was clearly important among the early inventors and entrepreneurs, who formed new companies in order to exploit their inventions. However, there were instances where demand predominated, and these certainly became more prevalent when innovation became 'routinized' within large firms. It is arguable even today that, whereas large firms with vast R&D expenditure account for the bulk of innovations, radical innovations often come from small firms.

Summary points   Concepts and processes

⟐ Technology applies scientific knowledge to practical purposes.
⟐ Inventions are new products or processes, while innovation covers

a broader range of improvements in products and ways of doing things.
⟐ Both science-push and demand-pull play roles in technological

innovation; for economies, commercialization of innovations contributes to economic growth.

Theories of technological innovation

Theories of technological innovation start from the assumption that innovation is vital to economic progress. In terms of competitive advantage, technological innovation, as Porter has pointed out, can create first-mover advantages, which governments can promote (see Chapter 4.) The importance of 'improvements in machines' was recognized by Adam Smith at the outset of his *Wealth of Nations*. However, for a long period, economic theorists tended to see technological change as an 'exogenous variable', that is, outside the traditional inputs of labour and capital. Against this background, Schumpeter stands out for his analysis of technological innovation as central to economic development.

Schumpeter's theory of industrial waves

Schumpeter's work spanned a long period, from 1912 to 1942. As industrial economies developed during that period, his analysis of the role of technological innovation evolved. From the outset in 1912, he stressed the importance of the individual entrepreneur in the innovative process. Schumpeter saw that innovation can encompass not just technical, but also marketing and organizational innovations. The key actors in the Industrial Revolution were both talented inventors and entrepreneurs, who often went into production, making (and improving) their own inventions. The cotton-spinning industry, for example, was transformed by the inventions of Arkwright, Hargreaves and Crompton in the late eighteenth century. Richard Arkwright, for one, embodied important qualities as inventor and entrepreneur, protecting and exploiting his patents, with a partner, Jedediah Strutt, providing needed capital for further investment. Large-scale machine production dramatically increased output and brought down prices.

Schumpeter saw the shift in technical innovation from the individual inventor to R&D specialist professionals within firms. Two developments were of particular importance. The first was the increasing importance of scientific research as the basis of innovation, and the second was the growing bureaucracy of large organizations, with their specialist R&D departments. He viewed changes that take place within capitalism as involving 'creative destruction'. New products, new methods of production, and new forms of organization emerge, 'revolutionizing economic structure, *from within*' (Schumpeter, 1942: 83 [Schumpeter's emphasis]).

He used the notion of business cycles, devised by the Russian economist Kondratieff, to describe successive 'waves' of economic development, in which technological innovation plays a crucial role. The first long wave was the Industrial Revolution and development of factory production (1780s–1840s) (see Table 10.1). The second wave was that of steam power and the growth of the railways, lasting until the 1890s. The third wave, which lasted until the Second World War, was dominated by electricity and steel. Following Schumpeter's death shortly after the war, theorists added a fourth wave, that of Fordist mass production (1940s–1990s) (see Chapter 5), and a fifth, that of microelectronics and computing, from the 1990s. Each Kondratieff wave is based on technological changes and their widespread diffusion in the economy, creating changes in investment opportunities and employment. While Schumpeter could not have foreseen the pace of technological change of recent decades, an enduring contribution of his analysis, which is echoed in more recent theorists, is the interdependence between technological innovation, economic progress and the social environment.

Table 10.1 **Summary of long waves of technical change**

Approximate timing	Kondratieff waves	Science, technology education and training
First 1780s–1840s	Industrial Revolution: factory production, for example in textiles	Apprenticeship; learning by doing; scientific societies
Second 1840s–1890s	Age of steam power and railways	Professional mechanical and civil engineers; institutes of technology; mass primary education
Third 1890s–1940s	Age of electricity and steel	Industrial R&D labs, national laboratories
Fourth 1940s–1990s	Age of mass production ('Fordism') of automobiles and synthetic materials	Large-scale industrial and government R&D; mass higher education
Fifth 1990s–	Age of microelectronics and computer networks; the internet	Data networks; R&D global networks; lifetime education and training

Source: Adapted from Freeman, C. and Soete, L. (1997) *The Economics of Industrial Innovation*, 3rd edn (London: Cassell) p. 19

Summary points Schumpeter's industrial waves

◆ Schumpeter shed light on the links between technological change, economic growth and the changing social environment.

◆ He likened the process of change within a capitalist system to 'creative destruction', whereby new products and processes have profound impacts on economic relationships.

Critical thinking

Is the creative genius a dying breed?

> Technological progress is increasingly becoming the business of teams of trained specialists who turn out what is required and make it work in predictable ways. The romance of earlier commercial adventure is rapidly wearing away, because so many more things can be strictly calculated that had of old to be visualized in a flash of genius. (Schumpeter, 1942, p. 132)

Is there still a role for the creative genius? In what type of organization is the intuitive innovator likely to be found?

Product life cycle and innovation

According to product life cycle theory (outlined in Chapter 2), the introduction of a new product by a firm depends on a large market in the firm's home country, which will bear the costs and risks of R&D. Demand from high-income consumers in the US in the 1950s and 60s thus resulted in a lead in consumer durables. The theory holds that this monopoly advantage is gradually whittled away as the product becomes standardized and production moves to less advanced countries. Maintaining competitive advantage requires continually introducing new products. The theory can be criticized for its static view of technology. More recent debate on the product cycle model points out that it overemphasizes consumer demand and misses the dynamic implications of technology development (Cantwell, 1989). As technology accumulates, innovation becomes diffused, and the 'technology gap' closes. A further shortcoming of the product cycle model is its focus on products independently of

▶ More online ... The OECD's website offers an innovation page at www.oecd.org, under the topic 'Science and Innovation'.

each other, with each new product seen as a radical innovation (Freeman and Soete, 1997). In reality, product innovations are interrelated, and technological changes evolve across ranges of products (see the opening case study of this chapter). Hence, the narrow focus of product cycle does not capture dynamic innovation processes.

Theories of how innovation is generated now take into account the diffusion of technology across the globe. Competitive positions of countries and firms may shift over relatively short time spans, as technological changes play out in markets. The technological lead of European countries before 1900 was eroded as the US (and later, Japan) caught up, and eventually surpassed European countries. European countries were then in the position of catching up. MNEs' geographical expansion has led post-war technological change, reshaping the competitive environment between firms and between countries. It is clear that industrial 'latecomers' have benefited from technology transfer, although, as we will see in this chapter, the diffusion of technology differs between different national environments.

Foreign direct investment (FDI) has brought about the globalization of production, but globalization of technological innovation has progressed more slowly. Large companies have tended to concentrate their R&D activities in their home countries, and only recently have begun locating specialized R&D in a variety of locations, to benefit from different areas of excellence in different localities. Automotive R&D, once dominated by the major carmakers, is now being undertaken more by specialist suppliers, who are responsible for nearly 60% of the industry's R&D. Considerable R&D investment in the motor industry now focuses on electric vehicles and reduction in emissions. Much of this research is taking place in emerging markets, especially China, which is rapidly increasing expenditure on clean technology R&D (Xiaomei Tan and Zhao Gang, 2009). Innovation capacity can contribute to economic development, but outcomes differ according to countries' differing systems of national innovation.

Summary points **Product life cycle theory and innovation**

◆ As conceived originally, product life cycle theory focused on the US, where innovation was driven by consumer demand.

◆ The global diffusion of technology and the rise of consumer societies around the world have led to a reassessment of how innovation takes place in a changing economic environment, focusing on both global and local factors in each location.

National systems of innovation

First Britain, then the US, and later Japan and Germany, have all been able to achieve high levels of technological innovation coupled with economic growth. It has long been recognized that the national environment is important in stimulating or inhibiting innovation. Writing in 1841, Friedrich List, in his *National System of Political Economy*, addressed ways in which Germany could catch up with England. Significantly, he emphasized the importance of both social and cultural factors and also government policy, in, for example, the protection of infant industries and the setting up of technical training institutes (Archibugi and Michie, 1997). Indeed, List anticipated many of the aspects of the national environment which were later to be grouped together under the term 'national system of innovation'. There is now a considerable body of literature on national systems, their different approaches to innovation and how they interact (see Tellis et al., 2009).

innovation system
the structures and institutions by which a country's innovation activities are encouraged and facilitated, both directly and indirectly

A national **innovation system** is broadly defined as the structures and institutions by which a country's innovation activities are encouraged and facilitated, both directly and indirectly. The term 'system' might imply that these institutions and policies are co-ordinated, when in fact levels of co-ordination vary between countries. The word 'network' has been used to describe the relevant linkages between companies, disciplines and institutions (Patel and Pavitt, 2000). Summing up these threads, Mowery and Oxley define national innovation system as 'the network of public and private institutions within an economy that fund and perform R&D, translate the results of R&D into commercial innovations and effect the diffusion of new technologies' (Mowery and Oxley, 1997: 154).

A national innovation system consists of both institutions and interactions, as highlighted in Figure 10.3. Educational and government inputs are more institutional in nature, while collaboration, scientific research and technology networking are more interactive. In practice, these dimensions are mutually reinforcing; for example, research institutions facilitate collaborations between education and industry.

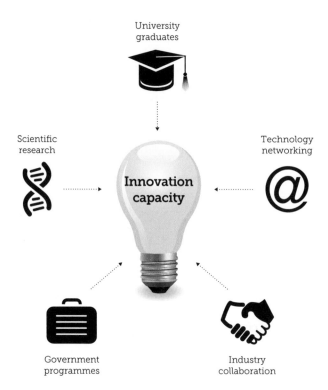

Figure 10.3 **Aspects of a national innovation system**

Key aspects of a national innovation system

Five key aspects of a national innovation system can be highlighted (Archibugi and Michie, 1997):

Education and training

Achieving high rates of participation in education at all levels, from primary through to higher education, helps to promote national economic growth. Spending on education differs markedly from country to country, as Figure 10.4 shows. The three countries that spend the most all have economies known for achievements in high technology industries. One might expect all the countries in the lower half of the chart to be developing nations, but note that Germany, a leading industrial power, is in this half. This suggests that just spending money is not the key to building innovation capacity. However, it might be worrying to Germans who feel that investment for future innovation capacity should be increased.

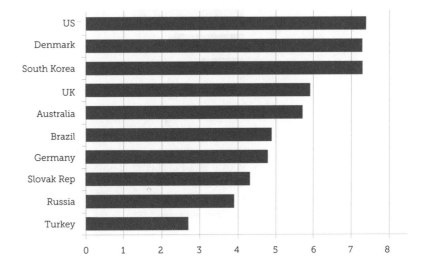

Figure 10.4 **Proportion of national wealth spent on education (all levels) as a percentage of GDP**

Source: OECD (2009)
Education at a Glance, 2009
indicators (Paris: OECD)

The proportion of students who complete first degrees is another indication of a country's educational achievement. Figure 10.5 provides some country comparisons, with percentages for women and men shown separately. Of these countries, Australia has the highest participation level, but, like the other three countries in the top half of this chart, many more women than men graduate from university. All the countries in this chart are important globally in industrial production and high-technology industries. China produces fewer graduates, only about 12% of the relevant age group in the country, but it should be remembered that China is catching up with these other countries: the number of graduates in China has doubled since 2000. Moreover, in 2007, 45% of China's graduates were in science and technology (OECD, 2009b). The average in the EU is 23%, while only 15% of US graduates are in science and technology.

Clearly, qualitative, as well as quantitative, issues are important, and governments are keenly aware of the need to encourage high-quality graduates in the new technologies such as IT and biotechnology. Learning covers a number of processes in addition to formal education. It includes learning-by-doing and interactive learning, which are influenced by social and cultural factors. Moreover, learning is increasingly perceived as a lifelong process of acquiring new skills and knowledge. Technological innovation relies on both institutionalized scientific research and interaction between people with different kinds of knowledge (Lundvall, 1992).

Science and technology capabilities

National authorities take decisions on what types of R&D to fund and how to meet the expenditure. Figure 10.6 shows the gross domestic spending on R&D as a

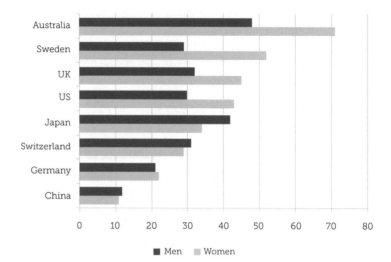

Figure 10.5 **Graduation rates at first-stage university level, by gender** (as a percentage of the relevant age cohort in the country)

Source: OECD (2009) Science, Technology and Industry Scoreboard, 2009 (Paris: OECD)

percentage of GDP in a number of countries. The richer countries tend to devote a higher percentage of GDP to R&D activities than the poorer ones. The percentage for China might seem low, but it, along with other emerging economies, is rapidly increasing R&D expenditure. South Korea's impressive showing is a factor in the success of its companies (see closing case study on Samsung). The bulk of funding for R&D is provided by businesses rather than governments. Governments, which often prioritize defence R&D, in general, fund under 10% of national R&D. In Russia, the government provides 55% of the funding for R&D, up from 50% in 1997. By contrast, in most countries, governments have reduced their contributions to R&D spending. The US is a good example – government spending came down from 14% to 9% from 1997 to 2007.

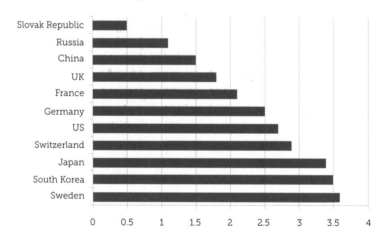

Figure 10.6 **Expenditure on R&D as a percentage of GDP**

Source: OECD (2009) Science, Technology and Industry Scoreboard 2009 (Paris: OECD)

Industrial structure

Large-scale investment in R&D is borne mainly by a country's large firms, as only they are able to undertake the long-term R&D programmes and the accompanying

► More online ... The OECD's full Science, Technology and Industry Scoreboard is at www.oecd.org

risks. Of course, simply spending a lot of money on R&D does not ensure successful innovation. Inter-firm rivalry and competition in home markets can lead to 'imitative' increases in R&D in particular product fields (Patel and Pavitt, 1994). Small firms can play a role, as has been the case in high-technology areas. The small start-up is flexible and less bureaucratic than the large established firm, and may be a rich source of ideas. Figure 10.7 shows the percentage of firms that produce new products in-house, comparing SMEs and large firms. In general, the large firms are more innovative. In France and Germany, over 50% of large firms produce new products in-house. Of these two countries, France has the more innovative SMEs. In Australia, levels of innovation are similar in both large firms and SMEs, but in the case of large firms, the level of innovation, which is similar to that of Poland, is lower than that in the other advanced economies shown on the chart.

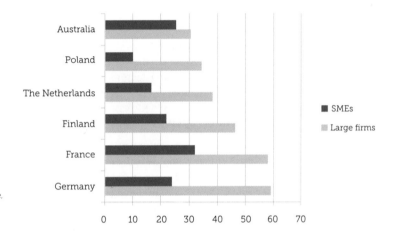

Figure 10.7 **In-house product innovators: comparing large firms and SMEs**
Percentages of total SMEs/large firms which produce new products in-house

Source: OECD (2009) Science, Technology and Industry Scoreboard (Paris: OECD)

Science and technology strengths and weaknesses

Countries differ in their areas of specialization and in the intensity of R&D activities. Where a country pursues a particular technological strength in an area of growing global importance, it stands to gain competitive advantage. Japan's intense investment in R&D in the fast-growing consumer electronics industry in the 1970s and 80s is an example. Japanese electronics firms overtook both European and US firms in taking out patents, both at home and in the US (Freeman, 1997). Many of Japan's technology SMEs remain global leaders in specialized areas of technology. India has targeted software development as an area of competitive advantage, and its government has fostered the growth in educational institutions which excel in this area.

Interactions within the innovation system

Interactions, whether formal co-ordination or informal networking, contribute to innovation activities within a country, and to their diffusion. Government guidance can be crucial in stimulating some industries to innovate – and discouraging others. The co-ordinating role of Japan's Ministry of International Trade and Industry is often cited for its pivotal role in the country's economic development. Strong state guidance in the Soviet Union, by contrast, was much less successful. There, separate research institutes for each industry sector had only weak links with each other. The Soviet system's concentration of R&D expenditure on military and space projects,

► More online ... The UN Industrial Development Organization (UNIDO) is at http://www.unido.org

coupled with the rigid command economy, left little scope for civilian innovation links to develop (Freeman, 1997). A more recent trend globally has been growing interaction between academic researchers and firms, as scientific research is playing a more important role in the development of many new technologies, for example, in life sciences.

Summary points National systems of innovation

◆ A national system of innovation encompasses, at the foundation level, education and training, especially in science and technology.

◆ Enhancing innovative capacity involves interactions between the academic community, businesses and governments.

◆ National innovation capacity can be a source of competitive advantage.

Critical thinking

Fostering technological capacities

Education systems tend to reflect the values of a society. To what extent can policies and resources encourage greater technological achievement within a society, and how does the national cultural environment play a part?

National innovation systems in context

There is no one model of innovation system that can be said to be superior in generating and diffusing technological innovation. While it is clear that innovation is linked to economic growth, countries display a good deal of diversity in their national innovation systems. Simple quantitative comparisons of R&D expenditure tell only a partial story. Social, cultural and historical differences have an influence on the ways in which learning, scientific curiosity, and entrepreneurial flair are allowed to flourish in national environments. Government initiatives can be influential. Huge investment in industrial R&D in Germany and Japan in the post-war period was crucial in their efforts to catch up economically.

The ability to assimilate and imitate innovations from elsewhere, as the basis of local innovative initiatives, has been a particular feature of Asian economic development. This process of technology transfer (defined in Chapter 2) holds out to all nations the possibility of benefiting from innovation. However, technical change has proceeded unevenly among countries and among individual companies. Adaptation of technology and use in local environments are still dependent on diverse national systems. Why are certain countries and certain firms innovative when others are not? Tellis et al. (2009) highlight four factors:

- The availability of skilled labour
- The availability of capital and financial resources generally
- The role of government and the national innovation system
- The role of culture, including national culture and corporate culture in particular firms

Although developed and developing countries are rapidly converging in the first two of the above factors, there is more divergence in the third, as it involves the evolution of a country's institutional environment. Innovation and diffusion of technology are in part governed by ownership structures of intellectual property, which are aspects of a country's legal system. Legal institutions themselves exist in a broader cultural environment. Many countries have similar IP legal protection in theory, but systems operate differently in practice.

Summary points National innovation systems in context

◗ Financial resources, skilled labour and government incentives all play a part in building innovative capacity within a country.

◗ The national culture and the corporate culture of individual companies also influence the

country's absorptive capacity and innovation potential.

Patents and other intellectual property rights

Patents are often referred to as a type of 'industrial' property, and patent activity is an indicator of levels of innovation (see Chapter 1). We should be cautious, though, not to read too much into patent statistics, as many innovations, such as informal and incremental improvements, fall outside patent activity. That said, patent statistics are an often-cited barometer of innovative activities.

Protection of property that exists in inventions and other products of human intellect has been the subject of heated policy debates from the days of the Industrial Revolution through to the present. Many would argue that technology should be freely available for anyone anywhere to use. Governments of industrialized countries, on the other hand, have long established policies for protecting **intellectual property (IP)**, in the belief that only by doing so will the incentive be provided for people to devote time and resources to innovation. Emerging economies are now following this example, with legal frameworks for the protection of IP.

From research and design through to testing, a new product can take many years before it reaches consumers. Those who support strong IP protection say that companies would be unwilling to commit resources in the absence of a system for granting exclusive rights over the product for a reasonable period of time. They acknowledge that limited monopolies are created, restricting competition, but argue that this is a price worth paying to ensure technical progress (Bainbridge, 1996). Many in developing countries, on the other hand, argue that they are effectively frozen out by these policies because of the concentration of intellectual property ownership in the industrialized countries. This is a recurring issue in relation to innovation policies, to which we will return when we look at technology transfer. In this section, we look at the nature of IP rights and how they come into being.

intellectual property (IP) property in intangible assets, such as patents, copyrights and trademarks, which can be legally protected from use by others unless permission is obtained from the owner

What is a patentable invention?

patentable invention a new product or process which can be applied industrially

The **patentable invention** is a new product or process which can be applied industrially. These basic requirements are similar across most countries, with some variations. In Europe, the main source of law is the European Patent Convention 1973 (EPC), which member states have incorporated into national law. (This has been adopted by EU states plus Switzerland, Monaco and Liechtenstein.) A European Patent Office was set up under the convention. In the UK, the relevant law is the Patents Act 1977. US patent law requires that the invention be 'useful', rather than 'industrially applicable', as required by the EPC. The requirement that the invention must be an industrial product or process rules out discoveries, scientific theories and mathematical methods, as they relate to knowledge and have no technical effect.

▶ More online ... The website of the UK Patent Office is http://www.patent.gov.uk
The European Union's site for intellectual and industrial property is http://europa.eu.int/ISPO/ecommerce/

Mere ideas or suggestions are also excluded, as a complete description of the invention must be submitted as part of the patent application. Moreover, the invention must not have been disclosed prior to the patent application: once disclosed, it becomes 'prior art' and can no longer be said to be new. Most inventions are not totally new products, but improvements on existing products. For a pharmaceutical drug, for example, a new patent can be obtained for a new dosage of one-a-week, rather than one-a-day. This can be a means of effectively extending the life of a patent. While we tend to think of only the most formal inventions as patentable, in fact the scope of potentially patentable inventions is expanding all the time, extending to software, microorganisms, and business methods.

Computer software and business methods are both patentable in the US, but only to a limited extent in Europe. In Europe a software-based invention is patentable if it has a 'technical effect'. This means that a new program affecting how the computer operates is patentable, whereas a computer game is not. The game, like most software, is protected by copyright. The expansion of software patents has been a trend in the US since software was recognized as patentable by the Supreme Court in 1981. In the US, a 'way of doing business' is patentable, whereas it would not be in Europe, although there are ways of getting around this restriction. The US has seen growing numbers of business methods patent applications, especially for e-commerce patents, such as Amazon.com's 'one-click' shopping method in 1999. The European Commission is considering widening European law, but many believe that the US has gone too far in granting monopoly protection where there is little justifiable case. They argue that it is difficult to see how a miracle cure for AIDS and an online retailer's system for repeat orders are at all comparable.

Summary points **The patentable invention**

◆ Inventions are at the heart of radical innovation. To qualify for a patent grant, the inventor must

demonstrate that the invention is new and can be applied industrially.

◆ The types of invention that qualify for a patent are being extended to areas such as business processes.

Patent rights in practice

patent type of intellectual property which gives its owner an exclusive right for a limited period, to exploit the invention, to license others to use it, and to stop all unauthorized exploitation of the invention

The **patent** gives its owner an exclusive right for a limited period to exploit the invention, to license others to use it, and to stop all unauthorized exploitation of the invention. Eighty per cent of patentholders are companies, not the actual inventors. The duration of a patent in the UK is four years, renewable up to 20 years. Renewal fees become steeper over time, and most inventions have been superseded by new technology long before the 20 years have expired. In the US, the normal duration is 20 years at the outset, with 'maintenance' fees payable at intervals. Being able to license the technology to other manufacturers entitles the patentholder to collect royalty fees agreed with the licensee. Much foreign direct investment relies on the licensing of technology. A patent may also be sold outright ('assigned') to someone else, who then is entitled to exploit it commercially. In common with other IP rights, 'exhaustion of rights' applies to patents. Under this principle, once the patentholder has consented to the marketing of the product in specific countries, he or she cannot prevent 'parallel imports', that is, importation of the product from another country, usually a lower-cost one. A consequence is that the owner of a

▶ More online ... The website for the World Intellectual Property Organization (WIPO) is http://www.wipo.int/ where information on the Patent Co-operation Treaty may be found

patent for a product sold in a number of countries might find it difficult to maintain price differentials between them.

For an inventor, the process of applying for a patent can be complicated, long and expensive. The process of patent office 'examination' of a patent application typically takes from two to four years. The help of expert professionals is almost always needed, stacking the odds against the individual inventor-entrepreneur. The simplest route for the inventor is to apply for a patent in his or her home country, but in that case, the patent granted will cover only that country, which most nowadays would find inadequate. There is no such thing as a global patent! For the multinational company with global markets, there are means available to alleviate the need to make separate applications in every country.

The European Patent Office (EPO) in Munich (established by the European Patent Convention) provides one route for patent protection. Application to the EPO allows the applicant to designate particular countries, typically eight, in which the patent will be valid. However, the grant will be a bundle of individual national patents, each of which must be translated into the national language, and enforced in national courts. The expense of translation into several languages adds considerably to the overall expense, making European patents several times more expensive than US or Japanese patents. For many years, businesses have pressed the European Commission for a simplified system which would allow a single application submitted in one language, making the process much more efficient and cheaper. Protracted negotiations have now made significant progress towards this goal, with the agreement of a draft regulation in 2009.

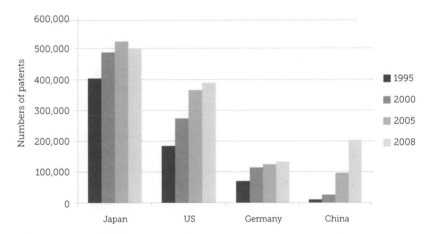

Figure 10.8 **PCT applications from major countries**

Source: WIPO statistics database, 2009, at www.wipo.int

An alternative route is offered by the Patent Co-operation Treaty (PCT) procedure, which covers over 100 countries. Under the PCT, the applicant makes one application to a regional office, and the process is divided into an 'international' phase and a 'national' phase. For the applicant with a global market in mind, there are considerable savings to be made in comparison with multiple individual country applications. The process is overseen by the World Intellectual Property Organization (WIPO) in Geneva.

Figure 10.8 sets out numbers of PCT patent applications from leading countries. Japan leads the world in PCT applications, followed by the US. The most dramatic increase in PCT applications is from China. Since 1995, Chinese applications have

Shake-up in the global pharmaceutical industry

The pharmaceutical industry has traditionally been divided into two camps: the cutting-edge, research-based companies who hold patents on most new medicines, and 'generic' producers who manufacture out-of-patent medicines for large markets. The elite pharmaceutical companies spend heavily on R&D and marketing, and charge high prices, which they justify by pointing to the need to keep up the flow of new medicines. As size and spending power have come to be equated, the industry has seen much consolidation: GlaxoSmithKline (GSK) was formed from several mergers. Merck took over Schering-Plough in 2009. The finances of these companies typically rely on a portfolio of drugs – sometimes only a handful – for which they enjoy the monopoly of patent protection, and for which they can charge premium prices. However, when patents run out or are successfully challenged in court, their owners' financial outlook can deteriorate quickly. The beneficiaries tend to be the generics companies, many of whom specialize in patent challenges. In the US – the world's largest drug market – generic makers' greatest legal breakthrough came in 1984, when legislation granted six months' exclusivity to the first company who successfully challenges an existing patent.

Since then, generic producers have prospered, notably companies such as Barr in the US. Outside the US, they grew strongly too, becoming global businesses. India abolished patents on products in the 1970s, to encourage domestic pharmaceutical companies. Although the country was compelled to reinstate patent protection as a condition of WTO membership in 2005, by then, the Indian firm Ranbaxy had grown into a global force. The world's largest generic producer, however, is Teva, an Israeli company whose aggressive CEO, a former general in the Israeli military, has pursued an acquisition strategy, seeking the benefits of high-volume production. One of his latest acquisitions was Barr, which brought Teva's portfolio of marketed products to over 500. Interestingly, Teva's most successful product, which generates a third of its profits, is not a generic, but a patented medicine for multiple sclerosis. However,

setbacks in clinical trials for a successor version could jeopardize this profit stream when the initial patent expires in 2012, giving Teva a taste of the problems facing research-based companies. This crossover, like the purchase of Barr, is indicative of the changes now taking place in global pharmaceutical markets.

Several factors are bringing about changes in the industry. The first is that the pace of scientific innovations leading to new drugs has slowed, which mainly affects the finances of the research-intensive companies. Increasingly, they have sought to acquire innovative SMEs, as in the biotechnology sector, or to acquire patent rights through licensing, to keep up the flow in the 'pipeline' of new drugs. A second factor is that regulators around the world have become stricter in assessing the risk of new medicines, insisting on longer, and more costly, clinical trials before approving a new drug. A third factor is that health systems are now feeling the financial constraints that have pervaded their wider domestic economies, forcing the pharmaceutical companies to lower their prices. Healthcare systems are also judging individual patient cases on the cost-effectiveness of a potential treatment. Healthcare reform in the US is contributing to this pressure, as new insurance schemes are rolled out to cover the millions of heretofore uninsured people.

Seeing their potential profits squeezed, the large pharmaceutical companies have engaged in widespread cost-cutting, including research budgets. They have also taken new strategic directions by acquiring generics businesses or forming strategic partnerships with them. Novartis of Switzerland bought generics company Hexal of Germany in 2005, merging the acquired business with its own Sandoz unit. Daiichi Sankyo of Japan purchased Ranbaxy, but encountered difficulties when drugs manufactured at two of Ranbaxy's factories were barred from the US by the Food and Drug Administration on safety grounds. Companies that decide to remain focused on patented medicines are diversifying into different types of treatment. Pfizer's purchase of Wyeth, largely for its specialist research in vaccines, is an example.

▶ More online ... Pfizer is at www.pfizer.com
GSK is at www.gsk.com
Ranbaxy is at www.ranbaxy.com

Cutting-edge scientific research is now taking place in a range of different organizations in diverse national settings, from SMEs to large multinationals

Source: Istock

Expansion into fast-growing emerging markets is a strategy common to both the research-based and generics businesses. Schering-Plough's businesses in China, Brazil and other emerging markets were among its attractions when Merck took it over. In developing countries generally, the generics producers are well placed. Their growing portfolios of medicines meet most of the needs of developing countries. However, since their breakthrough in the 1980s, generics companies have ridden 'piggyback' on the research-based companies. A tailing off in drug innovations is leading to a slimming of the research-based companies' portfolios, which will feed through to the generics companies. Moreover, the new biological drugs, to which many companies are now turning, are more complex and difficult to convert into generic versions. The two camps have somewhat converged, and both face an uphill march.

Sources: Jack, A. (2008) 'A bigger dose', *Financial Times*, 23 July; Jack, A. (2009) 'Pharma companies try different routes on rocky road to renewal', *Financial Times*, 13 March; Nakamoto, M. and Lamont, J. (2009) 'Daiichi profits hit by $4 bn Ranbaxy loss', *Financial Times*, 5 January; Rockoff, J. (2009) 'Merck to buy rival for $41 billion', *Wall Street Journal*, 10 March

Questions for discussion

◆ Why is the business model of traditional research-based pharmaceutical companies coming under pressure?
◆ What is the role of generics producers, and how is it changing?
◆ To what extent is basic scientific research likely to suffer setbacks in the current trends in the pharmaceutical industry?

▸ More online ... The US Patent and Trademark Office is at www.uspto.gov

risen from just over 10,000 to over 200,000. Recent years have seen a build-up of backlogs at official patent offices, as the bureaucratic processes fail to keep up with the pace of innovation (Intellectual Property Office, 2010). Where applications are to multiple patent offices, it should be possible to streamline the process and therefore speed up the award of patents. For example, if offices shared the work with each other, the duplication that now occurs could be avoided, offering potential savings in costs.

The US Patent and Trademark Office (USPTO) is the largest national patent office. It received over 485,000 applications for patents in 2008, and granted over 185,000 patents (US Patent and Trademark Office, 2009). The number of foreign applicants for US patents has risen significantly in recent years, as Figure 10.9 shows. Foreign applications now account for 51% of all US patents granted.

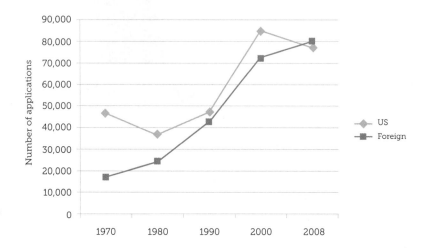

Figure 10.9 **US patent applications from US and foreign applicants**

Source: US patent statistics, 2009, at www.uspto.gov

Patent activity should be placed in perspective when looking at overall innovative behaviour. Patented inventions, however excellent, must be commercially viable and meet consumer needs. Capacity to build brands and establish reputation is as critical as winning products in achieving competitive advantage. Moreover, many innovations, such as new working practices, lie outside the category of patentable inventions.

Summary points Patent rights in practice

◆ The fact that patents are granted by national authorities can pose obstacles for inventors who wish to launch new products globally.

◆ There is some international co-operation in patent protection routes, to allow inventors to apply for multiple patents, such as through the Patent Co-operation Treaty.

Trade-related Aspects of Intellectual Property (TRIPS) multilateral international agreement on protection of intellectual property, which aims to bring national legal regimes into harmony

The Trade-related Aspects of Intellectual Property (TRIPS) agreement

There have been significant efforts to harmonize national laws on intellectual property rights through multilateral agreements. Following the Uruguay Round of GATT, the agreement on **Trade-related Aspects of Intellectual Property (TRIPS)** attempted to bring national legal regimes into harmony. Obligations of national treatment (equal treatment for foreign and domestic individuals and companies) and most-

▸ More online ... Information on TRIPS is at http://www.wto.org/english/tratop

favoured-nation treatment (non-discrimination between foreign individuals and companies) apply. These provisions took effect from 1996 for most countries, with transitional periods allowed for developing countries to comply. Most developing countries had a further five years, but the least developed countries had until 2006. TRIPS does not aim to make all countries conform to a single system, but to set certain 'minimum standards', with latitude for national variations. It specifies 20-year protection of patents on both process and products. In the controversial area of plants and animals, TRIPS provides that plant varieties must be patentable, but members may exclude certain types of plants and animal inventions. The TRIPS Council of the WTO monitors national laws for conformity. Disputes under TRIPS are settled through the WTO dispute settlement procedure.

TRIPS has come in for a great deal of criticism from developing countries. Critical areas for developing countries are new drugs to fight diseases such as AIDS, and new seeds for crops. Both areas rely on research in biotechnology, or life science technology. In industrial countries, the trend away from publicly funded research to private funding has brought the increasing domination of a few large multinationals in these areas. Many developing countries have become concerned about the grip of large MNEs in areas involving public goods.

Summary points **TRIPS**

◆ The aim of TRIPS is to harmonize the protection of intellectual property among the WTO's member states.

◆ The impact of TRIPS in developing countries has been to bring in more formal IP protection than they had had previously. While this benefits inventors generally, it

has been perceived as benefiting large MNEs in particular, as these global companies have a dominant position in patents in some areas, such as life sciences.

Technology transfer

technology transfer
process of acquiring technology from another country, especially in manufacturing, whereby skilled workers in the host country are able to learn from the foreign technology

Acquiring technology from other countries is known as **technology transfer**. While the term usually refers to transfers from the advanced economies to industrializing economies, it also covers transfers between industrialized countries. Technology transfer has been crucial to the processes of industrial growth and global integration. It is now recognized that technology transfer is not a simple one-way process, but more interactive and complex. Research has reopened basic issues of how knowledge and skills are acquired, and how imitation and innovation are interlinked.

Channels for international technology transfer

The post-war period has seen the emergence of four main channels of technology transfer. These are foreign direct investment, joint ventures and strategic alliances, licensing, and trade in capital goods (Mowery and Oxley, 1997). We look at each in turn.

FDI

FDI investment by MNEs is a major source of technology for developing countries. For the host country, the benefits derive from observing, imitating and applying the technologies, including the management methods. Spillover effects can include

MEET THE CEO

Kiran Mazumdar Shaw Chairman and Managing
Director of Biocon, the Indian biotechnology company

Starting a biotech company anywhere poses challenges for the technological entrepreneur, but for Kiran Mazumdar Shaw, starting up in India in the 1970s raised almost insurmountable hurdles. In her 20s, with a master brewer qualification from Australia, she had intended to go into the family business of brewing, but found it impossible to break into the male-dominated industry. She turned her scientific knowledge of fermentation and enzymes to biotechnology, but encountered more obstacles. As a woman, she had difficulty renting an office and hiring employees. Banks refused to lend to her without a male guarantor, and they were also sceptical about a start-up in biotechnology, which was new to them at the time. Nonetheless, she persevered, and, with the help of an Irish joint-venture partner, secured a bank loan to start Biocon in Bangalore in 1978.

The company grew from making enzymes for commercial purposes to more advanced scientific research, leading to more sophisticated products. But she needed more bank funding and again came up against the negative reactions of the banks. She says of that period, 'Technology is about innovation. I was all set to scale up and I was hitting a wall. I was in deep despair' (Yee, 2008). But she eventually secured a loan from the bank, ICICI, a large private-sector bank in India. Biocon was able to pursue research in biopharmaceuticals. Its IPO came in 2004. Most of its revenues now come from international sales.

In 2009, Biocon employed nearly 3,500 people, about half of whom are involved in R&D. The company describes itself on its website as 'delivering affordable innovation'. It has drawn on India's abundant pool of scientific researchers for its in-house R&D, for which it has 182 granted patents and 942 applications pending. It also carries out R&D for large pharmaceutical companies, benefiting from the low-cost advantages which India offers. Ms Shaw initially encountered scepticism from foreign companies over India's intellectual property protection, but Biocon's growing reputation has quelled their doubts. In 2009, it entered a collaborative arrangement with a US generic producer, Mylan, for making generic versions of biopharmaceutical drugs. The deal aims to aid Biocon in entering the highly regulated US market.

At the operating level, Biocon has developed manufacturing expertise, as well as expertise in incremental innovation, such as drug delivery systems, all with a view to creating affordable medicines and therapies. Its distinctive business model, combining elements from both the research-based and generic sectors, owes its direction to Ms Shaw. She says that the discrimination she encountered early in her career disappeared as the company became successful. She advises young women looking to become entrepreneurs themselves not to give up, saying, 'When you overcome challenges it makes you more confident' (Yee, 2008).

Sources: Yee, A. (2008) 'Tenacity in the face of prejudice', *Financial Times*, 15 October; Ahmed, R. (2009) 'Biocon signs pact with Mylan', *Wall Street Journal*, 29 June; Biocon website, at www.biocon.com

Kiran Mazumdar Shaw
Source: Biocon

linkages developed with domestic suppliers, but to exploit spillover effects requires incentives for local firms to adopt the new technologies. A recent trend among MNEs has been to relocate R&D activities from the home country to overseas locations, enhancing the parent company's overall innovative capacity. The late-industrializing countries of Asia and Latin America have benefited from FDI flows, mainly from the US and Japan. From the 1980s, outflows from newly industrialized countries, mainly South Korea, Taiwan, and China, have also increased, reflecting successful build-up of technological capabilities.

Joint ventures and strategic alliances

Collaborative innovation is a growing trend among firms in industrialized countries, and also between firms in industrializing and advanced economies. As costs of innovation have increased and R&D has become more specialized, companies see the benefits of marrying expertise and sharing costs. The joint venture is a favoured route for foreign investors in many countries. In welcoming FDI, China has insisted on joint ventures with Chinese partners, largely to gain benefits from the foreign partner's technological know-how. This policy has proved highly successful in promoting economic growth.

Technology licensing

The owner of a patent may license a foreign manufacturer to produce the product under licence, in return for royalties (see earlier discussion in Chapters 2 and 5). Many late-industrializing countries have relied heavily on licences for technology, particularly from the US and Japan. South Korea's spending on licences increased tenfold in the period 1982–91 (Mowery and Oxley, 1997). The age of technology transferred through licensing is significantly older than that transferred through FDI. Technology licensing to independent manufacturers, however, carries a risk of 'leakage' of IP, as there is less scope for control over operations than in an FDI project. Similarly, there is a risk of leakage of IP in joint ventures, but in these situations, the partner who owns important technology is in a stronger position to exert control through equity ownership.

Trade

Sometimes called 'embodied' technology transfer, the importation of machinery and equipment provides a means to assimilate the technology. By 'reverse engineering', discovering how a product has been made, it is possible to develop and refine the technology further. Japan's post-war industrial development is a good example of the benefits of imported technologies, which were assimilated and complemented by local R&D and engineering capabilities. Japanese firms similarly benefited from licensed technology, building on substantial investments in R&D and engineering (Bell and Pavitt, 1997). Importing foreign technology is not limited to imitation, but part of a larger process of technological accumulation (Lei and Bang, 2007).

Summary points Channels for international technology transfer

◆ FDI and joint ventures offer means whereby technology spillovers can lead to increased innovative activity in the host country.

◆ Technology licensing is perceived as advantageous mainly to the owner of the technology, with fewer spillover benefits in local economies.

◆ The import of capital goods can be a means of technology transfer, depending on the capabilities of the receiving country.

Technology diffusion and innovation

Technological diffusion was once thought to be the simple acquisition and adoption by developing countries of the technologies of developed countries, akin to adopting a set of 'blueprints', without any further creative contribution. It is now recognized that this view is oversimplified, in that the processes of diffusing technology are more dynamic, involving technical changes and adaptations to specific local conditions. Technological learning, or 'absorptive capacity', is at the heart of these processes. Formal education and training clearly play a part, but much learning is also acquired by doing, as in 'on the job' training. To benefit from technological accumulation, firms need to develop skills and know-how to improve the technology acquired from abroad. Japan and Germany are examples of countries that have combined imported technology with development of local technological capabilities. On the other hand, late-industrializing countries, while they have been able to increase productive capacity, have varied in their capacities for technological innovation. Manufacturers in some countries have benefited from importing advanced intermediary products, which help to stimulate domestic R&D activity (Lei and Bang, 2007). An example is South Korea, featured in the closing case study.

Some economies may seem to have become locked into sectors where competitiveness depends on low-wage production, and have been unable to break into the more knowledge-based sectors. Examples are the Latin American economies. A scale-intensive motor industry grew up in Argentina in the 1950s and 60s, along with the beginnings of specialist supplier industries, but these seemed not to have progressed further in the 1990s (Bell and Pavitt, 1997). To the extent that this is the case, economies are said to be 'path-dependent'. By contrast, some of the Asian late-industrializing economies have moved from labour-intensive sectors (which are supplier dominated) to sectors such as cars and consumer durables, and then to specialized equipment. Singapore is an example of this trajectory.

Activities of MNEs in expanding their global reach through FDI and licensing have been major contributors to the diffusion of technology. The choice of channel and the relationship between partners affects the ways in which proprietary technology is handled and the extent of diffusion. In equity joint ventures, where relations between the partners are of paramount importance, interactions in technology development can benefit both partners (Hagedoorn and Hesen, 2007). In licensing agreements, by contrast, the agreement is more strictly contractual. In this situation, there are fewer opportunities for long-term R&D collaboration. Still, the local manufacturer under a licence can benefit from the embedded technology, depending on the skills and expertise of the particular firm.

Summary points Technology diffusion and innovation

◆ The success of technology diffusion depends on local conditions in each country, often termed its 'absorptive capacity'.

◆ Also important is interaction between technology owners and hosts, as in FDI and joint ventures.

Critical thinking

Technology and development

What aspects of a country's innovation system are key to its ability to benefit from technological diffusion and nurture its domestic innovation capacities?

Technology and globalization

We have seen in this chapter that globalization of production has led to a diffusion of technology, but also that technological capacities still depend to a large extent on national innovation systems. Furthermore, technological innovation increasingly depends on links between scientific research and industrial R&D, both of which differ among national technological environments. R&D strategies of global companies aim to draw on sectoral specializations offered by specific countries. Globalization processes in both generating innovation and exploiting its fruits therefore highlight the continued role of national government policies. By providing incentives to companies for innovative activities, and supportive infrastructure such as industry–university partnerships, governments can attract the innovative activities that generate competitive advantages. It is for this reason that Michael Porter and others stress the importance of government in fostering innovation (Porter, 1998a).

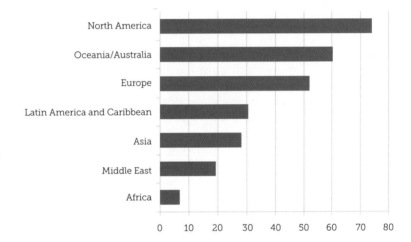

Figure 10.10 **Percentage of internet users out of total population in the world's regions**

Source: Internet world statistics, 2009, at www.internetworldstats.com

Countries that have concentrated on low-cost, labour-intensive manufacturing industries have been less successful in developing the more technologically advanced production systems. It is possible that businesses in these countries may find opportunities in the knowledge-intensive industries of the 'new economy', as it is often termed, where geographic location is less important than in, say, manufacturing. On the other hand, there is still wide divergence in internet usage across regions of the world, as Figure 10.10 shows. Asia now has by far the largest number of internet users, over 700 million. They account for 42% of the world's online population, but they make up just 19.4% of the total Asian population (see Figures 10.10 and 10.11). Internet penetration is highest in North America, at 74% of the population, but North Americans make up only 15% of the world's online population.

Poor developing countries risk falling further behind, opening up a 'digital divide' between rich and poor countries. IT diffusion in developing countries depends on investment in 'complementary assets' such as infrastructure (Shih et al., 2008). The completion of an undersea fibre-optic cable to Kenya in 2009 brought high-speed internet connecting South Africa, Tanzania, Kenya, Uganda and Mozambique to Europe and Asia. Costing $650 million and constructed over two years by an African company, Seacom, the new cable was hailed as opening the way for developing new-

▶ More online ... Seacom is at www.seacom.mu

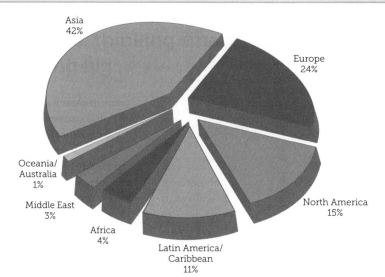

Figure 10.11 **World internet use** (percentages by region)

Source: Internet world statistics, 2009, at www. internetworldstats.com

economy opportunities. However, for users, the costs of internet access are far higher in developing countries than in developed ones.

In the new economy, as in the old, there are inequalities and exclusions, as well as opportunities. Erratic electricity supply is still a problem in many developing countries. Developing and transition economies in for example, Eastern Europe and Asia, have benefited from outsourcing. India is an example. It has become a host to call-centre operations, and its engineers and scientists are building computing, software and pharmaceutical businesses. Countries in the developing world have long histories of losing their highly skilled workers to the greater allure of opportunities in more advanced economies. However, growing opportunities in the large emerging economies are helping to redress the balance. India, for example, is seeing rising demand and rising salaries for high-technology workers.

Summary points Technology and globalization

◆ Globalization has seen a spread of R&D activities away from traditional centres to more diverse locations. Both local companies and foreign investors have seized on the innovation potential in the large emerging economies.

◆ National governments still play a crucial role in the technological environment.

◆ Regulatory frameworks and government oversight are areas in which governments are exerting influence over technology developments.

Conclusions

1   Technology is central to economic development and prosperity. Technological innovation can lead to competitive advantages in the world economy.

2   Innovation is a broad term, ranging from seemingly modest improvements in operations to radical new inventions that transform the way we live.

3   Technological development can be seen in terms of 'long waves' or cycles, each wave denoted by its dominant new technology, which transforms both methods of production and organizational structures. The current wave is that of microelectronics and computer networks.

4   The national system of innovation is defined as the institutions by which a country's innovation activities are encouraged and facilitated. Education and training, as well as industrial structures, are important components. Interactions, both formal and informal, are increasingly seen as contributing to innovation networks.

5   Patents are an indication of the amount of formal innovation in a society, and also the sources of innovation. Both products and processes, if new and industrially applicable, can be patented. Patent protection regimes are still essentially national.

6   Technology transfer represents a variety of means for acquiring technology from other countries. They include FDI, joint ventures, licensing, and trade in capital goods.

7   The diffusion of technology is increasingly seen as an interactive process, in which host countries can develop independent innovative capacities over time.

8   Domestic policies, often involving state support for technology initiatives, can help to foster innovation capacity within a national environment.

9   The impact of globalization of production on the generation of global technological innovation is much debated. R&D activities of MNEs are becoming more dispersed, benefiting from nation-specific specialisms.

10 There remains a divide between countries in which technological innovation is contributing to economic growth and those which are not as yet benefiting from the diffusion of technology. Lack of resources and infrastructure is one of the factors creating a 'digital gap'.

Review questions

1   Explain science-push and demand-pull in the development of new technology.

2   What is Schumpeter's view of technological innovation and waves of economic development?

3   Outline the elements of a national system of innovation. How relevant is the educational and training environment of the country?

4   Which countries have evolved particularly successful national innovation systems, and why?

5   Why are patents crucial to technological lead?

6   What are the conditions that must be satisfied before a patent may be obtained for a process or product?

7   Why is the TRIPS agreement said to be disadvantageous to developing countries?

8   Describe briefly the four ways in which technology transfer takes place, pointing to the advantages and disadvantages of each.

9   Why are some countries falling behind in the global diffusion of technology?

10 What are the benefits for an MNE in locating R&D activities in dispersed locations globally?

Key revision concepts

Diffusion of technology, p. 354; Globalization, p. 355; Innovation, p. 335; Innovation system, p. 340; Intellectual property rights, p. 345; Patentable invention, p. 345; R&D, p. 337; Spillover effects, p. 351; Technology licensing, p. 353; Technology transfer, p. 351

Assignments

◆ Assume you are advising a government of a developing economy. Report to the government on: (a) policies designed to bolster national innovative capacities; and (b) policies to gain maximum benefit from technology transfer afforded by its inward investors in manufacturing.

◆ To what extent is R&D becoming 'globalized', and in what ways may developing countries reap R&D advantages which could spill over into their domestic companies?

Further reading

Afuah, A. (2009) *Strategic Innovation* (London: Routledge).

Archibugi, D. and Michie, J. (1997) *Technology, Globalisation and Economic Performance* (Cambridge: Cambridge University Press).

Bainbridge, D. and Howell, C. (2008) *Intellectual Property Law* (London: Longman).

Castells, M. (2009) *The Rise of the Network Society*, 2nd edn with a new preface (Oxford: Wiley-Blackwell).

Freeman, C. and Soete, L. (1997) *The Economics of Industrial Innovation*, 3rd edn (London: Cassell).

Landes, D. (1998) *The Wealth and Poverty of Nations* (London: Abacus).

Tidd, J. and Bessant, J. (2009) *Managing Innovation: Integrating Technological, Market and Organizational Change*, 4th edn (London: John Wiley & Sons).

Westland, J.C. (2008) *Global Innovation Management* (Basingstoke: Palgrave Macmillan).

What lies behind Samsung's competitiveness?

Samsung Electronics, the flagship company of South Korea's Samsung conglomerate, is a company most competitors in the electronics sector fear – from Nokia, which has seen Samsung mobile phones grab market share to become the number 2 globally, to flatscreen TV makers who envy Samsung's number 1 position. It has overtaken prestigious Japanese rivals such as Sony, which have struggled in recent years. Its chief domestic rival, LG, which is older and larger, has seen its share of the TV market overtaken by Samsung. In a country that comes near the top of league tables for its depth of engineering education, the brightest and most talented graduates aspire to join Samsung. It has built a global reputation as a quality brand, although 'Korean' is hardly equated with 'German' in brand image. The brand seems to have remained untarnished despite the fact that its CEO, who has driven its global strategy, has been convicted of corruption and

recently served a two-year jail sentence, returning to the helm only in 2010.

Samsung's success has rested largely on the vision of its founder, Lee Byung-Chull, which, since his death in 1987, was enhanced and revised by his son, the current CEO, Lee Kun-Hee. Although more court cases for financial irregularities continue, it is likely that the second Mr Lee's son will take over to carry on the family empire. And 'empire' is the best way to describe the conglomerate, or, in Korean business terms, *chaebol*. From its founding in 1938, Lee B.-C. built the family fortunes on a range of businesses, from commodities to insurance. The electronics business dates from 1969, and was perhaps out of line with the others. With no background in technological industries, the company had to acquire technology while also seeking to build its own innovation capacity. A valuable asset was close ties with the government and friendly state-owned banks able to lend money cheaply. It thus

Manufacturing microchips, although seen by some global electronics brands as a non-core activity, has proved a winner for Samsung

Source: Istock

manoeuvered to buy technology from foreign competitors. During the 1970s and 80s, when South Korea enjoyed rapid economic growth, Samsung was able to expand in a protected domestic environment where it could make the most of its government links, and where foreign competitors were barred.

A turning point for Samsung came in 1978, when, again with little technological background of its own, it entered the semiconductor industry, manufacturing low-cost memory chips. With the intervention of the government, it obtained foreign technology from companies in the US and Japan, in return for access to the Korean market. Samsung went on to become the world's biggest producer of memory chips, used by computer manufacturers everywhere. It had produced its first TV in 1969, and was able to build up manufacturing capability in its protected home market, but aspired to become a global leader in TVs. Its first European assembly plant was opened in Portugal in 1982. Samsung's reputation for innovation rests heavily on the priorities of Lee K.-H., who, when he took over as CEO in 1987, invested heavily in R&D. Between 1987 and 1992, the company's profits more than doubled,

and much of this money was ploughed into R&D, including buying firms to acquire their technology.

Although the company's fortunes foundered in the Asian financial crisis, it has relied on its semiconductor business to sustain its financial position. In this respect, it differs from rivals such as LG. For a company in a sector that relies on innovation for competitive advantage, it is perhaps strange that the production of chips, which has now become commoditized, should be crucial. LG sold its chip business in 1999 after the Asian crisis. With fanfare appropriate for royal status, Samsung executives unveiled its new memory-chip plant near Seoul in 2010. The global fall in memory-chip prices, however, is causing the company to rethink its strategy once again. Another cloud on the horizon is that financial irregularities might threaten the Lee family's control.

Sources: *The Economist* (2009) 'Looking good?', 24 January; *The Economist* (2010) 'All in the family', 30 January; *The Economist* (2009) 'Crowning success', 6 June; Martin, S. (2010) 'Samsung Electronics profit tops $8 billion', *Industry Week*, 29 January, at www.industryweek.com; Wong, E. (2010) 'Samsung: Innovation sells in a recession', *Brand Week*, 10 March, at www.brandweek.com

Questions for discussion

◆ What are the main elements of Samsung's competitive strategy?
◆ How has the business climate in South Korea aided Samsung?
◆ What is Samsung's innovation strategy, and why has it been so successful?

CHAPTER **11**

ECOLOGY AND CLIMATE CHANGE

Outline of chapter

Introduction

Environmental degradation in context

Climate change
What is known about climate change?
Global co-operation to combat climate change
Climate change initiatives by governments: the implications for international business

Transboundary pollution and enery strategy

International legal frameworks for protecting the environment

Challenges of environmental protection for business
Sustainable development in the business context
Environmental management

EU initiatives on the environment

Sustainable consumption

Environmental protection and changing values

Conclusions

Learning objectives

1 To understand the nature and causes of the major environmental challenges, such as climate change and transboundary pollution
2 To appreciate interconnections between local, regional and global concerns
3 To gain insight into the role of governments and international co-operation in tackling environmental challenges
4 To identify at a practical level the initiatives businesses can take in environmental management and sustainable development strategy

Critical themes in this chapter

- **CSR and sustainability – corporate responsibilities in respect of environmental degradation and climate change**
- **Changing societies – impacts of environmental degradation on societies**
- **Multilayered environment – co-operation between states and with UN bodies to combat climate change**
- **Emerging economies – source of increasing carbon emissions; role at international level**

Rising emissions, like the smoke plumes from this refinery, are a challenge for both governments and businesses
Source: Istock

BYD is fired up – on batteries

BYD, whose motto is 'build your dreams', was the brainchild of Wang Chuan-Fu, who started his business in 1995 in Shenzhen, China, on funds raised from relatives. A chemist and engineer by background, his vision was to make rechargeable batteries that were reliable and affordable. He began by manufacturing batteries for mobile phones, aiming to capture market share from dominant Japanese manufacturers, Sony and Sanyo, whose imported batteries were expensive, not least because of Chinese import duties. By 2000, BYD overtook its Japanese rivals, and Wang went on to design handsets and parts for Motorola. BYD still makes 80% of Motorola's RAZR handsets, but Wang soon moved on to bigger challenges. He saw the car market taking off in China, and decided to diversify into car manufacturing. His opportunity came in 2003, when he bought a dying state-owned car company. Wang had little knowledge of cars, and while entrepreneurs are noted for taking risks that other people would not contemplate, Wang's entry into car manufacturing seemed ambitious even by entrepreneurial standards. However, he was soon manufacturing low-cost sedan cars and grabbing

Chinese market share from the established VW Jetta and Toyota Corolla. Meanwhile, his research was proceeding apace on his biggest career challenge: electric cars.

Wang was undaunted by the fact that many large MNEs with huge resources were also working on producing electric cars. Reducing greenhouse gas emissions has become a major element in combating climate change, and as China takes on a more influential role globally, its environmental policies are coming under the spotlight. Governments throughout the world are taking legislative initiatives to reduce the levels of permissible CO_2 emissions from motor vehicles. They are also concerned about dwindling oil supplies globally. Manufacturers are responding with a range of innovations to reduce emissions while maintaining the flexibility of the internal-combustion engine. The technology that has fired the greatest interest has been the lithium-ion battery. But these batteries are expensive and have disadvantages in terms of convenience and range. Recharging is slow and most have a range which makes them suitable only for city driving. The hybrid, with a back-up petrol

Going places: BYD has combined innovation and competitiveness to bring efficient, affordable electric cars closer to reality

Source: BYD

▸ More online ... BYD is at www.byd.com

engine, or a petrol engine that produces more electricity (the 'series' hybrid), is seen as a potential game changer. General Motors' Volt (Ampera in Europe) is one. At an estimated price of $40,000, it is still expensive, leaving much to play for in the innovation stakes.

The electric car is more efficient than the car powered by the internal-combustion engine. The latter can travel 1.5–2.5 km on a kilowatt-hour of energy. A hybrid can go up to 3.2 km, but a battery-powered car can go 6.5 km. Moreover, the energy that goes into an electric car is cheaper. The electricity used is generated on a large scale at power stations and is less wasteful than fuelling an individual car by filling it with petrol or diesel. Battery firms, often in conjunction with carmakers, are now rushing to develop lithium-ion batteries for cars. A Nissan-Renault-NEC partnership is launching a family car. BYD has lost no time in launching its own electric cars, the E3 and E6. Wang considers that his breakthrough technology based on new materials – the lithium-ion ferrous phosphate technology – will be a game changer. What is more, he aims to make the batteries 100% recyclable, using a non-toxic electrolyte fluid. His argument is that helping to solve problems of environmental degradation should not create more environmental problems.

Wang has won over one big convert, the respected US investor Warren Buffett, who took a 10% holding in BYD in April 2009, amounting to $230 million. Buffet, too, says he knows little about cars, but is impressed with Wang's drive and passion. The speed with which he has built up global market presence would be exceptional for an internet company. But for a manufacturing company whose business model is based on its own innovations, it is remarkable. BYD now has 130,000 employees in eleven factories: eight in China and one each in India, Hungary and Romania. For BYD, the dream of an affordable electric car is becoming a reality. Now, Wang is moving on to another big idea, enhanced solar panels. His Home Clean Power Solutions involves solar panels with built-in batteries to store power when the sun is not shining. In the supercharged world of BYD, the sun never seems to set.

Sources: Dyer, G. (2009) 'Chinese puzzle', *Financial Times*, 4 November; Gunther, M. (2009) 'Warren Buffett takes charge', *Fortune Magazine*, 13 April; *The Economist* (2009) 'The electric-fuel-trade acid test', 5 September

Questions for discussion

◆ What are the advantages and disadvantages of electric cars?
◆ Why would an American investor like Warren Buffett buy a large stake in a Chinese company like BYD?
◆ How does a relative newcomer such as BYD hope to compete against the established global carmakers in the electric-car market?

Introduction

Challenges posed by the environment are increasingly impacting on societies, governments and businesses. They include global warming, depletion of natural resources and pollution. These, and other, processes are detrimental to human well-being, and also harm plants and animals, both on the land and in the seas. While it may not be possible to bring back species that have become extinct or replace resources that have become exhausted, it is possible to slow down and control harmful processes, and with the aid of research, to find ways of combating the harmful effects. Whereas environmental issues were once seen as mainly local, they are increasingly perceived in the wider context of regional and global implications. Similarly, because it is about the public interest, the environment was once seen mainly as a matter of government concern, whereas the role of businesses – whether for bad or good – is now attracting more attention. Governments and businesses now co-operate in environmental protection, at national, regional and international levels. Often, this co-operation includes international organizations, both governmental and non-governmental (NGOs). The role of specialist environmental NGOs has been important in raising awareness of 'green' issues and also in promoting green alternatives to environmentally damaging activities. Greater weight has been given to these efforts by advances in scientific research, which have shed light on trends affecting the planet as a whole, and also provided details on the effects of different types of pollution in specific locations.

Much past and present environmental damage stems from the effects of economic development. These processes include industrialization, changes in farming methods and depletion of natural resources. As has been seen in Chapter 6, industrialization leads to urbanization, as rural dwellers flock to urban areas in search of work in new industries. While these twin processes began two centuries ago in the advanced economies, the centres of today's industrialization are in the developing world, and the processes are taking place much more quickly than in the first wave of industrialization. Moreover, current environmental changes are occurring in a context of unprecedented population pressures, mainly in the developing world. Protecting the environment, therefore, is now seen as part of a broad view of development, known as sustainable development, which takes into account not just the well-being of today's generation, but also the needs of future generations. Sustainable development is increasingly incorporated in the strategic thinking of international managers.

This chapter will first highlight the major environmental challenges, their causes and effects, both long term and short term. It will then look at responses to challenges at the level of business enterprises. Environmental management strategies adapted to sustainable development goals are evolving in a context of changing institutional and legal frameworks. Recent years have seen the increasing involvement of business players in both responses and initiatives in the area of environmental protection.

Environmental degradation in context

ecology the relationship between organisms and their environment, including changes in their distribution and numbers

Ecology focuses on the interactions between living organisms and their habitats. Organisms range from plant and animal life to human beings, in a variety of habitats, including urban centres as well as rural areas, forests, waterways and the sea. A

biodiversity the variety of living organisms and species co-existing in the same habitat

environmental degradation environmental change caused mainly by human activity, which has detrimental effects on ecological systems

change in any of these habitats impacts on the living creatures they support: the variety of living organisms (called **biodiversity**), their distribution and number are affected by even slight changes in environment. While environmental changes can occur naturally through changes in climate and weather, **environmental degradation** refers specifically to environmental change caused mainly by human activity (Held et al., 1999: 382). The development of agriculture in Europe and North America in the seventeenth and eighteenth centuries is an example which saw a huge expansion in the area of cultivated land, technological innovations and the emergence of capitalist market relationships in agriculture (Maddison, 2001). Forests were cut down, heathland was cleared, and numerous species of wildlife declined as their habitats were destroyed.

With the Industrial Revolution, the capacity for environmental degradation started to grow dramatically, in both intensity and geographic scope. Factory production relying on power sources like coal was joined by newer industries, including synthetic chemicals, which generated a mixture of old and new pollutants. As urban areas grew up around these industries, environmental problems also grew, posing threats to health associated with air pollution and poor access to clean water and sanitation. As Maddison points out, although city dwellers in the early period of industrialization enjoyed higher incomes than those in rural areas, their mortality rates were significantly higher, mainly due to the spread of infectious diseases, which took their greatest toll among infants and recent migrants (Maddison, 2001).

As Chapter 6 highlighted, almost all current population growth is taking place in the developing world, especially in Africa. In general, these countries' economies are heavily reliant on agriculture, but agriculture can be precarious, and is unlikely to promote sustained economic growth in today's world. Moreover, the effects of climate change, including extreme weather events and desertification, are taking their toll on agricultural production in the developing world. Meanwhile, there is growing demand for food from the large emerging economies, such as China and India, both of which are food importers. The world now faces stern challenges in growing enough food and managing its distribution.

Although industrial development has brought much-needed employment and income, it has also led to environmental degradation, including resource depletion and pollution. Major causes of environmental degradation are shown in Figure 11.1. As the figure shows, urbanization and modern consumer lifestyles have been central to these processes, leading to increased needs for power generation and transport. Industrial production requires land for factories, and also for housing and other services including roads and infrastructure. It is estimated that nearly 23% of all the world's cropland, pasture, forest and woodland have been degraded since the 1950s (World Bank, 2002). Similarly, in this period nearly one-fifth of all tropical forests have been cleared, most of them in the developing world (World Bank, 2002). Severe threats to biodiversity have resulted: many plants and animals are unique to particular areas and become extinct when the ecosystem is disrupted. Urbanization often encroaches into land that had been agricultural, while growing urban populations place greater pressure on supplies of food, water and energy. Burning fossil fuels such as coal is highly pollutant, and resources are finite. The result can be the stifling smogs which envelop cities in the developing world, causing health problems and increased burdens on health infrastructure.

The notion of 'global commons' in the atmosphere and the seas has led environmental researchers to view the entire planet as made up of interrelated ecosys-

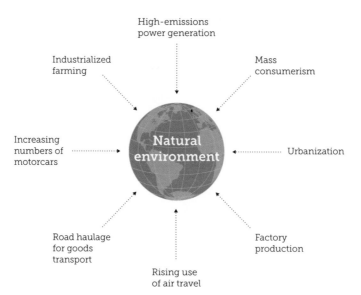

Figure 11.1 **Causes of environmental degradation**

tems, where actions in a specific location can have widely ramified impacts across the globe, some very unpredictable (Held et al., 1999: 378). Interconnections between local, regional and global phenomena are increasingly being revealed. For example, air pollution or waste dumped into a river from a single factory may travel long distances, heedless of national boundaries. In the wider picture, air pollution generated by industrial agglomeration, we now know, depletes the ozone layer of our atmosphere.

Large emerging economies are now enjoying growing prosperity, both from growth in their home countries and in their outward FDI. Like the expansion of MNEs from the developed world, these new global players are becoming enmeshed in the societies in which they operate, being called upon to manage conflicting agendas. A distinguishing feature of much recent global expansion by emerging MNEs has been their closeness to the state, often through state-owned or state-controlled companies. Governments in the Bric countries have tended to view economic development in their home countries as the top priority, and environmental damage as a price worth paying. Now, as the Bric countries have become global forces, and as the effects of just a few decades of industrialization become apparent, they realize that action must be taken to safeguard societies – and plan for more sustainable growth in the future. They face environmental pressures from three broad directions:

- From their own societies, where pollution threatens health and welfare
- From host societies, where similar health and environmental concerns arise
- From the international community, concerned that the developing countries take greater responsibility for global environmental damage

As we will see in the next section, the climate change debate has crystallized differing national perspectives, and thrown down immense challenges to businesses in all of the world's regions.

▶ More online ... The World Bank makes available research publications on 'environment and energy' under its research topics, on its website at www.worldbank.org

Summary points Environmental degradation in context

◆ Industrialization and urbanization have been major causes of environmental degradation, including pollution, depletion of natural resources and loss of plant and animal species.

◆ Currently, rapid economic growth in the large emerging economies presents a major threat of further environmental degradation.

◆ It is now recognized that the natural environment is a global, rather than strictly national, issue.

Critical thinking
Contradictions in the emerging economies
The large emerging markets are now facing pressures for greater environmental protection. To what extent are economic development and environmental protection incompatible?

Climate change

climate change any change in the climate over time, whether from natural causes or human activity

global warming global rise in temperatures, impacting on all forms of life, caused by the build-up of heat-trapping gases, or 'greenhouse gases' (GHG), in the earth's atmosphere

greenhouse gases (GHG) mixture of heat-trapping gases, mainly carbon dioxide (CO2), held to cause global warming

Climate change covers any change in the climate over time, whether from natural causes or human activity. Climate experts generally believe that we are now experiencing a slow process of **global warming**, caused by the build-up of heat-trapping gases, or **greenhouse gases (GHG)**, in the earth's atmosphere. In particular, carbon dioxide is to blame. Carbon dioxide (CO_2) emissions quadrupled over the second half of the twentieth century, a period of rapid economic growth in Europe, the US and Japan. The burning of fossil fuels, mainly in coal-fired power stations, is responsible for over half of greenhouse gas emissions globally. Factory production and its accompanying needs for transport and energy contribute to rises in emissions. These trends are pronounced in the world's large developing economies, where there is growing demand for the elements of modern consumer lifestyles, such as cars and air travel.

Shares of greenhouse gas emissions by region are given in Figure 11.2. Roughly taking North America and Europe together as developed regions, we see that emissions from these economies amount to 44% of the world total, whereas the other regions, predominantly developing and emerging economies, account for 56%. The largest share globally is that of Asia. Of course, the developing economies are home to much larger – and growing – populations than the developed world. Emissions per person in China and Brazil are about one-fifth those in the US. Emissions in India are lower still, less than half the emissions per person of the inhabitants of China. However, it is in these large emerging economies that emissions are increasing the most, as Figure 11.3 shows. Emissions are now 30% higher than they were in 1998, when the first climate change treaty, the Kyoto Protocol, was signed. Most of this growth has been in the developing world. Figure 11.3 gives a breakdown of this rise among regions and key individual economies. Germany stands out as having done most to reduce emissions, while China and India bear the main responsibility for growth in global emissions. Although the Kyoto Protocol did not include any provisions for limiting emissions in developing countries, the issue of these countries' emissions will be crucial to any future reductions in emissions globally.

▶ More online ... The US Energy Information Administration (EIA) is at www.eia.doe.gov

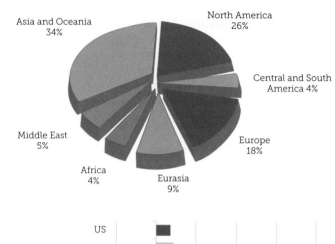

Figure 11.2 **Shares of greenhouse gas emissions by region**

Source: US Energy Information Administration (EIA), World emissions by country, 2009, at www.eia.doe.gov

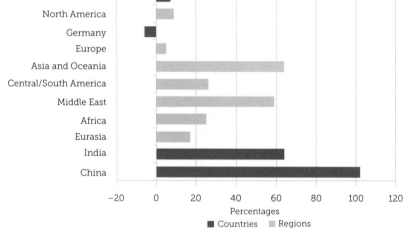

Figure 11.3 **Change in greenhouse gas emissions by major countries and regions, 1998–2009**

Source: US Energy Information Administration (EIA), World emissions by country, 2009, at www.eia.doe.gov

What is known about climate change?

Theories of climate change have been around over a hundred years, but only in the last two decades have scientists been able to monitor the changes with precision in a variety of locations. It is impossible to measure directly climate changes that took place before human civilization, but climate scientists are able to study a range of phenomena, such as rock and ancient Antarctic ice, which give them data on the earth's climate history. These studies show them the changes brought about by natural variations in CO_2. These data help them to assess current changes in the atmosphere, oceans, temperatures and rainfall. The UN established the Intergovernmental Panel on Climate Change (IPCC) in 1989, which assembled a panel of hundreds of scientists. Its aim was to bring together the scientific evidence about what changes are occurring, aiding governments to be in a better informed position to act. Their reports, in 1990, 1995 and 2000, have been influential in forming views about the nature and impacts of climate change. The research confirms the connection between increasing levels of CO_2 in the atmosphere and global warming.

The scientific data amassed by scientists suggest that global warming is a reality, and that it is happening because of human activity. However, there are sceptics who doubt the strength of the research, and there have been doubts about the rigour of the reports published by the IPCC. Apart from these doubts, there is uncertainty over

► More online … The Intergovernmental Panel on Climate Change is at http://www.ipcc.ch/

the rate of warming. By the end of the century, temperatures could rise by as little as 1.1 degrees C, which would represent only a limited threat to the planet, or as much as 6.4 degrees C, which could be catastrophic. The rate of increase in CO_2 equivalent emissions (CO_2 and other greenhouse gases) is the key factor in determining the extent of the rise. Before the Industrial Revolution these concentrations were 280 parts per million (ppm). The figure for 2009 has been estimated at 385 ppm. If the rise in emissions continues at the current rate, there is a 50% risk of a temperature increase of 5 degrees C globally (*The Economist*, 2009d). A rise on this scale would have severe impacts on ecology and human welfare.

The IPCC estimates that limiting the rise to 2 degrees above pre-industrial levels would be an attainable target. For the rise to be kept to this level requires that greenhouse gas emissions must not exceed a concentration of 450 ppm of carbon in the air. This means that there is very little leeway for further rise, and action needs to be taken urgently to slow the rise in emissions. Once released into the atmosphere, carbon dioxide can persist for a century, and there is no current technology to remove it on a large scale. The message of the climate scientists is therefore that steps must be taken to reduce emissions. There is a good deal of technology for reducing emissions and utilizing clean alternatives in many spheres of activity. However, implementing changes on a large scale involves government action to compel businesses and individuals to change their behaviour.

The effects of climate change are complex, as climate is more than just temperature, but includes interactions of temperatures with winds and rainfalls in different locations. Heatwaves, droughts, floods and hurricanes are all associated with climate change. It is estimated that all continents can expect shifts in their climate, and thus their ecology, as a result of global warming. Severe flooding can occur in some places, and desertification in others. Arid and semi-arid areas in Africa and Asia will have higher temperatures, causing loss of vegetation and depletion of water sources. Because the polar ice caps are melting, sea levels are rising. Island nations and low-lying regions, such as Bangladesh, risk becoming submerged beneath the sea, while the Sahara Desert in Africa is expanding. Subterranean aquifers are becoming depleted and rivers are drying up. Extremes of drought and flood, as well as extreme events such as storms, pose risks to agriculture and lead to insecurity of supplies of food and clean water. Agriculture is already becoming problematic in Australia because of drought, and agriculture in Spain, which supplies many European countries, would also be affected.

It has long been known that climate change poses serious threats to developing countries, mainly in Africa, which have fewer resources to cope with natural disasters or to change existing agricultural systems. It is now becoming apparent that rich countries are also vulnerable to floods, droughts, severe storms and rising sea levels. Although technologies, such as flood defences, exist, costs are great, and hurricanes can wreak havoc in the most advanced economies.

Summary points Causes and effects of climate change

● The increase in greenhouse gases in the earth's atmosphere, caused largely by the burning of fossil fuels, is a major factor in global warming.

● Impacts of global warming include rising sea levels, droughts, desertification, flooding and severe storms. Having more limited resources to combat these effects, developing countries are more at risk than developed ones.

● The UN's experts estimate that a rise of 2 degrees C is likely to occur, and that steps need to be taken urgently to keep the rise at this level, or below.

Balancing development and conservation: Brazil's dilemma

Deforestation is contributing to rising greenhouse gas emissions (GHGs) globally. Simply leaving trees standing is therefore a good way to limit emissions, but pressures to chop down trees for agriculture, roads and power stations are strong. The pressures are acutely felt in developing countries, where some of the largest areas of virgin forest are located. Brazil has some of the world's most extensive rainforests, and also a record of deforestation. Most of the damage is being caused by cattle ranching, which the land will sustain for just two to three years, before ranchers move on to cut down more trees. Encroachment for commodity crops for export, such as soya and sugar, is also prevalent, but varies with the market: when global prices are high and Brazil's currency is weak, deforestation rises.

A fast-growing Bric economy, Brazil is prioritizing economic development, to reduce poverty and improve living conditions. Its left-wing president, Luiz Inácio Lula da Silva (often referred to simply as 'Lula'), who has been in office since 2003, made protecting the environment central to his platform, appointing an aggressive environment minister, Ms Marina Silva, to combat deforestation. Her job was formidable, but Ms Silva was undaunted, having overcome the challenges of her own deprived upbringing in the Amazonian jungle, racked by poverty and forest diseases. Long ravaged by deforestation, Brazil's Amazonia is particularly vulnerable because of its deficient system of land title. There is no central land registry, and it is estimated that only 4% of the land is covered by a legal title. The rest is prone to land grabs by people simply helping themselves to land and hoping thereby to establish 'title' by occupation. The government of Mr da Silva

introduced a policy to give small plots to the people farming them and take over bigger plots under government ownership, to prevent deforestation. Deforestation peaked in 2004 at 27,000 square kilometres, but fell in the following years, a fall largely attributed to Ms Silva's efforts to rein in illegal logging and ranching. However, she resigned in 2008, in frustration that the president's development policies were putting the forest at greater risk. Since then, deforestation has again been on the rise. A recent source of threat has been the government's push for hydroelectric projects.

Brazil has one of the world's most extensive river systems, which has long been tamed to produce electricity, currently supplying 83.5% of the country's needs. Hydropower is clean and cheap, but must be managed efficiently and can be vulnerable when rainfall is low. Blackout disasters in 2001 and 2002 are remembered as factors in the preceding government's electoral defeat by Mr da Silva. Brazil needs to add capacity to cope with the estimated rise in consumption from 393,000 megawatt hours (MWh) in 2008 to 599,000 MWh in 2017. New projects are submitted to greater scrutiny for environmental impacts and disruption to communities than was the case in the past, especially in light of the government's concern that benefits must flow to the poor. New projects such as the Santo Antonio scheme use modern 'bulb turbines' which need less steep falls of water, and can be placed at intervals along the flow of a river.

Brazil reaps praise for its economic growth, but its image is tarnished by its record on deforestation, which has become a matter of global concern

Source: Istock

▶ More online ... A portal on global forests is www.forests.org
The Rainforest Alliance is at www.rainforest-alliance.org

Even so, the proposed Belo Monte project, the biggest so far, has angered environmentalists and drawn international attention, attracting filmmaker James Cameron, and stars of the film *Avatar* to protest alongside environmentalists.

The Belo Monte project would be the third biggest hydroelectric plant in the world, still behind the massive Three Gorges Dam in China. The Belo Monte project would flood 516 square kilometres, which is considered modest for such a big project, but its positioning along the Xingu, one of the main tributaries in the Amazon jungle, causes concern. The river's level will be lowered as it passes between reservations of indigenous peoples. Like other hydro projects, it would be subject to fluctuation in its output due to irregular rainfall, which could result in sharp falls in output.

Questions over the Belo Monte project have also come from the construction companies and their financiers who have expressed interest in building it. A government invitation to potential bidders imposed restrictive conditions: there is a cap of 70% of the electricity generated that can be sold to distribution companies, and the price is capped by the government. Given the restrictions, some large would-be bidders, including Brazilian construction companies, stayed away, fearing a meagre return on their investment. Despite a court ruling that revoked the project's environmental permit, the government was determined to proceed with the project, awarding the contract to a consortium led by a state-controlled hydroelectric company. Whether the project eventually goes ahead will, like the many Amazon initiatives in the past, depend on political resolve, with much riding on the outcome of elections in late 2010.

Constitutionally barred from standing for another term as president, the highly popular Mr da Silva chose the candidate he wished to succeed him, Dilma Rousseff, his chief of staff, who had been instrumental in his industrial development policies. However, his popularity did not automatically rub off onto Ms Rousseff. In the first round of voting, the former environment minister, Marina Silva, standing as a candidate for the small Green Party, received an unexpectedly high proportion of the votes, nearly 20%, which forced the election into a second round, as neither of the two main parties had an absolute majority. Although her share of the vote was not enough to take her into the second round, her electoral success, winning nearly 20 million votes, has drawn attention to the widespread concern within Brazil over environmental issues. In the final round, Ms Rousseff won with 56% of the vote. Although Brazilians are legally required to vote, there was a high abstention rate of nearly 22%.

Mr da Silva trumpeted the discovery of oil in the deep-sea area off Brazil's coast as a boost to fulfilling the country's energy needs. But the international spotlight also focuses on Brazil's environmental record. The country has always been reluctant to set targets for reducing carbon emissions, but it wishes to be seen as acting responsibly in international climate change forums. The 'other' Silva, backed by substantial public support, is taking this message forward in the post-Lula era.

Sources: Wheatley, J. (2009) 'Deforestation is the key for Latin Giant', *Financial Times*, 21 September; Crooks, E. (2009) 'Amazon dam comes under close scrutiny', *Financial Times*, 5 November; Wheatley, J. (2010) 'Anxious not to be tarred with a blackout brush', *Financial Times*, 6 May; *The Economist* (2010) 'Another Silva', 24 April; *The Economist* (2010) 'Power and the Xingu', 24 April; BBC news (2010) 'Brazil elects Dilma Rousseff as first female president', 1 November, at www.bbc.co.uk/news

Questions for discussion

◆ How have environmental and development goals clashed in Brazil?

◆ What policies are needed for slowing deforestation in Brazil?

◆ To what extent is Brazil in a good position to take a lead in international climate change policies?

▶ More online ... The home page of the Clean Development Mechanism is www.cdm.unfccc.int

Global co-operation to combat climate change

As in other spheres, such as trade, international co-operation relies on individual nations having the will and means to achieve goals which they share. The UN, like the WTO, can bring delegates to the negotiating table, but cannot force them to make an agreement or, if agreement is reached, to stick to it. The first climate change treaty was the Kyoto Protocol, which was signed in 1998 and came into legal force in 2005 despite non-ratification by the US, which was then the world's largest carbon emitter. The Kyoto Protocol contained a framework for international co-operation to deal with the effects of climate change. The treaty envisaged goals to be achieved by 2008–12, and laid the foundations for further treaty-making.

The Kyoto Protocol saw the world divided into developed and developing nations. Its provisions, including targets for reduction in emissions, were linked to these categories. This approach seemed appropriate at the time. Who in 1998 would have foreseen that China, a developing country, would become the world's largest emitter of greenhouse gases? Unfortunately, with hindsight, the treaty sowed the seeds of a rift among nations which has widened since then along political lines, making it difficult to bridge the gap in subsequent negotiations.

The Kyoto treaty set targets for the reduction in carbon dioxide emissions, focusing on the developed countries. The overall target was that by 2008–12, developed countries would reduce their combined GHG emissions to 5% below 1990 levels. There were no targets for developing countries. It introduced the principle of emissions trading, in the Clean Development Mechanism, allowing polluting industries simply to buy emission 'credits' from other countries, in order to meet their national targets without actually cutting emissions in their domestic economy. The emissions trading principle now looks inadequate to bring about the reductions needed. And the world picture regarding emissions now looks very different from 1998. The US continued to resist targets, as evidenced by its growing emissions (see Figure 11.3). President Obama, who came into office in January 2009, announced the US would set targets, but these would need to be passed by Congress, posing major hurdles. The main growth in emissions since 1998 has been from China and India, not included in the Kyoto targets.

Negotiations to agree a follow-up treaty to the Kyoto Protocol included all the major emitting countries. The process culminated in December 2009, in Copenhagen, with a final round of negotiations which was intended to reach an agreement on a new treaty. These efforts ended in acrimony, with representatives of developing and developed countries each accusing the other group of deliberately undermining attempts to reach consensus. China, whose influence among many developing countries is strong (due to its investment and trade links), was singled out as a key player in preventing the achievement of a binding agreement.

The Copenhagen meeting ended with an 'accord', reflecting a broad agreement on principles, but there was no consensus on the terms of a new treaty. The main points of the accord are summarized in Table 11.1. There were several positive points which came out of the meeting. It was agreed that both developing and developed countries would be included in the efforts to reduce global warming, and the goal of limiting warming to 2 degrees was agreed. Financial commitments from rich countries to help poor ones were announced, focusing especially on low-lying countries at most risk from rising sea levels. However, the accord included neither specific targets nor verification procedures. Because of the lack of consensus, the agreement had no legal force under UN rules. Moreover, it did not set a target date by which

Table 11.1 **Summary of the Copenhagen accord, 2009**

Discussion points	What was agreed in the Copenhagen accord
Long-term goal	To reduce global emissions to level which would see global warming rise less than 2 degrees
Who is covered?	Both developed and developing countries
Emissions reduction targets?	None specified
Verification procedures	Monitoring not agreed, largely because of difficulty of reaching agreement on monitoring in developing countries
Financing	Commitment of developed countries to fund technology transfer to developing countries; the sum would be $100 billion a year, from public and private sources
On deforestation	Recognition of importance of reducing deforestation, with commitment of financial resources from developed countries
Carbon markets	Mentioned, but not elaborated
Timetable for treaty?	None specified

commitments would be transformed into a treaty. This omission of a timetable was particularly disappointing for environmentalists, who had stressed the urgency of setting new emissions targets. A pessimistic interpretation would doubt the ability of countries to reach any concrete agreement in the form of a treaty which would bind all 193 UN members. Further negotiations were planned, but the political divide between countries seemed difficult to bridge, inevitably suggesting an analogy with the Doha trade talks, which went on intermittently for years without success (see Chapter 4).

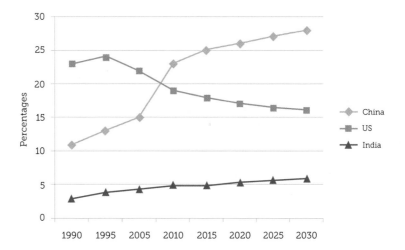

Figure 11.4 **Forecast growth in shares of global CO2 emissions**

Source: *Financial Times*, 25 November 2009

China was widely seen as the major 'winner' from the Copenhagen discussions. The absence of targets or international verification procedures benefits China above all. China is expected to produce nearly 30% of global carbon emissions by 2030 (see Figure 11.4), largely from its heavy dependence on coal-fired power generation, the

▶ More online ... The UN Framework Convention on Climate Change, which includes the Kyoto Protocol, is at http://unfccc.int Materials on climate change can be accessed via the World Wildlife Fund's website. Go to http://www.panda.org and click on 'climate change'.

capacity of which is set to more than double between 2007 and 2030 (Dyer and Harvey, 2009). Its government has announced policies to make changes in energy use and to shift to cleaner energy, but its economy remains carbon-intensive, and its commitments remain matters of national sovereignty, rather than part of an international legal framework.

Summary points Global co-operation to combat climate change

● The Kyoto Protocol of 1998 was a landmark treaty, introducing targets for emissions reductions by developed countries, and providing for an emissions trading scheme.

● As growth in emissions is now concentrated in the developing world, these countries are the focus of future global climate change negotiations. However, there is a political divide between developed and developing countries, which dims the prospect of a future treaty to reduce global emissions.

Climate change initiatives by governments: the implications for international business

Businesses appreciate that the threats posed by climate change demand action at the global level through intergovernmental co-operation. They can foresee that this will inevitably lead to stricter regulation, compelling them to make changes in the ways they operate. Businesses in every sector have watched astutely the developments of climate change negotiations such as Copenhagen, knowing the outcomes will imply strategy shifts to more low-carbon alternatives in their businesses. To plan these strategic changes, businesses need clear targets, certainty of regulatory procedures and a detailed timeframe for changes. Unfortunately, the Copenhagen process in 2009 yielded none of these. In its wake, business leaders lamented the fact that, although private-sector companies are crucial to achieving emissions reductions, there are as yet no details of what these will be or how rapidly they will come into force. Furthermore, companies are expected by governments to contribute huge sums to technology transfer to poor countries (see Table 11.1 above), but these commitments remain vague. A strong agreement to proceed to a treaty would have given businesses a clear indication of the future regulatory environment, but in the absence of agreement, they find it much harder to convince shareholders and other stakeholders that the extra costs involved in cleaner technology are justifiable.

Projects to develop green technology and renewable energy can be costly. Businesses in these sectors often work closely with governments. Government incentives and funding can be crucial in assessing the viability of a large project for a major energy company. In areas where there is a clear international regulatory system, businesses that operate across national borders can be assured that rules are consistent. When regulatory regimes remain national, there is inconsistency among locations, and there are also likely to be policy shifts when governments change. The current position with regard to emissions to curb global warming reflects this uncertainty. In such an environment, investors are disinclined to commit resources, and CEOs are disinclined to take on big projects. Nonetheless, legal obligation is only one reason, albeit a strong one, for undertaking greener strategies. Companies with strong CSR and stakeholder commitments will proceed with their own targets for reducing emissions despite the slowness of governments to bring in legislation. Companies with weak environmental records face issues of stakeholder objections and reputational risk. Moreover, there are many areas of environmental regulation on issues such as pollution which are already subject to international law.

Critical thinking
Climate change discord
Divergent viewpoints of developed and developing countries have dampened prospects of further climate change accords. What are the best solutions that can be realistically achieved, given the priorities of all the countries involved?

Transboundary pollution and energy strategy

transboundary pollution
the transmission of
pollutants through
the water, soil and
air from one national
jurisdiction to another

Transboundary pollution refers to the transmission of pollutants through water, soil and air from one national jurisdiction to another. The transmission may be intentional, as in the transport of hazardous waste, or it may be unintentional, as in an accident at a nuclear power plant.

Industrial enterprises have long been releasing waste into rivers and emissions like sulphur dioxide into the atmosphere. But only in the twentieth century was there a dramatic increase in the capacity for pollution on a large scale, with potential for devastating environmental effects. In addition, industries such as nuclear power generation raised the possibilities of catastrophic accident. The cataclysmic event that is usually cited as causing a shift in the environmental paradigm was the meltdown of the nuclear power station at Chernobyl in the former Soviet Union in 1986 (Landes, 1998). The fire, which burned for five days, released more than 50 tonnes of radioactive poison into the atmosphere, affecting Belarus, the Baltic states, and the Scandinavian countries. The disaster and the inept handling of the aftermath are cited as factors which contributed to the eventual collapse of the Soviet command economy (Landes, 1998).

Less dramatic has been the quiet destruction that acid rain has caused in the environment, becoming visible only when rivers and forests appear to be dying. 'Acid rain' is the term used to describe acid which falls out of the atmosphere. It may be wet, in the form of rain, fog and snow, affecting the soil on which plants and animals depend. Or it may be dry, in the form of acidic gases and particles, which blows onto buildings and trees and into homes. Its main components are sulphur dioxide and nitrogen oxides. It causes trees to gradually wither, buildings to decay and aquatic life to die. Aquatic ecosystems are particularly endangered. The burning of fossil fuels like coal for electricity is particularly blamed for acid rain. International co-operation for lowering acid rain emissions in Europe and North America has helped to reduce levels, but industrialization in the developing world has spread these problems to more countries.

Coal is still the dominant fuel worldwide, accounting for 44% of power generation globally, and expected to account for 77% of new energy capacity in the period to 2030 (International Energy Agency, 2009). While many countries in the developed world are shifting away from coal because of its carbon emissions and other environmental impacts, the developing world, particularly China and India, is burning increasing amounts of coal. China relies on coal-burning power stations for nearly 70% of its power, and India's power is 53% dependent on coal. As Figure 11.5 shows, China is the world's biggest coal producer, producing 38% of the world's annual output in 2008 (US Energy Information Agency, 2009). But its demand for coal, for both power generation and steelmaking, is so great that it became a net importer of coal in 2009. This is good news for the main exporting countries, like Australia, and the world's large mining companies, such as BHP Billiton. Of the countries shown in Figure 11.6, China and India are the two which stand out for the greatest increases in consumption. Demand in India is largely for power generation. The Indian government is building new coal-fired power stations to help supply electricity to the 40% of Indian homes which are still without. These new power stations will be in use for 30 to 40 years. In 1980, China and India consumed just one-fifth of the global output of coal; now they consume about one half, and by 2030, the proportion is expected to rise to two-thirds (Blas, 2010). The steep rise in coal consumption in China and India casts a shadow over international attempts to combat global warming and reduce pollution.

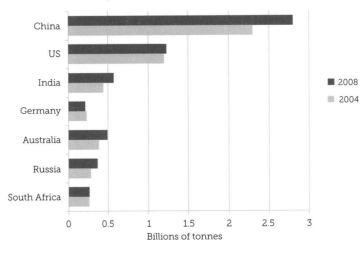

Figure 11.5 **Coal production of major producing countries**

Source: US Energy Information Agency, International energy statistics, 2009, at www.doe.gov

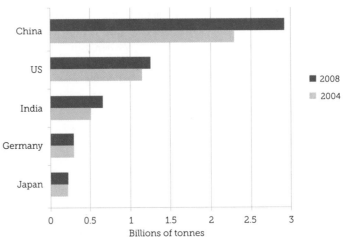

Figure 11.6 **Coal consumption of major consuming countries**

Source: US Energy Information Agency, International energy statistics, 2009, at www.doe.gov

Governments are now focusing on renewable sources of power generation, including wind turbines and solar power, offering opportunities for companies in these sectors. The case for nuclear power generation rests on its low level of emissions, combined with concerns over the depletion of non-renewable energy sources especially coal and oil. Some countries have invested heavily in nuclear capacity, as Figure 11.7 shows. Indeed, France's energy giant, EDF (Electricité de France), is in a

► More online ... The OECD's Nuclear Energy Agency is at www.nea.fr
EDF is at www.edfenergy.com

strong global position in building nuclear power stations. However, the expansion of nuclear power has brought risks. In 2004, an accident at a nuclear power station in Japan, in which four workers died, shook the confidence of the Japanese people in their nuclear industry. Risks have emerged with the growth in the nuclear reprocessing and recycling industries, combined with the need for safe treatment and storage of nuclear waste. Further, the safe transport of nuclear waste across land and sea, to reach reprocessing sites, has created new concerns, not just because of the risk of accidents, but also from the fear of terrorist attack. The risks associated with nuclear-related industries have become dispersed geographically as these industries have grown (see opening case study of Chapter 5). Although China is building nuclear power stations, its nuclear capacity in 2008 was only 1% of its overall power generation, and is expected to rise to 8.9% by 2030.

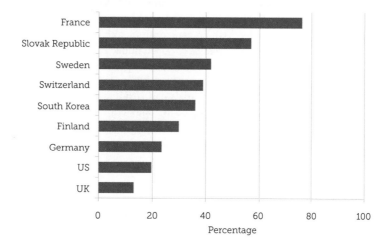

Figure 11.7 **Share of nuclear power in electricity generation, 2008**

Source: Nuclear Energy Agency (2009), Nuclear energy data, 2009, at www.nea.fr

Damage caused by transboundary pollution, whether intentional or unintentional, may be long-lasting, and, in some cases, the full extent of the damage is not apparent for many years. How to apportion responsibility and compel polluters to compensate (insofar as possible) for the harm they cause is complicated by the fact that different legal jurisdictions are involved. Often, the victims are in developing countries, with little in the way of resources to seek legal redress, especially if they must resort to litigation in another country, as was seen in the example of the Bhopal explosion, discussed in Chapter 8. The Indian government, in seeking to develop nuclear capacity, is drafting new stricter legislation for companies involved, taking into account the lessons learned from the Bhopal disaster. Co-operation between governments has led to numerous international regulatory regimes designed to monitor pollution and reduce the risk of accidents.

Summary points Transboundary pollution and energy strategy

◆ Transboundary pollution is mainly caused by industrial processes, including power generation.

◆ Demand for energy, especially in the emerging economies, is leading to increases in power generation capacity, largely in highly pollutant, coal-burning power stations.

◆ Due to its low emissions, nuclear energy is finding renewed favour with many governments, despite its safety risks and high costs.

▶ More online ... The Rio Declaration in full is at www.unep.org/Documents
ExxonMobil is at www.exxonmobil.com

> **Critical thinking**
>
> Is nuclear the answer?
>
> Nuclear power is becoming more popular as an alternative energy source for power generation, but environmentalists have long warned of the serious risks, especially as it is taken up by countries with weak regulatory systems. Do the benefits of nuclear outweigh the risks?

International legal frameworks for protecting the environment

The harmful effects of transboundary pollution on ecosystems and human well-being caused by industrial processes may emerge only gradually. By contrast, environmental disasters, such as the Exxon Valdez oil spill off the Alaskan coast in 1989 and the Chernobyl nuclear plant disaster in 1986, have an immediate impact, as well as lasting effects which can continue to harm the environment for many years. Such disasters have dramatically raised public consciousness of the need for co-operation between states. The United Nations Environment Programme (UNEP) dates from 1972. The UN Conference on Environment and Development (UNCED) produced a report in 1987, usually referred to as the Brundtland Report. It introduced the concept of **sustainable development**, which is 'development which meets the needs of present generations without compromising the ability of future generations to meet their own needs' (United Nations, 1987). This concept was at the heart of the Declaration on Environment and Development produced by the Rio Summit of 1992, sometimes referred to as the 'Earth Summit'.

sustainable development economic development which meets the needs of present generations without compromising the ability of future generations to meet their own needs

Table 11.2 **The Rio Declaration on Environment and Development, 1992** (selected key principles)

Principle 2	States have, in accordance with the UN Charter and the principles of international law, the sovereign right to exploit their own resources pursuant to their own environmental and development policies, and the responsibility to ensure that activities within their jurisdiction or control do not cause damage to the environment of other States or of areas beyond the limits of national jurisdiction.
Principle 3	The right to development must be fulfilled so as to equitably meet developmental and environmental needs of present and future generations.
Principle 5	All States and all people shall cooperate in the essential task of eradicating poverty as an indispensable requirement of sustainable development.
Principle 8	To achieve sustainable development and a higher quality of life for all people, States should reduce and eliminate unsustainable patterns of production and consumption and promote appropriate demographic policies.
Principle 13	States shall develop national law regarding liability and compensation for the victims of pollution and other environmental damage.
Principle 16	... the polluter should, in principle, bear the cost of pollution ...
Principle 25	Peace, development and environmental protection are interdependent and indivisible.

Source: UN Environment Programme, The Rio Declaration (1992), at www.unep.org

The main principles of the Rio Declaration appear in Table 11.2. The principles apply to a variety of activities and incidents, whether involving state agencies or

► More online ... The UN's biodiversity website is www.unep.org/themes/biodiversity

commercial enterprises. Note that, although the principle of state sovereignty over resources is acknowledged, it is qualified by the principle of sustainable development. The 'polluter-pays' principle is acknowledged, but when it comes to dispute resolution, the polluting state will seldom consent to international adjudication or arbitration. Principle 5 links sustainable development with poverty reduction. Critics have argued that this principle seems to indicate an underlying assumption of the Declaration that reducing poverty requires economic development, although the historical evidence suggests a more complex relationship than simple cause and effect (Castro, 2004). What is meant by 'poverty' is discussed in the next chapter, but it is relevant to note here that the definition includes dimensions other than purely economic ones, especially in the context of sustainable development. Moreover, as the benefits of market-based economic development are not spread evenly in societies, policies in relation to resource allocation and social priorities are factors in reducing poverty (Castro, 2004).

The Rio Summit of 1992 adopted the Convention on Biological Diversity and the Convention on Climate Change. The Biodiversity Convention aimed to protect and sustain biodiversity by a number of measures, including national monitoring of biodiversity, environmental impact assessments and national progress reports from individual countries. It reinforced the principle of sustainable development. In 1992, the UN also adopted a Convention on the Transboundary Effects of Industrial Accidents, placing an onus on states to take preventive steps and also to respond responsibly when accidents occur. A Convention on Nuclear Safety followed in 1994. While these international instruments focus on state responsibility for implementation of their provisions within their own jurisdictions, it should be noted that states vary in their commitment to prevent and control harmful activities. Developing countries, above all, may lack the resources to regulate environmental protection. Awareness of environmental implications by business enterprises is therefore a crucial factor in the environmental protection landscape. In particular, the responsibility of the large MNEs as important global players is increasingly recognized in environmental issues.

Summary points International legal frameworks

● The Rio Declaration of 1992 established the principle of sustainable development in environmental protection.

● UN conventions on biodiversity, transboundary pollution from industrial accidents, and nuclear safety date from the 1990s.

● UN member states bear responsibility for implementing international treaty obligations, but MNEs also bear environmental responsibilities, notably under the polluter-pays principle.

Challenges of environmental protection for businesses

Land, water and air are the components of the physical environment which have been affected by industrial processes associated with economic development. Managers have become accustomed to dealing with local pollution problems arising from their operations, entailing interaction with local community authorities. However, wider issues like climate change and biodiversity, while nonetheless real, seem remote, complex, and not susceptible to the usual means of resolution. What is more, scientific evidence is not always clear-cut, and regulatory regimes are still in the formative

► More online ... The UK Department for Environment, Food and Rural Affairs is at www.defra.gov.uk

stages, partly over difficulties of measurement and enforcement. It is largely down to lobbying – and more recently, the active involvement of 'green groups' – that environmental issues and climate change are now seen as urgent issues on the global agenda, engaging governments, corporations and consumers alike.

Sustainable development in the business context

Businesses are becoming more conscious of the need for new, cleaner technologies, partly because of growing social and ethical considerations, and also because of international instruments signed by governments. But how does a broad principle like sustainable development translate into a business strategy? The following statement provides some indication:

> For the business enterprise, sustainable development means adopting business strategies and activities that meet the needs of the enterprise and its stakeholders today while protecting, sustaining and enhancing the human and natural resources that will be needed in the future. (International Institute for Sustainable Development, 1992)

In terms of strategy, this statement is still rather general, but it does highlight the duty to stakeholders, and also the duty over both human and environmental resources. Companies now take a broader view of their 'environmental footprint', looking at all phases of their operations, from production processes to the nature of the products they sell, to assess whether they can be made more environmentally friendly. Consumers have been a source of pressure, creating new areas of demand in, for example, products which are recyclable. Environmental protection and economic efficiency, once seen as posing a dilemma of choice, are merging together, in that protecting the environment is now regarded as a primary object of the business, rather than as a constraint on business, as was felt in the past. Environmental issues are closely linked with social responsibility, and many businesses now publish sustainability reports on a regular basis.

Summary points Business strategy and sustainability

◆ Businesses now take a broad view of their environmental footprint, often as an aspect of social responsibility.

◆ Environmental protection, once seen as a drag on business, is now seen more positively as a benefit in stakeholder relations and long-term growth.

Environmental management

environmental management assessing environmental impacts and devising suitable strategies across a company's total operations

Environmental management, assessing environmental impact and devising suitable strategies, is now seen as central to companies' operations, especially in the industries which are by nature more pollutant. These include chemicals, mining, pulp and paper, iron and steel, and refineries. For the large MNEs using subcontracting and licensing arrangements, there is a question of how much control can be exerted on subcontractors in terms of environmental management. This question is often posed for MNEs operating in developing countries with weaker environmental protection laws.

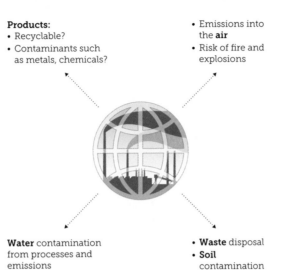

Products:
• Recyclable?
• Contaminants such
  as metals, chemicals?

• Emissions into
  the **air**
• Risk of fire and
  explosions

Figure 11.8 **Aspects
of environmental
management**

Water contamination
from processes and
emissions

• **Waste** disposal
• **Soil**
  contamination

Research and increased awareness of the damaging effects of climate change have impressed on businesses the need to look at the green implications of their operations, and especially their levels of emissions. One consideration is that reductions are likely to be required under future treaties, and it is preferable to get a head start. Another is that companies are in a position to take the lead in positive action to alleviate potentially harmful global warming, especially in industries that have high levels of emissions. Figure 11.8 shows the areas of environmental management in both processes and products. Industrial processes impact on the air, water and land, in the immediate location and often further afield. Emissions of gases, particle matter and chemicals can cause damaging air pollution. There are also risks of fires and explosions, which are high in some industries, especially in the energy sector.

In April 2010, there was an explosion in a BP-leased oil rig in the Gulf of Mexico, causing loss of life, atmospheric pollution, and damage to the sea (including fish and birds) from the resultant oil spill. BP was fined $87 million in 2009 for an explosion at one of its refineries, which cost 15 lives. The company's safety systems again came into question following the 2010 incident (see case study in Chapter 13). Contamination of water from industrial processes can affect all types of waterways, both surface and underground. Where water is becoming scarce, industrial use can be controversial, as whole communities can experience water shortages. Adapting processes to use less water, as well as reducing wastewater, has become a priority in industries which are heavy users of water.

Soil contamination and degradation are more localized than emissions into the atmosphere, but can have long-lasting impacts on the land, affecting its use for human habitation and agriculture. Waste disposal can be costly for firms, and in developing countries where environmental controls are weak, firms are more likely to be lax about how waste is disposed of than in more regulated environments. Ecuador is an example, where serious environmental degradation was caused by Texaco's operations in the 1970s and 80s. Because environmental restoration requirements agreed by the company with the Ecuadorian government were minimal, there was little inhabitants could do to make the company clean up and restore sites when they left the country in 1992 (Olsen, 2001). The Ecuadorians initiated legal proceedings against Chevron Texaco in the US courts in 1993, and an independent expert

▸ More online ... DuPont's website is www.dupont.com
The ISO is at www.iso.org

recommended the payment of $7–16 billion in compensation for the pollution damage. But the case was still in the trial stages in 2010, as Chevron continued to mount a robust defence of its legal position.

Surface disturbance, as well as waste disposal, is a factor in mining. Much of the world's coal reserves lie not in deep mines but near the surface, in opencast mines. Extracting this coal despoils the land, and the operations can be dispersed, affecting the ecology over large areas.

Cutting pollution, while it can be seen as a cost, is also a business opportunity. Much research is being carried out into changing the nature of consumer products, to make them less pollutant. As Figure 11.8 highlights, recycling is one aspect of greener products. Products that have been designed to be environmentally friendly use fewer metals and chemicals, and are easier to recycle. Large carmakers have committed considerable research effort into electric cars, with the help of government funding in many cases. Low-emission technologies have opened opportunities in the energy industry and also in a range of manufacturing industries. By 2004, DuPont, the large US chemicals company, had cut greenhouse emissions 69% below 1990 levels, and by 2007, they had been reduced by a further 9.5% (DuPont, 2008). DuPont has set itself targets on a number of environmental goals, including reducing its use of water, using more environmentally friendly vehicles, and introducing new products based on green technology. In its Sustainability Report of 2008, it reported water use down 10% and the introduction of 126 new products designed to promote a safer global environment (DuPont, 2008).

The extent to which businesses voluntarily set targets for emissions reductions affects global progress in combating climate change. Environmental reporting, detailing the ways in which a company's operations impact on the environment, has become an element in **triple-bottom-line reporting**. In addition to financial reporting, some companies report on social and environmental aspects of their operations, making up the three elements of triple-bottom-line reporting. While the latter two impact reports are voluntary, they are increasingly viewed by shareholders and other stakeholders as indicative of good governance. The International Organization for Standardization, which produces ISO standards, has developed a certification for standards of environmental management (ISO 14000). MNEs are finding that, in the new context of social responsibility, it is advantageous to integrate systems globally, wherever the location. DuPont reported in 2008 that 36% of its global sites had ISO 14000 certification.

triple-bottom-line reporting corporate reporting focusing on social and environmental aspects of the company, in addition to traditional financial information

Summary points Environmental management

◆ Environmental management involves looking at all aspects of a company's operations, assessing impacts of its processes and products on air quality, water and land.

◆ Changing processes and introducing new, greener products entail costs in terms of R&D, but are increasingly seen as justified in helping to achieve sustainable business models for the future.

Critical thinking
Environmental management and CSR
In what respects does environmental management simply make good business sense, and in what respects is it closer to a CSR perspective? Give examples from the different areas highlighted in Figure 11.8.

Khalid Al-Falih CEO of Saudi Aramco, the oil producer

When Khalid Al-Falih joined Saudi Aramco, which was to become his lifetime career, as a young man in 1979, he was sponsored to study for a BSc in Mechanical Engineering at Texas A&M University, which he completed in 1982. Both the priority on education and the links with America have been themes running through the history of Saudi Aramco. The company's origins date from an agreement in 1933 between the Saudi government and the Standard Oil Company of California, to explore for oil. Other agreements followed, notably with Standard Oil of New Jersey (now Exxon), before the Saudi government acquired 100% of the company in 1980. The co-operative manner in which assets and operations were gradually taken over by the national oil company is now seen as exemplary. Now the world's largest oil producer and exporter, Saudi Aramco has taken a lead in the responsible stewardship of its oil assets, both in terms of the country's development and in terms of global markets. Having taken over as CEO in 2009, Mr Al-Falih has been attentive to both perspectives.

The volatility of oil as a commodity immediately impacted on him when he took over as CEO. Oil had reached $150 a barrel and then suddenly fell to less than $35 when global financial and economic crisis struck. As he points out, oil exports account for 80–90% of Saudi Arabia's total revenues, and this 'dependence is not desirable' (Al-Falih, 2010). He sees both improved energy efficiency and diversification as strategic goals which the company and the country share. He argues that the country must move to become a more knowledge-based economy, with greater investment in education and research, not least because of the need to create jobs for young people. Four out of every 10 Saudis are 14 or younger, and 6 out of every 10 are under 25. He estimates that the country needs to create four million jobs over the next 10 years. This is a tall order, needing sustainable growth which stems from innovation and technology, rather than dependence on oil.

He points out that, although the world is gradually moving away from oil towards a more diverse energy mix, demand for oil is still expected to rise, from the current 86 million barrels per day (b/d) to 105–110 b/d by 2030. This is due mainly to demand from developing countries. Saudi Aramco recently expanded its capacity, so that production can be scaled up if global conditions require it. Mr Al-Falih warns of the complexities involved in developing unconventional sources of oil and sources in harsh environments, in contrast to Saudi Arabia's vast conventional reserves. He remains concerned not just about price and swings in demand, but also about the long-term impacts on societies. Saudi Aramco's corporate citizenship policy has extended into education and also into environmental stewardship. The company has taken initiatives in reducing lead in gasoline and producing low-sulphur diesel, as well as reducing emissions from plants. He points out proudly that the company issued its first green policy statement in 1963, long before green issues were perceived as aspects of corporate responsibility. He says he remains an optimist, but is not complacent about the tasks facing the nation, in which Saudi Aramco's role is pivotal.

Sources: England, A. (2009) 'Oil heavyweight ponders fast-changing landscape', *Financial Times*, 12 November; Hoyos, C. (2009) 'Expansion into lead position', *Financial Times*, 23 September; Al-Falih, K. (2010) 'Saudi Aramco and its role in Saudi Arabia's present and future', speech to the MIT Club of Saudi Arabia, Riyadh, 19 April, at www.saudiaramco.com

Khalid Al-Falih

Source: Saudi Aramco

EU initiatives on the environment

Governments in European countries and the EU itself have taken a lead in environmental protection measures, including 'economic instruments' such as fuel taxes, and market approaches such as emissions trading. The EU's greenhouse-gas emissions trading scheme began in 2005. Under the scheme, permits are given to individual plants, linked to emissions allocations. If the plant exceeds its target, it will have to buy permits from businesses which have not used all their allocations. Companies which are able to reduce their emissions by greater energy efficiency and cleaner technology stand to gain, as they are able to sell surplus permits to companies which have exceeded allocations. The latter companies, which include those who find it too expensive to convert to cleaner technology, face the added cost of permits. They may thus be encouraged to invest in cleaner technology.

The UK and Germany are roughly on target to meet Kyoto targets. UK emissions of the basket of greenhouse gases are expected to be about 22% below 1990 levels in 2010 (UK Department of Energy and Climate Change, 2010). This better-than-forecast reduction was due in part to the impact of economic recession in Britain. Taking into account economic recovery, the government expected to reach a target of 34% reduction from 1990 levels by 2020 (see Figure 11.9).

Figure 11.9 **UK greenhouse gas (GHG) emissions, including allowances from the EU emissions trading scheme** (measured by MtCO2e, or million tonnes of carbon equivalent)

Note: data beyond 2008 are forecasts. Allowances under the EU emissions trading scheme are taken into account from 2005 onwards.

Source: UK Department of Energy and Climate Change (2010), Energy and emissions projections at www.decc.gov.uk

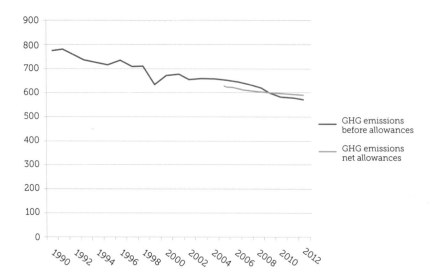

The EU has also embarked on a series of far-reaching measures in environmental legislation. Concern about the effects of excessive packaging on the environment dates back to the 1980s. In 1994, a directive on packaging and packaging waste recycling was enacted. It is reviewed at regular intervals, setting new targets for member states. The 2008 targets were 55% of packaging to be recycled and 60% waste to be recovered. These targets were met by most of the EU15 countries, but newer member states were given extended deadlines.

Critics argue that packaging is only a small part of the overall problem of increasing environmental awareness. Research in 2004 indicated that changing a four-wheel-drive SUV for a more fuel-efficient car would, in one year, save the same amount of energy as would recycling a family's bottles for 400 years (Houlder, 2004).

▶ More online ... The European Environment Agency is at www.eea.europa.eu
Consumer Focus, formerly the National Consumer Council, is at www.consumerfocus.org.uk

A new landfill directive aims to reduce the risk of polluting water and soil from land-fill sites. Hazardous and non-hazardous waste can no longer be disposed of jointly in landfill sites, and the categories of hazardous waste have expanded. Tyres, for example, cannot be disposed of in landfill sites. With fewer sites able to deal with hazardous waste, the costs of disposal are likely to rise. A growing problem is how to dispose of the mountain of old televisions, computers and other household electrical equipment; these are sources of heavy metals and organic pollutants. From 2005, the EU has required manufacturers and importers to take back and recycle these appliances, from mobile phones to washing machines. These requirements, which place the responsibility on the manufacturers, add to costs, but should create incentives to design products that are easier to recycle.

The polluter-pays principle was established in the EU's treaties, and a legal framework for implementing it was provided in a directive on environmental liability agreed in 2003. Under the directive, a company is liable for a variety of harms that might arise from its operations, including water or soil pollution, damage to biodiversity, and harm to human health. The company is responsible for repairing the damage insofar as possible. Of course, damage may be irreversible, and effects may take some time to emerge. The aim, as with the use of other mandatory legislation, is to encourage companies to take the environment into account at the planning stage, and to develop cleaner, less invasive, ways of operating. National authorities are required to report to the EU Commission on implementation of the directive within their states by 2013.

Summary points EU environmental initiatives

● The EU has been at the forefront of environmental legislation, in, for example, its emissions trading scheme and recycling directive.

● The polluter-pays principle has been enacted in the environmental liability directive, making companies responsible for harms which occur from their operations.

Sustainable consumption

When we think of consumers and green issues, we tend to think mainly of recycling waste and buying organic produce. However, green consumerism covers a wide range of lifestyle decisions. Besides shopping for environmentally friendly products and recycling, it covers using less pollutant transport, exploring eco-tourism for our holidays, and investing our money in socially responsible funds. In addressing the role of consumers in environmental issues, the UNEP focuses on a broad notion of **sustainable consumption**, which covers the many lifestyle decisions made by consumers which impact on the environment over the long term, whether directly or indirectly. In its research, Consumer Focus, a consumer body sponsored by the UK Department for Business, Innovation and Skills, has found that companies are increasingly making environmental claims for their products, and that consumers' expectations of products' and companies' environmental credentials are also on the rise. However, two-thirds of consumers found it difficult to know which products were better for the environment, and 58% thought that companies make green claims for their products simply in order to charge higher prices (Consumer Focus, 2009).

Sceptics about green consumerism argue that, even if consumers in rich countries change their buying habits to more environmentally friendly products, the effects will

sustainable consumption
principle that consumer lifestyle and purchasing decisions should take account of the environmental needs of future generations

be limited unless people are persuaded to consume less. They point out that improvements in products to make them less detrimental to the environment are often offset by growing demand. In transport, for example, although new cars are fuel-efficient, the growing number of vehicles on the roads cancels out the benefits of greater fuel efficiency. Carmakers are lured to the Bric countries. In these fast-growing economies, consumers are keen to acquire cars – and the new mobility they bring. With far fewer cars per inhabitant than the advanced economies, there is much scope for growth in these markets. Indeed, the Bric countries are viewed by car manufacturers as their main source of future profits, but what about the environmental consequences? As Figure 11.10 shows, China and India are the strongest growing car markets. By 2020, China is expected to have more than double the number of cars on US roads, but even if this phenomenal growth takes place, car penetration would still be less than half that in the US. There is one car for approximately every 1.2 people in the US; in China, by 2020, there would be one car for every 5–6 people (Wheatley, 2010).

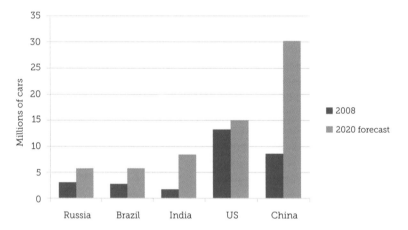

Figure 11.10 **Sales of new cars in key markets**

Source: *Financial Times*, 21 January 2010

For businesses, especially manufacturing firms, the notion of defining sustainable consumption as reduced consumption meets with little appeal. Similarly, for governments, reduced consumption is not likely to find favour. Reduced consumer spending tends to pose headaches, as highlighted in Chapter 3: reduced output is linked to decreases in employment, falling tax revenues and weak economic growth. Governments, however, are in a position to promote changes in consumer behaviour and changes in manufacturers' approaches which fall within the principle of sustainable consumption.

Summary points Sustainable consumption

◆ Consumers are open to green alternatives that do not radically alter their lifestyles, and are increasingly concerned over the environmental credentials of the products and services they buy and the companies behind them.

◆ Sustainable consumption arguably goes to the heart of modern consumer lifestyles, questioning the basic assumptions that consumers take for granted, such as the right to purchase a car or foreign holiday.

◆ Government legislation, rather than voluntary initiatives, is probably needed to make radical changes in consumer behaviour.

Critical thinking

The environmental bandwagon?

To what extent is there a risk that, in the welter of environmental claims for products and services, consumers become bewildered and ignore all the claims? What can a company do when consumers appear to resist paying extra for green products, suspicious of the claims made in advertising?

Environmental protection and changing values

Economic development based on industrialization and exploitation of resources is now an environmental issue for all countries, whatever their stage of economic development. Urbanization in developing countries, where infrastructure is struggling to catch up, is causing problems for provision of clean air, access to clean water and sanitation. Sprawling cities are also prone to suffer from food and energy shortages. Whereas these issues were once seen as matters of local concern, we now see them as global, involving sustainable development. Similarly, in areas of the world where population pressures and depletion of natural resources are causing hardship to both humans and other sentient beings such as wildlife, the issues are of global concern. Progress in tackling global environmental issues includes numerous regimes for international monitoring and co-operation among states to reach international agreements. Much of this progress can be attributed to NGOs, whose activities have raised the public's awareness of environmental issues.

Development has tended to be equated with western consumer lifestyles, dependent on cars, cheap air travel and throwaway appliances, all of which are becoming problematical in today's ecologically stressed environment. Should western consumerism be held up as a model for developing countries, including the vast swathes of China as yet untouched by modernity? As has been seen in this chapter, development, both past and present, tends to mean economic *growth*, with little heed for environmental consequences. What is added by the notion of sustainability may, at its most minimal interpretation, simply mean sustained economic growth, rather than sustaining the environment (Castro, 2004). However, a question mark hangs over sustained economic growth, as non-renewable energy resources become depleted. Given the observable effects of environmental degradation in today's world, failure to heed the ecological messages will jeopardize prospects of economic growth in the long term.

Summary points Environmental protection and changing values

◆ A conflict has emerged between global goals of sustainable development and the aims of many emerging economies to bring the benefits of western lifestyles to their populations.

◆ There is a risk that sustainable economic development has become equated with sustained economic growth, casting doubt on the needs to combat climate change and environmental degradation.

Conclusions

1 Environmental issues, including climate change, depletion of natural resources and pollution, are now seen as global issues, to be addressed by governments, businesses and consumers alike.

2 Human activity, particularly processes of industrialization and urbanization, result in environmental degradation such as pollution from emissions.

3 While promoting economic development in host societies, MNEs are enmeshed in the environmental consequences of their operations on societies.

4 Climate change, a process of global warming, is caused by a build-up of heat-trapping gases. Carbon dioxide emissions associated with industrialization are highlighted as a major factor.

5 International efforts to reduce global greenhouse gases took a step forward with the Kyoto Protocol, which aimed to reduce levels of these emissions to 1990 levels by 2008–12. However, even if these reductions are achieved, much further reduction is needed to have an impact on global warming.

6 The Copenhagen meeting to discuss a follow-up to the Kyoto Protocol in 2009 ended with an accord, but no legally binding agreement on targets to reduce emissions.

7 Transboundary pollution, such as acid rain, can have widely ramified impacts, needing co-operation between countries to reduce the levels.

8 While there is a strong case for nuclear power resting on its low level of emissions and concerns over the depletion of non-renewable energy sources, there remain concerns over its safety, including the nuclear reprocessing and recycling industries.

9 International legal frameworks now cover a variety of environmental issues. Most notably, the principles enunciated by the Rio Declaration in 1992 formed the basis of sustainable development policies.

10 Businesses face specific environmental challenges depending on their particular industry. In response, they now look at their 'environmental footprint' in a strategic light.

11 Environmental management addresses the specific environmental aspects of a firm's operations, including those of subcontractors. In some industries, such as extraction and mining, companies operating in host countries face challenges to operate according to international standards, rather than local standards, which are likely to be lower and weakly enforced.

12 The EU has taken a lead in environmental protection, particularly with new legislation on recycling and emissions trading.

13 Green consumerism, often considered to focus on buying environmentally friendly products, can be seen in the wider context of 'sustainable consumption', which impacts on a range of lifestyle decisions, including transport and recreation.

14 The challenges of sustainable development are particularly acute for the developing world, where development has been equated with the stereotypical western consumer lifestyle.

Review questions

1 In what ways do industrialization and urbanization impact on the environment?

2 What does environmental degradation refer to, and what are its effects?

3 What are the causes of climate change, and what are the effects of global warming?

4 What were the aims of the Kyoto Protocol, and why was the treaty significant in terms of progress towards international co-operation?

5 Why has transboundary pollution become a global concern? Give some examples of transboundary pollution, and examine ways of dealing with it through collaboration between countries.
6 Define 'sustainable development'. How does it differ from plain economic development?
7 What are the implications of sustainable development for business strategists?
8 What is meant by environmental management?
9 What initiatives are being taken by the EU in environmental protection?
10 How does a system of emissions trading work? What are the advantages and disadvantages of this type of system over a mandatory regulatory system in achieving targets for reducing emissions?
11 What is meant by 'sustainable consumption'? Are consumer attitudes in rich countries changing as a result of green campaigns and greater availability of information on environmental issues?
12 What are the challenges posed by a sustainable development agenda in the developing world?

Key revision concepts

Climate change, p. 367; Emissions trading scheme, p. 384; Environmental degradation, p. 365; Environmental management, p. 380; Global warming, p. 367; Greenhouse gases, p. 367; Sustainable consumption, p. 385; Sustainable development, p. 378; Transboundary pollution, p. 375; Triple-bottom-line reporting, p. 382

Assignments

◆ Assess the ways in which international co-operation to combat climate change is progressing.
◆ To what extent is sustainable development a realistic proposition for developing countries?

Further reading

Barrow, C.J. (1999) *Environmental Management: Principles and Practice* (Oxford: Routledge).
Bell, S. and McGillivray, D. (2008) *Environmental Law*, 7th edn (Oxford: OUP).
Blewitt, J. (2008) *Understanding Sustainable Development* (London: Earthscan Publications).
Daly, H.E. (1996) *Beyond Growth: The Economics of Sustainable Development* (Boston: Beacon).
Dresner, S. (2008) *The Principles of Sustainability*, 2nd edn (London: Earthscan).
Epstein, M. (2008) Making *Sustainability Work: Best Practices in Managing and Measuring Corporate, Social and Environmental Impacts* (Sheffield: Greenleaf Publishing).
Goldblatt, D. (1996) *Social Theory and the Environment* (Cambridge: Polity Press).
Hecht, A.D. (1999) 'The triad of sustainable development: Promoting sustainable development in developing countries', *Journal of Environment and Development*, 8: 111–32.
Landes, D. (1998) *The Wealth and Poverty of Nations* (London: Little, Brown and Company).

Oil companies scramble for stakes in Iraq's oilfields

War-torn Iraq urgently needs to revive its most important source of revenues, its oilfields, to help rebuild the country. The task is daunting. Iraq's oil ministry, embroiled in the political divides between different regions and groups, has been slow to set up a framework for the legal regulation of oil extraction. In the absence of a clear policy from the centre, foreign companies have moved into the semi-autonomous Kurdish region in the north, and are operating in the hope that a framework will follow. For the large oilfields in the rest of the country, the government's policy is to invite companies to bid for the rights to exploit the oilfields, in a series of auctions. For large oil companies, the situation presents unprecedented opportunities for accessing the precious resource, despite Iraq's unstable political situation.

Although accurate data are lacking, Iraq's massive oil reserves could be the third largest globally, following Saudi Arabia and Iran. The bulk of the world's oil reserves are controlled by the state-owned entities in the countries where they occur. Saudi Arabia, the world's leading oil exporter is one. And Iraq's oil industry was nationalized 40 years ago. But following the American-led invasion of Iraq and the overthrow of Saddam Hussein in 2003, the oil industry was left in limbo. Decades of underinvestment and neglect have left the country's oil production reliant on infrastructure dating from the 1960s in some areas. Production in 2010 was just 2.5 million barrels a day (b/d), whereas, with the right investment, production could be triple that figure. Making matters worse, Iraqi geologists and skilled engineers have sought work elsewhere, leaving the country short of the relevant skills. Recognizing the need to bring in the skills of foreign companies, the elected government of 2006 pledged to 'auction' the rights to exploit the oilfields.

The first of the government's oil auctions, in June 2009, for rights over the vast Rumaila field, disappointed most foreign companies. Iraq's oil ministry said it would pay only $2 a barrel to the oil

Map of Iraq

▸ More online ... Shell is at www.shell.com
Lukoil is at www.lukoil.com
Petronas is at www.petronas.com.my

companies once they had developed a field to its full potential production. The only bidders enticed by this offer were BP in a partnership with CNPC, the Chinese state oil company. It was a field BP had itself discovered back in 1952, and was confident of a reasonable return on the investment. Following consultations between the oil ministry and major energy companies, more deals followed. Eni of Italy, along with South Korea's Kogas and Occidental of the US obtained rights to develop the Zubair field. Eni, too, was confident it had achieved a good deal, with concessions on taxes that would improve the profitability of the project. The outcome was expected to be an increase in production at Zubair from 200,000 b/d to 1.1 million b/d. Lukoil of Russia teamed up with Statoil of Norway to obtain a contract to exploit the West Qurna 2 oilfield in the southern province of Basra. Lukoil had been here before. In 1997, it signed a deal which was later rescinded by Saddam Hussein.

Perhaps the biggest prize was the Majnoon oilfield, which could potentially produce 1.8 million b/d. The right to develop Majnoon went to the Anglo-Dutch energy company, Royal Dutch Shell. As the operator of the project, Shell holds a 45% share, while Petronas, Malaysia's state oil company, owns 30%. The rest is held by Iraq. The Iraq oil ministry was well pleased to have secured commitments from these companies, not least because of the need for modern technology to improve production and explore the fields fully. Iraq's reserves have not been surveyed and explored since the 1970s, and estimates dating from then are likely to be

conservative. However, turning potential output into a reality will require more than just technology.

The eastern fields and East Baghdad, where security risks are high, attracted less interest from foreign companies. Hanging over the prospects in all these locations is the volatile political situation in Iraq. A change of government could lead to new faces in the oil ministry, who might be inclined to argue that too many concessions have been given to foreigners. Elections in March 2010 failed to produce a clear winner, and the prime minister, Nouri al-Maliki, whose support is mainly from the Shia sect, stayed in office despite having won fewer seats than his nearest rival, Iyad Allawi, who has large support from the Sunni minority that formed the ascendant group under Saddam Hussein. Nine months after the elections, an agreement was reached on the formation of a coalition government under the leadership of Mr Maliki. However, key cabinet posts, including national security, remained unfilled due to lack of agreement, casting doubt on the long-term viability of the new government. There is a risk that continuing instability will set back the urgent task of rebuilding the country's oil infrastructure.

Sources: Hoyos, C. (2009) 'Shell winner of historic Iraqi oil auction', *Financial Times*, 13 December; Hoyos, C. (2009) 'Baghdad starts to rebuild its oil industry', *Financial Times*, 5 November; *The Economist* (2009) 'Deterring foreign investors', 26 September; *The Economist* (2010) 'The politicians wrangle as the nerves of the people jangle', 8 May; Kantner, J. (2009) 'Oil field project in Iraq won by Lukoil and Statoil', *New York Times*, 29 December; BBC news (2010) 'Iraqi parliament approves new government', 21 December, at www.bbc.co.uk/news

Questions for discussion

◆ In what ways is development of the oil industry linked with economic development in Iraq?

◆ Why is the situation presented by Iraq almost unique in terms of opportunities for foreign investment?

◆ What are the disadvantages of investing in Iraq's oilfields?

CHAPTER **12**

ETHICS AND SOCIAL RESPONSIBILITY

Outline of chapter

Learning objectives

1 To gain an overview of the foundations of ethical principles and how they are applied
2 To examine the elements of corporate social responsibility in theory and practice
3 To highlight the relationship between CSR and corporate governance
4 To assess social issues in developed and developing economies, with implications for CSR and sustainability

Critical themes in this chapter

- **Multilayered environment – national and international labour standards**
- **CSR and sustainability – ethical principles and CSR as integral to corporate strategy**
- **Changing societies – issues of poverty, hunger and health in developing economies**
- **Globalization – winners and losers in the global workforce**

What do western retailers and consumers know about the working conditions in factories where popular clothing items such as jeans are made?
Source: Istock

Cargill, the 'farm to fork' giant

Although Cargill's name might be unfamiliar, an ordinary person tucking into breakfast just about anywhere in the world is likely to be consuming a product that has been grown, processed or traded by this giant company. It produces pork which goes into the sausages, grows the soya which feeds livestock, processes the grain for bread products, grows and processes the oil which goes into spreads, and produces salt and seasonings for all types of processed foods. Our consumer's cocoa drink is likely to be made from cocoa and sugar traded by Cargill, as it is the world's largest trader of both these commodities. Even our breakfaster's cotton shirt is likely to be made from African cotton processed and traded by the company, although the name never appears on any labels.

Cargill is a private company founded in the US Midwest in 1865, a year more often remembered for the end of the American Civil War. The Cargill family still owns the company, which has grown into the world's largest trader of agricultural commodities. At the basic level, an agricultural trader typically buys produce from farmers, stores it, processes it and sells it to customers, who are likely to be food processors themselves. But buyers can also be governments and international agencies. When these activities become globalized, purchases and sales span the globe.

Cargill has invested heavily in vertical integration, controlling the supply chain in commodities. From its palm oil plantations, Cargill is both the largest exporter of palm oil to the US and the largest importer of palm oil into the US, where it is used in the production of processed food and cosmetics. For soya, another important commodity crop, especially for use in animal feeds, it supplies seeds and chemicals to farmers in Brazil. Crops are handled in its processing plants, and shipped from its own purpose-built port terminals. Cargill's size gives it considerable economic power over suppliers and customers. It has faced criticism for its potentially anti-competitive power over markets, as well as lack of transparency. As a result, it now keeps customers more informed about markets, including trends, such as imports of US corn by China and other

emerging markets. The growing consumption of meat in emerging markets, where people's eating preferences are becoming more westernized, is one of the trends which boost Cargill's business.

Cargill enjoyed nearly $117 billion in revenues in 2008, and employs 138,000 people in 67 countries. However, it has run into controversy in countries such as Indonesia and Brazil, where rainforests and sensitive ecological environments have been destroyed to make way for industrialized farming. Both palm oil and soya production typically involve destroying lowland rainforests. Cargill has been accused of clearing forests in Borneo for its plantations without the environmental impact assessment required by Indonesian law, even though it has subscribed to the Roundtable for Sustainable Palm Oil Principles (Rainforest Action Network, 3 May 2010). Its three plantations in Papua New Guinea also evoked criticism. Here, the company's labour scheme involved converting people who had been independent farmers into sharecroppers on fixed contracts with the company for their crops. The company was also alleged by NGOs to have been complicit in child labour practices. Promises of new roads and schools, which it made to local communities, failed to materialize (Gilbert, 2010). Cargill has sold the plantations in Papua New Guinea, stating that it is shifting its focus to Indonesia, which represents 'more value for our shareholders and customers' (Cargill, 2010).

In Brazil, a surge in deforestation in the Amazon has been attributed to Cargill's building soya refineries as well as port facilities deep into the Amazon rainforests (Vidal, 2006). The Brazilian government closed down Cargill's new port facility at Santarém on the Amazon River, for failure to report adequately on environmental impacts. However, the company has continued expanding its port facilities, enabling it to process growing quantities of soya and sugar. It now has six grain and sugar terminals in Brazil, and aims to quadruple the handling capacity of the Santarém port (Kassai, 2010). Most of the soya produced globally goes into feed for the livestock industry. Half the soya exported from the Amazon goes to Europe, where,

▸ More online ... Cargill is at www.cargill.com

The growing, processing and trading of commodity crops such as soya beans, featured here, are core activities for Cargill

Source: Istock

among other uses, it goes to feed chickens reared by Sun Valley, a Cargill wholly owned subsidiary in Britain, whose chickens are used in McDonald's Chicken McNuggets.

Cargill has a 'corporate responsibility' policy, notably without the inclusion of 'social' between the two words. It asserts that it is a good corporate citizen wherever it operates, and that it complies with national laws and principles of sustainability. Inhabitants of Indonesia, Papua New Guinea and Brazil might suggest otherwise.

Sources: Vidal, J. (2006) 'The 7,000 km journey that links Amazon destruction to fast food', *The Guardian*, 6 April; Rainforest Action Network, Report on Cargill's problems with palm oil, 3 May 2010, at http://action.ran.org; Gilbert, D. (2010) 'Cargill leaves a palm oil mess in Papua New Guinea', Rainforest Action Network, 24 February 2010, at http://action.ran.org; Cargill (2010) 'Cargill sells interest in Papua New Guinea palm oil plantations' Cargill news releases, 24 February, at www.cargill.com; Kassai, L. (2010) 'Cargill sees record soybean crop in Brazil, Argentina', *Businessweek*, 19 February, at www.businessweek.com; Blas, J. and Meyer, G. (2010a) 'Emerging markets retain appetite for western food', *Financial Times*, 19 May; Blas, J. and Meyer, G. (2010b) 'All you can eat', *Financial Times*, 19 May.

Questions for discussion

◆ What issues of corporate social responsibility are featured in this case study?
◆ Assess Cargill's CSR profile on each of the issues listed in the first question.

Introduction

At the start of this book, we posed some basic questions: 'What does the business exist to do?' and 'How should it go about achieving its goals?' We highlighted an obvious economic goal, to make money for the owners, but also suggested that businesses have a broader role in society. It is this broader role which is the focus of this chapter. It will be argued here that the business plays a multidimensional role in society, whether the firm's managers intend it to do so or not. This broader role can be seen through the eyes of stakeholder groups like customers and employees, and it can be viewed in even broader terms, for example in the context of climate change. Although the planet is not a stakeholder in the narrow sense, we tend nowadays to see the business organization as having responsibilities and duties to take positive action to combat climate change. Where do these duties come from, and how should businesses respond to this range of duties, both to stakeholders and wider global concerns? Does this imply that traditional economic goals are somehow less worthy? Many businesspeople would argue that social goals are for governments, and that the firm is best sticking to enterprise goals like selling goods and services.

This chapter unravels these different threads of thinking on the role of business in society. We begin by looking at how ethics influences both individual and group behaviour, and how ethical considerations permeate business activities. We discuss different perspectives of corporate social responsibility (CSR), assessing both the 'business case' and the ethical underpinning for companies in global business operations. We look at the role of the social enterprise as an example of the unequivocal commitment to social goals. For most businesses, CSR considerations are more peripheral. However, a shift in public expectations of businesses is taking place. In recent years, business ethics have come under the spotlight in a variety of situations, including corporate wrongdoings, such as breaches of human rights, and individual wrongdoing, such as bribery. Both what companies aim to achieve and how they go about it are coming more and more into the limelight in the areas of corporate governance, executive rewards and political activities. In a final section, we look at the growing interactions between governments and businesses in both funding and carrying out social aims.

Ethics: principles and practices

ethics system of values by which judgments of right and wrong behaviour are made

morality standards of behaviour considered right and wrong

Ethics focuses on systems of values by which judgments of right and wrong behaviour are made. The standards of behaviour so dictated are often termed standards of **morality**. As we found in Chapter 6, all national cultures have value systems, which dictate what is right and wrong within that culture. As businesses soon find when they become internationalized, values in one society may clash with those in another. Recall the case study on internet controls in Chapter 8, in which Google, by complying with Chinese internet censorship, was accused of acting unethically. This accusation was more pointed as the company has as its motto, 'Don't be evil'. This was a case of local law conflicting with ethical principles. The company could claim that acting morally in any location involves obeying the law, but accusations of unethical behaviour imply that there is some higher set of rules which should apply to individuals, companies and even governments.

Foundations of ethics

Google's dilemma in China focused on rights of the individual, particularly freedom of expression and association. The notion that respect for the individual human being is a source of ethical principles has deep historical roots, but the foundation of the modern debate goes back to differing perspectives which emerged in the Enlightenment of the eighteenth century. The individualist view, that each person has wants and needs which are pursued in a self-interested way, is at the heart of **utilitarianism**, which has been highly influential, especially in the English-speaking parts of the world. Based roughly on the ideas of Jeremy Bentham, utilitarianism focuses on the aggregate of individual goods. What is good overall is that which promotes the 'greatest happiness of the greatest number'. Sometimes referred to as the **consequentialist principle**, the test of the rightness or wrongness of an action depends on the results which flow from it (Quinton, 1989). The utilitarian favours minimal government interference in society, as the individual requires the maximum amount of liberty, defined as the absence of external constraints, to pursue his/her own goals. This view of human nature was taken up by the classical economists, notably Adam Smith, and has continued to underpin economists' assumption that free markets are the best way to maximize the overall prosperity of a society, by facilitating as many individuals as possible to fulfil their desires (Plamenatz, 1958: 173).

We would now criticize this view of the individual in society on a number of grounds. First, it does not seem to take into account that different cultures have different views of the individual human being. Secondly, it takes a narrow view of what human beings desire in life, focusing exclusively on rational acquisitiveness. We look at each of these criticisms in turn.

First, we now realize that different cultures have different value systems. This view, sometimes referred to as **ethical relativism**, holds that principles are not absolute, but depend on circumstances. Ethical relativism is perhaps a misleading term, as within a culture, right and wrong are clearly delineated. A more accurate term would be ethical **contextualism**, implying that ideas of right and wrong are real, but vary according to the particular belief system. That belief system can be a national culture, the culture of a distinctive people, or, as is often the case, a religion.

In many national environments, acting morally is associated with membership of a nation or state. In ancient Greece, being a citizen involved the capability of acting morally: slaves, not being citizens, were viewed as outside the *polis*, or community, and thus incapable of attaining virtue. It is common among religious believers to hold that their religion alone is the path to a righteous life, looking down on non-believers. Similarly, some state ideologies such as communism see themselves as the determinants of a society's values. Adopting a moralistic tone, communist political leaders are prone to extol the superiority of their social perspective over the hedonist, individualist values of western cultures, viewed as decadent. Still, individualist values are permeating countries like China as market forces become established. The clash of cultures is exemplified by the case of Google in China. Google is more at home in the freer environment of Hong Kong, with its legacy of western individualism.

Secondly, utilitarianism reduces human motivation to the appetitive element, underestimating the complexities of people's sense of social values, which influence their perceptions of right and wrong. The beliefs and feelings people hold stem in large part from their interactions in society:

utilitarianism philosophical thinking based on the individualist view of human nature that each person has wants and needs which are pursued in a self-interested way

consequentialist principle utilitarian principle that the test of the rightness or wrongness of an action depends on the results which flow from it

ethical relativism approach to ethics which holds that principles are not absolute, but dependent on circumstances

contextualism in ethical thinking, the principle that ideas of right and wrong stem from specific cultural environments

It is as social creatures that men acquire the standards and preferences out of which they build up for themselves images, however vague, however inarticulate, however changing, of what they are and would like to be, of how they live and would like to live. These are the images that give them a sense of position and of purpose in the world. (Plamenatz, 1958: 176)

We now appreciate the importance of community as a dimension of the individual's values and beliefs. European continental thinkers, notably Rousseau and Hegel, have long recognized the ethical dimension of the community. Contrasting views of liberty illustrate different concepts of the individual in society. Liberty in the negative sense, identified above in connection with the utilitarians, is about people having space to pursue their own personal goals. Liberty in the positive sense is about people being self-directed, being one's own master: 'I wish to be somebody, not nobody' (Berlin, 1958: 16). As Isaiah Berlin points out in the essay *Two Concepts of Liberty*, the two views of liberty would seem to be just two sides of the same coin. But historically, they have developed very differently. The theorists who emphasize self-realization have been accused of underestimating the dignity of the individual. They espouse a sense of community in which individual wills meld into a general will which is always right, even though individuals might not see it. This view of liberty is sometimes accused of opening the way for tyrants, and is at the base of much ideology that is reached for by authoritarian regimes to cloak themselves in legitimacy. Opposition to political tyrants has long rallied to the calls for freedoms of speech and association, famously articulated by one of the most notable of the utilitarians, John Stuart Mill, in his essay, *On Liberty* (1859).

Mill had difficulty in explaining how a sense of moral obligation arises from the greatest happiness principle, admitting that a person's conscience stems from education in the broad sense, and education can instil almost any values (Plamenatz, 1958: 139). Utilitarians have little interest in ethical principles, offering only general notions of feeling moral obligations towards others and also pointing to religious faith as a source of moral standards.

Do there exist ethical principles that aim to be universal, above national cultures and not dependent on religious values? Establishing how they arise and defining them has long been a concern of philosophers. They like to strip away religious, ideological, traditional and other sources of values, asking whether there is simply a 'human' basis for ethics. Immanuel Kant came closest to this approach with his postulate that 'every rational being exists as end in itself, not merely as means for arbitrary use by this will or that' (Kant, 1785). This notion of respect for every human being postulates human dignity as the guiding principle for behaviour. This principle is sometimes referred to as the **categorical imperative**. The ethical point of view is that pure egoistic action, with regard only for oneself is unethical, and that one ought to behave in a way that takes the needs and wants of others into account. This ethical principle is aimed particularly at the personal morality of the individual, but how does it translate to organizations, governments and whole societies?

categorical imperative ethical principle put forward by Kant, that respect for every human being should be the guiding principle for behaviour

Ethical behaviour can be conceived in a variety of ways, including obligations, duties, responsibilities, rights and justice. A person has an overall responsibility to act ethically, which imposes particular obligations, such as the duty not to harm other people. An individual also has human rights, such as the right to life. There are many dimensions to human well-being. Some of the main ones are food and shelter, education, health and the environment. The individual citizen needs food and shelter, but in many poor societies, even these minimal requirements of human existence are precarious. We would probably say that governments owe duties towards the population in respect of all these dimensions of human well-being. However, these needs are underprovided in many countries. International donors are sometimes confronted with the dilemma that governments of recipient countries spend the money on weapons rather than on programmes that would improve human well-being. The leaders of a poor country that receives international donor funds for food, but spends the money on weapons are acting unethically. Are firms which sell the weapons to such leaders also acting unethically? We examine the ethical context of business in the next section.

Summary points Foundations of ethics

● Individualism, with an emphasis on freedom to pursue one's own goals, is at the heart of utilitarian assumptions about human behaviour.

● Individualist assumptions are criticized for lack of social and ethical perspectives.

● Kant's principle of the categorical imperative aims towards universal standards by which individuals and organizations can be judged.

Ethics in business

Ethical principles arise in relation to both *what* the firm aims to do and *how* it goes about its activities. Many firms are successfully engaged in businesses like gambling, manufacturing tobacco products and making alcoholic drinks, all of which can become addictive, and could be considered unethical. These areas, like many types of activity that involve ethical principles, are the subject of laws in most countries. The firm that abides by the regulations regarding gambling, for example, is engaged in an activity for which there is clearly consumer demand, and, as long as it abides by the regulations that pertain to the industry, is acting legally. Most companies, such as alcoholic beverage companies, are highly aware of the ethical dimension of their activities, and present themselves as promoting responsible drinking among consumers. In most countries, there are restrictions on selling alcoholic drinks to children, but inevitably some traders are prepared to do so, aware they are probably not going to be caught.

Much of the focus of ethics in business is on how the firm operates, including its practices in relation to stakeholders. Is it truthful in its advertising messages, and does it particularly target children? Some of the major areas are set out in Figure 12.1. One area is transparency and honesty in communications with stakeholders and the public. Another major area is safety in a variety of contexts: safety in the workplace, safe products, and safety in operations to minimize the risk of accidents. Employment and labour issues are another big area. These cover the right of workers to join a trade union independent of management, and the right not to be discriminated against. Note that the aspects of ethics highlighted in the figure often overlap with law. For example, there are laws on truthfulness in advertising. We might be tempted to say that if the company abides by the law, that should be the extent of its obligation.

However, there are a couple of points that should be remembered regarding the overlap between law and ethics. First, legal regulation is usually confined to national jurisdictions, which vary in their standards and enforcement. In some developing countries, labour standards are lower than those that pertain in the developed world,

▸ More online … Gap's website for social responsibility is www.gapinc.com/socialresponsibility

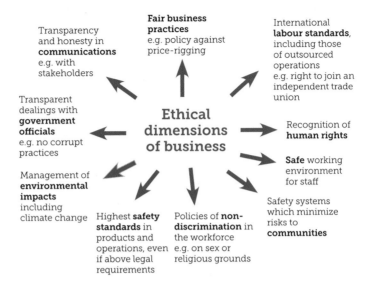

Figure 12.1 **Ethical dimensions of business**

and even these are likely to be weakly enforced, often for lack of resources. International labour standards are set by the ILO (see Chapter 8), and these tend to be higher than those set by national law. Companies such as Nike and Gap adhere to national labour standards in their outsourced manufacturing in Vietnam and Indonesia, but questions still arise about their ethical position, despite their adoption of CSR policies.

Secondly, legal compliance can be a grey area in many contexts. Here are three examples. Some companies, well aware of the law on, say, advertising, draft messages which rely on half-truths and suggestions: they might well mislead the consumer, but the firm can argue that it abided by the law in the strict sense. We might say they adhere to the letter of the law, but not its spirit. In fact, in matters of advertising, truthful but misleading statements are often found to be in breach of the rules. In a second example, companies can go to great lengths, usually with the help of professional tax consultants, to devise methods of reducing their liabilities to tax. They can claim to be complying with the law, but their sidestepping devices could be seen as unethical. Moreover, pure tax evasion schemes are in breach of the law in many countries. Google paid no tax on its £1.6 billion in earnings in the UK in 2008, by directing the money to its subsidiary in Ireland, where tax rates are much lower. Earnings from its other European operations, amounting to £5.9 billion, also flowed to Ireland, where the company paid £7.6 million in tax (Watts, 2009). Google has 800 employees in Britain. Had it paid UK tax on the British earnings, it would have faced a tax bill of £450 million just on the UK earnings. The company maintains it complies fully with tax laws, but ducking tax does not enhance its reputation for high ethical standards.

A third grey area occurs in situations such as industrial processes, in which the firm is obliged to observe the duty of **reasonable care**, which is the test for negligence. This can be interpreted in many ways, and in common law countries, there is a great deal of case law on what is meant by reasonable care. The firm is not expected to make operations 100% safe, which is impossible, but it is expected to take precautions which a reasonable person aware of the risks would take. There is a good deal of scope for differing interpretations of how safe an operation must be so as not to expose the employer to an accusation of negligence. Unfortunately, these issues are normally resolved in court after an accident has occurred. It is scant consolation for

reasonable care test used in law to determine whether a person has acted negligently

the victim or the victim's family that the employer was found to be negligent. Sometimes, safety devices would have incurred only small extra expenditure, but firms bent on cost-cutting would balk at the extra expense. By contrast, the firm with a strong ethical policy would take the view that the expense is justified, even if it reduces profits.

A final ethical dimension of business featured in Figure 12.1 is environmental management and the duty to combat climate change. Usually, duties are owed to a person or group, as in the examples just cited. But in the case of the environment, the position is less clear. As the figure shows, firms owe a duty to protect the environment from harm that affects workers and local communities. But the principle of sustainability (discussed in Chapter 11) goes further, resting on what can be termed **intergenerational justice**. This means that firms owe moral obligations to later generations, as *their* standards of living could be at risk if we do not take steps to reduce emissions (Dietz et al., 2008). This means that there is a potential conflict between the needs and wants of today's inhabitants and those of future inhabitants, involving firms in calculations of a possible trade-off between them.

intergenerational justice concept which underlies the principle of sustainability, implying that moral obligations are owed to future generations

Summary points Ethics in business

- Ethical principles apply to business goals and how they are achieved.
- Many ethical principles overlap with legal requirements, but ethical standards tend to be higher.

- The firm with a strong ethical stance will treat legal requirements as a minimum and consider that extra costs to ensure safety are justified.

- Protecting the environment is based on an ethical duty to future generations, encapsulated in the concept of sustainability.

Critical thinking

A duty to be good?

Many companies boast their strong ethical principles, yet go to lengths to offshore operations and tax liabilities. How, if at all, can this apparent inconsistency be justified?

Social responsibility of the firm

social responsibility the role of the organization in society, which implies duties to communities and the environment

MNEs have been the drivers of globalization, able to benefit from liberalization policies of national governments in many locations, to deepen interactions in a range of host communities, in addition to their ties in their home countries. As firms become active players in societies, they become part of communities. **Social responsibility** refers to the role of the firm in society, which entails obligations to stakeholders in local communities and to the environment. In some countries, such as Japan, the firm has traditionally been viewed as being part of society and having social roles in addition to its economic activities. For the Japanese employee, the job is more than merely a way of making a living, but a way of life in itself, tied up with the employee's sense of belonging.

In individualist western environments, the company has been viewed more narrowly, as performing an essentially economic role. Businesses have tended to feel that, so long as they adhered to existing legal obligations, they were free to focus on 'the bottom line', that is, profits and shareholder value. This simplistic view, which separates social responsibility concerns from business ones, has now given way to the view that companies, like individuals, are members of communities.

▶ More online ... Cargill's CSR policy is as www.cargill.com/corporate-responsibility

Two factors can be highlighted in bringing about this change in the approach to social responsibility. Firstly, while markets have delivered economic results, they have left out of the equation considerations of human and environmental values. The insertion of these concerns in social market economies is a recognition of market limitations. The human rights and environmental questions posed daily for large corporations, such as oil companies in developing states, also show the inadequacy of viewing business in isolation from the community. No longer can an MNE doing business in a developing country remain disengaged from the live community issues in its places of operation. Moreover, as we noted earlier, a minimal policy of obedience to national laws can fall well short of ethical principles. An example is Cargill, featured in the opening case study, which states that its corporate responsibility involves adherence to national laws.

Secondly, the sheer size of the world's global corporations now dwarfs many national economies. Questions of how they use this power in socially responsible ways are now being addressed to companies, as well as to governments. Cargill is a private company in the global food industry. It aims to deliver profits for its owners, but questions of social responsibility beyond legal compliance could also arise in the context of such a vital industry.

Theories of corporate social responsibility

Management theorists and corporate strategists for a number of years have been addressing the question of what the role of the company in society should be. While most now agree that its role extends beyond the purely economic dimension, there is much debate on the extent of this expanded social role, and how social performance can be measured. Adding complexity to the discussion is the reality that global companies operate in a number of different societies. Theories that attempt to define the company's responsibility to society are generally grouped together as theories of corporate social responsibility (CSR). These theories typically make reference to stakeholder groups, as well as to society in general. These concepts were introduced in Chapter 1, as they form one of the critical themes of this book, and have arisen in connection with a number of case studies (for example the takeover of Cadbury by Kraft in the closing case study of Chapter 9). Here we look at theories of CSR in conjunction with stakeholder theories, which have been the subject of academic focus in recent years (Mitchell et al., 1997).

A 'weak' theory of CSR focuses on philanthropic or charitable contributions and activities, which the firm engages in as an adjunct to its business activities: any costs are weighed against the benefit to be gained in terms of the firm's enhanced reputation as a good corporate citizen. On this view, CSR 'is fine, if you can afford it' (Freeman, 1984: 40). The concept of **corporate citizenship** visualizes the responsibility of the firm in the community as analogous to that of the individual citizen, entailing obligations to obey the law and pay taxes. As we have seen above, however, these obligations can be interpreted rather loosely. Critics of this approach argue that it is 'skin deep', entailing no rethinking of the firm's strategy and operations in terms of social issues – in theory, a company might be a socially responsible in this limited sense while exploiting its workforce and polluting the environment.

A stronger strategic approach to CSR is found in the work of A.B. Carroll. Carroll has devised a four-dimensional model of CSR (Carroll, 1991), which takes into account economic, legal, ethical and philanthropic dimensions (see Figure 12.2).

corporate citizenship concept which visualizes social responsibility of the firm in the community as analogous to that of the individual citizen, entailing obligations to obey the law and pay taxes

This model, which can be depicted as a pyramid, places the economic obligations of the company at the base, recognizing that the business must be economically profitable in order to survive. Above economic activities are legal responsibilities. Legal obligations cover many areas, including employment law, environmental law, and health and safety regulations. Of course, the law sets minimum standards, which differ from country to country. The firm with a strong CSR policy will aim to go beyond minimum legal standards. Carroll's model sees the need to rise above minimal legal requirements as an aspect of ethical responsibility, along with respect for ethical norms of the society in which the firm operates. The last element is **philanthropy**, such as charitable giving, which, while desirable, is less important than the other three – the icing on the cake. Carroll stresses that the model does not posit an inherent conflict between making profits and being socially responsible: for the manager, all four dimensions of the firm's responsibility should be central to corporate strategy.

philanthropy donation of resources to recipients deemed to be good causes in the eyes of the donor, with no expected material return

Figure 12.2 **Carroll's pyramid of corporate social responsibility**

Source: Adapted from Carroll, A.B. (1991) 'The pyramid of corporate social responsibility: Toward the moral management of organizational stakeholders', *Business Horizons*, 34: 42

stakeholder theory management theory which focuses on the many different groups and interests that affect the company

While Carroll's model provides an overall framework, analysis of the 'social' component of CSR is provided by **stakeholder theory**. (See Figure 1.1 for a diagram of stakeholder groups.) First developed by Edward Freeman, stakeholder theory points to the many different groups and interests that affect the company. Freeman defines them broadly as 'any group or individual which affects or is affected by the achievement of the organization's objectives' (Freeman, 1984: 46). Stakeholders may be classified according to the strength of their influence on the company, and how critical they are to the company's operational success at any given time. Some of these, such as shareholders and employees, are internal to the company, while suppliers, customers and the community in general are outside the organization itself, although these relationships may come to be seen as integral to the company's strategy. Situations in which stakeholder interests conflict with each other pose particular challenges for managers. For example, the decision to outsource a particular operation to a low-cost location will save money, but cause loss of employment in the company's home country, where most of its shareholders are likely to be located.

Summary points Theories of CSR

◆ A weak approach to CSR sees activities that benefit the community as 'extras', which the firm carries out on a voluntary basis.

◆ A stronger CSR theory goes to the heart of corporate strategy, viewing the firm's social and ethical stance as part of its way of doing business.

◆ Stakeholder theory is often seen as providing the social component of CSR approaches, although classifying stakeholders and assessing their importance tends to be seen mainly in economic terms.

Critical thinking

Corporate social responsibility

> Corporations are social institutions. If they don't serve society, they have no business existing. The argument that they serve society by making money and creating jobs is coming apart. (Mintzberg, in Skapinker, 2003)

What factors have caused the undermining of the purely economic view of the company's role, as identified by Mintzberg in this passage? To what extent does the view of the corporation as a social institution suggest a radical transformation in its role, or, alternatively, a reformulation of what corporations have always been doing?

CSR in practice

Many companies tend to subscribe to the weak notion of CSR, equating it with charitable giving and corporate citizenship. The 'social' element resides in the notion that, once the company has made lots of money, it is in a position to give some of it back to society. This view rests on a concept of CSR as being peripheral, not core to the business. However, many decisions a company takes, such as where to locate production, are both strategic and have a CSR dimension. Increasingly, managers appreciate this CSR dimension, especially in the context of corporate reputation. This is part of the **business case for CSR**. Also influential has been the principle of sustainability, mentioned earlier in the section on ethical principles.

While the sustainable business takes account of environmental impacts and climate change (discussed in Chapter 11), the concept of sustainability arguably extends to impacts on communities. Most companies now appreciate that their presence in a community entails positive duties. For example, if houses are destroyed to build a factory or engage in mining operations, the company is under an obligation to provide alternative housing for inhabitants, which is more than just minimal accommodation, but an attempt to preserve communities. Sustainability also applies to the company's overall business model. Some industries that rely on scarce natural resources are having to rethink their corporate goals in light of supply constraints and rising costs in the future. It is for this reason that companies in the oil industry, such as Saudi Aramco (whose CEO was featured in the last chapter), emphasize the need to diversify. As a state-owned company, Saudi Aramco's goals are closely aligned with those of the society, as the case study indicated.

The impact of CSR on corporate strategy takes in a number of stakeholder groups, including investors, consumers, employees and the community (McWilliams, 2001). McWilliams argues that, analysed in terms of costs and benefits, a business case for CSR can be based on a differentiation strategy and become a source of competitive advantage. Examples of CSR approaches in this context are:

business case for CSR argument that business goals will be met more successfully in the longer term through CSR than through a narrow focus on economic goals

▶ More online ... The RSPO website is www.rspo.org
The Fairtrade website is www.fairtrade.org.uk

- Products made from sustainable resources, for example recycled materials
- Products made through CSR-related processes, for example organic foods
- Advertising which provides information about CSR attributes, for example dolphin-free tuna labels
- Building brand reputation on CSR attributes

This approach supports a view of CSR based on market considerations, treating the choice of CSR attributes as a choice analogous to the other strategic choices a firm makes, in terms of the demand for the attribute and the costs of providing it. This 'instrumental' view of CSR is akin to the weak version of the theory mentioned at the start of this section, in that it rests the CSR case on business considerations rather than ethical ones. However, it does highlight the fact that demand exists and that it is coming from numerous stakeholder groups – an indication that social responsibility is one of the criteria guiding consumers and investors in their evaluation of corporate performance.

codes of practice
voluntary sets of rules devised by companies to guide their CSR, ethical and environmental practices

third-party verification
the use of outside specialist services or certification to monitor CSR and environmental performance

Many MNEs have in place voluntary **codes of practice** on CSR, ethical principles and environmental policies. These codes of practice contain stated aims which are not always carried through in practice. A way of assuring stakeholders of high corporate standards is **third-party verification**. Certification by specialist monitoring bodies is available across a wide range of industries, from organic produce to tourism. For example, the Fairtrade Foundation supports principles of sustainable agriculture and a fair return for farmers. Companies signing up to these principles can use the fair trade logo, which signifies to consumers the product is produced according to fair trade principles. In some sectors, however, certification is less effective. Large food companies, including Unilever and Procter & Gamble, have committed themselves to using sustainable palm oil, but the Roundtable on Sustainable Palm Oil (RSPO), as mentioned in the opening case study, has been only partially successful. Many of its member producers were found to have infringed either its standards or Indonesian law (see Meet the CEO feature in this chapter). Moreover, as processing of sustainable palm oil is not carried out in separate operations, the large food companies could not provide the public with assurances regarding sustainable production (*The Economist*, 2010b).

At intergovernmental level, more broadly based guidelines on CSR are being revised in light of the changing environment, in both economic terms and stakeholder expectations, as we find in the next section.

Summary points CSR in practice

◆ The business case for CSR now impacts on corporate strategy, especially in respect of corporate reputation.

◆ The principles of sustainable business also lead companies to consider long-term viability of their goals and operations.

◆ Voluntary codes of practice adopted by MNEs are of limited value in assessng CSR performance.

Reaching for international standards

There are now several sets of international CSR standards designed to guide MNEs in their international operations. Sponsored by intergovernmental organizations, which enjoy wide participation by both developing and developed countries, these state-

▸ More online ... The ILO's website is www.ilo.org
The website of the UN Global Compact is www.globalcompact.org

ments of CSR principles are increasingly recognized as setting the benchmarks in international CSR. We highlight three here. The three statements focus on broad principles, including human rights, working conditions, employment terms and environmental protection. Here is a brief summary of the main points of each:

- *OECD Guidelines for Multinational Enterprises* – Issued first in 1976, this was among the first statements of CSR principles. It was revised in 2000 and is being revised again in 2010. Participating in the revision are 11 non-OECD countries, mainly developing countries, in addition to the 30 OECD member states. Three areas are being highlighted in the 2010 revision. First, the responsibility of MNEs over the entire supply chain is highlighted as coming within the firm's sphere of influence, even though the companies are legally independent. Secondly, the guidelines stress human rights, addressing situations where host-country policies on human rights do not reach international standards, or where the host country has not ratified relevant UN human rights conventions. Thirdly, the guidelines address new environmental issues, including 'green growth' of economies, eco-innovation, biodiversity and sustainability.

- *International Labour Organization (ILO) Tripartite Declaration of Principles concerning MNEs and Social Policy (MNE Declaration)* – The ILO Declaration dates from 1977, and its fourth edition was issued in 2006. It covers five areas:

  1 General principles – These principles recognize the primacy of national law and urge respect for international conventions, for example on human rights.

  2 Employment – MNEs should provide employment for local people and not discriminate on grounds of race, colour, sex, religion, political opinion, national extraction or social origin.

  3 Training – MNEs should provide appropriate training for local workers in their operations.

  4 Conditions of work and life – MNEs should employ local people on terms not less favourable than those of local employers. MNEs should eliminate the worst forms of child labour, and observe international health and safety standards.

  5 Industrial relations – MNEs should recognize the freedom of association and right to organize among workers. Collective bargaining should be allowed, and there should be consultation with workers' representatives, as provided by national law. There should be conciliating mechanisms for settling industrial disputes, involving equal representation of employees and employers.

- *The UN Global Compact (UNGCO)* – Dating from 2000, this compact between governments, corporations and NGOs lists nine key principles from the Universal Declaration of Human Rights, the core standards of the ILO, and the Rio Declaration. They include support of human rights, the elimination of child labour, free trade unions and the elimination of environmental pollution. These are 'aspirational' rather than binding in their effects. The significance of the initiative is the bringing together of the major players in a single forum for debate about the issues. Nike, DaimlerChrysler, Unilever and Royal Dutch Shell were among the corporations that signed the accord, as were Amnesty International and the World Wildlife Fund. On its tenth anniversary, the UN Secretary General said, 'At first, the Compact was driven solely by morality. We asked businesses to do the right thing. Morality is still the driving force. But, today, the business community is coming to understand that principles and profits are two sides of the same coin' (UN Global Compact, 2010).

Companies seem to be responding to this line of thinking. The OECD commissioned a survey of companies in Europe, to assess whether their CSR approaches were either based on or inspired by international instruments. The findings, which appear in Figure 12.3, were based on 89 responses and a study of 281 other CSR and sustainability reports by companies.

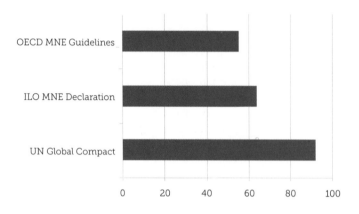

Figure 12.3 Basis of CSR approaches by companies in Europe
Percentage of companies responding 'yes' when asked, 'Is your CSR approach based on or inspired by international instruments?'

Source: *OECD Observer* (2009) 'OECD MNE Guidelines: A responsible business choice', No. 270/271, December 2008 – January 2009

International Organization for Standardization (ISO) body which oversees quality and environmental standards recognized across industries

The **International Organization for Standardization (ISO)** oversees quality and environmental standards recognized across industries. Its ISO 9000 is a recognized quality assurance standard, and the more recent ISO 1400 series applies to environmental standards (see Chapter 11). ISO is now producing its first guidance on social responsibility. Known as the ISO 26000 standards, this guidance will combine principles from the OECD, ILO and UN Global Compact.

The standards set out in this section are all voluntary, emphasizing the primary importance of national law. However, a strong lead by companies influences governments to change laws and raise standards. Moreover, stakeholders increasingly expect companies to maintain high ethical standards. The line between what is ethical and what is legal has become blurred. What is legal in a particular country, particularly a developing country, may not pass muster by international standards, which are now seen as providing the benchmarks for best practice.

Summary points International standards and CSR

● Internationally recognized CSR standards, involving a wide range of participating national delegations, are issued by the OECD, ILO and UN.

● These standards cover human rights, working conditions, employees' rights to organize, and environmental protection.

● While MNEs have in the past been content to adhere to national laws as the limit of their obligations, stakeholders increasingly expect adherence to international standards.

Critical thinking
International versus national standards
In what ways would companies enhance their CSR credentials among stakeholders globally by expressly embracing international standards?

CSR and corporate governance

In general, corporate boards are accountable to shareholders and other stakeholders through corporate governance mechanisms. However, as we highlighted in Chapter 1, every company is strongly influenced by the national environment of its home country and its own historical legacy. These factors are evident in its corporate culture, including perceptions of its role in society. In terms of corporate governance, corporate cultures diverge according to whether the company views its primary duty as maximizing shareholder value or achieving wider goals associated with the stakeholder perspective. In countries where liberal market capitalism retains a firm grip, shareholder value is perceived as paramount, and CSR tends to be marginalized or conceived in terms of enhancing shareholder value. In countries where social market values have dominated, as in Western Europe, the stakeholder perspective is more prevalent. In these countries, especially under the guidance of the EU Commission, liberal reforms have made headway. The EU has been influential in promoting more competitive markets in member states, in reducing state subsidies to businesses and in encouraging privatization of nationalized industries which have enjoyed monopolies in a number of sectors, such as telecommunications. That said, corporate governance in both the more shareholder-centred tradition and the stakeholder-centred tradition can be criticized on CSR grounds.

We found in Chapter 1 that even public companies have ownership structures that concentrate power in the hands of small group of insiders, often the founder's family and associates. Such power often stems from a dual-class share structure, in which the voting shares are concentrated in the ruling insiders. Ordinary shareholders may have little or no voting power on major issues. Insider control seems to be a phenomenon which crosses national borders. Numerous American, European and Asian companies, although divergent in corporate culture, have mechanisms which perpetuate a controlling group of shareholders. This control is typically exerted through appointments of executives and board members.

fiduciary duty duty of trust to act honestly and in the best interests of another; applies to the duty of directors owed to their company

All company directors, whether executive or non-executive, owe a duty to act always in the best interests of the company, known as **fiduciary duty**. Fiduciary duty denotes a position of trust. It is owed to the company as whole, but differing interpretations of the nature of fiduciary duties lead to differing views of corporate governance. In the Anglo-American tradition, the primacy of shareholders over other stakeholders leads directors to think of their duties rather narrowly as maximizing shareholder wealth. Indeed, this principle became the beacon of American capitalism. The spread of market values around the world owes much to the success of American companies. But with the financial crisis of 2008, the foundations on which the market model was built seemed to crumble (see Chapter 9). Weaknesses in corporate governance are now held to bear much of the responsibility for the persistence of high-risk strategies in many companies, despite the risks to the very shareholder value that the system was meant to uphold. The following are some of the specific weaknesses which emerged:

- Corporate boards tend to go along with the strategic decisions of executive directors, rather than act in an effective monitoring role. Although most boards have independent, non-executive directors, these part-time directors, while legally bearing the same fiduciary duties as full-time executives, tend to be compliant with management rather than be seen to 'rock the boat'.

MEET THE CEO

▸ More online ... Unilever is at www.unilever.com

Paul Polman CEO of Unilever, the consumer products company

When Paul Polman took over as CEO of Unilever, the company's shares went up on the news. In a sense, the company was breaking with tradition, appointing an outsider for the first time in its 80-year history. But Mr Polman was not just any outsider. He had spent most of his career of 27 years with P&G, Unilever's arch rival, followed by two years at Nestlé, another global giant in the food industry. His predecessor, Patrick Cescau, had spearheaded a turnaround at Unilever, which had rather lost its way competitively against its big rivals, despite its well-known brands such as Dove soap, Hellmans mayonnaise and Knorr soups. Polman wasted no time in making management changes to refocus the company on the consumer. He says, 'I do not work for the shareholder, to be honest; I work for the consumer, the customer ... I'm not driven and I don't drive this business model by shareholder value. I drive this business model by focusing on the consumer and customer in a responsible way, and I know that shareholder value can come' (Stern, 2010a).

Based in London, the company has become more streamlined and agile, abolishing the dual-listed structure that it inherited from its Anglo-Dutch past. Mr Polman is focusing on growth in emerging markets, where he sees the need to be adaptable in terms of products and to be able to respond quickly to new entrants. However, he also feels strongly that business models for the future will have to be more

sustainable, pointing out the concerns over rapidly depleting resources. Investors were initially sceptical, suspecting that performance would suffer. When he announced that he was doing away with short-term targets, Unilever's share price went down. He is philosophical, saying that he is seeking investors who appreciate a socially responsible business model, rather than those who are looking only for short-term performance. The right investors 'look at more numbers than just the balance sheet and the income statement ... It's not either results or responsibility, it's both ... It's doing good and doing well, which I don't see as a trade-off'(Stern, 2010b).

Mr Polman appreciates the difficulties in ethical sourcing of raw materials such as palm oil. The global market for palm oil has doubled in the last 15 years, largely because of increased demand from companies like Unilever. Palm oil production has been a major factor in deforestation in Indonesia and Malaysia. Unilever is committed to buying sustainable palm oil, and demonstrated its firm line by suspending trading with Sinar Mas, Indonesia's largest producer, for breaches of ethical standards, which occurred despite the fact that Sinar Mas is a member of the sustainable palm oil roundtable (RSPO). Mr Polman is hoping that other manufacturers and retailers will also take a hard line with producers, and that by 2015 all palm oil production will be sustainable. Although government action would be ideal, he feels that 'whilst waiting for governments to act there is still a huge amount that industry can do on its own' (Polman, 2010).

Sources: Stern, S. (2010a) 'Unilever chief backs criticism of shareholder primacy', *Financial Times*, 5 April; Stern, S. (2010b) 'The outsider in a hurry to shake up his company', *Financial Times*, 5 April; Mason, R. (2010) 'Unilever shares jump as it poaches Paul Polman as CEO from Nestlé', *The Telegraph*, 4 September; Polman, P. (2010) 'Redefining business success', paper given at *The Economist* Third Annual Sustainability Summit, London, 25 February

Paul Polman
Source: Unilever

- In corporate governance best practice, the positions of chairman of the board and CEO should be separate, but in practice, the roles are often combined, especially in the US. An effect is to give executive managers greater control over boards.
- Dominant shareholders exert control in many public companies (as highlighted in Chapter 1). They are in a strong position to influence voting and dictate strategy, leaving 'minority' ordinary shareholders in a weak position. Although there are legal protections for minority shareholders, especially when their interests are at stake, they have little influence on boards, and are usually unable, because of procedural hurdles, to put forward candidates to become directors.
- Committees of corporate boards, such as the remuneration (compensation) committee and audit committee, tend to be dominated by the insiders who control the company, despite having non-executive members. In theory, payment to managers through stock options and bonuses based on performance aligns managers' incentives more closely with owners, encouraging them to be more enterprise-minded. However, in practice, spiralling executive remuneration has come into the spotlight as an example of weak board oversight of managers.

CEOs of the 15 largest US companies earned 520 times more than the average worker in 2007, up from 360 times in 2003. Including share-based compensation, the average annual pay of US CEOs in 2007 was $24.5 million, up from $16 million in 2003 (ILO, 2008). This increase of 10% a year can be contrasted with the increase in pay of ordinary employees, which was just .7%. Dutch CEOs received even bigger rises, as Figure 12.4 shows. Interestingly, in the Netherlands, big increases were also enjoyed by executives generally, but not by ordinary Dutch workers. The huge compensation paid to executives in the US is largely attributable to share-based compensation. Dramatic increases in executive pay in the Netherlands can be largely attributed to the introduction of share-based compensation schemes (ILO, 2008).

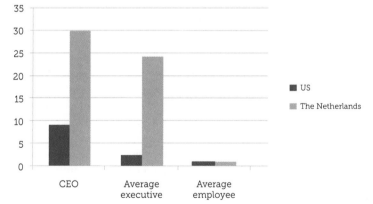

Figure 12.4 **Percentage annual increase in pay, 2003–2007: the US and the Netherlands**

Source: ILO (2008) *World of Work Report 2008* (Geneva: ILO)

Reforming corporate governance to promote greater accountability is a concern of governments, especially in sectors like banking, which have received large sums of public money. But the questions remain: to whom is accountability owed, and how is it best achieved? Stakeholder interests are usually associated with theories of management rather than corporate governance. In continental European countries, employee representatives play a role in governance, but these employee representatives tend to speak for members in the home country. Other stakeholders, including workers in international operations, do not enjoy the same participative role. Contrast this stakeholder perspective with the wider perspective of CSR. CSR principles encompass all stakeholders, environmental concerns and ethical principles. Only CSR principles would cause executives to think twice about changing the company's registration to an offshore location for the fiscal benefits like lower taxes.

Procedural reforms of corporate governance, such as changing voting systems for directors, will go only a limited way in persuading the investing public that companies are being run soundly and sustainably. A corporate culture of responsiveness, transparency and fairness to stakeholders is now expected of MNEs. Shareholders increasingly look beyond short-term financial criteria to long-term value creation, in which CSR and stakeholder perspectives come into play.

Summary points   CSR and corporate governance

◆ Liberal market models of corporate governance emphasize the primacy of shareholder wealth maximization, marginalizing CSR considerations.

◆ Stakeholder models of corporate governance involve participation by some stakeholders, such as employees, but not others.

◆ A change of corporate governance culture, away from short-term financial considerations towards one of social relevance is now perceived as a step towards more responsible corporate governance.

Critical thinking

CSR in the boardroom?

What difference would it make for raising ethical standards in practice if boards of directors were encouraged to think in terms of CSR rather than stakeholders?

The social enterprise

The social enterprise occupies the area between a for-profits business and a not-for-profits organization. Defined in Chapter 1, the social enterprise seeks to operate as a business and generate profits, but uses the profits for social causes. Its founders, known as social entrepreneurs, are committed to social causes, and see business means as conducive to that end. The social entrepreneur typically combines a market orientation with entrepreneurial zeal and a commitment to a particular cause. In some cases, the social enterprise operates in an area between mainstream business and government services. These enterprises are active in social service sectors, delivering services and providing jobs in local communities, often in areas of high unemployment. Housing, education, health and welfare advice for vulnerable groups are some of the sectors in which social enterprises operate in the UK. In many cases, they work alongside local and national government agencies. The social sector is expanding in many countries, partly because governments struggle to resource expanding welfare needs, for example the increasing numbers of older people with growing needs for care. However, the social enterprise is not a way of outsourcing social services, but rather of offering complementary services, often in conjunction with government agencies.

The social enterprise as an organization can take several forms, from registered charities to ordinary limited companies. The UK government introduced the

▶ More online ... The CIC regulator is at www.cicregulator.gov.uk
Global Easy Water Products (GEWP) is at www.gewp-india.com
An umbrella organization for UK social enterprises is the Social Enterprise Coalition, at www.socialenterprise.org.uk
The Social Finance bank is at www.socialfinance.org.uk

community interest company (CIC) a limited company set up to function as a social enterprise, which adheres to strict statutory requirements for adhering to social purposes

community interest company (CIC) in 2004, which allows the social entrepreneur to form a limited company, with strict requirements for adhering to social purposes. The Companies (Audit, Investigations and Community Enterprise) Act of 2004 provides a system of regulation of CICs, which assures the public that assets and profits are used for community purposes.

Social enterprises are also fulfilling needs in emerging economies, providing simple, affordable solutions adapted to local conditions. In India, home to over 100 million smallholder farmers living on less than $1 a day, water scarcity is a growing problem, but irrigation systems are expensive. A social entrepreneur, Global Easy Water Products (GEWP), devised a simple system based on the leaky hose principle, using bicycle tyre inner tubes and powered by a foot-pedal pump. It is cheap and adaptable, and, crucially, it is improving crop yields by 30–70%. Its business has become so successful that it has become a for-profit company.

The social sector offers many business opportunities for the innovative entrepreneur. The opening case study in Chapter 9 concerned microfinance, which has a strong social dimension. Microfinance has evolved from charitable organizations to social enterprises which are self-financing. Now, mainstream banks are also branching out into microfinance, demonstrating the potential for business at the 'base of the pyramid'. An example from the UK shows how a social enterprise grew out of a mainstream one. A private equity pioneer, Sir Ronald Cohen, whose group Apax Partners was one of the earliest private equity groups, has now shifted his attention to social financing. He has started a social investment bank, Social Finance, which aims to raise money from investors to fund social enterprises. He says, 'It is not enough to increase the standard of living at the high end. It is right at the same time to worry about those who are left behind' (*The Telegraph*, 2010).

Summary points The social enterprise

◆ The social enterprise links business activities with social goals.

◆ Social enterprises are growing in sectors such as welfare services which benefit communities.

Who is left behind, and why?

It was once thought, optimistically, that globalization would spread economic growth and prosperity from the advanced countries to the developing countries, eventually bringing benefits of a better quality of life to all. Since 1980, the gap between rich and poor within countries widened, as shown in Figure 12.5. The OECD has surveyed the wage gap between the highest 10% and the lowest 10% of people in member states, plus the three large emerging economies, Brazil, China and India. The gap had increased in 18 of the 20 countries surveyed, the largest gaps being in Brazil, China, India and the US. The gap was smallest in Belgium and the Nordic countries (ILO, 2008). The effects of the recent global financial crisis have exacerbated the impacts of widening inequalities, especially in poor developing countries.

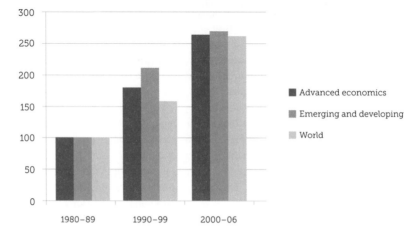

Figure 12.5 **Income inequalities since the 1980s**
The Gini coefficient index for the 1980s = 100

Source: ILO (2008)
World of Work Report 2008
(Geneva: ILO)

Winners and losers in the global workforce

Globalization has benefited some countries more than others. The Bric countries are often highlighted as among the winners, but for differing reasons. China, which has enjoyed the highest growth of the four, has benefited from export-oriented manufacturing industries. Other industrializing countries, such as Vietnam, have benefited for the same reason. Strong economic growth has helped these countries to reduce poverty, but within these societies, the winners have mainly been those in the manufacturing sector. Rural inhabitants have seen little in the way of greater prosperity, often relying on remittances sent from migrant factory workers in urban areas.

The lowering of tariff barriers has benefited the countries that rely heavily on exports, such as Brazil. Rises in the prices of commodities, including food and other natural resources, have aided growth in many countries. Brazil has made progress in reducing poverty, although the livelihoods of landless rural inhabitants remain precarious. Poorer developing countries, which cannot compete with Brazil's large agribusinesses, have seen less benefit from growing involvement in international trade. Although gaining as exporters from rising food prices, many poor countries, notably in sub-Saharan Africa, have struggled to meet rising prices of imports. Trade and FDI inflows to Africa (highlighted in Chapter 2) increased markedly in the post-2000 years, but declined in 2008–9 due to the global financial crisis.

For years, low-skilled workers in rich countries have seen jobs disappear in the global shift of manufacturing to low-cost locations. The process was highlighted in the case study in Chapter 2 on the global car industry. The global financial crisis has also resulted in rising unemployment. The ILO estimates that, globally, 20 million jobs were lost between the start of the financial crisis and the end of 2009 (ILO, 2009c). In addition, there are many workers in jobs that are insecure, especially short-term work, who join the ranks of the unemployed when the work runs out. In rich countries, public spending has soared, leaving governments nursing mounting budget deficits.

As we have seen, governments have come under pressure to bail out large companies like carmakers in the US, but pressures to alleviate the plight of the unemployed are also strong, if more diffuse. There has been a rise in the number of workers employed in the informal sector, especially in developing countries. These workers, a disproportionate number of whom are women, are particularly vulnerable, enjoying few of the welfare benefits, such as work-related injury benefits, which workers in the formal sector enjoy. Even in the formal sector, most countries offer only limited benefits to workers who have lost their jobs (see Figure 12.6).

In the advanced economies, only 49% of unemployed workers receive state benefits. Typically, unemployment benefit runs for just six months. However, long-term unemployment has become a concern. By May 2010, the number of unemployed in the US stood at 15 million (US Department of Labor, 2010). Of these, 46% were long-term unemployed, defined as jobless for 27 weeks or longer. Unemployment affects black Americans disproportionately: the unemployment rate among black people was 15.5%, whereas among white people it was 8.8%. In late June 2010, the US Congress faced an urgent request for legislative approval to extend unemployment benefits for a further six months beyond the existing 26-week limit. Although a good cause from the point of view of the out-of-work, it was controversial, as the measure would add billions to the already-huge budget deficit. Moreover, extending benefits for another six months is a temporary reprieve for many workers. The changing structure of global labour markets has been a major factor, made worse by the financial crisis.

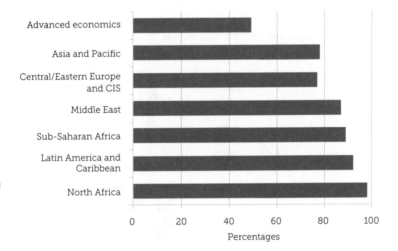

Figure 12.6 **Unemployed workers with no state benefits**

Source: ILO (2009) *World of Work 2009* (Geneva: ILO)

Large emerging economies suffered faltering growth due to the financial crisis, but were able to withstand the shocks. These countries generally have lower government debt burdens than those in the developed world. However, poor developing countries are more vulnerable. The World Bank observes that developing countries were struck particularly hard by the financial crisis, even though they were not part of the cause (World Bank, 2010). Higher food prices and unemployment have afflicted the poorest developing countries, where food is a major component of household spending. Sadly, child labour remains persistently high. In 2008, 306 million children globally, mainly in the 5–14 age group, were involved in economic activity, up from 211 million in 2000 (ILO, 2010). The increase was greatest in the countries of sub-Saharan Africa, up from 49 million in 2004 to 58 million in 2008. Here, children are 28.4% of the workforce. High levels of poverty and weak educational institutions are contributing factors. These factors have been highlighted by the UN in its initiatives to tackle the main challenges facing developing countries.

> More online ... The ILO's International Programme for the Elimination of Child Labour is at www.ilo.org/ipec/
> For the full text of the Millennium Development Goals, go to the website at www.un.org/millenniumgoals/

Summary points Left behind in a globalized world

● Globalization has benefited companies and groups of workers in countries favoured by location advantages of globalized production.

● Rising inequality has accompanied globalization, as the benefits have been spread unevenly within societies.

● The global financial crisis has resulted in widespread unemployment in both developed and developing countries.

Critical thinking
Global and national divides
In what ways is globalization leading to an urban/rural divide in many developing countries? Contrast these phenomena with the divides which have emerged in the US.

Development goals

In 2000, the UN Millennium Summit of world leaders set targets for reducing poverty, alleviating hunger and other goals in developing regions of the world. Collectively, these are the **Millennium Development Goals (MDGs)**. They were ambitious, aiming to halve the number of people living on less than $1 a day by 2015. Other targets were to halve the number of those undernourished and improve access to safe drinking water and sanitation. The main MDGs are highlighted in Figure 12.7.

Millennium Development Goals (MDGs) goals designated by the UN Millennium Summit of 2000, which set targets for improving human well-being in developing regions

Figure 12.7 **The UN's Millennium Development Goals**

The UN reports regularly on progress in each of these areas. By 2010, it was becoming clear which goals were likely to be achieved, giving some cause for encouragement, but lack of progress in some areas was disappointing (United Nations, 2010). The overall poverty reduction target is likely to be met. Although there are still 1.4 billion people living in extreme poverty, this number is expected to decrease to 920 million by 2015 – half the number in 1990. The target for reducing hunger is unlikely to be met, however. The number of undernourished people globally has risen, reaching close to a billion in 2009. Higher prices and poverty in poor countries meant that the poor had less access to food (see the case study which follows).

The target for access to drinking water is likely to be met, but there remains a large gap between urban and rural environments. Although access has improved, the safety of drinking water has become an issue in recent years, due mainly to agricultural and manufacturing activities which are causing pollution to surface and ground water in many countries. Another issue has been naturally occurring inorganic arsenic and other chemicals, a phenomenon in Bangladesh and other areas in South Asia. A lesson seems to be that care over safety must be given greater weight in infrastructure projects to improve access to water. Infrastructure weaknesses are also indicating that the target for improved sanitation is out of reach. Nearly half the population of developing regions is still without improved sanitation, which directly impacts on efforts to improve health and well-being. The problems are especially acute for young children and mothers. Although attention to the health of mothers and young children has improved, progress is uneven, and access to health services in rural areas remains a problem. In rural areas, children are twice as likely to be underweight as in urban areas. Largely because of donor funding, such as the Gates Foundation, progress is being made in reducing the incidence of HIV/Aids, and combating diseases like malaria and measles.

Progress in attaining educational goals has also been aided by donor funding. Although education is becoming more widely provided, especially in sub-Saharan Africa, there remain discrepancies. Boys are more likely than girls to go to school, and gender empowerment of women has made only limited progress in other spheres, such as political decision-making.

The UN points to both lack of resources and institutional weaknesses for the poor progress in areas covered by the MDGs. Weak systems of accountability are an aspect of poor governance which afflicts most developing countries. The UN also urges that more attention needs to be given to sustainable development (United Nations, 2010). The UN has long recognized the multiple dimensions of poverty and the interrelationships between poverty and other aspects of human development. Poverty in a narrow sense is simply inadequate income to sustain life, or 'income poverty'. It can also be viewed in broader terms, recognizing that human life is more than the economic dimension alone (recall the case study on Mexico in Chapter 5, which included the Mexican government's more nuanced definition of poverty). The UN coined the term, 'human poverty', to cover this broader spectrum of deprivation (United Nations, 2000: 73). It includes lack of capability to enjoy a long, healthy life, to be educated, and to have a decent standard of living. These more qualitative dimensions are captured in the UN's human development measures, which take into account life expectancy, healthcare and access to education. This broader view of deprivation's dimensions mirrors the distinction between economic development and sustainable development.

Sustainable development takes into account not just economic benefit, but the impact of environmental degradation, damage to ecosystems and loss of cultural goods. The UN's 2010 MDGs' Report found disappointing progress in achieving environmental sustainability goals (United Nations, 2010). The 2010 target for biodiversity conservation was already missed, and not enough was being done to protect key habitats of threatened species. These losses to ecosystems threaten societies' future prosperity and well-being.

Food security in the world: a safer future?

A sharp rise in food prices in 2007–8 sent nervous shivers around the world. Food is one of the world's most sensitive industries. In developing countries, where people spend 70% or more of their income on food, steep price rises globally can result in rising numbers of hungry people. Food shortages are associated with social unrest and political instability. The food crisis sparked riots in countries as disparate as Bangladesh and Honduras. In Madagascar, it even brought down the government. Governments around the world now take food security very seriously, and are taking steps to prevent, or at least cope with, future shocks. Following years of falling investment in agriculture in many countries, that is good news. But the less good news is that some of the measures now being taken might possibly make matters worse for global food security in the future.

Rising demand for food is a factor – but not the only one – in pushing up prices. Changing diets in emerging economies like China are leading to increased demand for meat. However, this in turn increases demand for grain, as rearing more livestock consumes greater quantities of grain on land which might otherwise be used for human food. Growing crops for biofuels has similar effects. The world is running out of arable farming land, and much of it is vulnerable to the effects of climate change, including drought and severe weather events. Crop yields have been going down for years, largely because government funding for R&D in agriculture has diminished around the world. The effects have been particularly devastating in developing countries, where growing populations and water scarcity strain agricultural resources. Governments are now waking up to the challenges.

In an apparent paradox, numerous emerging and developing countries with large agricultural sectors have become net importers of food, unable to meet rising home demand from domestic sources. China and India are both importers although both aspire to being self-sufficient. The situation in Senegal is particularly extreme. Here, although 75% of the population work in food production, the country imports 70% of its food. Senegal was another country to experience food riots in 2008.

Stung by price rises and market fluctuations that produce shocks, governments have prioritized food security, and many are turning away from dependence on markets. Some producing countries imposed export restrictions on grains in the food crisis. In 2008, two big rice producers, Thailand and Vietnam, banned exports. The impact of the ban was felt in the Philippines, one of the world's biggest importers of rice. There, the government reacted by doing large 'futures' deals to purchase 1.5 million tonnes of rice, which equates to about 5% of the total amount traded annually.

The removal of commodities from global markets has also taken the form of 'land grabs', by which countries that normally buy imports in the marketplace now do deals to lease or buy agricultural land in poorer countries. These new owners grow the crops and ship them back to their home populations. Saudi Arabia, China, South Korea and Kuwait have all made such deals. They are controversial, however, as much of the land they take over is in sub-Saharan Africa, where local people are vulnerable to food shortages, and are in receipt of food aid from the UN's World Food Programme. The UN estimates that the number of undernourished people globally, mainly in Asia and sub-Saharan Africa, reached over a billion in 2009.

Looking to the future, many governments now spend more on agricultural investment, boosting productive capacity, rather than looking to rely on food aid. Schemes include subsidizing inputs such as seeds and fertilizer, setting up seed banks, and helping farmers, many of whom run tiny operations, with financing. Malawi introduced a fertilizer subsidy, virtually giving fertilizer to the poorest farmers. This is an expensive programme, costing 4.2% of the country's GDP, but the results have been impressive. In 2005, Malawi imported 40% of its food, and in 2009, it exported more than half its output, exporting particularly to neighbouring Kenya, in the throes of

▶ More online ... The UN's world food programme is at www.wfp.org
Read about Malawi's fertilizer subsidy on the website of the Global Subsidies Initiative, at www.globalsubsidies.org

famine. Malawi had trebled its maize harvest in four years. But, of course, even if the government could find the money to continue the subsidy, fertilizer is not a sustainable solution, as it has long-term damaging environmental impacts. Agricultural R&D into drought-resistant crops perhaps holds out better hope for the future. In this respect, private-sector companies have a role to play, often working in partnership with governments and NGOs.

Sources: Blas, J. (2009) 'Global hunger forces itself to the top of political agenda', *Financial Times*, 10 November; Murray, S. (2009) 'The search for a fresh recipe', *Financial Times*, 16 October; Murray, S. (2010) 'How to feed people and save the planet', *Financial Times*, 27 January; *The Economist* (2009) 'If words were food, nobody would go hungry', 21 November

A combine harvester in action: global demand for grain, for both human and animal consumption, has soared, but crops are affected by uncertainties of weather and other factors, raising issues of food security in many countries

Source: Istock

Questions for discussion

◆ What factors are continuing to cause food shortages globally?
◆ Why are poor developing countries particularly vulnerable?
◆ To what extent are current policies sustainable, leading to greater food security in future?

Implications for CSR

The UN's Global Compact recognizes the responsibility of MNEs in improving human well-being and raising standards of living. We have seen that MNEs have tended to invoke national law in cases of working conditions and employment practices in developing countries. In many cases, these employees work for outsourcing companies, not the brand owner whose name appears on the manufactured products. Brand owners used to view these issues as outside their control, but, largely because of media attention and the activities of NGOs, brand owners and retailers can no longer wash their hands of responsibility for these workers. Stakeholders, including consumers and employees, are increasingly concerned about the negative perceptions of MNEs in many developing countries. Although western MNEs typically boast of their corporate citizenship profiles and point to their codes of ethics in foreign locations, differences between the rhetoric and the reality are often highlighted, as we found in the opening case study of this chapter.

A major reason for the failure of CSR to bring about real changes in the ways companies see their activities in communities is the attachment of many companies to shareholder wealth maximization, which often translates into the chase for short-term profits. A shift in corporate culture towards a more balanced stakeholder perspective could well lead to a dip in short-term profits. However, as the CEO highlighted in this chapter urges, the shift to a more sustainable way of doing business benefits shareholders in the longer term. But what about emerging-market MNEs, which are becoming more active in markets for corporate control? They are not steeped in the liberal market values of western counterparts. Indeed, in many developing countries, there has been a backlash against financial and trade liberalization, in light of the financial crisis which struck high-income countries (World Bank, 2010). Emerging-market MNEs, both state-controlled and private-sector companies, tend to have opaque corporate governance structures, in which family ties and informal links with political leaders are influential. Of course, the same can also be said of many western MNEs. However, western MNEs are now playing to a more critical home public, concerned about sustainability and social issues. Developing countries, too, are becoming more aware of social and environmental issues, and expectations of foreign investors are rising as host governments themselves take a more focused approach to development goals in their own societies.

Conclusions

1 The company's role in society raises a range of ethical issues for businesses, focusing on the moral content of behaviour, rather than solely on economic consequences.

2 Ethical considerations for international business arise in numerous contexts, including working conditions, human rights, discrimination in the workplace, environmental impacts and corrupt practices such as bribery.

3 Theories of corporate social responsibility (CSR) stress that companies' impact on society should become central to their strategy formation.

4 Assessing social interactions is often envisaged in terms of stakeholder groups, including investors, consumers, employees and society in general.

5 A firm's responsibilities can be considered in terms of four ascending levels: economic, legal, moral and philanthropic.

6 Weaknesses in corporate governance include domination by insider groups and minimal rights for ordinary shareholders.

7 Excesses such as spiralling executive pay and high-risk financial strategies are held up as emanating from an obsession with maximizing shareholder value, often in a short-term timeframe.

8 The social enterprise, which combines business activities with social goals, has become a viable vehicle in many sectors, especially in welfare services for vulnerable groups.

9 Workers who have benefited from globalization are in industries where global production networks have become highly developed. Poorly skilled workers in high-income countries have been among the main losers.

10 Although the UN's Millennium Development Goals (MDGs) have raised awareness of issues such as poverty and hunger, progress in alleviating them has been slow.

11 Economic development can be framed in a broader picture of human development, which takes in improvements in education, health and cultural well-being.

12 Social responsibility, including human rights, human development, and environmental protection, is now engaging managers of MNEs, responding to growing awareness of ethical and environmental issues by shareholders and consumers.

Review questions

1 In what ways have utilitarian principles influenced ethical thinking, and what are their shortcomings?

2 What are the ethical foundations of current thinking on corporate responsibility in societies, and in what areas of business activity are they relevant?

3 Describe Carroll's theory of CSR, and explain the role of stakeholders in Carroll's thinking.

4 What are the weaknesses of corporate codes of practice in relation to CSR?

5 In what ways can the recognition of international guidelines for CSR make companies more responsible in their international operations?

6 What are the criticisms of the shareholder model of corporate governance, and how can they be remedied?

7 Why is the social enterprise perceived as a way of providing services which governments struggle to fund?

8 What factors account for the gaps between the rich and poor within countries?

9 What areas of human well-being are highlighted by the MDGs, and which areas of the developing world are the main focus?

10 How is economic development contrasted with the broader concept of human development?

11 For an MNE, how can a CSR strategy promote goals such as the MDGs?

Key revision concepts

Categorical imperative, p. 397; Corporate citizenship, p. 401; CSR, p. 401; Ethics, p. 395; Fair trade initiatives, p. 404; Fiduciary duty, p. 407; Human poverty, p. 415; International labour standards, p. 405; Millennium development goals, p. 414; Philanthropy, p. 402; Social enterprise, p. 410; Third-party verification, p. 404; Utilitarianism, p. 396

Assignments

◆ Firms that have seen weakening financial performance might argue that they can no longer afford CSR, and that they must revert to a 'back to basics' competitive strategy. Assess the extent to which this is a valid argument in the current global environment.

◆ Many development goals look unlikely to be met in the poorest countries. How can the governments of developing countries best ensure that future globalization brings benefits for their societies as a whole?

Further reading

Allen, T. and Thomas, A. (2000) *Poverty and Development*, 2nd edn (Oxford: Oxford University Press).

Collier, P. (2008) *The Bottom Billion: Why the Poorest Countries are Failing and What Can be Done About It* (Oxford: OUP).

Crane, A., McWilliams, A., Matten, D. and Moon, J. (2009) *The Oxford Handbook of Corporate Social Responsibility* (Oxford: OUP).

Crane, A. and Matten, D. (2003) *Business Ethics* (Oxford: Oxford University Press).

Dehesa, Guillermo de la (2007) *What Do We Know About Globalization? Issues of Poverty and Income Distribution* (New Jersey: Wiley-Blackwell).

Hutton, W. and Giddens, A. (2000) *On the Edge: Living with Global Capitalism* (London: Jonathan Cape).

Kotler, P. (2004) *Corporate Social Responsibility* (London: John Wiley & Sons).

Meyer, A. (2000) *Contraction and Convergence: A Global Framework to Cope with Climate Change* (Newton Abbot: Green Books).

Melé, D. (2009) *Business Ethics in Action* (Basingstoke: Palgrave Macmillan).

Lomborg, B. (ed.) (2009) *Global Crises, Global Solutions: Costs and Benefits*, 2nd edn (Cambridge: Cambridge University Press).

Stiglitz, J. (2002) *Globalization and its Discontents* (London: Allen Lane).

Walmart: can bigger be better?

The mention of Walmart evokes a number of different images. **To millions of Americans, it means an efficient, low-cost retailer, especially appreciated when times are hard and household finances are strained. For Walmart employees, known as 'associates', of whom there are 1.4 million in the US** and another 600,000 worldwide, the company is associated with poor worker benefits, a slight taint of discrimination (lingering from multiple lawsuits by women employees in the US) and an anti-union bias. For environmentalists and NGOs concerned with social issues, Walmart evokes a negative image of factory production in countries such as China, where sustainability and CSR are in doubt. There is some truth in all these impressions of Walmart, but the company has strived in recent years to dispel the negative associations with sweatshop labour and unethical sourcing. Has it succeeded, or is it unrealistic for a company that has about 100,000 separate suppliers to ever guarantee sustainable principles applied across its supply chain?

Since its formation by Sam Walton in 1962, Walmart's low-cost strategy has been its hallmark, but cost-cutting is associated with poor ethical standards in the minds of many consumers. In 2005, Walmart launched its sustainability initiative, seeking to ensure that suppliers go along with its sustainability guidelines.

For Walmart, social responsibility is treated as an aspect of sustainability, highlighted in its Beijing Sustainability Summit of 2008, where it sought to engage its suppliers in committing to ethical policies. This was an achievement of Lee Scott, Walmart's former CEO, who sought to change Walmart's negative image. However, problems of child labour, forced labour, poor working conditions and lack of freedom of association (to organize in trade unions) are regularly perceived to be issues in the manufacturing centres of China. Walmart's Ethical Standards Manual for Suppliers was produced, and sustainability reports have followed. The Manual states that 'workers should be treated fairly and respectfully according to local laws and regulations' (Walmart, 2009: 22). Standards include a ban on child labour, defined as workers under the age of 14. They also stipulate that all overtime should be voluntary and that workers have a right to organize in a trade union of their choice and to engage in collective bargaining. However, in practice, monitoring and enforcement among thousands of suppliers present formidable challenges.

Walmart initially used its own auditors to visit factories, many on visits announced in advance. It now uses third-party auditors, many of whom work for a range of other western brand owners. Walmart employs a traffic light rating system, to report audit results. Green is the highest rating, where the factory has no violations or only low-risk ones. Yellow indicates medium risk, and orange is high risk. For yellow and orange ratings, work can carry

Pile it high and sell it cheaply: How sustainable and socially responsible is the business model made famous by Walmart?

Source: Istock

on and another audit will take place in 60 or 120 days. A red indicates such a high level of violations that the factory should be struck off the ethical suppliers list. In Walmart's 2010 results for China, only 3.3% of suppliers were rated green; 57.2% were rated yellow, and 35.5% were rated orange (Walmart, 2010a). These results suggest that much needs to be done to raise standards. Walmart observed that a factor was that its demands for large orders and urgent orders increased the need for overtime. Walmart's huge size gives it a dominant bargaining position with suppliers, who are under pressure to meet delivery targets, or risk losing their supply contract. There is an obvious tension between economic pressures and aspirations to behave ethically.

Walmart is not a company which is complacent about its market leadership. Its priorities, as headlined in its annual report, are growth around the world, leveraging to create greater competitive advantage and delivering strong returns to shareholders (Walmart, 2010b). The founder's family owns 40% of the company's shares, and is probably content that sales, although only 1% up in 2010, have continued to grow. The recession in the US has been a kind of blessing for Walmart, as its 'everyday low prices' are attracting middle-class customers who would once have considered the stores too down-market. Consider that, in 2009, one in every ten Americans received 'food stamps' (now in fact paid electronically) in the country's biggest-ever anti-hunger programme, the Supplemental Nutrition Assistance Program. The programme paid out $37.7 billion in 2009 to over 32 million people, much of the money finding its way to Walmart. Charitable organizations have also helped the needy, and Walmart has been keen to stress its contribution, through its charitable work in communities.

Its sights are now rising above its long relationship with America's low-income, largely rural, families, which have been the bedrock of its US businesses. Spurred by global ambitions, Walmart now sees growth coming mainly from its international division, especially emerging markets. In 2009, global sales exceeded $400 billion. Having accumulated $11.6 billion in cash in 2009, it was in a good position to go shopping. It bought a controlling share in Chile's largest retailer, D&S, and still had $8 billion left to spend on other acquisitions, as well as refurbishments of its US stores.

Under Lee Scott, who stepped down as CEO in 2009, Walmart's reputation improved. He realized that much of the criticism of the company was about its 'size and reach', and sought to turn this to advantage, becoming 'a trusted friend and ally to all' (*The Economist*, 2008). Like the company he headed, he was perhaps carried away by the rhetoric.

Sources: Walmart (2010a) Global Sustainability Report 2010 Progress update, at http://walmartstores.com; Walmart (2009) Ethical Standards Manual for Suppliers, at http://walmartstores.com; Walmart (2010b) Annual Report 2010, at http://walmartstores.com; Weitzman, H. (2009) 'Assistance soars in US as rich nations confront the needy', *Financial Times*, 7 April; Birchall, J. (2009) 'Walmart sees global sales break $400 billion barrier', *Financial Times*, 18 February; *The Economist* (2008) 'From bad to great', 29 November

Questions for discussion

- Assess Walmart from a CSR perspective.
- What are the ethical and CSR issues for outsourced manufacturing in low-cost locations such as Asian countries?
- To what extent are the tensions that exist in Walmart's business model indicative of those facing other companies that wish to improve their CSR credentials?

CRITICAL THEMES IN PERSPECTIVE

Outline of chapter

Learning objectives

1. To reflect on the critical themes developed throughout previous chapters
2. To appreciate interactions between unfolding themes in the current business environment globally
3. To assess the changing nature of globalization
4. To look forward to the new challenges for businesses, governments and societies

Critical themes in this chapter

- **A review of all the themes**
- **A look forward, featuring globalization and the role of the state**

At this job fair in China, people come in hope of finding work which brings both rewards and personal satisfaction. Will there be enough jobs to go around?

Source: Press Association

Shining a spotlight on working conditions at China's Foxconn

On 28th May 2010, just as Apple was anticipating a surge in publicity for its launch of the new iPad, it found itself at the centre of publicity of the unwanted variety. **Foxconn, the company which makes iPads and iPhones in China, was the focus of adverse reports of working conditions following the** suicides of a number of young factory workers on its assembly lines. Two Chinese reporters broke the story, and Foxconn swiftly brought a legal case against them for defamation, following which they received large fines. However, their case was taken up by Reporters without Borders, an NGO which promotes press freedom. Foxconn Technology, a subsidiary of Hon Hai of Taiwan, has become a major contract manufacturer for electronics companies, also manufacturing Dell computers, Sony Playstations and Amazon Kindle readers. However, Apple is its biggest customer. Foxconn's complex in Shenzhen employs 400,000 people, mostly migrant workers who live in dormitories provided by the company. The complex has been held up as a model of modern Chinese manufacturing prowess. Modern buildings, tree-lined avenues and facilities such as swimming pools for workers give the complex a campus appearance. Although the number of suicides is no higher than in the Chinese population as a whole, working conditions have been seen as a factor in the worrying incidence of suicides, which numbered 12 in the first six months of 2010.

Ma Xiangqian, aged 19, came from a poor village 800 miles to the west of Shenzhen. Like other migrant workers, he would be sending remittances back to his family. He started work for Foxconn in November 2009, on its production lines moulding metal and plastics. After a flare-up with his supervisor, he was put onto cleaning toilets in December. He took his life on 23 January 2010, by jumping from one of the high-rise dormitories. Records showed that he had worked 286 hours in the month before he died, 112 of them overtime, which is three times the legal limit of 36 hours a month. His pay, including overtime payment, was $1 an hour. His case was seen as typical. Among

complaints that emerged after his death were the military-style regime (in which workers were forbidden to speak to one another on the production line, which would result in a deduction from pay), verbal abuse by supervisors, humiliation and excessive overtime. For a large order for a customer, workers were known to work 13 consecutive days, getting sleep on the factory floor between shifts. For young migrant workers, living 8–10 in a dormitory room, there was little time or energy for any activity besides work. One worker reports that she shares a dormitory room with 12 others, with whom she cannot communicate as they all speak different dialects from her own. It is suspected that the company policy is to disperse people from the same province, who might group together to complain or organize a strike.

Foxconn responded quickly to global publicity over its working conditions. It raised pay dramatically, from $132 a month to $294 a month. It draped large nets around its buildings, and brought in trained counsellors to speak to workers. Terry Gou, Foxconn's billionaire chairman, denies that the company runs a sweatshop, in countering allegations similar to those which were targeted at Nike some years ago. Foxconn wishes its customers such as Apple to bear some of the increased labour costs, but such requests are not being favourably received. In a new agreement with Apple, it moved some of its production away from Shenzhen to its factories in north and central China, where labour costs are lower. But new contracts with global brand owners face some tense negotiations.

Industrialization has long been associated with grim factory conditions, as the history of early industrial production in Britain and the US shows. But today's young factory workers in China were mostly born in the 1990s, when their country was already witnessing industrialization and rising prosperity. They are better educated than their forebears, and aspire to a more fulfilling career than a stifling, regimented life which resembles a military regime more than a work environment. A leading academic of China's changing economy, Professor Huang Yasheng, says that China

▶ More online ... Foxconn is at www.foxconn.com
Reporters without Borders' website is at www.rsf.org

needs to find a new economic model based on innovation: 'The problem, though, is that those kinds of companies don't create a lot of opportunities for young, migrant workers' (Barbazoa, 2010). One team leader at Foxconn, who has worked for the company for six years, is leaving to set up a business with his brother – making candles for export.

Sources: Wong, S., Liu, J. and Culpan, T. (2010) 'Why Apple and others are nervous about Foxconn', *Business Week*, 3 June, at www.businessweek.com; Barbazoa, D. (2010) 'After suicides, scrutiny of China's grim factories', *New York Times*, 6 June; *The Economist* (2010) 'Socialist workers', 10 June; *Shenzhen Post* (2010) 'Foxconn suicides', 27 May, at www.szcpost.com; Hille, K. and Kwong, R. (2010) 'Foxconn wants clients to share wages burden', *Financial Times*, 8 June; Hille, K. (2010) 'Foxconn to move some of Apple production', *Financial Times*, 29 June

Along with smartphones and other similar products desired by consumers globally, this e-reader depends on outsourced manufacturing in low-cost countries. But with China's workers demanding better pay and conditions, how will outsourcing evolve?

Source: Istock

Questions for discussion

◆ What further can Foxconn do to improve employee relations?

◆ In what ways is the dependence on young migrant workers becoming unsustainable in China?

◆ To what extent, if any, should Apple, Sony and other brand owners whose products are manufactured by Foxconn be held responsible for the inhumane conditions in the factories?

Introduction

Eight critical themes have featured in the preceding chapters. Here we bring together the threads, forming an overall picture of how each theme is illustrated in different contexts. The links between these themes are also highlighted. The multilayered environment within which businesses operate has become more complex as more countries become active in the global economy. A greater diversity of economies is evident, as the spread of liberal market values, once assumed to be an inevitable component of globalization, has now given way to a more state-guided view of national economies. International risks, ever present in global markets, have taken on an added dimension as state players become active market participants. Both governments and businesses are more conscious of diverse risks facing societies, including the use of scarce resources, climate change and environmental degradation. As we have seen, businesses are sometimes more decisive than governments in confronting global problems, but government action often remains the key to making large-scale changes which can ensure a more sustainable future.

We therefore look forward in the second part of this chapter to the trends and issues which will capture the attention of decision-makers and influence business strategy in the future. In many industries, businesses have become accustomed to global supply chains, delivering both complex products like cars and relatively humble products like clothing and shoes to customers thousands of miles away. Scale economies have resulted in lower prices and greater accessibility for millions of consumers. However, this good news is now shading into uncertainties as workers, consumers and governments look more critically at the processes associated with globalization. National governments in emerging economies see industrialization as the route to economic development, but they now recognize the need to guide industrialization along sustainable principles. Moreover, international attention is falling increasingly on emerging economies, with expectations that they will recognize their responsibilities for acting to combat climate change and depletion of natural resources. Newer players are taking their places at the top tables of bodies such as the IMF and G20, marking a shift away from dominance by the western developed countries and Japan at the global level. Will these new players focus mainly on domestic competitiveness or take a longer view of global economic sustainability? This chapter will provide some clues.

Critical themes in retrospect

Here we look back at each of the critical themes in turn, bringing together discussion from earlier chapters. We begin with the two broadest, the multilayered environment and the multidimensional environment.

Multilayered environment

Layers of the business environment that have featured in this book were introduced in Figure 1.5. They are shown again in Figure 13.1. Every business operates in a local community and has local impacts, even those which see themselves as essentially global. With growing attention being paid to stakeholders, firms now recognize their roles in local communities. A manufacturing, agricultural or mining business employs local people and is involved with other aspects of the community. Compa-

▶ More online ... Microsoft is at www.microsoft.com
Google's investor relations site is http://investor.google.com

nies in other sectors, such as banks, exert more diffuse influences. The financial sector in London became a growth engine not just for London, but for Britain as a whole. The large banks discussed in Chapter 9 saw themselves mainly as global, but when financial crisis struck, they were viewed as national entities, many of which received national government aid. Britain had a light regulatory framework, which attracted financial services firms. Like many businesses featured in this book, location advantages played a big part in their choice of country. Ireland is another example we have featured for its location advantages, but its open economy was exposed to adverse global shocks when the financial crisis struck. For most companies, the legal and political environments are dictated by national legal frameworks. In addition, regional units, such as individual states in the US, impose a further level of law and regulation.

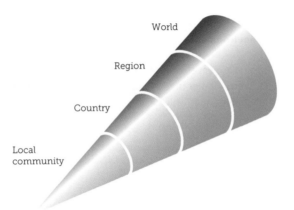

Figure 13.1 **Multiple layers of the business environment**

For an MNE that is widely ramified, multiple layers can give rise to great complexity. Facebook and Google are quintessentially global businesses, but both have encountered regulatory difficulties at national level, for example in privacy and copyright laws. Google has also been the subject of legal action at the regional level, as the EU has accused it of anti-competitive behaviour. Jostling with regulators, which Microsoft has experienced in numerous countries, awaits many global companies. And not just in western economies, which have long had bodies of antitrust law. A revelation to businesspeople everywhere has been the robust stance taken by the Chinese authorities to mergers and acquisitions which they deem to be anti-competitive. Google has also become embroiled with Chinese authorities, not for anti-competitive behaviour, as Google is still not a major player in China, but for compliance with censorship laws. One of its strategies for China has been to utilize the more open environment of Hong Kong, a special administrative region of China, to maintain Chinese operations. This is an example of turning a sub-national tier of authority into an opportunity.

Most companies view legal obligations as bounded by national laws, but the growth of international law, including international labour standards, now impacts on MNEs, especially those which are involved in outsourced manufacturing and other activities in developing countries. Awareness of international standards also affects retailers like Walmart. Walmart is now expanding internationally, bringing it into contact with governmental authorities in new markets, but its raised awareness of international standards stems mainly from stakeholders in the US, who have queried the operations of the company's suppliers in low-cost locations. Doubts also arise because adherence to national law can count for little if national enforcement mechanisms are not robust. The global company in the past became adroit at choosing locations in low-cost countries where regulatory burdens were light. In China, factory workers, most of whom are migrants, are gradually achieving improved wages, better conditions and better terms of employment. A consequence, however, is that China is losing its location advantages in industries which rely mainly on low-cost labour. These improvements for workers happened years ago in the advanced countries, such as the US, but many of these American workers effectively priced themselves out of jobs. The plight of the US automotive sector, featured in Chapter 2, shows all the layers of the environment: the impacts of local factors, such as the trade union environment; the national level, in the form of federal government aid; and the international level, in the globalization of the car industry.

Summary points The multilayered environment

- Multiple legal and regulatory layers can be viewed negatively as adding to the complexity of international business.

- However, diverse national environments contribute to location advantages which MNEs can exploit.

- Perceptions of local communities as stakeholders have become a focus of CSR policies, involving greater interaction with local and national authorities.

Multidimensional environment

The PEST framework (political, economic sociocultural and technological dimensions) was introduced in Chapter 1. It is a tool often used for analysing national environments, although, as we noted there, it does not capture all the relevant dimensions. To make it more complete, the legal dimension can be seen as an aspect of the political, and financial markets can be seen as part of the economic environment. But even with these additions, it does not take in the ecological environment. We have therefore devoted separate chapters to each of these, in recognition of their underlying concepts, an understanding of which is needed by all international managers. However, as the case studies show, in real-life business activities, these different dimensions usually interact with each other. Moreover, the different dimensions such as sociocultural and political, while often viewed as operating at national level, can in fact impact in any of the layers of the environment. Table 13.1 gives some examples.

Business strategists traditionally view economic factors as paramount, including trade and the competitive environment. This view was highlighted in Porter's five forces model (Chapter 5). We would now probably take a broader view of the dimensions, noting, for example, that cultural factors often play an influential role in determining a country's economic activities. Certainly, views about work and status are highly influenced by cultural values, which can have deep roots in a society. A country's political and technological environments, too, are coloured by cultural and social factors. An example highlighted in Chapter 5 is that of South Korea, where high levels of technological achievement, rooted in the scientific orientation in the education system, combine, perhaps paradoxically, with a traditional cultural environment in which family ties remain influential.

▶ More online ... Vale is at www.vale.com
Geely is at www.geely.com

Table 13.1 **Global and national environments**

Dimension	Global environment	National environment
Economic	Global and regional economic integration; globalization of production	National economic systems
Cultural	Media and internet penetration; consumer society and global markets	National and sub-national cultural, including linguistic and religious groupings
Social	International division of labour; international migration	National and sub-national social groupings, for example family and ethnic groups
Political	International and regional political interdependence and integration	National political systems; political parties in pluralist states
Legal	International law and practice (in, for example, human rights and environment); international tribunals	National legal systems, including national legislative processes and national judicial systems
Trade and competitive	Multilateral trade agreements (for example GATT); multilateral organizations (for example WTO); regional trade groupings	National strategic trade policy; bilateral trade agreements
Technological	Global R&D by MNEs and international bodies	National innovation systems
Financial	Global capital markets; international institutions (for example IMF and World Bank)	National financial systems, including banks and other financial institutions
Ecological	Climate change; international regulation	Resource depletion; environmental degradation; national regulation; national energy policies

To Vale of Brazil, an ambitious emerging-market mining company, Inco of Canada, which was rather inward-looking and complacent, seemed like a logical takeover target (Chapter 6). But Vale had not reckoned on the deep-seated culture of the Canadian workforce and its strong support in the local community. A breakdown in relations between the new employers and employees soon turned into a lengthy and bitter strike, in which there seemed to be little common ground on which to rebuild relations. As MNEs from emerging economies expand internationally, take-overs of firms in developed countries by developing country MNEs are becoming more common. Geely's takeover of Volvo is another (Chapter 2). In these cases, the cultural dimension looms large, as there is a potential clash between the more indi-vidualist culture of the acquired firm and the more collectivist culture of the acquirer. Similarly, the technological dimension rises up the agenda in such takeovers, as the target company is likely to have proprietary technology desired by the predator.

Familiar complaints of western firms seeking to do business in China are the weak protections afforded to their interests, including intellectual property, by the legal system, and the intrusive role of political authorities. This situation is probably the opposite of what many would be accustomed to in their home countries, and requires considerable adjustment. The situation also leads to uncertainties, as political and legal obstacles can emerge unpredictably. The upshot is that, despite the economic appeal of emerging markets like China, other aspects of the business environment are crucial, and can make the difference between a good investment and a costly mistake.

▶ More online ... The OECD's guide on sovereign wealth funds is at www.oecd.org

Summary points The multiple dimensions of the business environment

◆ Each of the dimensions of the environment provides insight into how societies and firms function.

◆ For business strategists, a consideration of all the dimensions provides a richer picture than a focus on simply economic factors, for example in choosing a potential market.

Role of the state

The state plays an important role in business in most countries, whether direct or indirect. In all countries, governments formulate macroeconomic policies on which the economy depends. In cultures where individualist freedoms predominate, the state is usually perceived as providing a smooth-functioning regulatory framework in which private enterprises can operate, which ensures that markets operate openly and fairly. This implies that the state is predominantly part of the business *environment*. However, a trend in both developed and developing countries has been for the state to take on greater roles, and in many cases, state-owned companies dominate whole sectors. Nonetheless, perceptions of the state's role in business differ markedly from country to country.

In western countries, the state has taken on an enlarged role in welfare services, a function which has expanded mainly since the Second World War. State-owned companies, which have been common in sectors such as public utilities and tele-communications, have been privatized in successive waves of liberalization, overseen in the EU by the European Commission. The recent financial crisis, which has seen governments taking over ailing companies in the private sector, rather runs against the cultural grain, and these companies, including banks and car companies, have been anxious to return to private-sector control.

In many emerging economies, by contrast, the state has driven economic development, both through state-owned companies and deals with foreign investors. In these countries, governments are typically more authoritarian than democratic, and tend to exert direct controls on markets. They undertake fewer social welfare programmes than governments in western countries (see Chapter 12), and tend not to be burdened with the high levels of public debt that western countries have accumulated. Many of the world's sovereign wealth funds, notably those from China and the Middle East, are active investors in global financial markets. The state player is a growing presence in the global economy, behaving like an 'ordinary' business in many contexts, and often listed on stock exchanges. However, these entities tend to operate through opaque control structures, shadowed by their political owners and masters.

Summary points Business and the state

◆ Governments determine macroeconomic policies, on which national economies depend.

◆ Although the state is conceived as playing an indirect role in regulating the business environment in countries such as the UK and US, governments in practice have taken on greater roles in business life in times of financial crisis.

◆ In many countries, especially emerging markets, the state plays a key role in guiding economic development. MNEs from these countries, often within the ambit of state control, are a growing influence in the global economy.

▶ More online ... Nestlé is at www.nestle.com
P&G is at www.pg.com

> **Critical thinking**
> Living with the state
> In what ways is the growing role of states a beneficial development in international business, and in what ways is it a threat?

Emerging economies

The Brics (Brazil, Russia, India and China) were introduced in Chapter 1, and have featured prominently in other chapters. 'Emerging economies' is rather vague as a category, as we highlighted from the outset. They are generally viewed as the fast-growing developing countries, mainly large countries with potentially large consumer markets. Their growth contrasts markedly with the rather lacklustre growth prospects in established western markets and Japan. India's growing industrial production, shown in Figure 13.2, is an example. With the exception of 2008, in the depth of the global financial crisis, India has achieved double-digit growth, showing strong rebound from the crisis. For these reasons, MNEs from all over the world are drawn to emerging economies, for both market and production opportunities. Many companies featured in the case studies of preceding chapters now target these countries for future growth. They include Nestlé (Chapter 2), Nokia (Chapter 2) and P&G (Chapter 4).

Figure 13.2 **Growth in India's industrial production**
Percentage change from the previous year. For 2005–9, the figure for September is given as an indicator; for 2010, the figure for May is given.

Source: Central Statistical Organization of India (2010), cited in Goyal, K. (2010) 'Industrial production for May; June wholesale-price data: India week ahead', 11 July, Bloomberg news at www.bloomberg.com

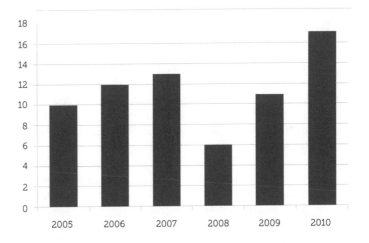

These economies have become both drivers and beneficiaries of globalization. China and India enjoy location advantages that have attracted FDI, although India has opened its doors to foreign investors much more cautiously than China did. On the other hand, emerging markets, and even the four Brics, are highly diverse. Brazil and India are democracies, with strong state guidance. China and Russia are governed by authoritarian rulers. Russia, often considered out of place with the other three, has suffered from slow growth, and, moreover, is classified by the UN as industrialized rather than developing. Arguably, Mexico, South Korea or Indonesia would have been more appropriate to highlight, but none of these is as potentially large a market as Russia.

Although the Brics do not represent a single development model, the recognition they now attract is highlighting their importance in the global economy. Other countries now clamour for similar recognition, South Africa among them. Recall that the

CEO of Zegna (Chapter 1) said it makes little sense to talk of China as emerging: it has already emerged. China remains a large market with growth potential, but he is now looking at newer emerging markets in Africa and the Middle East. Emerging economies grab our attention because they are the source of most of the future growth in the global economy, and their growing middle classes are fast catching up with consumer societies in the more developed regions of the world. MNEs from emerging economies are also branching out, investing and acquiring businesses around the world. Some we have featured that are not from Bric countries are SAB Miller of South Africa (Chapter 7) and Cemex of Mexico (Chapter 1).

Summary points The growing category of emerging economies

- Emerging economies are becoming global forces largely because they are fast-growing markets and their MNEs are rapidly expanding throughout the world.

- Emerging economies are diverse economically and politically, but in most cases strong state guidance of the economy is a characteristic.

- Besides the Brics, growing economies in Latin America, Asia and Africa are also considered emerging economies.

Changing societies

The most prominent changes occurring in societies in today's world are coming about because of economic development, in particular, industrialization. We like to think that these changes are for the good, bringing people more secure jobs, better health, longer life, better education and a healthier environment. However, as we have seen, industrialization connected with globalization benefits the sectors like manufacturing which are linked in global supply chains. Other sectors and their workers can fall behind, creating widening inequalities within societies. Poor working conditions in China's factories, shown in the opening case study of this chapter, indicate changing attitudes towards factory employment based on migrant labour. Issues of inequalities can occur just about anywhere. The passage of health-care legislation in the US brought the prospect of health insurance for the more than 43 million Americans who have lacked medical coverage. Astronomical executive salaries in the US can be contrasted with the precarious position of low-paid and unemployed people (Chapter 12). The number of people living in extreme poverty has diminished in China, but inequality is widening, and labour disputes are becoming common.

Urbanization is associated with industrialization, as evidenced by the rapid urbanization in emerging economies. China is rapidly increasing its urban housing stock. In theory, providing essential services and infrastructure for urban dwellers should be more efficient and sustainable than for rural inhabitants in scattered villages. However, much urbanization in developing countries is taking place as a result of exodus from the countryside, where people's livelihoods have become precarious, often due to drought or other impacts of climate change. For people living in slums and searching for work, life can be a continuous struggle. In its *Millennium Development Goals Report* of 2010, the UN found mixed progress in improving the conditions for urban populations (United Nations, 2010). The proportion of urban residents living in slums has fallen globally, from nearly 50% in 1990 to 33% in 2010, but the number of slum dwellers has gone up, from 657 million in 1990 to 828 million in 2010.

▸ More online ... Millennium Development Goals are at www.un.org/millenniumgoals/

Poor urban living conditions are worst in sub-Saharan Africa, and also in countries emerging from conflict (see Figure 13.3). The rise in slum dwellers in Western Asia is accounted for largely by Iraq. Here, 2.9 million people (17% of urban inhabitants) lived in slums in 2000, but following years of war, the number had risen to 10.7 million (53%) in 2010 (United Nations, 2010). Developing countries in Africa, which are experiencing high population growth, are looking to economic growth and job creation to emulate the success of the large emerging economies. Yet India, one of globalization's success stories, is still plagued by high levels of poverty, both urban and rural.

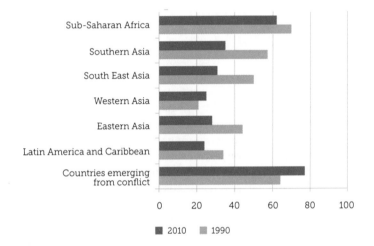

Figure 13.3 **Percentage of urban populations living in slums**

Source: United Nations (2010) *Millennium Development Goals Report 2010* (New York: UN)

Rural India seems a long way from the newly affluent middle classes in China's cities, enjoying new cars and foreign holidays in unprecedented numbers. China's rulers can point with pride to the fruits of economic development, but it has come at a cost. Chinese demand for energy, raw materials and food is a major factor in global markets, but environmental degradation and depletion of natural resources are becoming concerns for these educated classes. China's rulers see continued economic prosperity as the best guarantee of social stability, but, given the unevenness of that prosperity, local unrest is a continuing threat. We have asked to what extent Chinese people are content with the absence of democratic voice in their political system. Like most large countries, China is highly diverse culturally; separate languages and sense of identity denote different peoples, such as Tibetans, who have their own sense of nationhood. The notion of positive liberty (referred to in Chapter 12), which sees liberty as the right of a people to be free from the perceived oppression by outside rulers, is perhaps stronger in many places than the desire of individual citizens for a say at the ballot box.

Summary points **Changing societies**

◆ Industrialization and urbanization account for many of the changes taking place in societies, especially notable in developing and emerging economies.

◆ Growing middle classes in emerging markets seek all the trappings of consumer societies long taken for granted in western countries, such as new cars and foreign travel.

◆ Environmental degradation and depletion of resources suggest that the continued growth in consumer lifestyles could be unsustainable in the long term.

◆ China's uneven development and centralized authoritarian rule could yet prove an unstable mixture, as there are many disaffected groups, especially in China's diverse regions.

▸ More online ... BHP Billiton is at www.bhpbilliton.com
Cargill is at www.cargill.com

Critical thinking

Freedom to do what?

Western individualist cultures tend to see economic and political freedoms linked together, whereas in China, economic reforms have progressed markedly while the political system remains closed. China's leaders are banking on increasing prosperity to maintain their political hold. They can point to the fact that in western democracies, disillusionment with political leaders is common, evidenced by low turnout of voters in elections. To what extent might they have a valid point?

Globalization of industries

Globalization has been an overriding theme in a number of industries featured in this book, for example the car industry (Chapter 2) and the pharmaceutical industry (Chapters 3 and 10). In these cases, location advantages and scale economies have played a part. Both these industries have seen consolidation, resulting in the absorption of smaller companies by larger ones, which become even bigger. However, size and global reach do not guarantee success. Profits have been squeezed in both industries, and in the growing markets in emerging economies, there are intense competitive pressures. National authorities have strengthened regulatory frameworks in the pharmaceutical industry, largely in response to consumer safety issues. In the car industry, too, safety and quality issues have become a concern. Weak links can emerge in global supply chains, and companies such as Toyota, which built reputations on safety, have found it difficult to maintain quality systems when manufacturing takes place in diverse national environments. Hence, the success of large companies in globalized industries often depends on local factors. Does this suggest a backlash against globalization?

For MNEs, globalization has always rested on making the best use of specific locations for particular purposes. We saw that computing and pharmaceutical companies gravitated to Ireland for this reason – and many left when these advantages disappeared. Far from bringing about homogeneity, globalization has starkly revealed local differences. In global financial markets (Chapter 9), countries that opened their doors to short-term investors and derivatives markets were left exposed when these markets collapsed, whereas countries with more insular banking systems were not as affected. Having been rescued by the government in some cases, banks now face heavier regulation and are being encouraged to revert to a more traditional home-country-oriented banking model. Is this a sign of 'de-globalization', or withdrawal from global markets? Having been stung by excessive risk-taking, banks are being reminded by regulators to behave more cautiously, which implies fewer foreign adventures financed by borrowing.

We have also seen how consolidation in the mining industry has resulted in a few global players, but, in this situation, too, national governments can still stand in the way of corporate strategists. Recall the example of BHP Billiton (Chapter 4). A similar example, this time in agribusiness, is Cargill (Chapter 12), whose exit from palm oil plantations in Papua New Guinea was associated with legal obstacles in its path. Food production and trade in commodities have become global in scope. Yet, governments vie with markets in securing supplies for national needs. Globalization of food production has led to greater interdependence among countries. One of globalization's trademark characteristics, interdependence, does not spell a diminution of national or corporate forces, but a realization that self-sufficiency is not a sustainable option.

Summary points Globalization of industries

◆ Extended supply chains have exemplified globalization, benefiting from lowering of costs and scale economies.

◆ The risks associated with supply chains, including quality and safety, reveal that diverse national environments have led MNEs to re-examine how best to serve national markets.

◆ Globalized industries have seen considerable consolidation, resulting in a few powerful players. Although appearing to dwarf governments, they are still subject to national regulatory environments, which in some cases are becoming more stringent.

International risks

All businesses take risks to some extent, simply in the process of providing goods and services for customers. There is a constantly changing array of risks in the international environment, to which firms must adapt if they wish to operate internationally. Furthermore, firms that confine their activities to their home markets are not immune from international risks, for example, if they sell imported goods. As we have seen, just as success can create momentum across national boundaries, crises can also spread from country to country. No firm has a complete picture of all the relevant factors in every location, but understanding the dimensions of the environment in different national settings goes a long way towards building a sustainable global strategy.

Numerous types of environmental risks have been highlighted in these chapters. The major ones are shown in Table 13.2. Volatility in global financial markets has been one of the most frequently mentioned, but there are many others. Cultural and social risks often arise when a company acquires a foreign firm based in a country with a radically different cultural environment (Chapters 2 and 6). The technological environment is constantly changing. Today's winning product can be rapidly superseded by technological innovation, making it obsolete in a short

Table 13.2 **International risks for business**

Dimension	International risks
Economic	Price volatility in markets; economic downturn
Cultural	Cultural differences in diverse international locations
Social	Ethnic divisions; labour unrest in diverse locations
Political	Changes of government policies; greater control exerted by governments over private-sector companies; political instability
Legal	Changes in regulatory frameworks; weak rule of law in many locations
Trade and competitive	Rises in tariff and non-tariff trade barriers
Technological	New technologies which can alter an entire sector
Financial	Volatility in global markets, such as foreign exchange; financial crisis, such as a banking collapse, which can spread from country to country
Ecological	Climate change; depletion of natural resources

Oil spill in the Gulf of Mexico sparks a rethink of regulation in the oil industry

The Deepwater Horizon, an oil rig operated by BP in the Gulf of Mexico, 40 miles from the Louisiana coastline, exploded in April 2010, causing the deaths of 11 of the rig's crew of 126, and leading to an apparently out-of-control flow of oil from the sea bed. Gushing about 5,000 barrels of oil a day, the flow from the Macondo well posed threats to the environment, to livelihoods of those living in the states bordering the Gulf and to the livelihoods of people in the oil industry generally, who depend on continuing exploration and development of offshore oil reserves. Various types of equipment and techniques can be used to contain a blowout, but the task proved much more difficult in deepwater operations than in shallow oilfields. Deepwater drilling, although complex, has been viewed as a viable strategy in a world of shrinking oil reserves, but the Deepwater Horizon accident reopened the debate about its benefits and risks.

BP had a record of recent accidents which have been attributed to a weak safety culture. A fire at the Texas City refinery in 2005, which killed 15 workers, and an oil spill in 2006 from an Alaskan pipeline, formed a backdrop for the Deepwater Horizon accident. This poor safety record contributed in part to the public anger towards BP which erupted in the US. The US government stepped in to take charge of cleanup operations.

Appointing a retired Coast Guard Admiral to oversee operations, President Obama was keenly aware of criticism levelled at the federal government under his predecessor, President George W. Bush, following Hurricane Katrina in 2005, when the response seemed to be slow and uncoordinated. BP set aside money for payments for cleanup and damages, expected to run into billions. Its share price tumbled, and it has embarked on selling non-core assets in various locations to help fund the liabilities.

It took BP three months to cap the gushing well, during which time it drilled relief wells while trying various means of capping the main well. The extent of BP's legal liability for the disaster will be the subject of much litigation. It was the major shareholder in the consortium leasing the rig, the other two owners being Anadarko of the US (25%) and Mitsui of Japan (10%). The owner of the rig was Transocean, a Swiss company, and many of the workers on the site were Transocean employees. As in most complex negligence cases, questions of faulty equipment as well as how it is used

Rocked by an explosion at the Deepwater Horizon oil rig, BP and other oil companies are looking to improve their safety measures, under the more watchful eyes of regulators

Source: Press Association

come into play. A number of equipment manufacturers and service providers were involved. It is likely that liability will be shared among all these parties. Then, there is the question of whether inspection and regulatory frameworks were robust enough.

Although drilling in the Gulf of Mexico was widely believed to have a good safety record, federal records reveal a series of leaks, some of which were more serious than official statistics show (Mufson, 2010). The regulatory agency for deepwater drilling, the Minerals Management Service (MMS), has 60 inspectors to examine 4,000 facilities. The number of inspectors was

▶ More online ... BP is at www.bp.com
Transocean is at www.deepwater.com
Petrobras is at www.petrobras.com.br

55 in 1985, when there were just 65 deepwater wells. In 2009, there were 602. Over that period, oil production increased 3,000%. Apart from a dearth of inspectors, the MMS seemed to lack sufficiently precise guidelines to carry out inspections adequately (Kirchgaessner, 2010). The resulting lax regulation is held at least partly responsible for the disaster. A factor in the regulatory climate before the disaster was the strong influence of the American Petroleum Institute (API), an industry body which lobbies vigorously for growth in deepwater drilling.

The Gulf accounts for 30% of America's oil supply and 11% of its natural gas. Following the disaster, the government declared a six-month moratorium on further deepwater exploration in the Gulf of Mexico. This move was unwelcome news to the oil industry, and prompted other countries involved in deepwater oil exploration to re-examine their policies, but none followed the US in imposing a moratorium. They included Australia, Greenland, Norway, Canada, Libya, China, Brazil and Angola. Australia experienced an oil spill a few months before the Deepwater disaster, but its resources minister said, 'Shutting down the industry and putting the economy at risk does nothing to ensure safe oil exploration' (Hoyos et al., 2010).

Brazil and China are both active in deepwater oil exploration. Brazil's reserves are in waters which are deeper and more dangerous than those of the Gulf of Mexico. Its regulator is re-examining its rules, but they are generally seen as tougher than those of the MMS to begin with. Brazil is relying largely on its state-controlled oil company, Petrobras, which keeps its engineering expertise in-house, rather than rely on a multiplicity of service companies, as was the case with BP. Brazil feels it is thus better organized to mount an emergency operation more quickly than happened in the US. The Chinese state petroleum company CNOOC ordered checks on all its rigs after the Macondo disaster, but was not planning on scaling back its activities, which it feels have great potential for providing up to a quarter of China's demand for oil in the future. Royal Dutch Shell has also reviewed the safety of its operations in Nigeria. It already faces criticism from environmental groups in Nigeria, where oil spills are a common occurrence. The company is braced for more stringent controls, but the major

problems in the Nigerian environment have been oil theft and ethnic conflict.

At the time of the Deepwater disaster, a climate change bill was being considered by the US Congress, which would have introduced caps on carbon emissions. However, support for the bill was built on a fragile coalition of interests, which included legislators willing to go along with it only if more offshore drilling was contemplated. With the six-month moratorium in place, and question marks over future offshore drilling, the fragile consensus fell apart in July 2010. Instead, the energy bill focused on raising the legal limit on a company's liability for economic damage caused by an oil spill, from the current $75 million, to $10 billion. The climate change bill's supporters urge that in the long term, the country should be shifting to cleaner fuels, reducing reliance on extracting oil from highly dangerous deepwater fields near its shores, where human populations and wildlife are at risk.

Sources: Hoyos, C., Crooks, E. and McNulty, S. (2010) 'Oil companies resigned to tougher US rules on drilling', *Financial Times*, 22 July; Kirchgaessner, S. (2010) 'Regulator's inquiry into spill draws criticism', *Financial Times*, 18 June; Hook, L. (2010) 'China to step up exploring in deep water', *Financial Times*, 18 June; Stillman, A. (2010) 'Realism over risks replaces euphoria in Brazil's fledgling deep-sea industry, *Financial Times*, 20 July; *The Economist* (2010a) 'Deep trouble', 8 May; *The Economist* (2010b) 'Black storm rising', 8 May; Mufson, S. (2010) 'Federal records show a steady stream of oil spills in gulf since 1964', *The Washington Post*, 24 July

Questions for discussion

◆ What is the case for deepwater oil exploration, and are the risks justified?

◆ To what extent has BP suffered reputational damage, particularly in light of its previous poor safety record?

◆ How does regulation differ between countries where the oil industry is state-controlled and those where it is not?

space of time (Chapters 1 and 10). Risks often come intertwined with opportunities. Case studies on innovation in renewable energy sectors include Applied Materials in Chapter 10 and BYD batteries in Chapter 11. Risks such as global pandemics are a concern to governments, which look to the pharmaceutical industry to supply vaccines and medicines.

All markets, including commodities, energy and foreign exchange, experience ups and downs. Stock exchanges, too, can fluctuate dramatically. A firm can find the value of its traded shares drops suddenly, often because of external factors unconnected with the firm itself. Natural disasters and accidents can raise the risk profile throughout a sector. The explosion of the BP-leased oil rig in the deep waters of the Gulf of Mexico raised doubts about deep-sea drilling generally (as shown in the preceding case study). As a result, governments are looking more carefully at such operations, and stricter safety requirements could ensue.

The financial crisis of 2008 also led to government action to prevent future financial shocks and stabilize global markets. While such steps are conceived as preventive measures that discourage companies from engaging in excessive risk, government action is itself a kind of risk, which firms must increasingly take into account. In countries rich in natural resources and energy, MNEs are accustomed to negotiating exploration deals with governments, and have also become accustomed to subsequent political leaders wishing to change the terms. Many oil-rich countries present such risks. Iraq is one that was highlighted in a case study (Chapter 11).

Businesses and governments contend with the risks raised by scarce resources. Apart from energy needs, food security is an urgent concern. Growing populations in much of the developing world are putting pressures on food and water supplies, already under strain. Scientists project that food and energy production will need to increase by 50% over the next two decades to meet the needs of the additional 1.5 billion people living on the planet. We have discussed the risks of global warming associated with climate change, which are expected to impact severely in some of the poorest and most vulnerable countries. As we have seen, countries can rely on markets to meet essential needs, but a disaster such as widespread drought, which can send up global prices, is a major risk. Some countries therefore seek to secure supplies through intergovernmental deals, but these arrangements reduce the amounts traded in markets, pushing prices up further. A diminished faith in markets is understandable, especially following the crashes which have occurred in financial markets. But the spectre of protectionism and a retreat from free trade also carry risks that the weakest and most vulnerable countries will be disadvantaged.

Summary points International risks

- Markets of all descriptions, from commodities to finance, carry risks of volatility.
- MNEs operating in diverse cultures often face challenges in understanding and adapting to local differences.

- Technological innovations can spring up anywhere in the world, superseding existing technology in a short space of time.
- Government actions, often designed to shield populations from international risks, create risks for

firms doing business in a country. An example is more stringent regulatory requirements.

- The natural environment presents numerous risks, including depletion of resources and the impacts of climate change.

CSR and sustainability

Ethics and CSR are the focus of the preceding chapter, but they have featured throughout this book, as businesses encounter CSR issues in multifarious situations. Some are set out in the table below.

Table 13.3 **CSR and sustainability issues in dimensions of the environment**

Dimension	CSR implications
Economic	Economic efficiencies can conflict with sustainability principles
Cultural	Respect for local cultures; ethical practices in differing cultural environments
Social	Managing diversity in multi-ethnic societies; sensitivity in handling labour relations; treating workers in outsourced operations as stakeholders
Political	Corporate stance against bribery and corrupt practices; transparent dealings with political authorities
Legal	Adherence to national legal obligations; adherence to international labour standards
Trade and competitive	Stance against trading with oppressive regimes, such as Burma
Technological	Respect for IP rights, including patents and copyright
Financial	Transparency and compliance with tax laws in every location; compliance with sound corporate governance practices
Ecological	Promoting sustainable business models through reducing emissions and seeking to reduce dependence on scarce resources

FDI and outsourced manufacturing have lowered costs of many manufactured products, but strategies based on low wages in low-cost countries raise issues of ethics and CSR, as we saw in Chapter 12. Perceptions of poor working conditions, weak health and safety protection and breaches of human rights have troubled western MNEs, many of whom now issue guidelines for suppliers and publish reports on CSR performance. Nonetheless, delving beneath the surface, as we did in the case of Walmart, we found that practices fall short of lofty principles. Moreover, MNEs tend to see national laws, rather than international standards, as their benchmark for labour standards.

In many countries, practices such as bribery and child labour are tolerated, posing dilemmas for foreign investors. MNEs typically take a strong stance against these practices in theory, but are unable to control them in practice in many cases, especially where outside contractors and affiliate companies are operating relatively independently. Government censorship poses a dilemma for internet companies in many countries. An option is to exit the country, but, as Google found (Chapter 8), the prospect of exiting a large potential market makes little economic sense. Google suffered damage to its ethical reputation in the period when it complied with government censors. Its belated stance against the Chinese government was only partial, as it carried on operations in Hong Kong with a view to garnering mainland business.

In extreme cases, oppressive governments can be subject to sanctions from other countries. Burma's military dictators are subjected to sanctions by the US and EU. MNEs are wise to pull out or not to become involved. However, China, India, Singapore and Thailand all trade with Burma. Burma's natural resources, including oil and

▸ More online ... The Democratic Voice of Burma is at www.dvb.no
Chevron's position on Burma is explained on its website at www.chevron.com/globalissues/humanrights/myanmar

gas, are prized by foreign investors and generate large sums for Burma's military rulers. US oil giant Chevron still has operations in Burma, despite sanctions. India is eyeing Burmese locations for hydro projects that could generate electricity for Indian use, having encountered obstacles to such projects at home from domestic environmental and human rights groups (Wade, 2010). Burma's military leader was welcomed in an official visit to India in 2010, indicating the desire of the Indian government to strengthen ties, although the visit was condemned by human rights groups. China has made it a feature of its involvement in Africa that it does not take a critical approach to countries' political leadership.

China and India are both highlighted as leading sources of the growth in emissions of greenhouse gases (Chapter 11). Their governments are prioritizing economic growth; issues of sustainability, while acknowledged, are seen as subsidiary in practice. State-controlled companies and family companies with strong political ties are at the forefront of economic development in many emerging economies. Their governance and stakeholder perceptions are influenced by their ownership structures, often marked by closed management structures and little sense of accountability to a wider range of stakeholders.

Summary points   CSR and sustainability

◆ These issues arise in all facets of the business environment, as well as in the ways a company views its business purposes.
◆ Sociocultural and legal environments give rise to issues such as labour standards, bribery and human rights.
◆ Issues of sustainability arise in connection with a firm's environmental footprint.
◆ Companies that do business in countries ruled by military dictators or other authoritarian leaders risk suffering reputational damage.

Looking forward

Changes associated with globalization have been highlighted in the preceding review of each of the critical themes. Also prominent has been the role of national governments. In this section, we look at the changing balance between global and national forces, and their impacts on international business.

The changing configuration of globalization

Global strategies are being re-examined around the world, as companies weigh the risks of far-flung supply chains. Locating production near markets has been an outcome of this more cautious approach, often focusing on 'nearshoring' strategies to serve large markets. An example is locating manufacturing in Mexico to serve the US market. Similarly, western European markets are served by manufacturing in eastern European countries. For MNEs, knowing what to keep in-house and what to source from others, whether through external contracts or partnerships, has become an aspect of future strategies for global markets. Companies have rethought core competencies and the advantages of keeping key activities in-house. For some, the risks of leakage of intellectual property in joint venture and other strategic alliances is a continuing problem. For others, there are risks that supply-chain partners are

▸ More online ... Toyota is at www.toyota.com

unsound financially or struggle to maintain the right levels of quality. On the other hand, over-centralization carries risks for companies with global reach. Many pharmaceutical companies, despite long histories of keeping R&D in-house, are now relying on external sources for new ideas and investing in R&D in dispersed locations.

Quality problems forced Toyota to recall 8.5 million vehicles worldwide, causing the company to rethink its global strategy. The company has traditionally centralized its control at its headquarters in Japan, placing Japanese heads in charge of local factories worldwide. However, this rather cumbersome process has resulted in poor communications with local managers, which are partly to blame for lapses in quality. The company has now placed local managers in charge of many factories: 12 out of its 14 factories in the US now have non-Japanese bosses in place. The company has instituted a global quality committee, also with several non-Japanese members, to oversee global quality issues. However, Toyota as a company remains resolutely Japanese in its identity. All 38 members of its board are Japanese.

One of the recurring themes of this book is the shift in focus by MNEs away from established markets to emerging markets as the sources of future growth. Most of these markets are in fact low-cost economies. Western MNEs that set up export-oriented FDI in China for serving western markets are now shifting focus, looking to manufacture in China for the Chinese market. This can pose major challenges. Competition in China is generally based on price, to which domestic companies have astutely adapted, with products designed for Chinese domestic markets. Western brand owners find it difficult to compete on price, and western brands do not necessarily carry the same allure as they would in home markets. Moreover, as we have found, China has thriving businesses in items such as fake iPhones. Car manufacturers also anguish over the possible misuse of trademarks and other intellectual property. Western MNEs entering emerging markets must be prepared for a long journey in gaining market share, with risks along the way, as we found in the previous section.

Designing the right product for a new market is the challenge now gripping MNEs which are targeting African countries as the new emerging economies. Here, local competitors are also present, and price pressures are paramount, but consumer markets are less developed, and much retailing still takes place in informal settings. Western MNEs will find few of the new shopping malls that greet them in China, but here, too, the number of middle-class consumers is gradually increasing. Sourcing and manufacturing locally in these countries helps to keep down costs, and also helps the MNE to pursue a more viable CSR strategy, by employing local people and taking an active interest in the local environment.

At the new frontiers of globalization, weak institutional environments and large informal sectors in local economies create challenges for MNEs, but also offer opportunities, which can benefit both investors and local communities if managed sustainably.

Summary points **Changing globalization**

◆ Extended supply chains have led companies to re-examine global strategies, identifying core competencies.
◆ Decisions on what activities to keep in-house and what

to outsource are indicative of changing global strategies.
◆ MNEs are now focusing growth prospects on emerging markets, where middle classes are growing in spending power.

◆ New markets, especially those which are characterized by diverse cultures and weak institutional frameworks, pose challenges as well as opportunities for MNEs.

Critical thinking

De-globalization?

To what extent are changes taking place simply a retreat from globalization, which would more accurately be termed 'de-globalization'?

New challenges for national governments

When times are good and populations are enjoying growing prosperity, governments tend to bask in the mood of optimism, garnering plaudits from the general public for their policies. But when economies suffer downturns, public opinion tends to blame political leaders and governments. In truth, in today's global economy, in which national economies are interdependent, governments are seldom the chief architects of economic growth, nor the only culprits in economic downturn. Nonetheless, people look to governments to provide the foundations of both economic and social well-being. The main demands are shown in Figure 13.4.

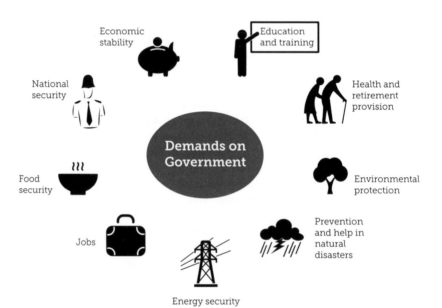

Figure 13.4 **Old and new demands on national governments**

There are now more demands on governments than ever before, as Figure 13.4 shows. Some are long recognized, such as the armed forces, which are responsible both for internal security and defence against external aggressors. Social provisions such as education of the young are also long established, but the figure also points to training, which can be needed at any time in a person's life, to learn vital new skills. Governments are now seen as taking some responsibility for these more vocational needs, traditionally viewed as the responsibility of businesses and individuals. Economic stability is highlighted, usually implying prudent monetary policies. However, active intervention to prop up failing firms is now accepted as necessary to maintain public confidence, and such measures have been resorted to in the most market-oriented economies. Health and retirement provision, such as pensions, are considered governmental responsibilities in some countries, especially those in western Europe, whereas in the US, businesses have traditionally shouldered much of the burden. The passage of universal healthcare legislation in the US signifies a shift towards government leadership in the area of individual healthcare, although financed through insurance schemes rather than a national health service, as exists in Western Europe.

In both developed and developing countries, food security is a priority. It includes protecting farmers' livelihoods, often through subsidies. Similarly, energy security is a preoccupation of governments. The rise of China, which is the source of growing demand for food and energy resources, has alerted other governments to the worrying possibilities of global shortages, to which some are responding with direct protectionist measures, including securing supplies through futures contracts. The growing risks from climate change have also heightened perceptions of food and water security. These newly recognized risks are associated with environmental protection in general. Extreme weather events and natural disasters can threaten not just homes and infrastructure, but a country's ability to grow food and produce energy. Governments face dilemmas of funding. For example, building flood defences costs huge sums in public money, and the risk of a flood disaster might be once in 50 or 100 years. By contrast, spending money on hospitals brings immediate and enduring benefits.

Another vexing demand on public money shown in Figure 13.4 is jobs, once thought to be the responsibility of individuals and businesses. However, in the era of globalization, the loss of a key factory in a community, resulting in large-scale job losses, is viewed as at least partly the responsibility of government. In many cases, governments have made incentive payments and other financial accommodation to foreign investors to attract employers in the first place. Although harsh in its effects, their departure to more advantageous locations in subsequent years is not unpredictable. Governments come under pressure to make payments to unemployed people. A new and worrying phenomenon (Chapter 12) is the growing number of long-term unemployed people. As noted above, retraining in new skills is now perceived to be a task of governments, especially for people whose jobs have migrated to other locations.

Summary points New challenges for governments

- Meeting aspirations for economic prosperity and social well-being has increasingly come to be expected of national governments.

- Securing strategic needs, such as food and energy, is often now viewed as a matter for government, too important to be left to private-sector firms.

- Job creation and training for new jobs, once seen as best provided by market forces, are now also viewed as a responsibility of government.

The shifting global balance of power

Globalization has often been depicted as spreading the values and workings of market economies around the world. However, as we have seen, although market mechanisms have sprung up in unlikely places, such as communist one-party states, the liberal, individualist values associated with market economies are noticeably absent. The growing economic power of emerging markets contrasts markedly with the rather stuttering economic growth in the developed world. Emerging countries are taking their place in the G20 and other forums (discussed in Chapter 4), where they now exert greater international political influence. However, it would be unwise simply to contrast their rise with the diminishing global influence of the established western powers and Japan.

China's economic growth has, in large measure, been facilitated by consumer spending in the advanced economies, particularly the US. But much of the consumer spending in the US has been funded by debt, which abruptly dried up with the financial crisis of 2008. China's growth model has been export-oriented, allowing it to build up huge trade surpluses. The US trade deficit with China amounted $42.3 billion in 2010. China is also the largest holder of US government bonds, its status as an important creditor further enhancing its global role. The flood of imports from China has benefited retailers like Walmart, but it can be seen as weakening job creation in the US, leading to lower income growth, which can weaken the US economy. In its own exports, the US excels in high-technology goods and services, such as aircraft, but it has not been very adept at high-volume exports of goods desired by consumers the world over. Only 4% of all American firms, and 14% of American manufacturers export anything at all. Eighty per cent of America's trade is conducted by just 1% of its firms (*The Economist*, 2010c). The US is seeking to increase its exports as a means of rebalancing its economy away from one of consumption and debt. It is hoping that it can sell more to the large emerging economies, which are gradually increasing their consumption. A rebalancing of the global economy would see greater consumption in emerging markets, benefiting exporters in countries like the US. An increase in exports, facilitated by a weak dollar, would be a significant contributor to its economic recovery. Growth in domestic demand is taking place in China, as Chinese consumers' spending power has accelerated. Japanese companies have been alert to this shift. Just as wage rises started to make China less attractive as a manufacturing location, the growing consumer market caught the attention of Japanese MNEs. China is now Japan's largest trading partner, absorbing 25% of Japanese exports.

Despite its brighter export prospects, the Japanese economy is still in the doldrums, and the government is nursing a huge budget deficit of nearly 8% of GDP. Germany remains an export leader, second only to China, but its economy, too, has struggled to control public spending and rein in budget deficits. Indeed, economic stimulus measures have seen increases in public spending, which the government, like others in the EU, hopes will boost economic growth. These countries, too, are looking to emerging markets for growth, as their domestic consumption remained lacklustre in the years following the financial crisis, largely because people were fearful for jobs.

Will emerging markets, with their new economic power, become the new powerhouses of globalization? It is worth remembering that all the Brics adopt some form of what might be called 'state capitalism'. China's rapid growth, often said to be based on a 'China model' that combines market mechanisms with authoritarian government, is sometimes pointed to as exemplifying a surer model of economic development than traditional capitalism, which other developing countries might emulate. Brazil and India, both democracies, have economic systems with strong socialist tendencies, which their governments see as central to their development models. Indeed, their leaders see their more statist models as having protected them from the worst effects of the economic crisis which afflicted the more liberal market economies. China's leaders are reluctant to boost domestic consumption through opening the economy to imports which compete with domestic producers. Import it does, as we have seen, absorbing raw materials and fuel, which are needed to generate growth. However, western business and political leaders see their own economies' prosperity dependent on emerging markets' importing more of the goods and services which they produce.

For the large emerging economies, as for the earlier industrializing economies, growing domestic companies are eager to do business in both their growing domestic markets and in exports. China's exports are moving up the value chain, to high-technology sectors in which they are building competitive advantage. Will they find markets in the world's older developed economies or mainly in other emerging economies? In order to sustain economic growth, the new powerhouses in emerging economies need markets in the developed world as much as they need growing domestic consumption. Globalization's lesson is that recognizing the interdependence of national economies is the most sustainable path towards prosperity for each of them.

Summary points Shifting balance of power

- Emerging economies are growing in global influence as their economies gain ground competitively.

- Many emerging economies are notable for state capitalism rather than market-oriented economic systems, leading to a tension between differing views of the state in society.

- Globalization has resulted in greater interdependence among businesses and governments. Economic diversity among both new and old national players is leading to a reformulation of state–market relations, as well as a rebalancing among national economic forces.

Critical thinking

Nationalism on the rise?

In a more interconnected world, there is obvious benefit in co-operation among sovereign states, but nationalism could be on the rise, as growing nations flex their muscles internationally. What are the risks of increased nationalism in today's world?

Conclusions

1 Layers of the global environment are becoming more complex, not diminishing, as national legal and political authorities become increasingly important.
2 Changes constantly take place in the differing dimensions of the environment; some changes, such as globalization of finance, happening more quickly than others.
3 The state is taking on a greater role in both developed and developing economies.
4 Emerging economies are the focus of attention for many MNEs because of their growth prospects and potentially large markets.
5 Industrialization and urbanization are bringing about the most dramatic changes in societies. While these processes improve well-being for many, they bring challenges for governments in terms of services and the environment.
6 Globalization has tended to reduce the number of global players in some industries, such as pharmaceuticals. In manufacturing, the use of global supply chains is associated with globalized production, built on location advantages in diverse regions.
7 There are risks in every dimension of the international environment, often heightened because of ripple effects in industries in which inter-firm ties and networks are prevalent.
8 CSR and sustainability issues are now perceived as relevant in every dimension of the business environment. However, perceptions of stakeholders and social responsibility differ from company to company, depending partly on the cultural environment of a firm's home country.
9 Looking forward, MNEs are now examining the risks of globalized production more critically, especially in the context of CSR issues.
10 National governments face challenges in meeting public expectations for societal and environmental well-being. While no country wishes to risk jeopardizing economic growth for environmental objectives, such as reducing emissions, the fast-growing economies are facing tough choices.
11 Emerging economies now see themselves as stepping into the limelight in international decision-making, but national goals, rather than international concerns, still loom large in the minds of political leaders.

Review questions

1 Which layers of the international business environment are the most important for a firm hoping to enter a new market?
2 Which dimension of the business environment is likely to cause the greatest challenges for a firm entering a joint venture with a foreign partner?
3 In what ways are the political and legal environments intertwined?
4 In what ways are developing economies carving out a bigger role for the state in economic development?
5 What role is envisaged for the state in market economies? How is this changing?
6 What aspects of emerging economies' business climate pose challenges for foreign MNEs?
7 What are the positive aspects of industrialization, and what are the negative aspects?
8 In which regions of the world is urbanization posing the sternest challenges, and why?
9 What aspects of global supply chains pose risks for businesses, and how can these be mitigated?

10 What types of international risk have become greater due to globalization processes, and why?

11 In what ways are CSR issues affected by the national environment of a firm's home country, and how does this hold it back from conceiving a global CSR approach?

12 National governments in emerging economies are sometimes accused of putting growth before the environment. To what extent is this a fair criticism?

13 Emerging economies are now more important players in intergovernmental organizations, but this does not necessarily imply greater international consensus on the pressing global issues. Why?

Key revision concepts

Globalization, p. 434; International risks, p. 435; Global balance of power, p. 443; Interdependence of national economies, p. 443; State capitalism, p. 430; Sustainability, p. 439

Assignments

◆ Assess the role of the Bric countries in the global political and legal environments.
◆ Assess the changes taking place in business approaches to sustainability, including the roles of NGOs and national governments in influencing business strategy.

Further reading

Aqtmael, A. van (2008) *The Emerging Markets Century: How a New Breed of World-Class Companies is Overtaking the World* (New York: Simon & Schuster).

Findlay, R. (2010) *Power and Plenty: Trade, War and the World Economy in the Second Millennium* (Princeton: Princeton University Press).

Halliday, F. and Ozkirimli, U. (2000) *Theories of Nationalism: A Critical Introduction* (Basingstoke: Palgrave Macmillan).

Harvey, D. (2010) *The Enigma of Capital: and the Crises of Capitalism* (London: Profile Books).

Huang, Yasheng (2008) *Capitalism with Chinese Characteristics: Entrepreneurship and the State* (Cambridge: Cambridge University Press).

Obi, C. and Cheru, F. (2010) *The Rise of China and India in Africa: Challenges, Opportunities and Critical Interventions* (London: Zed Books).

Rodrik, D. (2007) *One Economics, Many Recipes* (Princeton: Princeton University Press).

Rotberg, R. (ed.) (2008) *China into Africa: Trade, Aid and Influence* (Washington, DC: Brookings Institution).

Rothermund, D. (2009) *India: The Rise of an Asian Giant* (New Haven: Yale University Press).

Santos-Paulino, U. and Wan, G. (2010) *The Rise of China and India: Impacts, Prospects and Implications* (Basingstoke: Palgrave Macmillan).

Sen, A. (2009) *The Idea of Justice* (London: Allen Lane).

APPENDIX
ATLAS

1	Netherlands	7	Slovenia	13	Serbia	
2	Belgium	8	Croatia	14	Albania	
3	Luxembourg	9	Slovakia	15	Macedonia	
4	Switzerland	10	Hungary	16	Moldova	
5	Czech Republic	11	Bosnia & Hercegovina	17	Armenia	
6	Austria	12	Montenegro	18	Azerbaijan	

THE WORLD

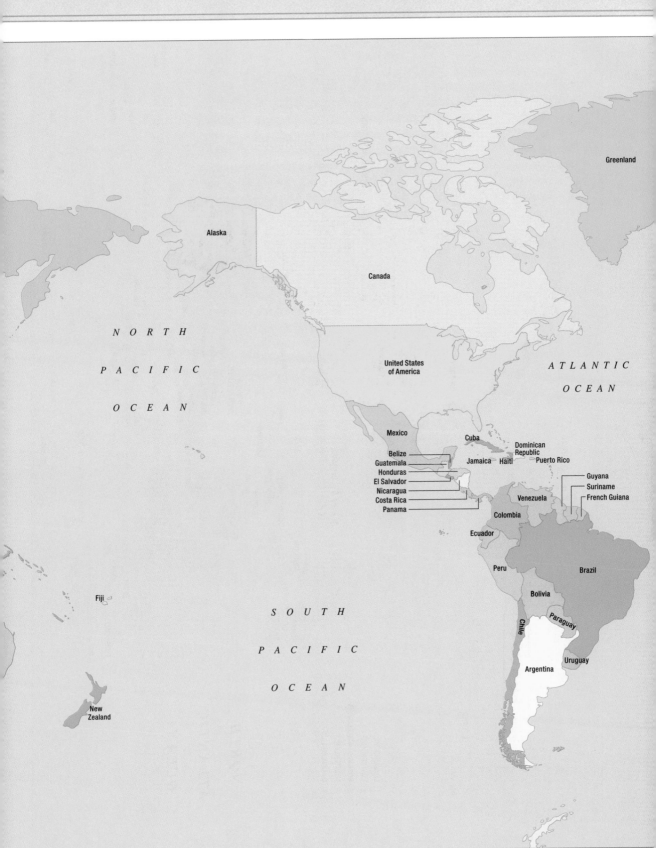

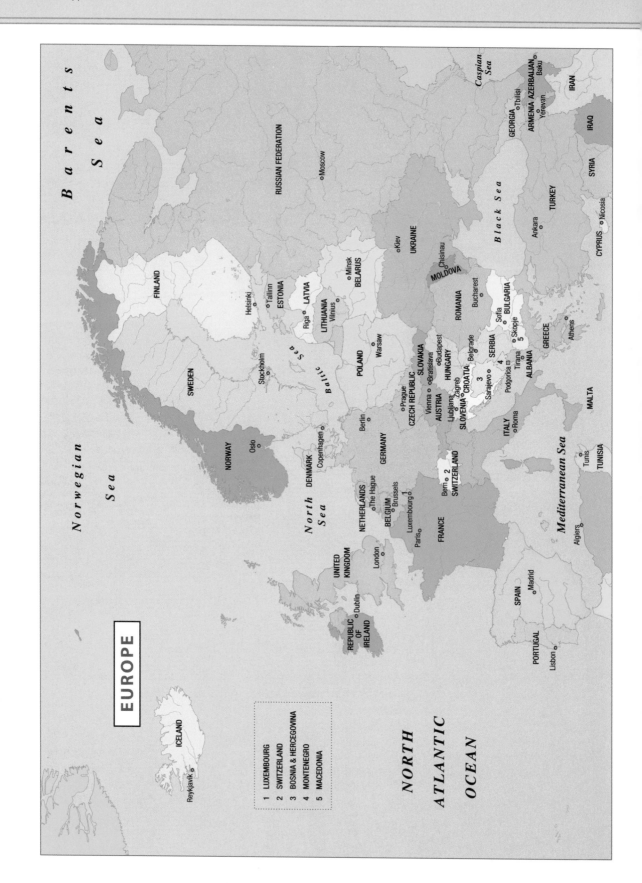

EUROPE

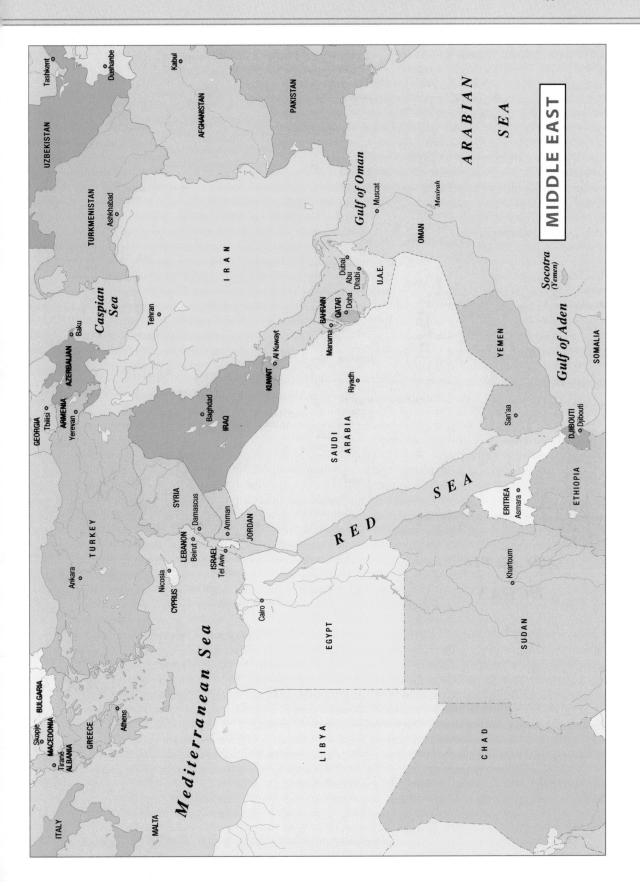

MIDDLE EAST

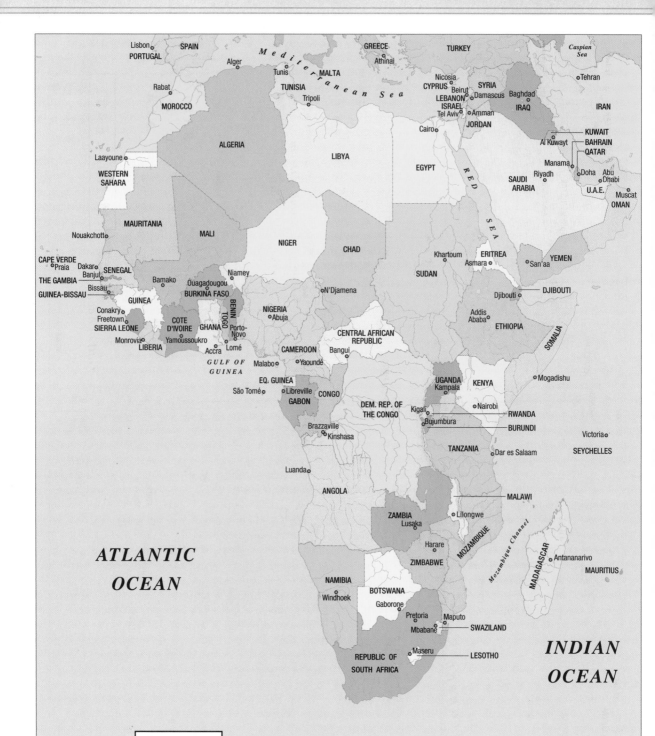

AFRICA

GUATEMALA
San Salvador
EL SALVADOR
Tegucigalpa
NICARAGUA
Managua
San José
COSTA RICA
PANAMA
Panama
City

CARIBBEAN SEA

ST. LUCIA
ST. VINCENT &
THE GRENADINES
GRENADA
Caracas
VENEZUELA

BARBADOS
Bridgetown
TRINIDAD
& TOBAGO
Port of Spain

Georgetown
COLOMBIA
Bogotá
GUYANA
Paramaribo
SURINAME
Cayenne
FRENCH
GUIANA

Quito
ECUADOR

PERU

Lima

BRAZIL

Brasilia

La Paz   BOLIVIA

Sucre
(Legal Capital)

SOUTH AMERICA

PARAGUAY
Asunción

SOUTH
PACIFIC
OCEAN

CHILE

Santiago

ARGENTINA

URUGUAY

Buenos Aires   Montevideo

SOUTH
ATLANTIC
OCEAN

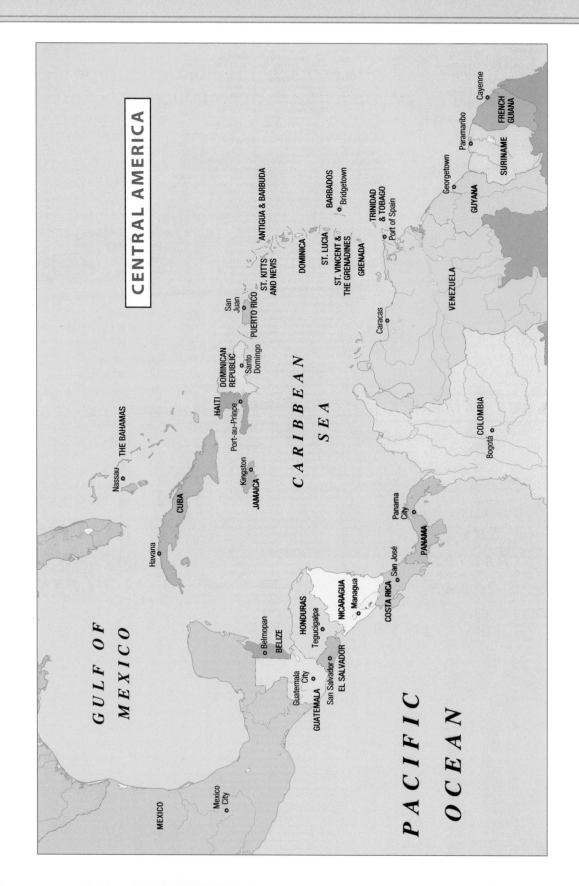

CENTRAL AMERICA

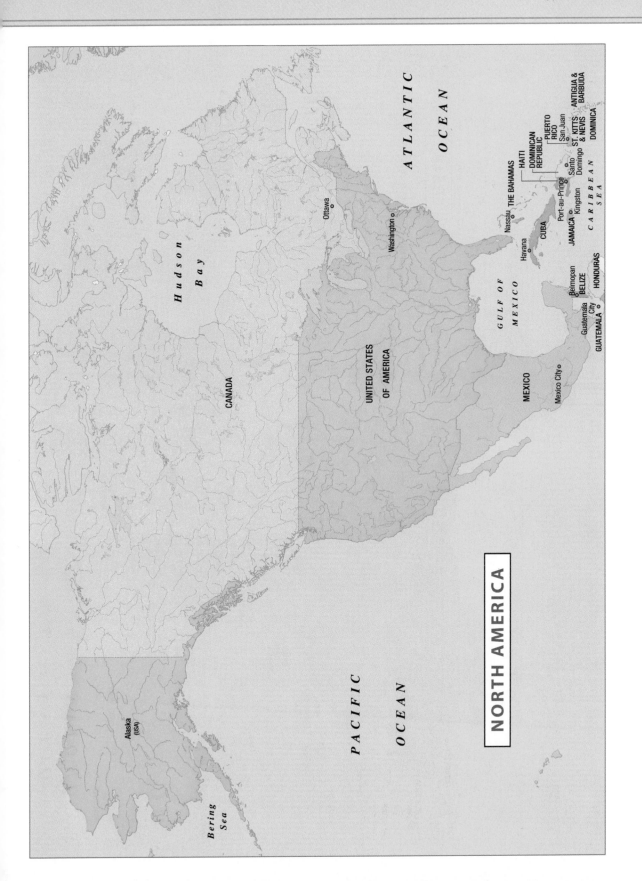

NORTH AMERICA

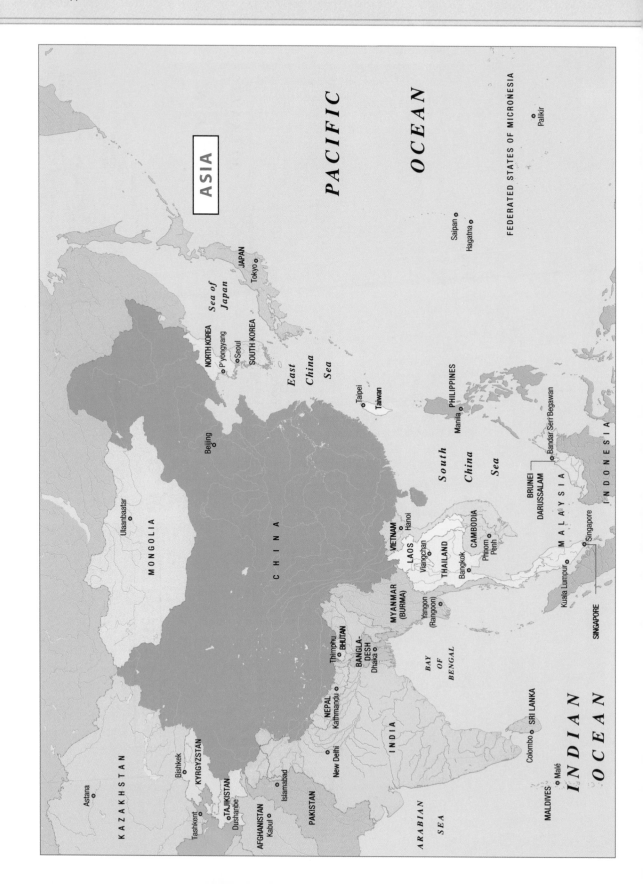

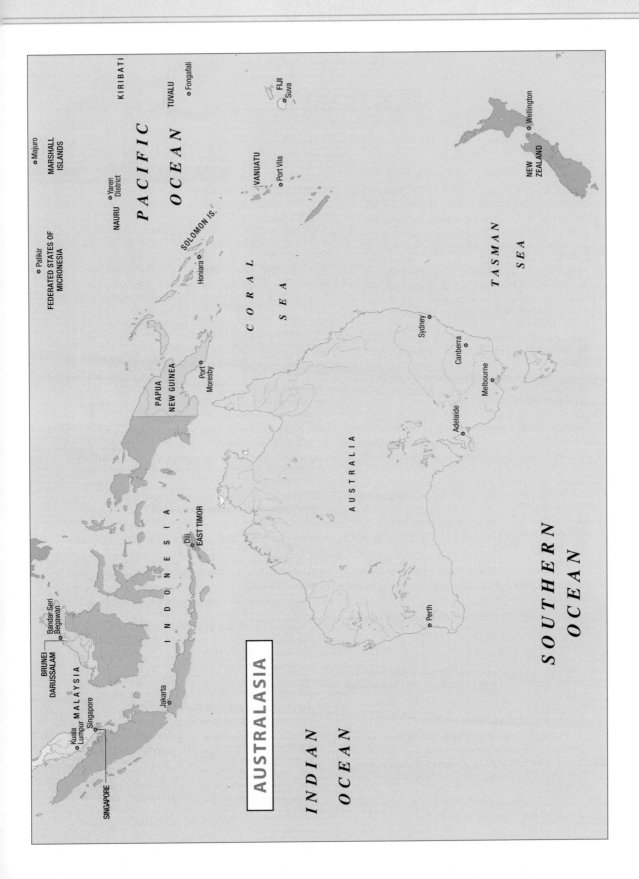

GLOSSARY

A

absolute advantage enjoyed by a country which is more efficient at producing a particular product than any other country

acquisition type of FDI in which an investor purchases an existing company in a foreign location

affiliates organizations connected through ownership or other strategic ties to an MNE

Andean Community South American free trade area

anti-dumping rules WTO rules which allow anti-dumping duties to be imposed on the exporting country by the importing country, in order to protect local producers from unfair competition

arbitrage financial activities which involve making profits from the buying and selling of currencies, commodities or other assets

arbitration the submission of a legal dispute to a named person or organization in accordance with a contractual agreement; an alternative to litigation

area divisions company divisions based on geographical regions of the world, adapting strategy to local conditions

arm's length contracting business dealings between people who interact only for the purpose of doing business with each other

Asia-Pacific Economic Cooperation Group (Apec) co-operation agreement of economies bordering on the Pacific

assimilation in an acquisition by one firm of another, compelling the acquired company to conform to the culture and practices of the new owner

assimilation of cultures process by which minority cultures become integrated into the mainstream culture of a nation

Association of South East Asian Nations (Asean) co-operation agreement of South East Asian countries

authoritarianism rule by a single leader or group of individuals, often sustained by ideology associated with a one-party state

B

balance of payments credit and debit transactions between a country's residents (including companies) and those of other countries

bilateral agreement an agreement between two countries, often for reciprocal trade terms

biodiversity the variety of living organisms and species co-existing in the same habitat

bond a loan instrument which promises to pay a specific sum of money on a fixed date, and to pay interest at stated intervals

born-global firm SME which aims to become global from the outset, often in a high-technology sector

Bretton Woods agreement agreement between Allied nations in the aftermath of the Second World War, which was intended to bring about exchange rate stability; established the IMF and World Bank

Bric countries collective reference to Brazil, Russia, India and China, which are grouped together loosely as emerging economies

Buddhism Asian religion based on the teachings of Buddha

business any type of economic activity in which goods or services (or a combination of the two) are supplied in exchange for some payment, usually money

business case for CSR argument that business goals will be met more successfully in the longer term through CSR than through a narrow focus on economic goals

C

capital account in connection with an economy, account based on transactions involving the sale and purchase of assets, such as investment in shares

caste system social stratification system based on birth; associated with Hinduism

categorical imperative ethical principle put forward by Kant, that respect for every human being should be the guiding principle for behaviour

chaebol family-dominated industrial conglomerates characteristic of business organizations in South Korea

checks and balances system by which the three branches of government (legislative, executive and judicial) share legal authority and accountability

chief executive officer (CEO) the company's senior executive, who oversees its management and is accountable to the board of directors

Christianity monotheistic religion based on belief in Jesus Christ, whose teachings are in the Bible

civil (or private) law in any legal system, the law pertaining to relations between private individuals and companies

civil law tradition legal system based on comprehensive legal codes which form the basic law

civil society sphere of activities in society in which citizens are free to pursue personal goals and form associations

climate change any change in the climate over time, whether from natural causes or human activity

Climate Change Panel UN body which brings together research on climate change and makes recommendations for action by member states

coalition government government composed of two or more parties, usually arising in situations where no single party has obtained a majority of seats in legislative elections

codes of practice voluntary sets of rules devised by companies to guide their CSR, ethical and environmental practices

co-determination principle of stakeholder participation in corporate governance, usually involving a two-tier board, with employee representation on the supervisory board

common law tradition legal system based chiefly on accumulated case law in decided judgments, through a system of binding precedents

common market regional grouping in which member states enjoy free movement of goods, labour and capital

community interest company (CIC) a limited company set up to function as a social enterprise, which adheres to strict statutory requirements for adhering to social purposes

company a legal form of an organization which has a separate legal identity from its owner(s); also called a 'corporation'

comparative advantage enjoyed by a country where production of a particular product involves greater relative advantage than would be possible anywhere else

competition law area of law which concerns rules against abuse of a dominant position and unfair trading practices by one or more firms

competitive advantage theory (devised by Porter) that international competitiveness depends on four major factors: demand conditions, factor conditions, firm strategy and supporting industries

competitive strategy a firm's business strategy which focuses on advantages of particular products and particular markets

Confucianism ancient Chinese ethical and philosophical system based on the teachings of Confucius

conglomerate large, diversified company, in which there is no single identifiable core business

consequentialist principle utilitarian principle that the test of the rightness or wrongness of an action depends on the results which flow from it

consolidation in an industry, a pattern of larger firms taking over smaller ones, which results in a few large companies

constitutionalism set of rules, grounded in a society's shared beliefs, about the source of authority in the state and its institutional forms

consumer price index (CPI) index which tracks the percentage rise or fall in prices, with reference to a specific starting point in time

contextualism in ethical thinking, the principle that ideas of right and wrong stem from specific cultural environments

core competencies capabilities of a firm to maintain innovative and competitive edge

corporate citizenship concept which visualizes social responsibility of the firm in the community as analogous to that of the individual citizen, entailing obligations to obey the law and pay taxes

corporate governance a company's structures and processes for decision-making at the highest level

corporate social responsibility (CSR) an approach to business which recognizes that the organization has responsibilities in society beyond the economic role, extending to legal, ethical, environmental and philanthropic roles

corporate strategy strategy which focuses on the overriding goals of the company, embracing its values and culture

criminal law body of laws which designate offences and set out legal procedure for prosecution of those charged with violations

culture shared, learned values, norms of behaviour, means of communication and other outward expressions which distinguish one group of people from another

current account in connection with an economy, account based on trade in goods (the merchandise trade account), services (the services account), and profits and interest earned from overseas assets

customs union regional grouping in which member states remove all trade barriers among themselves and adopt a common set of external barriers

D

deflation decline in prices in an economy, associated with recession and falling demand

democracy system of elected government, based on fair and free elections and universal suffrage

demographic change changes in whole populations brought about by rises and falls in the birth rate and death rate, as well as by migration of people

depression situation in which an economy deteriorates significantly, diminishing by one tenth in size

derivative financial instrument whose value is dependent on another asset class, such as stock

developed countries countries whose economies have become industrialized and have reached high income levels

developing countries countries in the process of industrialization and building technological capacity

directors people appointed by the company to bear ultimate responsibility for the company's activities

diversification corporate strategy whereby a company acquires businesses in a range of different sectors

dumping sale of goods abroad at below the price charged for comparable goods in the producing country

E

East African Community (EAC) common market of East African countries

eclectic paradigm theory of FDI devised by Dunning, based on three sets of advantages: ownership (O), location (L) and internalization (I); also known as the 'OLI paradigm'

ecology the relationship between organisms and their environment, including changes in their distribution and numbers

Economic Community of West African States (Ecowas) organization for co-operation among West African states

economic development can refer to any change in a country's overall balance of economic activities, but usually refers to industrialization and resultant changes in society

economic growth a country's increase in national income over time; negative growth occurs where the economy is contracting

economic union regional grouping in which member states unify all their policies, including monetary, fiscal and welfare policies

emergent strategy theory devised by Mintzberg, which focuses on firm strategy adapting over time, rather than following a deliberate plan

emerging economies/markets fast-growing developing countries

entrepreneur a person who starts up a business and imbues it with the energy and drive necessary to compete in markets

environmental degradation environmental change caused mainly by human activity, which has detrimental effects on ecological systems

environmental management assessing environmental impacts and devising suitable strategies across a company's total operations

equity in corporate finance, the share capital of a company

ethical relativism approach to ethics which holds that principles are not absolute, but dependent on circumstances

ethics system of values by which judgments of right and wrong behaviour are made

ethnocentric an unquestioning belief that one's own national culture and ways of doings things are the best

Eurobond a bond denominated in a currency other than the one of the country in which it is issued

European Court of Human Rights (ECHR) court established by the Council of Europe, which hears cases of alleged breaches of the European Convention on Human Rights, brought by individuals in member states

European Court of Justice (ECJ) highest court for interpreting EU law

European Economic Area (EEA) grouping of the European Free Trade Area (EFTA) and the EU

European Free Trade Area (EFTA) grouping formed in 1960 by countries not signed up to the Treaty of Rome (which created what is now the EU)

European Monetary Union (EMU) EU programme centred on the single currency and an independent central bank, which sets monetary policy for eurozone member states

European Union (EU) regional grouping of European countries which evolved from trade agreements to deeper economic integration

eurozone member states in the EU which have satisfied the Maastricht criteria and joined the EMU

executive directors directors who actively manage the company

export selling products in a country other than the one in which they were made

F

FDI inflows aggregate value of investments that flow into a country

FDI inward stock the total value of foreign investments that a country has attracted

FDI outflows aggregate value of investments from a country's organizations to overseas destinations

FDI outward stock the total value of foreign investments made by a country's nationals

federal system system of government in which authority is divided between the centre and regional units

fiduciary duty duty of trust to act honestly and in the best interests of another; applies to the duty of directors owed to their company

finance and accounting business function which concerns control over the revenues and outgoings of the business, aiming to balance the books and to generate sufficient profits for the future health of the firm

first-mover advantages precept that countries or firms which are first to produce a new product gain an advantage in markets that makes it virtually impossible for others to catch up

fiscal policy budgetary policies for balancing public spending with taxation and other income

five forces model in Porter's theory of competitive strategy, an analysis of an industry based on buyers, suppliers, potential entrants and possible substitute products

flexible mass production model of manufacturing which combines the benefits of flexibility with those of scale economies

Fordism approach to an industrial organization based on large factories producing standardized products for mass consumption, named after the automobile magnate Henry Ford

foreign direct investment (FDI) mode of internationalization in which a firm invests in productive assets in a foreign country, acquiring them wholly or partly and using this ownership stake to exert control on operations

for-profit organizations businesses that aim to make money

franchising business agreement by which a business uses the brand, products and business format of another firm under licence

free trade agreement (FTA) any agreement between countries which aims to liberalize trade among them; often bilateral or regional

free trade area or bloc a group of countries which have joined in a regional trade agreement

functional approach organizational structure based on business functions, such as finance, HRM and marketing

functional strategies a firm's strategy pertaining to each functional area, such as marketing, which contributes to achieving corporate goals

functions activities of a business which form part of the overall process of providing a product for a customer

futures contract contract to carry out a particular transaction on a designated date in the future

G

G20 grouping of 20 developed, developing and emerging economies, brought together by the IMF in 1999, which meets regularly, focusing mainly on financial stability

General Agreement on Tariffs and Trade (GATT) series of multilateral agreements on reducing trade barriers

geocentric organization which aims to focus on global corporate goals, but allowing for local responses and adaptation

globalization processes by which products, people, companies, money and information are able to move quickly around the world

globalization of markets MNEs' ability to serve consumers across the world, taking account of different products for different national markets

globalized production MNEs' ability to locate different stages of production in the most advantageous location

global model in Bartlett and Ghoshal's typology, a model of the international company based on centralized control

global warming global rise in temperatures, impacting on all forms of life, caused by the build-up of heat-trapping gases, or 'greenhouse gases' (GHG), in the earth's atmosphere

gold standard the setting of exchange rates based on the value of gold (from the 1870s to 1914)

government structures and processes of the state by which laws are made and administered; also refers to the particular officeholders at any given time

greenfield investment FDI which focuses on a new project, such as a factory, in a foreign location

greenhouse gases (GHG) mixture of heat-trapping gases, mainly carbon dioxide (CO_2), held to cause global warming

gross domestic product (GDP) the value of the total economic activity produced within a country in a single year, including both domestic and foreign producers

gross national income (GNI) the total income from all the final products and services produced by a national economy within a single year

Group of Seven (G7) grouping of 7 advanced economies (US, Canada, UK, France, Germany, Italy, and Japan); with the addition of Russia, it is known as the G8

guanxi personal relations which establish trust and mutual obligations necessary for business in China

H

hedge a financial tool or arrangement which insures a firm against adverse currency movements in its international financial activities

hedge fund investment fund managed by an individual or firm, which is active in all types of securities markets

high-context culture culture in which communication relies heavily on the behavioural dimension, such as 'body language'

Hinduism polytheistic religion whose followers are concentrated in India

holding company company, often referred to as the 'parent' company, which owns a number of subsidiaries

horizontal integration mergers or acquisitions between two or more companies in the same industry

human resource management (HRM) all aspects of the management of people in the organization, including recruitment, training, and rewarding the workforce

human rights basic, universal rights enjoyed by all individuals, which transcend social and cultural differences

I

ideology all-encompassing system of beliefs and values, or 'world-view'

import the purchase of goods or services from a buyer in another country

import quota a barrier to trade which consists of limiting the quantity of an imported product that can legally enter a country

import substitution approach to economic development which favours producing goods for domestic consumption that otherwise would have been imported

industrialization transformation of an economy from mainly agricultural production for domestic consumption to one based on factory production, with potential for export

inflation the continuing general rise in prices in an economy

initial public offering (IPO) first offering by a company of its shares to the public on a stock exchange; also known as 'flotation'

innovation activities which seek improvements and new ways of doing things

innovation system the structures and institutions by which a country's innovation activities are encouraged and facilitated, both directly and indirectly

intangible assets rights over products, such as trademarks and patents, which can be exploited commercially; they can be contrasted with tangible assets

integration in an acquisition of one firm by another, the blending of the two cultures into a single organizational culture

intellectual property (IP) property in intangible assets, such as patents, copyrights and trademarks, which can be legally protected from use by others unless permission is obtained from the owner

interconnectedness improved communications across national borders, facilitated mainly by advances in technology, computing and the internet

interdependence links based on complementarities and co-operation between two or more countries or organizations

intergenerational justice concept which underlies the principle of sustainability, implying that moral obligations are owed to future generations

intermediate goods components and parts which cross national borders before being made into final products

international business business activities that straddle two or more countries

International Court of Justice (ICJ) UN-sponsored international court which hears legal cases relating to member states

International Criminal Court (ICC) court established under the auspices of the UN and the International Court of Justice, which hears cases involving crimes against humanity and war crimes

international law body of rules recognized by the international community as governing relations between sovereign states

international model in Bartlett and Ghoshal's typology, a model of the international company based on decentralized subsidiaries

International Monetary Fund (IMF) agency of the UN which oversees the international monetary and financial systems

International Organization for Standardization (ISO) body which overseas quality and environmental standards recognized across industries

invention product or process which can be described as 'new', in that it makes a significant qualitative leap forward from the state of existing knowledge

Islam monotheistic religion based on the teachings of the prophet Muhammad, as revealed in the Koran; followers are referred to as Muslims

J

joint venture an agreement between companies to form a new entity to carry out a business purpose, often an FDI project judicial system system of courts, usually divided between civil courts and criminal courts

just-in-time (JIT) manufacturing system of manufacturing which relies on a continuous flow of materials

K

kaizen management philosophy of continuous improvement, involving the entire workforce

keiretsu grouping of Japanese companies, characterized by inter-firm ties and cross-shareholdings

L

law rule or body of rules perceived as binding because it emanates from state authorities with powers of enforcement

lean production systems and techniques of production enabling companies to reduce waste, leading to greater flexibility in production processes

least developed countries the world's poorest developing countries, mainly in sub-Saharan Africa

legal risk uncertainties surrounding legal liabilities, their implementation in differing legal systems, and the observance of fairness and impartiality in judicial proceedings in differing locations

legislation laws enacted by law-making processes set out in national constitutions; also known as statute law

legislative assembly body of elected representatives within a state, which has law-making responsibilities

leveraged buy-out (LBO) acquisition of a company's equity by a firm or group of individuals, financed by borrowing

liberal market economy capitalist economic system in which supply and demand, as well as prices, are determined by free markets

licence legal agreement by which a firm (the licensor) grants permission to another firm (the licensee) to use its property, notably intellectual property such as patents and trademarks

limited liability principle that the shareholder is liable up to the amount invested in the company

litigation the use of judicial procedures and the court system to bring claims for damages and other remedies in legal cases

local content requirements trade policy which requires foreign investors to use local component suppliers in, for example, manufacturing

location advantages inherent advantages of country or region, such as access to transport and low labour costs

low-context culture culture in which communication is clear and direct, rather than relying on patterns of behaviour

M

macroeconomics the study of national economies

management process of planning, organizing, leading and controlling the work of organization members

manufacturing under licence production of products by a firm by agreement with the owner of their patents, trademarks or other intellectual property

market a location where exchange transactions take place, either with formal standing or informally

marketing satisfying the needs and expectations of customers; includes a range of related activities, such as product offering, branding, advertising, pricing, and distribution of goods

matrix structure organizational structure involving two lines of authority, such as area and product divisions

Mercosur South American common market

merger coming together of two or more companies to form a new company

microeconomics the study of economic activity at the level of individuals and firms

migration movement of people from one place to another, which can be within a country or between countries, with a view to making a new life in the new location

Millennium Development Goals (MDGs) goals designated by the UN Millennium Summit of 2000, which set targets for improving human well-being in developing regions

mixed economy economic system which combines market elements with state controls

modes of internationalization methods by which companies expand internationally, such as FDI

monetary policy economic policies for determining the amount of money in supply, rates of interest, and exchange rates

monopoly domination by one firm of the market for particular goods or services, enabling the firm to determine price and supply

morality standards of behaviour considered right and wrong

most-favoured-nation principle (MFN) GATT principle by which the most favourable tariff treatment negotiated with one country is extended to similar goods from all countries

multidivisional structure organizational structure with decentralized divisions based on product lines or geographical areas

multilateral agreement international agreement signed by many countries, usually in the form of a treaty which creates legal obligations

multinational enterprise (MNE) an organization which acquires ownership or other contractual ties in other organizations (including companies and unincorporated businesses) outside its home country

multinational model in Bartlett and Ghoshal's typology, a model of the international company based on autonomous national units

multi-party system system in which many political parties represent a wide spectrum of views, and where the government is likely to be a coalition of parties

N

nation-state social, administrative and territorial unit into which the world's peoples are divided

national budget balance the extent to which public spending is balanced by receipts from taxes and other sources; budget deficits are common

national culture distinctive values and behavioural norms which distinguish one nation from other

national debt the total debt accumulated by a central government's borrowings over the years

nearshoring type of FDI or outsourcing by which a firm invests in operations in a lower-cost location near to a major market

negligence breach of a duty to take reasonable care which causes injury or other harm to another person or organization

non-executive directors part-time company directors who are independent of the firm's management and owners

non-governmental organization (NGO) voluntary organization formed by private individuals for a particular shared purpose

North American Free Trade Agreement (Nafta) free trade area comprising the US, Canada and Mexico

not-for-profit organizations organizations such as charities, which exist for the purpose of promoting good causes, rather than to make a profit

O

offshoring contracting out of a business process, usually to a low-cost location; often carrying negative connotations

oligopoly an industry dominated by a few very large firms

operations the entire process of producing and delivering a product to a consumer; covers tangible goods and services, and often a combination of both

Organisation for Economic Co-operation and Development (OECD) organization of the world's main developed economies, which supports market economies and democratic institutions

organization two or more people who work together in a structured way to achieve a specific goal or set of goals

organizational culture an organization's values, behavioural norms and management style; also known as 'corporate culture'

outsourced production agreement between a brand owner and a manufacturer to make the firm's branded products under licence

outsourcing the process by which an owner contracts out to another firm a business process, such as product manufacturing or a business service, usually under a licence agreement

ownership advantages resources specific to a firm, such as patents, which can be exploited for competitive advantage

P

parliamentary system system of government in which voters directly elect members of parliament, from whom a prime minister is chosen

patent type of intellectual property which gives its owner an exclusive right for a limited period, to exploit the invention, to license others to use it, and to stop all unauthorized exploitation of the invention

patentable invention a new product or process which can be applied industrially

pegged exchange rate exchange rate which links the value of a currency to that of another, usually stronger, currency

PEST analysis of a national environment which stands for political, economic, social and technological dimensions

philanthropy donation of resources to recipients deemed to be good causes in the eyes of the donor, with no expected material return

planned economy economic system based on total state ownership of the means of production, in which the state controls prices and output

pluralism existence in society of a multiplicity of groups and interests independent of the state, characterized by freedom of association; includes political parties and independent trade unions

political party organization of people with similar political perspectives, which aims to put forward candidates for office and influence government policies

political risk uncertainties associated with the exercise of governmental power within a country, and from external forces

politics processes by which a social group allocates the exercise of power and authority for the group as a whole

polycentric openness to other cultures and ways of doing things

portfolio investment buying shares or other securities in a number of companies internationally, with a view to making financial gains on the investments

presidential system system of government in which the head of the executive branch, the president, is elected by the voters, either directly or through an electoral college (as in the US)

primary production agriculture, mining and fishing

private equity fund investment fund managed on behalf of wealthy investors, which engages mainly in buy-out activities

private international law the body of law for determining questions of which national law prevails in cases between individuals and companies in different countries

private limited company company whose shares are not publicly traded on a stock exchange

privatization process of transforming a state-owned enterprise into a public company and selling off a proportion of shares to the public, usually while retaining a stake and a controlling interest by the government

product divisions company divisions based on products, which co-ordinate product strategy globally

product liability the liability of a producer of a defective product to consumers harmed by the product; can extend to suppliers

product life cycle theory theory of the evolution of a product in stages, from innovation in its home market to dissemination and production in overseas markets

product recall withdrawal of a product from the marketplace due to defects which might cause harm to consumers

proportional representation system of electoral representation in which seats are allocated in proportion to the votes obtained by each party

protectionism government trade policy of favouring home producers and discouraging imports

public company company which lists on a stock exchange and offers shares to the public

public law body of law covering relations between citizens and the state

pull factors factors in a country which attract foreign investors

purchasing power parity (PPP) means of estimating the number of units of the foreign currency that would be needed to buy goods or services equivalent to those that the US dollar would buy in the US

push factors factors in a company's home country which persuade it to seek growth potential overseas

R

reasonable care test used in law to determine whether a person has acted negligently

recession two consecutive quarters of negative economic growth in an economy

referendum example of direct democracy, in which electors cast a vote on a particular issue

regionalization growing economic links and co-operation within a geographic region, both on the part of businesses and governments

regional trade agreement (RTA) free trade agreement among a number of countries in the same broad geographic region

relational contracting business dealings in which personal relations between the parties are more important than formal written agreements

religion set of beliefs and moral precepts which guide people in their lives; often contained in sacred scriptures and propounded by spiritual leaders

remittances money sent by migrant workers back to their families in their home location

research and development (R&D) seeking new knowledge and applications which can lead to new and improved products or processes

resource-based theory theory of the firm based on analysis of three sets of resources: physical, human and organizational

rights issue for a company, a means of raising capital whereby existing investors are asked to increase their investment

rule of law principle of supremacy of the law over both governments and citizens, entailing equality before the law and an independent judiciary

S

secondary production industrial production, concentrated in factories

segment in marketing, a group of identifiable consumers, such as an age group, socio-economic group or culturally distinct group

separation of powers in systems of government, the division between legislative, executive and judicial functions, or branches, with checks and balances to prevent one branch becoming dominant

shareholders legal owners of a company, known as 'members', who enjoy rights such as receiving dividends from company profits

Shari'a the authoritative source of Islamic law

small-to-medium size enterprise (SME) business ranging from micro-enterprises of just one person to firms with up to 249 employees

social contributions charges levied by governments on businesses and other taxpayers to help finance social spending

social enterprise an enterprise that lies somewhere between the for-profit and not-for-profit organization, aiming to make money, but using it mainly for social causes

social market economy capitalist market economy with a strong social justice dimension, including substantial welfare state provisions

social responsibility the role of the organization in society, which implies duties to communities and the environment

sole trader the person who is in business on his or her own account, also referred to as a self-employed person

sovereignty supreme legal authority in the state; also mutual recognition of states in international relations

sovereign wealth fund entity controlled by a government, which invests state funds and pursues an investment strategy; often active global financial markets

spillover effects benefits to local firms in host countries from FDI, including technological capabilities and local supply contracts

stakeholder broad category including individuals, groups and even society generally, that exerts influence on the company or that the company is in a position to influence

stakeholder theory management theory which focuses on the many different groups and interests that affect the company

stock exchange market in which shares in public companies and other securities are traded

structure the design of organization through which the enterprise is administered

subculture minority culture in a society, often associated with immigrant communities

subsidiary company a company owned wholly or substantially by another company, which is in a position to exert control

subsidies payments from public funds to support domestic industries; can also be export subsidies to home producers to bolster a country's exports

sustainability the principle that business should be carried out in ways which do not cause a detriment to the ability of future generations to fulfil their needs

sustainable consumption principle that consumer lifestyle and purchasing decisions should take account of the environmental needs of future generations

sustainable development economic development which meets the needs of present generations without compromising the ability of future generations to meet their own needs

SWOT analysis strategic tool used by businesses to assess the organization's strengths, weaknesses, opportunities and threats

T

tangible assets physical assets such as machinery and stock

tariff tax imposed by governments on traded goods and services, usually imports but can also be on exports

technology methodical application of scientific knowledge to practical purposes

technology transfer process of acquiring technology from another country, especially in manufacturing, whereby skilled workers in the host country are able to learn from the foreign technology

terrorism action by an individual or group intended to inflict dramatic and deadly injury on civilians and create an atmosphere of fear, generally for a political or ideological purpose

tertiary sector the third type of economic activity (following primary and secondary) which consists of services, such as financial services

third-party verification the use of outside specialist services or certification to monitor CSR and environmental performance

tort in common law countries, branch of law which concerns obligations not to cause harm to others in society

Trade-related Aspects of Intellectual Property (TRIPS) multilateral international agreement on protection of intellectual property, which aims to bring national legal regimes into harmony

transboundary pollution the transmission of pollutants through the water, soil and air from one national jurisdiction to another

transition economies economies such as those of Eastern Europe and the CIS (Commonwealth of Independent States, including Russia) which are making the transition from planned economies to market-based economies

transnational corporation (TNC) a company which owns and controls operations in one or more countries other than its home country

transnational model in Bartlett and Ghoshal's typology, a model of the international company balanced between the centre and subsidiaries

treaties instruments of international law; may be multilateral, involving many countries, or bilateral, between two countries

triad countries advanced economies of North America, the EU and Japan; Australia and New Zealand are also in this category

triple-bottom-line reporting corporate reporting focusing on social and environmental aspects of the company, in addition to traditional financial information

two-party system political system in which there are two major political parties, alternating between government and opposition

U

unemployment the percentage of people in the country's labour force who are willing to work but are without jobs

unitary system system of authority within a state in which all authority radiates out from the centre

United Nations (UN) the world's largest and most authoritative intergovernmental organization

urbanization process of large-scale shift of populations from rural areas to cities

utilitarianism philosophical thinking based on the individualist view of human nature that each person has wants and needs which are pursued in a self-interested way

V

value chain concept which identifies the value created at each stage in a production process

vertical integration acquisitions of firms in successive stages of production

voluntary export restraint (VER) tool of government trade policy by which trading partners wishing to export into a country are encouraged to limit their exports, or else incur the imposition of tariffs or import quotas

W

World Bank organization established in the aftermath of the Second World War, to fund development projects and broader development programmes

World Trade Organization (WTO) successor organization to the GATT, set up to regulate world trade and settle trade disputes among member countries

REFERENCES

Archibugi, D. and Michie, J. (1997) 'Technological globalisation and national systems of innovation: an introduction', in Archibugi, D. and Michie, J (eds) *Technology, Globalisation and Economic Performance* (Cambridge: Cambridge University Press), pp. 1–23.

Arnold, J. (2008) 'Do tax structures affect aggregate economic growth?' OECD Working paper ECD/WKP(2008)51.

Bainbridge, D. (1996) *Intellectual Property*, 3rd edn (London: Pitman Publishing).

Balassa, B. (1962) *The Theory of Economic Integration* (London: Allen & Unwin).

Barney, J. (1991) 'Firm resources and sustained competitive advantage', *Journal of Management*, 17(1): 99–120.

Bartlett, C.A. and Ghoshal, S. (1990) 'Matrix management: not a structure, a frame of mind', *Harvard Business Review*, 90(4): 138–45.

Bartlett, C.A. and Ghoshal, S. (1998) *Managing Across Borders: A Transnational Solution*, 2nd edn (London: Random House).

Beetham, D. (1991) *The Legitimation of Power* (Basingstoke: Macmillan – now Palgrave Macmillan).

Bell, M. and Pavitt, K. (1997) 'Technological accumulation and industrial growth: contrasts between developed and developing countries', in Archibugi, D. and Michie, J. (eds) *Technology, Globalisation and Economic Performance* (Cambridge: Cambridge University Press), pp. 83–137.

Berlin, I. (1958) *Two Concepts of Liberty* (Oxford: OUP).

Bhagwati, J. (2006) 'Why Asia must opt for open regionalism on trade', *Financial Times*, 16 April.

Blas, J. (2010) 'A market re-emerges', *Financial Times*, 14 April.

Boseley, S. (2008) '151,000 civilians killed since Iraqi invasion', *The Guardian*, 10 January.

Birkinshaw, J. (2000) 'The structures behind global companies', in Mastering Management, Part 10, *Financial Times*, 4 December.

Bradshaw, M.J. (1996) 'The prospects for the post-socialist economies', in Daniels, P.W. and Lever, W.F. (eds) *The Global Economy in Transition* (Harlow: Addison Wesley), pp. 263–88.

Buckley, N. (2006) 'Self-confident state re-enters world stage', *Financial Times*, 21 April.

Cantwell, J. (1989) *Technological Innovation and Multinational Corporations* (Oxford: Blackwell).

Carroll, A.B. (1991) 'The pyramid of corporate social responsibility: toward the moral management of organizational stakeholders', *Business Horizons*, 34: 39–48.

Castells, M. (2000) *The Rise of the Network Society*, 2nd edn (Oxford: Blackwell).

Castro, C. (2004) 'Sustainable development: mainstream and critical perspectives', *Organization & Environment*, 17(2): 195–225.

Catholic News Agency (2009) The Vatican Yearbook 2008, at www.catholicagency.com.

Chandler, A. (1990) *Strategy and Structure: Chapters in the History of the Industrial Enterprise* (Cambridge, MA: The MIT Press).

Charkham, J. (1994) *Keeping Good Company: A Study of Corporate Governance in Five Countries* (Oxford: OUP).

Coates, D. (1999) 'Why do growth rates differ', *New Political Economy*, 4(1): 77–95.

Collier, P. (2008) *The Bottom Billion* (Oxford: OUP).

Consumer Focus (2009) Green Expectations, www.consumerfocus.org.uk

De Haan, A. (1999) 'Livelihoods and poverty: the role of migration – a critical review of the migration literature', *The Journal of Development Studies*, 36(2): 1–47.

Diamond, L. (1996) 'Is the third wave over?' *Journal of Democracy*, 7(3): 21–39.

Diamond, L. (2008) 'The democratic rollback: the resurgence of the predatory state', *Foreign Affairs*, 87(2): 36–48.

Dicken, P. (2003) *Global Shift*, 4th edn (London: Sage Publications).

Dietz, S., Hepburn, C. and Stern, N. (2008) 'Economics, ethics and climate change', Conference paper, Climate Change and Social Justice Conference, Department of Politics and International Relations, University of Oxford.

Dunning, J.H. (1993) *Multinational Enterprises and the Global Economy* (Wokingham: Addison Wesley).

DuPont (2008) Sustainability Progress Report 2008, at www2.dupont.com/sustainability.

Dyer, G. (2009) 'The dragon stirs', *Financial Times*, 25 September.

Dyer, G. and Harvey, F. (2009) 'A high-wire act', *Financial Times*, 25 November.

Economist, The (2009a) 'Currency contortions', 19 December.

Economist, The (2009b) 'Athenian dances', 19 December.

Economist, The (2009c) 'No Mariachis, please', 14 February.

Economist, The (2009d) 'Getting warmer', 5 December.

Economist, The (2010a) 'The gods strike back', 13 February.

Economist, The (2010b) 'The other oil spill', 26 June.

Economist, The (2010c) 'Export or die', 3 April.

Eichengreen, B. (1996) *Globalizing Capital: A History of the International Monetary System* (Princeton: Princeton University Press).

Eichengreen, B., Bordo, M., Klingebiel, D. and Soledad, M. (2000) 'Is the crisis problem growing more severe?' at www.econ.berkeley.edu.

European Commission (2008) Eurostat database: GDP per capita for member states, at http://eurostat.ec;. europa.eu

Freeman, C. (1997) 'The national system of innovation in historical perspective', in Archibugi, D. and Michie, J. (eds) *Technology, Globalisation and Economic Performance* (Cambridge: Cambridge University Press), pp. 24–49.

Freeman, C. and Soete, L. (1997) *The Economics of Industrial Innovation*, 3rd edn (London: Cassell).

Freeman, R.E. (1984) *Strategic Management: A Stakeholder Approach* (Boston, MA: Pitman).

Gerlach, M. (1991) *Alliance Capitalism: The Social Organization of Japanese Business* (Berkeley: University of California Press).

Gilpin, R. (2000) *The Challenge of Global Capitalism: The World Economy in the 21st Century* (Princeton: Princeton University Press).

Grant, J. and Mackenzie, M. (2010) 'Ghost in the machine', *Financial Times*, 18 February.

Hagedoorn, J. and Hesen, G. (2007) 'Contract law and the governance of inter-firm technology partnerships – an analysis of different modes of partnering and their contractual implications', *Journal of Management Studies*, 44(3): 342–66.

Hall, M.R. and Hall, E.T. (1960) 'The silent language of overseas business', *Harvard Business Review*, 38(3): 87–95.

Harrison, J., Bosse, D. and Phillips, A. (2010) 'Managing for stakeholders, stakeholder utility functions and competitive advantage', *Strategic Management Journal*, 31: 58–74.

Hawthorn, J. (1993) 'Sub-Saharan Africa', in Held, D. (ed.) *Prospects for Democracy* (Cambridge: Polity Press), pp. 330–54.

Held, D., McGrew, A., Goldblatt, D. and Perraton, J. (1999) *Global Transformations: Politics, Economics and Culture* (Cambridge: Polity Press).

Hirst, P. and Thompson, G. (1999) Globalization in Question, 2nd edn (Cambridge: Polity Press).

Hofstede, G. (1994) *Cultures and Organizations: Software of the Mind* (London: HarperCollins).

Hofstede, G. (1996) 'Images of Europe: past, present and future' in Joynt, P. and Warner, M. (eds) *Managing Across Cultures: Issues and Perspectives* (London: International Thomson Business Press), pp. 147–65.

Houlder, V. (2004) 'Industry says the environmental case overlooks consumer responsibilities', *Financial Times*, 28 February.

Hughes, J. (2009) 'In death do we part', *Financial Times*, 9 July.

Husted, B. and Salazar, J. (2006) 'Taking Friedman seriously: maximizing profits and social performance', *Journal of Management Studies*, 43(1): 75–91.

Hymer, S. (1975) 'The multinational corporation and the law of uneven development', in Radice, H. (ed.) *International Firms and Modern Imperialism* (Harmondsworth: Penguin).

ILO (International Labour Organization) (2008) *World of Work Report 2008: Income Inequalities in the Age of Financial Globalization* (Geneva: ILO).

ILO (2009a) 'Employment and unemployment', at www.ilo.org/global.

ILO (2009b) *Global Unemployment Trends* (Geneva: ILO).

ILO (2009c) World of Work Report 2009, at www.ilo.org.

ILO (2010) Global child labour developments: Measuring trends for 2004 to 2008, at www.ilo.org.

IMF (2009) World Economic Outlook database, 2009, at www.imf.org.

Intellectual Property Office (2010) *Patent Backlogs and Mutual Recognition* (London: London Economics).

International Energy Agency (IEA) (2009) World Energy Outlook 2009, at www.worldenergyoutlook.org.

International Institute for Sustainable Development (1992) 'Business strategies for sustainable development', at www.iisd.org.

Inter-Parliamentary Union (2010) Women in national legislatures, at www.ipu.org.

Johnson, C. (1982) *MITI and the Japanese Miracle* (Stanford: Stanford University Press).

Juergensmeyer, M. (2003) *Terror in the Mind of God: The Global Rise of Religious Violence*, 3rd edn (Berkeley: University of California Press).

Kant, I. (1785) *Groundwork of the Metaphysic of Morals*, cited in Körner, S. (1955) *Kant* (Harmondsworth: Penguin).

Kapstein, E.B. (1994) *Governing the Global Economy: International Finance and the State* (Cambridge, MA: Harvard University Press).

Kirkpatrick, G. (2009) 'The corporate governance lessons from the financial crisis', OECD report in Financial Market Trends series, at www.oecd.org.

Knight, G. and Cavusgil, S. (2004) 'Innovation, organizational capabilities, and the born-global firm', *Journal of International Business Studies*, 35(2): 124–41.

Krugman, P. (1994) *Rethinking International Trade* (Cambridge, MA: MIT Press).

Krugman, P. (1999) *The Return of Depression Economics* (Harmondsworth: Penguin).

Kynge, J. (2009) 'China's growth dictates a fresh view of the way the world works', *Financial Times*, 20 March.

Lamy, P. (2007) 'Multilateral or bilateral agreements: which way to go?' Speech of 17 January at summit of the Confederation of Indian Industries, Bangalore, India, at www.wto.org.

Landes, D. (1998) *The Wealth and Poverty of Nations* (London: Little, Brown and Company).

Lei Zhu and Bang Nam Jeon (2007) 'International R&D spillovers: trade, FDI and information technology as spillover channels', *Review of International Economics*, 15(5): 955–76.

Leys, S., translator and editor (1997) *Analects of Confucius* (New York: W.W. Norton & Co.).

Linz, J. (1993) 'Perils of presidentialism', in Diamond, L. and Plattner, MF. (eds) *The Global Resurgence of Democracy* (Baltimore: The Johns Hopkins University Press), pp. 108–26.

Linz, J. and Stepan, A. (1997) 'Towards consolidated democracies', *Journal of Democracy*, 7(2): 14–33.

List, F. ([1841] 2005) *National System of Political Economy: History*, Vol. 1 (New York: Cosimo Inc.).

Lundvall, B.-A. (ed.) (1992) *National Systems of Innovation* (London: Pinter).

Maddison, A. (2001) *The World Economy: A Millennial Perspective* (Paris: OECD).

Mahbubani, K. (2009) 'Lessons for the west from Asian capitalism', in The Future of Capitalism, *Financial Times*, 12 May.

Mazower, M. (2010) *No Enchanted Palace: The End of Empire and the Ideological Origins of the United Nations* (Princeton: Princeton University Press).

McGregor, R. (2001) 'Legal evolution with strings attached', *Financial Times*, 2 May.

McGregor, R. (2009) 'The party organiser', *Financial Times*, 1 October.

McWilliams, A. (2001) 'Corporate social responsibility: a theory of the firm perspective', *Academy of Management Review*, 26(1): 117–28.

Michie, J. and Kitson, M. (eds) (1995) *Managing the Global Economy* (Oxford: OUP).

Mikesell, R.F. (2000) 'Bretton Woods – original intentions and current problems', *Contemporary Economic Policy*, 18(4): 404–15.

Mill, J.S. ([1859] 1947) *On Liberty*, edited by A. Castell (New York: Appleton-Century-Crofts Inc.).

Mintzberg, H. (2000) *The Rise and Fall of Strategic Planning* (Harlow: Pearson Education).

Mintzberg, H., Ahlstrand, B. and Lampell, J. (2009) *Strategy Safari*, 2nd edn (Harlow: Pearson Education).

Mitchell, R.K., Agle, B.R. and Wood, D.J. (1997) 'Toward a theory of stakeholder identification and salience: defining the principle of who and what really counts', *Academy of Management Review*, 22(4): 853–86.

Moens, G. and Gillies, P. (1998) *International Trade and Business: Law, Policy and Ethics* (Sydney: Cavendish Publishing).

Mowery, D.C. and Oxley, J. (1997) 'Inward technology transfer and competitiveness' in Archibugi, D. and Michie, J. (eds) *Technology, Globalisation and Economic Performance* (Cambridge: Cambridge University Press), pp. 138–71.

Nathan, A. (2009) 'China since Tiananmen: authoritarian impermanence', *Journal of Democracy*, 20(3): 37–40.

OECD (Organisation for Economic Co-operation and Development) (2000) 'Cross-border trade in financial services: economics and regulation', *Financial Market Trends*, 75, March.

OECD (2004) Principles of Corporate Governance, at www.oecd.org.

OECD (2005) *Oslo Manual: Guideline for Collecting and Interpreting Innovation and Data*, 3rd edn (Paris: OECD).

OECD (2009a) *Agricultural Policies in OECD countries: Monitoring and Evaluation* (Paris: OECD).

OECD (2009b) *Science, Technology and Industry Scoreboard, 2009* (Paris: OECD).

Ohmae, K. (1995) *The End of the Nation State* (London: HarperCollins).

Ohmae, K. (2000) *The Invisible Continent: Four Strategic Imperatives of the New Economy* (London: Nicholas Brealey Publishing).

Olsen, J.E. (2001) 'Environmental problems and ethical jurisdictions: the case concerning Texaco in Ecuador', *Business Ethics: A European Review*, 10(1): 71–7.

Onodera, O. (2008) 'Trade and innovation project: a synthesis paper', OECD Trade Policy Working Paper No. 72 (Paris: OECD).

Palmisano, S. (2008) 'The global consumer gives small companies a big reach', *Financial Times*, 6 May.

Patel, P. and Pavit, K. (1994) 'National innovation systems: why they are important and how they might be measured and compared', *Economics of Innovation and New Technology*, 3: 77–95.

Patel, P. and Pavitt, K. (2000) 'National systems of innovation under strain: the internationalization of corporate R&D', in Barrell, R., Mason, G. and O'Mahony, M. (eds) *Productivity, Innovation and Economic Performance* (Cambridge: Cambridge University Press), pp. 217–35.

Peel, M. and Croft, J. (2010) 'Case closed', *Financial Times*, 16 April.

Perlmutter, H. (1969) 'The tortuous evolution of the multinational corporation', *Columbia Journal of World Business*, 4: 9–18.

Phelps, E. (2009) 'Uncertainty bedevils the best system', in The Future of Capitalism, *Financial Times*, 12 May.

Piercy, N. and Giles, W. (1989) 'Making SWOT analysis work', *Marketing Intelligence and Planning*, 7(5): 5–7.

Plamenatz, J. (1958) *The English Utilitarians*, 2nd edn (Oxford: Blackwell).

Plattner, M. (2010) 'Populism, pluralism and liberal democracy', *Journal of Democracy*, 21(1): 81–92.

Pontusson, J. (1997) 'Between neo-liberalism and the German model: Swedish capitalism in transition', in Crouch, C. and Streeck, W. (eds) *Political Economy of Modern Capitalism* (London: Sage), pp. 55–70.

Porter, M. (1998a) *The Competitive Advantage of Nations* (Basingstoke: Macmillan – now Palgrave Macmillan).

Porter, M. (1998b) *On Competition* (Boston, MA: Harvard Business Review Publishing).

Porter, M. (1998c) *Competitive Strategy: Techniques for Analyzing Industries and Competitors* (with new introduction) (New York: Free Press).

Porter, M. (2008) 'The five competitive forces that shape strategy' updated version in *Harvard Business Review*, January 2008, pp. 78–93.

Prahalad, C.K. (2009) *The Fortune at the Bottom of the Pyramid* (Philadelphia, PA: Warton School Publishing).

Prahalad, C.K. and Hamel, G. (1990) 'The core competence of the corporation', *Harvard Business Review* 68(3): 79–91.

Pugh, D.S. (1997) 'Introduction to the fourth edition', in Pugh, D.S. (ed.) *Organization Theory: Selected Readings* (Harmondsworth: Penguin), pp. xi–xiii.

Quinton, A. (1989) *Utilitarian Ethics* (Chicago: Open Court Publishing).

Ravallion, M. (2009) 'The developing world's bulging (but vulnerable) "middle class"', World Bank Policy Research Working Paper 4816, at www.worldbank.org.

Ricardo, David ([1817]1973) *Principles of Economy and Taxation* (London: Dent).

Rodrik, D. (2009) *One Economics: Many Recipes* (Princeton: Princeton University Press).

Sabel, C.E. (1994) 'Flexible specialization and the re-emergence of regional economics', in Amin, A. (ed.) *Post-Fordism: A Reader* (Oxford: Blackwell), pp. 101–56.

Sartori, G. (1997) 'Understanding pluralism', *Journal of Democracy*, 8(4): 58–69.

Schumpeter, J.A. (1942) *Capitalism, Socialism and Democracy* (New York: Harper & Row, 1975 edn), originally published in 1942.

Sell, S. (2000) 'Big business and the new trade agreements' in Stubbs, R. and Underhill, G., *Political Economy and the Changing Global Order*, 2nd edn (Oxford: OUP).

Sen, A. (2009) 'Adam Smith's market never stood alone', in The Future of Capitalism, *Financial Times*, 12 May.

Shih, E., Kraemer, K. and Dedrick, J. (2008) 'IT diffusion in developing countries', *Communications of the ACM*, 51(2): 43–8.

Singh, A. (1999) '"Asian capitalism" and the financial crisis', in Michie, J. and Grieve Smith, J. (eds) *Global Instability: The Political Economy of World Economic Governance* (London: Routledge).

SIPRI (Stockholm International Peace Research Institute) (2009) 2009 Year Book, at www.sipri.org.

Skapinker, M. (2003) 'In search of a balanced society', *Financial Times*, 16 September.

Smith, A. ([1776]1950) *An Inquiry into the Nature and Causes of the Wealth of Nations* (London: Methuen).

Stiglitz, J. (2000) 'The insider', *New Republic*, 222(16/17): 56–60.

Stiglitz, J. (2002) *Globalization and its Discontents* (London: Allen Lane).

Stoner, J. and Freeman, R. (1992) *Management*, 5th edn (New Jersey: Prentice Hall).

Streeck, W. (1997) 'German capitalism: does it exist? Can it survive?' *New Political Economy* 2(2): 237–56.

Tait, N. (2009) 'Elements in common mask widely varying enforcement firepower', *Financial Times*, 30 November.

Telegraph, The (2010) 'Sir Ronald Cohen: Capitalism has its consequences', 26 June.

Tellis, G., Prabhu, J. and Chandy, R. (2009) 'Radical innovation across nations: the preeminence of corporate culture' *Journal of Marketing*, April, 73: 3–23.

Terpstra, V. and David, K. (1991) *The Cultural Environment of International Business* (Cincinnati: South-Western Publishing Co.).

Time (1986) 'The Courts vs Apartheid', 25 August, at www.time.com.

Towers Perrin (2009) 2009 Update on US tort cost trends, at www.towersperrin.com.

Trompenaars, F. (1994) *Riding the Waves of Culture* (New York: Irwin).

UK Department of Energy and Climate Change (2010), Energy and emissions projections, at www.decc.gov.uk.

UNCTAD (2009) *Trade and Development Report 2008* (Geneva: United Nations).

UNDP (2009) *Human Development Report 2009* (Basingstoke: Palgrave Macmillan).

United Nations (1987) Report of the World Commission on Environment and Development: Our Common Future (the Brundtland Report), at www.un-documents.net.

United Nations (1999) *World Investment Report 1999* (Geneva: United Nations).

United Nations (2000) *Human Development Report 2000* (Oxford: OUP).

United Nations (2003) *World Investment Report 2003* (Geneva: United Nations).

United Nations (2007) World Urbanization Prospects, 2007 revision, at http://esa.un.org.

United Nations (2008a) *World Investment Report 2008* (Geneva: United Nations).

United Nations (2008b) *Millennium Development Goals Report 2008* (New York: United Nations).

United Nations (2010) *Millennium Development Goals Report 2010* (New York: United Nations).

United Nations Policy Working Group (2002) Report of the Policy Working Group on the United Nations and Terrorism, Ref. A/57/273, at www.un.org/terrorism/.

UN Global Compact (2010) Address by UN Secretary General to Global Compact summit leaders, New York, 24 June, at www.unglobalcompact.org

UN Population Division (2008), World Population Prospects, 2008 revision, at www.un.org.

US Census Bureau (2009) Income, Poverty and Health Insurance Coverage in the US: 2008; 10 September, at www.census.gov.

US Defense Department (2007) Base Structure Report, at www.defense.gov/pubs/BSR_2007.

US Department of Labor (2010) 'The employment situation, May 2010', Bureau of Labor Statistics, at www.bis.gov/.

US Energy Information Agency, International energy statistics, 2009, at www.doe.gov.

US Patent and Trademark Office (USPTO) US patent statistics, 2009, at www.uspto.gov.

US Trade Representative's Office (2009) Trade statistics, at www.ustr.gov.

Valukas, A. (2010) Report of the Examiner into Lehman Brothers bankruptcy, US Bankruptcy Court Southern District of New York, Chapter 11 case number 08-13555(JMP), 11 March.

Vitols, S. (2000) 'Globalization: a fundamental change to the German model' in Stubbs, R. and Undershill, G (eds) *Political Economy and the Changing Global Order*, 2nd edn (Oxford: OUP), pp. 373–81.

Wade, F. (2010) 'India trade dampens Burma sanctions', Democratic Voice of Burma, 19 July, at www.dvb.no.

Waters, M. (2001) *Globalization*, 2nd edn (London: Routledge).

Watts, R. (2009) 'Google pays no tax on £1.6 billion in Britain', *The Times*, 20 December.

Wells, L.T. (ed.) (1972) *The Product Life Cycle and International Trade* (Boston, MA: Harvard Business School Press).

Wheatley, J. (2010) 'Promise of growth lures carmakers', *Financial Times*, 21 January.

Whipp, L. (2009) 'Optimism over China proves infectious with its neighbours', *Financial Times*, 21 July.

World Bank (2000) World Development Report 1999–2000, at www.worldbank.org.

World Bank (2002) World Development Report 2003, at www.worldbank.org.

World Bank (2009) Migration and Development Brief 10, 13 July, at www.worldbank.org.

World Bank (2010) Global Economic Prospects 2010, at www.worldbank.org.

World Economic Forum (2009a) *Global Risks 2009* (Geneva: World Economic Forum).

World Economic Forum (2009b) Global Competitiveness Report 2009–10, at www.weforum.org.

World Economic Forum (2009c) *Transforming Pensions and Healthcare in a Rapidly Ageing World* (Geneva: WEF).

World Federation of Exchanges (2010), 10-year Review, at www.world-exchanges.org.

WTO (2009) International trade statistics, at www.wto.org.

Xiaomei Tan and Zhao Gang (2009) 'An emerging revolution: clean technology research, development and innovation in China', World Resources Institute, WRI Working Paper at www.wri.org.

Zimmerer, T., Scarborough, N. and Wilson, D. (2007) *Essentials of Entrepreneurship and Small Business Management*, 5th edn (New Jersey: Prentice Hall).

Zweigert, K. and Kötz, H. (1998) *Introduction to Comparative Law*, 3rd edn (Oxford: Clarendon Press).

INDEX OF ORGANIZATIONS

INDEX OF PEOPLE

SUBJECT INDEX

Printed in China